Top Ten Supermarket Chains Ranked by Sales

Supermarket Chain	1984 Rank	1980 Rank	1970 Rank	1960 Rank
Safeway	1	1	2	2
Kroger	2	2	3	3
American Stores	3	5	5	4
Lucky Stores	4	4	8	17
Winn-Dixie	5	6	9	7
Great Atlantic & Pacific	6	3	1	1
Albertson's	7	9	17	a
Supermarkets General	8	10	12	a
Grand Union	9	8	10	8
Stop and Shop	10	12	13	13

a Not listed in "50 Largest Merchandising Firms."

Source: "50 Largest Merchandising Firms" and "50 Largest Retailing Companies," Fortune *(August 1961), (May 1971), (July 13, 1981), and (June 10, 1985).*

Financial Performance Data on Supermarket Chains, Selected Years

Financial Data	1983–1984	1980–1981	1975–1976	1970–1971	1965–1966
Gross margin	23.89	22.03	21.22	21.39	22.32
Total expenses (including interest)	23.28	21.41	21.31	21.20	21.38
Net operating profit	0.61	0.62	−0.09	0.19	0.94
Other income or deductions	0.93	0.84	1.27	1.54	1.46
Total net earnings before inc. taxes	1.54	1.46	1.18	1.73	2.40
Total net earnings after inc. taxes	0.94	0.90	0.62	0.86	1.31

Source: "Annual Report of the Grocery Industry," Progressive Grocer, *various issues.*

Largest Retail Advertisers, 1983–1984

Retailer	Major Business	Advertising Rank	Advertising-to-Sales Ratio (%)
Sears, Roebuck	General merchandise	1	2.2
K mart	General merchandise	2	2.2
McDonald's	Fast food	3	4.4
J. C. Penney	General merchandise	4	2.5
Tandy	Electronics, computers	5	6.7
Batus	General merchandise	6	2.4
Burger King	Fast food	7	3.8
Wendy's	Fast food	8	3.4
Dayton Hudson	General merchandise	9	0.3
Southland	Convenience store	10	0.3
Imasco USA	Fast food	11	1.7
Household International	General merchandise	12	0.4
Federated Department Stores	General merchandise	13	0.3
American Stores	Supermarket	14	0.2
Safeway	Supermarket	15	0.1

Source: "100 Leading National Advertisers," Advertising Age *(September 14, 1984); and "Second 100 Leading National Advertisers,"* Advertising Age *(June 13, 1985).*

Retail Management
A Strategic Approach

Barry Berman
Hofstra University

Retail

A Strategic

Joel R. Evans
Hofstra University

Management

Approach

THIRD EDITION

Macmillan Publishing Company
New York
Collier Macmillan Publishers
London

Cover photos reprinted by permission of Rouse Company, International Business Machines Corporation, K mart, M. O'Neil Company, and Jack Gifford.

Copyright © 1986, Macmillan Publishing Company, a division of Macmillan, Inc.

Printed in the United States of America

Earlier edition (s), entitled Retail Management: A Strategic Approach copyright © 1979, © 1983 by Macmillan Publishing Company

Macmillan Publishing Company
866 Third Avenue, New York, New York 10022
Collier Macmillan Canada, Inc.

Library of Congress Cataloging in Publication Data

Berman, Barry.
  Retail management.

  Includes bibliographies and indexes.
  1. Retail trade—Management.   I. Evans, Joel R.
II. Title.
HF5429.B45   1986   658.8'7   85-24008
ISBN 0-02-308620-3

Printing: 3 4 5 6 7 8   Year: 6 7 8 9 0 1 2 3 4

ISBN 0-02-308620-3

To Linda, Glenna, and Lisa
To Linda, Jennifer, and Stacey

Thank you for your continuing patience and understanding.

Preface

We are gratified by the continuing response to this text, as evidenced by adoptions at more than 375 colleges and universities. In this third edition, we have set out to retain the material and features most desired by professors and students, add new material and features requested by professors and students, keep the book as current as possible, and maintain the length of prior editions.

As in earlier editions, the concepts of a strategic approach and a retail strategy form the foundation of *Retail Management: A Strategic Approach*. As defined in the text, a strategic approach "concentrates on planning to meet objectives and satisfy the retailing concept." A retail strategy is "the overall plan that guides the firm—a framework of action for a retail establishment. It outlines the philosophy, objectives, consumer market, overall and specific activities, and control mechanisms for a retailer." The major goals of our text are to enable the reader to become a good retail planner and decision maker and to help focus on change and adaptation to change.

The book is designed as a one-semester text for a beginning student of retailing. In most cases such a student will have already been introduced to marketing principles. We strongly believe that retailing should be viewed as one aspect of marketing and not distinct from it.

These significant features have been retained from earlier editions:

1. A career orientation, with actual career ladders and a thorough discussion of ownership and employment alternatives and an appendix on careers in retailing.
2. A decision-making orientation, with many flowcharts, figures, tables, and pictures.
3. A real-world approach that focuses on retailers such as McDonald's, Sears, A&P, Toys 'R' Us, Safeway, and The Limited.
4. Full coverage of all major retailing topics—including consumer behavior, marketing research, store location, service retailing, the retail audit, retail institutions, international retailing, and retailing in a changing environment.
5. Thirty-two end-of-chapter cases involving a wide range of retailers.
6. Up-to-date information gathered from such sources as *Progressive Grocer, Chain Store Age, Stores, Merchandising, Business Week, Journal of Retailing, Journal of*

Marketing, the *National Retail Merchants Association*, and the *1982 Census of Retail Trade*.

7. A 17-chapter organization. This structure allows the text to be covered conveniently in a one-semester course.
8. Numerous questions at the end of each chapter in the text.
9. An appendix explaining how to solve case studies, following Chapter 1.
10. An appendix on franchising, following Chapter 3.
11. End-of-text appendixes: careers in retailing, firms with retailing positions for college graduates, and glossary.
12. A comprehensive companion text in retailing *(Applying Retail Management: A Strategic Approach)* that contains chapter objectives, questions, readings, exercises, and an appendix on retail mathematics.

These features have been added for the third edition:

- An eight-page color photo essay in Chapter 1, showing the scope of retailing.
- All new chapter-opening vignettes, based on real companies and situations.
- New or expanded coverage of entrepreneurial characteristics, store positioning, buying clubs, direct marketing, retail information systems, computerization, human resource management, inventory control, gross margin return on investment (GMROI), performance measures, productivity, and video-ordering systems.
- Eighteen new end-of-chapter cases, several by distinguished colleagues.
- Five new comprehensive cases at the end of the text. These cover a wide range of retailing concepts and institutional types.

As mentioned, *Retail Management: A Strategic Approach* is divided into seventeen chapters. Chapter 1 acquaints the reader with the framework of retailing and available careers within retailing. The growth and success of Toys 'R' Us, Dayton Hudson, and Joe's Camera Store (an independent retailer) illustrate the concept of strategic retailing, the orientation of the text.

Chapter 2 introduces and explains the retail strategy process and its stages: situation analysis, objectives, identification of consumer characteristics and needs, overall strategy, specific activities, control, and feedback.

Chapters 3 and 4 examine the institutions of retailing. In Chapter 3, independent retailers, chain stores, franchises, leased departments, vertical marketing systems, and consumer cooperatives are described. In Chapter 4, retail institutions are analyzed on the basis of retail strategy mix (convenience store, conventional supermarket, combination store, superstore, box store, warehouse store, specialty store, variety store, department store, full-line discount store, retail catalog showroom, off-price chain, factory outlet, buying club, and flea market), nonstore retailing (vending machines, direct-to-home selling, and direct marketing), and service versus product retailing.

Chapters 5 and 6 relate consumer behavior and marketing research to retailing. In Chapter 5, the consumer's decision process, factors affecting the process, and types of decision processes are detailed. In Chapter 6, the marketing research process, secondary data, primary data, and the retail information system are examined.

Chapters 7 and 8 explain how a store location is chosen. Chapter 7 concentrates on trading-area analysis and characteristics of trading areas. Government and other data that describe trading area attributes are discussed. Chapter 8 deals with the selection of a specific store site from among several types of locations.

Chapter 9 describes how to set up a retail organization, organizational patterns in retailing, and human resource management.

Chapters 10 and 11 explore merchandise planning and management. Chapter 10 is involved with the merchandise buying and handling process (which includes all aspects, from setting up a buying organization to negotiating the purchase and to re-evaluating on a regular basis) and the basic merchandise decisions of what, how much, when, and where to buy merchandise. Chapter 11 covers the financial aspects of retailing and centers on inventory valuation, merchandise forecasting and budgeting, unit control systems, and financial inventory control. Numerous computations are illustrated in this chapter.

Chapters 12 and 13 discuss communicating with the customer. In Chapter 12, store atmosphere, customer services, and community relations are described. In Chapter 13, elements of the retail promotional mix, planning the retail promotional strategy, and reviewing and revising the promotional plan are described.

Chapter 14 examines pricing: factors affecting retail pricing (the consumer, the government, suppliers, and competition) and the development of a retail price strategy. Numerous computations are explained.

Chapter 15 examines planning by a service retailer and considers the special problems or considerations that occur when selling or renting a service rather than selling a physical product. Strategic concepts are applied to service retailing.

Chapter 16 concentrates on integrating and controlling the retail strategy. Planning and opportunity analysis, performance measures, productivity, uses of technology, and retail auditing are each discussed.

In Chapter 17, the changing environment is presented. Trends in demographics, life-styles, consumerism, technology, retail institutions, and the international environment of retailing are evaluated.

Five comprehensive cases are placed after Chapter 17. These are followed by three appendixes: careers in retailing, a listing of 175 retail employers, and a 400-item glossary.

A complete teaching package is available for instructors.

Acknowledgments

Many people have assisted us in the preparation of this book, and to them we extend our warmest appreciation.

We thank these colleagues for contributing cases:

Jack Gifford, Miami University of Ohio
Laurence Jacobs, University of Hawaii
Marvin A. Jolson, University of Maryland
Michael V. Laric, University of Baltimore
Kevin F. McCrohan, George Mason University
John Roman, Rochester Institute of Technology
Franklin Rubenstein, Retail Management Consultant
Steven J. Shaw, University of South Carolina
Elaine Sherman, Hofstra University
Robert J. Small, University of Hawaii
William A. Staples, University of Houston at Clear Lake City
Robert A. Swerdlow, Lamar University

We thank the following reviewers, who have reacted to this or earlier editions of the text. Each of these reviewers provided us with perceptive reviews that helped us crystallize our thoughts:

Ramon Avila, Ball State University
Stephen Batory, Bloomsburg University
Joseph Belonax, Western Michigan University
Ronald Bernard, Diablo Valley College
John J. Buckley, Orange County Community College
Peter T. Doukas, Westchester Community College
Jack D. Eure, Jr., Southwest Texas State University
Myron Gable, Shippensburg University
Linda L. Golden, University of Texas at Austin
Mary Higby, Eastern Michigan University

Marvin A. Jolson, University of Maryland
J. Ford Laumer, Jr., Auburn University
John Lloyd, Monroe Community College
James O. McCann, Henry Ford Community College
Curtis Reierson, Baylor University
Steven J. Shaw, University of South Carolina
Gladys S. Sherdell, Montgomery College
John E. Swan, University of Alabama in Birmingham
Lillian Werner, University of Minnesota
Kaylene Williams, University of Delaware
Terrell G. Williams, Utah State University

Special thanks and acknowledgment are due to Bill Oldsey, our fine Macmillan editor. We are also indebted to Ed Neve, Chip Price, Dave Horvath, Steve Vana-Paxhia, Bob Doran, Leo Malek, Gwen Larson, Holly Reid McLaughlin, and Bob Pirrung of Macmillan; Laurie Olson, our conscientious research assistant; and Linda Berman for compiling the index.

Barry Berman
Joel R. Evans
Hofstra University

Contents

4

Retail Institutions: Part II 87

5

Consumer Behavior: Understanding the Decision Process 122

6 Marketing Research in Retailing 155

Choosing a Store Location: Trading-Area Analysis   187

Choosing a Store Location: Site Selection   216

9

Retail Organization and Human Resource Management   244

10 Merchandise Planning and Management: Buying and Handling 280

11 Merchandise Planning and Management: Financial 320

12 Communicating with the Customer: Establishing and Maintaining a Store Image   357

17 The Changing Environment of Retailing   527

Retail
Management
A Strategic Approach

1

An Introduction to Retailing

Chapter Objectives

1. To explain the characteristics and significance of retailing
2. To provide an overview of careers in retailing
3. To examine the principles of retail strategy and show several applications of strategic planning in retailing
4. To relate the marketing concept to retailing

In 1960, Tom Monaghan and his brother Jim raised $500 and bought a small Italian restaurant near Eastern Michigan University in Ypsilanti. Soon thereafter, Jim left the business and Tom found another partner. They opened new outlets near the University of Michigan, Ann Arbor, and Central Michigan University, Mount Pleasant. But by 1965, Tom was on his own and several thousands of dollars in debt. At that point, he deleted every menu item except pizza, began specializing in takeout and delivery service, and created a new company name. Today, Domino's Pizza Inc. has annual sales of more than $625 million through its nearly 2,000 units; and Tom Monaghan plans to have 5,000 units in his chain by 1987.

These are just a few of the factors that have led to Domino's huge success:

- Domino's concentrates on one product line, pizza.
- Growth has been aided through franchising arrangements. Domino's charges a $160,000 initial fee and an annual fee per outlet of $3,500 plus 5.5 per cent of sales.
- Domino's has a clear competitive advantage—free delivery. It guarantees delivery of a hot pizza within 30 minutes of an order being called in. The customer gets the pizza at no charge if delivery is not made on time.

• Consumer satisfaction surveys are conducted regularly.[1]

It is clear that Tom Monaghan understands the special characteristics of retailing and has applied a unique strategy to achieve his goals.

The Framework of Retailing

Retailing can be defined as those business activities that involve the sale of goods and services to the ultimate (final) consumer for personal, family, or household use. It is the final stage in a channel of distribution.

Students are prone to think of retailing as involving only the sale of tangible (physical) goods. It is important to realize that retailing also encompasses the sale of services. A service may be the shopper's primary purchase (insurance, airline ticket); or it may be part of the shopper's purchase of a good (delivery, warranty, credit).

Retailing does not have to involve the use of a store. Mail order, direct selling to consumers in their homes, and vending machines fit within the scope of retailing.

Finally, retailing does not have to include a "retailer." Manufacturers, importers, and wholesalers are acting as retailers when they sell their products or services to the ultimate consumer. On the other hand, purchases made by manufacturers and wholesalers for use in conjunction with their businesses are not part of retailing.

The color photo portfolio following page 6 illustrates the stimulating and diverse nature of retailing and its associated activities.

Special Characteristics of Retailing

There are special characteristics that distinguish retailing from other areas of marketing. The average size of a sales transaction for retailers is less than for manufacturers. Final consumers make many unplanned purchases; those who buy for resale or for use in manufacturing products are more systematic and plan ahead. Most retail customers must be drawn to a store location; salespeople regularly visit manufacturers to initiate and consummate transactions. Each of these factors imposes special requirements on retail firms.

Average sales transactions in 1983 were $21.00 for department stores, about $40.00 for specialty stores, $2.25 for convenience stores (not counting gasoline), and $13.46 in chain supermarkets. These low average sales create a need to tightly control the costs associated with each transaction (such as credit verification, delivery, and bagging) and to increase impulse and suggestion selling. However, low average sales and high costs cannot always be controlled. For example, 63 per cent of department store sales and 57 per cent of specialty store sales are on credit.[2]

Inventory management is difficult when there are many transactions with a number of different customers. As an illustration, while the average chain supermarket had

---

[1]Bernie Whalen, " 'People-Oriented' Marketing Delivers Lots of Dough for Domino's," *Marketing News* (March 16, 1984), Section 2, pp. 4–5; and "Pizza Chains Toughest Turf," *New York Times* (February 18, 1985), pp. D1, D5.
[2]David P. Schulz, "FOR: Financial and Operating Results," *Stores* (November 1984), p. 5; "51st Annual Report of the Grocery Industry," *Progressive Grocer* (April 1984), p. 98; and Francis C. Brown III, "Convenience Stores Moving to Diversify," *Wall Street Journal* (September 12, 1984), p. 35.

$7.4 million in sales during 1983, it also had 10,052 weekly transactions.[3] The large number of transactions makes it harder to determine the levels of existing stock and the popularity of various brands, sizes, and prices of merchandise. A wholesaler, who sells items in substantial quantities to fewer customers, does not have these problems.

Many retail transactions involve unplanned or impulse purchases. For example, surveys indicate that 40 per cent of drugstore purchases are completely unplanned; yet the average drugstore shopper spends less than 15 minutes in the store per visit.[4] This signifies the importance of point-of-purchase displays, attractive store layouts, well-organized stores, and promotions in newspapers and store windows. Cosmetics, current fashions, and new products can be sold as impulse items if they are placed in visible, high-traffic locations in the store. The retailer's ability to forecast, budget, and order merchandise is lessened when consumers buy many products in an unplanned manner.

Retail customers normally visit a store. The number of customers, the average sale size, the unplanned nature of purchases, and the consumers' desire for privacy are all reasons for the popularity of stores. Because shoppers must be attracted to a store, retailers need to consider factors such as location, transportation facilities, store hours, assortment, parking, and advertising.

Reasons for Studying Retailing

Among the major reasons for studying the field of retailing are its impact on the economy, its functions in distribution, and its relationship with firms that sell products to retailers for their resale or use. These factors are discussed in this section. A fourth, and most important, element for students of retailing is the broad range of career opportunities, which are described separately in the following section.

The Impact of Retailing on the Economy

Retailing is a significant factor in the economy of the United States. Retail sales and employment are substantial percentages of total U.S. sales and employment. In addition, a large number of college graduates pursue careers in retailing.

According to the Department of Commerce, 1983 retail store sales (including mail order) were about $1.2 trillion. Vending machine and direct-to-home selling added revenues of $24 billion. Personal consumption expenditures on services (not all retail) were almost $1.1 trillion. Table 1-1 shows retail store sales by kind of business from 1974 through 1983.

Table 1-2 shows the twenty-five largest retailers in the United States for 1983. These twenty-five retailers accounted for about $215 billion in annual sales (about 18 per cent of total U.S. retail store sales) and employed over 2.5 million workers. Department stores (Federated, May, etc.), supermarkets (including Safeway and Kroger), variety stores (e.g., Woolworth), and convenience stores (such as Southland, which operates 7-Eleven) are among the wide variety of retail types represented in Table 1-2.

Retailing is a major source of employment. According to the Department of Labor, about 17 per cent of the nonagricultural labor force was employed in retailing during

[3]"51st Annual Report of the Grocery Industry," p. 44.
[4]*Walgreen's Annual Report, 1984,* p. 8.

Table 1-1
Retail Store Sales by Kind of Business, 1974–83
(Millions of Dollars)

Type of Retailing	1974	1975	1976	1977	1978	1979	1980	1981	1982	1983	Per Cent Increase 1974–83
All retail stores	540,988	588,146	657,375	725,220	807,426	900,558	962,816	1,047,573	1,075,679	1,174,033	117
Durable good stores, total	169,417	182,966	217,805	248,692	278,617	302,357	292,811	316,020	320,868	381,538	125
Automotive group	96,504	106,616	129,754	149,952	166,139	174,662	158,276	173,922	182,390	219,876	128
Furniture and appliance group	25,950	26,921	30,021	33,176	36,928	42,789	44,939	46,462	46,513	53,981	108
Lumber, building materials, and hardware group	22,357	22,995	27,933	33,214	38,592	44,320	43,683	44,800	42,544	59,871	168
Nondurable goods stores, total	371,571	405,180	439,570	476,528	528,809	598,201	670,005	731,553	754,811	792,495	113
General merchandise group	71,159	75,711	81,756	90,686	103,321	110,282	115,733	127,948	131,282	143,491	102
Department stores*	55,449	59,437	65,651	73,647	84,112	89,152	93,345	103,672	107,030	117,323	112
Variety stores	7,746	8,025	7,199	7,095	7,370	8,062	8,180	8,705	8,735	9,122	18
Apparel group	28,896	31,315	33,717	35,565	40,489	43,422	46,188	50,270	51,991	55,915	94
Men's and boys' wear stores	5,939	6,355	6,535	6,943	7,498	7,819	7,813	8,152	8,110	8,422	42
Women's apparel, accessory stores	11,240	12,374	13,382	13,458	15,740	16,707	17,184	18,553	19,288	21,659	93
Family and other apparel stores	6,191	6,647	7,224	8,055	8,311	8,785	9,796	10,682	10,830	12,844	107
Shoe stores	4,358	4,633	5,033	5,650	6,618	7,688	8,307	9,279	9,854	9,538	119
Gasoline service stations	43,022	47,547	51,949	56,468	60,648	75,325	97,434	108,231	104,633	105,374	145
Eating and drinking places	44,673	51,067	57,211	63,276	71,869	82,270	90,367	98,585	107,357	114,837	157
Food group	125,955	138,371	147,972	157,941	175,700	199,210	222,687	241,102	252,802	258,964	106
Drug and proprietary stores	18,444	19,872	21,620	23,196	25,378	28,173	30,613	33,593	35,849	39,845	116
Liquor stores	11,001	11,809	12,357	12,967	13,767	15,551	17,507	18,631	19,031	20,422	86

*Beginning in 1979, mail-order data are included in department store sales.

Source: Bureau of the Census, U.S. Department of Commerce.

Table 1-2
The Twenty-Five Largest Retailing Companies, 1983

1983 Rank	Company	Sales (thousands)	Net Income (thousands)	Employees*
1	Sears Roebuck	$ 35,882,900	$1,342,200	450,000
2	K mart	18,597,900	492,300	250,000
3	Safeway Stores	18,585,217	183,303	162,088
4	Kroger	15,236,013	127,079	161,986
5	J. C. Penney	12,078,000	467,000	175,000
6	Southland	8,772,067	131,768	60,800
7	Federated Department Stores	8,689,579	338,342	123,700
8	Lucky Stores	8,388,155	105,400	65,000
9	American Stores	7,983,677	117,902	60,000†
10	Household International	7,911,900	206,400	77,000
11	Winn-Dixie Stores	7,018,605	113,460	66,500
12	Dayton Hudson	6,963,255	245,457	100,000†
13	Montgomery Ward	6,003,000	54,000	78,500†
14	Jewel Companies	5,723,522	83,053	36,600
15	Batus	5,523,191	258,560	64,000†
16	F. W. Woolworth	5,456,000	118,000	114,600
17	Wal-Mart	4,743,744	196,244	62,000
18	Great Atlantic & Pacific Tea	4,607,817	31,211‡	40,000
19	Albertson's	4,279,331	70,281	34,000
20	May Department Stores	4,229,400	187,000	70,200
21	Melville	3,923,200	176,260	68,143
22	Associated Dry Goods	3,717,827	115,520	59,000
23	Allied Stores	3,675,873	128,471	62,000†
24	Carter Hawley Hale Stores	3,632,662	67,485	58,000
25	Grand Union	3,519,341	226	30,800
	Totals	$215,142,176	$5,356,922	2,529,917

*Year-end total unless followed by a dagger (†) in which case average for year.
‡Reflects an extraordinary credit.

Source: "The 50 Largest Retailing Companies," Fortune (June 11, 1984), pp. 186–187. Reprinted from The FORTUNE Directory by permission; © 1984 Time Inc. All rights reserved.

1983. This figure understates the actual number of people employed in retailing because it does not include seasonal employees, proprietors, or unreported workers in a family business or partnership. The largest employers are eating and drinking places, food stores, general merchandise stores, apparel and accessory stores, and furniture and home furnishing stores.

From another perspective—costs—retailing is a significant field of study. On the average, about 42 per cent of every sales dollar goes to department and specialty store retailers as compensation for the activities they perform.[5] A change in retail efficiency would therefore have a great impact on consumers and the economy. Price levels and product assortment are also affected by retailer competence.

[5]Schulz, "FOR: Financial and Operating Results," p. 16.

Retail Functions in Distribution

Retailing plays an important part in the distribution of products, acting as an intermediary between manufacturers and/or wholesalers and the final consumer. The retailer collects an assortment of goods and services and sells them to customers. This procedure is called the **sorting process.**[6] The typical manufacturer would like to produce one type of item and sell the entire inventory to one buyer. The typical customer wants to choose from among a variety of products and purchase a limited quantity. Through the sorting process, a retailer bridges the gap between manufacturers and customers.

The retailer satisfies manufacturers by purchasing their limited range of products in large quantities. In this way, the manufacturer maximizes efficiency. The retailer satisfies customers by offering a wide variety of products or services (collected from a number of manufacturers) and selling them in small quantities.[7] The consumer is able to choose and buy whatever quantity is desired, all in one transaction. Also, wide assortments enable buyers to undertake one-stop shopping.

Another distribution function that retailers perform is the dissemination of information to customers and other channel members (manufacturers, wholesalers). Customers are informed about the availability of goods and services, the characteristics of goods and services, store location, store hours, sales, and so on. Manufacturers, wholesalers, and others are informed about sales forecasts, delays in shipping, customer complaints, defective products, inventory turnover (by style, color, size), and so on. Many goods and services have been revised by manufacturers on the basis of interviews with retailers.

For small manufacturers, retailers can provide valuable assistance by shipping, storing, marking, advertising, and prepaying for merchandise. On the other hand, small retailers need the same type of help from their suppliers. The number of functions performed by the retailer has a direct bearing on markup requirements.

When manufacturers such as IBM, Sherwin-Williams, and Tandy (Radio Shack) operate their own retail facilities, they need to understand the full range of retailing functions so as to better compete with traditional retailers. As an illustration, IBM had some difficulties when opening its IBM Product Centers. These problems included a poor record-keeping system, an unattractive decor, and improper staffing. IBM corrected its strategy by installing point-of-sale systems, changing store designs, implementing a sales training program, and making the centers look like "a place where you can get a deal."[8]

The Relationships Among Retailers and Their Suppliers

It is essential that the complex relationships among retailers and their suppliers be understood. On the one hand, retailers are part of a channel of distribution; and manufacturers and wholesalers must be concerned about coverage of the consumer market, adequate product displays, consumer services, store hours, and retailer reliability. On the other hand, retailers are major customers of goods and services such as items for

---

[6]This concept was formally introduced by Wroe Alderson, *Marketing Behavior and Executive Action* (Homewood, Ill.: Richard D. Irwin, 1957), pp. 199–211.

[7]The breaking-bulk function can be shown in the derivation of the term *retailing*. It is based on the Old French word *retailler*, which means "to cut up."

[8]Peter Petre, "IBM: Misadventures in the Retail Jungle," *Fortune* (July 23, 1984), p. 80.

Retailing involves all types of businesses that interact with final consumers. It includes everything from the corner drugstore to a large clothing-store chain. The camera department in the on-campus store of the Rochester Institute of Technology is shown here. Photo courtesy of the RIT Communication Arts Department.

Since the majority of retailers operate in a very competitive environment, it is important that they thoroughly understand customer needs and satisfy them through a distinctive offering of goods and services. At Store 24, Inc. in Waltham, Massachusetts, this means "we're here to serve you." Photo courtesy of Selame Design.

A number of supermarket chains are opening new superstores to sustain their growth and improve profit margins. In comparison with traditional supermarkets, these superstores are much larger, stock many more nonfood items, and have higher profit margins. The housewares department in Safeway's Arlington, Texas, superstore is shown here. Photo courtesy of Safeway Stores, Inc.

To protect themselves against competition from discounters, department stores are remodeling outlets, designing boutiques in stores, and increasing scrambled merchandising. The latter occurs when a store adds goods or services unrelated to its original business, such as this restaurant in a Famous-Barr department store. Photo courtesy of Pat Gifford.

One of the most important decisions a retailer makes involves the choice of a store location. As a result, in recent years, a variety of declining central business districts have been revitalized to attract and retain retailers and their customers. A very successful renovation is Faneuil Hall in Boston, shown here. Photo courtesy of Rouse Company.

Planned shopping centers are centrally owned or managed, based on balanced tenancy, and surrounded by parking. These centers have some type of anchor store and a mix of smaller outlets. Large regional centers, such as the King of Prussia center in Pennsylvania, often feature fountains and other attractive displays. Photo courtesy of Jack Gifford.

Human resource management is a key ingredient in a successful retail strategy. Qualified, motivated employees must be recruited, selected, trained, compensated, and supervised. At Kentucky Fried Chicken, employees are trained through a combination of formal manuals and on-the-job training, using chainwide methods. Photo courtesy of Kentucky Fried Chicken.

Since virtually all the personnel in a retail firm—from the supermarket cashier shown here to senior-level executives—interact with consumers, it is essential that customer courtesy and company policies be properly communicated. Employees should represent "their" store. Photo courtesy of International Business Machines Corporation.

Inventory shrinkage consists of shortages due to customer shoplifting, employee theft, and inventory record-keeping. It is estimated that inventory shrinkage costs retailers over $26 billion each year. To reduce this figure, retailers are turning to sophisticated surveillance systems, such as the Sensormatic system shown in action. Photo courtesy of Sensormatic Electronics Corporation.

When planning a product assortment strategy, retailers need to consider the combination of manufacturer, dealer, and generic brands that they carry. At J. C. Penney, a greater emphasis is being placed on designer clothing as the firm upgrades its image. Shown here are fashions by Halston. Photo courtesy of J. C. Penney.

A store image is defined in the shopper's mind by both functional qualities and psychological attributes. It is based on physical, personnel, product, price, service, and other factors. The Saks Fifth Avenue upscale image is exhibited by this distinctive storefront for its Oakbrook, Illinois, outlet. Photo courtesy of Jack Gifford.

Within their stores, retailers need to carefully plan floor space and the arrangement of individual products—as well as displays for these items. In the linen department at K mart, a gridiron layout is used in conjunction with ensemble and end-aisle displays. The result is efficiency and visual excitement. Photo courtesy of K mart.

A balanced promotion strategy often involves a mix of advertising, publicity, personal selling, and sales promotion. Advertising can draw customers into a store, while personal selling can be used to demonstrate products, answer questions, and clinch sales (as shown here). Photo courtesy of International Business Machines Corporation.

Community relations enable retailers to contribute to the quality of life in the neighborhoods in which they are located. They may also result in favorable publicity. At the Harborplace Shopping Center in Baltimore, Maryland, community relations include cooperation with the United Way. Photo courtesy of Rouse Company.

Retailers must set prices that achieve profitability for the firm and satisfy customers, while adapting to various constraints. Today, many retailers use diverse pricing tactics. At this Jewel supermarket, generic brands are carried for price-conscious consumers. Higher-priced manufacturer brands are sold to other consumers. Photo courtesy of Jack Gifford.

In planning for the future, many retailers are placing a priority on improving productivity through the computerization of routine retail functions. IBM programmable store systems feature numeric and alphameric displays and automate sales, transactions, reports, etc. Photo courtesy of International Business Machines Corporation.

resale, store fixtures, data-processing equipment, management consulting, and insurance.

Frequently, retailers and their suppliers have divergent viewpoints, which need to be reconciled. Unless suppliers are aware of the characteristics and needs of retailers, they cannot develop good rapport with them; and as long as competitive forces exist, retailers will select suppliers who understand and react to their needs. The following examples illustrate several key issues in retailer/supplier relationships:

- Product image—Samsung Electronics is a Korean manufacturer of televisions and related products. While U.S. retailers view Samsung products as promotional items and emphasize low prices on them to generate store traffic, the manufacturer wants its products to be priced at the same levels as popular Japanese models in order to develop a high-quality image.[9]
- Display space—Norelco was unable to secure adequate display space for a line of light bulbs in grocery stores, which account for over one-half of light bulb sales. General Electric has dominated the light bulb market for more than 40 years, and grocery stores generally want to carry only one brand and deal with only one supplier.[10]
- Inventory management—Because of the snowless winters of 1979–80 and 1980–81, many retailers ended up with three years of inventory for snowblowers by Winter 1982. As a result, thousands of retailers stopped buying Toro and other snowblowers. To remedy this, Toro improved its inventory support program for dealers. In addition, its "Sno risk" program encourages consumers to purchase snowblowers by offering a Toro-sponsored rebate program in case snowfall is very low.[11]
- Product pricing—Just before the 1984 Christmas holiday season, IBM announced a series of discounts and rebates on personal computers that reduced the prices paid by retailers by up to 8 per cent. Retailers were upset by the discount plan, since it reduced the value of their existing inventories (which had been building up during a slack period) and came during a time when they were not planning additional orders.[12]
- Franchise agreements—Large automobile fleet buyers such as Hertz are able to purchase cars for as much as $800 less per unit than the automakers' own franchised dealers. These dealers argue that this practice undermines their ability to do business and gives fleet buyers an unfair advantage when selling used cars.[13]
- Product distribution to unauthorized firms—Recently, Phillips–Van Heusen took out full-page ads in trade newspapers to discourage retailers from reselling its apparel to discounters. The ads stated: "If you cheapen our brand, we won't sell to you." Phillips–Van Heusen remains concerned that the customer service, displays, and store image of off-price retailers are incompatible with its marketing goals.[14]

[9]Douglas R. Sease and Steven P. Galente, "Korean Video-Recorder Makers Vow Not to Sell Cheaply in the U.S. but Retailers Have Other Ideas," *Wall Street Journal* (December 21, 1984), p. 23.
[10]Karen Austin Carlson and Thomas V. Bonoma, "North American Philips Lighting Corp: Project Shopping Cart," Harvard Business School Case Services, 9-582-100.
[11]Richard Gibson, "Toro Breaks Out of Slump After Taking Drastic Action," *Wall Street Journal* (January 23, 1985), p. 6.
[12]Marci Jo Williams, "Computer Squeeze," *Fortune* (November 26, 1984), pp. 135–136.
[13]Amal Hag and William Celis III, "Auto Dealers Seeking Legislative Support to End Detroit's Discounts to Fleet Buyers," *Wall Street Journal* (May 16, 1984), p. 35.
[14]Claudia Ricci, "Discount Business Booms, Pleasing Buyers, Irking Department Stores," *Wall Street Journal* (May 3, 1983), pp. 35, 45.

Manufacturers of products used by retailers must also have a knowledge of retailing. For example, a store fixture manufacturer has to understand the requirements of the retailer. Store layout, linear feet of shelf space, self-service merchandising, routing of customer traffic, and storage specifications are some of the criteria used in the selection of store fixtures. Knowledge of basic retailing principles, as well as the special factors relative to a given type of retailer, are necessary for the fixture manufacturer to succeed.

Firms that sell services, such as store insurance, to retailers benefit from an understanding of retailing. Inventory valuation, construction costs of facilities, crime rates, and depreciation are some of the factors that must be examined. For example, how should merchandise that has been marked down in price be appraised if there is a fire? Or how much will fire insurance premiums be reduced if sprinklers are installed in a store?

Careers in Retailing

As pointed out previously, retailing is a major source of employment. A person looking for a career in retailing has two broad possibilities: owning a business or working for an employer. One alternative does not preclude the other. Many retailers open their own outlets after getting experience as employees. A person can also choose franchising, which has elements of both enterpreneurship and managerial assistance. Franchising is discussed in Chapter 3.

Owning a Business

Owning a retail establishment is quite popular, and many opportunities exist. About 79 per cent of all retail outlets are sole proprietorships. In addition, many of today's retail giants started out as independent stores. J. C. Penney, R. H. Macy's, K mart, Wickes, Abraham & Straus, Filene's, Levitz, Toys 'R' Us, Lazarus, McDonald's, and Sears are examples of this phenomenon. See Figure 1-1 for a chronology of K mart (formerly S. S. Kresge).

Too often, people overlook the possibility of owning a retail business. In a number of cases, initial investments can be quite modest (several thousand dollars). For example, mail-order, vending-machine, direct-to-home selling, and many service retailers require relatively low initial investments. In addition, financing may be available from banks, manufacturers, store fixture firms, wholesalers, and equipment companies. Chapter 2 contains an in-depth discussion of starting and operating a retail business.

A small retailer has several advantages. All resources are tailored to the needs of a specific customer category. Personal management and service are provided by the owner. Some of the problems facing large retailers are eliminated or minimized. There are no unions, no antitrust legislation, and no executive turnover.

A small retailer also encounters disadvantages. Because of cost factors, advertising on television usually is not possible, and much computer technology cannot be utilized. The owner-operator works long hours. Large chains can also underprice the small retailer because of their volume purchases.

A Chronology of the K mart Corporation
(formerly S. S. Kresge Company) 1897–1985

1897	Sebastian S. Kresge entered the dimestore business, buying half interest with J. G. McCrory in a store in Memphis, Tenn., with $8,000 in savings.
1904-1909	Company grew from 4 to 42 dimestores.
1921	Kresge green front stores, to sell items costing 25¢ to $1.00, came into existence. They abutted Kresge dimestores. Other dimestore chains followed this lead and the "dollar store" was born.
1935	The company reached its dimestore peak with 745 units and started phasing out the green front division by physically joining green front stores and dimestores to make variety stores.
1952	Kresge began opening stores in shopping centers.
1962	The first K mart discount department store opened in a suburb of Detroit in March. Seventeen others opened the same year.
1966	Founder Sebastian S. Kresge died at the age of 99.
1967	Sales climbed to $1,385,706,000 — a 25% increase over the 1966 record. K mart discount department stores numbered 217, Jupiter discount stores 117, and Kresge variety stores 614.
1973	Kresge acquired Planned Marketing Associates, Inc., a Dallas, Tex., based insurance company.
1976	The Kresge Company became the second largest nonfood retailer based in the United States with fiscal year sales of $8.4 billion, a 23.8% increase over fiscal 1975.
1976	Kresge opened an unprecedented 271 K marts. The total number of stores in operation was 1,647; 1,206 were K marts.
1977	The name of the Kresge Company changed to the K mart Corporation by shareholders at the May 17 Annual Meeting. In fiscal 1976, K mart sales accounted for 94.5% of the company's domestic consolidated sales.
1980	K mart signed a licensing agreement with Daiei, the largest retailer in Japan, to develop a mass merchandising operation in Japan.
1980	Furr's Cafeterias were acquired.
1981	The 2,000th K mart store opened.
1982	The first Designer Depot specialty apparel store opened.
1983	K mart acquired Bishop Buffets.
1984	Home Centers of America (now Builders Square) and WaldenBooks were acquired.
1985	Financial and banking services were expanded. Pay Less Drug Stores were acquired.

Source: *K mart Fact Sheet*, October 29, 1984.

Figure 1-1

Opportunities as an Employee

Employment in retailing is not confined to buying and merchandising. Career opportunities with retail firms encompass such areas as advertising, public relations, credit analysis, sales forecasting, corporate planning, warehouse management, personnel management, auditing, marketing research, customer services, store design and layout, and site selection.

To a certain degree, the type of position sought should be matched with the type of retailer likely to have such a position. For example, chain stores and franchises have real-estate divisions. Department stores and chain stores have large personnel departments. Mail-order houses and catalog showrooms have large production departments.

For new college graduates, the executive training programs of larger retailers offer good learning experiences and the potential for substantial advancement. These retailers often offer careers in merchandising and nonmerchandising areas. Because department stores are a good source for first jobs, the discussion in the remainder of this section centers on their training programs and career paths.[15]

A college graduate hired by a large department store typically enters a training program (which may last from three months to a full year or more), designed to train him or her to run a merchandise department. The training program often involves on-the-job and classroom experiences. On-the-job training usually includes handling merchandise records, reordering stock, planning displays, and supervising salespeople. Classroom activities normally include learning how to evaluate vendors, analyze computer reports, forecast fashion trends, and administer store policy.

At the completion of the initial training program, the employee is designated as assistant department manager or assistant buyer. An assistant department manager or assistant buyer works under the direction of a department manager or buyer and analyzes sales, assists in purchasing goods, handles reorders, and assists in displays. The assistant department manager supervises personnel and learns store operations, whereas the assistant buyer is more involved in purchasing decisions than operations. Depending on store philosophy, either type of assistant may follow the same type of career path, or the assistant department manager may progress up the store management ladder and the assistant buyer up the buying ladder.

The responsibilities and duties of an assistant depend on the department manager's (buyer's) willingness to delegate and teach. They also depend on the autonomy given to the manager (buyer) to design and implement strategies. In a situation where the manager (buyer) has the authority to make decisions, the assistant will usually be given greater responsibility. When a store operates under a centralized management philosophy, the manager (buyer) is limited in his or her responsibilities, as is the assistant. Furthermore, the assistant will gain more experience if he or she is located in a store near a wholesale market center and can make trips to the market to buy merchandise.

The next step in the career path is to department manager or buyer. This position can be viewed as entrepreneurial, the running of a business. The manager or buyer selects merchandise, develops a promotional campaign, decides which merchandise to reorder, oversees departmental personnel, and supervises recordkeeping. In some stores, manager and buyer are synonymous terms. In others, the distinction is as explained

---

[15]See Susan Bass, "Retailing: Basic Analysis," *Standard & Poor's Industry Surveys* (January 26, 1984), Section 2, pp. R136–139, for a discussion of the training programs of Garfinckel's, Jordan Marsh, K mart, and J. C. Penney.

above for an assistant. Generally, an assistant is considered for promotion to manager or buyer after two years.

Large stores have additional levels of personnel to plan, supervise, and control merchandise departments. On the store management side, there can be group managers, store managers, vice-presidents of branches, and so on. On the buying side, there can be divisional managers, vice-presidents of merchandising, and so on.

Selected career paths at Abraham & Straus (a department store chain), J. C. Penney, Osco (a drugstore chain), and Giant Food are shown in Figures 1-2 through 1-5. At each succeeding step in these career ladders, a manager gains additional responsibility and authority.

A Career Path at Abraham & Straus

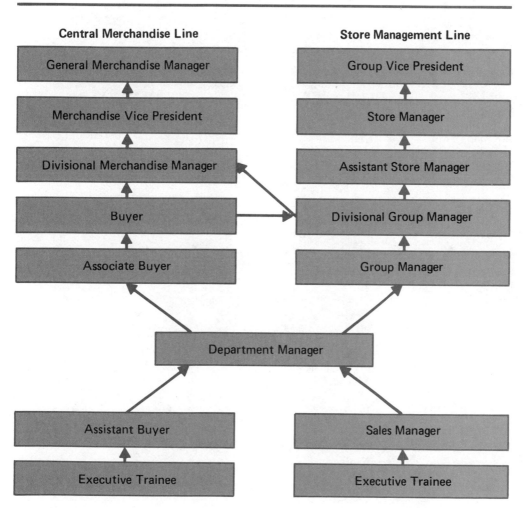

Source: *Rate Yourself as a Retail Executive* (New York: Abraham & Straus), p. 9. Reprinted by permission. Abraham & Straus is a division of Federated Stores.

Figure 1-2

A Merchandising Career Path at J.C. Penney

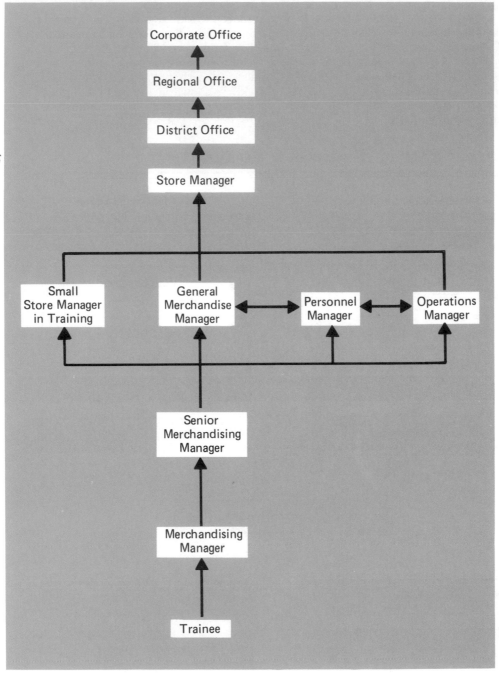

Source: *J.C. Penney Stores.* Reprinted by permission.

Figure 1-3

An Osco Drugstore Management Career Path

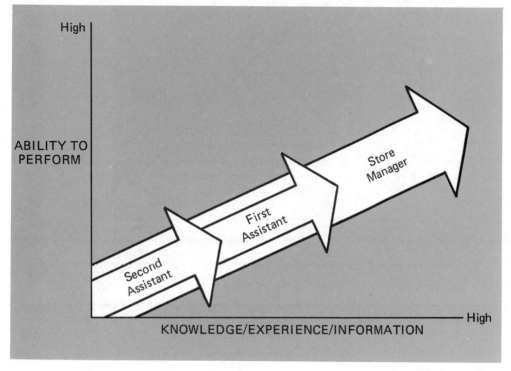

Source: *Osco Drug Career Opportunities* (a division of Jewel Companies). Reprinted by permission.

Figure 1-4

The speed of promotions, compensation levels, and maximum attainable positions depend on the abilities and ambitions of the employees at these and other large retailers. In addition, more and more retailers are looking for college graduates. See Table 1-3 for 1983 base-salary ranges for various retail positions. See also Appendix A on retail careers.

Retail Strategy in Action

A **retail strategy** is the overall plan that guides the firm. It has an influence on the retailer's business activities and his or her response to market forces, such as competition or the economy. Any retailer, regardless of size or type, can and should utilize the following principles of strategic planning:

1. Systematically evaluate one's environment to ascertain opportunities and constraints.
2. Determine competitive strengths and weaknesses.
3. Establish company objectives.
4. Develop long-range planning.
5. Implement an integrated combination of variables (such as location, product lines, displays, and pricing) to achieve objectives.

A Career Development Program at Giant Food

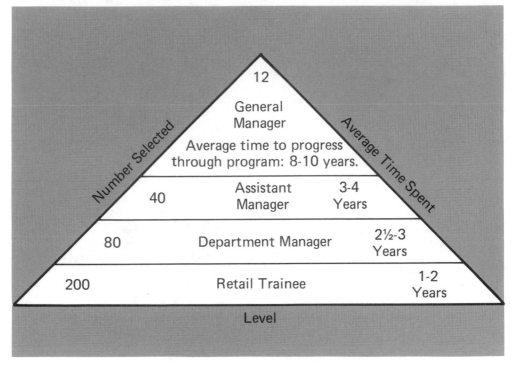

Source: *Giant Career Development Program: Steps to Future Success.* Reprinted by permission.

Figure 1-5

6. Evaluate performance and create contingency plans in the event that problems occur and objectives are not attained.

This section will examine portions of the strategic plans of Toys 'R' Us, Dayton Hudson, and Joe's Camera Store (a local camera shop). These firms have been selected because they represent diversity in retailing. They differ in size and structure and use different strategies. These retailers also illustrate the variety of career opportunities.

Toys 'R' Us: A Unique Approach to Retailing[16]

Toys 'R' Us is the nation's largest toy retailer, with 1984 sales of $1.3 billion and an estimated 11 per cent of the U. S. toy market. 1984 sales were 175 per cent above the 1980 level; and 1984 net profit as a per cent of sales was a healthy 7 per cent.

[16]Much of the material has been drawn from Subrata N. Chakravarty, "Toys 'R' Fun," *Forbes* (March 28, 1983), pp. 58, 60; Bob Davis, "Toy Sales Brisk Growth Eases but Sellers See a Record Year," *Wall Street Journal* (December 20, 1984), p. 4; Peter Kerr, "The New Game at Toys-R-Us," *New York Times* (September 4, 1983), p. F.7; Kenneth Labich, "Toys 'R' Us Moves in on Kiddie Couture," *Fortune* (November 26, 1984), p. 135; Claudia Ricci, "Children's Wear Retailers Brace for Competition from Toys 'R' Us," *Wall Street Journal* (August 25, 1983), p. 21; *Toys 'R' Us Form 10K, 1984;* and "Who Gets the Most Pay?" *Forbes* (June 4, 1984), pp. 98, 140.

Table 1-3
1983 Compensation for Established Personnel in Selected Retailing Positions

Position	Compensation Range
Assistant buyer	$14,000–$25,000+
Department sales manager	$14,000–$25,000+
Display worker	$15,000–$30,000+
Downtown store manager	$15,000–$50,000
District store manager	$15,000–$50,000
Marketing research worker	$18,000–$35,000
Suburban store manager	$20,000–$40,000+
Regional store manager	$20,000–$80,000
Director of advertising	$20,000–$100,000+
Public relations specialist	$22,000–$36,000
Buyer	$23,000–$35,000+
Divisional merchandising manager	$23,000–$80,000
Senior buyer	$25,000–$70,000+
Top personnel executive	$25,000–$75,000+
Top store manager	$25,000–$90,000
Top operations executive	$25,000–$90,000+
Top financial executive	$25,000–$100,000+
General merchandising manager	$30,000–$100,000+
Executive vice-president	$100,000–$300,000+
President	$100,000–$400,000+
Chief executive officer and chairperson	$200,000–$600,000

Sources: Updated from Harry Brown, Robert Bartlett, and Andrew Minstein, Executive Compensation Survey of the Retail Industry *(New York: National Retail Merchants Association, Personnel Division, 1977), p. 12;* Occupational Outlook Handbook, *1984–1985 Edition (Washington, D.C.: U.S. Government Printing Office, Bureau of Labor Statistics, March 1984), pp. 27–28, 194–196; "Executive Compensation Survey,"* Business Week *(May 7, 1984), pp. 110–111; Janine Linden, "Retailing: A Hard Sell Industry,"* Business Week's Guide to Careers *(December 1984– January 1985), pp. 56–58; and Susan Bass, "Retailing: Basic Analysis,"* Standard & Poor's Industry Surveys *(January 26, 1984), Section 2, pp. R136–R139.*

Charles Lazarus, the founder and current chairman of the board of Toys 'R' Us, began his career in retailing in 1948 by selling baby furniture in Washington, D.C. He soon found that customers were asking him for toys, which he began to stock; and unlike baby furniture, toys encouraged repeat store visits by customers. At that point, Lazarus devised the company's unique approach to toy retailing by developing a supermarket format with wide aisles and shopping carts. Sales grew rapidly.

In 1966, Lazarus sold Toys 'R' Us to Interstate Stores for $7.5 million in cash. However, poor management and overexpansion into discount stores forced Interstate into bankruptcy in 1974 and brought Lazarus back into control of Toys 'R' Us. He quickly returned the chain to profitability and strong growth. During the two-year period 1982–83, Lazarus' compensation exceeded $44 million, a reward for his role in the success of Toys 'R' Us.

These are some of the factors leading to the accomplishments of Toys 'R' Us:

- Although the company makes over half of its annual sales in the fourth quarter (particularly during the six weeks before Christmas), it maintains a year-round inventory of toys. In contrast, department stores shrink or eliminate the toy department directly after Christmas. As a result, Toys 'R' Us maintains a high level of customer loyalty and is able to get early indications of popular new toys.
- Toys 'R' Us stores offer customers an extensive selection by carrying 18,000 items.
- Orders are placed in February (an off-season for manufacturers) to secure better purchase terms. Normally, Toys 'R' Us has up to 12 months to pay for these purchases.
- Floor space is used effectively and efficiently. Items are arranged in stores according to blueprints; and most outlets have identical displays and layouts. This facilitates some operations and eases shopping for customers. Stores typically utilize vertical merchandising with their 16-foot ceilings and occupy 45,000 square feet of space.
- The size of Toys 'R' Us gives it delivery priority on fast-selling merchandise.
- The firm has an aggressive pricing policy, although it is not a discounter.
- A computer system logs sales item by item, store by store, and actual versus projected. Items with better than average sales performance are expanded; those with poor results are marked down.
- When adding new stores, Toys 'R' Us operates on a regional basis by opening several stores and a warehouse distribution center to serve a promising market area. This gives the company important promotion and distribution advantages.

The growth prospects for Toys 'R' Us are excellent for two major reasons. First, there are many potential locations still untapped by the firm. Toys 'R' Us is not represented in six of the top twenty U.S. retail markets. It has only recently opened outlets in Boston, Miami, and Philadelphia. The company has a file of more than 300 locations identified as future store sites and it is currently increasing its total square footage at the the rate of 18 per cent each year.

Second, Toys 'R' Us has recently entered the children's clothing market with its Kids 'R' Us discount stores. Unlike Toys 'R' Us outlets, which feature a warehouse format, Kids 'R' Us outlets are carpeted and include play areas, music videos, funhouse mirrors, and soft rock music. Kids 'R' Us stores are several times larger than most clothing discounters and have a larger selection of in-season, name-brand clothing and accessories for children up to age 12. These stores do not handle irregular or off-season merchandise, as do most off-price retailers.

Department stores are watching Kids 'R' Us carefully, since they are not pleased that it carries in-season merchandise and sells items at discount. Recently, Toys 'R' Us sued Federated Department Stores and two clothing manufacturers, alleging a conspiracy to prevent Kids 'R' Us from buying products. The suit was settled out of court, and Kids 'R' Us is not having difficulty obtaining merchandise now.

Overall, Charles Lazarus and Toys 'R' Us have done a good job of applying strategic planning principles. The initial focus of Lazarus' baby furniture company was altered to take advantage of growth opportunities, an innovative merchandising concept was enacted and refined, a modern computer system provides a lot of information for decisions, and there is a well-thought-out expansion program. The strategy of Toys 'R' Us is so effective that it dominates toy retailing and is an emerging threat to children's clothing retailers.

Dayton Hudson: A Strong Commitment to Its Customers[17]

Dayton Hudson is the fifth largest general merchandise retailer in the United States with 1983 sales of almost $7 billion. Over a 14-year period, its total number of stores rose from 100 to more than 1,000 and its retail square footage grew from 14 million to 40 million.

The company has divided its stores into four distinct categories:

- Target—an upscale discount store chain. Two-thirds of sales are from convenience-oriented durables and one-third is from fashion merchanidse.
- Mervyn's—a highly promotional, popular-priced, value-oriented department store chain. It features national-brand and private-label apparel, accessories, and household merchandise.
- Department stores—Dayton's and Hudson's. These are traditional department store chains.
- Specialty merchandise—B. Dalton Bookseller (a bookstore chain) and Lechmere (a home and leisure products store chain).

A recent one-year experiment with Plum's, a four-store upscale discount apparel chain, ended when the stores failed to meet performance goals. Said a company spokesperson, "The projected size and rate of return doesn't equal that of other expansion opportunities already available to us through Dayton Hudson's established growth companies."

Dayton Hudson's mission statement gives it a clear focus and direction as a company:

> Dayton Hudson is a diversified national retailer whose business is to serve the American consumer through the retailing of dominant assortments of merchandise that represent quality, fashion, and value.

The company's overriding objective is to be premier in every facet of its business. To achieve this objective, Dayton Hudson subscribes to the operating principles shown in Figure 1-6.

According to Dayton Hudson's chief executive, "Words like discounter, off-price, and highly promotional don't mean anything to the customer. What she cares about is value and consistency of product. You abandon that customer and you pay for it." Therefore, Dayton Hudson is intent on providing value to its customers in terms of extensive assortments, merchandise quality, shopping environment, fashion timeliness, "hassle-free" shopping, and competitive pricing.

Dayton Hudson's current five-year plan calls for a $3.3 billion expansion program. Of this amount, $1.5 billion is going to Mervyn's for 142 new stores and $1 billion is going to Target for seventy-two new stores. The department stores division is receiving only $300 million, while $500 million is allocated to B. Dalton and Lechmere. Dayton Hudson estimates that Melvyn's and Target will soon contribute 70 per cent of earnings.

---

[17]Much of the material has been drawn from *Dayton Hudson Corporation Annual Report, 1983;* M. Howard Gelfand, "Dayton Hudson Keeps Its Vision," *Advertising Age* (July 9, 1984), pp. 4, 46; Frank James, "Dayton Hudson Will End Test in Discounting," *Wall Street Journal* (February 22, 1984), p. 4; Kenneth A. Macke, "Managing Change: How Dayton Hudson Meets the Challenge," *Journal of Business Strategy*, Vol. 4 (Summer 1983), pp. 78–81; and Jeffrey A. Trachtenberg, "Never Mind the High Road," *Forbes* (December 3, 1984), pp. 174, 176–177.

Dayton Hudson's Operating Principles

1.	A return-on-investment and growth orientation guide the allocation of resources within the firm and provide a foundation for the company's financial planning.
2.	Strategic planning is viewed as an ongoing process. Managers devote one day each month to strategic issues.
3.	The firm believes in decentralized decision making. Each store group receives operating autonomy.
4.	Decision making is participatory; there is a consensus style of management.
5.	Support systems enable early detection of emerging problems.
6.	Management is rewarded based on a comparison of actual performance with company objectives.

Source: Kenneth A. Macke, "Managing Change: How Dayton Hudson Meets The Challenge," *Journal of Business Strategy*, Vol. 4 (Summer 1983), pp. 78–81.

Figure 1-6

It is clear that Dayton Hudson is committed to its customers and to ongoing strategic planning. It has distinct store groups, well-defined objectives, operating principles which view strategic planning as a continuous process, an allocation of resources based on opportunities, and a willingness to abandon a business (e.g., Plum's) when early indications are that goals will not be met.

Joe's Camera Store: Adding a One-Hour Film-Processing Service[18]

Joe's Camera Store is a full-service, independently owned camera shop that offers a good selection of cameras, slide projectors, film, film processing, and photographic accessories. The store is located in a suburban shopping center about 20 miles from a major downtown shopping district known for its discount retailers (who also engage in heavy mail-order sales).

[18]Joe's is a composite camera retailer based on material drawn from Gay Jervey, " 'Gray Market' Hits Camera, Watch Sales," *Advertising Age* (August 15, 1983), pp. 3, 62; Raymond A. Joseph, "One-Hour Photo Processors Face Bitter Fight for Survival," *Wall Street Journal* (March 12, 1984) p. 31, "One-Hour Film Processors Leave Photo Kiosks in a Blur," *Business Week* (January 23, 1984), p. 44; Lynn Reiling, "Flat Growth Causes Photofinishers to Seek New Marketing Approaches," *Marketing News* (October 12, 1984), pp. 16–17; and "Speed Is the Trend in Photo Finishing," *Newsday* (February 13, 1984), Business, pp. 1, 13.

Over the years, Joe's Camera Store has done well, in large part due to its comprehensive and integrated strategy:

- Individual attention is given to each customer. Either Joe or one of his three employees is always available to demonstrate cameras or provide advice on picture taking. According to Joe Newton, the owner, "we will never sell a camera or equipment unless the customer is sure it is the right model for him or her and understands how to use it. Customer service is crucial for us."
- A one-price policy is used; and bargaining is not encouraged nor permitted. While Joe's prices are 10 to 20 per cent higher than those charged by downtown discounters, its prices are honest and represent the full-service orientation. Joe's does not surprise customers with hidden charges (such as pricing separately for the bulb and tray in a slide projector); and the discounters are reluctant to demonstrate cameras or compare different models.
- Joe's only carries photographic equipment purchased from manufacturers' authorized distributors. Many competitors purchase imported items from unauthorized distributors overseas. The "gray market" cameras stocked by competitors are priced very low (sometimes below an authorized distributor's wholesale price); however, they usually do not have a standard warranty and will not be repaired by authorized U.S. distributors. Joe's and its distributors honor all U.S. warranties; and Joe's offers an extra one-year store warranty on all 35mm cameras and more expensive products (those over $100) at no charge.
- Joe's has a good store location. It is situated in a medium-sized shopping center anchored by a branch outlet of a major department store chain. The shopping center is off a heavily trafficked highway in a middle-class residential community. Special events, such as photography exhibits, add to the attractiveness of the center. Parking is plentiful.

About six months ago, Joe Newton did a complete analysis of his store. He determined that camera, slide projector, and related sales were continuing to rise satisfactorily. However, film and film-processing sales were not meeting expectations. Joe was concerned about this for several reasons. First, film and film processing represent about 20 per cent of total store sales and almost 25 per cent of store profits. Second, film and film-processing sales are necessary for Joe's to generate adequate traffic into the store; once in the store, consumers frequently buy batteries, camera cases, extra lenses, and so on, and see displays for new models. Third, Joe's uses customer names on film-processing receipts to develop a mailing list for advertisements and promotions, and to study the store's trading area.

After much thought and discussions with customers, Joe's decided to enter the one-hour film-processing business. According to industry reports, one-hour-processing sales are growing 25 per cent annually compared with 10 per cent for regular film processing. Furthermore, since the large pharmacy in its shopping center recently introduced one-hour film processing, Joe's views this as a defensive measure. Newton is convinced people would rather have their film processed in a camera store than in a store unrelated to the camera business.

Joe's acquired a Kis S.A. one-hour film-processing machine for $32,900. This machine requires only 25 square feet of space and is one-tenth the size of traditional machines. It can process 50 to 60 rolls of film per day. By charging $7.50 per 24-exposure roll of film, Joe's earns a gross profit of $5.80 per roll (chemicals and paper cost $1.70). Joe's estimates that it will process an average of 9,000 rolls each year, about 35 rolls per day. This will yield an annual gross profit of $52,200 and enable the machine to be paid off within eight months.

After several months, the new film-processing service is performing as expected. Film and film-processing sales are up (Joe's continues to offer regular processing for those customers desiring it, in addition to the one-hour service). Customer store traffic has improved.

By examining the procedures followed by Joe's Camera Store, it should be evident that strategic planning in retailing is equally applicable to small retailers and those with a service orientation. Joe Newton systematically evaluates his environment, employs an integrated approach (including outlining his competitive advantages), understands that his business includes both goods (cameras) and services (film processing), regularly surveys customers, and is willing to respond to competition.

The Marketing Concept Applied to Retailing

Each of the firms described here has shown a willingness to adjust its retail strategy in response to consumer preferences. Toys 'R' Us carefully monitors sales to determine fast-selling toys and has opened Kids 'R' Us to take advantage of growth opportunities. Dayton Hudson's plans are based on providing value—as defined by its customers. Joe's Camera Store offers a range of services for its customers and encourages a dialogue with them.

In addition to a customer orientation, each of the companies utilizes a coordinated, companywide approach to strategy development and implementation and expresses a profit orientation. These three principles form the marketing concept, a notion first introduced by the General Electric Company.

The marketing concept can be transformed into the retailing concept and should be understood and used by all retailers. The **retailing concept** has these elements:

1. Customer orientation—A retailer must determine the characteristics and needs of customers.
2. Coordinated effort—A retailer must integrate all plans and activities to maximize efficiency.
3. Profit orientation—A retailer must strive to generate sales while attaining acceptable profits.

Unfortunately, the retailing concept is not understood and used by all retailers. Many are indifferent to customer needs, plan haphazardly, and increase sales at the expense of profits. Too often, retailers are not receptive to change or new customer services are ignored by retailers, or one retailer initiates a new strategy and competitors blindly follow. Some retailers do not research their customers but rely on the reports of vendors or their own past sales.

A retailer is able to adopt the retailing concept fairly easily. Customer characteristics and needs are researched. Integrated short-run and long-run plans are developed. Changes in customers, the economy, competition, and so on are monitored. Plans are based on profitability, rather than on sales expansion or stability.

The retailing concept is a guide to company strategy. It does not deal with a firm's internal capabilities or competitive advantages but offers a broad framework for planning.

Description of the Format of the Text

There are various approaches to the study of retailing: a functional approach, which focuses on the activities retailers must perform (such as buying, pricing, personnel practices); an institutional approach, which describes the various types of retail establishments and their development; and a strategic approach, which concentrates on planning to meet objectives and satisfy the retailing concept.

This book will study retailing from each perspective, but it focuses on the **strategic approach.** The underlying principle is that a retail firm needs to plan and revise its plans continually in order to adapt to a changing environment. Environmental opportunities and constraints must be considered. Strategic management constantly forces a retailer to evaluate competition, economic factors, changes in customers, legal restrictions, and so on. A retailer will succeed when his or her competitive strengths are matched with the opportunities presented in the environment.

A strategic analysis of retailing has three major advantages over a functional or institutional format:

1. The strategic approach views retailing from a dynamic perspective. The emphasis on a changing retail environment (and the necessary shifts in strategy to succeed in the new environment) shows the importance of monitoring it.
2. The strategic approach highlights the idea that a retailer's environment offers opportunities and constraints.
3. The strategic approach focuses on planning for the future as well as analyzing the past.

Chapters 2 through 4 form the foundation for the remainder of the book. Chapter 2 outlines the construction of a retail strategy based on the retailing concept and a firm's resources. Chapters 3 and 4 identify the various types of retail institutions and discuss their development, from a strategic perspective.

An Introduction to Retailing: A Summary

Retailing, the business activities involving the sale of goods and services to the final consumer, is a significant field to study. It has many special characteristics (low average sales, unplanned purchases, and customer visits to a store). The impact of retailing on the economy is quite powerful. Retailing performs many distribution functions, especially gathering assortments and selling small quantities. There are special relationships with suppliers.

There are many career opportunities, either as an owner or as an employee. The potential for advancement (promotion and salary) is substantial. Many large retailers have extensive management training programs, which are open to college graduates.

To be successful, a retailer must use strategic planning. Several examples of successful strategies have been presented. All retailers should understand and implement the retailing concept (customer orientation, integrated effort, and profit orientation) in conjunction with their strategies.

Retailing can be studied from a functional, institutional, or strategic perspective. The strategic approach to retailing (planning to meet objectives) forms the basis for this book.

Questions for Discussion

1. Explain the key elements in the definition of retailing.
2. Show how the special characteristics of retailing offer unique opportunities and problems for retailers. Why do impulse purchases present an opportunity as well as a problem?
3. What are three statistics that show the importance of retailing in the U.S. economy?
4. Describe the sorting process from the manufacturer's perspective. From the retailer's perspective.
5. Explain how an optician would gather a stock of lenses, frames, eyeglass cases, and so on. What services are the customers given?
6. What aspects of retailing would it be important for a cash register manufacturer to learn? Why?
7. Comment on the statement that "A retailer is not interested in pushing one brand over another, because this does not increase overall business."
8. Evaluate Phillips–Van Heusen's practice of discouraging retailers from reselling its apparel to discounters by running ads stating "If you cheapen our brand, we won't sell to you."
9. List five retail employment careers aside from buying and merchandising.
10. Describe the responsibilities of an assistant buyer.
11. Name the broad elements of strategic planning. Show how a person desiring to start a small business can employ strategic planning.
12. What are the common factors in the strategies of Toys 'R' Us and Joe's Camera Store?
13. Define the retailing concept. Apply it to a neighborhood dry cleaner.
14. Differentiate among the following approaches to the study of retailing:
    a. Functional
    b. Institutional
    c. Strategic

Appendix on How to Solve a Case Study

The information contained in this appendix is intended to give the reader some insights into the analysis of case studies. A case study is a collection of facts and data based on a real or hypothetical problem-oriented business situation.

The objective of a case study is to develop one's ability in the solving of complex business problems, using a logical framework. The problems within a case are generally not unique to a specific individual, company, or industry, and they frequently deal with more than one element of a retail strategy. Sometimes the material presented within a case can be in conflict. For example, two managers can disagree about a strategy; statistics can be contradictory; or there can be several interpretations of the same information.

In all case studies, the reader must analyze the material presented and state which specific actions best resolve the major issues or problems present. These actions must reflect the information contained in the case and the environment facing the firm.

Steps in Solving a Case Study

Retailing case studies revolve around the identification of problems and the presentation and evaluation of proposed solutions. Any analysis of a case study must include the following sequential steps:

1. Presentation of the facts surrounding the case.
2. Identification of the problem(s).
3. Listing of alternative solutions to the problem(s).
4. Evaluation of alternative solutions.
5. Recommendation of the best solution.

23

Presentation of the Facts Surrounding the Case

It is helpful to read the case several times until one is familiar with the information contained therein. Rereadings often aid the reader to understand facts, possible strategies, or questions that need clarification that were not apparent earlier. It is important to pay particular attention to exhibits, tables, charts, and diagrams. Often data can reveal vital information when translated into percentages or compared with prior years.

In answering the case, the reader should assume that he or she is a retailing consultant hired by the company. Although facts and figures should be accepted as true, statements, judgments, and decisions made by the individuals in the case should be questioned, especially when not supported by facts or figures—or when one individual disagrees with another.

During the first and subsequent readings of the case, the reader should

- Underline important facts.
- Interpret all figures and charts.
- Question comments made by individuals.
- Judge the rationality of past and current decisions.
- Develop a list of questions whose answers would be useful in resolving the retailer's problem(s).

Identification of the Problem(s)

Many times, the facts surrounding a case point out problems such as a decline in market share, poor profitability, excess inventories, and increased bad debts. As a retailing consultant, the reader must identify the major cause(s) of the problem(s) and substantiate them using the material contained in the case. In some instances, the analyst must delve deeply because the key problem(s) and their causes may not be immediately evident.

Listing of Alternative Solutions to the Problem(s)

Next, alternative solutions to the specific key and peripheral retail problems, defined in the previous step, are stated. These solutions are examined on the basis of appropriateness to the company and the situation. Thus, an advertising strategy for a small mail-order retailer would not be appropriate for a large retailer operating exclusively in planned shopping centers.

Solutions should take into account factors such as

- Product or service category.
- Objectives.
- Target market.
- Overall strategy.
- Product assortment.
- Competition.
- Legal restrictions.
- Financial capabilities.
- Personnel capabilities.
- Sources of supply.

Evaluation of Alternative Solutions

Each proposed solution must be evaluated, based on the facts surrounding the case, the key problems, and the environment of the firm. Specific criteria should be used, and each alternative should be analyzed on the basis of these criteria. The ramifications and risks associated with each solution should also be considered. Important information and statistics not included in the case should be mentioned.

Recommendation of the Best Solution

The solution to the case should not be a summary of the case. The analysis will be critiqued on the extent to which it shows an understanding of the dynamics of the problem rather than on which specific solution is chosen.

Be precise about which alternative is most desirable for the retailer in his or her current context. Remember that the objective of case study analysis is the learning of a logical reasoning process applied to retailing. A written report must demonstrate this process.

2

Retail Strategy: Owning or Managing a Business

Chapter Objectives

1. To define retail strategy and show its importance
2. To explain the elements of a retail strategy: situation analysis, objectives, identification of consumer characteristics and needs, overall strategy, specific activities, control, and feedback
3. To consider retail strategy as a series of integrated steps
4. To enumerate the controllable and uncontrollable variables involved in retail strategy
5. To examine retail strategic planning in a variety of situations

Lucky Stores, based in Dublin, California, is one of the leading retailers in the United States, with annual sales of about $8.5 billion. While Lucky operates department stores and apparel, automotive, and fabric specialty stores, its food stores account for two-thirds of sales volume.

Like more and more retailers, Lucky is now placing greater emphasis on strategic planning to guide the firm:

> Lucky is committed to strategic and long-term planning in all segments of our business. The ability to make informed strategic decisions about Corporate policy and objectives, competitive positioning, resource allocation, and asset redeployment allows the Company to establish a clear direction for the future. Strategic planning helps ensure that current operating decisions are consistent with our long-term direction.
>
> Each year, the Company goes through a planning process that reconfirms our strategy and long-range plans, and gives direction to our implementation planning for the coming year. This annual review is necessary because of rapid changes in customer desires and competitive situations.

Strategic planning and our planning process do not eliminate business risk, but they do enable the Company to understand risk and select from a variety of options the most appropriate alternatives for the future. This in turn allows management to take actions that have the greatest probability of maintaining a superior level of return for our shareholders.[1]

Overview

Retail strategy is defined as an overall plan or framework of action for a retail establishment. Ideally this plan will be at least one year in duration and will outline the philosophy, objectives, consumer market, overall and specific activities, and control mechanisms of the retailer over the length of the plan. Without a predefined and well-integrated strategy, the firm may flounder and be unable to cope with the environment that surrounds it.

A retail strategy has several attractive features. First, it provides a thorough analysis of the requirements for different types of retailing. Second, it outlines the objectives of the retailer. Third, a firm is shown how it can differentiate itself from competitors and develop an offering that appeals to a group of customers. Fourth, the retailer is forced to study the legal, economic, and competitive environments. Fifth, the total efforts of the company are coordinated. Sixth, crises are anticipated and often avoided.

Strategic planning can be conducted by the owner of the firm, by professional management, or a combination of the two. When one moves up a retail career ladder, a key measure of performance and advancement potential is whether increased planning responsibility is undertaken and how well it is completed.

It is important to note that the steps in a retail strategy are interdependent, and often a firm will start off with a general plan that will become more specific as alternatives, payoffs, and so on become clearer. In this chapter we concentrate on the development of a comprehensive, integrated retail strategy, as shown in Figure 2-1.[2]

Situation Analysis

Situation analysis is the objective evaluation of the opportunities and potential problems facing a retailer. It seeks to answer two general questions: Where is the retailer now? In what direction should the retailer be headed? To a retailer, situation analysis means defining a philosophy of business, outlining (in broad terms) the product or service category to be sold, and evaluating ownership alternatives.

Philosophy of Business

A **philosophy of business** is a firm's understanding of its role in the business system; it is reflected in general attitudes toward consumers, employees, competitors, govern-

---

[1] *Lucky Stores Corporate Profile 1984*, p. 16. See also "Lucky: Shooting for a New Service Niche," *Progressive Grocer* (October 1984), p. 42.
[2] For interesting articles on retail strategy planning, see Bert Rosenbloom, "Strategic Planning in Retailing: Prospects and Problems," *Journal of Retailing*, Vol. 56 (Spring 1980), pp. 107–120; Robert F. Lusch and Michael G. Harvey, "A Framework for Retail Planning," *Business*, Vol. 33 (October–December 1983), pp. 20–26; and Isadore Barmash, "How They Plan," *Stores* (September 1983), pp. 7–15.

Development of a Retail Strategy

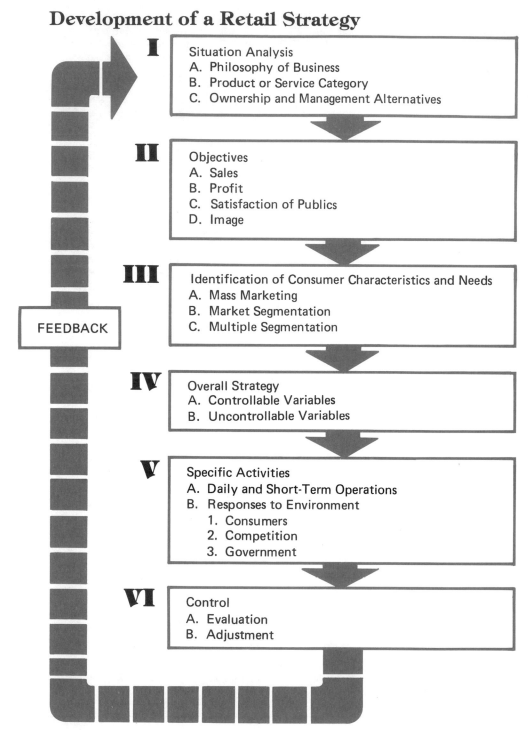

I Situation Analysis
A. Philosophy of Business
B. Product or Service Category
C. Ownership and Management Alternatives

II Objectives
A. Sales
B. Profit
C. Satisfaction of Publics
D. Image

III Identification of Consumer Characteristics and Needs
A. Mass Marketing
B. Market Segmentation
C. Multiple Segmentation

IV Overall Strategy
A. Controllable Variables
B. Uncontrollable Variables

V Specific Activities
A. Daily and Short-Term Operations
B. Responses to Environment
   1. Consumers
   2. Competition
   3. Government

VI Control
A. Evaluation
B. Adjustment

FEEDBACK

Figure 2-1

ment, and others. A philosophy of business enables the retailer to create a consumer following and distinguish itself from competitors.

For example, McDonald's philosophy of business is based on providing budget-conscious families with high-quality food, quick service, clean surroundings, and a wholesome environment. Sears' philosophy is reflected in its slogan: "There's more for your life at Sears." As the world's largest retailer, Sears attracts middle-class consumers to its extensive offerings of products and services, and it is establishing several hundred "stores of the future." Avis, in recognition of its second-place ranking in the automobile rental market, coined a slogan that summarizes its philosophy: "We try harder." Figure 2-2 shows the "principles of doing business" of Lands' End, a large mail-order retailer.

principles of doing business.

Principle 1.

We do everything we can to make our products better. We improve material, and add back features and construction details that others have taken out over the years. We never reduce the quality of a product to make it cheaper.

Principle 2.

We price our products fairly and honestly. We do not, have not, and will not participate in the common retailing practice of inflating markups to set up a future phony "sale."

Principle 3.

We accept any return, for any reason, at any time. Our products are guaranteed. No fine print. No arguments. We mean exactly what we say: GUARANTEED. PERIOD.

Principle 4.

We ship faster than anyone we know of. We ship items in stock the day after we receive the order. At the height of the last Christmas season the longest time an order was in the house was 36 hours, excepting monograms which took another 12 hours.

Principle 5.

We believe that what is best for our customer is best for all of us. Everyone here understands that concept. Our sales and service people are trained to know our products, and to be friendly and helpful. They are urged to take all the time necessary to take care of you. We even pay for your call, for whatever reason you call.

Gary Comer, President

Principle 6.

We are able to sell at lower prices because we have eliminated middlemen; because we don't buy branded merchandise with high protected markups; and because we have placed our contracts with manufacturers who have proved that they are cost conscious and efficient.

Principle 7.

We are able to sell at lower prices because we operate efficiently. Our people are hard working, intelligent and share in the success of the company.

Principle 8.

We are able to sell at lower prices because we support no fancy emporiums with their high overhead. Our main location is in the middle of a 40-acre cornfield in rural Wisconsin. We still operate our first location in Chicago's Near North tannery district.

Reprinted by permission.

Figure 2-2

A firm's philosophy is a long-term commitment to a type of business and a place in the market. One major decision a retailer must make is whether to organize around a physical product or service or according to consumer needs. For example, a retailer entering the lumber business must decide whether to stock a line of bathroom vanities along with raw lumber products. Probably, this retailer would determine not to carry the vanities because they are unconnected with the perceived business. However, a retailer who views the lumberyard as a do-it-yourself home-improvement center would see the bathroom vanities as a natural extension of business.

In the first case, the retailer has a product- or service-oriented philosophy of business. The retailer in the second instance has a philosophy of satisfying a certain type of consumer (the do-it-yourselfer). This store will carry any merchandise that the consumer, not the storekeeper, desires. A retailer must consider his or her philosophy and his or her reasons for entering business and examine the alternative approaches available.

Although the development of a philosophy is the first step in a retailer's planning process, it should be noted that this process is continually reviewed and adjusted to reflect changing company objectives and a dynamic retail environment.

Product or Service Category

Before a prospective retailer is able to design a well-defined marketing plan, he or she must determine the product and/or service category that the firm will sell. Figure 2-3 shows the diversity of product and service categories from which a retailer can choose.

The potential retailer should select a type of business that will allow him or her to match personal abilities, financial resources, and time resources with those required by the business.

Personal abilities depend on an individual's aptitudes—the preference for a type of business and the potential to do well; education—formal learning about retail practices and policies; and experience—practical learning about retail practices and policies.

A retailer must have an aptitude for the business he or she chooses to enter. For example, the retailer who wants to run his or her own store, who likes to use initiative, and who has the ability to react quickly to competitive developments will be suited for a different type of situation than the retailer who depends on others for advice and does not like to make decisions. The first retailer should enter business as an independent operator, in a dynamic business such as fashion; the second retailer should look for partners or a franchise and a business that is relatively static, like a car wash. In addition, some retailers enjoy close personal interaction with their customers; these would dislike the impersonality of a pure discount or self-service operation. Still, others enjoy the impersonality of mail-order retailing. These illustrations show the importance of aptitude in the selection of a type of business.

Education and experience requirements are clearly specified in certain fields and are enforced by federal or state laws. Insurance brokers, stockbrokers, real-estate brokers, barbers, beauticians, certified public accountants, pharmacists, and opticians represent a good cross section of the kinds of retailers who must satisfy minimum educational and/or experience standards. Professional competency must be demonstrated. For instance, a real-estate broker must be licensed. This licensing involves an analysis of the individual's ethical character, as well as an examination of the person's knowledge of real-estate practice and law. (However, designation as a broker does not depend on the ability to sell, keep good financial records, or negotiate with buyers and sellers.)

Selected Kinds of Retail Product and Service Establishments

Product Establishments

Durable Goods Stores

Automotive group
   Motor vehicle dealers
   Auto supply stores
Furniture and appliance group
   Furniture and home furnishing stores
   Household appliance and radio-TV
   stores
Lumber, building, and hardware group
   Lumber and building materials dealers
   Hardware stores
Jewelry stores

Nondurable Goods Stores

Apparel group
   Men's and boys' wear stores
   Women's apparel and accessory stores
   Shoe stores
Food group
   Grocery stores
General merchandise group with non-
  stores
   Department stores
   Variety stores
   Mail order
Eating and drinking places
Gasoline service stations
Drug and proprietary stores
Liquor stores

Service Establishments

Amusement Services

   Motion picture theaters
   Orchestras and entertainers
   Bowling, pool, billiards
   Dance halls, studios, schools
   Clubs, baseball
   Clubs, football
   Racing, automobile
   Racing, dog
   Racing, horses
   Golf courses, public
   Skating rinks
   Amusement parks
   Carnivals and circuses
   Fairs
   Coin-operated amusement devices

Hotel Services

   Hotels
   Motels, motor hotels
   Trailer parks
   Camps, recreational

Personal Services

   Laundries and dry cleaning
   Beauty shops
   Barber shops
   Photographic studios
   Shoe shine, shoe repair, and hat cleaning
   Funeral services, crematories

Repair Services

   Automobile repair
   Automobile parking
   Truck, car, trailer rental
   Car wash
   Radio-television appliances
   Other electrical appliances
   Furniture
   Watch and jewelry
   Welding

Source: *Census of Business.*

Figure 2-3

Some skills can be learned through education and/or experience; other skills are inborn. Potential retailers must be able to examine their personal skills and match them with the requirements of a business. This is a difficult process that involves insight into oneself and careful, honest reflection. Strengths and weaknesses must be assessed and evaluated in this matching process. Partnerships may arise when two or more parties possess complementary skills. A person with extensive selling experience and ability will often join someone possessing the operational skills necessary to open a store. Each partner has valuable skills but cannot operate the store without the expertise of the other.

A second major consideration in the selection of a product or service category for a retail business is the level of **financial resources** required. Many enterprises, especially new, independent ones, fail because the owners do not correctly estimate the financial resources needed to succeed. Figure 2-4 outlines some of the financial investments for a new retail venture.

Financial Investments for a New Retail Venture

Use of Funds	Source of Funds
Land and Building (lease or purchase)	Personal savings, bank loan, commercial finance company
Inventory	Personal savings, manufacturer credit, commercial finance company, sales revenues
Fixtures (including: display cases, storage facilities, signs, lighting, carpeting, etc.)	Personal savings, manufacturer credit, bank loan, commercial finance company
Equipment (including: cash register, marking machine, office equipment, computers, etc.)	Personal savings, manufacturer credit, bank loan, commercial finance company
Personnel (including: salespersons, cashiers, stockpersons, etc.)	Personal savings, bank loan, sales revenues
Promotion	Personal savings, sales revenues
Personal Drawing Account	Personal savings, life insurance loan

Miscellaneous:
   Equipment Repair
   Credit Sales (bad debts)
   Professional Services
   Repayment of Loans
	Personal savings, manufacturer and wholesaler credit, bank credit plan, bank loan, commercial finance company

Figure 2-4

Table 2-1
Financial Requirements for a Used-Car Dealer

Total investments (first year)	
Lease (10 years, $35,000 per year)	$ 35,000
Beginning inventory (fifty cars, average cost of $4,000)	200,000
Replacement inventory (fifty cars, average cost of $4,000)*	200,000
Fixtures and equipment (includes painting, paneling, carpeting, lighting, signs, heating and air-conditioning system, electronic cash register, service bay)	20,000
Replacement parts	10,000
Personnel (one mechanic)	24,000
Promotion (brochures and newspaper advertising)	12,000
Drawing account (to cover owner's personal expenses for one year; all selling and operating functions except mechanical ones performed by the owner)	25,000
Accountant	4,000
Miscellaneous (including loan payments)	60,000
Profit (projected)	10,000
	$600,000
Source of funds	
Personal savings	$100,000
Bank loan	150,000
Sales revenues (based on expected sales of fifty cars, average price of $7,000)	350,000
	$600,000

*Assumes that fifty cars are sold during the year. As each type of car is sold, a replacement is bought by the dealer and placed into inventory. At the end of the year, inventory on hand remains at fifty units.

New retailers frequently underestimate the needs for a drawing account, shown in Figure 2-4. This drawing account is used for the personal needs of the retailer and his or her family during the early, unprofitable stage of a business. Housing, clothing, food, medical, and other personal expenses are paid from this account. Because very few new retail stores are immediately profitable, the budget for the venture must include personal expenditures.

The costs of renovating an existing facility are also often underestimated by the new retailer. It is common for undercapitalized (low on funds) retailers to invest initially in only essential renovations. Other improvements are made when the firm is prospering, and the costs for these alterations are paid out of profits. Although this practice does reduce the initial investment, it can give the store a poor image.

Merchandise width and depth of assortment, as well as the types of products sold, have an impact on the financial outlay required of a new retailer. The use of a partnership or a franchise agreement will also have an effect on the initial investment.

Table 2-1 provides a description of the financial resources and requirements of a hypothetical used-car dealer. Table 2-2 shows inventory costs and revenues for this retailer.[3]

[3]For an in-depth look at how used-car dealers apply retail strategies, see Francis C. Brown III, "Independent Used-Car Dealers Are Trying New Ways to Respond to Stiff Competition," *Wall Street Journal* (August 14, 1984), p. 33.

Table 2-2
Analysis of Beginning Inventory Costs and Expected First Year Sales Revenues by Type of Car for a Used-Car Dealer

Type of Car	Number of Cars In Beginning Inventory	Average Cost	Average Selling Price	Total Cost of Beginning Inventory	Annual Total Revenue*
Subcompact	10	$2,500	$ 4,375	$ 25,000	$ 43,750
Compact	14	3,500	6,125	49,000	85,750
Intermediate	15	4,500	7,875	67,500	118,125
Full-size/luxury	6	6,000	10,500	36,000	63,000
Station wagon/van	5	4,500	7,875	22,500	39,375
	50	$4,000	$ 7,000	$200,000	$350,000

*Fifty cars are sold during the year. As each type of car is sold, a replacement is bought by the dealer and placed into inventory. At the end of the year, inventory on hand remains at fifty units.

The initial personal savings investment of $100,000 required to enter this type of business would force many potential retailers to rethink the choice of product category as well as the intended format of the retail organization. First, the plans for a fifty car inventory reflect the entrepreneur's desire to have a balanced product line. However, if the dealer described in Tables 2-1 and 2-2 concentrates on subcompact, compact, and intermediate cars, he or she can become more specialized and be able to reduce significantly the size of the inventory. This would lead to lower investment costs. Second, the entering used-car dealer can also reduce the initial investment by seeking a location that has facilities that do not have to be modified—for example, the site of another used-car dealer. Third, fewer financial resources are needed if the dealer enters into a partnership, which would allow the costs (as well as the profits) to be shared.

The **time demands** on retail entrepreneurs differ significantly by product or service category. Customer groups require varying amounts of service, and the time required of the entrepreneur will be influenced by his or her ability to delegate activities to others.

A firm such as a major appliance store must be open during evening hours because appliance purchases are usually made jointly by the husband and the wife (evening hours being convenient for these types of customers). The mom-and-pop grocery store or a convenience food store sells its greatest volume when supermarkets are closed; therefore evening and weekend hours must be maintained. Gift shops, sporting goods stores, house painters, and others have extreme seasonal shifts in business and are forced to keep long hours during the prime seasons. On the other hand, mail-order firms (which can process orders during any part of the day) have much more flexible hours.

The ability or inability of a retailer to delegate duties also affects the number of hours worked. Some types of businesses are organized on the basis of involvement by the owner. These include coin-operated laundromats, hotels and motels, and car rental agencies. The emphasis on advertising, extensive financial controls, and self-service allows these retailers to minimize their time investments. Other types of businesses require the active involvement of the owners. Beauty parlors, barber shops, butcher shops, luncheonettes, and jewelry stores are examples of time-consuming businesses.

Intensive owner participation can be caused by several factors. First, the owner may be the major worker, and consumers are attracted by his or her skills (the major competitive advantage of the store). In this case, the delegation of work to others will diminish consumer loyalty. Associated with this aspect is the personal service that only an owner can give to certain customers. Second, many smaller stores are undercapitalized. Therefore, the owner and his or her family must operate the store because there are insufficient funds to hire employees. Third, a business that operates on a cash basis and has weak financial controls requires the owner to be on the premises to avoid being cheated. In a small store with poor inventory procedures, it is difficult to match sales with reductions in inventory levels. Therefore, it is easy for employees to pocket cash sales if not watched by the owner.

A common error is to assume that the retailer works only when the store is open. For many retailers, off-hours activities are necessary. A butcher must go to the meat wholesaler at least once a week to make purchases. (Meat wholesalers are busiest between 3 and 6 A.M.) In a luncheonette, foods must be prepared before the store opens. The jeweler specializing in diamonds must go to the city's diamond exchange to examine and negotiate for merchandise. An antique dealer often spends weekdays hunting for goods. The small storekeeper sweeps, stocks shelves, and does the books during the hours the store is closed.

The prospective retailer should examine his or her own time preferences in terms of stability versus seasonality (some would rather work 40 hours per week for 48 weeks a year; others would rather work 80 hours per week for 24 weeks a year and relax the balance of the year); ideal working hours (days and times); and the level of personal involvement (absentee ownership or on-site management).

Table 2-3 presents a profile of the small business entrepreneur, based on a number

Table 2-3
A Profile of the Small Business Entrepreneur

Characteristics

50% have parents who owned a business.
35% were age 30 or less when they started their first ownership venture.
35% have a college degree or more.
About two-thirds had at least three full-time jobs before setting up their own business.
About one-third operate businesses that handle products/services that are different from
 their prior work experiences.
60% deal with customers similar to those from their prior work experiences.
Almost three-fourths supervised employees prior to beginning their own businesses.
More than a third devote at least 11 hours a day to their businesses.
85% are married.

Attitudes

91% would still choose to own a business if they were starting over.
18% would recommend that their children go into their business.
54% view their accountant as the most valuable outside source of information.
55% believe that work experience is the best preparation for ownership.
70% feel that the the entrepreneurial spirit in the United States has declined or remained
 the same in recent years.
80% experience stress related to work.
89% are optimistic.

Sources: Arnold C. Cooper, "Entrepreneurship: Starting a New Business," National Federation of Independent Business Research and Education Foundation, 1983; and Small Business Speaks: The Chemical Bank Report (New York: Chemical Bank, 1983).

of characteristics. The data in this table are derived from two studies that together surveyed almost 3,000 owners.[4]

Ownership and Management Alternatives

A very important part of situation analysis is the assessment of ownership and management alternatives. Ownership decisions include whether to operate as a sole proprietorship, partnership, or corporation as well as determining whether to start a new business, buy an existing business, or become a franchisee. Management alternatives include owner-manager versus professional manager and centralized versus decentralized structures.

A **sole proprietorship** is an unincorporated retail firm owned by one person. All benefits, profits, risks, and costs accrue to the single owner. A **partnership** is an unincorporated retail firm owned by two or more persons, each of whom has a financial interest. The partners share benefits, profits, risks, and costs. A **corporation** is a retail firm that is formally incorporated under state laws. It is established as a legal entity separate from the individual stockholders. The advantages and disadvantages of these ownership forms are summarized in Figure 2-5.

Starting a new business offers a retailer flexibility in location, operations, product lines, and consumer markets. It may also mean construction or renovation costs, time lags until the business is ready to open, and establishing an inventory of goods. Buying an existing business enables a retailer to acquire an established location and customer following. It also means that the strategy will be less flexible. Becoming a franchisee allows a retailer to combine independent ownership with cooperative advertising, franchisor management assistance, thorough strategy planning, and a well-known company name. On the other hand, it means very rigid operational restrictions. A thorough discussion of franchising appears in Chapter 3. Figure 2-6 shows the attributes of these purchase forms; and Figure 2-7 provides a checklist of questions to consider when purchasing an existing retail business.[5]

Strategically, the management format chosen has an additional impact on decision making. With an owner-manager system, planning tends to be less formal and more intuitive, and many functions tend to be reserved for the owner-manager (such as employee supervision). With a professional manager system, planning tends to be more formal and systematic. However, the professional manager is usually more constrained in his or her authority than the owner-manager. In a centralized structure, decision-making authority is limited to top management or ownership; in a decentralized structure, managers in individual departments have major input into decisions. Regardless of management format, a retailer is best able to develop and enact a successful strategy only if there is ample information and communication.

[4]See also David E. Gumpert and David P. Boyd, "The Loneliness of the Small-Business Owner," *Harvard Business Review*, Vol. 62 (November–December 1984), pp. 18–24.

[5]For more information on retail ownership, see John H. Hand and William P. Lloyd, "Determining the Value of a Small Business," *MSU Business Topics*, Vol. 28 (Summer 1980), pp. 5–10; Isadore Barmash, "Opportunity," *Stores* (June 1981), pp. 11–20; Sanford L. Jacobs, " 'Unrealistic Expectations' Pose Problems for Sellers of Firms," *Wall Street Journal* (August 20, 1984), p. 17; and Sanford L. Jacobs, "Partnerships Are Easy to Start but Not Easy to Keep Going," *Wall Street Journal* (April 15, 1985), p. 31.

Retail Ownership Forms

	Sole Proprietorship	Partnership	Corporation
Advantages	Simple to form Control by single owner Flexible operations Easiest to dissolve Single taxation	Shared responsibility and costs Expertise of two or more owners Greater capability to raise funds Simpler to form than corporation Single taxation	Greatest capacity for raising funds through sale of stock Claims of creditors cannot be made against individuals Easy to transfer ownership Long-term legal existence Greatest use of professional management Clearcut operating authority with corporate officers
Disadvantages	Personal liability of owner Limited capital Limited expertise	Personal liability of owners Dissolving of partnership upon death of a partner or a disagreement Actions of one partner bind all partners Less ability to raise capital than corporation	Double taxation (corporation and dividends) Increased government regulation Complexity and costs of establishing a corporation Depersonalization Separation of ownership and management

Figure 2-5

Alternatives in Purchasing a Retail Business

	Starting a New Business	Buying an Existing Business	Becoming a Franchisee
Advantages	Flexibility in selecting product lines, customers, store location, etc.	Established name, customer following, building and fixtures, and personnel staff	Established name and customer following
	Tailored to owner's desires and strengths	Ongoing sales	Management training
		Immediacy	Site selection by franchisor
		Possible financing from seller at favorable interest rates	Cooperative advertising and buying
			Regional or national image
Disadvantages	Start-up costs	Older fixtures	Contractual agreements limiting product lines and specifying operations
	Time lag before opening	Inflexibility of building and personnel	
	Time until profitability	Possibility of saturated market	Possibility of termination by franchisor
	No established name and following		Tying agreements with franchisor
	No established supplier realtionships		

Figure 2-6

Objectives

After situation analysis, the objectives of a firm are developed. **Objectives** are the goals, long-run and short-run, that a retailer hopes to attain. The statement of clear objectives helps to mold a strategy and translate the company philosophy into action. A retailer may be concerned with one or more of the following objectives: sales (including growth, stability, market share); profit (including level, return on investment, efficiency); satisfaction of publics (including stockholders and consumers); and image (including customer and industry perceptions). Each of these objectives is sought by many retailers. Some retailers attempt to achieve all of the objectives; most select a few and attempt to achieve these well.

A Checklist for Purchasing a Retail Business

These questions should be considered when purchasing an existing retail business:

1. Why is the seller placing the business up for sale?

2. How much are you paying for goodwill (The cost of the business above its tangible asset value)?

3. Have sales, inventory levels, and profit figures been confirmed by your accountant?

4. Will the seller introduce you to his/her customers and stay on during the transition period?

5. Will the seller sign a statement that he/she will not open a directly-competing business in the same trading area for a reasonable time period?

6. If sales are seasonal, are you purchasing the business at the right time of year?

7. In the purchase of the business, are you assuming existing debts of the seller?

8. Who receives proceeds from transactions made prior to the sale of the business but not yet paid by creditors?

9. What is the length of the lease if property is rented?

10. If property is to be purchased along with the business, has it been inspected by a professional engineer?

11. How modern are the storefront and store fixtures?

12. Is inventory fresh? Does it contain a full merchandise assortment?

13. Are advertising policy, customer service policy, and pricing policy of the past owner similar to yours? Can you continue old policies?

14. If the business is to be part of a chain, is the new unit compatible with existing units? How much trading area overlap is there with existing stores?

15. Has a lawyer examined the proposed contract?

16. What effect will owning this business have on your life-style and on your family relationships?

Figure 2-7

Sales

Sales objectives are those concerned with the sales volume of a retailer. Growth, stability, and/or market share are the sales objectives most often sought by retailers.

Some retailers set sales growth as a top priority. Under this objective, a firm is interested in expanding operations and increasing sales. There is less emphasis on short-run profits. The assumption is that investments in the present will yield profits in the future. A small or large retailer that does well often becomes interested in opening new units and increasing sales volume.

However, too active a pursuit of expansion can result in problems. Many retailers who are successful in their current business fail when they open new units. Management skills and the "personal touch" are sometimes lost with improper expansion. Sales growth is a legitimate goal for large and small retailers, but growth should not be too fast or exclude the consideration of other objectives.

Stability in annual sales and profits is the objective of a wide range of retailers. These companies place their emphasis on maintaining their sales volume, market share, price lines, and so on. Small retailers are often interested in stable sales that will enable them to make a satisfactory living every year, without the pressure of downswings or upsurges. Other retailers develop a loyal following of consumers and are not intent on expanding but on maintaining the services that have attracted the original consumers.

Another objective of many retailers is proper market share. Market share is the percentage of total industry sales contributed by one company. In retailing, market share is usually an objective only for large retailers or retail chains.[6] The small retailer is more concerned with competition across the street or down the block than with total sales in a metropolitan area.

Sales objectives may be expressed in dollars and units. To achieve its dollar objectives, a retailer can employ a discount strategy (low prices and high unit sales), a moderate strategy (medium prices and medium unit sales), or a prestige strategy (high prices and low unit sales). In the long run, the use of sales units as an indicator of performance is important. Dollar sales over a two- to three-year period may be difficult to compare because of changing retail prices and the rate of inflation. However, sales in units are relatively easy to compare from year to year. A company with dollar sales of $200,000 in 1980 and $300,000 in 1985 might assume that it is doing very well, until unit figures are computed—10,000 in 1980 and 8,000 in 1985.

Profit

Profitability means that the retailer wants to attain at least a minimum level of profits during a designated time period, usually a year. Profits may be expressed in dollars or as a percentage of sales. For a retailer having yearly sales of $5 million and total yearly costs of $4,200,000, profits in dollars are $800,000, and profits as a percentage of sales are 16 per cent. If the profit objectives of the firm are equal to or less than $800,000, or 16 per cent, the retailer is satisfied. If the profit objectives are greater than $800,000, or 16 per cent, the retailer has not attained the minimum desired level of profits and is therefore dissatisfied.

[6]Isadore Barmash, "Chasing Market Share," *Stores* (March 1982), pp. 9–13.

Retailers who invest large capital expenditures in land, buildings, equipment, and so on often have return on investment (ROI) as a company objective. Return on investment is the relationship between company profits and investment in capital items. This statistic is used in the same manner as the profit statistic. A satisfactory rate of return is predefined by the company, and this rate is compared with the actual rate of return at the end of the year or other designated time period. If a company has annual sales of $5 million and expenditures (including the long-term payment of capital items) of $4 million, the yearly profit is $1 million. Assume that the cost of land, buildings, and equipment is $10 million. Then ROI equals $1 million/$10 million, or 10 per cent per year. The company's ROI objective would have to be 10 per cent or less per year for it to be satisfied.

Increased efficiency in selling is an objective of many retailers. Efficiency may be expressed as $1-$ (selling expenses/company sales). The larger this figure, the more efficient the firm. A retailer with sales of $2 million and selling expenses of $1 million has an efficiency rating of 50 per cent ($[1-(\$1$ million/$\$2$ million$)]$). Fifty cents of every sales dollar are contributed to nonselling costs such as merchandise purchases and profits, and 50 cents go for selling expenses. The retailer might set as an objective for next year an increase in selling efficiency to 80 per cent. On sales of $2 million, selling expenses would have to be reduced to $400,000 ($[1-(\$400,000/\$2$ million$)]$). In this instance, 80 cents of every sales dollar are contributed to nonselling costs and profits; only 20 cents go for selling expenses. The increase in efficiency will lead to an overall increase in the retailer's profits.

Satisfaction of Publics

A retailer is often concerned with **satisfying his or her publics,** including stockholders, consumers, suppliers, employees, and government. Stockholder satisfaction is a vital objective for any retail establishment that is publicly owned. It is up to store management to set and attain goals that are consistent with the wishes of stockholders. Many companies have policies that lead to small annual increases in sales and profits (because these goals can be sustained over the long run and indicate good management), rather than policies of introducing innovative ideas that might lead to peaks and valleys in company sales and profits (indicating poor management). Stable earnings for the store lead to stable dividends for stockholders.

Consumer satisfaction with the total retail offering is an objective that most firms are practicing today, although many have acknowledged this only recently. It is crucial for the company to satisfy the consumer and not to adopt a policy of caveat emptor, "Let the buyer beware." Retailers must be willing to take criticism and adjust to the desires of the consumer. They can easily accomplish this by gearing a company's philosophy and objectives to the consumer. If the consumer is satisfied, the other objectives will be accomplished. Despite the inclusion of consumer satisfaction as a stated objective for today's retailers, the importance of this objective ranks low for many, large and small alike. The other objectives cited rate higher in the list of priorities.

Good supplier relations are important. A retailer must understand and work with suppliers, such as manufacturers and wholesalers, if favorable prices, new products, good return policies, prompt shipments, and cooperation are to be received. Because suppliers perform many functions for small retailers, good relations are particularly important for them.

Favorable employee relations are crucial to the performance of a retailer, whether the retailer is small or large. Positive employee morale leads to less absenteeism, better performance, and lower turnover. Employee relations can be improved through effective selection, training, and motivation.

Because federal, state, and local governments all impose restrictions on retailers, it is important to understand and react to these policies. In some cases, retailers are able to influence government regulations by acting singly or as members of large groups, such as trade associations or chambers of commerce.

Image (Store Positioning)

Image refers to how a firm is viewed by consumers and others. A firm may be viewed as progressive or conservative, ethical or unethical, caring of consumers or indifferent, economical or high priced, and so on. A retailer is concerned with the way the company is viewed and sets as an objective the creation of the image that he or she wants consumers to have. The key to a successful image is that the consumer views the store in the manner the retailer intends.

Store positioning enables a retailer to determine how consumers perceive the company relative to its retail category and its competitors. For example, a retailer selling women's clothing could be positioned as an upscale specialty store, a department store, or a discount specialty store and it could be positioned in relation to any nearby retailers selling women's clothing.

As shown in Figure 2-8, Mandy's Women's Shop is positioned as an upscale specialty store. This is a small retail category, but it has loyal customers and high profit margins. Mandy's is well positioned for its category, having a very good fashion/price mix. Of Mandy's five competitors, two are upscale specialty stores, one is a department store, and two are discount specialty stores.

For some of the retailing giants, such as Sears or Safeway Stores, industry leadership is an important objective. Industry leadership means two major benefits for a company. First, company image is improved because consumers place the company on a higher plateau than its competitors. Second, other retailers will follow pricing and other strategies of the leader, and imitation is the best kind of flattery. Another subsidiary benefit is the internal satisfaction that accompanies being "Number One," and this encourages all to work harder.

Selection of Objectives

The objective or objectives that a retailer selects will have a great impact on the development of an overall strategy. The retailer who clearly defines objectives, and develops a strategy to achieve them, improves chances for success.

An example of a store that has clearly specified its objectives and has established a strategy to attain them is Wal-Mart, a discount chain that operates largely in rural communities of 5,000 to 15,000 people in nineteen states in the South and Southwest. Wal-Mart's sales growth plans call for doubling sales every two to three years. It opens between 100 and 125 new stores a year and recently has begun to open stores in medium-sized cities. In addition, Wal-Mart has attained sales growth averaging 17 per

A Store Positioning Map for Mandy's Women's Shop

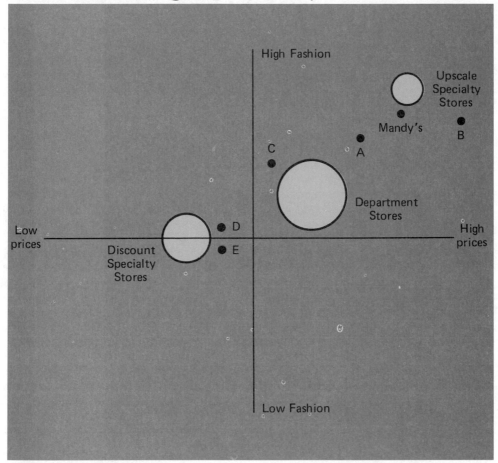

Consumers' perception of store positioning for a retail category. The size of the circle refers to the relative size of the category for women's clothing.

Consumers' perception of Mandy's and five of its competitors (A–E).

Figure 2-8

cent in the stores that are at least one year old. This is double the industry average. Growth is due to Wal-Mart's choice of towns (which other merchants tend to avoid), its knowledge of local markets, and new institutional formats such as buying clubs (Sam's Wholesale Club).[7]

[7]Isadore Barmash, "The Hot Ticket in Retailing," *New York Times* (July 1, 1984), p. F4; Hank Gilman, "Rural Retailing Chains Prosper by Combining Service, Sophistication," *Wall Street Journal* (July 2, 1984), pp. 1, 12; and John Nielsen, "Shopping at the Club," *Fortune* (December 24, 1984), pp. 91–92.

Identification of Consumer Characteristics and Needs

Next, the retailer or prospective retailer must determine the characteristics and needs of consumers. The consumer group that a retailer tries to satisfy is called the **target market.** In selecting this target market, the retailer can employ either of three techniques: to sell products to a broad spectrum of consumers, the **mass market;** to zero in on one specific market, **market segmentation;** or to use **multiple-segmentation** strategies in which the retailer attempts to capture several market segments at the same time, using different offerings for each.

Conventional supermarkets and traditional shoe stores such as Thom McAn are examples of retailers that define their target markets in very broad terms. These stores have several different product lines and stock many kinds of items at a variety of prices. On the other hand, the small boutique or a fruit or vegetable store exemplifies the retailer who selects a well-defined and narrow consumer group. Both of these outlets have a narrow product assortment and pricing scheme because they attract a certain type of customer, not everyone. Most department stores seek multiple market segments. These stores cater to several different groups of consumers and provide unique products and services for each group. For example, women's clothing may be subdivided into several distinctive boutiques scattered throughout a department store. Large retail chains frequently have divisions that appeal to different market segments. Associated Dry Goods operates the fashion-oriented Lord & Taylor as well as the discount-oriented Caldor. See Figure 2-9 for the strategy implications of selecting a target market.

The selection and clear statement of a target market give direction to a store's overall location, merchandise, price, and promotion efforts; enable the firm to stress its competitive advantages; and direct the financial requirements of the retailer. Although all of these are important, the concept of competitive advantage is too often overlooked. The choice of a target market and its satisfaction by a unique retail offering are necessary for success. Some examples will demonstrate this point.

Saks Fifth Avenue defines its target market as the upper-class, status-conscious consumer, whereas K mart defines its target market as the middle-class, value-conscious consumer. Factory outlets cater to price-conscious consumers, whereas small clothing stores concentrate on consumers interested in the personal touch. National gasoline-station chains seek consumers who value a total car-service offering; small, independent gasoline stations attract buyers interested in only the lowest prices for gasoline. The key to the success of each of these companies is their ability to define their customers and cater to their needs in a distinctive manner.

The strategy development of a boutique will show the importance of a well-defined target market from an overall perspective. The owner of the boutique has defined her target market as women who are 24 to 35 years old, who reside within a five-mile radius of the store, and who desire youth-oriented clothing. By knowing the target market, the owner is able to develop a strategy different from her competitors. The merchandise is stylish sportswear, jeans, tops, and so on, in junior sizes 5 to 14. Credit cards, layaway plans, and liberal return policies are used. Direct-mail ads are sent to past customers, and ads are taken in the local fashion newspaper. The sportswear lines are popularly priced. Misses' sizes, conservative fashions, high-priced dresses, and daily newspaper ads are not invested in by the boutique. They are not appropriate for the target market.

Methods for Selecting a Target Market

Strategy Implications	Mass Marketing	Market Segmentation	Multiple Segmentation
Location	near a large population base	near a small or medium population base	near a large population base
Products	wide assortment of medium-quality items	deep assortment of high-quality or low-quality items	distinct products aimed at each market segment
Promotion	mass advertising	direct mail, subscription	different media and messages for each segment
Price	"popular prices"	high or low	high, medium and low—depending on market segment
Strategy Emphasis	one general, "middle-of-the road" strategy directed at a large homogeneous (similar) group of consumers	one specific strategy directed at a specific, limited group of customers	several specific strategies, each directed at different (heterogeneous) groups of consumers

Figure 2-9

With an understanding of the consumer market, a retailer is able to do three things: identify the characteristics and desires of various potential markets; decide whether to use mass marketing, market segmentation, or multiple segmentation; and develop an overall retailing strategy. A discussion of this last point takes place in the next section.

Overall Strategy

After situation analysis, setting objectives, and selecting a consumer market, the retailer is ready to develop an overall strategy. This strategy involves two areas: those aspects of business that the retailer can directly affect (such as store hours and sales help) and those to which the retailer must adapt (such as laws, the economy, and competition).

The former are called **controllable variables,** and the latter are called **uncontrollable variables.** Retailers must develop their strategies with both of these variables in mind.

Controllable Variables

The controllable parts of retail strategy are broken down into the following categories of decision making: store location and operations; product and/or service offerings; store image and promotion; and pricing. Each of these variables is depicted in Figure 2-10. A successful strategy is predicated on an integrated approach to these four areas. A consistent, unified strategy must be developed.

Retail Strategy: Controllable Variables

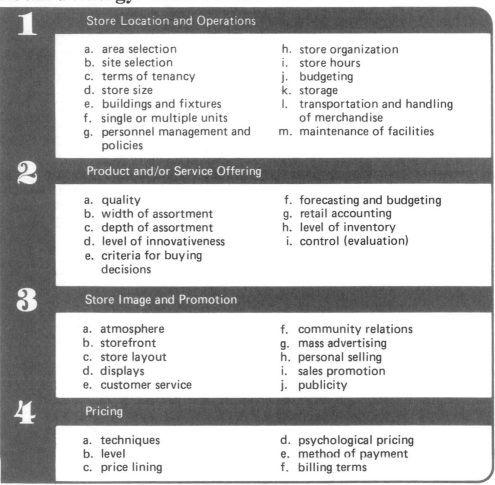

1 Store Location and Operations

a. area selection
b. site selection
c. terms of tenancy
d. store size
e. buildings and fixtures
f. single or multiple units
g. personnel management and policies
h. store organization
i. store hours
j. budgeting
k. storage
l. transportation and handling of merchandise
m. maintenance of facilities

2 Product and/or Service Offering

a. quality
b. width of assortment
c. depth of assortment
d. level of innovativeness
e. criteria for buying decisions
f. forecasting and budgeting
g. retail accounting
h. level of inventory
i. control (evaluation)

3 Store Image and Promotion

a. atmosphere
b. storefront
c. store layout
d. displays
e. customer service
f. community relations
g. mass advertising
h. personal selling
i. sales promotion
j. publicity

4 Pricing

a. techniques
b. level
c. price lining
d. psychological pricing
e. method of payment
f. billing terms

Figure 2-10

A retailer has several store-location and operations decisions to make. The general area and the specific site must be determined. Competitors, transportation, population density, type of neighborhood, nearness to suppliers, and so on should all be considered when one is picking a store location. The terms of tenancy (such as rent, flexibility, and length of contract) must be evaluated, and a build, buy, or rent decision must be made. The store size, type of building, and fixtures need to be chosen. The use of multiple outlets, an increasing phenomenon in today's retailing environment, must be considered if expansion is an objective of the firm. Each of these aspects of location can provide problems if not adequately defined in the strategy phrase.

Store operations decisions involve personnel management and policies (hiring, training, compensating, supervising, and so on); store organization (organization chart and line of command); store hours (days and times); budgeting for operations; storage (where and retailer versus manufacturer controlled); transportation and handling (how and retailer versus manufacturer controlled); and maintenance of facilities.

The second area of strategic decision making is the product and/or service offering. The general product or service quality of the establishment must be ascertained. Decisions are necessary about the width of the assortment (the number of different product categories that a store handles) and the depth of the assortment (the completeness of stock within a given product category). Policies should be set outlining how innovative the store is going to be in the introduction of new products or services. Criteria for buying decisions (how often, terms, and so on) need to be established. Forecasting, budgeting, and retail accounting procedures must be developed. The level of inventory (average stock on hand) must be ascertained for each type of product that is stocked. Finally, the retailer must institute control or evaluation procedures in order to measure the success or failure of each product or service offered for sale.

The third broad area of retail decision making involves the establishment of a store image and the utilization of promotional techniques. As mentioned earlier in this chapter, store image is critical to the success of a retailer. If the target market does not perceive the store in the manner intended by the store, then it cannot succeed. Therefore, a distinctive image (consistent with the desires of the target market) must be sought. This image can be created through the use of several techniques.

Store atmosphere represents the store's physical appearance relative to the image that is sought. A prestige store creates and upholds its image through plush carpeting, wide aisles, attractive displays, and hidden price tags. A discounter creates and upholds image through bare floors, crowded displays, obvious price tags, and self-service. Color arrangements, scents, music, and type of sales personnel also contribute to a store's image. The construction of a storefront (the physical exterior) contributes to the image or atmosphere of the store. It is the first part of the store that a consumer sees. Store layout and displays (the arrangement and positioning of merchandise within a store) are other contributors to atmosphere.

Customer services and community relations should also be used as tools in creating a favorable store image. Customer services including parking, gift wrapping, liberal return policy, extended store hours during special seasons, layaway plans, alterations, use of credit cards, and telephone and mail sales.

Proper use of promotional techniques can help lead to profitable retailing. These techniques can range from very inexpensive, door-to-door flyers for a supermarket or takeout restaurant to very expensive, national advertising campaigns for a franchise chain. Three types of paid promotion are available to retailers. Mass advertising (television, radio, magazines, billboards, direct mail, and most often, newspapers) allows the retailer to direct one message at a large number of consumers. Personal selling enables the retailer to have a one-to-one relationship with consumers. Sales promotions provide added persuasion in attracting and satisfying the customer. Sales promotions include coupons, special sales, contests, point-of-purchase displays, shopping bags, balloons, matches, skywriting, and so on. In addition to these forms of paid promotion, retailers can obtain free publicity through community service and other projects.

The fourth area of retail strategy involves pricing decisions. The retailer must choose from among several pricing techniques (such as leading, following, cost-plus, and demand-oriented). He or she must decide what level of prices to charge: low, medium, or high. Which of these levels is consistent with the store's image and the quality of the products or services offered? The number of prices for any item category should be determined. For example, how many prices of candy should a luncheonette carry? This concept is called price lining. Psychological pricing may also be used; this requires a thorough understanding of the consumer and his or her willingness to pay high prices for certain items, such as cosmetics. The method of payment, such as cash only or cash plus credit, must be planned. Many retailers allow credit purchases today. The major exception is the supermarket industry (because of the already low profit margins of supermarkets). Even small delicatessens and cleaning stores allow credit on an informal, personal basis. Billing terms must also be determined: length of deferred payments and the resultant interest charges; the use of COD; discounts for cash or early payments.

The preceding discussion has outlined the controllable portions of the retailing strategy. Store location and operations, product and/or service offerings, store image and promotion, and pricing all fall within the control of the retailer. The retailer should plan these areas after defining the product or service area, examining the characteristics and desires of the target market, and understanding the uncontrollable aspects of the environment. A discussion of these uncontrollable variables follows.[8]

Uncontrollable Variables

The uncontrollable parts of retailing strategy can be divided into several categories: the consumer, competition, technology, economic conditions, seasonality, and legal restrictions. These are depicted in Figure 2-11. Retailers must adapt the controllable parts of their strategies to satisfy the elements beyond their immediate control. The uncontrollable nature of these variables is explained as follows.

Once a retailer has defined a target market, the product or service offering must be adapted accordingly. A successful retailer realizes that he or she cannot alter demographic trends, change life-style patterns, impose tastes, or "force" products or services on consumers. Rather, the retailer should understand the characteristics and needs of consumers and develop an offering consistent with these attributes. Selecting a target market is within the control of the retailer, but a retailer cannot sell products or servces that are beyond the price range of the consumer, that are not wanted, or that are not displayed in the proper manner. The total retail offering must be oriented toward satisfying the target market.

---

[8]A retailer's ability to understand and predict the effects of controllable and uncontrollable variables is enhanced by the use of marketing research. Marketing research in retailing is described in Chapter 6.

Retail Strategy: Uncontrollable Variables

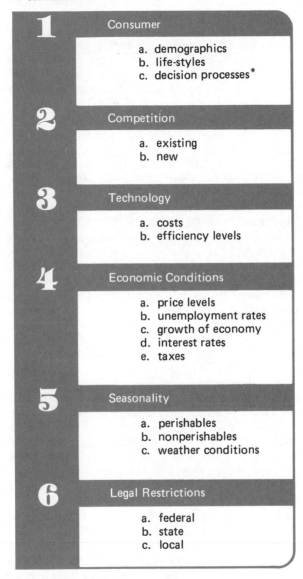

1 Consumer
- a. demographics
- b. life-styles
- c. decision processes*

2 Competition
- a. existing
- b. new

3 Technology
- a. costs
- b. efficiency levels

4 Economic Conditions
- a. price levels
- b. unemployment rates
- c. growth of economy
- d. interest rates
- e. taxes

5 Seasonality
- a. perishables
- b. nonperishables
- c. weather conditions

6 Legal Restrictions
- a. federal
- b. state
- c. local

*Discussed in Chapter 5.

Figure 2-11

After the type of business is selected and the store's location chosen, there is little that most retailers can do to limit the entry of competitors. In fact, the success of an existing retailer will encourage the entry of new retailers or cause established retailers to modify their product lines to reflect popular trends. The growth of competition often forces a retailer to re-examine overall strategy—including the definition of the target market and the product–service mix—to ensure that a competitive advantage is maintained. An error that too many retailers make is to assume that being first in a location is a sufficient competitive advantage in fighting off new entrants. A continued willingness to satisfy the target market better than any other retailer is essential.

In today's world of retailing, technology is rapidly advancing. Complex computer systems are now in use for inventory control and checkout operations. Electronic surveillance is used to reduce shoplifting. The Universal Product Code, in moderate use at the present time, is revolutionizing merchandise handling and inventory control. More efficient warehousing and transporting of merchandise have been developed. Mail and telephone selling are more popular than ever before. However, it should be recognized that some of these improvements are expensive and may be best suited to large retailers.

It is difficult for the small retailer to keep up with the technological changes in handling, marking, and ringing up sales. Accordingly, the ability to keep prices near those of large competitors must suffer. The only feasible way the small retailer can survive, in the face of decreasing efficiency relative to the competition, is to provide more personalized and more diversified services. A small retailer must accept some of the technological changes as being beyond his or her grasp and adapt the controllable strategy to make up for this.

Economic conditions are beyond the control of any retailers. Inflation, unemployment, interest rates, tax levels, and changes in the Gross National Product (GNP) are elements of the environment that a retailer must cope with and cannot change. In delineating the controllable aspects of strategy, the retailer must consider and adjust to forecasts about international, national, state, and local economies.

Another constraint on certain types of retailers is the seasonality of products or services and the possibility that unpredictable weather changes will play havoc with sales forecasts. Retailers of sports equipment, clothing, fresh food, and others cannot control the seasonality of their products or bad weather. As a service example, travel agencies are hard-pressed to maintain a high level of sales during off-seasons.

A solution to this uncontrollable part of strategy planning is for retailers to diversify their sales offerings. A product or service line containing items that are popular in each season of the year could be developed. For instance, a sporting goods retailer can carry ski equipment and snowmobiles in the winter, baseball and golf equipment in the spring, scuba equipment and fishing gear in the summer, and basketball and football supplies in the fall. In this way the effects of seasonality are minimized by planning the controllable part of retail strategy.

Finally, all retailers should be familiar with the federal, state, and local legal restrictions placed on them. Figure 2-12 shows how the controllable aspects of the retailing strategy are affected by the legal environment. A brief discussion of legislation at the three levels of government (federal, state, and local) follows.[9]

At the federal level, legislation began in 1890 with the Sherman Act, which was designed to reduce monopolies and restraints of trade. The Clayton Act (1914) was enacted to strengthen the Sherman Act. Also in 1914, the Federal Trade Commission

[9]For additional information, see Consuelo L. Kertz, "Keeping Legal," *Sales & Marketing Management* (October 11, 1982), pp. 53–55, "The Crazy Quilt of Blue Laws," *New York Times* (August 29, 1984), p. C6; Mary Williams, "Pennsylvania Weighs Selling Liquor Stores," *Wall Street Journal* (December 14, 1983), p. 33; and Diana Solis, "If You Want to Make a Retailer Red-Hot, Talk About Blue Laws," *Wall Street Journal* (February 4, 1985), p. 25.

was established to deal with unfair trade practices and consumer complaints. In the 1930s, the Robinson-Patman Act (1936) and the Miller-Tydings Act (1937) were passed. Both of these laws were aimed at protecting small retailers after the Depression. The Robinson-Patman Act was enacted because of the discounts A&P was getting in the purchase of its products. The Miller-Tydings Act (fair trade) attempted to limit discounting on the part of large retailers by forcing all retailers to sell fair-traded items at the same prices. The fair trade law has now been removed in all states.

The Anti-Merger Act was passed in 1950 to limit mergers between large retailers. The 1960s and 1970s saw an onslaught of consumer protection acts in such areas as door-to-door sales, product labeling, product safety, product packaging, consumer credit, and product warranty and guarantee. Although these acts are mostly oriented toward manufacturers, they affect retailers who use deceptive selling practices and/or sell private-label merchandise. The 1980s have been a period of deregulation and self-regulation, allowing retailers much greater freedom in their strategies and operations.

At the state and local levels, there are many restrictions placed on retailers. Zoning laws prohibit retailers from operating at certain locations and require building specifications to be met. Construction, fire, elevator, smoking, and other codes are placed on retailers by the state and city. Minimum resale laws require that specified items cannot be sold for less than a floor price. Blue laws limit the hours that retailers can conduct business. Other ordinances, called Green River laws, restrict direct-to-home selling. In addition, various licenses necessary for operation are under the jurisdiction of the state or city. Also, many states and municipalities are involved in consumer protection, and they police retailers from this vantage point.

A retailer who voluntarily adheres to the spirit and the letter of the law is one who will maintain a consumer following and is less likely to attract government attention. A retailing strategy must be established in a manner that satisfies all three levels of government. For further information, the reader should contact the Federal Trade Commission, state and local regulatory agencies, the National Retail Merchants Association (NRMA), or the local Better Business Bureau.

Integrating Overall Strategy

At this point, the retailer has completed the development of an overall strategy. The product or service category of business has been selected. A target market of consumers has been designated and studied according to its characteristics and desires. The retailer has made long-range decisions concerning each of the following: store location and operations, product and/or service offerings, store image and promotion, and pricing. These elements have been developed in a unified manner and have taken into consideration several factors that are beyond the immediate control of the retailer: the consumer, competition, technology, economic conditions, seasonality, and legal restrictions. Now the retailer is ready to undertake the specific activities necessary to carry out this strategy.

Specific Activities

Short-run decisions have to be made and implemented for each controllable component of the retail strategy outlined in the preceding section and in Figure 2-10. These actions

The Impact of Legislation on Retailing*

A. The Impact upon Store Location and Operations

1. *zoning laws* — these restrict the choice of locations and the type of facilities that can be constructed
2. *blue laws* — these restrict the days and hours that retailers can operate
3. *local ordinances* — these involve licensing and fire, smoking, capacity, and other regulations
4. *personnel laws* — these involve the hiring, promoting, and firing of employees in a fair manner
5. *antitrust laws* — these limit mergers and expansion
6. *franchise agreements* — franchisee must abide by legal precedents concerning purchase requirements, customer service levels, etc.
7. *leases and mortgages* — lessee or mortgagee must abide by the clauses and stipulations in the tenancy document

B. The Impact upon Product and/or Service Offerings

1. *patents and copyrights* — exclusive rights in the sale of products or services for a specified period of time
2. *trademark* — exclusive rights to the name and symbol representing the store
3. *Robinson-Patman Act* — limits ability of large retailers to elicit discounts in the purchase of merchandise
4. *product safety laws* — these inhibit retailers from selling new products that have not been fully tested, or which have been declared unsafe
5. *product liability* — retailers can be sued if they sell defective products
6. *warranty and guarantee laws* — if a retailer offers its own warranty, it must adhere to federal standards
7. *mail and telephone sales* — there are restrictions on the items that may be sold in this format
8. *delivery laws* — some states enforce penalties against late deliveries
9. *inventory laws* — these mandate that a retailer have adequate stock when running a sale
10. *labeling laws* — merchandise must be correctly labeled and priced, and displayed as such
11. *lemon laws* — these specify consumer rights if new products, usually autos, require continuing repairs

C. The Impact upon Store Image and Promotion

1. *truth in advertising, labeling, and packaging laws* — these require retailers to be truthful and not to omit information

Figure 2-12

The Impact of Legislation on Retailing* (continued)

C. *The Impact upon Store Image and Promotion (continued)*

2. *truth in credit laws* — these require the consumer to be fully informed of all terms when buying on credit. Recently, credit legislation has expanded to include equal opportunity in borrowing

3. *loss leaders* — in some areas, it is illegal to sell an item below cost, even if the consumer is not deceived

4. *bait-and-switch* — it is not legal to lure a customer into a store to buy an inexpensive item and then try to switch the customer to a higher-priced item through pressure selling

5. *door-to-door sales* — there are many restrictions on this type of selling (i.e., Green River Ordinances)

6. *cooling-off laws* — these allow customers to cancel completed sales orders, usually apply to door-to-door sales, and allow cancellation within 3 days of contract date

7. *other restrictions* — some items are not allowed to be advertised in certain media. For example, there are no cigarette ads on radio or television

D. *The Impact upon Pricing*

1. *unit pricing laws* — in some areas, for certain types of retailers, the price per unit must be displayed

2. *correct marking* — discounted and sale items must be marked with the correct price. It is not sufficient to have the sale price only noted in the store window

3. *dual pricing* — this occurs when the same item has two different prices on different containers. When there is inflation, old stock is frequently priced lower than new stock. In some areas, dual pricing is illegal. Only one price per item is allowed

4. *collusion* — it is not legal to discuss selling price with competitors under any circumstances. This is now enforced with stiff fines and sometimes with jail sentences

5. *sales* — a sale is defined as a reduction in price from the retailer's normal selling price. Anything else called a sale is illegal

6. *minimum-price laws* — products cannot be sold for less than their cost plus an allowance for retailer's overhead

7. *item price removal laws* — these require that prices be marked on both individual items and on store shelves

---

*This table is broad in nature and purposely omits a law-by-law description. Many laws are state or locally oriented and apply only to certain areas; the laws in each locale differ widely. The intent is to give the reader some understanding of the current legal environment as it affects retail management. For more specifics, contact the sources named in the chapter.

are called **tactics** and involve the daily and short-run operations of a retailer. Once the store location has been selected and general operating guidelines have been set, tactical decisions must be made.

Arrangement of departments, contraction and expansion of departments, maintenance of facilities, hiring and firing of personnel, changes in store hours, warehousing, and so on are all areas requiring constant tactical decision making. The sale of specific product categories and the exact assortments within each category must be consistently revised, and new buying decisions often arise. The creation and continuance of a store image require constant analysis and adaptation. Store layout may be altered to provide a store with a "new look" or to help sell slow-moving merchandise. Promotional campaigns must change according to season or type of product advertised. Customer services may vary according to season and product line, for example. Pricing decisions are required to push slow-moving merchandise or add lower-priced items to the assortment. Each of these elements and others are subject to review and refinement.

Retailers must be responsive to the uncontrollable environment that surrounds them. Consumer demands, competitive actions, and government restrictions especially need to be considered in the retailer's tactical decisions. The essence of successful retailing is constructing a sound strategy and "fine tuning" it as changes occur. A retailer who stands still is often moving backward. Alterations in the basic strategy are often necessary as the uncontrollable environment changes. A comprehensive discussion of tactical decision making appears in Chapters 7 through 15.

Control

As already noted, retail strategy and tactics should be evaluated and revised on a continuous basis. A semiannual or annual review of the company should take place, with the strategy and tactics (steps IV and V, Figure 2-1) that have been developed and employed evaluated against the philosophy of business and the firm's objectives (steps I and II, Figure 2-1). This procedure is called a **retail audit,** a systematic procedure for analyzing the performance of a retail establishment. The retailing audit is explained in Chapter 16.

After the performance of a retailer is compared with objectives, the strengths and weaknesses of the company are revealed. The elements of the retail strategy that have gone well should be left alone, and the elements that have been conducted poorly should be revised, consistent with the firm's philosophy and objectives. Minor adjustments are desired because major changes in a retailer's operations will only confuse and intimidate customers. The adjustments that are undertaken should be evaluated during the next retail audit.

Feedback

During each stage in the development of a retail strategy, management receives signals or cues as to the success of that part of the strategy. These signals or cues are called **feedback.** Some forms of positive feedback are increased sales, no problems with the government, employee satisfaction, and status in the community. Some forms of negative feedback are declining sales, shoplifting, governmental interference, excessive inventories, and consumer complaints.

When feedback occurs, the retailer should determine the causes of it. Then emphasis should be placed on the elements of the strategy that are working well, and changes should be made in those elements of the strategy that are causing problems. A retailer should look for these signals or cues, because he or she can take immediate action without waiting for the semiannual or annual retailing audit. See the feedback arrow in Figure 2-1.

Retail Strategy—Owning or Managing a Business: A Summary

This chapter has concentrated on the development of a retail strategy, which has been defined as the overall plan or framework of action for a retail establishment. A retail strategy should contain a situation analysis, objectives, consumer markets, overall strategy, specific activities, control, and feedback. These elements are shown in Figure 2-1.

Situation analysis is the objective evaluation of the opportunities and potential problems facing a retailer. It seeks to determine where the retailer is now and in what direction he or she should be headed. Situation analysis consists of defining the firm's philosophy of business, outlining the product or service category to be sold, and evaluating ownership alternatives. A philosophy of business is a long-term commitment to a type of business and place in the market. The product or service category sold depends on personal abilities, financial resources, and time resources. Ownership and management alternatives are selected from sole proprietorship, partnership, or a corporation; starting a new business, buying an existing business, or becoming a franchisee; owner-manager or professional manager; and centralized or decentralized.

Objectives are the long-run and short-term goals of the retailer. Retailers may be interested in one or more objectives: sales (including growth, stability, and market share); profit (including level, return on investment, and efficiency); satisfaction of publics (including stockholders and consumers); and image (including customer and industry perceptions).

The characteristics and needs of consumers are determined. The consumer group that a retailer seeks to satisfy is known as the target market. In appealing to the target market, a retailer can use mass marketing, whereby a wide assortment of medium-priced products is sold to a broad spectrum of customers; market segmentation, whereby one product offering is sold to a very specific consumer group (segment); or multiple segmentation, whereby two or more distinct product offerings are sold to two or more distinct consumer segments.

Next, an overall retail strategy is constructed. Understanding the potential consumer market is a prerequisite to building a successful strategy. It is especially important to understand the consumer from the perspective of the product or service category that the retailer is interested in selling. In developing an overall strategy the retailer must consider both the controllable elements (store location and layout, product and/or service offering, store image and promotion, and pricing) and the uncontrollable elements (the consumer, competition, technology, economic conditions, seasonality, and legal restrictions) of strategy when making and implementing decisions.

After the overall strategy has been developed, the retailer must implement the specific activities (controllable aspects) of the plan. Daily and short-run decisions, called tactics, must be made. These decisions are subject to control (an evaluation and adjustment of the strategy and the tactics) on a continuous, systematic basis. The retailer must also be constantly alert for signals or cues, known as feedback, that reveal the success or failure at each step in the retail strategy.

Throughout the remainder of the text, the development of retail strategy will be detailed. Chapters 3 and 4 lay the framework, by explaining the types of institutions that exist in retailing and the strategic implications of each. Chapters 5 and 6 examine consumer behavior and the role of research in retailing. Chapters 7 through 14 concentrate on the specific retail activities outlined in Figure 2-10. Chapter 15 discusses the unique aspects of service retailing. Chapter 16 describes the integrating and control processes. Chapter 17 examines emerging trends in retailing.

Questions for Discussion

1. Why is it necessary to develop a well-integrated retail strategy?
2. What is meant by situation analysis? What is a philosophy of business?
3. How will aptitudes, education, and experience guide a prospective retailer in the selection of a product or service category?
4. Explain why new retailers frequently underestimate the financial requirements of a business.
5. Comment on the profile of the small business entrepreneur shown in Table 2-3.
6. In what situation is a sole proprietorship, partnership, or corporation the preferred ownership format?
7. Jack Watson is a 35-year-old former shoe salesman. Jack has saved $30,000 and wants to open his own retail shoe store. How do you think Jack would respond to the questions in Figure 2-7? What further information about Jack is needed?
8. Describe the objectives a retailer may seek. Do most firms have only one objective or several? Explain.
9. Give examples of retailers using mass marketing, market segmentation, and multiple segmentation. Relate your answer to the concept of store positioning.
10. What are some of the alternatives a retailer has in the planning of store location and operations, product and/or service offerings, store image and promotion, and pricing?
11. How should a retailer react to each of the uncontrollable factors that face him or her: consumer, competition, technology, economic conditions, seasonality, and legal restrictions?
12. Describe how a retailer would use fine tuning.
13. Detail the control phase of retail strategy development.
14. How can a retailer properly use feedback?
15. Should a small retailer plan a strategy differently from a large retailer? Why or why not?

CASES

1. Bill Janis: Evaluating a Business Opportunity

Bill Janis, a recent college graduate, is seeking to purchase a business with the financial assistance of his father. Bill has always been an entrepreneurial type, is fascinated with retailing, and has a high energy level. He is keeping in mind these criteria in the search for an appropriate opportunity:

- Bill does not want to become a franchisee. He does not want to pay franchising fees, contribute to a national advertising program, or have his ability to manage a business restricted.
- Bill wants to purchase an established business that has not met its full potential. In this way, the risks of failing will be reduced. He will consider a moderately successful firm that has absentee management or a complacent owner; this will allow him to apply his talents.
- Bill wants a service-based business, since service retailers are growing at a faster rate than product-based retailers. A service firm also requires less inventory investment.
- Bill wants a business with some barriers to entry. He does not want to look at upholstery and carpet-cleaning firms or 60-minute film-processing studios, since they require little training and capital investments. He wants to avoid oversaturation and price competition.
- Bill wants to own the real estate on which his firm is located. This will allow him to use depreciation as an expense, control maintenance, and be free from concerns about lease renewal.

Table 1
The Characteristics of Otto's Super Wash (as Noted by Bill Janis)

1. This is an older car wash; it is not brushless. Such a car wash can cause scuff marks on autos, and may break car antennas or damage loose molding. Some equipment (e.g., drying machine) does not function well. Since the equipment is not state-of-the-art, car buffing, undercarriage washing, and other services cannot be offered.

2. The car wash handles about 1,000 cars in an average week. It is open Monday through Saturday, 8 A.M. to 6 P.M. There are three full-time employees.

3. Prices are low: $2 for exterior only; $3 for full service (interior vacuuming, windows cleaned, ashtrays emptied; $1 extra for hot wax). These prices may be difficult to raise.

4. Business is heaviest on Fridays and Saturdays and two to three days after major snowfalls.

5. The car wash is located on a heavily trafficked road. It is highly visible and easy to reach by passing vehicles.

6. Otto will provide financing. A $100,000 down payment is required. A $300,000 15-year loan will have to be taken.

7. A real-estate appraiser values the car wash's property at $200,000. This does not include the value of the car wash itself.

8. If a renovation is undertaken, the car wash would have to be closed for a month. The renovation would cost $35,000 to $75,000, depending on the modifications.

Table 2
Selected Financial Data on Otto's Super Wash, Latest Year

Revenues:		
Exterior-only washes	$70,000	
Full-service washes	60,000	
Wax applications	27,000	
		$157,000
Expenses:		
Wages/fringes	$45,000	
Equipment repair	18,000	
Wax/water treatment chemicals	12,000	
Property taxes	7,000	
Property repairs	5,000	
Electricity	5,000	
Property and liability insurance	4,000	
		$ 96,000
Net profit before taxes		$ 61,000

For the past year, Bill has examined the car wash industry and several individual firms within a 30-mile radius of his house. In particular, Bill likes several aspects of this business. One, the average sale is between $4 and $5 and many customers pay extra for car buffing, premium wax, motor steaming, and other services. Two, zoning restrictions and the limited availability of large, prime locations often limit competitors' entry. Three, little technical expertise, except for equipment repair, is required. Four, absentee ownership is prevalent; this represents good potential for Bill.

About three weeks ago, Bill saw this ad in his daily newspaper: "Car Wash. Exterior/interior. One owner for 25 years. Excellent location, includes land and building. $100,000 down. Call Otto's Super Wash. 555-1155." The next day, he visited the car wash and jotted down detailed notes based on a conversation with the owner, Otto Franke. Bill was also provided with Otto's most recent financial statement, which was verified by Bill's accountant. See Tables 1 and 2.

The total purchase price for the car wash is $400,000, which seems reasonable to Bill. Otto is willing to provide him with a $300,000 loan at a 12 per cent interest rate. The loan would be fully repaid after 15 years.

Questions

1. Comment on Bill's criteria for selecting an appropriate opportunity.
2. Evaluate the information contained in Tables 1 and 2. On the basis of the facts presented in the case, should Bill make an offer for the car wash?
3. What other kinds of information should Bill acquire before making a decision?
4. If Bill buys the car wash, what kind of strategy should he employ? Refer to Figure 2-1 in your answer.

2. Allied Stores: Following a Progressive Strategy*

Allied Stores operates thirty separate department and specialty store divisions, with almost 600 stores in forty-five states. Among Allied's best-known chains are Jordan Marsh, Bonwit Teller, Joske's, Garfinckel's, Brooks Brothers, Maas Brothers, and Plymouth Shops. In 1983, sales were $3.7 billion; and net profit as a percentage of sales was 3.5 per cent.

Allied Stores has positioned itself to "serve a customer who is searching for better-quality, fashion-right merchandise at competitive prices." Its retail strategy is consistent with this approach.

In its department stores, Allied features a "wide assortment of excellent-quality, fashionable merchandise at reasonable prices, virtually anything you might want in the way of ready-to-wear and furnishings for your home." Department store chains are frequently clustered in order to economize purchases, maximize promotion efforts, and serve an entire region. For example, Jordan Marsh has twelve stores in Massachusetts, two in New Hampshire, and one each in Rhode Island and Maine. Allied is a leader in using downtown, flagship stores to spur inner-city revitalization in locales such as Miami and Minneapolis–St. Paul.

After abandoning its Almart–J. B. Hunter discount division in 1979, Allied has decided to let price-conscious consumers shop elsewhere. At a time when many other traditional retailers have invested in discount operations (Dayton Hudson's Target, Federated Department Stores' Gold Circle and Filene's Basement, and Associated Dry Goods' Loehmann's and Caldor), Allied has no discount or off-price chains. Furthermore, it does not have "bargain basements" in its stores. As Allied's chief executive noted, "I don't want the whole pie. I want only the part that is the sweetest and the most satisfying."

Up until 1979, Allied Stores did not operate any specialty stores. At that time it acquired Bonwit Teller and Plymouth Shops. Since then, it has acquired several other specialty chains. In 1983, specialty stores accounted for 18 per cent of overall Allied sales. Its interest in specialty store retailing is due to several factors. First, these stores are targeted at specific market segments (e.g., Ann Taylor appeals to fashion-conscious women, while Plymouth Shops caters to career-oriented women who desire moderate prices). Second, specialty stores are more flexible in terms of the locations they can occupy, in terms of store size and population. Third, these stores concentrate on narrow product lines, with great depth of assortment. Fourth, expansion is less costly than for department stores. Fifth, specialty stores complement the sales of department stores for Allied; they do not replace them.

To facilitate decision making, Allied uses an automated merchandise reporting system to identify and control merchandise; all of its stores use the system. In addition, senior executives have computer terminals to evaluate sales, operating profits, expenses, and other aspects of every store division. Return on investment and return on net worth are the major measures used to gauge performance. Finances are carefully allocated to divisions and stores that are the most productive, while the least productive units are consolidated or divested.

*The material in this case is drawn from Isadore Barmash, "Vague Frustrations of a Retailing Career," *New York Times* (June 10, 1984), Section 3, p. 6; Jean A. Briggs, "Is Discounting Done For?" *Forbes* (August 15, 1983), pp. 40, 42; and Thomas M. Macioce, "Diversification—A Strategy for Retailing," lecture presented at Syracuse University, Syracuse, N.Y. (March 29, 1984).

Through it all, Allied Stores remains committed to its philosophy of business: "We are all looking for businesses that will increase our sales and improve the profitability of our organizations while providing an essential service to the customer."

Questions

1. Evaluate Allied Stores' decision not to pursue price-conscious customers.
2. How do the basic strategies for department stores and specialty stores differ? How are they the same?
3. Describe in detail five objectives that Allied could set for the next three years.
4. What uncontrollable factors are most likely to affect Allied's performance? Why?

Retail Institutions: Part I

Chapter Objectives

1. To describe retail institutions and the ways in which they can be classified
2. To study retail institutions classified by ownership type and examine the overall sizes and characteristics of each type
3. To explore the methods used by manufacturers, wholesalers, and retailers to obtain channel control

One of the fastest-growing areas of retailing is franchising, because it enables small proprietors to combine the attributes of independent ownership with the clout of a large chain. It also allows franchisors to expand rapidly and retain some control over operations.

However, sometimes franchisors and their franchisees do not agree on marketing factors, such as the use of uniform advertising in all markets. Franchisors are very supportive of "one-voice advertising," as these comments indicate:

> We don't want to see the image we've spent years carving out diminished on the local level.

> There's only so much room in people's minds for an image of an advertiser. The more diffuse the message, the less effective it is.

Franchisees respond:

> We want someone who will research the local market and react quickly.

> We want a campaign that is tailored to our unique market and competitive situation.[1]

Autonomy/control is just one of the many factors retailers must consider when evaluating alternative ownership arrangements.

[1]Ronald Alsop, "Ad Agencies Press Franchisees to Join National Campaigns," *Wall Street Journal* (January 17, 1985), p. 29.

Overview

The term **retail institution** refers to the basic format or structure of a business. The diversity of retail operations can be shown by a comparison of different insitutional forms. This chapter and the next will examine retail institutions from a variety of perspectives.

An institutional study of retailers shows the relative sizes of different forms of retailing; outlines the characteristics of various retail forms; reveals the impact of economic, social, political, and competitive environments on given institutional forms; provides the reader with knowledge of specific institutional forms which is helpful in career decisions; and provides a good background for understanding and applying retail strategy.

Classifying Retail Institutions

Retail institutions can be analyzed from the following perspectives: ownership, retail strategy mix, nonstore operations, and service versus product retailing. Figure 3-1 contains a breakdown of each category.

The classifications are not mutually exclusive; that is, a retail institution may be correctly placed in more than one such classification. For example, a department store unit may be part of a chain, may accept mail-order sales, and will have a specific retail strategy mix.

It is important to note that the data presented in this chapter and the next one must be interpreted carefully. Because the terms may not be mutually exclusive, great care should be taken if one combines tables to obtain aggregate sales because double counting may occur. Although an attempt has been made to use as many current statistics as possible, not all data correspond to a common date.

Retail Institutions Categorized by Ownership

A great deal of diversity of retail institutions appears within the ownership category. For example, retail institutions may be independently owned, chain-owned, franchisee-operated, owned by manufacturers or wholesalers, or consumer-owned.

Although retail institutions are primarily small (according to the *1982 Census of Retail Trade*, about 48 per cent of all retail institutions had two or fewer paid employees, and about 79 per cent of all retail firms operated only one establishment), retailing also includes large institutions. The five largest retail institutions, according to *Fortune's 1984 Directory*, had an average of about 240,000 employees and average sales in excess of $20 billion during 1983.

Independent

An **independent** retailer owns only one retail unit. In the United States, retailing primarily comprises a great many small, owner-operated independents. The high number of independent retailers is associated with the ease of entry into the marketplace.

A Classification Method for Retail Institutions

I **By** **Ownership**	a. Independent b. Chain c. Franchise d. Leased department e. Vertical marketing system f. Consumer cooperative	
II **By Retail** **Strategy Mix**	a. Convenience store b. Conventional supermarket c. Combination store d. Superstore e. Box (limited line) store f. Warehouse outlet g. Specialty store h. Variety store i. Department store j. Full-line discount store k. Retail catalog showroom l. Off-price chain m. Factory outlet n. Buying club o. Flea market	Food-based retailers General merchandise retailers
III **By Nonstore** **Retailing**	a. Vending machine b. Direct-to-home selling c. Direct marketing	
IV **By Service vs.** **Product** **Retailing**	a. Rented good b. Owned good c. Nongood	

Figure 3-1

Because of low capital requirements and no, or relatively simple, licensing provisions, entry for small retailers is easy. The investment per worker in retailing is significantly lower than that of manufacturing establishments. The licensing of retailers, although more stringent in recent years, is still a routine task.

The ease of entry into retailing is reflected by the low market shares of the leading firms in various retail categories as a percentage of total category sales. For example, the four largest retail food chains and the four largest general merchandise stores account for only about 17 and 28 per cent of sales in their respective merchandise groupings.

The relative ease of entry generates a greater degree of competition. However, it is also undoubtedly an important factor in the high rate of retail business failures. In 1983, 30.2 per cent of the retailers in business three or fewer years failed; 54.1 per cent of those in business five or fewer years failed.[2,3] The early 1980s were a very difficult period for retailers due to layoffs and unemployment in several key industries.[4]

Competitive Advantages and Disadvantages of Independents

Independent retailers have a variety of advantages and disadvantages facing them. Among the advantages are flexibility, low investments, specialization, direct control of strategy, image, uniformity, independence, and entrepreneurial drive.

Independent retailers have a great deal of flexibility when choosing store locations and developing strategy. Because only one store location is involved, a detailed list of specifications can be derived from the best location and a thorough search undertaken. Uniform location standards are not developed, as they are for chain stores, and the independent does not have to worry about being too close to other company stores.

In setting strategy, independents have great latitude in selecting customer markets. Because many independents have modest goals, small portions of the overall customer market may be selected rather than the mass market. Product assortments, prices, store hours, and so on, are then set consistently with the market.

Because independents run only one store, investment costs for leases, fixtures, employees, and merchandise can be held down. In addition, there is no duplication of stock or personnel functions. Responsibilities are also clearly delineated within the store.

Many independents are able to operate as specialists and so develop skills in a particular area. These stores can then be more efficient and can attract customers interested in specialized retailers.

Independent retailers can exert strong control over their strategies because only one store must be managed, and the owner-operator is usually on the premises. Decision making is usually centralized, and the layers of management personnel are minimized.

There is a certain image attached to independents, particularly small ones, that

---

[2]*1982–1983 Business Failure Record* (New York: Dun & Bradstreet, 1985), p. 13.

[3]Dun & Bradstreet defines business failures as firms involved in court proceedings or in voluntary actions resulting in losses to creditors.

[4]*The Small Business Economy—1981* (Washington, D.C.: National Federation of Independent Business, March 1982).

chains would have difficulty in capturing. This is the image of a friendly, personalized retailer who provides an intimate atmosphere.

Independents are able to sustain uniformity because only one geographic market is served and one strategy (store hours, product assortment, prices, sales personnel, promotion, and so on) carried out. For example, there cannot be problems because two branch stores are selling identical items at different prices.

An independent retailer has "independence." The owner-operator is generally in full control and does not have to worry about stockholders, meetings of the board of directors, and labor unrest. For example, independents are often free from union work rules and seniority regulations. This can materially affect labor productivity.[5]

As a last major advantage, independents have a strong entrepreneurial drive. They have a personal investment in a business, success or failure has substantial implications, and there is a high degree of ego involvement.

Among the disadvantages of independent retailing are limits in bargaining power, little economies of scale, intensiveness of labor, reduced access to media, overdependence on the boss, and little time and resources for planning.

When bargaining with suppliers, independents do not have much power because they often buy in small quantities. Therefore, in many instances, independents must pay high prices and accept standard merchandise instead of custom-made items. Some independents, like hardware stores, form buying groups to increase their power in dealing with suppliers.

Independents are usually unable to establish economies of scale (low per unit costs due to the handling of many units at one time) in buying and maintaining inventory. Because of demand and financial constraints, small assortments of items are purchased several times per year rather than large orders once or twice per year. This means that transportation, ordering, and handling costs are high.

Store operations for independents are very labor intensive. There is little computerization. Ordering, taking inventory, marking merchandise, ringing up sales, and bookkeeping are generally done manually. Manual operations are time consuming and less efficient than computer tabulations (which are expensive in terms of initial investment).

Because of the costs of television and the large geographic coverage of magazines (too large for independents), independent retailers are limited in their access to advertising media and sometimes pay abnormally high fees as compared to regular users. However, a creative independent has a number of promotion tools available (see Chapter 13).

An important problem for independents—particularly small, family-run businesses—is an overdependence on the owner. In too many cases, all decisions are made by this person, and no continuity of management is stipulated for the time the owner-boss is ill or on vacation or retires. Long-run success and employee morale can be affected by overdependence on the owner.

Another critical problem for independent retailers is the limited amount of time and resources allocated to long-run planning. Because the owner is intimately involved in the day-to-day running of the store, adaptation to new legislation, new products, and/or new competitors often suffers.

---

[5]See John Merwin, "A Piece of the Action," *Forbes* (September 24, 1984), pp. 146–148ff.

Table 3-1
Retail Firm Size, 1982, 1977, 1972

	Number of Firms	Establishments as Per Cent of Total*			Sales as Per Cent of Total*			Payroll as Per Cent of Total*		
	1982	1982	1977	1972	1982	1977	1972	1982	1977	1972
U.S. total	1,572,792	100.0	100.0	100.0	100.0	100.0	100.0	100.0	100.0	100.0
Single unit total	1,521,846	79.1	82.1	84.7	47.7	52.0	54.9	47.0	49.2	51.4
Multiunit total	50,946	20.9	17.9	15.2	52.3	48.0	45.1	53.0	50.8	48.6
2 to 4 units	41,612	5.2	4.6	4.4	8.1	7.3	7.0	9.1	8.5	8.4
5 to 9 units	5,505	1.8	1.8	1.4	3.6	3.3	3.0	3.8	3.7	3.4
10 to 24 units	2,422	1.8	1.7	1.3	4.0	3.6	3.5	4.0	3.9	3.6
25 to 99 units	1,031	2.5	2.2	1.8	7.1	6.7	6.3	6.7	6.5	6.4
100 or more units	376	9.5	7.7	6.1	29.5	26.9	25.3	29.3	28.3	26.8

*Rounding errors appear in some of the percentages.
Source: 1982 Census of Retail Trade; *and authors' estimates.*

Chain

A **chain** can be defined as multiple retail units under common ownership, that utilize centralized purchasing and decision making.

Table 3-1 provides data on the number of establishments, sales volume, and payroll (as a percentage of the U.S. total) for firms of differing numbers of units during 1972, 1977, and 1982. It is clear from this table that the relative strength of chains is great. In 1982, multiunit firms comprised 20.9 per cent of retail establishments, but 52 per cent of retail sales and 53 per cent of total retail payrolls. Most multiunit retail firms had a small number of establishments (of the 50,946 multiunit firms, 41,612, or 82 per cent, had two to four units; 92 per cent of all multiunit firms had nine or fewer establishments). It is important to note that a large percentage of the sales of multiunits were made through grocery stores and department stores.

During the 10-year period from 1972 to 1982, the percentage of total retail sales made by multiunit retailers increased substantially. A look at Table 3-1 reveals that this increase is due largely to retailers operating 100 or more units. For this category, the sales as a percentage of total retail sales have gone up sharply. As of 1982, only 376 retailers operated with 100 or more units; however, those retailers accounted for about 30 per cent of all retail sales in the United States. As an example, in the pharmaceutical area, the five leading drugstore chains accounted for 22.4 per cent of total industry sales and operated an average of 1,078 units in 1983.[6]

The distribution of multiestablishment firms differs by kind of business. See Table 3-2. In 1982, multiestablishment firms accounted for 98.5 percent of all department store sales, 87.7 per cent of variety store sales, and 75.7 per cent of grocery store sales. In contrast, they accounted for 48.0 per cent of the sales for gasoline service stations, 41.0 per cent of the sales for furniture stores, and 32.5 per cent of the sales for liquor stores.

[6]Isadore Barmash, "The New Look in Drugstores," *New York Times* (January 25, 1985), pp. D1, D7.

Table 3-2
Percentage Distribution of Sales by Number of Units
per Firm for Selected Kinds of Retailers, 1982

	Retail Trade Total	Department Store	Variety Store	Grocery Store	Gasoline Service Station	Women's Ready-to-Wear Store	Furniture Store	Liquor Store
Single unit	47.7	1.5	12.3	24.3	52.0	26.8	59.0	67.5
Multiple units	52.3	98.5	87.7	75.7	48.0	73.2	41.0	32.5
2 to 9 units	11.7	4.1	3.4	12.2	11.9	16.1	24.9	11.2
10 or more units	40.6	94.4	84.3	63.5	36.1	57.1	16.1	21.3
Total units	100.0	100.0	100.0	100.0	100.0	100.0	100.0	100.0

Source: 1982 Census of Retail Trade.

Chains operating 100 or more retail establishments were predominantly made up of grocery stores, gas service stations, variety stores, drugstores, shoe stores, and auto accessory dealers. A more precise breakdown of these large chains is contained in Table 3-3.

Competitive Advantages and Disadvantages of Chains

There are several competitive advantages for chain stores: bargaining power, wholesale function efficiencies, multiple-store efficiencies, computerization, access to media, well-defined management, and long-run planning.[7]

A large chain has bargaining power when dealing with a manufacturer. The chain can threaten the manufacturer with loss of business unless the retailer is given a dis-

Table 3-3
Firms Owning 100 or More Retail Establishments by Selected Kinds of
Business, Number of Establishments, and Number of Firms, 1982

Kind of Business	Number of Establishments	Operated by Number of Firms	Average Number of Establishments/Firm
Grocery stores	26,966	61	442
Gas service stations	14,914	45	331
Variety stores	5,072	12	423
Drugstores	9,726	22	442
Shoe stores	18,281	25	731
Tires, batteries, and accessories	5,658	9	629
Total	80,617	174	463

Source: 1982 Census of Retail Trade.

[7]See Richard T. Hise, J. Patrick Kelly, Myron Gable, and James B. McDonald, "Factors Affecting the Performance of Individual Chain Store Units: An Empirical Analysis," *Journal of Retailing*, Vol. 59 (Summer 1983), pp. 22–39.

count below the prevailing market price. This is true despite the existence of Robinson-Patman pricing legislation that bans this practice. Whether or not bargaining power is used, it does exist, and suppliers are aware that the elimination of a large retailer as a customer could lead to losses or even bankruptcy.

A chain can achieve cost efficiencies through the performance of wholesale functions. Buying, shipping, storing, and other wholesale activities can be performed by the retailer. Wholesale salespeople can be eliminated and the volume of orders can be increased. The costs of products bought by chains have been found to be significantly lower than for independents.

Efficiency in multiple-store operations can be attained through lower costs of securing capital, lower rental costs, and centralized decision making. It is typical for a ladies' apparel chain or a shoe chain to give central office personnel authority and responsibility for buying, pricing, and promotion functions. Centralized decision making may result in economies from buying large quantities, as well as from the elimination of market trips by individual branch store managers or more specialized personnel.

Chain stores, because of their resources and number of transactions, are able to use computers in ordering merchandise, taking inventory, forecasting, ringing up sales, and bookkeeping. This use of computers increases efficiency and reduces overall costs.

Chains, particularly national or regional ones, can take advantage of a variety of media, from television to magazines to traditional newspapers. Large sales volume and geographic coverage of the market allow chains to utilize all forms of media.

Most chains have well-defined management philosophies, whether centralized or decentralized. Overall strategies are clearly delineated, and the responsibilities of employees are clearly outlined. In addition, continuity is assured when managerial personnel are absent or retire.

Finally, many chain stores expend considerable time and resources in long-run planning. Frequently specific personnel are assigned to long-term planning on a permanent basis. Opportunities and constraints are also carefully monitored.

Chain stores do have a number of disadvantages: inflexibility, high investments, lack of control, and limited independence.

Once a chain store is well established, its flexibility is limited. Adequate, non-overlapping store locations may be difficult to find. A consistent strategy must be maintained throughout all of the branches; prices, promotions, and product assortments must be similar for each store. For chains that use centralized decision making, there may be difficulty in adapting to local needs, such as taking into account differences in life-styles among city, suburban, and rural customers.

For chains, investment costs are high. Multiple-store leases, fixtures, product assortments, and employees are involved. The purchase of any merchandise may be costly because a number of store branches must be stocked.

Managerial control can present a problem for chains, especially for those having geographically dispersed branches. Top management cannot maintain the control over each branch that an independent owner has over his or her single outlet. Lack of communication and time delays in making and enacting decisions are two particular problems.

Personnel in large chains have limited independence. In many cases, there are several layers of management, unionized employees, stockholders, and boards of directors.

Franchising

Franchising is defined as a contractual arrangement between a franchisor (who may be a manufacturer, a wholesaler, or a service sponsor) and a retail franchisee, which allows the franchisee to conduct a given form of business under an established name and according to a given pattern of business. In a typical franchise arrangement, the franchisee pays an initial fee and a monthly percentage of gross sales in exchange for the exclusive rights to sell goods and services in a specified geographic area. Franchising represents a retail organizational form in which small businesspeople can benefit by being part of a large, multiunit chain-type retail institution.

There are two broad types of franchising arrangements: product/trademark franchising and business format franchising. In a product/trademark franchising arrangement, franchised dealers acquire the identity of their suppliers by agreeing to sell the latter's products and/or operate under the suppliers' names. These franchised dealers operate relatively autonomously from the suppliers. Although they must adhere to certain operating rules, they set store hours, choose locations, determine store facilities and displays, and otherwise run their stores. Examples of product/trademark franchises are auto dealers and many gasoline service stations.

With business format franchising, there is a more active relationship between the franchisor and the franchisee. The franchisee receives assistance on site location, quality control, accounting systems, startup practices, management training, and responding to problems—in addition to the right to sell goods and services. The use of prototype stores, standardized merchandise lines, and cooperative advertising enable business format franchises to achieve a level of coordination previously found only in chains. Since the 1950s, the major growth in franchising has involved business format arrangements. These arrangements are common for restaurants and other food outlets, real estate, and rental services.

Although many variations in franchising exist, McDonald's is a good example of a business format franchise arrangement. The company provides each new franchisee with an intensive training program at its "Hamburger U," a detailed operations manual (complete down to the most minute facets of running machinery), regular visits by field service managers, and repeat trips to Hamburger U for brush-up training courses. In return for these rights and privileges, the McDonald's Corporation receives $300,000 and more for a long-term agreement to operate a franchise. A large down payment is required, and a McDonald's franchisee pays a royalty fee, based on gross sales, to the franchisor.

Size and Structural Arrangements

Retail franchising began in the United States in 1865 when the Singer Sewing Machine Company first franchised its dealers. However, retail franchising did not become popular until undercapitalized automobile manufacturers started utilizing franchising to expand their distribution systems in the early 1900s.[8] Although the automobile industry still accounts for about 52 per cent of all franchise sales, there are few retail industry

[8]Jacob Goodman, "Franchisor–Franchisee Relation Requires Delicate Balance," *Marketing News* (February 17, 1984), p. 4.

Table 3-4
1984 Retail Franchise Sales

	Sales (billions)	Per Cent of Sales
Auto and truck dealers	$208.9	52.1
Gasoline service stations	106.2	26.5
Restaurants (all types)	44.1	11.0
Convenience stores	11.3	2.8
Auto products stores	5.8	1.4
Other retailing	24.9	6.2
All franchises	$401.2	100.0

Source: Franchising in the Economy: 1982–1984 *(Washington, D.C.: U.S. Department of Commerce, 1984), p. 12.*

groups that have not been affected by franchising's growth. In 1984, franchising accounted for $401 billion in retail sales, or about 32 percent of 1984's total retail store sales. Overall, 86 per cent of franchising sales (both retail and nonretail) were made by franchisee-owned units and 14 per cent were made by company-owned outlets.[9] Table 3-4 shows 1984 retail franchise sales.

Three types of structural arrangements involving retail franchises can be distinguished: manufacturer-retailer, wholesaler-retailer, and service sponsor-retailer. These arrangements are explained and illustrated in Figure 3-2.

Competitive Advantages and Disadvantages of Franchising

The franchisee receives several benefits by investing in a successful franchise operation. First, an individual businessperson can own and operate a retail enterprise with a relatively small capital investment. Second, the franchisee acquires a well-known name and product line. Third, standard operating procedures and management skills are taught. Fourth, a cooperative marketing program is employed (e.g., national advertising) that could not otherwise be afforded. Fifth, the franchisee obtains exclusive selling rights for a specified geographical territory. Sixth, purchases may be made more cheaply because of volume.

Some potential problems exist for franchisees. First, oversaturation occurs when too many franchisees are located in one geographic area; therefore, the sales and profits of each unit are adversely affected. Second, because of the overzealous selling of franchises, the income potential and required managerial ability, initiative, and investment of a franchise unit may be incorrectly stated.[10] Third, a franchisee may be locked into a tying agreement whereby purchases must be made through the franchisor or certain approved vendors. Fourth, cancellation provisions may give the franchisor the right to cancel a franchise if any provision of the franchise agreement is not met. Fifth, in some industries, franchise agreements are of short duration. Sixth, under most franchise contracts, royalties are a percentage of gross sales, regardless of the franchisees' profits.

[9]*Franchising in the Economy: 1982–1984* (Washington, D.C.: U.S. Department of Commerce, 1984), pp. 12–13.
[10]See John R. Nevin, Shelby D. Hunt, and Michael G. Levas," Legal Remedies for Deceptive and Unfair Practices in Franchising," *Journal of Macromarketing*, Vol. 1 (Spring 1981), pp. 23–34.

Franchising Structural Arrangements

	Types of Retail Structural Arrangements	Examples of Structural Arrangements	
A.	**Manufacturer-Retailer** Manufacturer gives right (through licensing arrangement) for independent businessperson to sell products subject to conditions.	*Car/Truck Manufacturer* General Motors Ford Chrysler American Motors	*Petroleum Refiners* Exxon Mobil *Farm Equipment* John Deere
B.	**Wholesaler-Retailer** 1. Voluntary—wholesaler organizes a franchise system and grants franchises to individual stores. 2. Cooperative—retailers set up a franchise cooperative by owning and operating a wholesale organization.	VOLUNTARY *Auto* Western Auto COOPERATIVE *Grocery* Foodtown Key Food Shop Rite	*Electronics* Radio Shack *Hardware* Ace True Value
C.	**Service Sponsor-Retailer** Service firm licenses retailer to provide specific service package to ultimate consumer.	*Auto Rental* Avis Hertz National *Fast Food* McDonald's Burger King Dunkin' Donuts Wendy's International House of Pancakes Dairy Queen Kentucky Fried Chicken Carvel Baskin-Robbins	*Motels* Holiday Inn Howard Johnson *Employment Agencies* Manpower Kelly Girl *Lawn Care* Lawn-A-Mat Lawn King Chem Lawn *Automobile Repair* Midas Muffler Lee Myles

Figure 3-2

These six factors result in **constrained decision making,** whereby the franchisor can exclude franchisees from or limit their involvement in the decision-making process.

In an effort to curb unfair franchisor sales practices, in 1979, the Federal Trade Commission introduced a rule entitled "Disclosure Requirements and Business Opportunities." This rule applies to all franchisors in the United States and is intended to provide potential franchisees with adequate information prior to making an investment.[11] In addition, a number of states have enacted fair practice laws stipulating that franchisors may not terminate, cancel, or fail to renew a franchise without sufficient cause.[12] Arizona, California, Indiana, New Jersey, Virginia, Washington, and Wisconsin are among the states with fair practice laws. Furthermore, fifteen states require that franchise offerings be registered.[13]

The franchisor accrues many benefits by selling individual franchises. First, a national chain can be developed more quickly and with a smaller investment on the part of the franchisor. Second, qualifications for franchise ownership can be set and enforced. Third, money is obtained when goods are delivered rather than when they are sold. Fourth, agreements can be drawn up that require franchisees to abide by stringent regulations set by the franchisor. Fifth, because franchisees are owners and not employees, they have a greater incentive to work hard. Sixth, after a franchisee has paid for the franchise, the franchisor also receives royalties or sells products to the individual proprietors.

A franchisor may also face potential problems. First, individual franchisees can ruin the overall image and reputation of the franchise because standards are not maintained. Second, lack of uniformity adversely affects customer loyalty. Third, intrafranchise competition is not desirable. Fourth, the resale value of individual units is injured if franchisees perform poorly. Fifth, an ineffective franchise unit directly injures the franchisor's profitability from the sales of services, materials, or products to franchisees, or from royalty fees.

Additional information on franchising is contained in the appendix following this chapter.

Leased Department

A **leased department** is a department in a retail store—usually a department, discount, or specialty store—that is rented to an outside party. The proprietor of a leased department is responsible for all aspects of its operations (including fixtures) and normally pays the store a percentage of sales as rent. The store imposes various stipulations on the leased department to ensure overall consistency and coordination.

In traditional department stores, leased departments have been used to broaden merchandise or service offerings into product areas requiring highly specialized skills or knowledge not possessed by the internal store organization. Consequently, leased departments operate in areas that tend to be on the fringe of the department store's

---

[11]Philip S. Gutis, "The Stunning Franchise Explosion," *New York Times* (January 20, 1985), Section 3, p. 4.

[12]See John R. Nevin, Shelby D. Hunt, and Robert W. Ruekert, "The Impact of Fair Practice Laws on a Franchising Channel of Distribution," *MSU Business Topics*, Vol. 28 (Summer 1980), p. 28.

[13]Thomas O'Donnell, "Franchising: No Entrepreneurs Need Apply," *Forbes* (December 3, 1984), p. 130. Also see Eugene Carlson, "Michigan Seeks Better Image with a New Franchising Law," *Wall Street Journal* (March 26, 1985), p. 33.

product lines. Departments most commonly leased to outside organizations include beauty salons, photographic studios, millinery, shoes, jewelry, watch repairs, shoe repairs, and sewing machines.[14]

The situation differs for leased departments in discount stores, whose early growth, in many cases, depended heavily on leasing a number of departments to specialized operators. Discount store operators choose to lease departments for the following major reasons:

- Store operators sometimes lack merchandising ability in product lines that could be supported in general-merchandise discount stores.
- Operators often lack the financial ability to support the inventory investment necessary to enter various product lines that could be leased to others.
- Ambitious store operators desire to enlarge their market niche by providing one-stop shopping services for customers.
- The administrative and operating problems of selecting, training, and maintaining a merchandising staff for all departments is avoided by the leasing of certain departments.
- The leased department is often a source of working capital, because revenue is available daily from the central checkout operation but is retained by the storekeeper until the end of specified accounting periods, when a settlement is made with the leased-department operators.[15]

From the outside proprietors' perspective, there are several reasons for becoming leased-department operators:

- Discount stores have a high traffic potential.
- The investment is lower than normally required because of shared facilities, such as a central checkout area.
- There are economies of scale (volume savings) in pooled advertising, central air-conditioning, and central parking services.[16]

A leased department can be viewed from two perspectives: as an element in a shopping center and as a part of a franchise system. In the shopping center context, the leased department is renting an area with a given traffic flow to conduct its business. The leased-department operator must examine the character of the traffic and its relationship to the chosen consumer market. The lessor must examine the extent to which the department will either create additional traffic or be a parasite and live off the traffic generated by other parts of the store. The franchise analogy relates to the leased department's ability to blend with the merchandise philosophy of other merchants and the need to set a broad policy for all departments, so that an entire store's reputation is not injured by one operator.

An example of a successful long-term lease arrangement is one utilized by the CPI Corporation and Sears. For more than twenty years, CPI has operated photographic studios in Sears stores. In exchange for the use of 300 square feet of space in each of

---

[14]See Marcie Lynn Avram "A Lessee for the Floor Covering Department?" *Stores* (June 1983), pp. 16–17.
[15]William R. Davidson, Alton F. Doody, and James R. Lowry, "Leased Departments as a Major Force in the Growth of Discount Store Retailing," *Journal of Marketing*, Vol. 34 (January 1970), p. 41.
[16]Ibid., p. 42.

well over 600 Sears stores, CPI pays Sears 15 per cent of its gross sales. CPI generates annual sales of $450 per square foot, compared with Sears' overall average of $291. CPI's agreement with Sears can be terminated by Sears on sixty days' notice.[17]

Vertical Marketing System

Products are normally distributed through one of the three types of marketing channels, or systems, depicted in Figure 3-3.

In most instances, individual retailers or chains do not own manufacturing or wholesaling facilities and do not perform these functions. For this arrangement, manufacturers seek out wholesalers, who seek out retailers to stock and sell products. This is **independent channel ownership.**

There are other cases in which two channel members are able to perform all the

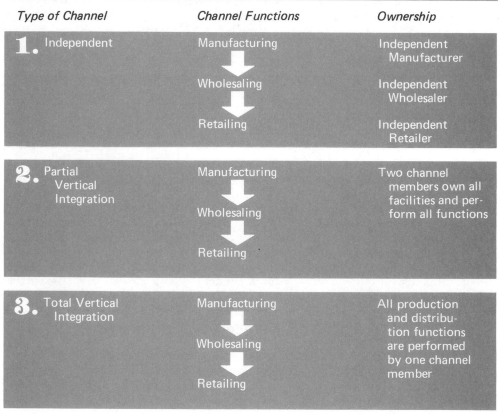

Figure 3-3

[17]John A. Byrne, "Profit from Portraits," *Forbes* (June 6, 1983), pp. 107–108.

production and marketing functions without the aid of the third. The most common form of this marketing channel arrangement occurs when a manufacturer and a retailer are able to accomplish shipping, storing, and other intermediate marketing activities in the absence of an independently owned wholesaler. This is **partial vertical integration.**

Total vertical integration occurs when successive stages of production and distribution are contained under single ownership. This allows one firm to own all facilities, perform all functions, and deal directly with the consumer. It is this type of channel that will now be examined.

Although the majority of retailers purchase goods and services from manufacturers and wholesalers they do not own, in several important cases all the stages of manufacturing and marketing are combined under single ownership. Sherwin-Williams Paint Company owns and operates more than 1,500 retail outlets.[18] Sears obtains a substantial proportion of its products from manufacturing facilities in which it has an equity interest. For example, in 1983, Sears owned over 30 per cent of the Roper Corporation (a manufacturer of ranges and mowers), over 30 per cent of DeSoto Incorporated (maker of paints and detergents), and over 20 per cent of the Kellwood Company (maker of apparel and soft goods.)[19] Hartmarx, a clothing manufacturer, owns and operates several hundred men's and women's specialty shops.[20]

Many food chains, such as Kroger and Southland (7-Eleven), manufacture dairy, baked goods, ice cream, and other products. At Kroger, one-sixth of the food sold is company produced. Southland has one of the country's largest dairies—with eleven regional brands.[21]

A company that is vertically integrated can achieve many objectives, such as self-sufficiency, lower costs through elimination of middlemen, direct contact with the consumer, greater bargaining power when dealing with outside suppliers or retailers, a sense of achievement because the total product or service process is controlled, and time efficiencies in orders and deliveries. For example, Tandy makes most of the products for its Radio Shack stores. As a result, it is able to maximize product visibility, improve staff product knowledge, stock and display a full and distinctive product line, and control retail prices.[22]

However, there may be some difficulties associated with vertical integration. In particular, the firm may not have expertise in both manufacturing and retailing operations. As an illustration, after one evaluation of its candy-making operations, Kroger's chief executive reached this conclusion: "We can make candy as *good* as anyone. We just can't make it as efficiently."[23]

In addition to the ownership of manufacturing, wholesaling, and retail facilities by one member of a channel (as in a totally integrated marketing system), a company can control a channel because of economic, political, or legal power; superior knowledge; or promotional tactics. **Channel control** occurs when one member of a channel is able to impose its will on other independent channel members. Manufacturers, wholesalers,

---

[18]Paul Ingrassia, "Sherwin-Williams Makes Big Turn Around Under Chairman's Aggressive Leadership," *Wall Street Journal* (December 14, 1983), p. 33.
[19]*Sears, Roebuck and Company Form 10K*, for fiscal year ended December 31, 1983, p. 4.
[20]*Hartmarx 1983 Annual Report*.
[21]Bill Saporito, "Kroger, The New King of Supermarketing," *Fortune* (February 21, 1983), p. 76; and "The Case of U.S. vs. Southland," *Business Week* (November 21, 1983), p. 108.
[22]"The Chains Take Over Computer Retailing," *Business Week* (November 7, 1983), p. 90.
[23]Saporito, "Kroger, The New King of Supermarketing," pp. 75–76.

and retailers each have a combination of control tactics available to them, apart from ownership of other members.[24]

Manufacturers can exert control through franchising, whereby the franchisee's marketing program comes under close scrutiny; developing strong brand loyalty, wherein retailers are forced to stock merchandise because of consumer pressure; preticketing merchandise, thereby designating suggested list or selling prices; and exclusive distribution, whereby the retailer voluntarily agrees to adhere to given standards in exchange for sole distribution rights in a geographic area.

Wholesalers have the ability to exert control over manufacturers and retailers. If the wholesaler is large, its business is important, and pressure can be applied to suppliers and buyers. Wholesalers can introduce their own private brands, and circumvent manufacturers. A franchise system and/or brand loyalty can also be developed to control the distribution system.

Retailers are able to exert control over other channel members in the following instances: a large proportion of a manufacturer's output is sold to one retailer, private branding is employed, or economic power (large gross sales) exists.

When one retailer represents a large percentage of a manufacturer's sales volume, channel control may be applied. For example, there are a number of independent companies from whom Sears purchases a large proportion of its output. One such company is Armstrong Rubber (manufacturer of tires and tubes), which makes a large amount of its sales through Sears. As a result, Sears has a very strong bargaining position.

Store brands or private labels enable a retailer to possess channel control, improve competitive positioning, and raise profit margins. Eighty-five per cent of the merchandise purchased by J. C. Penney is specifically made for the company. At Sakowitz, Dayton's, Nordstrom, and Lord & Taylor department stores, from 20 to 40 per cent of apparel purchases involve private labels. Even at K mart, which stresses manufacturer brands, 25 per cent of merchandise is privately branded.[25]

Through private labeling, retailers gain significant power over wholesalers and manufacturers by attaining brand loyalty for their goods, converting it to store loyalty, and causing merchandise to be made to specifications. Private labeling thus enables retailers to switch vendors (sellers) with no impact on their customer loyalty as long as the same product specifications are followed. The threat of switching vendors (with no offsetting impact on the private brand sales) is often adequate action to get a manufacturer into line on a retailer's price, delivery, or terms request.

It is important to note that channel control in many cases has significant advantages for the controlled party, as well as the leader. Long-term relationships allow for scheduling efficiencies and enable vendors to obtain bank loans (because of presold inventories). Some economies result because many activities are eliminated, simplified, or repositioned. Advertising, financing, and billing are drastically simplified, and many functions, such as merchandise marking, can be performed by the manufacturer.

---

[24]See Andy Paszter, "Justice Department Guidelines Support Most Marketing Restrictions by Makers," *Wall Street Journal* (January 24, 1985), p. 12; and Leslie Maitland Werner, "U.S. Issues Guidelines on 'Vertical' Accords," *New York Times* (January 24, 1985), pp. D1, D17.

[25]*J. C. Penney Merchandise*, p. 3; Ann Morrison, "The Upshot of Off-Price," *Fortune* (June 13, 1983), p. 129; Steve Weiner, "Caught in a Cross-Fire, Brand-Apparel Makers Design Their Defenses," *Wall Street Journal* (January 24, 1984), pp. 1, 17; *Associated Dry Goods Corp. 1983 Annual Report*, p. 68; and "What 'Discount' Doesn't Mean at K mart," company press release.

Consumer Cooperative

A **consumer cooperative** is a retail establishment characterized by consumer ownership. A group of consumers invests, receives stock certificates, elects officers, manages the operations, and shares the profits or savings that accrue.

Consumers have formed cooperatives based on three fundamental concepts: (1) consumers can perform the retailing function better than existing institutions, (2) existing retail institutions are inadequately fulfilling consumers' needs, and (3) existing retailers make excessive profits.

Consumer cooperatives have been most prevalent in the food category, particularly with produce items. Yet food cooperatives account for well under 1 per cent of total supermarket retail sales and supermarket produce sales. Heating oil cooperatives have recently been formed in the Northeastern part of the United States, where oil is the primary home heating fuel.

Many consumer food cooperatives operate in the following manner. Weekly, participants develop lists of products they want to order. These lists are collated and large orders placed. Members go on buying trips, make sure that goods are assembled for delivery, and arrange for shipping. After goods are received, they are marked and packaged for pick up by these members who have submitted orders. Members pay when they pick up their orders. Because a cooperative's tasks are divisible, each work assignment usually consists of a single responsibility (such as purchasing, bookkeeping, order collating), which is rotated among cooperative members.

Smaller cooperatives have not grown further because they involve a lot of customer initiative; consumers are not experts in buying, handling, and distributing items; selling prices have not provided the desired savings in many instances; and the functions can be time consuming.

The Cooperative League estimates that there are about 5,000 food cooperatives in the United States, ranging from small buying clubs to large supermarket-style outlets. Annual sales are between $500 million and $1 billion. The largest food cooperative is the Consumers Co-Op of Berkeley, California, with sales of $58 million in 1984 (down from $84 million in 1980) and six outlets.[26]

Retail Institutions—Part I: A Summary

Retail institutions can be classified by ownership, by retail strategy mix, by nonstore retailing, and by service versus product retailing. This classification system is not mutually exclusive; that is, a retail institution can be correctly placed in more than one such classification. This chapter analyzed retail institutions as categorized by ownership: independents, chains, franchising, leased departments, vertical marketing systems, and consumer cooperatives.

Most retail establishments can be classified as being independent, as 79 per cent of all retail establishments are single unit in ownership. The large number of independent retailers is associated with the ease of entry into the marketplace. Among the

[26]Andrew Pollack, "Food Co-Ops in a Struggle," *New York Times* (February 23, 1985), pp. 29, 40.

competitive advantages of independents are flexibility, low investment, specialization, direct control of strategy, image, uniformity, independence, and entrepreneurial spirit.

Retail chains are comprised of multiple retail units under common ownership that utilize centralized purchasing and decision making. Chains make up 21 per cent of all retail establishments, and they account for 52 per cent of total retail sales. Chain stores have several distinct advantages: bargaining power, wholesale function efficiencies, multiple-store efficiencies, computerization, access to media, well-defined management, and long-range planning.

A franchise is defined as a contractual arrangement in which the franchisor (who may be a wholesaler, a manufacturer, or a service sponsor) awards a franchisee the right to conduct a given form of business according to an established pattern. Franchises account for about 32 per cent of retail sales. A franchise system allows owners of small businesses to benefit from the experience, buying capabilities, and image of a large, multiunit retail institution. A common characteristic of franchising is constrained decision making, reflected in cancellation provisions, short-term franchise agreements, or tying agreements.

A leased department is a department in a retail store—generally a discount, department, or specialty store—that is rented to an outside party. The proprietor of a leased department is responsible for all aspects of its operation and normally pays the store a percentage of sales as rent. Departments commonly leased to outside organizations include beauty salons, photographic studios, millinery, shoes, jewelry, and watch repair.

Vertical marketing occurs when successive stages of production and distribution are contained under single ownership. A vertically integrated firm can achieve many objectives, such as self-sufficiency, lower costs through elimination of middlemen and direct contact with the consumer, greater bargaining power when dealing with outside suppliers or retailers, a sense of achievement because the total product or service process is controlled, and time efficiencies in orders and deliveries. In addition to the ownership of manufacturing, wholesaling, and retail facilities by one member of a channel, a company can control a channel because of economic, political, or legal power; superior knowledge; or promotional tactics.

A consumer cooperative is a retail establishment characterized by consumer ownership. A group of consumers invests, receives stock certificates, elects officers, manages the operations, and shares the profits or savings that accrue. Consumer cooperatives have been most prevalent in the food category, particularly with produce items.

Questions for Discussion

1. What are the characteristics of each of the ownership forms discussed in this chapter?
2. May a retailer be categorized by more than one ownership form? Explain your answer.
3. Why are there so many small, independent retailers?
4. How can an independent retailer overcome the problem of overdependence on the owner?
5. Compare the advantages and disadvantages of independents versus chains.
6. What problems might an independent face if it tries to develop into a chain?
7. Do you expect chains to continue their dominance in the future? Why or why not?
8. Distinguish between chain ownership and franchising.

9. What are the advantages and disadvantages of franchising for the franchisee? For the franchisor?
10. Which factors would you use to compare alternative franchising opportunities?
11. Why would a department store want to lease space to an outside operator rather than run a business, such as a beauty salon, itself?
12. What are some of the disadvantages that may occur with total vertical integration?
13. Under which circumstances are retailers likely to be able to exert a great deal of channel control? Very little channel control?
14. Why have consumer cooperatives not expanded rapidly? Can this be changed?

CASES

1. Tandy Corporation: Competing for Home-Computer Sales*

Tandy Corporation, the parent company of Radio Shack, makes and sells its own brands of merchandise (e.g., Realistic, Radio Shack) through a network of nearly 9,000 company-owned or affiliated stores. Tandy markets radios, telephones, electronic games, television antennas, electrical components, and a host of other related items as well as personal computers.

Tandy entered the personal computer market in 1977, after the CB radio craze ended. By 1984, it was selling personal computers through 731 traditional Radio Shack outlets and 429 Radio Shack Computer Centers; and computer sales and software accounted for over a third of overall company revenues. However, during this period, Tandy's market share fell drastically and its profit margins dropped significantly as competition intensified.

In 1984, there were about 3,700 retail computer specialty stores in the United States. This figure does not include traditional Radio Shack outlets, mass merchants such as Sears and K mart, toy stores such as Toys 'R' Us, office-supply stores, and others. In addition, manufacturers such as IBM employ their own sales forces. Of the 3,700 computer specialty stores, 28 per cent were franchise outlets, 23 per cent were single-location independents, 20 per cent were small retailer-owned chains, 19 per cent were manufacturer-owned chains, and 10 per cent were larger retailer-owned chains.

By making products and selling them through its own stores, Tandy has gained some important advantages over other firms:

- Brand exclusivity is maintained. Tandy brands are only available through its stores.
- More profits are retained within the company.
- There is better control over merchandise distribution, point-of-purchase displays, salesperson training, advertising, and prices.
- Distribution for new products is assured.
- The proper image can be projected at all levels (manufacturing and retailing).

*This case was prepared and written by Professor Michael V. Laric, University of Baltimore, Baltimore, Maryland. Material in this case is drawn from Peter W. Barnes, "Tandy's Shifting Sales Strategy," *New York Times* (August 19, 1984), Section 3, pp. 1, 26; and John Marcom, Jr., and Frederic M. Biddle, "Computer Dealers That Are Selling Top Brands Gain Big Edge in Market," *Wall Street Journal* (August 23, 1984), p. 25.

Despite these advantages, Tandy is experiencing a variety of problems with its computer stores:

- Consumers like to shop in outlets carrying many computer brands. This is not possible with Tandy stores, which do not sell IBM, Apple, or any other nonTandy brand.
- By 1988, there will be an estimated 7,000 retail computer specialty stores. Since Tandy is not planning to increase the number of stores it has carrying computers, Radio Shack computers will be available in fewer than 1,200 outlets (including traditional Radio Shack stores). This will limit sales potential.
- Traditional Radio Shack stores offer a limited number of computer models (due to cramped space) and are not very conducive to consumer shopping. They appeal more to hobbyists.
- Many retail computer specialty stores have trained their salespeople better than Tandy has. Whereas Tandy requires its computer salespeople to have 100 hours of training, retailers such as Sears require personnel to have at least five full weeks of product-line training.
- IBM, Apple, and other manufacturers offer their dealers financial backing, advertising support, training programs, and service support.

Tandy intends to continue with its integrated marketing system, despite the preceding issues. However, to increase its market penetration, the firm has just begun a novel approach. It is recruiting a sales force that will make in-home presentations to young families with children.

Questions

1. Outline the pros and cons of independent retailing, chain retailing, and a vertical marketing system for computer stores.
2. Should Tandy begin franchising Radio Shack Computer Center outlets to increase its market penetration? Why or why not?
3. Should Tandy begin operating leased departments for its computer stores in department stores? Why or why not?
4. Evaluate Tandy's decision to hire a sales force to make in-home presentations to young families with children.

---

2. Coastal Grocers Versus McGrath's: Power In the Relationship Between Wholesalers and Retailers*

Kenneth McGrath is the owner of a convenience food store in Spokane, Washington. Since opening in 1975 he has seen his sales grow from $75,000 to $780,000 in 1985. At this time he was fairly comfortable. He was paying himself a salary of $35,000 per year and was enjoying a net return of 4.45 per cent on sales.

Early in 1980 he had joined Coastal Grocers, a large cooperative wholesaler in the Northwest. At that time Coastal Grocers was a retailer-sponsored organization consisting of approximately forty other independent retailers such as McGrath. Basi-

*This case was prepared and written by Professor Kevin F. McCrohan, George Mason University, Fairfax, Virginia.

cally, the cooperative served to purchase in bulk for its members and to arrange delivery. To a limited extent, the cooperative also conducted joint promotional efforts aimed at informing consumers of the advantages of dealing with cooperative members. Ken felt that he had certainly benefited from the buying power the cooperative afforded him and he supposed that the promotional efforts could not hurt.

When he had initially joined Coastal, its delivery schedule was much to his liking. Although not perfect, the 11:30 A.M. delivery was not that disruptive to customers and did not require him to take a checker off his or her duties during the busy afternoon or evening hours.

However, Coastal had hired an outside consultant who had revised the store distribution plan to make it more efficient. The cooperative membership had grown by thirty members within the past two years and all the members had agreed that the old system, which had grown by pieces, was very inefficient. The new store distribution plan resulted in the total lowest delivery cost for the cooperative and therefore benefited all members. Unfortunately for Ken this schedule provided him with a 5:00 P.M. delivery. Since a good portion of Ken's business occurs between 4:00 P.M. and 7:00 P.M., as people return from work, this delivery time disrupts customers, parking, and the assignment of cashiers.

Discussions of this delivery schedule between Ken and Tara Murphy, Coastal's vice-president for marketing, were very lengthy and less than cordial. Tara pointed out that deliveries at any other time would increase delivery costs for everyone. Ken noted that his costs had increased with the new schedule.

Ken knew that the cooperative provided him with numerous advantages which he would lose if he were to leave it. Since Coastal did buying in bulk and was controlled by the members, Ken enjoyed a degree of autonomy over most merchandising decisions that would in all probability be lost were he to deal through another wholesaler. Additionally, of all the wholesaler-retailer arrangements open to him, he knew that the cooperative arrangement provided him with more power over the wholesaler's decisions. However, he also knew that the other arrangements provided him more power over wholesaler logistics and service. This was of course the issue which was presently causing him problems.

After much consideration, Ken told Tara that the present schedule was too disruptive to his operation and that his continued membership in the cooperative hinged on a change in the delivery schedule. Tara told Ken that there was absolutely nothing that she could do. The schedule was known to all the members and if a change was allowed for Ken, everyone—with the exception of those getting deliveries at 8:00 A.M.—would request a change. She also pointed out that the cooperative was nearing the size, ninety to one hundred firms, when it would be arranging for additional delivery equipment and would be redesigning the delivery schedule at that time.

Ken told Tara to contact him when that time came, but as of now he was out of the cooperative. He also pointed out that his leaving decreased the efficiency of the new delivery schedule and that everybody's costs would now increase because the consultant had come up with such an unrealistic delivery time.

Questions

1. Do you agree with McGrath's decision? Explain your answer.
2. Do you agree with Coastal's decision? Explain your answer.

Appendix on Franchising

This appendix on franchising is provided because of the substantial growth of franchising and the interest in it. The appendix goes beyond the discussion of franchising in Chapter 3 and presents material on managerial issues in franchising and the tensions between franchisors and franchisees.

Between 1974 and 1983, total annual franchising sales more than doubled. In 1983, franchisee-owned stores had average sales of slightly over $1 million; company-owned units averaged $628,000. As of 1984, nearly 1,800 companies (with several hundred thousand establishments) were engaged in franchising. Currently, about 7 per cent of the U.S. labor force either is employed by a franchise or owns one. The Department of Commerce predicts that one-half of total retail sales will be accounted for by franchising by the year 2000.[1]

Managerial Issues in Franchising

Franchising appeals to many owners of small businesses for a variety of reasons. One, most franchises have standard operating methods that can be readily learned. Franchisors often have training facilities where franchisees are taught how to operate equipment, manage employees, maintain records, and improve customer relations. Two, a new outlet of a nationally advertised franchise (such as Midas Muffler, Avis, or Chem Lawn) can develop a large customer following rather quickly and easily, because of the reputation of the franchisor. Three, some franchises are aimed at passive investors who do not have time to devote to active day-to-day management. Four, according to the International Franchise Association, the failure rate for franchisees is much lower than for retailers in general. Only about 5 per cent of franchised retailers fail; when fran-

---

[1]Philip S. Gutis, "The Stunning Franchise Explosion," *New York Times* (January 20, 1985), Section 3, p. 4; and *Franchising in the Economy: 1982–1984* (Washington, D.C.: U.S. Department of Commerce, 1984), p. 13.

chisees run into trouble, their outlets may be sold to other operators or taken back by the franchisor.[2]

In return for these and other benefits described in Chapter 3, franchisees typically pay one-time franchise fees and continuing royalty and advertising fees. The range of these fees varies widely. For example, Wendy's International (a well-known fast-food franchise company) has this approximate cost schedule for each restaurant a franchise contracts to build:[3]

Technical assistance fee	$ 20,000–$ 20,000
Land	$100,000–$300,000
Building	$175,000–$225,000
Site improvement	$ 50,000–$150,000
Equipment	$135,000–$160,000
Miscellaneous (initial inventory, working capital, corporate taxes, insurance, utility deposit, licenses)	$ 32,000–$ 49,000
Total	$512,000–$904,000

On an ongoing basis, Wendy's franchisees must also pay 4 per cent royalty fees on gross sales, a 1.5 per cent of sales contribution for national advertising, and a 2.5 per cent of sales contribution for local and regional advertising—a total of 8 per cent of sales.[4]

In contrast, Insty-Prints, a quick-printing franchisor, charges franchisees a non-refundable $8,000 franchise fee, a royalty of 3 per cent of sales (payable monthly), and an additional 2 per cent of sales for advertising. Mr. Build, a home-remodeling franchisor, charges $7,900, 6 per cent of sales, and $300 a month for a national advertising fund.[5]

In addition to monetary payments, a franchisor can enforce detailed standards covering every aspect of business, such as signs, product freshness, merchandise selection, employee uniforms, and so on. These standards must be adhered to by franchisees. The franchisor's concern for systemwide uniformity and the franchisee's desire to conduct his or her own business sometimes lead to conflict.

Franchise outlets can be purchased directly from the franchisor, from a master franchisee, or a current franchisee. The franchisor directly sells either new locations or company-owned units (some of which may have been taken back from unsuccessful franchisees). In some cases, the franchisor sells the right to develop outlets in an entire county to a master franchisee, who then deals with individual franchisees. A current franchisee generally has the right to sell his or her unit providing that it is first offered to the franchisor, that the purchaser meets all the franchisor's financial and other criteria, and that the purchaser undergoes a comprehensive training program.

Figure 1 contains a checklist by which potential franchisees can evaluate opportunities. When using this checklist, the prospective franchisee should obtain financial statements from the franchisor and survey existing customers and franchise operators.

[2]Thomas O'Donnell, "Franchising: No Entrepreneurs Need Apply," *Forbes* (December 3, 1984), p. 128.
[3]Wendy's International, March 1984.
[4]*Wendy's International, Inc. Form 10K*, for the fiscal year ending December 31, 1983, pp. 4–5.
[5]Sanford L. Jacobs, "Operating a Franchise Often Pays, but Demands Are Great," *Wall Street Journal* (November 3, 1980), p. 33; and Curtis Hartman, "The Conversion of Skip Kelley," *Inc.* (February 1984), p. 41.

A Checklist for Prospective Franchisees to Evaluate Franchise Opportunities

1. What are the required franchisor fees: initial fee, advertising appropriations, and royalties?

2. What degree of technical knowledge is required of the franchisee?

3. What is the required investment in time by the franchisee? Does the franchisee have to be actively involved in the day-to-day operations of the franchise?

4. What is the extent of control of a franchise by a franchisor in terms of materials purchased, sales quotas, space requirements, pricing, the range of goods to be sold, required inventory levels, and so on?

5. Can the franchisee accept the regimentation and rules of the franchisor?

6. Are the costs of required supplies and materials purchased from the franchisor at market value, above market value, or below market value?

7. What degree of brand recognition do consumers have of the franchise? Does the franchisor have a national advertising program?

8. What reputation does the franchise have among consumers, and among current franchisees?

9. What are the level and quality of services provided by the franchisor to franchisees: site selection, training, bookkeeping, human relations, equipment maintenance, and trouble-shooting?

10. What is the franchisor policy in terminating franchisees? What are the conditions of franchise termination? What is the rate of franchise termination and nonrenewal?

11. What is the franchisor's legal history?

12. What is the length of the franchise agreement?

13. What is the failure rate of existing franchises?

14. What is the franchisor's policy with regard to company-owned and franchisee-owned franchises?

15. What policy does the franchisor have in allowing franchisees to sell their business?

16. What is the franchisor policy with regard to territorial protection for existing franchisees with regard to new franchisees and new company-owned establishments?

17. What is the earning potential of the franchise during the first year? The first five years?

Figure 1

Tensions Between Franchisors and Franchisees

For a variety of reasons, tensions exist between many franchisors and their franchisees. Franchisors become displeased when franchisees do not maintain a proper image, refuse to contribute to voluntary advertising campaigns, seek to carry competing brands, and do not adhere to operating guidelines. Franchisees become displeased when new outlets are opened nearby, fees are viewed as too high, operations are too tightly controlled, and the franchisor does not employ a good marketing program.[6]

Tensions can lead to disagreements, conflicts, and even litigation. Potential negative franchisor actions include terminating the franchise agreement; limiting promotional and sales support; and creating unnecessary red tape for orders, information requests, and warranty work. Potential negative franchisee actions include terminating the franchise agreement, adding competitors' product lines, refusing to promote products, and not complying with franchisor information requests.[7]

While franchising has historically been categorized by the franchisor's possessing more power than the franchisee, this power inequality has been reduced. First, a number of franchisees have joined together to increase their power. For example, the Midas Dealers' Association represents about 80 per cent of the franchisees running Midas muffler repair outlets. The association recently negotiated a plan to protect existing units, when Midas began a large expansion program.[8] Second, a number of umbrella organizations representing franchisees, such as the California Franchise Council and the National Franchise Association Coalition, have been formed. Third, many franchisees now operate more than one outlet, giving them greater clout. The major oil producers fear that multiunit gasoline stations can amass enough power to purchase gas from independent suppliers.[9] Fourth, there has been a substantial rise in litigation between franchisors and their franchisees.

Figure 2 shows the sources of tension between franchisors and franchisees. Improved communication and cooperation will be necessary to resolve these issues.

[6]See William Renforth, "Legal Hassles of Franchising Are Commensurate with Business and Marketing Sophistication of Franchisees," *Marketing News* (February 17, 1984), p. 8.
[7]Stanley D. Sibley and Donald A. Michie, "An Exploratory Investigation of Cooperation in a Franchise Channel," *Journal of Retailing*, Vol. 58 (Winter 1982), p. 28.
[8]Tegi Agins, "Owning Franchises Has Pluses, but Wealth Isn't Guaranteed," *Wall Street Journal* (October 22, 1984), p. 33.
[9]Emily Sachar, "Exercising the Franchise," *Newsday* (February 14, 1983), pp. B1, B13.

Causes of Tension Between Franchisors and Franchisees

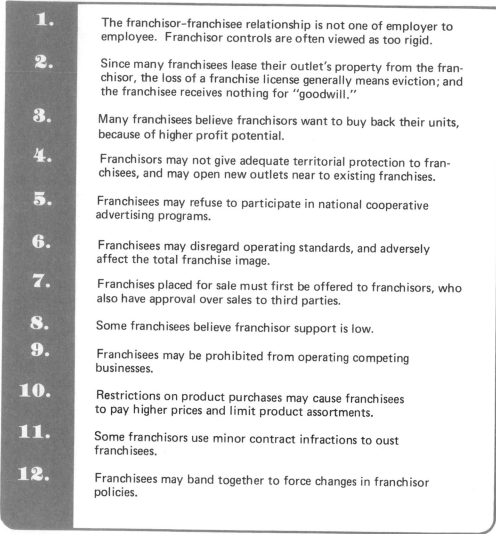

1. The franchisor–franchisee relationship is not one of employer to employee. Franchisor controls are often viewed as too rigid.

2. Since many franchisees lease their outlet's property from the franchisor, the loss of a franchise license generally means eviction; and the franchisee receives nothing for "goodwill."

3. Many franchisees believe franchisors want to buy back their units, because of higher profit potential.

4. Franchisors may not give adequate territorial protection to franchisees, and may open new outlets near to existing franchises.

5. Franchisees may refuse to participate in national cooperative advertising programs.

6. Franchisees may disregard operating standards, and adversely affect the total franchise image.

7. Franchises placed for sale must first be offered to franchisors, who also have approval over sales to third parties.

8. Some franchisees believe franchisor support is low.

9. Franchisees may be prohibited from operating competing businesses.

10. Restrictions on product purchases may cause franchisees to pay higher prices and limit product assortments.

11. Some franchisors use minor contract infractions to oust franchisees.

12. Franchisees may band together to force changes in franchisor policies.

Figure 2

4

Retail Institutions: Part II

Chapter Objectives

1. To examine retail institutions classified by strategy mix
2. To study the wheel of retailing, scrambled merchandising, and the retail life cycle and how they explain the performance and evolution of strategy mixes
3. To describe retail institutions categorized by nonstore retailing and by service versus product retailing
4. To provide a synopsis of the retail institutions described in Chapters 3 and 4

In 1982, Bill Isackson sold Ross Stores, his six-unit San Francisco clothing store chain, to U.S. Venture Partners (a company run by a number of experienced former retail executives). At that time, sales were $15 million annually, although Ross Stores had been in business for 25 years. New management at Ross immediately converted the chain to off-price retailing. By 1984, revenues reached $200 million, and there were sixty-six stores (including locations in Seattle, Phoenix, and Texas). The chain expects sales to continue their rapid increase:

> We think the off-price retailer flourished during and because of the recession. But we think that the basis for the kind of store, where solid value is offered, is going to be a long-term prospect in retailing.

Ross' strategy mix incorporates many standard practices followed by off-price chains. Prices are low, 20 to 60 per cent off suggested list prices. Outlets are frequently situated in free-standing locations abandoned by other retailers and in strip centers where other stores' leases have expired. Store sites are leased to hold down capital investments. Women's apparel represents about two-thirds of its merchandise mix.

Ross also employs some practices that are distinctive for an off-price chain. A liberal return policy is offered. Bank credit cards are accepted, as are personal checks. Sales personnel are employed. Merchandise is displayed in an attractive (though "no frills") manner. The central display area is carpeted.[1]

Overview

In the preceding chapter, retail institutions were described by ownership form. In this chapter we view retail institutions from three other perspectives: retail strategy mix, nonstore retailing, and service versus product retailing.

Retail Institutions Categorized by Strategy Mix

A retailer can be classified by his or her strategy mix. The **strategy mix** is composed of location, product, service, promotion, and price variables. Store location refers to placement in a geographic area and a locational format (such as a shopping center versus an isolated store). Product refers to the width (number of different product lines) and depth (selection within any one product line) of assortment and the quality of merchandise. Service refers to the level and quality of sales personnel, credit, return policies, delivery, and so on. Promotion refers to the use of displays, advertising, sales promotions, and personal selling. Price refers to the retailer's comparative strategy: prestige pricing, creating a quality image through high prices; competitive pricing, setting prices at the level of one's rivals; or penetration pricing, underpricing other retailers to attract value-conscious consumers.

By combining these five elements, a retailer can develop a unique strategy. The strategy mixes of fifteen types of retailers, divided into food-based and general merchandise categories, are shown in Table 4-1. Each mix is different because of its combination of location, product, service, promotion, and price.

Before examining each strategy mix shown in Table 4-1, three important concepts that help explain the performance and evolution of these mixes are detailed: the wheel of retailing, scrambled merchandising, and the retail life cycle. In particular these concepts are useful in describing the performance of existing retailers, predicting new retail institutions, determining the impact of new institutions on existing retailers, and forecasting how existing retailers are likely to respond to change.[2]

According to the **wheel-of-retailing** theory, retail innovators often first appear as low-price operators with low profit-margin requirements. As time passes, the innovators upgrade their product offerings, facilities, and services (by obtaining high-rent locations, offering credit and delivery, and so on), and prices must rise accordingly. As

---

[1]"California's Off-Price Phenom Focuses on $1 Billion in Sales," *Chain Store Age Executive* (January 1985), pp. 92, 99.

[2]See Malcolm P. McNair and Eleanor G. May, *The Evolution of Retail Institutions in the U.S.* (Cambridge, Mass.: Marketing Science Institute, 1976); Rom J. Markin and Calvin P. Duncan, "The Transformation of Retail Institutions: Beyond the Wheel of Retailing and Life Cycle Theories," *Journal of Macromarketing*, Vol. 1 (Spring 1981), pp. 58–66; and E. Terry Deiderick and H. Robert Dodge, "The Wheel of Retailing Rotates and Moves," in John Summey et al. (Editors), *Marketing: Theories and Concepts for an Era of Change* (Carbondale, Ill.: Southern Marketing Association, 1983), pp. 149–152.

these innovators mature, they become vulnerable to new discount retailers with lower cost structures, hence the wheel of retailing:[3]

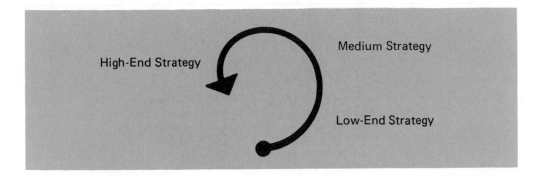

The wheel of retailing is based on four basic hypotheses:

1. There are many price-sensitive shoppers willing to trade services, wide selections, and convenient locations for lower prices.
2. Price-sensitive shoppers are often not store loyal and are willing to switch to stores offering lower prices. Other, prestige-sensitive customers like to shop at stores with high-end strategies.
3. New institutions are frequently able to implement lower operating costs than existing institutions.
4. Retailers typically move up the wheel to increase sales, broaden the target market, and improve store image.

During the 1950s and again in the 1970s, prices in department stores rose to levels that encouraged the growth of two institutional forms: the full-line discount store and the retail catalog showroom. These retailers were able to emphasize low prices because of such cost-cutting techniques as a small sales force, poor location, inexpensive fixtures, high stock turnover, and only cash or check payments for goods.

As discount stores and retail catalog showrooms succeeded, they looked to develop into more traditional types of stores. This meant enlarging the sales force, improving the location, upgrading fixtures, carrying lower-turnover merchandise, and granting credit. These improvements led to higher costs, which, in turn, led to higher prices. In the 1980s the wheel of retailing has again been functioning as newer types of discounters, such as off-price chains, factory outlets, and flea markets have expanded to satisfy the needs of the price-conscious consumer.

Figure 4-1 shows the alternatives a retailer faces when considering a strategy. Through this dichotomy, one can differentiate between the two extreme cases of strategy emphasis: low-end and high-end. This figure illustrates the opposite spectrums of

[3]The pioneering works on the wheel of retailing are Malcolm P. McNair, "Significant Trends and Developments in the Postwar Period," in A. B. Smith (Editor), *Competitive Distribution in a Free High Level Economy and Its Implications for the University* (Pittsburgh, Pa.: University of Pittsburgh Press, 1958), pp. 17–18; and Stanley Hollander, "The Wheel of Retailing," *Journal of Marketing*, Vol. 25 (July 1960), pp. 37–42.

Table 4-1
Retail Strategy Mixes

Type of Retailer	Location	Product	Service	Promotion	Price
Food-based					
Convenience store	Neighborhood	Medium width and narrow depth of assortment; average quality	Limited	Little	Above average
Conventional supermarket	Neighborhood	Extensive width and depth of assortment; average quality; national, private, and generic brands	Limited	Heavy use of newspapers, flyers, and coupons; self-service	Competitive
Combination store	Community shopping center or isolated site	Full selection of supermarket and drugstore products or drugstore and general merchandise; average quality	Limited	Heavy use of newspapers and flyers; self-service	Competitive
Superstore	Community shopping center or isolated site	Full assortment of supermarket items, plus health and beauty aids and general merchandise	Limited	Heavy use of newspapers and flyers; self-service	Competitive
Box (limited line) store	Neighborhood	Narrow width and depth of assortment; no perishables; few national brands	Very low	Little or none	Very low
Warehouse store	Secondary site, often in industrial area	Narrow width and depth; emphasis on national brands purchased at discounts	Very low	Little or none	Very low
General Merchandise					
Specialty store	Central business district or shopping center	Very narrow width of assortment; extensive depth of assortment; average to good quality	High level and quality	Heavy use of displays; extensive sales force	Prestige or competitive

Table 4-1 (*continued*)
Retail Strategy Mixes

Type of Retailer	Location	Product	Service	Promotion	Price
Variety store	Central business district, shopping center, or isolated store	Good width and depth of assortment; below average to average quality	Limited	Heavy use of newspapers; self-service	Competitive
Department store	Central business district, shopping center, or isolated store	Extensive width and depth of assortment; average to good quality	Good to excellent	Heavy use of ads; catalogs; direct mail; personal selling	Competitive or prestige
Full-line discount store	Central business district, shopping center, or isolated store	Very good width and depth of assortment; average to good quality	Below average to average	Heavy use of newspapers; price oriented; limited sales force	Penetration or competitive
Retail catalog showroom	Central business district, shopping center, or isolated store	Good width and depth of assortment; average to good quality	Little or low	Heavy use of catalogs; little advertising; self-service	Penetration or competitive
Off-price chain	Suburban shopping strip or isolated store	Moderate width, but poor depth of assortment; average to good quality; low continuity	Little	Use of newspapers; brands not advertised; limited sales force	Penetration or competitive
Factory outlet	Out-of-the-way site or discount mall	Moderate width, but poor depth of assortment; some irregular merchandise; low continuity	Very low	Little; self-service	Penetration
Buying club	Isolated store or secondary site (industrial park)	Moderate width, but poor depth of assortment; low continuity	Very low	Little; some direct mail; limited sales force	Penetration
Flea market	Isolated site, race track, arena, or parking lot	Extensive width, but poor depth of assortment; variable quality; low continuity	Very low	Limited; self-service	Penetration

Retail Strategy Alternatives

Low-End Strategy	High-End Strategy
a. low rental location — side street	a. high rental shopping center or central business district location
b. no services or services charged at additional fee (or services may be limited to credit and returns)	b. elaborate services available included in price, such as: credit decorating delivery gift-wrapping alterations lay-away
c. spartan fixtures and displays	c. elaborate fixtures and displays
d. simple retail personnel organization	d. elaborate retail personnel organization
e. price emphasis in promotion	e. no price emphasis in promotion
f. self-service or high sales per store personnel ratio	f. product demonstration, low sales per store personnel ratio
g. crowded store interior	g. spacious store interior
h. most merchandise visible	h. most merchandise in back room

Figure 4-1

the wheel of retailing. The wheel-of-retailing theory suggests that established retailers should be cautious in adding services or in converting strategy from low-end to high-end. Because price-conscious shoppers are not usually store loyal, they are likely to switch to lower-priced stores. Furthermore, retailers may be eliminating the competitive advantages that have led to profitability.

Whereas the wheel of retailing focuses on strategy changes based on prices and service levels, scrambled merchandising refers to a retailer's width of assortment. **Scrambled merchandising** occurs when a retailer increases its width of assortment by adding product lines that are unrelated to each other and to the firm's original business.

Scrambled merchandising has become popular in recent years for three major reasons: retailers like to cater to a large portion of overall family needs; unrelated merchandise may be fast-selling or have high profit margins; and consumers are attracted to one-stop buying.

It is important to note the contagious nature of scrambled merchandising. For example, drugstores, full-line discounters, bookstores, and automobile parts stores are affected by scrambled merchandising on the part of supermarkets. In 1983, almost 10 per cent of supermarket sales volume was from general merchandise, health and beauty aids, and other nongrocery items, such as pharmacy products and money orders.[4] When

---

[4]"Supermarket Sales by Category," *Progressive Grocer* (July 1984), p. 42. See also Glenn Snyder, "Safeway Fine Tunes Its Nonfoods Mix," *Progressive Grocer* (August 1984), pp. 75–86; and Glenn Snyder, "Nonfoods Win a Place in the 'King's' Court," *Progressive Grocer* (January 1985), pp. 71–76.

a supermarket branches out into nonfood items (because it desires larger gross-profit margins and consumers want one-stop shopping), a void may be created in other stores' sales. These stores are then forced to scramble their merchandise with other items, such as toys, housewares, and home improvement products. This creates a void for additional stores, which are also forced to scramble.

The growth of scrambled merchandising means that competition between different retail institutions is increasing, and distribution costs for manufacturers are rising as sales are dispersed among more retailers. There are other limits to successful scrambled merchandising, especially when one considers the lack of buying, selling, or servicing expertise retailers have with regard to many of the items they carry. In addition, low turnover may occur if too many product lines are stocked.

The third concept for analyzing retail strategy performance and evolution is the **retail life cycle.** This theory assumes that retail institutions, like products, pass through an identifiable life cycle that has four stages: innovation, accelerated development, maturity, and decline.[5] The direction and speed of institutional changes can be interpreted from this theory.

During the first stage of the life cycle, innovation, there is a strong departure from existing retail institutions. A retailer in this stage alters at least one element of the retail mix significantly from that of traditional competitors. In this stage, sales and then profits rise rapidly for the innovator.

An example of an institution in the innovation stage is cable television retailing, whereby consumers order merchandise from their homes by punching product code numbers into home computer consoles and indicating the quantity desired. Computers process orders, arrange deliveries, and send bills. Cable television retailing now has limited use but is expected to expand rapidly as more areas become wired.

In the second stage, accelerated development, both the sales and profits of a retail institution exhibit rapid growth. Innovative retailers expand their geographic bases of operations and newer firms enter the field. Toward the end of accelerated development, cost pressures begin to affect profits. Costs cover a large staff, a more complex inventory system, and extensive controls.

For example, in the 1980s, many retailers have introduced off-price apparel chain stores to service price-conscious consumers. The stores have minimal services (such as no alterations, no delivery, community dressing rooms, and no layaway). They sell national brands and rely on overproduction and canceled orders. In 1984, off-price chain sales reached $9.5 billion, up from $3 billion in 1979.[6]

The third stage, maturity, is characterized by a slowdown in sales growth for the institutional type. This is brought on by inadequate management skills to direct big companies, saturation of the market, and/or competition from newer forms of retailers.

Retail catalog showrooms are in maturity. After annual sales increases of 24 per cent from 1975 to 1979, annual sales growth slowed to an annual average of 8 per cent between 1980 and 1984.[7]

The final stage in the life cycle is decline. In some cases, this stage leads to termination of the institutional form; in others, decline can be avoided or postponed by repositioning the institution.

---

[5]The material on the retail life cycle is drawn from William R. Davidson, Albert D. Bates, and Stephen J. Bass, "The Retail Life Cycle," *Harvard Business Review,* Vol. 54 (November–December 1976), pp. 89–96.
[6]Leslie Schulz, "Taking on the Off-Pricers," *Inc.* (January 1985), p. 25.
[7]Katherine Strauss Burger and Roberta Janasz, "Industry's Volume Should Pass $10 Billion Mark in '84," *Catalog Showroom Business* (September 1984), p. 3.

For example, closed-door membership stores were formed to enable customers to pay discount prices for merchandise that was subject to fair trade laws (requiring all retailers to have uniform prices). When national fair trade laws were removed, closed-door membership stores declined and eventually went out of business, because other retailers were able to offer competitive prices and had better customer followings.

Conventional supermarkets have been able to slow their decline by locating new units in shopping centers and suburbs, redesigning interiors, expanding store hours, maintaining low prices, closing unprofitable units, developing in-house bakeries, relying on scrambled merchandising, and/or converting to larger superstores.

Overall, the retail life-cycle concept explains how retailers should respond as their institutions evolve. Expansion should be the focus in the initial stages; administration and operations become relevant in maturity; and adaptation is essential at the end of the life cycle. Table 4-2 summarizes the retail life cycle.

Table 4-2
The Retail Life Cycle

	Area or Subject of Concern	1 Innovation	2 Accelerated Development	3 Maturity	4 Decline
Market characteristics	Number of competitors	Very few	Moderate	Many direct competitors; moderate indirect competition	Moderate direct competition; many indirect competitors
	Rate of sales growth	Very rapid	Rapid	Moderate to slow	Slow or negative
	Level of profitability	Low to moderate	High	Moderate	Very low
	Duration of new innovations	3–5 years	5–8 years	Indefinite	Indefinite
Appropriate retailer actions	Investment/ growth/risk decisions	Investment minimization, high risks accepted	High level of investment to sustain growth	Tightly controlled growth in untapped markets	Marginal capital expenditures and only when essential
	Central management concerns	Concept refinement through adjustment and experimentation	Establishing a pre-emptive market position	Excess capacity and "overstoring," prolonging maturity and revising the retail concept	Engaging in a "run-out" strategy
	Use of management control techniques	Minimal	Moderate	Extensive	Moderate
	Most successful management style	Entrepreneurial	Centralized	"Professional"	Caretaker

Source: Adapted from William R. Davidson, Albert D. Bates, and Stephen J. Bass, "The Retail Life Cycle," Harvard Business Review, *Vol. 54 (November–December 1976), p. 92. Reprinted with permission. Copyright © 1976 by the President and Fellows of Harvard College; all rights reserved.*

Food-Based Retailers

As shown in Table 4-1, there are six basic strategy mixes for food-based retailers: convenience store, conventional supermarket, combination store, superstore, box (limited line) store, and warehouse store.

Convenience Store

A **convenience store** is usually a food-oriented store that is well located, is open long hours, and carries a limited number of items. This type of retailer is small (1,000 to 4,000 square feet of floor space compared to 17,000 for a supermarket), has above-average prices, and provides average to above-average services.

In 1957, there were 500 convenience stores; during 1960, 2,500 such stores existed; as of 1971, there were 13,600 stores; and by 1983, 40,400 convenience stores were operating. Sales of such stores increased from $357 million in 1960 to $2.9 billion in 1971 and to $25 billion in 1983 (including gasoline). During 1983, they accounted for 6.3 per cent of U.S. grocery sales. The average convenience store had sales of over $408,000 in 1983.[8]

While milk, eggs, and bread once accounted for the major portion of a convenience store's sales, sandwiches, canned beer, and magazines are now also key items. In addition, gasoline contributes about 40 per cent of total convenience store sales, up from 0 per cent in 1970 and 23 per cent in 1980.[9] Other important trends include convenience stores adding automatic teller machines and fast-food items, and the increase in the size of the average supermarket making the convenience store a more attractive place to shop for some consumers.[10]

The largest single operator of convenience outlets is 7-Eleven Stores, whose Southland Corporation owned and controlled about 7,400 stores with $8.7 billion in sales during 1983. These stores generally carry a balanced inventory of dairy, bakery, beverage, tobacco, frozen-food, delicatessen, grocery, nonfood, and limited produce items as well as gasoline (which yields 16 per cent of sales).[11]

The convenience store's natural market advantage is its usefulness for fill-in merchandise when a shopper does not want to encounter long lines, or when a shopper needs merchandise and the typical supermarket may be closed. One half the goods sold by 7-Eleven are consumed within 30 minutes. The typical customer is young and male and returns an average of more than four times per week. This customer spends about $2.25 per visit.[12]

Because of limited shelf space, convenience stores receive about 70 deliveries each week, and higher prices reflect those handling costs. Convenience stores achieve a gross margin of 31 per cent, versus 20 per cent for supermarkets, because their customers are less price sensitive.[13] Many supermarkets are responding to convenience stores by opening for 24 hours, seven days a week.

[8]"51st Annual Report of the Grocery Industry," *Progressive Grocer* (April 1984), p. 44.
[9]Carol E. Curtis, "Mobil Wants to Be Your Milkman," *Forbes* (February 13, 1984), pp. 44–45; and Pamela G. Hollie, "Southland's Successful Mix," *New York Times* (February 25, 1983), pp. D1, D3.
[10]Craig Endicott, "Life in the Fast-Food Lane," *Advertising Age* (October 10, 1983), pp. M-32, M-34; and "Circle K Aiming for Tops in Convenience," *Advertising Age* (April 2, 1984), pp. 4, 55.
[11]"The 50 Largest Retailing Companies," *Fortune* (June 11, 1984), pp. 186–187; and "Southland Rolls Epic, Tests Fast-Food Units," *Advertising Age* (February 6, 1984), p. 6.
[12]*1982 Major Market Study* (Dallas, Tex.: 7-Eleven Research Department, 1982); and Francis C. Brown III, "Convenience Stores Moving to Diversify," *Wall Street Journal* (September 12, 1984), p. 35.
[13]"51st Annual Report of the Grocery Industry," p. 96.

Leading convenience stores are 7-Eleven, Circle K, and National Convenience Stores. In addition, Mobil, Atlantic Richfield (Arco), Texaco, and other oil producers have begun converting traditional gasoline stations to convenience stores.

Conventional Supermarket

The Food Marketing Institute defines a **supermarket** as a self-service food store with grocery, meat, and produce departments and minimum annual sales of $2 million.[14] Included in this definition are conventional supermarkets, combination stores, superstores, box (limited line) stores, and warehouse stores.

A **conventional supermarket** is a departmentalized food store that emphasizes a wide range of food and related products; sales of general merchandise are limited. It started as a retail institution in the 1930s. At this time, it was realized that only a large-scale operation would enable a retailer to combine volume sales, self-service, and low prices. The self-service concept allowed supermarkets to cut costs as well as increase volume. Personnel costs were reduced, and impulse buying increased.

The automobile and the refrigerator contributed to the supermarket's success by lowering travel costs and adding to the life span of perishable items. Easy parking and lower prices (for consumers buying in bulk) were marketing strategies used by the supermarket to exploit these inventions.

Since 1962, overall supermarket sales have stabilized at about 72 to 77 per cent of total U.S. grocery sales, with conventional supermarkets now responsible for 63 per cent of total supermarket sales. In 1983, conventional supermarkets operated 22,625 stores and had sales of $119 billion.[15] Chains account for the majority of sales. The largest chains are Safeway, Kroger, American Stores, Lucky Stores, Winn-Dixie, and A & P. Most independent supermarkets are affiliated with cooperative or voluntary organizations such as IGA, Red and White, Super Valu, and Clover Farm.

Conventional supermarkets have generally relied on high inventory turnover (volume sales). Their profit margins are very low. One study found average gross margins (selling prices less merchandise costs) to be 20 per cent of sales and net operating profits to be 1.2 per cent of sales.[16]

Conventional supermarkets are facing intense competition from other types of food stores. Convenience stores offer greater convenience, combination stores and superstores provide more assortment and variety, and box and warehouse stores have lower prices. Over the last five years, more than 5,500 conventional supermarket outlets have closed. In 1983, 41.2 per cent of the new supermarket outlets opened were superstores, 8.4 per cent were warehouse stores, and 2.6 per cent were box stores.[17] The emerging supermarket formats are discussed next.

Combination Store

A **combination store** is a conventional supermarket in which general merchandise accounts for 30 to 40 per cent of sales. The introduction of food-based combination stores

[14]Prior to 1981, supermarkets included food stores with annual sales of at least $1 million. This should be noted when comparing data before and after 1981.
[15]"51st Annual Report of the Grocery Industry," p. 144.
[16]Ibid., pp. 92, 97.
[17]Winston Williams, "The New Supermarket Takes Shape," *New York Times* (September 2, 1984), Section 3, p. 1; and "Store Formats Emerge as Competitive Weapons," *Chain Store Age Executive* (July 1984), pp. 29–30.

can be traced to the late 1960s and early 1970s when common checkout areas were developed for separate supermarkets and drugstores or general merchandise stores.

The growth of food-based combination stores can be attributed to two major factors. First, one-stop shopping is appealing to consumers, and broader assortments enhance it. Second, supermarkets are patronized much more frequently than drugstores or general merchandise stores; by establishing combination stores, drug items and general merchandise are purchased more often.

In 1983, there were 650 combination stores with annual sales of $8.5 billion. One of the largest such chains is Jewel/Osco, a California-based group of supermarket/drugstore combination stores; and Giant Food has recently introduced a 64,000 square-foot prototype combination food/pharmacy store in Rockville, Maryland.[18]

Superstore

A **superstore** is a large food-based retailer that is much more diversified than either a supermarket or combination store. Superstores typically carry garden supplies, televisions, clothing, wine, boutique items, bakery products, and household appliances and offer specialty services such as in-house bakeries and takeout operations in addition to a full line of supermarket items. Whereas the conventional supermarket occupies 15,000 to 20,000 square feet, a superstore utilizes 30,000 or more square feet. Some superstores may occupy 100,000 square feet. In 1983, there were 3,575 superstores in the United States with sales of $44 billion.[19]

Superstores cater to one-stop shoppers, capitalize on nonfood sales, rely on improved transportation networks, and maximize profit margins. However, they require substantial investments, may be difficult to locate in proper facilities, and assume that store managers can handle widely divergent product lines. Safeway, Kroger, and Supermarkets General (Pathmark) are three of the many supermarket chains rapidly expanding the number of superstores they operate.

Box (Limited Line) Store

The **box (limited line) store** is a food-based discounter that focuses on a small selection of items, restricted hours of operation, few services, and limited national brands. There are usually fewer than 1,500 items, no refrigerated perishables, and one size and brand per item. Price marking is on the shelf or on overhead signs. Items are displayed in cut cases. Customers do their own bagging. Checks are not accepted. Box stores depend on aggressively priced private-label or controlled brands. They aim to price merchandise 20 to 30 per cent below supermarkets.

The box store concept originated in Europe around 1970 and was exported to the United States in 1975–76. The growth of these stores has not been as high as anticipated. Traditional supermarkets, in many cases, have matched box store prices. Some customers are loyal to national brands. And, box stores cannot fulfill one-stop shopping needs.

---

[18]"51st Annual Report of the Grocery Industry," p. 144; and Janet Meyers, "Giant Never Sleeps in Washington Market," *Advertising Age* (February 11, 1985), pp. 4, 82.

[19]Ibid. See also Ronald Tanner, "Minyard Picks Up the Pace," *Progressive Grocer* (November 1984), pp. 67–76; Ronald Tanner, "Pick 'n Save: Making It Famous in Milwaukee," *Progressive Grocer* (February 1985), pp. 61–69; and Robert E. O'Neill, "Publix: New Face, New Challenge," *Progressive Grocer* (January 1985), pp. 55–58.

There were about 450 box stores in the United States in 1983 with sales of $1.7 billion.[20] Among the leading box operators are Jewel T Discount and Aldi.

Warehouse Store

A **warehouse store** is a discounter that offers a moderate number of food items in a no-frills setting. Warehouse stores appeal to one-stop food shoppers, unlike box stores. These stores concentrate on special purchases of national brands. They use cut-case displays, provide little service, post prices on shelves, and are situated in secondary locations (such as industrial districts).

Warehouse stores begin in the late 1970s. By 1983, there were 2,250 stores with $15.5 billion in sales.[21] Today, there are three warehouse store formats in terms of size: from 15,000 to 25,000 square feet, from 25,000 to 35,000 square feet, and from 50,000 to 65,000 square feet.

The largest store is known as a super warehouse. It has weekly sales of $400,000 and contains a variety of departments, including produce. High ceilings are used to accommodate pallet loads of groceries. Shipments are made directly to the store. Customers pack their own groceries. Super warehouses can be profitable at 14 per cent gross margins versus 20 per cent for conventional supermarkets.[22] Major super warehouse chains are Food 4 Less (Fleming Companies), Super Plus (A&P), and Cub Foods (Super Valu).

A potential problem, which may limit the growth of warehouse stores, is the lack of brand continuity. Because products are purchased by the stores when special deals are available, brands may be temporarily or permanently out of stock.

Table 4-3 provides operating data for convenience stores, conventional supermarkets, combination stores, superstores, box stores, and warehouse stores.

General Merchandise Retailers

As shown in Table 4-1, there are nine basic strategy mixes for general merchandise retailers: specialty store, variety store, department store, full-line discount store, retail catalog showroom, off-price chain, factory outlet, buying club, and flea market.

Specialty Store

The **specialty store** concentrates on selling one merchandise line, such as apparel and its accessories, sewing machines, or high-fidelity equipment. In contrast to a mass-marketing orientation, specialty stores carry a narrow, but deep, assortment of products and tailor their strategy toward selective market segments. This enables specialty stores to maintain better product selection and sales expertise than competitors, which are often department stores.

Consumers shop at specialty stores so they will not be confronted with racks of merchandise, they will not have to search through several departments for the same

[20]Ibid.; and authors' estimates.
[21]Ibid.
[22]Jacquelyn Bivins, "Is It a Store? Is It a Grocery? It's a Super Warehouse!" *Chain Store Age Executive* (August 1983), p. 18; and "Super Warehouses 'Chomp' into the Food Business," *Business Week* (April 16, 1984), p. 72.

Table 4-3
Operating Data for Food-Based Retailers, 1983

Factor	Convenience Store*	Conventional Supermarket	Combination Store	Superstore	Box (Limited Line) Store	Warehouse Store†
Number of stores	40,400	22,625	650	3,575	450	2,250
Total annual sales (millions)	$16,500	$119,370	$8,450	$44,125	$1,710	$15,515
Average annual sales per store	$408,415	$5,276,020	$13,000,000	$12,342,655	$3,800,000	$6,895,555
Weekly sales per store	$7,855	$101,460	$250,000	$237,360	$73,075	$132,605
Average store selling area (square feet)	3,500	17,000	30,000 min.	30,000 min.	9,000	18,000
Number of checkouts per store	1+	7	9+	9+	3	7+
Gross margin (%)	31	20	25	23	12	16
Number of items stocked per store	3,100	8,000–12,000	20,000+	25,000+	Under 1,500	8,000+
Emphasis	Daily fill-in needs: dairy, bakery, tobacco, magazines, gas	Food; 5% of volume from general merchandise	General merchandise 30–40% of sales	Wide range of foods and nonfood items; often 24-hour operation	Low prices; few or no perishables	Low prices; variable assortments; may or may not stock perishables

*Excludes sales of gasoline (1983 total sales were $25 billion).
†Can vary in size. A typical 15,000–25,000-square-foot warehouse store is represented in the table.

Source: "51st Annual Report of the Grocery Industry," Progressive Grocer (April 1984), p. 44; Safeway Stores, "Presentation to the New York Society of Security Analysts" (March 1, 1984); Wayne H. Bud Fisher, "Forecasting the Future of Supermarket Formats," Progressive Grocer (November 1983), pp. 73–74; Winston Williams, "The New Supermarket Takes Shape," New York Times (September 2, 1984), Section 3, p. 6; and authors' estimates.

types of merchandise, they can select from small assortments chosen for them, and there are no crowds. The appeal of the specialty store has created problems for department stores. Because of this, department stores are placing increased emphasis on boutiques and specialty shops within the department stores themselves.

In total, specialty stores have annual sales of $60 billion and account for 40 to 50 per cent of general merchandise sales. Among the leading apparel stores are The Limited, Casual Corner, and Paul Harris, which appeal to fashion-oriented young women; Petrie's, Miller-Wohl, and Charming Shopper, which are aimed at low-income,

Table 4-4
Selected Operating Results for Specialty Stores with Annual Sales over $1 Million, 1983

Net sales (% gain over previous year)	10.0
Average gross sale	about $40.00
Terms of sale (%)	
Cash	44.2
In-house credit	40.9
Outside cards	14.9
Cumulative markon (%)	51.6
Markdowns (%)	16.1
Stock shortages (%)	2.0
Gross margins (owned retail departments—%)	43.5
Total company gross margin (%)	41.6
Sales per square foot	$152.10
Stock turns (times)	3.0
Pretax earnings (%)	3.1
Net operating expenses (%)	39.0

Source: David P. Schulz, "FOR: Financial and Operating Results," Stores (November 1984), pp. 5–6; and authors' estimates. Copyright National Retail Merchants Association 1984. Reprinted by permission.

price-conscious women; Lane Bryant (now a division of The Limited), which features large and tall clothing sizes; and The Gap, a unisex jeans chain. National nonapparel chains include Radio Shack, Thom McAn Shoes, and Zale Jewelers.

Recently, some of the best-known fashion designers (such as Georgio Armani, Ralph Lauren, Norma Kamali, and Hanae Mori) have opened their own specialty stores. A number of factors have contributed to this trend: designer interest in improving public awareness, fear that wide distribution can hurt their image, and the desire to control store atmosphere. In some cases, boutiques have been licensed, with the licensees providing the investment and the designer selecting sites, hiring decorators, and choosing the store manager.[23]

Table 4-4 contains selected 1983 operating data for specialty stores with annual sales over $1 million.

Variety Store

The Bureau of Census defines a **variety store** as a form of retailing that handles a wide assortment of low- and popularly-priced goods, such as stationery, gift items, women's accessories, toilet articles, light hardware, toys, housewares, and confectionary. Sales are usually on a cash basis. There are open displays and few sales personnel. Variety stores do not carry complete lines of merchandise, are not departmentalized, and do not deliver merchandise.

In 1983, variety stores accounted for $9.1 billion of sales, about 6.4 per cent of general merchandise sales and 0.8 per cent of total retail store sales. F. W. Woolworth, the country's sixteenth largest retailer, dominates the variety store category. Its 1,230 traditional Woolworth outlets had U.S. sales of $3.1 billion in 1983, almost 60 per cent

[23]Pamela G. Hollie, "Designers Turn to Boutiques," *New York Times* (June 14, 1984), pp. D1, D4.

of overall company sales.[24] At Woolworth's variety stores, the strongest departments are health and beauty aids, housewares, stationery, greeting cards, toys, books, and candy.

From 1974 to 1983, variety store sales grew by the lowest rate of any retail category compiled by the Department of Commerce. This was attributable to the bankruptcy of W. T. Grant in 1976, the movement of variety stores into discounting, and the scrambled merchandising of drug and supermarket chains.

Of the major original variety store chains, only F. W. Woolworth, G. C. Murphy, and McCrory retain a solid commitment to that business. Most others, among them S. S. Kresge (now K mart), Nichols, Barner's, and Duckwall-ALCO have virtually abandoned variety stores in favor of their discount operations.[25] Even Woolworth is accelerating its expansion into specialty retailing operations.

Department Store

A **department store** is a large retailing business unit that handles an extensive variety (width and depth) of products and is organized into separate departments for purposes of buying, promotion, service, and control. Product quality ranges from average to quite good. Pricing is usually competitive or prestige. Service varies from moderate sales help, credit, delivery, and so on to high levels of each.

The Bureau of the Census defines a department store on the basis of three characteristics. First, at least twenty-five people must be employed. Second, the merchandise assortment must include some items in each of these lines: dry goods and household items, family wearing apparel, and furniture, home furnishings, appliances, radios, and TV sets. Third, if sales are less than $10 million per year, no more than 80 per cent of the sales can come from any one of the lines. If sales are greater than $10 million, there is no limitation on the percentage of sales for any line, as long as the combined sales of the smallest two lines are at least $1 million.

Some department stores (such as Dayton's, Macy's, and Gimbel's) sell dry goods, family wearing apparel, and furniture and appliances. Others (such as Lord & Taylor and Saks Fifth Avenue) place more emphasis on wearing apparel and do not carry home appliances. Many department stores have substantial private-label and mail-order sales. Total 1983 department store sales were $117 billion, including mail order. This represented about 10 per cent of all retail store sales.

A department store has the greatest assortment of any retailer, provides a variety of customer services, dominates the stores around it, is frequently a fashion leader, and has strong credit-card penetration. Department stores have used innovative marketing strategies over the years. The first type of retailer to advertise prices was a department store. The first retailer to develop a one-price policy (all consumers paying the same price for a given quantity) was a department store. Totally automated checkout facilities have been readily adopted by department stores. Strong product guarantees have been given to customers. Decentralized management principles have been adopted. Finally, the department store has been quick to use suburban shopping center facilities while simultaneously altering its strategy to maintain central business district profitability. Branch units yield a large per cent of total department store sales.

[24]*F. W. Woolworth 1983 Annual Report*, pp. 8, 23.
[25]Jacquelin Bivins, "F. W. Woolworth: Turning Back the Clock?" *Chain Store Age Executive* (October 1983), pp. 29–30 ff.

Table 4-5
*Selected Operating Results for Department Stores
with Annual Sales over $1 Million, 1983*

Net sales (% gain over previous year)	10.5
Average gross sale	$21.00
Terms of sale (%)	
Cash	37.0
In-house credit	52.5
Outside cards	10.5
Cumulative markon (%)	47.9
Markdowns (%)	13.8
Stock shortages (%)	1.7
Gross margins (owned-retail departments—%)	42.0
Total company gross margin (%)	39.8
Sales per square foot ($)	135.60
Stock turns (times)	3.1
Pretax earnings (%)	5.8
Net operating expenses (%)	35.5

*Source: David P. Schulz, "FOR: Financial and Operating Results," Stores
(November 1984), p. 5. Copyright National Retail Merchants Association
1984. Reprinted by permission.*

Many department stores are parts of large diversified chains, such as Federated, Dayton Hudson, May, Carter Hawley Hale, R. H. Macy, Allied Stores, Batus, Associated Dry Goods, and Mercantile. These chains own everything from specialty stores to supermarkets. In addition, unlike Sears and J. C. Penney, which employ single store names nationwide, these chains operate under several department store names in order to appeal to distinct market segments.

Table 4-5 contains selected operating results for department stores with annual sales over $1 million during 1983. The data in this table can be compared with those in Table 4-4, for specialty stores. For example, the average department store sale was much lower ($21.00 versus $40.00). In-house credit was more significant for department stores (52.5 versus 40.9 per cent of sales). Although gross margins and stock turns were similar, sales per square foot were higher for specialty stores.

Department stores are now facing strong competition on various fronts. First, the geographic expansion of some aggressive department store chains is placing these outlets into direct competition with existing stores. This has occurred in Dallas and Miami with the entry of Bloomingdale's.[26] Second, Sears and J. C. Penney have embarked on significant store renovation programs and are increasing their fashion emphasis to attract more upscale consumers.[27] Third, off-price chains have been taking customers away from department stores by featuring branded merchandise at low prices. Fourth, specialty stores are competing on the basis of distinctive product lines, strong store image, a better selection, and an attractive atmosphere.

A number of strategies are being adopted by department stores to protect their position in the market. These include developing more private-label merchandise, so that customer loyalty can be generated and normal markups can be taken (without the

[26]Jolie B. Solomon, "Federated Stores Set to Catch Up to Rivals in Retail Revolution," *Wall Street Journal* (April 5, 1984), pp. 1, 24.
[27]Steve Weiner, "Large Retailers Are Changing Strategy, Image by Remodeling Stores, Upgrading Product Lines," *Wall Street Journal* (July 10, 1984), p. 2.

fear of being undercut by off-price chains);[28] refusing to deal with suppliers that sell to discounters; opening their own off-price chains; showing a greater interest in fashion leadership; running sales more frequently; and moving toward a boutique (store-within-a-store) orientation. At Macy's, "We try to think of each of our departments as a specialty store so that each has an appropriate ambience and personality." This approach is viewed as a return to what a department store originally was—a collection of independent shops.[29]

Full-Line Discount Store

A **full-line discount store** is characterized by these features:

* A broad merchandise assortment, including both hard and soft goods, which in scope (but not in price) resembles the department store's. Less fashion-sensitive merchandise is carried.
* A relatively low operating-cost ratio. Gross total expenses average 25 per cent of sales, much lower than for specialty and department stores.
* Credit sales of 12 to 25 per cent of total sales, compared with over 50 per cent for department stores.
* Relatively inexpensive buildings, equipment, and fixtures.
* Low-rent locations.
* Emphasis on self-service.
* Heavy promotion of national-brand merchandise.
* Frequent use of leased departments.

Table 4-6 outlines the operating results of discount stores during 1982–1983.

Table 4-6
Selected Operating Results for Self-Service Discount Department Stores 1982–83

	Per Cent of Sales
Gross margin	28.26
Leased department income	0.41
Gross income	28.67
Total expenses	24.74
Net operating profit	3.93
Other income or deductions	−1.00
Earnings before income taxes	2.93
Federal and state income taxes	1.27
Net earnings after taxes	1.66

Source: "Retailing: Basic Analysis," Standard & Poor's Industry Surveys (January 26, 1984), Section 2, p. R 120. Reprinted by permission.

[28]Jean A. Briggs, "Is Discounting Done For?" *Forbes* (August 13, 1983), pp. 40, 42; and Penney Gill, "Hitting Home: Off-Price Linens," *Stores* (May 1983), pp. 56–62.
[29]Subratu N. Chakravarty, "The Per-Square Foot Approach," *Forbes* (January 31, 1983), pp. 33–34.

The major expansion of full-line discount stores occurred in the 1960s when they began to merchandise nationally advertised hard goods at considerable price reductions over conventional outlets. These lower prices were made possible through higher sales volume, self-service, and minimum consumer service. The mass-merchandising tactics of discounters allowed them to operate with lower gross-profit margins.

From 1962 to 1972, full-line discount store sales rose from about $6 billion to over $28 billion annually. In 1984, full-line discount store sales reached $79.2 billion, and there were 8,109 stores. Five merchandise categories accounted for about half of full-line discount store sales: women's apparel, 18.1 per cent; men's and boy's wear, 10.4 per cent; housewares, 8 per cent; consumer electronics, 7.4 per cent; and health and beauty aids, 7 per cent.[30]

In recent years, some full-line discounters have fallen on hard times. Both Korvette and the Treasury Store division of J. C. Penney closed in 1980; and in 1982, Woolworth wrote off $325 million when it closed all 336 of its Woolco discount stores.[31] These store terminations were caused by two key factors. First, full-line discounters sell much of their merchandise to lower-income, blue-collar consumers. This group has been particularly affected by the recessions that have occurred in the past decade. Second, a range of competitors has taken business away from full-line discounters. Retail catalog showrooms attract shoppers interested in jewelry, housewares, and gift items. Off-price chains, factory outlets, and flea markets attract shoppers looking for wearing apparel. Some of these competitors carry nationally advertised garments that full-line discounters cannot acquire because of department store pressure on manufacturers (full-line discount stores are frequently located near department stores).

Some full-line discounters have revised their strategies. For example, K mart has increased the soft goods lines it carries, now has its own color and fabric coordinators, and more quickly responds to fashion trends.[32]

Retail Catalog Showroom

A **retail catalog showroom** is an operation in which the consumer selects merchandise from a catalog and shops at a warehouse. In some instances, the shopper not only selects the merchandise by number but also writes up the sales order. Usually, all the goods are stored out of the shoppers' reach; the closed inventory rooms may encompass up to two-thirds of the outlet's space.

Retail catalog showrooms need to make actual merchandise decisions months in advance of sale due to catalog preparation lead time. They attempt to make long-term price and delivery arrangements with many suppliers to reduce the impact of inflation, to minimize changes in catalog selling prices, and to assure adequate stocks of merchandise.

The sales mix is an important part of a retail catalog showroom's overall strategy. Five categories (jewelry, electronics, housewares, gifts, and watches) account for close to 70 per cent of overall sales. Jewelry alone accounted for 28 per cent of overall 1983 sales. While the gross profit margins on product categories such as personal care, photography, housewares, electronics, hardware, and tools were below 20 per cent,

[30]"Census '84–'85: Merchandising Profiles," *Discount Store News* (July 23, 1984), pp. 18, 67.
[31]Claudia Ricci, "Woolworth Sets Woolco Closing for $325 Million," *Wall Street Journal* (September 27, 1982), p. 8.
[32] Steve Weiner, "K mart Upgrades Clothing Lines to Draw More Customers and Change Firm's Image," *Wall Street Journal* (April 3, 1984), p. 35.

the profit margins on jewelry were close to 50 per cent.[33] Retail catalog showrooms do not normally stock soft goods such as apparel.

The success of the catalog showroom is the result of its ability to cut costs below those of other types of retailers:

- Losses from shoplifting are low because goods are kept in a stockroom.
- Payroll expenses are low. There are few salespeople; products are not demonstrated; customers write up orders; and products are not assembled or delivered.
- Store decoration costs are low because 60 per cent of floor space is in the warehouse area.
- By avoiding clothes and other high-fashion items, showrooms eliminate the worry of style changes and size complexities, which makes reordering easier.
- Since 95 per cent of buyers preshop in catalogs at home, there is less need for displays and sales assistance.[34]
- Catalogs generally cost the showroom up to about $2.60 each to print and distribute. Catalogs and flyers are the major advertising expense.

Retail catalog showroom sales were $10.7 billion in 1984. These sales were distributed among 2,055 outlets.[35] Major catalog showrooms include Best Products, Service Merchandise, Consumers Distributing, and Ardan.

Despite their success, retail catalog showrooms now face some potential problems. Many other retailers are aggressively cutting prices. Catalog showroom advertising expenses have recently risen because of the increased use of flyers and newspaper ads. Pricing is difficult because catalogs must be prepared far in advance. During inflationary periods, costs change more frequently than catalogs are printed. For example, the cost of gold (which is highly variable) greatly affects jewelry prices. The showrooms have to weigh price increases against reduced profit margins. Finally, rental costs are rising as showrooms seek out more costly shopping center locations.

The retail catalog showroom industry is now undergoing consolidation. While there were 1,100 companies in 1971, there are now 300 firms. Fewer than 40 companies account for 90 per cent of showroom sales. Recent acquisitions include Best Products' purchase of Modern Merchandising and Basco; and Service Merchandising's purchase of Sam Solomon, H. J. Wilson, and Ellman's.[36]

Off-Price Chain

An **off-price chain** features brand name (sometimes designer label) apparel, footwear (primarily women's and family), linens, fabrics, and housewares and sells them at low prices in an austere, limited-service environment. It frequently utilizes community dressing rooms, centralized checkout counters, no gift wrapping, extra charges for alterations, and no delivery. Merchandise is bought opportunistically, when special deals occur. Other retailers' canceled orders, manufacturers' irregulars and overruns,

---

[33]"Market '84 Audit," *Catalog Showroom Business* (September 1984), p. 47.

[34]"Tenth Annual Catalog Showroom Business Consumer Audit '84," *Catalog Showroom Business* (May 1984), p. 57.

[35]"Market '84 Audit," pp. 3, 37

[36]Jacquelyn Bivins, "Fewer Players on the Oligopoly Board," *Chain Store Age Executive* (June 1983), p. 17; and Jim Montgomery, "Two Firms Agree to Sale to Service Merchandise Co.," *Wall Street Journal* (April 9, 1985), p. 5.

and end-of-season merchandise are often purchased for one-fifth to one-fourth of their original wholesale prices.[37]

Off-price chains usually compete for the same type of shoppers as department stores—married suburban females, aged 30 to 39, with children and household incomes of $35,000. Off-price stores are geared to upscale customers who know brands and price levels.[38]

The most important part of the strategy of off-price chains involves the buying of merchandise and establishing long-term relationships with suppliers. To succeed, the chains must secure large quantities of merchandise at reduced wholesale prices and have a regular flow of goods into stores.

In some cases, the manufacturer seeks out the off-price chain in order to sell samples and products that have not done well (this generally occurs three to four weeks after the beginning of a season) and/or merchandise remaining on hand near the end of a season. In this way, the manufacturer has access to quick cash, obtains a market for close-outs and discontinued items, and encourages a relationship with a retailer who promises not to mention brand names or prices in ads (so as not to alienate a department store or specialty store client). Also, off-price chains are usually less demanding than department stores in terms of the credit and advertising allowances requested from suppliers. According to an executive at T. J. Maxx, a major off-price chain:

> A vendor looks forward to a T. J. Maxx coming in, buying a ton of merchandise, not caring about the colors and sizes, not threatening to return it, paying on time, and wanting it sent to one location, not all over the country. It's kind of tough for vendors to walk away from that.[39]

In other cases, off-price chains employ a more active buying strategy. Instead of waiting for close-outs and canceled orders, they convince manufacturers to make garments during off-seasons and pay cash for items before they are produced (or delivered).[40]

In 1984 sales of off-price chains were estimated at $8.5 billion, about 6 per cent of total U.S. apparel and footwear sales.[41] Table 4-7 identifies the ten largest off-price chains for 1983. It is essential to note that many of these chains are owned by traditional retailers, despite the concerns these retailers have expressed about the competition provided by off-price stores.

Much of the excitement about off-price chains is due to their recent rapid growth, as reflected by an annual sales growth rate of 23 per cent from 1979 to 1984, and their impact on department and specialty stores. While off-price chains have gross margins of about 33 per cent, compared with gross margins of 42 to 44 per cent for department and specialty stores, they are able to generate 8 to 10 stock turns per year (about three times greater than traditional stores) and an 8 per cent pretax profit as a percentage of sales (two to four times greater than traditional stores).[42] The increasing development of off-price shopping centers is also adding to their competitive strength.

[37]"Off-Price Name Brand Apparel Retailing: Who's Doing It and How," *Stores* (May 1983), p. 27.
[38]Ann M. Morrison, "The Upshot of Off Price," *Fortune* (June 13, 1983), pp. 122–124.
[39]Ibid., p. 124.
[40]Walter McQuade, "The Man Who Makes Millions on Mistakes," *Fortune* (September 6, 1982), p. 112.
[41]Schulz, "Taking on the Off-Pricers," p. 25.
[42]Gill, "Hitting Home: Off-Price Linens," p. 56; and Isadore Barmash, "A Revolution in American Shopping," *New York Times* (October 23, 1983), Section 3, pp. 1, 28.

Table 4-7

The Top Off-Price Apparel Chains, 1983

Chain (Parent Firm)	Sales (millions)	Number of Outlets
Marshalls (Melville (Corp)	$1,100	175
T. J. Maxx/Hit or Miss (Zayre Corp.)	755	471
Loehmann's Inc. (Associated Dry Goods)	275	70
Pic-A-Dilly (Lucky Stores)	210	271
Syms, Inc.	185	11
Burlington Coat Factory	200	46
J. Brannam (Woolworth)	75	38
T. H. Mandy (U.S. Shoe)	200	122
Dress Barn, Inc.	44	70
Rose Stores	80	26

Source: Eric C. Peterson, "Off Price," Stores *(May 1984), p. 47. Copyright National Retail Merchants Association 1984. Reprinted by permission.*

Factory Outlet

A **factory outlet** is a manufacturer-owned store that sells the manufacturer's closeouts, canceled orders, discontinued merchandise, and irregulars. Manufacturers' interest in outlet stores is increasing for three basic reasons. First, a manufacturer can control where discounted merchandise is sold. By locating outlets in out-of-the-way locations, in depressed areas, or in areas with low sales penetration of the firm's brands, factory outlet sales are unlikely to affect a manufacturer's key customers (which may be specialty and department stores). Second, these outlets can be profitable despite prices up to 50 per cent less than customary retail prices. This occurs because of low operating costs, such as few services, low rent, limited displays, and plain store fixtures. In addition, the manufacturer does not have to compensate wholesalers and/or retailers.

Third, through factory outlets, manufacturers can control the visibility of the stores, establish promotional policies, remove labels, and be sure that discontinued items and irregulars are disposed of properly. As the president of Phillips–Van Heusen noted, factory outlets represent "the only way in which a brand can keep clean" and not be sold through discounters competing with traditional stores.[43]

Recently, factory outlets have begun to locate in clusters or in outlet malls to expand customer traffic and utilize cooperative advertising. There are currently factory outlet malls in Tennessee, Georgia, New York, Connecticut, Florida, and other states. It is estimated that 1980 factory outlet sales were about $1 billion.[44] Examples of manufacturers operating factory outlets are Warnaco (maker of Hathaway Shirts, White Stag sportswear, and Warner's lingerie) with seven stores, Phillips–Van Heusen with twenty-six stores, U.S. Shoe Corp. with thirty Bannister Shoe stores, and Hamilton Clock with three stores.

When determining whether to enter into or expand factory outlets, manufacturers need to be cautious. They must evaluate their expertise in retailing, dollar investment costs, impact on existing retailers who buy from them, and the response of final customers. Certainly, manufacturers will not want to jeopardize their products' sales at full retail prices.

[43]Claudia Ricci, "Discount Business Booms, Pleasing Buyers, Irking Department Stores," *Wall Street Journal* (May 3, 1983), p. 35.
[44]Isadore Barmash, "Outlets," *Stores* (June 1982), p. 13.

Buying Club

A **buying club** (sometimes known as a warehouse club) straddles the line between wholesaling and retailing. The major portion of sales, usually about 60 per cent, comes from small businesses that pay nominal membership fees and buy goods at wholesale prices. About 40 per cent of sales are to individual consumers for their personal use; they are charged 5 per cent above wholesale prices. Although many clubs require consumers to belong to a union or service group or be a municipal employee, in reality, eligibility is defined so broadly as to exclude few consumers. Membership fees are about $25 for small businesses; individual consumers receive free membership.[45]

The buying club is a derivative of the membership-based discounter that was common in the United States in the 1950s and 1960s and of the giant European supermarket that caters to small food and drug retailers.[46] The operating strategy of a buying club centers on the use of little or no advertising (but direct mail is often employed), opportunistic buying (with no continuity of merchandise and limited selections), an industrial park location, plain fixtures, wide aisles (to allow forklift trucks to have access to shelves), concrete floors, no delivery, no credit, and merchandise sent directly from manufacturers to store outlets.

By providing few services, achieving a stock turnover rate of eighteen times a year, paying low rent, and generating high sales volume per square foot (four to five times higher than a typical department store), buying clubs are able to earn a profit on gross margins of 10 per cent—versus 28 per cent for full-line discount stores. At one major buying club chain, Price Club, sales are comprised of sundries (28 per cent), food (22 per cent), appliances and housewares (20 per cent), hard lines (16 per cent), liquor (7 per cent), and soft goods (7 per cent). Other large buying clubs are Zayre's BJ's Wholesale Club, Wal-Mart's Sam's Wholesale Club, and the Pay 'n Save Corporation. Total retail sales in buying clubs were expected to be almost $4 billion in 1985 (up from $1.5 billion in 1984).[47]

Flea Market

The **flea market** is rooted in the centuries-old tradition of street selling—shoppers touch, sample, and haggle over goods of all kinds. Once, flea markets sold only antiques, bric-a-bracs, and assorted used merchandise. Today, flea markets sell new merchandise such as clothing, foods, housewares, and cosmetics. Flea markets are normally located in sites not associated with retailing: race tracks, stadiums, drive-in movie parking lots, and former supermarket and department store outlets. They may be indoor or outdoor.

Individual retailers rent space on a daily, weekly, or seasonal basis. For example, one sizable flea market rents 20-foot by 40-foot spaces for $20 to $40 or more per day, depending on the location. Some flea markets impose a parking fee or admission charge for final customers.

[45]John Nielsen, "Shopping at the Club," *Fortune* (December 24, 1984), pp. 91–92; and Molly Brauer, "Sam's: Setting a Fast Pace," *Chain Store Age Executive* (August 1983), pp. 20–21.

[46]Frank E. James, "Big Warehouse Outlets Break Traditional Rules of Retailing," *Wall Street Journal* (December 22, 1983), p. 27.

[47]Brad Altman, "Price Club's Angle: For Members Only," *Chain Store Age Executive* (May 1983), p. 44; Hortense Leon, "Discount Warehouses Open New Doors," *Advertising Age* (August 9, 1984), pp. 18–19; Amy Dunkin, Todd Mason, and Teresa Carson, "Boom Times in a Bargain Hunter's Paradise," *Business Week* (March 11, 1985), pp. 116, 120; and Molly Brauer, "Membership Retailing Trend Taking Off," *Chain Store Age Executive* (November 1984), p. 17.

No specific government or trade association data exist, but one source estimates there were about 200 major flea markets in the United States in 1980. Inflation, the rising popularity of Sunday shopping, the broadened product mix of flea markets, and the acceptance of flea markets by customers have all contributed to the growth of this retail institution. The largest flea markets in the United States operate at Roosevelt Raceway in Long Island, New York (which has 1,600 merchants and draws as many as 35,000 people to the 15,000 car parking lot), and the Rose Bowl Flea Market in Pasadena, California (which attracts up to 40,000 people per day).[48]

Traditional merchants are not happy about flea markets. They believe flea markets represent an unfair method of competition because suppliers are often unaware that their merchandise is sold there, operating costs are extremely low, state and federal taxes can be easily avoided, private-label merchandise and seconds can be misrepresented, and shoppers may purchase items at flea markets and then return them to traditional retailers for refunds. Furthermore, flea markets may cause traffic congestion.

The popularity of off-price chains, factory outlets, buying clubs, and flea markets can be explained by the wheel of retailing. All these institutions are low-cost retailers that appeal to price-conscious consumers who have not been satisfied with other retailers who have added services, raised prices, and moved through the wheel.

Retail Institutions Categorized by Nonstore Sales

Nonstore retailing refers to retailers who do not possess conventional facilities—for example, storefront, in-store selling, displays of merchandise, and so on. Vending machine, direct-to-home selling, and direct marketing are the major types of nonstore retailing. Shopping through cable television ordering systems is covered in Chapter 17 ("The Changing Environment of Retailing"). In 1983, nonstore retailing accounted for approximately $174 billion in sales.

Vending Machine

A **vending machine** is a retail institution that involves coin-operated machinery. The vending machine eliminates the use of sales personnel, allows for around-the-clock sales, and can be placed outside or inside a store. Although these advantages seem to indicate rapid growth and success for vending machines, there have been problems. Among the most important are high costs, breakdown of machines, theft, vandalism, stockouts, and image (low-quality convenience items). An additional problem, exact change, has been solved in recent years with the introduction of the dollar-bill changer. The introduction of the Susan B. Anthony dollar coin had a negligible effect on the industry because of its lack of consumer acceptance. In 1983, vending machines had an average net profit before tax of only 1.5 per cent; and operating expenses were 54.4 per cent of sales.[49]

---

[48]Isadore Barmash, "Flea Markets: New Retail Force," *New York Times* (November 24, 1980), p. D1; and Rita Reif, "Flea Markets in Season All over Region," *New York Times* (June 12, 1981), pp. C1, C15. See also Elaine Sherman, Kevin McCrohan, and James D. Smith, "Informal Retailing: An Analysis of Products, Attitudes, and Expectations," in Elizabeth Hirschman and Morris Holbrook (Editors), *Advances in Consumer Research* Vol. XII (Provo, Utah: Association for Consumer Research, 1985), pp. 204–208.

[49]"1984 Census of the Industry," *Vending Times* (July 1984), p. 44.

Vending machine sales are centered around a fairly narrow product line. Beverages and cigarettes account for 70 per cent of sales, while nonfood items yield less than 7 per cent of sales. About 36 per cent of vending machine sales are in plants and factories, in hospitals, and on college campuses. The consumers' reluctance to purchase hosiery and other staple apparel items from vending machines has been shown in a variety of experiments with these products. In 1983, vending machine sales were $14.8 billion.[50] Major vending machine operators are Canteen Corporation and ARA Services.

To improve productivity, vending machine operators are applying a variety of innovations. For example, microprocessors are being used in machines to track consumer preferences, trace malfunctions, and record deposits. Some firms are also equipping their machines with voice synthesizers that are programmed to say "Thank you, come again" or "Your change is 15 cents."

Direct-to-Home Selling

Direct-to-home selling involves personal contact with consumers in their homes. Cosmetics, vacuum cleaners, encyclopedias, dairy products, and newspapers are kinds of merchandise that have been successfully sold in this manner. In 1983, direct-to-home selling accounted for about $9.3 billion in sales and employed over 5 million people.[51]

There are several advantages with direct-to-home selling. First, a personal touch is used in dealing with consumers. Second, a complete demonstration can be made. Third, the consumer is more relaxed in his or her home. Fourth, this is a very convenient way of shopping, especially for shut-ins. Fifth, a small business can be operated with low overhead costs.

There also are several disadvantages with direct-to-home selling. First, many consumers are suspicious and will not open their doors to salespeople. This reaction has been partially overcome by firms such as Mary Kay and Tupperware, which use community residents and a party atmosphere rather than a strict door-to-door approach. However, even a party plan requires networks of relationships with family, friends, and neighbors.

Second, selling costs are high because of travel requirements and low productivity. Third, many legal restrictions have been placed on direct-to-home retailing because of deceptive selling practices. Fourth, the images of some products sold direct-to-home are low. Precontacting customers, referrals, and greater advertising are responses to these problems. Because of the negative connotation of "door-to-door," these retailers have adopted the phrase "direct-to-home."

Fifth, improved job opportunities in other fields and an upswing in the economy generally reduce the number of qualified recruits interested in direct-to-home selling and increase the number of part-time salespeople who take other jobs. Revenues for direct selling companies largely depend on the number of sales representatives employed, not on the size of the market. It is common for major U.S. direct selling firms

---

[50]Ibid.; and *Vending and Food Service Management* (Chicago: National Association of the Vending Machine Industry, 1984), p. 4.

[51]Dean Rotbart and Laurie P. Cohen, "The Party at Mary Kay Isn't Quite So Lively These Days as Recruiting of Saleswomen Falls Off," *Wall Street Journal* (October 28, 1983), p. 12.

to reach less than one-half of their potential customers. Sixth, the growth in working women has reduced the interest and availability of this group as consumers.[52]

It is often assumed that direct-to-home selling is inexpensive because of the absence of costs associated with a store, such as rent, fixtures, light, and heating. However, training, supervision, and compensation costs are high for direct-to-home sales. In addition, turnover is quite rapid.

Contributing to the costs of direct-to-home sales are high commission rates and relatively low productivity per salesperson. For example, Avon had 425,000 active representatives in the United States in 1983. Sales representatives earned a commission of between 35 and 50 per cent of sales depending on performance. These representatives were supervised by 7,500 district managers. The average Avon representative is a housewife selling part time. Turnover is so significant that Avon sometimes has to sign up 600,000 new recruits per year to maintain the average size of its sales force. Recently, Avon began rewarding salespeople for bringing in new recruits; yet more than one-third of U.S. households are not served by Avon representatives.[53]

Dominant direct-selling firms are Avon (cosmetics), Mary Kay (cosmetics), Amway (home-cleaning supplies), Shaklee (vitamins and health foods), Encyclopedia Britannica, Tupperware (plastic dishes and food containers), Consolidated Foods' Electrolux (vacuum cleaners), and Scott and Fetzer's World Book (encyclopedias) and Kirby (vacuum cleaners).

Large department stores are also involved in direct-to-home selling. For example, J. C. Penney has trained decorator consultants who sell a complete line of furnishings in the home. These decorators are invited by consumers and sell products not available in Penney stores.

Direct Marketing

Direct marketing is a form of retailing in which a customer is first exposed to a nonpersonal medium (such as direct mail, conventional or cable television, radio, magazines, or coupons) or contacted by telephone and then orders products by mail or telephone (usually through a toll-free 800 number). Simmons Market Research Bureau estimated that retail direct marketing totaled $172 billion in 1984, with one-half of the U.S. households it studied doing some shopping at home. The majority of direct marketing orders involved gift purchases, apparel, magazine subscriptions, and home accessories.[54]

Direct marketing has several strong points. First, costs are reduced: initial investment costs are low; a mail-order business can be operated out of a garage or basement; inventory levels are minimal; no fixtures or displays are needed; a prime location is unnecessary; store hours do not have to be maintained; and a personal sales

[52]Pat Sloan, "Avon Ladies Toughen Up Sales Pitch," *Advertising Age* (March 12, 1984), p. 12; Gwen Kinkead, "Tupperware's Party Times Are Over," *Fortune* (February 20, 1984), pp. 113–114ff; Bill Saporito, "A Door-to-Door Bell Ringer," *Fortune* (December 10, 1984), pp. 83–84, 88; and Jo Ellen Daily and Mark N. Vamos, "How Tupperware Hopes to Liven Up the Party," *Business Week* (February 25, 1985), pp. 108–109.
[53]Sloan, "Avon Ladies Toughen Up Sales Pitch," p. 12; *Avon Products Inc. Form 10K*, dated December 31, 1983; and Jo An Paganetti, "An American Best Seller's Story Is Still 'Direct'," *Advertising Age* (March 19, 1984), p. M-4.
[54]"Direct Marketing Sales Far Outpace Estimates," *Marketing News* (November 23, 1984), pp. 1, 8.

force is not needed. Second, a large geographic area can be covered. Third, it is possible for a firm to offer lower prices because of its reduced costs relative to a store retailer. Fourth, the consumer is given a convenient method of shopping. There are no crowds, parking difficulties, or lines at cash registers.

Fifth, a traditional store-based retailer can use direct marketing to supplement its regular business and expand its geographic trading area (even becoming a national retailer) without adding outlets. Sixth, a direct marketer is able to target its efforts at specific customer market segments. Seventh, a consumer can legally avoid sales tax by purchasing items from direct marketers who do not operate retail facilities in the consumer's state.

There are some limitations to direct marketing, but they are not as critical as the problems that face direct-to-home sellers. First, merchandise cannot be examined prior to its purchase by a consumer. Thus, the range of items sold via direct marketing is usually more limited than that sold in stores. Also, direct marketers need liberal return policies to attract and maintain customers. Second, prospective retailers may underestimate entry costs. Catalogs are costly, with printing and mailing costs easily being $2 to $3 or more per catalog. A computer system may be required to track shipments, monitor purchases and returns, and keep mailing lists current. A 24-hour telephone staff may be necessary.[55]

Third, since most catalogs are delivered by third-class mail, the profitability of direct marketers is highly sensitive to postal rates and to the costs of paper stock. Fourth, even the most successful catalogs draw purchases from less than 10 per cent of recipients. The high costs and relatively low response rates have caused some merchants to charge for their catalogs (with the fee usually reimbursed after the first order is placed) or to limit catalogs to customers previously meeting minimum purchase amounts. Fifth, direct marketing clutter still exists. In 1983, almost 7 billion catalogs were mailed—nearly 80 apiece for every U.S. household. Sixth, some unscrupulous direct marketers have given the industry a poor image because of delays in delivery and the shipment of damaged goods. Seventh, because catalogs are prepared six months to a year in advance, prices and styles may be difficult to plan.[56]

The "30-day rule" is a federal regulation that greatly affects direct marketers. This regulation requires that mail-order merchants ship orders within 30 days after their receipt or notify customers of delays. If an order cannot be shipped within 60 days, the customer must be given a specific delivery date and offered the option of canceling the order and obtaining a refund or continuing to wait for the order to be filled.

Direct marketers can be divided into two general categories: general merchandise and specialty merchandise. General-merchandise firms offer a full line of products and sell everything from clothing to heavy appliances. Sears, Spiegel, Montgomery Ward, and J. C. Penney are examples of general-merchandise direct marketers. Specialty-merchandise firms concentrate on a narrow product line, like their specialty store

[55]Richard Greene, "A Boutique in Your Living Room," *Forbes* (May 7, 1984), p. 91.
[56]Laundra Saunders, "Direct Mail," *Forbes* (May 7, 1984), p. 94; Hank Gilman, "Catalog Merchants Posting Bigger Gains for Christmas than Traditional Retailers," *Wall Street Journal* (December 23, 1984), p. 7; Frank E. James, "Good Return and Refund Policies Are Vital to Successful Christmas Shopping by Mail," *Wall Street Journal* (November 26, 1984), p. 37; Wendy Kimbrell and Lewis Lazare, "Sears Book Gets Breezy Look," *Advertising Age* (July 9, 1984), p. 24; Steve Weiner, "Sears Is Charging Some Customers $4 for Popular Book," *Wall Street Journal* (April 13, 1984), p. 16; "Mail Order Industry Is Fighting the Old, Sleazy Image on Several Fronts," *Marketing News* (July 8, 1983), p. 1; and William M. Bulkeley, "Buying Computers by Mail Saves Money, but Don't Expect Quick Repairs or Help," *Wall Street Journal* (January 29, 1985), p. 35.

counterparts. Book-of-the-Month Club, Spencer Gifts, L. L. Bean, Franklin Mint, and Time, Inc. are just a few of the several thousand specialty-merchandise direct marketers operating in the United States.

Sustained growth for direct marketing is projected for several reasons:

- The increased emphasis on the standardization and branding of products is reducing the risk of consumer buying on the basis of a catalog description.
- Extended travel time, heavy traffic, and inadequate parking are avoided when consumers respond to direct-marketing efforts.
- Consumer interest in convenience and the difficulty in setting aside time for shopping are expected to continue.
- Direct marketers are rapidly improving their skills and efficiency; they are much more effective than ever before.
- Technological breakthroughs are broadening the opportunities for direct marketers. These breakthroughs include in-home computer ordering systems and computerized inventory systems.
- Many direct marketers operate 24-hour service for telephone orders.

Retail Institutions Categorized by Service Versus Product Retailing

From a definitional perspective, **service retailing** involves the sale of services rather than goods to the final consumer. As noted in Chapter 1, the total sales of all U.S. services (retail and nonretail) in 1983 were about $1.1 trillion. For example, 1983 sales for hotels, motels, personal services, health care (not hospital), auto repair, amusement parks, and miscellaneous repair services amounted to $164 billion.

Service retailing involves "a market transaction by an enterprise or entrepreneur where the object of the market transaction is other than the transfer of ownership (and title, if any) of a tangible commodity." There are three types of service retailing: **rented-goods services,** in which customers rent and use products; **owned-goods services,** in which products owned by consumers are repaired, improved, or maintained; and **non-goods services,** in which intangible personal services (rather than products) are offered to consumers as "experiential possessions."[57]

Some examples of rented-goods services are Hertz Rent-a-Car, carpet cleaner rentals from a supermarket, and apartment rentals. In each case, a tangible product is leased for a fee for a specified period of time. The consumer may enjoy the use of the product, but ownership is not obtained and the product must be returned when the rental period is up.

Owned-goods services involve an alteration of some type in a product already owned by the customer. Examples are repair services (automobile, watch, plumbing, appliance, and so on), lawn care, car wash, furniture upholstering, and dry cleaning. In this category, a service is provided to improve an owned good, and the retailer undertaking the service never owns the product.

---

[57]Robert C. Judd, "The Structure and Classification of the Service Market," unpublished Ph.D. dissertation, University of Wisconsin, 1962, p. 21; and Robert C. Judd, "The Case for Redefining Services," *Journal of Marketing*, Vol. 28 (January 1964), p. 59.

Nongoods services are those where no tangible products are involved, and the retailer offers personal services requiring the use of his or her time for a fee. Some examples are baby-sitter, stock broker, tutor, travel guide, personal care (doctor, barber, beautician, and so on), and real estate broker. In each instance, a personal service is provided, the seller offers his or her expertise for a specified period of time, and a fee is paid for the service. Many nongoods services could be performed by the consumer if he or she so desired (an obvious exception is a medical checkup).

The marketing characteristics of services differ significantly from those of products, as shown by the following list:

- Services are sometimes expressed as rates, fees, admissions, charges, tuition, and so on, and not in terms of price.
- The buyer of a service is often called a client and not a customer.
- Service firms are highly differentiated in their approaches to marketing.
- Surpluses cannot be inventoried; therefore, services are highly perishable.
- Some services are nonprofit in nature.
- Many services are marketed in a professional or formal manner.
- Standards are not precise, because many services cannot be mass produced.
- Price-setting practices vary greatly.
- It is difficult to apply the economic concepts of supply and demand, and costs are also difficult to apply because of the intangible nature of services.
- Few service chains have existed (but this is now changing rapidly—examples are Century 21 Real Estate and H&R Block Tax Service), and concentration in the service sector is relatively small.
- Many service retailers do not understand that their services must be marketed; being available does not guarantee business.
- Symbolism derives from how well a service is performed rather than from ownership of a product.[58]

Figure 4-2 contains a detailed, but not exhaustive, list of services available. It should be noted that although some services have not been commonly considered a part of retailing (such as medical, dental, legal, and educational), they should be. Each entails a service purchased by a final consumer.

Chapter 15 presents a detailed discussion of strategy development for a service retailer.

Retail Institutions: A Synopsis

In Chapters 3 and 4, retail institutions have been categorized and explained from four different perspectives: ownership, retail strategy mix, nonstore retailing, and service versus product retailing. None of these four classifications is all-encompassing or mu-

---

[58]See, for example, G. Lynn Shostack, "Designing Services That Deliver," *Harvard Business Review*, Vol. 62 (January–February 1984), pp. 133–139.

Selected Retail Services

Amusement park	Insurance agency
Automobile maintenance and repair	Interior decorating
Appraisal	Landscaping
Appliance repair	Laundromat
Baby-sitting	Law
Banking	Medicine
Barber shop	Movie theater
Beauty salon	Parking
Bell-hop	Plumbing
Car wash	Radio and TV
Chauffeur	Recreation facilities
Consulting engineer	Rental
Country clubs	Residential real estate broker
Custom alterations	Restaurant
Dance studio	Shoe repair
Dentistry	Sports tickets
Dry cleaner	Stock broker
Education	Tax preparation
Employment agency	Telephone answering
Film processing	Transportation
Floor and furniture refinishing	Trash collection
Funeral parlor	Travel
Health spa	Watch repair
Home cleaning	Window cleaning
Hotel and motel	Yard maintenance
House painter	

Source: Drawn in large part from the *Census of Business.*

Figure 4-2

tually exclusive. The intention is to provide the reader with several bases for understanding the field of retailing.

What is most apparent is the range of retail institutions. Retail ownership can vary from a small, independent store to a leased department to a franchise to a large chain store. Retail strategy mixes run the gamut from a convenience store (limited variety, medium prices, and limited services) to a full-line department store (wide variety, medium to high prices, and extensive services). Nonstore retailing can involve vending machines, direct-to-home selling, and direct marketing. This form of retailing can include total personal contact (a lengthy in-home sales visit) or the absence of personal contact (mail-order sales). Service retailing, because of its intangibility, is different from product retailing.

It is important to understand principles such as channel control, the wheel of retailing, scrambled merchandising, and the retail life cycle. Although channel control may be achieved by ownership of a complete marketing channel, it also refers to the use of private labeling, persuasion, preticketing of prices, and so on. This principle can contribute to a better understanding of the different objectives of retailers, manufacturers, and wholesalers, as well as the dynamics of decision making among these groups.

The wheel of retailing provides an explanation for much of the recent growth in newer types of discounters and should be useful in predicting the nature of future institutions. The current lack of distinction between some traditional full-line discount stores and full-line department stores, in terms of overall levels of customer service and the quality of retail locations, has been predicted by this concept.

The scrambled-merchandising principle shows the successes and problems associated with expanding product lines and the impact on competing retailers. Today, scrambled merchandising is used by almost all retailers, as they attempt to maintain or expand sales. It is suggested that there are limits to scrambled merchandising, and beyond these limits retailers will face serious problems.

The retail life cycle explains the stages that retail institutions pass through and the appropriate strategic responses at each stage. The stages in the life cycle are innovation, accelerated development, maturity, and decline. Because life cycles appear to be accelerating, as a result of competition and environmental factors, it is becoming more difficult to sustain long-run growth and profitability.

The reader should realize that some of the statements made in these two chapters do not coincide with "commonsense" feelings toward retail institutions. For example, commonsense would not predict high administrative costs for some nonstore retailers such as vending machines, high pretax profits as a percentage of sales for off-price chains, or the growth of factory outlets. Thus, the reader should look at retail research and not jump to premature conclusions.

Retail Institutions—Part II: A Summary

Retail stores have alternatives concerning their strategic mixes. A firm can locate at a high-rent shopping center, a low-rent isolated site, or a combination of the two. A retailer can sell many different types of products (width of assortment) and/or it can sell many varieties within one product line (depth of assortment). On the other hand, a firm may carry only one product line and/or sell only one brand or size within the product line. A retailer can provide no services or a wealth of them. In the former instance, operations involve self-service, cash payments, and no delivery. For the latter, operations involve sales personnel, credit, delivery, gift wrapping, dining facilities, and so on. A retailer can promote extensively, using newspapers, television, radio, personal selling, and so on, or a retailer can use minimal promotion and count on the other elements to draw customers. Last, a retailer can sell merchandise at a high price (prestige), a low price (penetration), or a competitive price. A combination of these prices can be used. However, prestige and penetration pricing within one store will damage the store's image.

All strategy components must be consistent. In this chapter, fifteen types of retailers were examined by strategy mix: convenience store, conventional supermarket, combination store, superstore, box store, and warehouse store (food based); and specialty store, variety store, department store, full-line discount store, retail catalog showroom, off-price chain, factory outlet, buying club, and flea market (general merchandise).

Three forms of nonstore retailing were discussed: vending machine, direct-to-home selling, and direct marketing. Nonstore retailing contributes well over $174 billion annually. A vending machine involves coin-operated retailing. Sales personnel are eliminated. Sales can be made around the clock if the machine is located outside a store. But rental and labor costs are high, and the machines need constant repair. Theft is a problem, and only a limited variety of products can be sold.

Direct-to-home selling involves sales made to consumers in their homes. A personal approach is used. Demonstrations may be convenient. The owner of a small business can operate with low overhead costs. On the other hand, consumers are suspicious of direct-to-home salespeople. Selling costs are high because of extensive recruitment, supervision, and compensation. Productivity is low. There are many legal restrictions to this form of selling. The image of direct-to-home products and salespeople often is low.

Direct marketing occurs when a consumer is contacted (or reached) by a nonpersonal medium or telephone and then orders items by mail or telephone. With this form of nonstore retailing, a large trading area can be covered at minimal cost. A personal sales force, prime store location, merchandise displays, and store hours are not important. The customers shop in a convenient and inexpensive manner. Direct marketing can supplement the regular business of a store retailer. There are some negative aspects of mail-order retailing. Consumers cannot examine merchandise or receive personal assistance. Not all types of merchandise will be bought through the mail or by telephone. Slow delivery and underhanded businesspeople also inhibit the growth of direct marketing.

Service retailing can involve rented goods, owned goods, and nongoods. The unique aspects of service retailing include fee pricing, nonstorage of surpluses, imprecise standards, and symbolism. Chapter 15 deals with service retailing.

Questions for Discussion

1. Explain the wheel of retailing. Is it applicable today?
2. Develop a low-end strategy for a major appliance retailer. Include location, product, service, promotion, and price.
3. The appliance retailer in Question 2 wants to upgrade to a high-end strategy. Outline the proper strategy. What are the risks facing this retailer?
4. Why have supermarkets been the leaders in scrambled merchandising?
5. Can retailers prosper without using scrambled merchandising? Why or why not?
6. How can retail institutions postpone the decline phase of the retail life cycle?
7. Contrast the strategies of convenience stores, conventional supermarkets, superstores, and warehouse stores. Is there room for each in the marketplace? Explain your answer.
8. How should full-line discount stores and department stores distinguish between one another?
9. Differentiate between off-price chains and factory outlets. Which of the two has a better future? Why?

10. Describe and evaluate a flea market near your university or college.
11. Do you agree that nonstore retailing will continue to grow? Explain your answer.
12. What are some of the problems involved in nonstore retailing?
13. What criteria should a small retailer use in selecting a nonstore retailing form? A large retailer?
14. Distinguish among the three types of service retailing.
15. Is the nature of rental retailing significantly different from that of nongoods retailing? Explain your answer.

CASES

1. Foodland: Countering a Supermarket Industry Trend*

The Karolick family has sold groceries in Bentleyville, Pennsylvania, a blue-collar coal mining town with a population of 2,250, for more than sixty years. In 1969, the Karolicks built a 22,000 square-foot supermarket named Foodland. In planning for Foodland, the Karolicks visited over 200 grocery stores throughout the United States.

Foodland is providing a variety of services, an attractive atmosphere, and comfortable shopping experience while the supermarket industry is moving toward greater self-service, an austere atmosphere, and a routinized shopping experience. As Tom Karolick, Jr. stated:

> We're in a little coal-mining town, but people here like something nice, too. They like to be catered to. There's a market for warehouse-type grocery stores, but no one store can be everything to everyone. There always will be people who like to shop somewhere nice. It comes down to the market segment you want to go after.

Foodland's customer services are stressed. Many employees have been with the store since it opened; they make a determined effort to know and accommodate customers. The employees offer information, respond to customers' special orders, and engage in friendly conversations. Foodland has a bakery and a hot deli to facilitate one-stop shopping.

The atmosphere at Foodland is quite warm. Soft colors and indirect lighting are utilized, in contrast to bright colors and lighting in traditional supermarkets and the newer warehouse stores. Antique scales and shopping carts as well as other unusual grocery equipment are displayed throughout the store to enhance the atmosphere. Functional displays are modern, yet blend into the "subdued" atmosphere of Foodland. Said Tom Karolick, Jr.:

> We have a large frozen food section that also happens to be the warmest place in the store. The freezer area in supermarkets usually is pretty cold, but the low ceiling in that area of our store keeps the heat closer to the floor. The whole store is wallpapered, and there's a ceiling-to-floor woodland scene at the checkout counters, instead of a wall of glass. It's very serene.

*The material in this case is drawn from Kevin Higgins, "Supermarket in Small, Coal-Mining Town Rejects Box-Store Trend, Gives Shoppers Touch of Class," *Marketing News* (March 19, 1982), p. 6.

Table 1
Analysts' Questions Regarding Foodland

1. Can a city with a population of 2,250 support a large supermarket?
2. What proportion of the population is price sensitive?
3. Would Foodland's customers trade atmosphere for lower prices?
4. Is Foodland cost effective?
5. Is Foodland vulnerable to environmental changes, such as the economy or competition?
6. How would Foodland respond to the entry of a warehouse-type grocery store?

The interior layout at Foodland also encourages customer shopping rather than rushed or routinized behavior. Displays are less rectangular and more varied, whereas traditional supermarkets move their customers through stores in a smooth rectangular flow.

While outside analysts praise the Karolick's well-conceived and implemented plans at Foodland, they do raise several questions about the long-term potential of the store. These questions are summarized in Table 1.

Questions

1. Evaluate Foodland's approach in relation to the food retailing trends cited in this chapter.
2. By enacting Foodland's strategy mix, what do the Karolicks believe are the major reasons that consumers have for selecting a supermarket? Do you agree? Explain your answer.
3. Could a national supermarket chain enter Bentleyville and successfully compete with Foodland? Why or why not?
4. What impact would economic factors have on Foodland? Explain your answer.

2. Retail Catalog Showrooms: Analyzing the Characteristics of Customers and Noncustomers*

Annually for the last decade, *Catalog Showroom Business* magazine has surveyed retail catalog showroom shoppers to determine their attitudes toward this retail institution. In 1984, 400 catalog showroom shoppers in four major markets (New York, Florida, Minneapolis–St. Paul, and Los Angeles) were interviewed at a variety of times and days. In addition, 100 noncustomers were interviewed; these people patronized a shopping center containing a catalog showroom, but chose to shop at other types of stores on the day interviewed. Table 1 presents selected findings from the 1984 *Catalog Showroom Business* survey.

*The material in this case is drawn from Katherine Strauss and Roberta Janasz, "10th Annual Consumer Audit '84," *Catalog Showroom Business* (May 1984), pp. 51–55ff.

Table 1
Selected Characteristics of Customers and Noncustomers of Retail Catalog Showrooms

A. *Customers* (those shopping in a catalog showroom on the day interviewed)

Why do you like to shop at this showroom?*

	Males	Females
Low prices	68.4%	70.3%
Convenient location	44.4%	37.3%
Good selection of merchandise	26.5%	25.4%
Pleasant shopping environment	15.4%	20.4%
Good sales service	12.8%	19.0%

What don't you like about shopping in this showroom?*

	Males	Females
No complaints	72.6%	68.1%
Too crowded/long lines	8.5%	15.1%
Credit/check approval	6.0%	4.7%

How often do you shop in this showroom?

	Males	Females
At least once a week	1.7%	1.8%
2 or 3 times a month	6.8%	4.2%
Once a month	13.5%	15.9%

Which of the following type of merchandise did you buy here today?*

	Males	Females
Housewares	29.3%	32.6%
Giftware	3.4%	10.6%
Electronics	26.7%	15.4%

B. *Noncustomers* (those not shopping in a catalog showroom on the day interviewed)

Why do you like to shop at other stores?*

	Males	Females
Low prices	6.5%	2.9%
Convenient location	41.9%	30.9%
Good selection of merchandise	61.3%	55.9%
Pleasant shopping environment	35.5%	64.7%
Good sales service	16.1%	7.4%

What don't you like about shopping here?*

	Males	Females
No complaints	51.6%	55.2%
Too crowded/long lines	9.7%	20.9%
Credit/check approval	3.2%	3.0%

Table 1 *(continued)*
Selected Characteristics of Customers and Noncustomers of Retail Catalog Showrooms

How often do you shop in catalog showrooms?

	Males	Females
At least once a week	0%	0%
2 or 3 times a month	0%	5.5%
Once a month	4.2%	9.1%

Do you ever shop in catalog showrooms?

	Males	Females
Yes	77.4%	79.7%
No	22.6%	20.3%

*This is a multiple-response question; the sum of all responses can exceed 100 per cent.

Reprinted by permission.

Questions

1. Analyze the data in Table 1 on the basis of the retail strategy mix offered by retail catalog showrooms.
2. Relate the wheel-of-retailing concept to the findings of this survey.
3. What are the basic differences shown in Table 1 between males and females? Customers and noncustomers? Explain the implications of these differences.
4. What other questions could be asked to enable retail catalog showrooms to improve their strategy?

5

Consumer Behavior: Understanding the Decision Process

Chapter Objectives

1. To examine consumer behavior as it relates to retailing
2. To explain the stages in the consumer's decision process: stimulus, problem awareness, information search, evaluation of alternatives, purchase, and postpurchase behavior
3. To describe the factors affecting the consumer's decision process: demographics and lifestyle
4. To study the types of decision processes
5. To view the decision process from a strategic retailing perspective

During 1984, Simmons Market Research Bureau conducted an analysis of the in-home shopping behavior of consumers. Its study covered orders placed with vendors by mail or by phone after the consumer received a piece of mail, saw a direct-response advertisement, or was called. These are some of the findings from the Simmons study:

- One-fourth of orders are placed on Mondays; and this figure drops steadily throughout the week. Only 5 per cent of orders are placed on Sunday.
- The most popular items are apparel, magazine subscriptions, and home accessories.
- Nearly half of orders are in response to catalogs and direct-mail advertisements. Just 3 per cent are in response to television commercials.
- Over 30 per cent of the households report receiving four or more pieces of mail (of all types) daily.

- About half of the households report that they listen to all advertising phone calls. Seven per cent hang up on all such calls.
- Increased in-home shopping would be motivated by lower prices, the elimination of shipping charges, faster delivery, easier return procedures, and so on.
- Seven per cent of households are extremely satisfied with in-home shopping, and 43 per cent are very satisfied. This compares with 15 per cent and 51 per cent, respectively, for in-store shopping.[1]

By examining and responding to these findings about consumers, direct marketers can improve their retailing efforts.

Overview

A retailer's ability to develop a sound strategy depends on an understanding of consumer behavior. **Consumer behavior** can be defined as "the process whereby individuals decide whether, what, when, where, how, and from whom to purchase goods and services."[2] In this chapter, the consumer's decision-making process (and the impact of demographics and life-style upon it) will be described and analyzed from a strategic retailing perspective. This decision process shows the steps a consumer goes through in purchasing a product or service and the implications for retailers.

Before the steps in the consumer's decision process are explained, three brief illustrations will show how retailers can use this important concept.

Macy's is a department store that carries a fairly extensive selection of high-fidelity equipment, which is sold predominantly to novices. These customers are attracted to Macy's for several reasons: the security provided by a well-known, reliable store name; the emphasis on systems selling (receiver, turntable, and speakers sold together to ensure matched equipment); the availability of nationally advertised brands; and a liberal return policy.

Mark Holtz owns an appliance store specializing in large items (such as refrigerators, washing machines, dishwashers, and ranges). Store hours are 9:30 A.M. to 9:00 P.M., Monday through Friday, and 9:30 A.M. to 6:00 P.M. on Saturday. Holtz is closed on Sunday because he likes to spend the day with his family. However, Mark has just seen a new consumer research study and may have to open on Sundays. This study reveals that large appliances are bought by husbands and wives shopping together, and couples prefer the leisurely pace of Sunday to the hustle and bustle of midweek, evening shopping.

Blonder Pontiac is a medium-sized Pontiac dealership in Los Angeles, California. Murray Blonder, the owner, mails a questionnaire to all buyers one week after their purchase of a car. According to Blonder, "The sale of an automobile should not be viewed as ending with a purchase. Too many retailers feel that the absence of a complaint means customer satisfaction. By using my survey techniques, I can find out my strengths and weaknesses and take quick corrective action. A truly satisfied customer will send his or her friends to my dealership."

---

[1]Stan Rapp, "Simmons Study Takes Peek at In-Home Purchasing Transactions," *Direct Marketing* (December 1984), pp. 36–40.
[2]C. Glenn Walters, *Consumer Behavior: Theory and Practice*, Third Edition (Homewood, Ill.: Richard D. Irwin, 1978), p. 7.

Each of these examples shows how a retailer can develop a sound strategy, based on an understanding of the consumer's decision process. Macy's understands the motives and apprehensions of its high-fidelity customers and reacts accordingly. Mark Holtz realizes that Sunday hours are necessary for the sale of large appliances and contemplates changing his retail strategy. Murray Blonder is aware that customer feedback is important and works to get this feedback.

Through a formal analysis of the consumer's decision process, a base for retail strategy development (in any context) is provided.

The Decision Process

A **consumer's decision process** is comprised of two parts, the process itself and factors affecting the process. The decision process consists of six basic steps: stimulus, problem awareness, informative search, evaluation of alternatives, purchase, and postpurchase behavior. Factors that affect the process are a consumer's demographics and life-style. The total consumer decision-making process is shown in Figure 5-1. The elements in the decision process are listed in Table 5-1.

When a customer buys a product or service, he or she goes through this decision process. In some situations, all six steps in the process are used; in others, only a few

The Consumer's Decision-Making Process

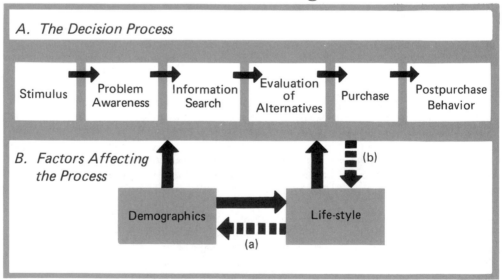

NOTE: Solid arrows connect all the elements in the decision process and show the impact of demographics and life-style upon the process.

Dotted arrows show feedback. (a) shows the impact of life-style on certain demographics, such as family size, location, and marital status. (b) shows the impact of a purchase on elements of life-style, such as social class, reference groups, experience, and performance.

Figure 5-1

Table 5-1
Elements in the Consumer's Decision Process

A. The Decision Process

Stimulus:
  Social
  Commercial
  Physical
Problem awareness:
  Recognition of shortage
  Recognition of unfulfilled desire
Information search:
  List of possible alternatives
    Internal (memory)
    External (commercial, noncommercial, social)
  Characteristics of each alternative
    Internal (memory)
    External (commercial, noncommercial, social)
Evaluation of alternatives:
  Criteria for decision
  Importance of each criterion
  Ranking of alternatives
  Choice of product or service
Purchase:
  Place of purchase
    Store choice (location, layout, service, sales help, image, level of prices, etc.)
    Nonstore choice (image, level of prices, hours, convenience, etc.)
  Terms (price, method of payment)
  Availability (stock-on-hand, delivery)
Postpurchase behavior:
  Further purchase(s)
  Re-evaluation (satisfaction versus dissatisfaction)

B. Factors Affecting the Process*

Demographics:	
Age	Height
Education	Weight
Income	Mobility
Occupation	Location
Gender	Possessions
Marital status	Type of dwelling
Family size	Race and religion

Life-style:	
Activities	Family life cycle
Interests	Experience
Opinions	Personality
Culture	Motives
Social class	Performance
Reference groups	Importance of purchase
Class consciousness	Time constraints

*This listing is for illustrative purposes only and is not meant to be all-inclusive. It is further realized that some life-style elements may be considered demographics by others.

of the steps are utilized. For example, a consumer who has previously and satisfactorily purchased luggage at a local luggage store may not use the same extensive decision process as a customer who has never bought luggage before.

The decision process outlined in Figure 5-1 assumes that the end result is a purchase of a good or service by the consumer. It is important to realize that at any point in the process a potential customer may decide not to buy, and the process then stops at this point. The product or service may be unnecessary, unsatisfactory, or too expensive.

Before considering the different ways in which the consumer uses the decision process, the entire process depicted in Figure 5-1 and Table 5-1 will be explained.

Stimulus

A **stimulus** is a cue (social or commercial) or a drive (physical) meant to motivate or arouse a person to act. When one talks with friends, fellow employees, professors, and so on, **social cues** are received. These cues may activate behavior. Some examples of social cues are:

"Gee Ed, I hear that the Tivoli Theater has a good movie. Let's go."

"We haven't been to a football game in a long time, and the Super Bowl is next month. Let's get tickets tomorrow."

"It's Thursday. Please meet me at the supermarket."

"Alice, I found an excellent new hair salon. You should really try it."

Each of these cues is a hint at arousing some action, which the individual on the receiving end may ignore, treat as unimportant, or follow through on. The distinguishing attribute of a social cue is that it comes from an interpersonal, noncommercial source.

A second type of stimulus is a **commercial cue.** This is a message that is sponsored by a retailer, a manufacturer, a wholesaler, or some other seller. The objective of a commercial cue is to interest a consumer in a particular store, product, or service. Advertisements, sales pitches, and point-of-purchase displays are commercial stimuli. Some examples of commercial cues are:

"Our store is going out of business. If you are thinking about a winter coat, *now* is the time for a bargain."

"When was the last time you treated yourself to a night on the town? At the Palace, we will wine and dine you with service fit for royalty."

"Holiday Health Spas. A younger, healthier, more attractive you. You'll love the new you. *They'll* love the new you."

"*My Fair Lady*. Last 7 performances of this revival."

These cues have the same objective as social stimuli, the creation of excitement about an object, a person, an idea, and so on as the first step in a decision process.

However, commercial cues may not be regarded as highly as social ones by consumers because the messages are seller-controlled. A consumer may receive a cue differently when a friend rather than a salesperson makes a suggestion.

A third type of stimulus is a **physical drive.** This occurs when a person's physical senses are affected. Pain, hunger, thirst, cold, heat, and fear lead to physical reactions. If the stimulus is weak, it may be ignored. A strong physical drive, however, normally impels some type of action. Examples of physical drives are:

"My eyes really hurt when I woke up last Thursday morning. I knew that I had to think about making an appointment with an eye doctor."

"It's five after one. My stomach is awfully noisy. Another homework problem and I'll break for lunch.

"We've been driving for five hours, and I am really thirsty. We better stop for a soda before my tongue falls out."

"When I went out yesterday, it was 80 degrees. Today, it's 45. I'm freezing. And, I don't even have a winter coat."

"This summer has been a real scorcher. Last night, I tossed and turned. I couldn't sleep at all."

"My car broke down. I was afraid that I would be late for my job interview."

In each of these cases, the person's physical senses are affected, and a desire to act is created. However, the remaining steps in the decision process help determine whether a person will actually act or just think about acting.

A potential consumer may be exposed to any or all three stimuli for any product or service. If a person is aroused, he or she will go on to the next step in the decision process. If a person is not sufficiently aroused, he or she will ignore the stimulus. This terminates the decision process for the given product or service.

Problem Awareness

At the **problem awareness** stage in the decision process, the consumer not only has been aroused by social, commercial, and/or physical stimuli but also recognizes that the product or service under consideration may solve a problem of shortage or unfulfilled desire.

A consumer moves from the stimulus to the problem awareness stage because of a motivation or desire for a product (service). It is sometimes difficult to determine why a consumer is motivated, especially because many consumers buy the same product for different reasons (price, image, quality, durability, and so on); a consumer may not know his or her own motivation (subconscious); and consumers may not tell a retailer their real reasons for buying a product or service.

Recognition of shortage occurs when a consumer discovers that a product or service needs to be repurchased. Products may wear out (automobile, refrigerator, watch, clothing), or the consumer may run out of items (milk, bread, tissues, cigarettes). Services are required when products wear down (repair of automobile, refrigerator, watch) or services wear out (hair cutting, lawn mowing, car washing). In each instance, the consumer needs to replenish products or services. Examples of stimuli interacting with problem awareness (recognition of shortage) are:

"The sun is strong today. I'll need protection for my eyes *(stimulus)*, but my old sunglasses are broken *(recognition of shortage)*."

"Why did I have to get a flat tire *(stimulus)*? I don't even have a spare *(recognition of shortage)*."

"Debbie said that she didn't like the way my hair looked *(stimulus)*. Maybe it is too long *(recognition of shortage)*."

"I really want a cough drop *(stimulus)*. But I gave my last one to Herb *(recognition of shortage)*."

If the people in the preceding examples feel that their problems are important enough for further action, they will continue to the next step in the decision process. Should these people think about their shortages and then shrug them off, the decision process will end and no purchase will be made.

Recognition of unfulfilled desire occurs when a consumer becomes aware of a product or service that has not been purchased before. The product or service may improve the person's looks, self-image, status, and so on in a way that the person has not tried before (hair transplant, cosmetic surgery, charm school, health spa, European vacation), or it may offer new, unheard of performance characteristics (self-cleaning oven, pot-cleaning dishwasher, pocket computer). In this situation, the consumer is aroused by the desire to improve himself or herself and considers the necessity to fulfill these dreams. Examples of stimuli interacting with problem awareness (recognition of unfulfilled desires) are:

HENRY: "We've been married thirty-one years and have never been on a real vacation *(stimulus)*."

BARBARA: "Why can't we go on a trip where it's sunny and the sand is beautiful *(recognition of unfulfilled desire)*?"

"I don't like the way I look. My hair, my face—I just don't like anything *(stimulus)*. Why don't I find a good plastic surgeon and have cosmetic surgery. Then I'll be the life of the party *(recognition of unfulfilled desire)*."

"One of the reasons I hate to cook is that I dislike washing pots *(stimulus)*. General Electric just came out with a line of dishwashers that do a great job of cleaning pots as well as dishes *(recognition of unfulfilled desire)*."

"All my friends eat at good restaurants and have fine meals at least once a week, but I eat at fast-food houses *(stimulus)*. Just once, I'd like to go into a restaurant, have a maitre d' show me to a table, drink a bottle of fine wine, and enjoy a delicious meal *(recognition of unfulfilled desire)*."

Most consumers are more hesitant to react to unfulfilled desires than to shortages. There are more risks and the benefits are more indeterminate. This is especially true when the consumer has had substantial satisfactory experience with the product or service to be replaced. When a consumer feels that he or she must satisfy an unfulfilled desire, the remaining steps in the purchase process are undertaken.

Whether the consumer is aware of a problem of shortage or a problem of unfulfilled desire, he or she will act only if it is perceived as a problem worth solving. An unworthy problem will not be acted on, and the decision process will terminate. A strong stimulus does not mean the presence of a worthy problem. For instance:

"The sun is strong today. I'll need protection for my eyes. My old sunglasses are broken, but I can tape the frame together."

"Debbie said that she didn't like the way my hair looked, but she would criticize Robert Redford."

"I really want a cigarette, but it's dangerous to my health. Maybe I'll give up smoking."

HENRY: "We've been married 31 years and have never been on a real vacation."

BARBARA: "You're just dreaming again. You know that you enjoy working in your garden more than travel."

Information Search

After the consumer decides that the shortage or unfulfilled desire is worth further consideration, information is sought. The **information search** involves two parts: (1) gathering a list of alternative products or services that will solve the problem at hand, and (2) determining the characteristics of each alternative.

First, the consumer compiles a list of alternative products or services that solve the problem stated in the previous step of the decision process. This list does not have to be very formal nor even in written form. It may be a group of items that the consumer thinks about. The key is that the consumer amasses a list of the relevant solutions to his or her problem. This aspect of information search may be internal or external.

A consumer with a lot of purchasing experience (in the specific area) will normally utilize an internal search of his or her memory to determine the products or services that would be satisfactory for the solution of the given problem. A typical thought process of this type is:

"It's raining *(stimulus)*. My old raincoat is torn; I really need a new one *(problem awareness)*. The question is: Will I buy a London Fog, a Botany 500, or a Harbor Master raincoat *(internal search for listing alternatives)?*"

A consumer with little purchasing experience will usually use an external search to develop a list of products or services that would solve the given problem. This external search can involve commercial sources (mass media, salespeople), noncommercial sources (*Consumer Reports*, government publications), and social sources (family, friends, colleagues). In this instance, the consumer seeks information outside of his or her memory. Examples of commercial, noncommercial, and social sources of information used in the listing of alternatives are:

"Our roof is leaking *(stimulus)*. This house is getting on my nerves. Let's look for a new one *(problem awareness)*. Sunday's edition of the *Gazette* will have a listing of all the new houses in our area. We should use it to develop a list of possibilities *(commercial source for listing alternatives)."*

"It just cost me $400 for a new transmission. I am worried that the car will break down again *(stimulus)*. Now is the time to look for a new car before this one breaks down again *(problem awareness)*. *Consumer Reports* lists the new-model cars in its next issue. Let's get that issue and see what's going to be available this year *(noncommercial source for listing alternatives)."*

ALICE: "We haven't eaten out in a long time. I'm in the mood to have a good meal tonight *(stimulus)."*

DEAN: "You're right, I didn't realize how long it has been since we have gone out *(problem awareness)*. Where should we go?"

ALICE: "We can go to the Mandarin Inn, the Elm Tree restaurant, the Swan Club, or the Homestead *(social source for listing alternatives)."*

The second type of information a consumer gathers concerns the characteristics of each alternative. Once the various product or service alternatives are known, the consumer must determine the attributes of each. This kind of information may be obtained internally (memory) or externally (commercial, noncommercial, social), in much the same manner as the list of alternatives is generated.

An experienced consumer will search his or her memory for the attributes (pros and cons) of each product or service alternative:

"It's raining *(stimulus)*. I need a new raincoat because my old one is torn *(problem awareness)*. I want to choose from among London Fog, Botany 500, and Harbor Master *(list of alternatives)*. London Fog makes a fine product, but it's rather expensive. Botany 500 makes a fine product, but I can't get it in my area. Harbor Master makes an equally fine product, but I have trouble with the fit *(internal search for characteristics of alternatives)."*

The consumer with little experience or a lot of uncertainty will search externally for information about each alternative under consideration. Commercial, noncommercial, and social sources are available for the collection of information about product or service attributes:

"My wife and I want to go to Europe this summer for a vacation *(stimulus and problem recognition)*. Your ad mentioned six different packages *(list of alternatives)*. Please explain the details and costs of each one *(commercial source for characteristics of alternatives)."*

"As I am interested in a new refrigerator *(stimulus and problem recognition)*, I want to read *Consumer Reports*. Not only are all models listed, but every one is described in depth *(noncommercial source for list and characteristics of alternatives)."*

"OK, I agree that we should go to the Mandarin Inn, the Elm Tree Restaurant, the Swan Club, or the Homestead *(stimulus, problem awareness, and list of alternatives)*. But let's consider the quality of food, service, and prices before we make a decision *(social source for characteristics of alternatives.)"*

The extent to which a consumer searches for information depends, in part, on the consumer's perception of the risk attached to the purchase of a specific product or service. Risk varies among individuals. For some, it is inconsequential; for others, it is quite important.

Perceived risk is related to the probability of making a wrong decision and the consequences of an incorrect decision. The five major elements of risk are:

1. Economic risk—How much money is lost if the wrong decision is made?
2. Performance risk—Will the product perform as expected?
3. Social risk—Will friends and relatives view the product or service in a positive manner?
4. Physical risk—Will the product be safe?
5. Psychological risk—Will the product affect my self-esteem?

The retailer's role in a search process is to provide the consumer with enough information to evaluate alternative products, thereby reducing the consumer's perceived risk. Point-of-purchase advertising, product displays, and knowledgeable sales personnel provide consumers with the information they need to make decisions.

Now that the consumer's search for information is completed, it must be determined if the shortage or unfulfilled desire can be satisfied by any of the alternatives. When one or more products or services is found satisfactory, the consumer moves to the next step in the decision process. However, the consumer will discontinue the process should no satisfactory products or services be found. For example, when all restaurants are too expensive or all vacations are unappealing, the consumer will not continue the purchase process.

Evaluation of Alternatives

At this point, the consumer has enough information to select one product or service alternative from the list of choices. Sometimes this is quite easy, if one alternative is clearly superior to the others across all attributes. A product that is excellent quality and has a low price will be the easy choice over more expensive, average-quality items.

Often the selection is not that simple, and the consumer must carefully **evaluate the alternatives** before making a decision. When two or more alternatives are attractive, the consumer will determine what criteria (attributes) to evaluate and the relative importance of the criteria (attributes). Then the alternatives will be ranked, and a choice will be made.

Criteria for a decision are those product or service attributes that the consumer desires. These criteria may include price, quality, fit, color, durability, and warranty. The consumer sets standards for these characteristics and evaluates each alternative according to its ability to meet the standards. The importance of each criterion is also determined by the consumer. The various attributes of the product or service are of differing importance to each consumer. As an example, for some consumers, the initial price may be more important than the operating costs (as measured by electrical consumption) of a new air conditioner. In selecting a brand of air conditioner, this type of consumer will choose a less expensive product that consumes a lot of energy over a more expensive, more efficient product.

Next the consumer ranks the alternatives (from favorite to least favorite) and selects one product or service from among the list of alternatives. The following illustration will show the entire process of evaluating alternatives:

> Judy and Larry had talked about visiting California for several years. This year they finally decided they would leave Vermont for the first time and go to California. They talked with friends, read newspapers, and consulted with a travel agent. Three alternatives were available: a 14-day Amtrak trip, a 17-day car trip, or a 10-day plane trip. Judy and Larry agreed that their choice of a trip would depend on cost, time available for sightseeing, and sightseeing. Cost was important, but the time available for sightseeing and the sightseeing itself were more important. The Amtrak trip was the cheapest; the plane trip was the most expensive. The car trip left the least time for sightseeing; the plane trip provided the most. The car trip was the best for sightseeing because it was so flexible; the Amtrak trip provided the worst sightseeing because it included a fixed itinerary. Judy and Larry decided that on the basis of their criteria, and the order of these criteria, the plane trip was the best available alternative. The Amtrak trip was the worst.

For some products or services, it is difficult to evaluate the characteristics of the available alternatives (because the items are technical, poorly labeled, new, and so on). In this instance, consumers often use price, brand name, or store name as an indicator of a product's overall quality, and they choose a product or service based on this criterion.

Once a consumer examines the attributes of the alternatives and ranks the alternatives, the product or service that is most satisfactory is then chosen. In situations where no alternative proves to be adequate, a decision not to purchase is made.

Purchase

Following a determination of the best product or service from the list of alternatives, the consumer is ready for the **purchase act**—an exchange of money or a promise to pay for ownership of a product or service. Decision making still goes on during this step in the process. From a retailing perspective, the purchase act may be the most crucial aspect of the decision process because the consumer is mainly concerned with three factors: place of purchase, terms, and availability.

The consumer must determine where to buy the product or service. Place of purchase may be a store or a nonstore location. Many more items are bought at store locations (department, drug, furniture, and so on) than at nonstore locations (home, work, school, and so on). The place of purchase is evaluated in the same manner as the product or the service itself. The alternative places of purchase are listed, their characteristics defined, and a ranking computed. The most desirable place of purchase is then used.

Criteria for store selection include store location, store layout, service, sales help, store image, and level of prices. Criteria for the selection of a nonstore retailer include image, level of prices, hours, and convenience. The consumer will shop with the store or nonstore retailer that offers the best combination of criteria, as defined by the consumer.

The consumer is also interested in the terms of purchase and the availability of the product or service. The terms of purchase are the price and method of payment. Price is the dollar amount of a product or service that the consumer must pay to achieve ownership or use. Method of payment is the way the price must be paid (cash, short-term credit, long-term credit). Availability relates to stock-on-hand and delivery. Stock-on-hand is the amount of an item that the place of purchase has in its inventory. Delivery is the time span between the order and the receipt of an item and the ease with which an item is transported to its place of use.

When the consumer is satisfied with these three components of the purchase act, the product or service will be bought. When there is dissatisfaction with place of purchase, terms of purchase, and/or availability, the consumer may not buy the product or the service even though there is contentment with the product or the service itself. The following are examples of both situations:

> Jenny was interested in buying a new sofa to complete her living-room set. She already had two chairs and a coffee table, but until now, Jenny could not afford a new sofa. She knew exactly what she wanted, a Sealy convertible (Model 155). The questions were where to buy the sofa, how to pay for it, how soon it could be delivered, and how it would be delivered. Jenny selected the Living Room Store from among four possible stores and bought the sofa. She never considered buying by telephone or mail, because she didn't trust nonpersonal shopping. The Living Room Store provided Jenny with what she wanted. She received good service at a convenient location. A special discount was given for a cash payment. Because the sofa was in stock, it was delivered within one week. Delivery was included in the sofa's price.

> Ken wanted to buy a stereo system. He knew what system to get and had saved $100 for a down payment. But after a month of trying to buy the stereo, Ken gave up in disgust. He explained why: "The system I wanted was sold in only three stores in my neighborhood and through a mail-order house. Two of the stores overpriced the stereo by about $75. The third store had a really good price, $399; but the owner insisted that I pay in cash. In addition, I would have had to drive to their warehouse fifty miles away and pick up the system myself. The mail-order company had a really good deal—low price, credit, and delivery. But they ran out of the model I was interested in and told me the wait would be four months. After I heard that, I just gave up. My portable eight-track player will have to suffice."

Postpurchase Behavior

Following the purchase of a product or service, the consumer is involved in **postpurchase behavior**. This behavior falls into either of two categories: further purchases or re-evaluation. In many situations, buying one product or service leads to further purchases. For instance, the purchase of an automobile leads to buying insurance. The purchase of a new suit may be accompanied by the purchase of a new shirt and tie. Buying a stereo system will require records or tapes to play on it. Therefore, it can be stated that some purchases provide the impetus for others, and the decision process continues until the last purchase is made. Characteristics of the supplementary items are noted and the alternatives ranked, just as in the decision process for the original item. A retailer who utilizes scrambled merchandising by stocking nonrelated items may also stimulate a shopper to further purchases once the primary product or service is bought.

A warning: the retailer should carefully evaluate his or her expansion of product lines (related or nonrelated). The skills necessary to obtain a supplemental purchase may not be similar to those required for the major product or service category. For example, real-estate and property insurance sales involve different skills; television sales and service contracts need different abilities; and muffler repairs and transmission overhauls are quite dissimilar.

The consumer will also re-evaluate the purchase of a product or service. Does the product or service perform as promised? Do the actual attributes of the product or service match the expectations the consumer had of these attributes? Satisfaction may mean contentment, repurchase when the product or service wears out, and favorable conversations with friends interested in the same product or service. Dissatisfaction may mean unhappiness, brand or store switching when the product or service wears out, and unfavorable conversations with friends interested in the same product or service.

The latter situation (dissatisfaction) is the result of **cognitive dissonance**, doubt that the correct decision has been made. The consumer may regret that the purchase was made at all or may wish that another alternative from the list had been chosen. To overcome cognitive dissonance and dissatisfaction, the retailer must realize that the purchase process does not end with the purchase. Aftercare of the consumer (telephone call, service call, advertisement) may be as important as anything the retailer can do to complete the sale. When items are expensive and/or important to the consumer, aftercare takes on added significance, because the consumer really wants to be right. In addition, the more alternatives from which to choose, the greater the doubt after the decision is made and the more the importance of aftercare.

Many retailers acknowledge that consumers often have doubts and second thoughts about recent purchases. Wanamaker and others pioneered the concept of a money-back guarantee, so that customers could return merchandise if doubts or second thoughts became too great.

Realistic selling and advertising campaigns minimize dissatisfaction because consumers' expectations will not exceed reality. If overly high expectations are created, the consumer becomes unhappy because the product or service does not perform at the level promised. The coupling of an honest sales presentation with good aftercare of the consumer should reduce or eliminate cognitive dissonance and dissatisfaction.

The Decision Process: Selected Retail Research Findings

The components of the decision process have been investigated in a variety of retail settings. In this section, some examples of retail research involving the decision process are presented. If a retailer understands and uses the components of the decision process, he or she is better able to develop a strategy that will satisfy consumers.

It should be pointed out that the results of the studies described in this and later sections may be limited to the specific product categories/retailer groups that were investigated. Nonetheless, the reader is shown applications of the decision process in actual retail situations.

Information Search

A study of urban shoppers for cosmetics found that the type of information sought depends on the type of shopper:

- A special shopper (who looks for discounts) emphasizes samples, print ads, and home-oriented magazines.
- A brand-loyal consumer relies on newspaper and magazine ads, and salespeople. Information on competing brands is not sought.

- A store-loyal consumer seeks information from salespeople but not friends or neighbors. The brands carried by a store are important.
- A problem-solving consumer utilizes television, friends, and salespeople. All kinds of information are sought.
- A psychosocializing consumer relies on friends and neighbors but also looks at television and print ads.
- A name-conscious consumer is interested in well-known stores, uses print ads and salespeople, and looks to fashion, news, and business media.[3]

Two recent studies of perceived risk yielded these findings. An analysis of consumers shopping at discount stores and catalog showrooms discovered that consumers are least inclined to purchase high social–low economic risk products; they are more likely to buy low social–high economic risk products.[4] Consumers of color televisions, automobile tires, and radios like to reduce risk by purchasing well-known brands from well-known retailers.[5]

Evaluation of Alternatives

An important aspect in the consumer's evaluation of alternatives are the criteria set by the consumer. In selecting food stores, a study determined that consumers rate low prices, pleasant shopping experience/helpful personnel/good service, one-stop shopping, the clear marking of prices on individual items, and the variety of store brands and lower-priced products as the most important criteria. A comparison of supermarket shoppers and warehouse store shoppers reveals that the former are less interested in low prices, but much more interested in marking prices on individual items and the variety of store brands.[6]

A survey of women beauty salon customers found that frequent patrons are most interested in the quality of work, cleanliness, flexibility in scheduling appointments, cost, and adherence to the schedule. On the other hand, less-frequent patrons are most concerned about the quality of work, cost, operator's knowledge of style trends, cleanliness, and friendliness of the operator.[7]

In-Store Behavior

A consumer's in-store shopping behavior is affected by factors such as sales personnel, displays, price posting, and stockouts. Retailers need to develop their strategies to take these factors into account.

Studies on retail sales personnel show that customers react more favorably if salespeople are perceived as being like themselves. This is particularly true for the racial

[3]George P. Moschis, "Shopping Orientations and Consumer Use of Information," *Journal of Retailing*, Vol. 52 (Summer 1976), pp. 61–70ff. See also, Ralph W. Jackson and Jeffrey K. Sager, "An Inventory of Shopper Typologies: Research Directions and Strategic Implications," in John C. Crawford and James R. Lumpkin (Editors), *1983 Proceedings of the Southwestern Marketing Association*, pp. 206–209.
[4]Pradeep K. Korgaonkar, "Consumer Preferences for Catalog Showrooms and Discount Stores: The Moderating Role of Product Risk," *Journal of Retailing*, Vol. 58 (Fall 1982), pp. 76–88.
[5]Robert L. Taylor and C. P. Rao, "An Empirical Study of Perceived Risk and Confidence: The Effects of Brand and Store Reputation," in John C. Crawford and James R. Lumpkin (Editors), *1983 Proceedings of the Southwestern Marketing Association*, pp. 14–18.
[6]"What's Important in Choosing a Store," *Progressive Grocer* (October 1983), pp. 36–37, 52.
[7]Hazel F. Ezell and Phillip J. Ward, "Differentiating Between Frequent and Less-Frequent Patrons of Beauty Salons: A Focus on Working Women," in John Summey et al. (Editors), *Marketing: Theories and Concepts for an Era of Change* (Carbondale, Ill.: Southern Marketing Association, 1983), pp. 68–71.

similarity of the customer and the salesperson.[8] As product complexity increases, consumers place greater emphasis on the salesperson's product expertise, empathy, trustworthiness, personal appearance, credibility, and professionalism.[9]

A study on in-store displays in supermarkets found that the value of these displays varies widely by product category. However, for all but one of twelve products examined, in-store displays increase sales. In-store displays have the greatest impact for hand and body lotions, shampoo, salad dressings, canned fruit drinks, and trash bags. They are least effective for toilet tissue, carbonated beverages, headache remedies, heavy-duty detergents, and ready-to-eat cereals (all products that are extensively advertised).[10]

In-store behavior is also affected by stockouts of merchandise. A recent study determined that stockouts cause consumers to have a lower store image, less satisfaction with purchase behavior, and reduced purchase intentions for particular product categories. Sales shoppers are much less sensitive to stockouts than nonsale shoppers. Stockout behavior does vary by product category.[11]

Consumer Satisfaction/Dissatisfaction

Retailers are extremely interested in the causes of consumer satisfaction and dissatisfaction in order to optimize their strategies. A study of department store consumers found that satisfaction with the shopping experience is most influenced by store salespersons, special store sales, the products/services purchased at the store, the store environment, and the value–price relationships offered by the store.[12]

A study of electric food mixer consumers discovered that shoppers usually select the brand providing the most information. Those consumers buying brands for which there is little information tend to be more dissatisfied with their purchases than those buying brands for which there is ample information. Consumers assume undisclosed information is less favorable than that which is disclosed.[13]

According to a third study, there are several significant differences between complainers (those who have actively complained once or more during the past year) and noncomplainers. Complainers are more likely to be male, actively engage in comparison shopping, believe that many products break or go wrong soon after purchase, and feel that most companies do not handle complaints properly. Nonetheless, more complainers also believe that consumers are better treated by business today than in the past.[14]

[8]Ishmael P. Akaah, "Dyadic Similarity and Its Influence on Customer Preferences: An Experimental Study," in Richard P. Bagozzi et al. (Editors), *Marketing in the 80's* (Chicago: American Marketing Association, 1980), pp. 114–117.

[9]Ronald E. Michaels, "Differences in Customer Expectations Concerning Salesperson Characteristics Across Products of Varying Complexity," in Kenneth Bernhardt et al. (Editors), *The Changing Marketing Environment: New Theories and Applications* (Chicago: American Marketing Association, 1981), pp. 131–134.

[10]"Display Effectiveness: An Evaluation," *Nielsen Researcher* (Number 2, 1983), pp. 2–8.

[11]Paul H. Zinzer and Jack A. Lesser, "An Empirical Evaluation of the Role of Stock-Out on Shopper Patronage Processes," in Richard P. Bagozzi et al. (Editors), *Marketing in the 80's*, (Chicago: American Marketing Association, 1980), pp. 221–224.

[12]Robert A. Westbrook, "Sources of Consumer Satisfaction with Retail Outlets," *Journal of Retailing*, Vol. 57 (Fall 1981), pp. 68–85.

[13]W. E. Patton III, "Brand Choice and Varying Quantity of Information," *Journal of Business Research*, Vol. 12 (1984), pp. 75–85.

[14]Mel S. Moyer, "Characteristics of Consumer Complainants: Implications for Marketing and Public Policy," *Journal of Public Policy and Marketing*, Vol. 3 (1984), pp. 67–84.

Factors Affecting the Process

The factors that affect the consumer's decision process have been described and categorized by a variety of authors. Of most importance to strategy-oriented retailers is the impact of demographics and life-style on the purchase process. These two factors have a major effect on the way a consumer thinks and acts, and they incorporate broad classifications of important terms.

The study of demographics and life-style dimensions is particularly important for a retailer interested in market segmentation. Because different consumer groups may react differently to a stimulus, the retailer must identify (demographics and life-style) his or her target market and construct a strategy to satisfy it. By knowing how demographics and life-style variables affect the decision process, a retailer can fine-tune the retail mix to cater to the market.

Why do two or more people use the decision process in exactly the same way? Or, why do two or more people use the decision process in quite diverse ways? It is important to answer both questions because retail strategy must adapt to the consumer's decision process.

Demographics

Demographics are easily identifiable and measurable population statistics. Table 5-1 contains a comprehensive, but not all-inclusive, list of the demographics that affect a consumer's decision process. Consumers with different demographic profiles (combinations of all demographic statistics) act dissimilarly.

Young consumers seek more information than older consumers. They have little experience and are uncertain. Commercial, noncommercial, and social sources of information are sought by young customers to determine the products that are appropriate, the characteristics they possess, and the best choice. Older consumers are habitual and tend to repeat purchases. New information is less important for them, and the purchase process is completed quickly. Older consumers will usually not be persuaded to try a new product unless a social source has recommended it. Commercial and noncommercial sources do not have a strong effect on older consumers for new products. Younger customers may be more willing to try new types of merchandise and services than older customers. Therefore, a store with a target market of older customers probably should maintain limited product assortments and a high level of national brands.

The college-educated consumer uses the decision process more thoroughly than less-educated consumers. Noncommercial and social sources of information are especially sought by the college-educated consumer. This consumer is aware of the various types of information that are available and utilizes them. Advertising and selling that are honest and provide knowledge will attract the well-educated consumer, who conducts a complete search of alternatives and their characteristics before making a decision. New items, properly promoted, can be sold to the college-educated consumer. Less-educated consumers spend little time searching for or evaluating information. Commercial and social sources are used, noncommercial sources are not. New products or services are bought more infrequently by less-educated consumers. Education has an impact on the consumer, because it shapes his or her outlook and objectives. The service retailer, such as a travel agent, is particularly interested in defining the educational level of clients. As another example, the toy retailer is concerned with the education of customers because it becomes an important criterion in the purchase of children's toys (the toy's educational value).

The middle-income consumer uses the decision process more thoroughly than any other income group. Lower-income consumers frequently buy national (manufacturers') brands and do not look at the full range of alternatives. National brands provide consistency and security in product choice. Upper-income consumers do look at a variety of products or services before purchasing. The information search is not as intense as that of the middle-income consumer because price is not an important factor, and an unsatisfactory product can often be replaced. The middle-income consumer is concerned with price and uses a detailed search process for listing and evaluating alternatives. Noncommercial and social sources are very important to this group. A retailer who seeks the low-income market should offer lower-priced merchandise as well as extensive credit. A retailer aiming at the more affluent consumer must develop a total offering: service, status, assortment, price, and so on.

A consumer's occupation may be placed in one of two basic categories: white collar or blue collar. White-collar consumers (office workers or professionals) often utilize the decision process more completely than blue-collar consumers (craftspeople, machine operators, and so on). The white-collar consumer knows of the available information sources and uses them more than the blue-collar consumer, who is not as aware of information and product or service alternatives. The white-collar consumer relies on noncommercial sources to a greater extent than the blue-collar consumer, who uses commercial sources.

The gender of the consumer has an impact on the purchase process. On the average, women are more likely to be the decision makers for foods and beverages (nonalcoholic), health care items, housewares, and pet foods. Men are more likely to be the decision makers for gasoline, alcoholic beverages, tobacco products, and automobiles. Both men and women are decision makers for products such as appliances, cameras, and watches. Information sources should be directed toward the consumer making the decision, although it should be pointed out that married couples share decision making for expensive, important items even though one party may have the greater influence.

A consumer's marital status affects the decision process in much the same way as family size. A single person looks for and evaluates information independently. Commercial, noncommercial, and social sources of information are directed at one decision maker. A married couple may act independently or dependently, according to the importance of the product or service and the effect of the item on both parties. For important, expensive items, both spouses seek and evaluate information. The information source should be directed at both parties. When items are inexpensive and unimportant, one spouse will seek and evaluate information in the same manner as a single person. The process is usually longer and more thorough if two parties are involved.

As family size increases, the length of the decision process increases. For families of two or more people, information is usually collected and analyzed by more than one party. In this case, the decision process may have three stages. First, family members confer about the possible product or service. Second, information is collected, often independently. Third, family members confer again and reach a purchase decision. With a larger family, the retailer can use several different types of promotion addressed to various family members. Clothing, furniture, automobile, travel, and other retailers can segment their markets on the basis of family size.

The physical attributes of consumers influence the decision process for items like clothing. A consumer of average height and weight spends less time deciding on a purchase than a person who is very short or very tall and overweight or underweight. For the nonaverage consumer, the search for acceptable alternatives may be lengthy, and availability may be limited. The average consumer has a much wider selection from which to choose and many stores that carry the sought after merchandise. Convenience is possible. An informative segmentation campaign will appeal to the nonaverage consumer, with special emphasis on the availability of alternatives.

Mobility affects the decision process in a different way than other demographics. A person who changes residences frequently emphasizes commercial and noncommercial sources of information because social sources are unknown. The decision about where to make a purchase also requires a great deal of investigation for a mobile person. A nonmobile consumer depends on social and commercial sources. This person is usually store-loyal and hesitant to try new products or services. The mobility rate of the target market is helpful to some retailers. Hardware stores, drugstores, moving companies, repair services, lodging facilites, and so on should be actively involved in pursuing the mobile consumer.

The location of consumers has an influence on the purchase process. Rural and suburban consumers tend to do a lot of shopping at one time. Detailed lists are compiled beforehand, and shopping may last for several hours. Social and commercial sources of information are dominant for these consumers. The availability of merchandise is also important. Urban consumers shop more often, with less time spent on each occasion. There are unplanned purchases made by this consumer, and these require in-store promotion. Store location is important to urban shoppers, who are unwilling to spend the same time traveling as their rural and suburban counterparts. It must be determined if the market is widely dispersed (a large trading area) or densely populated (a small trading area). A dispersed market will require longer store hours, delivery services, parking, one-stop shopping, and more advertising than a market that is densely populated.

The possessions of a consumer have a significant effect on the purchase process. When a product is replaced or ownership is expanded (e.g., a new record is added to the collection), the consumer does not rely heavily on the search aspect of the purchase process. Problem awareness and availability are the key elements for this consumer. If the consumer is buying a new item, the entire purchase process is utilized. Information on alternatives is compiled and analyzed, and considerable time is expended.

The possessions that a consumer currently has are quite useful in predicting future behavior because the chances are good that a consumer will repeat purchase behavior. Knowledge of who owns certain types of products and how long they have been owned is valuable to the retailer because he or she can relate ownership to other demographics and thereby adjust the retail offering. Analysis of credit card sales can be used to obtain this information.

The type of dwelling the consumer lives in affects the decision process. Homeowners are more concerned with the permanence and quality of products for the home than apartment dwellers, who view the apartment as a temporary residence. The homeowner spends time looking for and evaluating products that are to be used in the home. The apartment dweller spends less time on products that become part of the home (e.g., wallpaper, storm windows, air conditioners) but will devote time to movable objects (e.g., furniture, television). Knowing the consumer's type of dwelling is a crucial factor for some types of retailers, such as lumberyards, interior decorators, and hardware stores.

Race and religion influence the purchasing process. There have been numerous studies on the interaction between race or religion and purchasing behavior. The results of these studies are quite diverse. However, if a racial or religious group is an important part of a retailer's target market, its methods of decision making should be examined.

This discussion has been quite general in nature. It might be an oversimplification if applied directly to the marketplace because differences in decision making have been related to only single demographic variables. In reality, a consumer has a demographic (and life-style) profile that consists of many attributes, including age, education, marital status, and occupation. A person may be twenty-eight years old, college-educated, single, and a carpenter. It is the composite of these variables that influences behavior. Because of the multidimensional characteristics of people, it may be difficult to predict behavior.

Life-Style

A person's demographic background has a strong influence on the life-style, or way of living, that the person adopts. In turn, the person's life-style has a significant effect on the purchasing process. One definition of **life-style** is the way in which an individual lives and spends time and money.[15] Table 5-1 contains a comprehensive, but not all-inclusive, listing of the elements of life-style. Consumers with different life-styles act dissimilarly in their use of the purchasing process.

In recent years, marketers—and more hesitantly, retailers—have examined the consumer as he or she functions in the environment. From this examination, a description of consumer life-styles has developed. Life-styles encompass much of the demographic information already detailed here and integrate it with consumer behavior and attitudes. If the retailer is able to determine and understand the life-styles of the target market, he or she has a powerful tool with which to make decisions.

The consumer's activities, interests, and opinions (**AIO**) can be used to analyze life-styles and their impact on purchase behavior.[16] Activities, interests, and opinions are especially useful when they can be related to demographic data. Grouping people according to these three criteria will reveal substantial differences in product usage, time spent shopping, enjoyment of shopping experience, location and hours of the store, and so on. A typical consumer AIO survey would include questions on membership, hobbies, travel, shopping, work, and entertainment (activities); involvement in the home, the family, and the community (interests); and feelings about economics, politics, and advertising (opinions). The use of the AIO measurement has also been called psychographics; it is in the early stages of development.

Culture, social class, reference groups, and class consciousness are social dimensions of life-style that have an impact on purchasing behavior. A **culture** is a group of

---

[15]James F. Engel and Roger D. Blackwell, *Consumer Behavior*, Fourth Edition (Hinsdale, Ill.: Dryden Press, 1982), p. 188.
[16]William D. Wells and Douglas J. Tigert, "Activities, Interests, Opinions," *Journal of Advertising Research*, Vol. 11 (August 1971), pp. 27–35.

people sharing a distinctive heritage. A **social class system** is the ranking of people within a culture. A **reference group** is a group that influences a person's thoughts and/ or actions. **Class consciousness** is the extent to which social status is desired and pursued.

A person's culture affects the importance of family, religion, education, and other concepts. North Americans act differently than South Americans or Europeans because of their cultural heritage. In the United States, purchasing decisions are more decentralized; religion has a declining impact on behavior (e.g., the repeal of many Sunday blue laws); and advanced education is a valued commodity. From a retailing perspective, the norms or standards of behavior that are influenced by culture are most important. Culture has an impact on all aspects of the purchasing process.

Within a culture, people are divided into various social classes. See Figure 5-2. These classes, which are based on income, occupation, education, dwelling, and so on, separate society into divisions so that people with similar values and life-styles are grouped together. The use of the purchasing process varies greatly among classes. For example, lower-class consumers have limited information sources and seek local, friendly retailers. Middle-class consumers utilize media information and extensive search. They are willing to shop out of their neighborhoods. Upper-class consumers use media information and shop at prestige stores.

For products or services that are conspicuous, reference groups have an important role in the purchasing process. A reference group may be aspirational, membership, or dissociative. An aspirational group is one to which a person does not belong but wishes to belong (fraternity, social club, professional club). A membership group is one to which the person does belong (family, union, PTA). A dissociative group is one to which the person does not belong—and he or she wants it to stay that way ("losers," unhealthy people, unemployed). Those reference groups that are face-to-face (e.g., one's family) have the most impact on the purchasing process. The different types and uses of reference groups need to be understood. As an example, one's neighbors are a membership reference group. However, a retailer must distinguish between the use of neighbors as a reference group by suburbanites and the use by city dwellers. The suburbanite will follow his or her neighbors and know them much better. City dwellers are more independent and know little about their neighbors.

Class consciousness helps determine a consumer's use of reference groups and the importance of prestige purchases. Those consumers who are not class-conscious rely on personal or family criteria. Consumers who are class-conscious—either maintainers (reliance on membership groups) or strivers (reliance on aspirational groups)—are concerned about the social status of products, services, and stores. Then the purchasing process includes social sources of information and an evaluation of the social benefits as well as the physical benefits of the product or service.

The **family life cycle** (see Figure 5-3) shows how a typical family evolves from bachelorhood to marriage to children to solitary retirement. At each stage in the family life cycle, needs and income change. Accordingly the use of the purchase process varies. In the early stages, the full process is used often because new and major purchases are made. During the middle and later parts of the cycle, two things happen. First, intrafamily communication increases as a source of information and evaluation of alternatives. Second, the entire process is used less often because many products are repurchased and little information and decision making are necessary. In addition to the traditional family life cycle shown in Figure 5-3, retailers need to plan for the increasing

The Social Class Structure in the United States

Class	Size	Characteristics
Upper–Upper	Less than 1%	Social elite. Inherited wealth. Exclusive neighborhood. Summer home. Children attend best schools. Money not important in purchases. Secure in status.
Lower–Upper	Combined with Upper–Upper equals 3%	Highest income level. Earned wealth. Often professionals. Social mobility. "Nouveaux riche." College educated, not at the best schools. Seek the best for children. Active in social affairs. Value material possessions. Not secure in position. "Conspicuous consumption." Money not important in purchases.
Upper–Middle	12%	Career-oriented. Successful professionals and businesspeople. Earnings over $30,000. Status based on occupation and earnings. Education important. Most educated in society. Not from prestige schools. Demanding of children. Quality products purchased. Careful but conspicuous. Attractive home. Nice clothing. "Gracious living."

Lower–Middle
  a. Prosperous
  b. Core
  c. Poor but honorable
	35%	"Typical American." Respectable. Conscientious. Obedient. Church-going. Conservative. Home ownership is sought. Do-it-yourselfers. Neat. Work at shopping. Price sensitive. Variety of low-level white-collar occupations. Incomes from $10,000 to $25,000. Purchases related to income and occupation. College for children.

Upper–Lower	40%	Routine existence. Blue-collar occupations. Limited education. Seek job security. Income can overlap with lower-middle. Life of wife monotonous. Child-oriented. But poor understanding of children. Impulsive for new purchases. Brand loyal for regular items. "National brands." Little social contact. Not status-oriented. Protective against lower-lower.
Lower–Lower	10%	Present-oriented. Impulsive. Overpay. Use credit. Poor education. Limited information. Unemployed or most menial jobs. Large market for foods. Poor housing.

Sources: This table is derived, in large part, from James F. Engel and Roger D. Blackwell. *Consumer Behavior,* Fourth Edition (Hinsdale, Ill.: Dryden Press, 1982), pp. 128–129; and Terrell G. Williams, *Consumer Behavior: Fundamentals and Strategies* (St. Paul: West Publishing, 1982), pp. 194–196.

Figure 5-2

Applying The Traditional Family Life Cycle
To Retail Decision Making

Stage in Cycle	Characteristics	Relevance for Retailing
Bachelor	Independent. Young. Early stage of career. Low earnings. Low discretionary income.	Clothing. Automobile. Stereo. Travel. Restaurants. Entertainment. Appeal to status.
Newly Married	Two incomes. Relative independence. Present- and future-oriented.	Furnishing apartment. Travel. Clothing. Durables. Appeal to enjoyment and togetherness.
Full Nest I	Youngest child under 6. One income. Limited independence. Future-oriented.	Products and services geared to child. Family use items. Practicality of items. Durability. Safety. Drugs. Appeal to economy.
Full Nest II	Youngest child over 6, but dependent. One-and-a-half incomes. Husband established in career. Limited independence. Future-oriented.	Savings. Home. Education. Family vacations. Child oriented products. Some interest in luxuries. Appeal to comfort and long-range enjoyment.
Full Nest III	Youngest child living at home, but independent. Highest income level. Independent. Thoughts of retirement.	Education. Expensive durables for children. Replacement and improvement of parents' durables. Appeal to comfort and luxury.
Empty Nest I	No children at home. Independent. Good income. Thoughts of self and retirement.	Retirement home. Travel. Clothing. Entertainment. Luxuries. Appeal to self-gratification.
Empty Nest II	Retirement. Limited income and expenses. Present-oriented.	Travel. Recreation. Living in new home. Drugs and health items. Little interest in luxuries. Appeal to comfort at a low price.
Sole Survivor I	Only one spouse alive. Actively employed. Present oriented. Good income.	Immersion in job and friends leads to opportunities in travel, clothing, health, and recreation areas. Appeal to productive citizen.
Sole Survivor II	Only one spouse alive. Retired. Feeling of futility. Poor income.	Travel. Recreation. Drugs. Security. Appeal to economy and social activity.

Figure 5-3

number of single adults, divorced and widowed adults, single-parent families, and childless couples.[17]

As the consumer becomes experienced, the utilization of the entire decision process declines. A new consumer uses the process much more thoroughly than an experienced shopper. For example, a new resident of a city or town will more carefully investigate the retailers selling refrigerators than a lifelong resident, who is familiar with the attributes of each retailer.

Personality, motives, and performance are individual dimensions of life-style that have an impact on purchasing behavior. A **personality** is the sum total of an individual's traits which make that individual unique. **Motives** are an individual's reasons for behavior. **Performance** is how well a person carries out his or her roles (e.g., worker, consumer, citizen, parent).

A consumer's personality traits affect the purchase process. For an impatient person, the process is short. For someone with little self-confidence, the process is long. A loner and a show-off seek different types of information. Postpurchase satisfaction is very important to a status-seeker.

Consumers have different motives (reasons) when they buy products. As an example, when choosing a department store in which to shop, one consumer may consider convenience and low prices most important. A second consumer may select the store on the basis of assortment. And still a third customer wants to minimize risk and chooses the store that sells national brands. Each person has different goals in shopping (time, prices, choice, and risk) and acts accordingly. Motives are critical when the consumer ranks alternatives and makes a final decision. Motives do change in different situations (e.g., reasons for renting versus buying a summer home).

A person's performance in various roles determines his or her social acceptance and influences the purchasing process. A good worker, parent, citizen, and so on is accepted by his or her peers. This person looks to peers for information, shops at popular stores, and buys socially approved products. A poor worker, parent, citizen, and so on is not accepted by his or her peers. This person can have one of several reactions: to emulate peers in an attempt to win their respect, to withdraw and become a loner, or to seek to overshadow peers (shop at better stores, buy better products). Each of these reactions is possible and will result in a different application of the purchasing process.

Lastly, the importance of the purchase and time constraints have an impact on the consumer's decision process. When a purchase is important, financially or socially, the consumer uses the decision process more carefully than when the purchase is not important. For example, the consumer who considers a grandfather clock an important purchase may look at the selections in several stores; the consumer who wants a grandfather clock but views it as just one more piece of furniture may look in only one store.

The consumer's use of the decision process is limited by the time available. Although a person may like to gather a lot of information before making a purchase, lack of time may minimize or prohibit this. If the consumer has little time for the decision process, he or she must rely on past experience. When experience does not exist, the consumer makes a decision and faces an increased possibility of dissatisfaction.

[17]See, for example, Patrick E. Murphy and William A. Staples, "A Modernized Family Life Cycle," *Journal of Consumer Research*, Vol. 6 (June 1979), pp. 12–22; and James M. Sinkula, "A Look at Some Shopping Orientations in Single Parent Households," in Russell W. Belk et al. (Editors), *1984 AMA Educators' Proceedings* (Chicago: American Marketing Association, 1984), pp. 22–25.

Factors Affecting the Process: Selected Retail Research Findings

The demographics and life-style variables that have been discussed offer excellent means of segmenting a market. It is important for a retailer to understand the composition of different consumer groups and the reactions of these distinct groups to the retailing mix.

Although the demographic and life-style variables were detailed separately in the previous sections, the research findings in these areas will be combined because the two variables complement each other in predicting behavior.

The current retail research on demographics and life-styles is divided into several subsections. As in the case of decision process research, the reader should realize that the examples are only illustrations of how demographics and life-style influence behavior.

Shopper Profiles

There has been considerable research into describing the profiles of consumers who patronize malls, department stores, clothing stores, and grocery stores.

A study on mall-prone and mall-avoiding consumers found that shoppers who enjoy patronizing malls are younger and live in a smaller community than mall avoiders. Mall-prone consumers are also more interested in store variety, mall facilities, innovative retailers, and credit usage.[18]

Another study found that frequent department-store shoppers can be defined on the basis of demographics, activities, interests, and opinions, and media usage. Overall, frequent shoppers are younger, better educated, and have a higher income than less frequent shoppers. They are active in vacationing, interested in fashion, and believe in a modern family structure. They also are frequent magazine readers and enjoy other media.[19]

A comparison of consumers who described themselves as clothing fashion leaders and fashion followers revealed that more leaders are age 18 to 24, are single, enjoy shopping, are not cost conscious, and are not practical. Fashion leaders rate themselves as more sophisticated, modern, unique, willing to take chances, creative, and sociable than fashion followers.[20]

An analysis of grocery shoppers showed that they could be classified into involved, apathetic, convenience, and price groups. Involved shoppers have positive images of their favorite stores; believe prices are low, advertising is good, and convenience and quality are high at these stores; are oldest and most likely to be married; and are the least store loyal. Apathetic shoppers have negative attitudes, are skeptical about value and advertising, are the youngest, and are store loyal. Convenience shoppers represent the largest category, trade off price for convenience, are the most store loyal, and are

---

[18]Jon M. Hawes, David E. Jordan, Jr., and James R. Lumpkin, "An Exploratory Study of the Mall-Prone Shopper," in John Summey et al. (Editors), *Marketing: Theories and Concepts for an Era of Change* (Carbondale, Ill.: Southern Marketing Association, 1983), pp. 135–138.
[19]Melvin R. Crask and Fred D. Reynolds, "An Indepth Profile of the Department Store Shopper," *Journal of Retailing*, Vol. 54 (Summer 1978), pp. 23–32.
[20]Jonathan Gutman and Michael K. Mills, "Fashion Life Style, Self-Concept, Shopping Orientation, and Store Patronage: An Integrative Analysis," *Journal of Retailing*, Vol. 58 (Summer 1982), pp. 64–86.

the most likely to shop at high-price stores. Price shoppers trade convenience and some quality for low prices, rely on newspaper advertisements, and have a low degree of store loyalty.[21]

In-Home Shopping

Studies done on in-home shoppers reveal some surprising results. The in-home shopper is not always a captive audience. Shopping is often discretionary, not necessary. Convenience in ordering one item, without traveling for it, is important. In-home shoppers are also active store shoppers, and they are affluent and well educated.[22] Catalog shoppers are self-confident, younger, and venturesome. They like in-store shopping but have low opinions of local shopping conditions. For many catalog shoppers, time is not an important shopping variable.[23]

When appealing to in-home shoppers, the retailer should realize the differences between in-home and store purchases. In particular, in-home shoppers have a limited ability to comparison shop; cannot touch, feel, handle, or examine products firsthand; are concerned about service; usually do not have a salesperson from whom information can be acquired; and may have difficulty in making sense out of a product's physical dimensions.[24] Also, the retailer needs to understand how consumer behavior is affected by electronic in-home shopping rather than by catalog. For example, more comparative shopping is done via catalog than by an electronic system.[25]

Outshopping

Outshopping (out-of-hometown shopping) is important for both local and surrounding retailers. The former want to minimize this behavior, whereas the latter want to maximize it. Outshoppers are often male, young, members of a large family, new to the community, less than college-educated, and low income.[26] This is important information for suburban shopping centers.

Outshoppers differ in their life-styles from those who patronize neighborhood or hometown stores. Outshoppers enjoy fine foods, like to travel out-of-town, are active, like to change stores, and read out-of-town newspapers more than hometown shoppers. They also downplay hometown stores and compliment out-of-town stores.[27]

Outshoppers have the same basic reasons for patronizing out-of-town shopping areas whether they reside in small or large communities. Among these reasons are easy

[21]Robert H. Williams, John J. Painter, and Herbert R. Nicholas, "A Policy-Oriented Typology of Grocery Shoppers," *Journal of Retailing*, Vol. 54 (Spring 1978), pp. 27–42.

[22]Peter L. Gillett, "A Profile of In-Home Shoppers," *Journal of Marketing*, Vol. 34 (July 1970), pp. 40–45; and Peter L. Gillett, "In-Home Shoppers—An Overview," *Journal of Marketing*, Vol. 40 (October 1976), pp. 81–88.

[23]Fred D. Reynolds, "An Analysis of Catalog Buying Behavior," *Journal of Marketing*, Vol. 38 (July 1974), pp. 47–51.

[24]Shirley Mitchell, "Eager Marketers May Overlook Consumers Not So Eager for 'Shopless Shopping'," *Marketing News* (December 12, 1980), p. 20.

[25]Subhash Sharma, William O. Bearden, and Jesse E. Teel, "Differential Effects of In-Home Shopping Methods," *Journal of Retailing*, Vol. 59 (Winter 1983), pp. 29–51.

[26]A. Coskun Samli and Ernest B. Uhr, "The Outshopping Spectrum: Key for Analyzing Intermarket Leakages," *Journal of Retailing*, Vol. 50 (Summer 1974), pp. 70–78ff.

[27]Fred D. Reynolds and William R. Darden, "Intermarket Patronage: A Psychographic Study of Consumer Outshoppers," *Journal of Marketing*, Vol. 36 (October 1972), pp. 50–54; and N. G. Papadopoulos, "Consumer Outshopping Research: Review and Extension," *Journal of Retailing*, Vol. 56 (Winter 1980), pp. 41–58.

access, liberal credit terms, store diversity, product assortments, prices, the presence of large chain outlets, entertainment facilities, customer services, and product quality.[28]

Manufacturer, Dealer, and Generic Brands

During recent years many retailers have increased the sales of dealer (private) brands and generic brands at the expense of manufacturers' (national) brands. At Sears and J. C. Penney, where dealer brands are being de-emphasized, these brands still account for the major portion of sales. Generic brands have had their greatest success with pharmaceutical and supermarket products. In total, dealer brands and generic brands account for about 28 per cent of supermarket sales, with generics rising from 0 per cent of sales in 1977 to over 4 per cent today.[29]

Studies of supermarket customers buying generics show these shoppers to be younger, upscale, employed in good jobs, from larger families (children), and well educated. They shop frequently, have a high product usage rate, generally purchase lower-priced items, and have a high level of store loyalty. These consumers believe they will be better off financially in the future, are willing to try unknown brands, and are confident about their performance.[30]

Types of Decision Processes

In the preceding two sections, the consumer's entire decision-making process was described. The decision process and the factors affecting it were detailed. Two important conclusions must be drawn from this discussion. First, each time a consumer buys a product or service, he or she uses the decision process. Often the process is used subconsciously and the consumer is not even aware of its use. Second, the decision process is used differently in variant situations. One situation may require the thorough use of each step in the process; another situation may allow the consumer to concentrate on certain steps and omit others.

There are three types of decision processes: extended decision making, limited decision making, and routine decision making. These are explained next.

Extended Decision Making

Extended decision making occurs when a consumer makes full use of the decision process shown in Figure 5-1 and Table 5-1. Much time is spent on information search

[28]A. Coskun Samli, Glen Riecken, and Ugur Yavas, "Intermarket Shopping Behavior and the Small Community: Problems and Prospects of a Widespread Phenomenon," *Journal of the Academy of Marketing Science*, Vol. 11 (Winter 1983), pp. 1–14; and R. Eric Reidenbach, M. Bixby Cooper, and Mary Carolyn Harrison, "A Factor Analytic Comparison of Outshopping Behavior in Larger Retail Trade Areas," *Journal of the Academy of Marketing Science*, Vol. 12 (Spring 1984), pp. 145–158.

[29]Arthur C. Nielsen, Jr., "The Development of Industry Brands and Distributors' Brands in Europe and the United States," *Nielsen Researcher* (Number 2, 1984), pp. 2–19.

[30]Kenneth R. Evans and Richard F. Beltramini, "An Integrative Assessment of Consumers of Generic Products: Retail Marketing Strategy Considerations," in Patrick E. Murphy et al. (Editors), *1983 AMA Educators' Proceedings* (Chicago: American Marketing Association, 1983), pp. 257–261; Martha R. McEnally and Jon M. Hawes, "The Market for Generic Brand Grocery Products: A Review and Extension," *Journal of Marketing*, Vol. 48 (Winter 1984), pp. 75–83; and Ken Kono, "Psychographic Profile of Generics Buyers," in Patrick E. Murphy et al. (Editors), *1983 AMA Educators' Proceedings* (Chicago: American Marketing Association, 1983), pp. 11–15.

and evaluation of alternatives before a purchase is made. In this category are expensive, complex products or services with which the consumer has had little or no experience. Risk, financial and social, is high. Examples of products or services requiring extended decision making are a college, a house, and a first car.

At any point in the purchasing process, the consumer can stop, and for expensive, complex items, this occurs quite often. The factors affecting the process have their greatest impact for products or services that require extended decision making. Demographic and life-style factors (such as age, education, income, marital status, activities, experience, and social class) have an important influence on the use of extended decision making. Risk and uncertainty always lead to increased information seeking, evaluation, and re-evaluation.

Limited Decision Making

Limited decision making occurs when a consumer uses each of the steps in the purchase process but does not need to spend a great deal of time on each of the steps. This type of decision making requires less time than extended decision making because the consumer probably has some experience. In this category are items that the consumer has purchased before, but not regularly. Risk is moderate, and the consumer is willing to spend some time shopping. The thoroughness with which the decision process is used depends mostly on the prior experience of the consumer. Emphasis would probably be on the evaluation of known alternatives according to consumer desires and standards, although the information search is also important for some. Examples of products requiring limited decision making are a second car, clothing, a vacation, and gifts.

The factors affecting the process have an impact on decision making, but the effect becomes less as risk decreases and experience increases. Income, the importance of the purchase, and motives play very strong roles in the uses of limited decision making.

Routine Decision Making

Routine decision making takes place when the consumer buys because of habit and skips steps in the purchasing process. The consumer is willing to spend no time on shopping, and the same brands are usually repurchased. In this category are items that are purchased regularly. These products or services have little risk for the consumer because of experience. The key step for this type of decision making is problem awareness. When the consumer realizes that the product or service is depleted, a repurchase is made. Information search, evaluation of alternatives, and postpurchase behavior have less importance than in limited or extended decision making. These steps will not be undertaken as long as the consumer is satisfied. However, the retailer must continue to reinforce this habitual response through promotional effort and other elements of the retail mix. Examples of products or services requiring routine decision making are weekly groceries, newspapers, and haircuts.

The factors affecting the process have little impact in routine situations. Problem awareness almost inevitably leads to a purchase.

Because consumers like to reduce risk and the use of detailed choice processes, most purchases are made by routine or limited decision making. Few involve extended decision making. As experience increases and the complexity and price of a product or service decrease, the consumer moves toward routine decision making.

Types of Decision Processes:
Retail Implications and Selected Research Findings

Extended decision making must be understood by retailers selling expensive, complex goods and services, such as automobile dealers, computer stores, and real estate brokers. A great deal of information must be provided in order for the consumer to react favorably. Mass media, store displays, and salespeople are crucial and should be geared to providing information, with less emphasis on persuasion.

Limited decision making must be understood by shopping stores, such as department stores and specialty stores, that carry goods and services which the consumer has bought before. The internal environment of the store is very important. Store displays and sales personnel should be oriented toward providing information and persuasion. Assortment is important.

Routine decision making must be understood by retailers such as supermarkets, dry cleaners, and fast-food restaurants. The following are required: good location, adequate store hours, store displays, and most important—product availability. Mass advertising should be reminder-oriented. Salespeople have little impact, except for completing the purchase act.

Although little retail research has been conducted on the types of decision processes, shopping and travel time, impulse purchases, and store loyalty have been investigated.

The consumer's willingness to spend time shopping has been studied by retailers. For example, banking customers can be divided into convenience- and service-oriented types. Convenience customers bank where they shop and are not concerned about rates and services. Service customers look at bank image and the availability of better rates and loans and are less interested in bank location.[31] In supermarket shopping, females are more likely than males to make a shopping list, check supermarket ads, and use coupons. Males are more likely to buy impulse items and spend a greater amount.[32] When apparel shoppers are under time pressure, store familiarity, immediate salesperson attention, and product assortment take on added importance.[33]

In the selection of a shopping center, consumers consider driving time and the attractiveness of the center (measured by store image, store space, and product assortment). When driving time increases, the number of consumers decreases, and as store space and product assortment increase, the willingness to travel increases.[34]

Mapping is a relatively new concept for evaluating the trading area of a store. With this technique, the retailer determines the distances consumers are likely to travel to get to the store, the population density of the geographic area surrounding the store, and the travel patterns and times from various locations. Then a map is drawn showing these factors.

---

[31]W. Thomas Anderson, Jr., Eli P. Cox III, and David G. Fulcher, "Bank Selection Decisions and Market Segmentation," *Journal of Marketing*, Vol. 40 (January 1976), pp. 40–45.

[32]Mary Johnson, "Consumer Watch: Cooking, Cleaning, Shopping—The Manly Things to Do," *Progressive Grocer* (July 1983), p. 19.

[33]Bruce E. Mattison, "Situational Influences on Store Choice," *Journal of Retailing*, Vol. 58 (Fall 1982), pp. 46–58.

[34]William E. Cox, Jr., and Ernest F. Cooke, "Other Dimensions Involved in Shopping Center Preference," *Journal of Marketing*, Vol. 34 (October 1970), pp. 12–17; and John R. Nevin and Michael J. Houston, "Image as a Component of Attraction to Intraurban Shopping Areas," *Journal of Retailing*, Vol. 56 (Spring 1980), pp. 77–93.

Impulse purchases involve products the consumer does not plan to buy on a specific trip to a store. Behavior is similar to that in routine decision making; there is no time spent shopping and the key step is problem awareness. Impulse purchases are more susceptible to in-store displays than preplanned purchases. One study found that discount-store shoppers are more likely to make impulse purchases, but department-store shoppers are apt to make more costly impulse purchases. This study also discovered that situational variables (store environment, and product and trip-specific factors) have a greater impact on impulse purchases than shopper characteristics.[35] Another study determined that impulse purchases in a department store vary by product category. Impulse purchases are high for costume jewelry, bakery products, women's sportswear, curtains/draperies, women's/girls' footwear, and meals and snacks. Impulse purchases are much lower for women's lingerie, cosmetics and toiletries, men's clothing, and books and stationery.[36] A third study, of grocery store shopping, found that almost half of purchases are unplanned and can be heavily influenced by in-store displays.[37]

When **store loyalty** exists, the consumer regularly patronizes a particular store. Store-loyal consumers tend to be time-conscious, use entertainment media, like local shopping, are fashion followers, do not rely on credit, and are not involved with out-shopping.[38] Retailers can plan by defining the consumers whose loyalty is sought, determining the benefits desired by these consumers, specifying the consumers' personal characteristics, and formulating an appropriate strategy.[39] In a service setting, such as automobile repair, satisfaction with service quality often leads to store loyalty. Price has little bearing on decisions.[40]

Consumer Behavior—Understanding the Decision Process: A Summary

In order to plan a retail strategy properly, a retailer must understand the consumer and adapt his or her retailing mix accordingly. One way of analyzing the consumer is through the use of the decision process. This process shows how a consumer becomes aware of and informed about products and services and then shops for them.

A stimulus (social, commercial, or physical) arouses the consumer to act. If the stimulus is successful, it causes the person to become aware of a problem. Either a shortage exists, or recognition of an unfulfilled desire occurs. The consumer then starts an information search. A list of possible alternatives is developed from memory or external searching (commercial, noncommercial, or social). The characteristics of each alternative are determined from memory or external searching (commercial, noncom-

---

[35]V. Kanti Prasad, "Unplanned Buying in Two Retail Settings," *Journal of Retailing*, Vol. 51 (Fall 1975), pp. 3–12.

[36]Danny H. Bellenger, Dan H. Robertson, and Elizabeth C. Hirschman, "Impulse Buying Varies by Product," *Journal of Advertising Research*, Vol. 18 (December 1978), pp. 15–18.

[37]"Display Effectiveness: An Evaluation," p. 2.

[38]Fred D. Reynolds, William R. Darden, and Warren S. Martin, "Developing an Image of the Store-Loyal Customer," *Journal of Retailing*, Vol. 50 (Winter 1974–75), pp. 73–84.

[39]Kenneth E. Miller and Kent L. Granzin, "Simultaneous Loyalty and Benefit Segmentation of Retail Store Customers," *Journal of Retailing*, Vol. 55 (Spring 1979), pp. 47–60.

[40]Gabriel J. Biehal, "Consumers' Prior Experiences and Perceptions in Auto Repair Choice," *Journal of Marketing*, Vol. 47 (Summer 1983), pp. 82–91.

mercial, or social). At this point, the alternatives are evaluated. The criteria for the decision are established. The importance of each criterion is stated. The alternatives are ranked, and a choice is made. The purchasing act is completed. The place of purchase is selected. The terms of purchase are established. Availability is ascertained. After the purchase, postpurchase behavior occurs. The consumer may make further, dependent purchases. The performance of the product or service is re-evaluated.

While the consumer is moving through the purchasing process, several factors affect him or her. These factors can be categorized as demographics and life-style. Demographics are easily identifiable and measurable population statistics, such as age, education, income, occupation, gender, marital status, family size, height, weight, mobility, location, possessions, type of dwelling, race, and religion. Life-style characteristics are variables that define a person's way of life, such as activities, interests, opinions, culture, social class, reference groups, class consciousness, family life cycle, experience, personality, motives, performance, importance of purchase, and time constraints.

The purchasing process may be used in three ways: extended decision making for new or complex products; limited decision making for shopping items; and routine decision making for convenience items.

Questions for Discussion

1. Why should a retailer understand and adapt to the consumer's decision process?
2. Describe how the consumer's decision process operates for each of the following: a television, life insurance, a new magazine, and tickets to a movie.
3. For each of the products or services contained in Question 2, which elements of the decision process are most important for retailers? Develop appropriate strategies.
4. Which type of stimulus (social, commercial, or physical) is most effective? Why?
5. Will a purchase be made without the problem awareness stage? Can a retailer "force" problem awareness?
6. What are the two types of problem awareness? Should a retailer's strategy be the same for both? Why or why not?
7. Do consumers ever skip the evaluation of alternatives stage of the decision process? Explain your answer.
8. What criteria do consumers use in selecting among alternatives? Are the criteria always the same?
9. What elements in the retail strategy can close sales or lose them at the point of purchase?
10. Explain cognitive dissonance. What can a retailer do to overcome it?
11. How do demographics and life-style affect the consumer's use of the decision process? Describe the relevance of these factors to retail strategy development.
12. Define extended, limited, and routine decision making. How should retailers react to these different uses of the purchasing process?
13. Can all types of retailers profit through the study of the decision process? Explain your answer.
14. What are the difficulties in using the consumer's decision process as a basis for retail strategy?

CASES

1. Al's Landscape Service: The Importance of Understanding Consumer Behavior*

Al's Landscape Service is located in Hawaii. It is one of several firms offering a full complement of landscaping services, including pest control, tree and bush trimming, planting, lawn and tree fertilization, and sprinkler installation and repair.

Although Al's prices are 20 to 25 per cent above what a homeowner would pay if he or she individually contracted for each service the company performs, Al's customers benefit from his experience, the convenience of dealing with one vendor, employing a firm that is bonded and insured, early detection and correction of lawn and tree disease, and Al's personally inspecting each job. Table 1 lists the services most frequently provided by Al's Landscape Service.

Al very much wants to expand his business. This would enable him to utilize more automated equipment, advertise more effectively in certain media, and increase sales and profits. As a result, Al sponsored a study to find out about the consumer behavior involved in landscape services. These are the key findings of his study:

- The average consumer is uninformed about the benefits of specific landscape services. They do not understand the differences between plastic and brass sprinkler heads, the need for soil analysis, and the specific pests that are controlled through chemical treatment.
- Family members typically have divided responsibilities relative to dealing with lawn maintenance suppliers. While the husband gives approval for the job, the wife usually observes the work and notes the need for additional services or lawn problems to be corrected.
- Two major market segments are the "perfectionist" and the "just get by" customer. The perfectionist desires the best lawn on the block and is very knowledgeable about lawns. The "just get by" customer views yardwork as a necessary evil, is price sensitive, and does not believe in programmed maintenance. Landscape services are hired on a one-time basis when an emergency arises.

Table 1
The Services Most Frequently Provided by Al's Landscaping Service

- Lawn fertilization
- Lawn, tree, and bush pest control
- Complete landscape installation
- Weed control (certified contractor)
- Tree and bush trimming
- Tree fertilization through root feeding
- Construction of ornamental walks and walls
- Design, installation, and repair of sprinkler systems
- Soil fumigation (certified contractor)
- Planting shrubs

*This case was prepared and written by Mr. Robert J. Small and Professor Laurence Jacobs, University of Hawaii, Honolulu, Hawaii.

- Consumers have high loyalty to their landscapers and are not prone to consider switching if services are viewed to be satisfactory. The average consumer is more concerned with dependability and price than with the quality of lawn care.
- The most important source of new landscape accounts is word-of-mouth communication from satisfied customers. Word of mouth is responsible for 50 to 60 per cent of new accounts. Telephone classified advertising and direct mail are also important.

Al is very much concerned about competing against family-owned landscape businesses (which typically mow lawns, cut bushes, apply lawn fertilizers, and perform other limited landscaping services). In many cases, these firms can undercut Al's price by 40 to 50 per cent due to their use of family members, not having necessary licenses, and refraining from the purchase of necessary liability and worker's compensation insurance.

Questions

1. What are the implications of the consumer behavior analysis for Al's strategy?
2. Which market segment is Al best equipped to reach? Why?
3. Contrast the consumer decision processes used to select landscaping services by "perfectionist" consumers and "just get by" consumers.
4. Develop a plan for Al to increase his business and to compete successfully against limited-service, family-owned landscape businesses. Incorporate the information contained in the consumer behavior study.

---

2. Encyclopedias: The Emergence of Store Retailing*

In 1980, more than 1.2 million encyclopedias of all types were sold. The two leaders were World Book and Encyclopedia Britannica. By 1983, annual sales were close to $500 million. Until recently, no major full-length encyclopedias were sold exclusively through stores; and some encyclopedias were not available at all in retail stores. Direct-to-home retailing was, and still is, the dominant method for selling major encyclopedias. However, changes are slowly occurring in the retailing of encyclopedias.

The Academic American Encyclopedia became the first full-length multiple-volume encyclopedia to be sold exclusively in book and department stores when it was introduced in September 1980. Store retailers are pleased with this development. A spokesperson for Stix, Baer, & Fuller, a major St. Louis department store commented: "The set sold well in all our stores, from the lowest income level area to the highest, which came as a complete surprise." An executive of B. Dalton Bookseller said: "It has certainly been a good move for us."

The strategy for Academic American contained a number of components. It was introduced in six markets, with plans to expand to at least thirty by 1982. More than $10 million in advertising was spent in 1981. A thorough training program was provided to sales personnel in each store. Point-of-purchase brochures were distrib-

*The material in this case is drawn from Penny Gill, "Bought Any Good Books Lately? Or, How Some Stores Are Selling Encyclopedias," *Stores* (July 1981), pp. 41–43.

uted. The encyclopedia was priced at a low $450, compared with $1,200 for Britannica. Yet retailers were able to attain a 50 per cent markup (much higher than that of other encyclopedias).

In addition, Academic American's management realized the complexity of the consumer's decision process for this product:

> Our philosophy is that consumers may examine an encyclopedia at retail on several shopping trips before actually deciding to buy. So we want to provide them with as much information, through sales staff and printed material, as possible.

Both World Book and Encyclopedia Britannica have begun to use store retailing as a supplement to their traditional direct-to-home sales. World Book has a cooperative arrangement with B. Dalton and pays it a per cent of sales for the space it occupies. B. Dalton is happy to be selling both Academic American and World Book, because the store receives high profit margins from the former and high brand recognition from the latter.

Britannica has taken a different approach. It has its own sales force set up portable displays in shopping malls, Montgomery Ward stores, and WaldenBooks stores. Sales are not made in these store settings; instead, Britannica uses the stores to generate more efficiently customer leads for sales personnel. Britannica also uses a back-to-school sweepstakes in conjunction with WaldenBooks.

Questions

1. Explain the consumer's decision process for encyclopedias.
2. How does the place of purchase, in-home versus in-store, affect the consumer's decision process for encyclopedias?
3. Compare the consumer's decision process for inexpensive encyclopedias sold in supermarkets with the process for Academic American in book and department stores. What are the implications of this for retailers?
4. Can the retailing approach of Academic American succeed? Why or why not?

6

Marketing Research in Retailing

Chapter Objectives

1. To describe marketing research as it applies to retailing
2. To discuss the problems involved with nonsystematic research
3. To explain the marketing research process: problem definition, secondary data search, generation of primary data (if necessary), data analysis, recommendations, and implementation of findings
4. To examine the retail information system, its components, and advances in information processing

The On-Site Research Company is one of a number of specialized marketing research firms that make their services available to retailers. On-Site Research has developed a procedure that enables wide-angle, time-lapse cameras to observe and monitor in-store traffic patterns, merchandising effectiveness, and consumer behavior. Shoppers are not aware that they are being observed.

Recently, On-Site Research completed observation studies for CBS Records and Channel Home Centers. In the CBS project, the traffic patterns and behavior of consumers in a record store were viewed. CBS learned that displays are more effective when they are placed along the consumer's shopping route through the store. Displays near checkout counters are often blocked by those waiting on line; and they cannot be read. Aisle signs can inhibit the flow of in-store traffic if they are placed too far out from the shelves. Also, CBS was able to examine the actions of shoplifters and consider methods to reduce pilferage. In the Channel project, the emphasis was on entry–exit traffic patterns and the effectiveness of point-of-purchase displays. Channel learned a lot about spatial efficiency.[1]

By using mechanical observation and/or various other marketing research tools, retailers can acquire a lot of information that will assist them in making decisions.

Overview

Marketing research in retailing is the systematic collection and analysis of data relating to retailing strategy. Whether one is developing a new strategy or modifying an existing one, marketing research should be used.

Various aspects of retailing can be researched, such as store location, store management and operations, product and service offerings, store image and promotion, and pricing. Examples of research in these and other areas will be provided throughout the chapter.

Research is useful because it reduces a retailer's risk. Without research, risk is higher, because an incorrect strategy decision may occur based on little information or on information gathered nonsystematically.

The extent of research activity should, to a large degree, be determined by the level of risk involved in a decision. For instance, there is considerable risk for a department store considering a new branch store location. There is much less risk where a retailer is deciding whether a store should carry a new line of slacks. For the branch-store location problem, several thousand dollars for research and many months of study may be necessary. In the case of ordering new slacks, limited research is probably sufficient.

Marketing research should be a continuous process, yielding information for planning and control. Unless research is done on a continuous basis, it often becomes concerned with day-to-day problems (crises) as opposed to the long-range strategy-planning needs of the retailer.

Retail Strategies Based on Nonsystematic Research

Retailers are often tempted to rely on nonsystematic measures in evaluating strategies because of time constraints, cost constraints, or lack of research capabilities. Examples of nonsystematic attempts at research include the following:

1. The use of intuition (e.g., "My gut reaction is to order 100 dozen quartz watches and sell them for $50 each as Christmas gifts.")
2. A continuation of what was done before (e.g., "I have never sold jewelry on credit. Why should I do so now?")
3. The copying of a successful competitor's strategy (e.g., "Bloomingdale's has had great success with the sale of gourmet foods. We should stock and promote these products.")

---

[1]"Lights . . . Action . . . Camera: Keeping an Eye on Business," *Chain Store Age Executive* (February 1985), p. 58.

4. The development of strategy from speaking to a few individuals about their perceptions (e.g., "My friends Bill and Mary feel that my prices are too high. I ought to lower them to improve sales and profits.")
5. The assumption that past trends will continue into the future (e.g., "The wholesale prices of calculators have fallen off 25 per cent in the last year. I will wait another six months to make a purchase and get a really low price. I can then underprice my competitors, who are buying now.")

In this section, several decisions made by retailers who have not used systematic research are described, and their strategic errors are analyzed.

A movie theater charges $4.00 for tickets throughout the entire week. The manager cannot understand why attendance is poor during weekday afternoons. The theater manager thinks that because all patrons are seeing the same movie, the prices should be the same for a Monday matinee as for a Saturday evening show. However, a research study would indicate that people prefer Saturday evening performances and would pay more to see a movie at this time. Weekday customers have to be attracted, and a lower price is one means of doing so.

A toy store orders conservatively for the holiday season because the previous year's sales were poor. The store sells out a month before the peak of the season and additional merchandise cannot be delivered to the store in time for holiday sale. The toy store uses a technique familiar to many companies: incremental budgeting. Under this policy, a percentage is added or subtracted from the previous year's budget to arrive at the present year's budget. In this instance, the store owner assumed that the previous year's poor sales would occur again. However, a survey of consumers would have revealed a new degree of optimism and an increased desire to give gifts. A research-based retailer would have planned his or her inventory accordingly.

A chain bookstore decides to open a new branch unit seventy miles away from its closest store. The decision is based on the growing population in the area and the current absence of an outlet by the chain. After a year, the new store is attaining only 40 per cent of its expected business. A subsequent study by the chain reveals that the store name (and image) was relatively unknown in the area and that the choice of advertising media was incorrect. In planning the new branch, these two important factors were not researched.

A mail-order retailer is doing well selling appliances, televisions, and needlepoint patterns. Recent expansion into furniture and stereo systems has yielded poor results. This retailer has developed a good reputation in its traditional product lines and has attracted loyal customers. He feels that the time is ripe for expansion into other product lines to capitalize on his name and customer goodwill. However, the retailer has not conducted research on the consumer behavior of mail-order customers. People will buy standard, branded merchandise through the mail; they will not buy most furniture and stereos (both of which must be seen and handled) via the mail. These items must be experienced or tried out before a purchase.

A florist cuts the price of two-day-old flowers from $3.00 to $0.75. They don't sell. The florist cuts the prices of older flowers because they have a short life expectancy. She assumes that bargain-hunting consumers will buy these flowers as gifts or floral arrangements. What the florist does not realize (because of no research) is that consumers perceive the older flowers to be of inferior quality, color, and smell. The reduced price is actually too low and turns off customers!

The conclusion to be drawn from these examples is that nonsystematic means of collecting and/or analyzing data can cause a retailer to develop an inappropriate strategy.

The Marketing Research Process

Marketing research in retailing involves a series of activities: the definition of the problem to be solved, examination of secondary (published) data sources, generation of primary data (if necessary), analysis of data, recommendations, and implementation of findings. It is not a single act. The use of this process will enable the retailer to collect and evaluate data systematically for the resolution of strategy decisions.

Figure 6-1 outlines the research process. Note that each of the activities is conducted sequentially. For instance, secondary data cannot be examined until after the problem is defined. The dashed line around the primary data suggests that primary data need to be generated only when the secondary data search does not yield enough information to make a strategy decision. The components of the research project are described next.

Problem definition involves a clear statement of the topic to be investigated. What information does the retailer want to obtain in order to make a decision? Without a clear statement of the topic to be researched, mounds of irrelevant and confusing data

The Research Process in Retailing

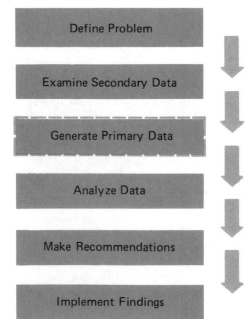

Figure 6-1

could be collected. Some examples of problem definition for a downtown shoe retailer are:

1. "Of three potential new store locations, which should I choose?"
2. "What store hours should I keep?"
3. "How can we improve the sales of our men's shoes?"
4. "Why is my competitor doing well? How can I draw customers away from this store?"

It is important to note from these examples that research problems differ in their nature. Whereas the first problem relates to evaluating three alternative locations and is fairly structured, the third problem is much less structured.

After the research problem has been defined, **secondary data** sources are examined. Secondary data are those that have already been gathered for purposes other than solving the problem currently under investigation. Secondary data may be internal (company records) or external (government reports, trade publications). Secondary data sources will be described in the following section.

Primary data are those collected to solve the specific problem under investigation. This type of data may be developed through surveys, experiments, observations, and simulation. Primary data will be discussed more fully later in the chapter.

Through the generation of secondary and/or primary data, the following types of information can be gathered for the problems defined previously:

Problem Definition	Information Needed to Solve Problem
1. Which store location?	1. Access to transportation, traffic, consumer profiles, rent, store size, and types of competition are compiled from government reports, trade publications, and observation by the owner for each of the three potential store locations.
2. What store hours?	2. Local ordinances for store hours are obtained, as are the hours for neighboring and competing stores. Consumer attitudes are determined.
3. How to improve sales of shoes?	3. Competitors' product offerings and prices are noted. A consumer survey in a nearby mall is conducted.
4. People shopping at a competitor's store?	4. Extensive information about the competitor is gathered. Consumers leaving the competitor's store are questioned.

In some instances, primary data are collected; in others, secondary data are used. For some, both are used. Two points are noteworthy. First, the diversity of data collection (types and costs) is great. Second, only data that are relevant to the problem under investigation should be amassed.

After the secondary and/or primary data are developed, **data analysis** must be performed in terms of the defined problem. The alternative solutions should be clearly outlined. For example:

Problem Definition	Alternative Solutions
1. Which store location?	1. Each store location is ranked for all of the criteria (access to transportation, traffic, consumer profiles, rent, store size, and types of competition).
2. What store hours?	2. The advantages and disadvantages of different store hours are compared (in terms of increased sales and increased costs).
3. How to improve sales of shoes?	3. Alternative strategies to boost shoe sales are analyzed and ranked.
4. People shopping at a competitor's store?	4. The reasons for the competitor's success are studied, and possible reactions are listed.

Then the advantages and disadvantages of each alternative are enumerated. See Table 6-1.

At this point, **recommendations** are made. What strategy should the retailer use to solve best his or her problem? From the alternatives, which is best? Table 6-1 shows the recommendations for the problems discussed throughout this section.

Last, but not least in importance, is the **implementation** of the recommended strategy. If research is to replace intuition in the development of a retail strategy, a good retailer will follow the recommendations of marketing research even if they appear to contradict his or her ideas.

Secondary Data Sources

Advantages and Disadvantages of Secondary Data

Secondary data (information previously gathered for other purposes) have several advantages over primary data. The assembly of data is inexpensive. Company records, trade journals, government publications, and so on, are all inexpensive to use. No data collection forms, interviewers, and tabulations are needed.

Secondary data can be collected quickly. Company or library records can be analyzed immediately, whereas the generation of primary data may take up to several months.

For many retailing problems, several sources of secondary data are available. These allow a company to receive many perspectives and large quantities of data. With a primary study, limited data and only one perspective are obtained.

A secondary source may possess information that the retailer would otherwise be unable to get. For example, government publications often have statistics that no private company could otherwise acquire. Furthermore, the data contained in government literature may be more honest and accurate than a private company could receive.

Table 6-1
Research-Based Recommendations

Problem	Alternative	Pros and Cons of Alternatives	Recommendation
1. Which store location?	Site A.	Best transportation, traffic, and consumer profiles. Highest rent. Smallest store space. Extensive competition.	Site A: the many advantages far outweigh the disadvantages.
	Site B.	Poorest transportation, traffic, and consumer profiles. Lowest rent. Largest store space. No competition.	
	Site C.	Intermediate on all criteria.	
2. What store hours?	9 A.M.–8 P.M.	Hours maintained by neighboring stores. Not early enough for customers. No legal violations.	7 A.M.–6 P.M.: satisfy customers and show results of informal survey to other merchants.
	7 A.M.–6 P.M.	Hours desired by customers. Violation of voluntary retail dealers' agreement. No legal violations.	
3. How to improve sales of shoes?	Increased assortment.	Will attract and satisfy many more customers. High costs. High level of inventory. Reduces turnover for many items.	Lower prices and add advertisements: additional customers offset higher costs and lower margins; combination best expands business.
	Drop some lines and specialize.	Will attract and satisfy a specific consumer market. Excludes many segments. Costs and inventory reduced.	
	Reduce prices.	Unit sales increase. Markup and profit per item decline.	
	Advertise.	Will increase traffic and new customers. High costs.	
4. People shopping at a competitor's store?	Reduce price, increase inventories, add salespeople.	Similar to successful strategy of competitor. Will increase costs and appeal to a different consumer market (old customers may be lost). Imitation.	Modernize facilities and improve image: competitive advantages are retained and improved; poor strategy to imitate competitor and lose present customers.
	Modernize facilities and advertise high-quality image.	Maintains old customers and attracts new ones with a distinctive image. Expensive and time consuming.	

When secondary data are assembled by a source such as *Progressive Grocer*, A. C. Nielsen, *Business Week*, or the federal government, the results are believable. Each of these sources has a high level of credibility and a reputation for thoroughness.

Often a retailer may have only a rough idea of the problems that he or she wants to investigate. In this instance, a search of secondary data may help the retailer to define the problem more specifically. In addition, background information about a problem can be gathered from secondary sources before the primary study is undertaken.

Although the use of secondary data has many advantages, there are also several disadvantages. Available data may not suit the purposes of the current study because they have been collected for other purposes. The units of measurement may be different. A retailer normally needs local demographic and other types of information.

However, neighborhood statistics are rarely found in secondary sources (which contain federal, state, and city statistics). Data may be categorized in an unusable fashion. For example, a gasoline station owner is interested in the number of local citizens having automobiles. He wants this information broken down by year and model, so that he can stock parts. The motor vehicle bureau can provide statistics on the models but not the mileage driven.

Secondary data may be dated. Because the information has already been assembled for another purpose, it may have outlived its usefulness. The conclusions reached five or even two years ago may not be valid today. As an example, the *Census of Population* is conducted every 10 years. The last one was done in 1980, and the statistics contained in this census are rapidly becoming outdated. In addition, there is often a long time delay between the completion of the census and the release of data.

The accuracy of secondary data must be evaluated. The retailer must determine whether the data have been compiled in an unbiased, objective manner. The objectives of the original study, the data collection techniques, and the method of analysis should each be examined for bias. Determination of bias is especially important when the research has been undertaken by a company that has a stake in the study's findings. The supporting evidence (raw data) should be read as well as summary reports. In addition, some secondary data sources have low levels of accuracy.

The source of secondary data can be a disadvantage as well as an advantage. A partisan, profit-making company usually does not provide competitors with information that will hurt it. Generalities and omissions should be noted by the retailer. Also some sources are known for their poor data collection techniques, and these should be avoided. When conflicting data are found, it is important to distinguish among sources and select the one with the best reputation for accuracy. Conflicting results presented by equally accurate sources may lead a retailer into primary research (the collection of his or her own data).

Finally, the reliability of secondary data is not always known. Reliability is the ability to replicate a study and get the same outcome. In retailing, many research projects are not retested; therefore, the user of secondary data is hoping that the results from one narrow study are applicable to his or her problem.

A retailer who desires information to solve a problem has many criteria to consider when contemplating the use of secondary data. Low costs, speed, and access to materials are weighed against improper fit, out-of-date statistics, and accuracy of data.

Whether secondary data solve the retailer's problem or not, their low cost and immediate availability require that primary data not be collected until after a thorough search of secondary data. If secondary sources prove unsatisfactory or incomplete, then primary data should be collected.

In the following section, a variety of secondary data sources for retailers are detailed.

Sources of Secondary Data

There are different types of secondary data. The major distinctions are between internal and external retail data. Internal secondary data are obtainable within the company. External secondary data must be collected from sources outside the firm.

Internal Secondary Data

Before spending time and money searching for external secondary data or primary data, the retailer should look at the information that is available inside his or her company. Table 6-2 shows some of the major sources of internal data.

At the beginning of the year, most retailers develop budgets for the next twelve months of the year. These budgets, based on sales forecasts, outline planned expenditures during the coming year. The retail budget and a store's performance in the attainment of budgetary goals (adherence to the outlined plan of expenditures) are good sources for secondary data.

Retailers often use sales figures as indicators of success. For many retailers, these figures are accurately and rapidly available through point-of-sale cash registers. By examining the sales of each store, department, item, and salesperson and comparing these sales with prior time periods, a retailer gets a feeling of growth or contraction. But this feeling, and an overdependence on sales data, may be misleading. Increased sales do not always lead to increased profits. To be valuable, sales data should be used in conjunction with profit-and-loss statistics.

A retailer's profit-and-loss statements reveal a great deal of information. If profit goals have been set, actual achievements can be measured against these goals. Trends in company success can be determined over time. Profits can be analyzed by store, department, item, and salesperson. A detailed breakdown of profits and losses can show strengths and weaknesses in retail operations and management and can lead to improvements.

Customer billings provide a host of information. A retailer is able to learn about inventory movement, sales made by different personnel, peak selling times, and sales volume. For credit customers, the retailer is able to examine sales by geographic area, outstanding debts, length of repayment time, types of purchases made, and demographic data. Company invoices show the retailer his or her own past purchase history and allow the retailer to evaluate this performance against budgetary or other goals.

Inventory records show the levels of merchandise carried by a retailer throughout the year and the movement of this merchandise. Knowledge of the lead time necessary to place and receive orders from suppliers and of the amounts of safety stock (excess merchandise kept on hand to avoid running out) held at different times during the year aid in inventory planning. These are valuable sources of secondary data.

If the retailer conducts market research, the research report should be retained for future use. When the report is used initially, it is primary data. However, later reference to the report is secondary in nature (because the report is no longer being employed for its "primary" purpose). A thorough report should have some validity in

Table 6-2
Selected Internal Secondary Data Sources

Budgets
Sales figures
Profit-and-loss statements
Customer billings
Inventory records
Prior research reports
Written reports

the future unless conditions change drastically; although, the datedness of the report must be noted.

Written reports are another source of internal secondary data. The reports may be composed by management, buyers, sales personnel, stockroom workers, and so on. Customer attitudes, complaints, suggestions, and problem areas are examples of the kinds of information available through written reports. With proper direction, all phases of retail management can be improved through formal report procedures.

External Secondary Data

After checking internal sources of information, a retailer should consult external secondary data sources if his or her problem has not yet been solved. External secondary data sources are broken down into government and nongovernment categories.

In order to use either form of external secondary data, a retailer must be familiar with the available reference guides. A reference guide contains a listing of written materials on a subject (*Business Periodicals Index* lists important business references) or a wide range of subjects (*Monthly Catalog of United States Government Publications* lists all federal government publications) for a specified time period. Listings within

Table 6-3
Selected Reference Guides to External Secondary Data

ABI/INFORM (data base). Covers 550 journals in business/management. In 300 core journals, all major articles are indexed and abstracted.

Business Periodicals Index. Monthly, except for July. Cumulations quarterly, semiannually, and annually. Subject index of approximately 120 U.S. and British periodicals.

Catalog of U.S. Census Publications. Monthly, with an annual cumulation.

Lorna M. Daniells, *Business Reference Sources* (Boston: Baker Library, 1979); and "Note on Sources of External Marketing Data" (Boston: Harvard Business School, 1980), 9-580-107 (revised June 1984).

Encyclopedia of Associations (Detroit: Gale Research Co., 1980).

Encyclopedia of Business Information Sources (Detroit: Gale Research Co., 1980).

Journal of Marketing. Quarterly. Provides an annotated bibliography arranged by subject.

Management Contents (data base). Indexes and abstracts articles in over 700 business/management periodicals.

Marketing Information Guide. (Garden City, N.Y.: Hoke Communications). Monthly, with a semiannual index. Annotated list of selected marketing material.

Measuring Markets: A Guide to the Use of Federal and State Statistical Data (Washington, D.C.: U.S. Industry and Trade Administration, 1979).

Monthly Catalog of United States Government Publications. Monthly, with subject index. Lists publications of all branches of government.

New York Times Index. Semimonthly with subject index and annual cumulation.

Predicasts F&S Index. Weekly, with monthly, quarterly, and annual cumulations. Covers industries and companies.

Public Affairs Information Service Index. Weekly, with cumulations five times a year and annually. Indexes more than 1,000 periodicals.

Reader's Guide to Periodical Literature. Semimonthly and annual. Indexes over 125 publications.

Martha Farnsworth Riche, "1984 Demographic Services Directory," *American Demographics* (January 1984), pp. 32–41.

Wall Street Journal Index. Monthly, with annual cumulation.

the guides are usually by subject or topic heading. Table 6-3 contains selected reference guides, chosen because of their importance to retailers. These guides include government and nongovernment sources and encompass thousands of publications. They are available in any business library or large library.

The government distributes a wide range of statistics and descriptive materials. Table 6-4 shows some selected government publications. The items detailed in this table should be in any business library or medium-sized library. In their totality, these publications provide a wealth of information on retail trade, consumer profiles, transportation, and so on.

Government agencies, such as the Federal Trade Commission, also provide a variety of pamphlets and booklets on topics like franchising, unit pricing, deceptive advertising, and credit policies. The Small Business Administration helps smaller retailers, providing literature and managerial advice. The pamphlets or booklets are either distributed free of charge or sold for a nominal fee. The *Monthly Catalog of United States Government Publications* contains a listing of these materials.

Nongovernment secondary data come in a variety of forms, most of which are listed in reference guides. Three forms of nongovernment data are noted: regular periodicals; books, monographs, and other nonregular publications; and commercial research houses. Table 6-5 contains a listing of these sources.

The regular periodicals are available in business libraries or via personal subscrip-

Table 6-4
Selected Sources of External Secondary Data: Government

Census of Business, Retail Trade (1982). Statistics for almost 100 store classifications by metropolitan region. Data include multiple ownership, employment, products and services, and sales.

Census of Service Industries (1982). Similar to *Census of Business, Retail Trade* but covers 200 service industries. Data include form of organization, size, geographic area, and reports on specific service industries.

Census of Housing (1980). Statistics on types of structures, appliances, rent paid, race of occupants, size of dwelling, etc., by city block for larger cities.

Census of Population (1980). Population statistics by state, county, city, metropolitan area, and census tract (a highly urban area of 4,000 within a large city). Data include age, income, sex, education, job, etc.

Consumer Expenditure Survey (1980–1981). Survey of consumer expenditures used in revising the Consumer Price Index.

County and City Data Book (Washington, D.C.: Superintendent of Documents, Government Printing Office, 1977). Statistics on population, income, education, etc., for every city and county over 25,000.

Monthly Urban Review. Monthly data from the Bureau of Labor Statistics, including employment, salaries, consumer price index, wholesale price index, etc.

State and Metropolitan Area Data Book (Washington, D.C.: Superintendent of Documents, Government Printing Office, 1981). Statistics of the United States, each state, and each Standard Metropolitan Statistical Area.

Statistical Abstract (Washington, D.C.: Superintendent of Documents, Government Printing Office, annual). The standard annual summary of U.S. statistics.

Survey of Current Business. Monthly, with weekly supplements. On all aspects of business, as reported by the Department of Commerce.

Other. Registration data (births, deaths, automobile registrations, etc.) Available through a variety of federal, state, and local agencies.

Table 6-5
Selected Sources of External Secondary Data: Nongovernment

Regular Periodicals

Advertising Age. Semiweekly magazine of advertising, with applications to retailing.
Business Week. Weekly magazine, with articles on all phases of business.
Catalog Showroom Business. Monthly, on trends in catalog showrooms.
Chain Store Age (Executive Edition). Monthly, catering to chain store information.
Chain Store Age (General Merchandise Edition). Monthly, includes articles on general merchandise retailing.
Direct Marketing. Monthly, articles on direct marketing, direct mail, and promotion.
Discount Merchandising. Monthly, with articles on discount store management.
Drug Store News. Biweekly, with articles on current trends, health and beauty aids, productivity statistics.
Fortune. Semimonthly magazine, with articles on all phases of business.
Journal of Advertising Research. Bimonthly, includes articles on advertising in retailing.
Harvard Business Review. Bimonthly, with articles on all aspects of business.
Journal of Marketing. Quarterly, developments in all areas of marketing.
Journal of Marketing Research. Quarterly, research developments in all areas of marketing.
Journal of Retailing. Quarterly, developments in all aspects of retailing.
Merchandising. Monthly, with articles on appliance and electronics retailing.
Progressive Grocer. Monthly, emphasis on trends in food retailing.
Restaurant Business. Eighteen times per year, developments in restaurant field.
Retail Control. Monthly, with focus on credit, store security, and inventory management.
Sales & Marketing Management. Monthly, of interest to retailers: annual survey of buyer power by county (based on income, retail sales, and population in each county).
Stores. Monthly, with emphasis on department stores, specialty stores, and off-price retailing.
Supermarket Business. Monthly, with articles on supermarket retailing.
Supermarket News. Weekly, includes articles on market share, changes in markets, financial data on supermarket industry.
Women's Wear Daily. Five times per week, emphasis on fashion information.
Other periodicals. Regular publications for retailers in areas such as hardware, supermarket, franchising, furniture, and department stores.

Books, Monographs, and Other Nonregular Publications*

The following publish a variety of information pertaining to retailing:
American Management Association.
American Marketing Association.
Better Business Bureau.
Chamber of Commerce.
Conference Board.
Direct Marketing Association.
Food Marketing Institute.
International Association of Chain Stores.
International Council of Shopping Centers.
International Franchise Association.
Marketing Science Institute.
National Mass Retailing Institute.
National Retail Furniture Association.
National Retail Hardware Association.
National Retail Merchants Association.

Table 6-5 *(continued)*
Selected Sources of External Secondary Data: Nongovernment

Point-of-Purchase Advertising Institute.
Radio Advertising Bureau.
Super Market Institute.

Commercial Data†

More specialized information can be obtained from these private companies:
A. C. Nielsen. Conducts a Retail Index service. Continuous data on food, drug, cosmetic, tobacco, toiletry, other products sold in food stores and drugstores.
Audits and Surveys. Provides a physical audit of merchandise in stores.
Market Research Corporation of America. Examines purchasing behavior via a large consumer panel. Consumer and store data computed.
R. L. Polk. Provides mailing lists and automobile registrations.
Selling Area—Marketing, Inc. (SAMI). Gathers information on the flow of products to retail outlets.
Standard Rate and Data Service. Collects information on advertising rates for various media. Consumer data include income, retail sales, etc.

*Many other sources may be found in any business library.
†This is a sampling of commercial researchers. Others may be found in the classified section of local telephone directories.

tions. Some of the periodicals are quite broad in scope *(Business Week, Fortune, Journal of Marketing)* and discuss a great number of different business topics. Other periodicals are more specialized in their coverage *(Chain Store Age, Journal of Retailing, Stores)* and deal only with topics of concern to retailers. Solutions to a retail problem may be found in both the broad and the narrow publications. However, it is important that readers of periodicals understand the differences in orientation and quality among the various publications.

Regular periodicals contain articles on all aspects of retailing and provide insights for strategy development. Following is a discussion of some examples of the kinds of information found in this literature. These examples are intended to provide an overview of the types of information available and are not exhaustive.

Many aspects of store location are examined in the regularly published literature. Computer-based models for site selection,[2] the drawing power of stores,[3] and store saturation[4] are some of the store location topics that have been researched.

Store management and operations are analyzed. Among the related topics that have been examined in the regularly published literature are the conflicts between

[2]Michael F. Goodchild, "ILACS: A Location-Allocation Model for Retail Site Selection," *Journal of Retailing*, Vol. 60 (Spring 1984), pp. 84–100.
[3]David A. Gautschi, "Specification of Patronage Models for Retail Center Choice," *Journal of Marketing Research*, Vol. 18 (May 1981), pp. 162–174; John R. Nevin and Ruth A. Smith, "The Predictive Accuracy of a Retail Gravitation Model: An Empirical Evaluation," in Kenneth Bernhardt, et al. (Editors), *The Changing Marketing Environment: New Theories and Applications* (Chicago: American Marketing Association, 1981), pp. 27–30; and Glen E. Weisbrod, Robert J. Parcells, and Clifford Kern, "A Disaggregate Model for Predicting Shopping Area Market Attraction," *Journal of Retailing*, Vol. 60 (Spring 1984), pp. 65–83.
[4]Charles A. Ingene and Robert F. Lusch, "Market Selection Decisions for Department Stores," *Journal of Retailing*, Vol. 56 (Fall 1980), pp. 21–40.

shopping center managers and retailers,[5] store managers' perceptions of consumers,[6] employee staffing,[7] employee job satisfaction,[8] and the use of strategic management techniques in retailing.[9]

A broad range of secondary data is available for product and/or service offering decisions. Fashion products and their life cycles,[10] merchandising strategy,[11] expanding financial services in traditional retail stores,[12] product line sales by store type,[13] financial results,[14] and new methods to curb shoplifting[15] are some of the subjects covered in regularly published magazines and journals.

The retailer may find the secondary data on store image and promotion to be helpful. A sampling of the research conducted in this area includes the effects of store displays on sales,[16] store image and positioning,[17] sales promotion,[18] customer relations,[19] and salesperson effectiveness.[20]

Pricing strategies are also described and evaluated in regularly published periodicals. Some illustrations of retail pricing topics examined in articles include the link between advertising and price competition,[21] price deals,[22] product line pricing,[23] and unit pricing.[24]

[5]Leonard J. Konopa and Ronald L. Zallocco, "A Study of Conflict Between Shopping Center Managers and Retailers Within Regional Shopping Centers," *Journal of the Academy of Marketing Science*, Vol. 9 (Summer 1981), pp. 274–287.

[6]Michael F. O'Neill and Del I. Hawkins, "Managerial Bias in Anticipated Images of Competing Shopping Areas," *Journal of Business Research*, Vol. 8 (December 1980), pp. 419–428.

[7]Myron Gable, Karen R. Gillespie, and Martin Topol, "The Current Status of Women in Department Store Retailing: An Update," *Journal of Retailing*, Vol. 60 (Summer 1984), pp. 86–104.

[8]R. Kenneth Teas, "A Test of a Model of Department Store Salespeople's Job Satisfaction," *Journal of Retailing*, Vol. 57 (Spring 1981), pp. 3–25; and J. Patrick Kelly, Myron Gable, and Richard T. Hise, "Conflict, Clarity, Tension, and Satisfaction in Chain Store Manager Roles," *Journal of Retailing*, Vol. 57 (Spring 1981), pp. 27–42.

[9]Glen S. Omura and M. Bixby Cooper, "Three Strategic Planning Techniques for Retailers," *Business*, Vol. 33 (January–March 1983), pp. 2–8.

[10]George B. Sproles, "Analyzing Fashion Life Cycles—Principles and Perspectives," *Journal of Marketing*, Vol. 45 (Fall 1981), pp. 116–124.

[11]Morris Holbrook, "On the Importance of Using Real Products in Research on Merchandising Strategy," *Journal of Retailing*, Vol. 59 (Spring 1983), pp. 4–20.

[12]Marian Burk Rothman, "A New Look at Services," *Stores* (May 1980), pp. 56–57.

[13]Fabian Linden, "Retail 1980: Illusion and Reality," *Across the Board* (January 1981), pp. 61–63.

[14]David P. Schulz, "FOR: Financial and Operating Results," *Stores* (November 1984), p. 5.

[15]Jane Sasseen, "Stopping Roast Rustlers," *Forbes* (May 23, 1983), pp. 58–59.

[16]"Display Effectiveness: An Evaluation," *Nielsen Researcher* (Number 2, 1983), pp. 2–8.

[17]Jacob Jacoby, "Linking Brand and Retailer Images–Do the Potential Risks Outweigh the Potential Benefits?" *Journal of Retailing*, Vol. 60 (Summer 1984), pp. 105–122.

[18]"Sales Promotion," *Advertising Age* (October 25, 1984), pp. 11–47.

[19]"Customer Relations," *Progressive Grocer* (April 1981), pp. 115–116; and Dale R. Harley, "Customer Satisfaction Tracking Improves Sales, Productivity, Morale of Retail Chains," *Marketing News* (June 22, 1984), p. 15.

[20]Alan J. Dubinsky and Steven J. Skinner, "Impact of Job Characteristics on Retail Salespeople's Reactions to Their Jobs," *Journal of Retailing*, Vol. 60 (Summer 1984), pp. 35–62.

[21]Paul W. Farris, "Advertising's Link with Retail Price Competition," *Harvard Business Review*, Vol. 59 (January–February 1981), pp. 40–44; and J. B. Wilkinson, J. Barry Mason, and Christie H. Paksoy," Assessing the Impact of Short-Term Supermarket Strategy Variables," *Journal of Marketing Research*, Vol. 19 (February 1982), pp. 72–86.

[22]Robert C. Blattberg, Gary D. Epen, and Joshua Lieberman, "A Theoretical and Empirical Evaluation of Price Deals for Consumer Durables," *Journal of Marketing*, Vol. 45 (Winter 1981), pp. 116–129.

[23]David J. Reibstein and Herbert Gatignon, "Optimal Product Line Pricing: The Influence of Elasticities and Cross-Elasticities," *Journal of Marketing Research*, Vol. 21 (August 1984), pp. 259–267.

[24]David A. Aaker and Gary T. Ford, "Unit Pricing Ten Years Later: A Replication," *Journal of Marketing*, Vol. 47 (Winter 1983), pp. 118–122.

A number of nonprofit organizations publish books, monographs, and other non-regular literature. Some organizations (American Management Association, American Marketing Association) disseminate information in the hope of increasing the level of knowledge and awareness of their readers. Other organizations (Better Business Bureau, Chamber of Commerce) are interested in improving the public's image of business and in self-governance by industry. These associations distribute literature to acquaint companies with efficient and legal practices. Yet another type of organization (National Retail Merchants Association) functions as a retail spokesperson and lobbyist, fighting for practices in the best interests of retailers. This association sends out information about current practices and new developments in retailing.

Each of these organizations publishes and distributes materials for a nominal fee or free of charge. In addition to the groups listed in Table 6-5, numerous other retail associations exist, and these can be discovered through contact with the National Retail Merchants Association.

The last external secondary data source is the commercial research house that conducts ongoing studies and makes the results of these studies available to many clients for a fee. The fee can be quite low, or it can range into the thousands of dollars, depending on the complexity of the problem. This type of research is secondary when the retailer acts as a subscriber and does not request specific studies pertaining only to his or her company.

Several of the large commercial houses that specialize in secondary data for retailers are shown in Table 6-5. The companies provide a host of subscription services at much lower costs (and probably with greater expertise) than the retailer would incur if the data were collected only for his or her primary use.

Primary Data Sources

Advantages and Disadvantages of Primary Data

After a retailer has exhausted the available secondary data, his or her problem may still not be solved. In this instance, primary data (those collected for the solution of the specific problem at hand) are necessary. In cases where secondary data research is sufficient, primary data are not collected.

There are several advantages of primary data. They are collected to fit the specific purposes of the retailer. The units of measure and the data categories are also designed to satisfy the problem under investigation. The data are current. In addition, the retailer either personally collects the data or hires an outside party for the study. Therefore, the source is known and controlled, and the methodology is constructed for the specific study. There are no conflicting data from different sources, and the reliability of the research can be determined, if desired. When secondary data do not solve the problem, the collection and analysis of primary data is the only alternative.

There are several disadvantages of primary data. They are more expensive to obtain than secondary data. The collection is more time consuming. Some types of information cannot be acquired by an individual retailer. If only primary data are collected, the perspective may be limited. In some cases, irrelevant information is collected when the retailer does not state the problem specifically enough.

A retailer who desires information for solving a problem has many criteria to consider when evaluating the use of primary data. Specificity, currentness, and reliability are weighed against high costs, time, and limited access to materials. Benefits of research must be weighed against the costs.

In the following subsection, a diversity of primary data sources for retailers is explained.

Sources of Primary Data

The first decision to be made in the collection of primary data is who will undertake it. A retailer can personally gather the data (internal) or hire a research company (external). Internal data collection is usually quicker and cheaper. External data collection is usually more objective and formalized.

Second, a sampling methodology is specified. Instead of gathering data from all stores, all products, all customers, and so on, a retailer can obtain accurate information by studying a sample of stores, products, or customers. Sampling saves time and money.

There are two broad sampling approaches: probability and nonprobability. In a probability (random) sample, every store, product, or customer has an equal or known probability of being chosen for study. In a nonprobability sample, the stores, products, or customers are chosen by the researcher because of judgment or convenience. The probability sample is more accurate but is also more costly and difficult to undertake. A further discussion of sampling is beyond the scope of this book.

Third, the retailer must choose among four basic types of primary data collection: survey, observation, experiment, and simulation. All of these methods are capable of generating data for each of the elements of a retail strategy.

Survey

The **survey** is a research technique with which information is systematically gathered from respondents by communicating with them. A survey may be conducted in person, over the telephone, or via the mail. In almost all cases, a questionnaire is used.

A personal survey is face-to-face, flexible, and able to elicit lengthy responses. In addition, any ambiguity in the questionnaire can be explained. It is expensive, and interviewer bias is possible (the interviewer may affect the results by suggesting ideas to the respondent). A telephone survey is fast and relatively inexpensive. Responses are usually short, and nonresponse may be a problem. It must be verified that the desired respondent is contacted. A mail survey can reach a wide range of respondents, has no interviewer bias, and is relatively inexpensive. Slowness of return and participation by incorrect respondents are the major problems. Each of the survey techniques may suffer from nonresponse, although this is most true of a mail survey. The technique that is chosen depends upon the objectives and the needs of the research project.

The retailer must also decide whether the survey is to be nondisguised or disguised. In a **nondisguised survey,** the respondent is told the real purpose of the study. In a **disguised survey,** the respondent is not told the real purpose of the study. For example, it may be inappropriate to divulge the purpose of the study or its sponsor if a retailer is interested in the consumer's perception of the store's image. Otherwise, the respondent may answer what he or she thinks the interviewer wants to hear.

Survey techniques are used in a variety of retail settings, as the following illustrations will show. Figures 6-2 and 6-3 show two nondisguised surveys. A movie theater owner uses the questions in Figure 6-2 to determine the market's behavior and atti-

A Survey on Behavior and Attitudes Toward Movies

1. Do you ever go out to see a movie? ☐ Yes
☐ No

IF NO, PLEASE DO NOT ANSWER ANY MORE QUESTIONS.

2. During the year, about how many movies do you go to see? _____

3. Please rank your movie preferences. Let 1 be your favorite type of movie and 6 your least favorite.

☐ Comedy   ☐ Musical

☐ Drama   ☐ Mystery

☐ Love Story ☐ Science Fiction

4. Please describe why you go out to see a movie.

_____

_____

_____

_____

5. Please rank the factors you consider in the selection of a movie theater. Let 1 be the most important factor and 7 the least important.

☐ Cleanliness of Theater
☐ Location of Theater
☐ The Movie Playing at the Theater
☐ Parking
☐ Refreshments
☐ Ticket Prices
☐ Time Schedule of the Theater

6. Are there any reasons why you do not go to see more movies?

☐ Yes

☐ No

IF YES, PLEASE EXPLAIN.

_____

_____

_____

Figure 6-2

An Attitudinal Survey for a Department Store

Please indicate how you feel about each of the following statements describing Macy's Department Store. For each statement, indicate your level of agreement or disagreement by checking the appropriate space. We are interested in your honest opinions about Macy's.

	Strongly agree	Agree	Neither agree nor disagree	Disagree	Strongly disagree
1. Macy's has a wide assortment of items.	___	___	___	___	___
2. The products carried are of high quality.	___	___	___	___	___
3. Macy's is very dependable.	___	___	___	___	___
4. The employees are quite helpful.	___	___	___	___	___
5. Prices are high.	___	___	___	___	___
6. Macy's is old-fashioned.	___	___	___	___	___
7. Delivery service is prompt and reliable.	___	___	___	___	___
8. The displays in the store are confusing.	___	___	___	___	___
9. Macy's is a friendly store.	___	___	___	___	___
10. When Macy's runs a sale, real bargains can be found.	___	___	___	___	___

Figure 6-3

tudes. The questions in Figure 6-3 are used to ascertain the attitudes of shoppers toward Macy's. In both surveys, the respondents (those answering the questions) are told the real purposes of the studies, and questionnaire forms are used to enter responses.

Disguised surveys are used to gather information about consumer attitudes or personalities without revealing the true intent of the studies. These surveys may utilize word associations, sentence completions, cartoon analysis, and/or questions. Figure

Picture Analysis for a Restaurant

Figure 6-4

6-4 contains an example of a picture analysis study. The respondent is asked to describe the woman and the restaurant represented in the picture. The respondent is not told that the answer actually describes herself.[25]

The **semantic differential** (a list of bipolar adjective scales) is a survey technique that may be disguised or nondisguised, depending on whether the respondent is told the true purpose of the study. In the semantic differential, a respondent is asked to rate a store(s) on several criteria. Each criterion is evaluated along a bipolar adjective scale, such as good–bad or clean–dirty. By computing the average rating of all respondents for each criterion, an overall store profile can be developed.

An example of a semantic differential appears in Figure 6-5. Store A is a prestige, high-quality furniture store, and Store B is a medium-quality, family-run furniture store. The semantic differential reveals the overall images of each furniture retailer and graphically portrays them.

Another survey research tool that is becoming popular is **multidimensional scaling.** For this type of research, attitudinal data are collected so that an overall store rating can be developed (rather than a profile of several individual characteristics). A statistical

[25]Adapted from Burton H. Marcus, "Image Variation and the Multi-unit Establishment," *Journal of Retailing,* Vol. 48 (Summer 1972), pp. 29–43.

A Semantic Differential for Two Furniture Stores

Please check the blanks that best indicate your feelings about Stores A and B.

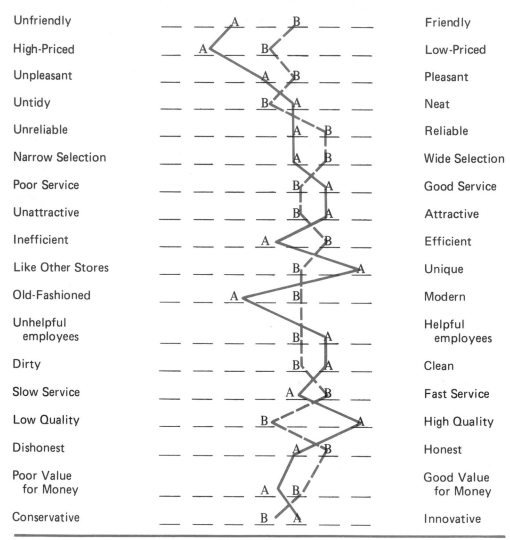

Unfriendly	Friendly
High-Priced	Low-Priced
Unpleasant	Pleasant
Untidy	Neat
Unreliable	Reliable
Narrow Selection	Wide Selection
Poor Service	Good Service
Unattractive	Attractive
Inefficient	Efficient
Like Other Stores	Unique
Old-Fashioned	Modern
Unhelpful employees	Helpful employees
Dirty	Clean
Slow Service	Fast Service
Low Quality	High Quality
Dishonest	Honest
Poor Value for Money	Good Value for Money
Conservative	Innovative

Figure 6-5

description of this technique is beyond the scope of the text,[26] but Figure 6-6 shows how multidimensional scaling can be used to construct single overall ratings. In this

[26]For good discussions on multidimensional scaling in retailing, see Ricardo Singson, "Multidimensional Scaling Analysis of Store Image and Shopping Behavior," *Journal of Retailing*, Vol. 51 (Summer 1975), pp. 38–52ff; Raj Arora, "Consumer Involvement in Retail Store Positioning," *Journal of the Academy of Marketing Science*, Vol. 10 (Spring 1982), pp. 109–124; and Pradeep K. Korgaonkar and Kamal El Sheshai, "Assessing Retail Competition with Multidimensional Scaling," *Business*, Vol. 32 (April–June 1982), pp. 30–33.

Multidimensional Scaling Applied to Drugstores

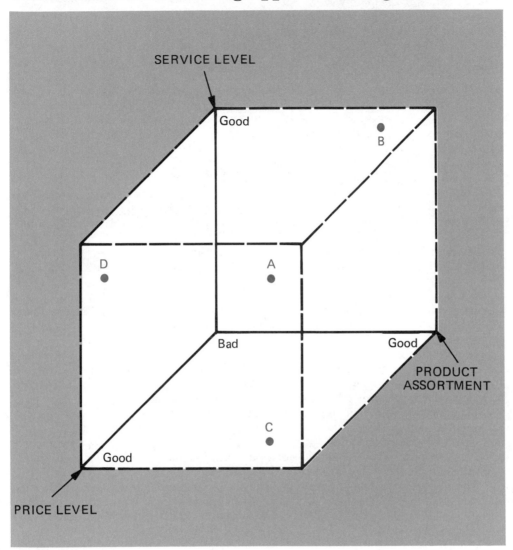

Figure 6-6

example, service level, product assortment, and price level are the major criteria used in establishing profiles for four competing drugstores. These ratings define the consumer's perceptions of each store, show the strengths and weaknesses of each store, and aid in strategy development and modification.

From Figure 6-6, these conclusions can be reached. Drugstore A is rated as good on all three criteria; it is the best liked store. Drugstore B is equal to A in terms of service level and product assortment; it is viewed as having high (bad) prices. Drugstore C is equal to A in terms of product assortment and price level; it is viewed as providing bad service. Drugstore D is equal to A in terms of service level and price level; it is viewed as having a bad product assortment. Drugstores B, C, and D need to improve their strategies to compete with A.

Other types of survey techniques also can be utilized, but those described here should provide the reader with a sense of the usefulness of this primary data procedure.

Observation

Observation is a form of research in which present behavior or the results of past behavior are observed and recorded. People are not questioned. Observation does not require the cooperation of respondents, and interviewer or question biases are minimized. In many instances, observation is used in actual situations, eliminating the influences of artificial environments. The major disadvantage of using observation (by itself) is that attitudes cannot be obtained.

Examples of the use of observation by retailers include: determining the quality of sales personnel presentations (through use of a mystery shopper), measuring related item buying by consumers, determining store activity (by time of day and day of week), traffic counts (to measure new locations), and determining the proportion of shopping-center patrons using public transportation.

When a retailer utilizes observation, several decisions are necessary: natural or contrived, disguised or nondisguised, structured or unstructured, direct or indirect, and observers or mechanical devices.

Natural observation occurs when a person is viewed entering, shopping in, and leaving a store. Contrived observation takes place when observers pose as customers to determine a salesperson's "pitch" or a special display is set up for the observation of shoppers' reactions.

In disguised observation, the shopper is not aware that he or she is being watched. A two-way mirror or hidden camera provides disguised observation. With nondisguised observation, the participant knows that he or she is being observed. An example would be a department manager's observing the sales behavior of an employee.

Structured observation requires the observer to watch for and note specific behavior. Unstructured observation demands that the observer watch and note all actions performed by the person under study. An example of unstructured observation is a drugstore researcher's watching the total purchasing behavior of customers to determine the actions they take and the items they buy.

The observer watches the present behavior of people in direct observation. The observer examines evidence of past behavior in indirect observation. Litter in garbage dumps and food cans in consumer pantries are examples of items that would be analyzed via indirect observation.

Human observation is natural and may be disguised, but the observer may record biased notations or interpretations, and may miss behavior. Mechanical observation eliminates viewer bias and does not miss any behavior. A movie camera that films in-store behavior is an example of mechanical observation.

Experiment

An **experiment** is a type of research in which one or more factors are manipulated under controlled conditions. A factor may be price, store layout, a shelf display, or store hours. In an experiment, just the factor under investigation is manipulated; all other factors remain constant. For example, if a retailer is interested in finding out the effects of a price change on item sales, only the price factor is varied (e.g., make this week's price $0.99, next week's $1.19, then compare unit sales for each week). The other elements of the retail strategy remain the same. This way, only the effect of the price change is measured.

An experiment may utilize survey or observation techniques to record information. In a survey, questions are asked about the experiment: How does A differ from B? Did you buy product A because of its new shelf display? Are you buying extra ice cream because it's on sale? In an observation, behavior is observed during the experiment: the sales of product X increased by 20 per cent when a new display was used; ice cream sales went up by 25 per cent during a special sale.

Survey and observation techniques are experimental if they take place under controlled conditions. When a survey asks broad attitudinal questions or observation of unstructured behavior occurs, an experimental procedure is not being utilized. In a retail setting, an experiment is difficult to undertake because many factors beyond the control of the retailer (such as weather, competition, and the economy) may influence the results. On the other hand, a well-controlled experiment is quite accurate.

The major advantage of an experiment is its ability to show cause and effect (e.g., a lower price equals higher sales). It is also systematically structured and implemented. The major disadvantages are high costs, contrived settings, and uncontrollable factors.

Simulation

Simulation is a type of experiment defined as "the act of creating a complex model to resemble a real process or system, and running and experimenting with the model in the hope of learning something about the real system."[27] To phrase this in simple terms, simulation is a computer-based technique that manipulates retailing factors on paper rather than in a real setting. A model of the controllable and uncontrollable factors (and their interactions) facing the retailer is constructed. These factors are then manipulated via a computer to determine their effects on the overall retail strategy. Simulation will become more popular for retailers as their level of mathematical and computer sophistication increases.

Further discussion of this research tool is beyond the scope of this text. The concept has been introduced to show its availability and utility. It is somewhat difficult to use. However, no consumer cooperation is needed, and many different factors and combinations of factors can be manipulated.

The Retail Information System

As stated earlier in the chapter, retailers should not approach marketing research as a one-shot solution to a single problem. Rather, the collection of useful information should be viewed as an ongoing, well-integrated process or system. A **retail information system** anticipates the information needs of retail managers; collects, organizes, and stores relevant data on a continuous basis; and directs the flow of information to the proper retail decision makers.

[27]Philip Kotler and Randall L. Schultz, "Marketing Simulations: Review and Prospect," *Journal of Business*, Vol. 43 (July 1970), p. 238.

A Retail Information System

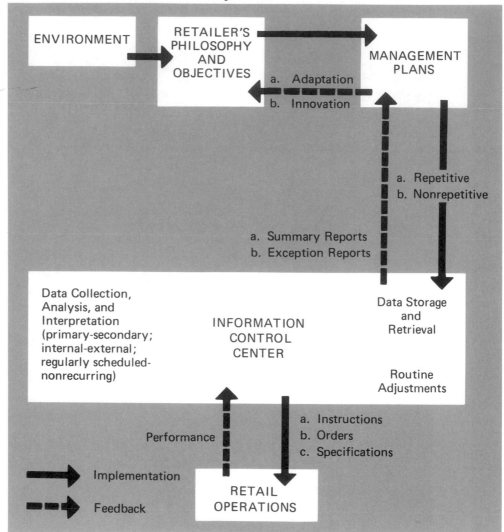

Source: Adapted from Fremont E. Kast and James E. Rosenzweig, *Organization and Management: A Systems and Contingency Approach*, Third Edition (New York: McGraw-Hill, 1979), p. 356. Reprinted by permission.

Figure 6-7

Figure 6-7 presents a retail information system. In this system, a retailer begins with the determination of his or her business philosophy and objectives. The philosophy and objectives are influenced by the environment (such as competitors, economy, and government).

The retailer's philosophy and objectives provide very broad guidelines, which direct management planning. Some management plans are repetitive (routine) and in the long run may require little re-evaluation. Other plans are nonrepetitive (nonroutine) and will require careful evaluation each time they arise.

Once the retail strategy is outlined, the data needed to implement it are collected, analyzed, and interpreted. If the data are already available, they are retrieved from storage in the company's files. Exact instructions, orders, and specifications are then determined and put into operation.

After the retailer starts operating, performance results are fed back into the information center and evaluated against preset standards. Data are retrieved from files, or further data are collected. Routine adjustments are implemented immediately. Summary reports and exception reports (explanations of deviations from expected performance) are sent to top management. When necessary, the retailer adapts to performance results in a way that affects his or her philosophy or objectives (such as changing the store's image). An innovative reaction may also require a change in philosophy or objectives (such as sacrificing short-run profits to introduce a new, computerized checkout counter).

All types of information remain stored in the information control center for future and ongoing use. The control center is integrated into the short-run and long-run planning and operations of the company. Information is not gathered sporadically and haphazardly. It is gathered systematically, consistent with management objectives, plans, and operations.

Having a retail information system offers several advantages. First, information collection is organized and broad in perspective. Second, data are continuously collected and stored before a crisis occurs (when time is limited). Third, the elements of retail strategy can be coordinated. Fourth, new strategies are developed more quickly. Fifth, quantitative results are obtainable, and cost-benefit analysis can be conducted. However, developing a retail information system is not easy. It requires high initial time and manpower investments. Complex decision making is necessary.[28]

As computer technology has become both more sophisticated and less expensive, greater numbers of retailers (of all types) have developed comprehensive information systems. For example, in 1978, only about 200 supermarkets used computerized scanning systems; by 1986, over 11,000 supermarkets (representing 50 per cent of total grocery store sales) will have installed such systems.[29] In the mid-1970s, the computerized systems were used only to reduce clerical cashier errors and improve inventory control. Today, the systems form the foundations for retail information systems and are involved with consumer surveys, ordering, transfers of merchandise between stores, and other diverse activities.

A recent major study of retailers with annual sales of $1 million or more revealed these characteristics about retail information systems:

- Many information systems fall under the jurisdiction of the financial area of the retailer.
- A formal, written annual plan is often produced for information systems departments.
- Microcomputers are used by most companies using information systems analysis.
- Retailers spend between 0.5 and 1.5 per cent of sales on their information systems efforts.
- Substantial growth in the use of retail information systems is expected.[30]

---

[28]See Fitzhugh L. Corr, "Scanners in Marketing Research: Paradise (Almost)," *Marketing News* (January 4, 1985), pp. 1, 15.
[29]"Scanning for Dollars," *Chain Store Age Executive* (July 1983), p. 80.
[30]"POS Applications: Retail Checklist," *Stores* (June 1984), pp. 82, 84.

Table 6-6
Retail Information Systems Efforts Planned for Development or Improvement Between 1984 and 1986

| | Per Cent of Firms Planning to Develop or Improve Systems* | | | | | | | |
| | By Sales | | | By Type of Store | | | | |
Types of Systems	Under $100 Million	$100–500 Million	Over $500 Million	Mass Merch. Stores	Dept. Stores	Specialty Stores	Comb./ Grocery Stores	All Partici-pants
Point of sales	62	51	73	75	36	61	64	58
Distribution	42	49	59	45	36	51	64	48
Purchase order management	73	59	41	45	64	61	64	58
Sales reporting/analysis	54	24	36	30	23	49	18	35
Financial planning	23	22	23	40	23	19	9	23
General ledger	46	32	18	40	27	35	9	31
Accounts payable	42	37	23	35	32	40	18	34
Accounts receivable	4	12	9	10	18	5	0	8
Inventory control	69	56	55	55	64	70	27	60
Stock replenishment	58	54	46	65	50	51	46	53
Payroll	12	22	18	20	14	12	36	17
Human resources/ personnel	8	34	36	40	32	7	64	26
Store level (in-store systems)	46	34	68	45	41	44	64	46
Other	12	2	18	10	0	14	0	8
None	0	0	0	0	0	2	0	1

*This was a multiple response question. Totals will not equal 100%.

Source: "POS Applications: Retail Wishlist," Stores (June 1984), p. 82. Copyright National Retail Merchants Association 1984. Reprinted by permission.

Table 6-6 shows the expectations of the retailers regarding their continuing development and improvement of information systems during the period 1984–86. There are many differences among retailers on the basis of sales and type of stores operated.

The development of retail information systems can be divided into two categories: food and general merchandise. Food retailers rely on the Universal Product Code (UPC) system. Under the UPC system, products are marked with thick and thin vertical lines, which represent each product's inventory code. The lines are read by optical scanning equipment at the checkout counter. Information can be stored and monitored on an item-by-item and store-by-store basis.

These systems are being used by both large and small retailers, as these two examples show. Giant Food is a major supermarket chain headquartered in Washington, D.C. Through a UPC-based system, its computers are linked directly to its distribution network. As a result, Giant saves about $1.6 million in ordering costs annually.[31] Dick's Supermarkets is a chain of five stores in Wisconsin that installed electronic cash registers in all its units in 1975; it has upgraded the system regularly since then. Dick's now uses an IBM System 36 computer network. Because of its system, Dick's

[31]J. Barry Mason and Morris L. Mayer, "Retail Merchandise Information Systems for the 1980's," *Journal of Retailing*, Vol. 56 (Spring 1980), pp. 64–65.

has been able to conduct frequent experiments (e.g., what size of an item sells best?) and increase sales and profits significantly.[32]

In general, food retailers expect their information systems to provide better merchandising information, better pricing information, improved inventory controls, more information on consumer tastes and characteristics, faster checkouts, increased store and labor productivity, and a reduction in incorrectly rung up purchases.[33]

Commercial research houses are offering many services to food retailers based on UPC information, such as BehaviorScan by Information Resources, Inc., and ScanTrack by A. C. Nielsen.[34] Both of these services report sales, prices, store characteristics, and consumer household information for products within UPC categories using data gathered from selected grocery stores that utilize electronic cash registers. BehaviorScan also conducts more intensive research, because its consumers receive all their television programming through a cable hookup and this behavior can be monitored.

The Optical Character Recognition (OCR-A) system has been developed for nonfood retailers. In an OCR-A system, product information and a computer strip are placed on the price tags attached to products. This information is readable by both humans and machines. One very extensive OCR-A-based system is operated by J. C. Penney. Most of its items are OCR-A marked; and all credit-card sales are routed through terminals. With its system, J. C. Penney operates a merchandise management cycle, provides reports for all levels of management, stores data for every sales transaction, and monitors sales and inventory by product category.[35]

While OCR-A is intended as a universal system, it has not received the acceptance level of the UPC system. Less than 30 per cent of department stores use an OCR-A system; the figure is much lower for other types of stores.[36] A number of nonfood retailers have developed their own product coding systems using multipart tags (such as the type made by Kimball) rather than rely on OCR-A. They believe OCR-A to be too limiting, do not want vendors to print OCR-A tags with preset retail prices, need a mechanism for revising selling prices, and have found the OCR-A and UPC systems to be incompatible (since some general merchandise retailers also sell food items).

For example, Woolworth has implemented a visual electronic ordering (VEO) system in 1,250 stores. This system allows hand-held scanning wands to read bar-coded product labels adhered to display counters. Through the VEO system, Woolworth has reduced order turnaround time from two weeks to five days.[37] County Seat, a large Minneapolis-based apparel chain, has electronic point-of-sales terminals in each store. The terminals process data on unit sales, prices, credits, shipments, physical inventory counts, exchanges and returns, price changes, employee discounts, and payroll hours. The system monitors millions of stock numbers and prints over 200 reports. County

[32]Michael Friedman, "ScanLab Scores with Scan Data at Store Level," *Chain Store Age Executive* (July 1984), pp. 106, 111–113.

[33]"Hard Savings an MIS Statistic Now," *Chain Store Age Executive* (October 1980), pp. 50, 57; "New NRMA Study Documents POS Benefits," *Stores* (March 1982), pp. 14–16; and "Supermarket Sales Manual: 1984," *Progressive Grocer* (July 1984), p. 41.

[34]Robert E. O'Neill, "How to Sell Your Scanning Data," *Progressive Grocer* (February 1983), pp. 63–67; Scott Hume, "BehaviorScan Links Purchasing, TV Viewing," *Advertising Age* (January 2, 1984), p. 33; and Kevin Higgins, "High-Tech Research Firm Is Hit with Advertisers and Investors," *Marketing News* (March 2, 1984), pp. 1, 28.

[35]Marian Burk Rothman, "Making It Work," *Stores* (October 1980), pp. 38–39; and "New Possibilities for POS," *Chain Store Age Executive* (January 1984), p. 57.

[36]"This Magic Wand Is Slightly Bent," *Sales & Marketing Management* (September 12, 1983), pp. 24, 26.

[37]"Woolworth's Wanding Is Made to Order," *Chain Store Age Executive* (April 1984), p. 52.

Seat also receives information about fashion planning, activity by market, stock-on-hand comparisons by store, and an exception report on forecasting errors.[38]

Altman's, Bamberger's, Mervyn's, Sears, Montgomery Ward, and Strawbridge & Clothier are among other retailers who are using retail information systems.[39] OCR-A and UPC systems are discussed further in Chapter 11 ("Merchandise Planning and Management: Financial").

Marketing Research in Retailing: A Summary

The successful development and implementation of a retailing strategy depends on good information. The use of sound marketing research techniques (the systematic collection and analysis of data related to retail strategy) enables a retailer to generate good information. Retailers who rely only on intuition increase their probabilities of failure.

Marketing research is comprised of several steps: problem definition, secondary data search, collection of primary data (if necessary), analysis of data, recommendations, and implementation of findings.

Secondary data offer several advantages: they are inexpensive, can be collected quickly, have several sources, and may provide otherwise unattainable information. Some sources are quite credible (believable). And when the problem is ill defined, a secondary data search can clarify it. There are several disadvantages to secondary data. They may not suit the purposes of the study. The units of measurement and the categories of data may not be specific enough. Information may be dated and/or inaccurate. The source may be disreputable, and several sources may offer conflicting results. In addition, the data may not be reliable.

Secondary data should always be consulted before primary data. Internal secondary data come from company sources. External secondary data come from sources outside the company. These data are available from government and nongovernment sources. Reference guides, regularly published periodicals, nonregular publications, and commercial research firms are external secondary data sources.

Primary data have several advantages. They are specific and current. The data are collected and categorized with the measures desired. The methodology is known. There are no conflicting data. The level of reliability can be determined. When secondary data do not exist, primary data are the only alternative. The disadvantages of primary data are costs, time, limited access, narrow perspective, and irrelevant information.

Primary research may be done internally or externally. Four types of primary data collection are available: survey (personal, telephone, or mail), observation (natural-contrived, observer-mechanical), experiment, and simulation. Each technique has its advantages and disadvantages.

The retail information system is an integrated, ongoing structure that directs the flow of information. Research should not be viewed as a one-time occurrence, but as a continuous process. Increasingly, retailers are developing and implementing information systems.

---

[38]"More Data, Faster: County Seat," *Stores* (March 1981), pp. 56–58.
[39]See David Schulz, "New Functions," *Stores* (March 1984), pp. 68, 70; and "Series/1s Lay a POS Foundation at Ward," *Retail Technology* (January 1985), Section Two, pp. 4, 8.

Questions for Discussion

1. Define *marketing research.* How would you define *retailing research?*
2. At the beginning of this chapter, several unsuccessful strategies were described. What types of research would you recommend for each of the retailers?
   a. Movie theater
   b. Toy store
   c. Chain bookstore
   d. Mail-order retailer
   e. Florist
3. What are the steps in the research process? May any of these steps be skipped?
4. Explain the advantages and disadvantages of secondary data.
5. What are the major sources of internal secondary data? What kinds of information are available from these sources?
6. How may a retailer use reference guides?
7. What types of information are available from government sources?
8. Distinguish among regular periodicals, nonregular publications, and commercial data sources.
9. Under what circumstances should a retailer collect primary data?
10. Why would a retailer want to use a disguised survey?
11. How do Figure 6-5 (semantic differential) and Figure 6-6 (multidimensional scaling) differ?
12. Under what circumstances would the following types of observations be utilized?
    a. Contrived
    b. Nondisguised
    c. Unstructured
    d. Indirect
13. What is a retail information system?
14. Why do you think that smaller retailers have not yet adopted the retail information system in great numbers?
15. What can result if a retailer does not use research?

CASES

1. Arco: Using Marketing Research as a Basis for Changing a Customer Credit Policy*

In the early 1980s, the Atlantic Richfield Company (ARCO) found the overall consumer demand for gasoline to be declining due to a combination of higher prices, personal conservation, and government-mandated automotive fuel-economy improvements. According to its senior vice-president of marketing: "When you have

*The material in this case is drawn from George H. Babikian, "How Arco Used Marketing Research to Go 'Cash Only in a Plastic Society'," *Marketing News* (January 6, 1984), Section 1, pp. 1, 27.

decreasing demand, you have excess capacity in a shrinking market. That spells trauma."

As a result, Arco undertook an examination of its credit-card operation to determine if a change in policy would enable it to reduce its costs to be more competitive with self-service stations and with low-price, high-volume independent gas chains (those not owned by oil producers). At the time Arco conducted its research, credit costs were its second largest gas station expense item (after payroll) at $73 million a year (nearly 9 cents per gallon) and increasing.

Through research, Arco identified the five alternative strategies shown in Table 1 to lower credit costs. After analyzing the results of its own data collection and a study completed by Opinion Research Corporation, Arco concluded that two-thirds of the gasoline-buying public never used credit cards and that only one-sixth of the gasoline-buying public could be defined as dedicated credit users. Accordingly, Arco decided to adopt alternative 5 in Table 1—a cash-only policy.

Arco's cash-only policy resulted in lost sales shortly after introduction. Marketing research found that the firm was not doing a good job in presenting its low-price message to consumers. Arco then revised its commercials, using the theme "Don't 'buy' gasoline, 'shop' for gas. You could be missing a bargain." This message proved effective, and sales per station and national market share rose considerably.

Arco is now conducting additional research on consumer pricing. For example, a recent study revealed that half of the people who use full-service gas stations do not have any idea what they pay for gas or what the service is costing them.

Table 1
Arco's Strategy Options to Lower Credit Costs

1. *A bank credit card dedicated to gasoline-buying purposes.* While consumers indicate they would utilize such a card, the plan would only partially reduce credit costs. The program would also require a major marketing campaign to implement.

2. *Regular bank credit cards and travel-and-entertainment credit cards.* Marketing research shows consumers would resist using these cards for gasoline purchases. The cards would not encourage brand loyalty. Arco dealers would still have to pay a service fee on these cards.

3. *A dual-pricing or discount-for-cash program.* In this plan credit-card users would pay higher prices for the use of this service. This is confusing to customers; and many consumers would avoid buying gas on credit.

4. *An annual fee for credit-card usage.* Marketing research shows that more than 80 per cent of Arco cardholders would cancel their credit cards if a $20 yearly fee is charged. Two-thirds of cardholders say they would cancel their credit cards even if the $20 fee would result in lower gasoline prices.

5. *A cash-only policy which eliminates credit cards.* Two-thirds of Arco's credit customers say they would stay with Arco if a 3-cent-a-gallon savings would be passed on to them due to the elimination of credit.

Questions

1. What secondary data sources could Arco have used to gather further information on the credit alternatives contained in Table 1?
2. Develop a semantic differential that could be used to compare Arco with gas stations offering credit for their customers.
3. Describe how observation could be used to evaluate consumer willingness to pay more for credit. What are the benefits of natural, disguised observation in this situation?
4. What types of information on pricing should Arco have in its retail information system? Explain how this information would be compiled, stored, and retrieved.

2. World of Shoes: Learning from Industry and Company Data

Dan Bell owns and operates a chain of fifty shoe stores, with headquarters in Los Angeles, California. All of the stores operate under the World of Shoes name and are located in regional shopping centers. The stores cater to the whole family: men, women, and children. In 1985, chainwide sales exceeded $12 million for the first time. Nationally, retail sales of footwear were more than $25 billion in 1985.

A typical World of Shoes store occupies 2,500 square feet of space, with 1,500 square feet devoted to selling. It competes with two to three department stores, half a dozen shoe stores, and assorted other stores (e.g., variety stores, clothing stores, sporting goods stores) in each regional shopping center. The assortment of shoes and accessories, such as socks and shoe care products, is extensive. Prices are moderate to low, and compare quite favorably to competitors'.

World of Shoes features a self-service format, similar to that used by Fayva. Sales personnel are available to answer questions, replace stock, and receive payment. The self-service approach keeps prices low and encourages browsing. It is a mass-market oriented strategy, which relies on extensive television and newspaper advertising.

As the chain has expanded, Bell has become increasingly dissatisfied with the information available to him for planning and evaluation. Accordingly, he has launched a three-step program to improve the quality and quantity of information for World of Shoes.

First, Bell established a three-person marketing research department at company headquarters. The department is responsible for assembling internal data, conducting research studies, and monitoring the published data of organizations such as the American Footwear Industries Association and the National Retail Merchants Association. The department recently presented its initial major findings, a comparison of World of Shoes operations with those of the industry. See Table 1.

Second, a computerized cash-register system is being installed. Each shoe store is to receive two electronic cash registers, which have the capacity to record sales, compute inventory levels, determine unit sales and average sales, and enact many other functions. Data will be collected, analyzed, and distributed to individual stores through the office of the vice-president of merchandising. Bell hopes to be able to fully apply the system by the end of 1986.

Table 1
The Retail Shoe Industry in the Western United States, 1985

	World of Shoes	Department Stores	Family Shoe Stores
Sales per store	$240,000	$200,000	$190,000
Sales per square foot of selling space	$160	$145	$150
Per cent of sales to			
Men	20	15	25
Women	65	75	55
Children	15	10	20
Average prices for shoes			
Men	$38	$45	$43
Women	$35	$43	$38
Children	$20	$25	$22
Inventory turnover	Moderate	Low	Moderate
Stock shortages (% of sales)	2.0	1.2	1.0
Gross margin (% of sales)	30	40	40
Net profit (% of sales)	7	6	8

Third, Dan Bell has just hired an outside consultant to set up a retail information system for the World of Shoes. Bell wants the information system to include internal data by store unit, special reports and research projects, government and trade association data, vendor specifications and data, employee records, and company forecasts.

Questions

1. Evaluate Bell's overall plan and each of the specific elements for improving the information capability of World of Shoes.
2. Analyze the data in Table 1. What are the implications for World of Shoes?
3. If Dan Bell hired you as the consultant to set up a retail information system, what steps would you follow?
4. Develop a retail information system flowchart that includes the data requested by Bell. [Sources of data and output.]

Choosing a Store Location: Trading-Area Analysis

Chapter Objectives

1. To examine the importance of store location for a retailer
2. To analyze the major factors involved in selecting a trading area
3. To study the various sources of data available for trading-area analysis
4. To describe different methods of evaluating trading areas and store saturation

Ames Department Stores operates about 175 full-line discount stores in eleven states from Main to Virginia. Since Ames intends to increase the number of stores in its chain by 10 per cent each year for the "forseeable future," selecting proper store locations is essential. Accordingly, Ames now uses a computerized system to analyze trading areas.

Ames' system was developed in several stages. First, the trading areas surrounding existing stores were defined geographically by zip code. Demographic information on population size, income, number of households, occupations, education, and so on were acquired from Donnelly Marketing Information Services. Second, Ames outlined the trading-area profiles for successful stores. Third, Ames provided Control Data Business Information Services with detailed internal and external data; these data were processed by Control Data using a computerized statistical program. Fourth, each new broad trading area that Ames considers is evaluated by the computer model, which generates a four-page report.

Not only are Ames' executives able to pinpoint good trading areas through the computer system, they are also able to ascertain the type of store that would do best in a particular trading area: "We've developed a system that scans our data base and tells us which of our store models is most similar to others in that market. Our competitors don't have anything like that because we developed that capability ourselves."[1]

Overview

One of the most crucial decisions a retailer makes involves the selection of a store location. This chapter and Chapter 8 explain why store location is so critical and describe the steps a retailer should take when choosing a location for his or her store and deciding whether to build, lease, or purchase facilities.

The Importance of Location to a Retailer

The importance of store location to a retailer cannot be overestimated. Whereas a good location can minimize the problems caused by certain merchandising deficiencies, a poor location can be such a liability that even the most able merchant is unable to overcome it.[2]

The selection of a store location requires extensive decision making because of its long-term nature and large investment requirements. Leases of five years or less are common in poorer retailing locations, but leases in good shopping centers or shopping district locations are usually at least ten years. It is not uncommon for a supermarket location to be leased for fifteen, twenty, or even thirty years. Department stores and large specialty shops, which locate on major downtown thoroughfares, have been known to sign ninety-nine year leases.

Therefore, it is clear that even a retailer who seeks to minimize his or her financial investment by leasing (rather than owning a building and land) can have a commitment of hundreds of thousands of dollars. In addition to the lease, the retailer must spend money for new lighting, fixtures, storefront renovation, and so on.

Store location is the least flexible element of the retailer's strategy. Advertising, prices, services, and product assortment can be changed rather quickly if the environment (consumers, competition, economy) requires a new retailing strategy. However, location cannot be easily adjusted because of long-term lease agreements; and, in some instances, a retailer is prohibited from renting the location to another party during the term of the agreement. If a retailer does break a lease, he or she may be liable for damages incurred by the property owner. In addition, a retail facility such as a department store cannot easily be converted into another type of retail operation.

The retailer who owns property may also find it difficult to change locations. He or she would have to find an acceptable buyer and perhaps assist the buyer in financing the property. A financial loss may result.

---

[1]"Ames Uses Computer System to Select Store Sites," *Chain Store Age Executive* (November 1984), p. 57.
[2]"Why Site Selection," *Chain Store Age Executive* (January 1983), pp. 29–37.

All retailers who move from one location to another face three potential problems. First, some loyal customers and employees may be lost; the greater the distance between the old and the new locations, the greater the loss. Second, the new location may not possess the same characteristics that originally made the store a success. Third, existing store fixtures and improvements at the old location cannot be switched to the new location; their remaining value is lost if they have not been fully depreciated.

The location of a store has a strong impact on short-run and long-run planning. In the short run, the choice of a store location may influence many strategic factors. For example, a store that locates in a downtown area populated by office buildings may have little pedestrian traffic on weekends. Therefore, it may be inappropriate to sell major appliances at this location (because these items are purchased jointly by husbands and wives). The retailer who selects this downtown location would either have to close on weekends and not stock certain types of merchandise or have to remain open on weekends and try to attract customers to the area by using extensive promotional campaigns and/or aggressive pricing.

The retailer who closes on the weekend is adapting merchandising policy to the characteristics of the location. The retailer who stays open on weekends is investing additional resources in an attempt to alter customer buying habits. It is possible that the latter store is able to trade off increased merchandising costs against lower rent. In any event, a retailer trying to overcome the location faces greater risks than a retailer adapting to the location.

In the long run, the selection of a store location affects the retailer's overall strategy. The retailer must constantly study and monitor the environment and adjust strategy (in anticipation of market changes). By examining the characteristics of customers and the distances they travel to the store and by watching the entry and exit of competitors, the retailer can gauge changes and react accordingly. A retailer needs to choose a store location that is consistent with the philosophy of business, objectives, and target market. Furthermore, a strategy mix (product assortment, promotion, prices, and so on) must be developed that is appropriate for the chosen location. This mix must be adjusted as the environment surrounding the store changes.[3]

In the choice of location, retailers must make these decisions:

1. Evaluate alternate geographic areas in terms of the characteristics of residents and existing retailers.
2. Determine whether to locate in an isolated store, an unplanned business district, or a planned shopping center within the geographic area.
3. Select the general isolated store, unplanned business district, or planned shopping-center location.
4. Analyze alternate sites contained in the specified retail location type.

This chapter concentrates on step 1. Chapter 8 details steps 2, 3, and 4. The selection of a store location must be viewed as a process involving each of these four steps.

---

[3]See Craig E. Cina, "Selecting Store Locations: A Market-Driven Approach," *Marketing News* (September 14, 1984), p. 41.

Trading-Area Analysis

A **trading area** is "the geographic area from which a store draws its customers."[4] It is also defined as

> A district whose size is usually determined by the boundaries within which it is economical in terms of volume and cost for a marketing unit or group to sell and/or deliver a good or service.[5]

The description of a trading area is the first stage in the analysis of a retail store location. Clear delineation of the trading area provides the retailer with several benefits:

1. The demographic and socioeconomic characteristics of consumers can be detailed once the trading area is specified. Government and other published data can be utilized to obtain this information. For an existing store, it can be determined if the current retail strategy matches the needs of consumers. The study of a proposed trading area reveals the market opportunities that exist and the retail strategy necessary for success.
2. The focus of promotional activities can be ascertained. For example, a retailer who finds that 95 per cent of customers live within a three-mile radius of the store would have a considerable amount of waste if he or she advertised in a newspaper with a citywide audience. To avoid wasted circulation, the retailer should evaluate the media coverage pattern of an existing or proposed location.[6]
3. It can be determined whether a proposed branch store will service a new population or take away business from existing stores in the chain or franchise.[7] For example, a supermarket chain currently has an outlet in Jackson, Mississippi. This outlet has a trading area of two miles. The chain is considering an additional location, three miles from its Jackson store. Figure 7-1 shows the distinct markets and overlap of the two outlets. The shaded portion represents the **trading area overlap** between the stores; the same customers are served by both branches.

    The chain needs to find out the overall net increase in sales if it adds the proposed location shown in Figure 7-1 (total revised sales of existing store + total sales of new store − total previous sales of existing store). Management must also consider that a competitor may open at the new location if expansion does not take place, and lost sales would occur.
4. The proper number of outlets operated by a chain retailer in a geographic area can be calculated. How many outlets should a bank, a travel agency, and so on, situate

---

[4]Manuel D. Plotkin, "The Use of Credit Accounts and Computers in Determining Store Trading Areas," in Frederick E. Webster, Jr. (Editor), *New Directions in Marketing: Proceedings of the 48th National Conference of the American Marketing Association* (Chicago: American Marketing Association, 1965), p. 271.
[5]Ralph S. Alexander (Chairman), *Marketing Definitions: A Glossary of Marketing Terms* (Chicago: American Marketing Association, 1960), p. 22.
[6]See David L. Huff and Roland T. Rust, "Measuring the Congruence of Market Areas," *Journal of Marketing*, Vol. 48 (Winter 1984), pp. 68–74.
[7]See Dale D. Achabal, Wilpen L. Gorr, and Vijay Mahajan, "MULTILOC: A Multiple Store Location Decision Model," *Journal of Retailing*, Vol. 58 (Summer 1982), pp. 5–25.

The Trading Areas of Current and Proposed Supermarket Outlets

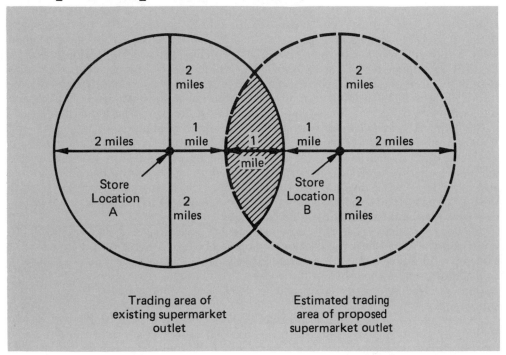

Trading area of existing supermarket outlet

Estimated trading area of proposed supermarket outlet

Figure 7-1

in an area to provide adequate service for its customers (without raising investment costs too much)?[8]

5. Geographic weaknesses are highlighted. For instance, a suburban chamber of commerce conducted a trading-area analysis and discovered that a significant number of people residing south of town did not shop there. A more thorough study revealed that there was a dangerous railroad crossing on the southern outskirts of town, and residents were afraid to cross it. The chamber of commerce exerted political pressure to make the crossing safer and was able to increase shopping in the suburb.

6. Other factors can be described and evaluated. Competition, availability of financial institutions, transportation, availability of labor, location of suppliers, legal restrictions, and projected growth can each be ascertained after the trading area is clearly specified.

[8]C. Samuel Craig and Avijit Ghosh, "Covering Approaches to Retail Facility Location," in Russell W. Belk et al. (Editors), *1984 AMA Educators' Proceedings* (Chicago: American Marketing Association, 1984), pp. 195–199.

The Size and Shape of Trading Areas

A trading area is comprised of three parts: primary, secondary, and fringe. The **primary trading area** encompasses 55 to 70 per cent of a store's customers. It is the area closest to the store and possesses the highest density of customers to population and per capita sales. There is a minimum of overlap with other trading areas (intra- and interstore).

The **secondary trading area** contains an additional 15 to 25 per cent of a store's customers. It is located outside the primary area, and customers are more widely dispersed. The **fringe trading area** includes all the remaining customers, and they are the most widely dispersed. For example, a discount-store chain reported that its outlets have a primary trading area of four miles, a secondary trading area of four miles, and a fringe trading area of eight miles.[9]

Figure 7-2 contains an illustration of a trading area. Trading areas do not have to follow this concentric or circular pattern. They adjust to the environment.[10] The size and shape of a trading area are determined by a variety of factors, among them: store type, store size, the location of competitors, travel time and traffic barriers (toll bridge or a poor road), and availability of media.

Two types of stores can have different drawing powers even though they are both located in the same shopping district or shopping center. One store can offer a wide assortment of merchandise, promote extensively, and create a strong image. This store could have a trading area two to three times that of a weaker competitor. As an illustration, the trading area for a convenience food store is much smaller than that for a supermarket.[11]

One type of store, called a **parasite,** does not create its own traffic and has no trading area of its own. The store depends on customers who are drawn into the area for other reasons. A magazine stand located in a hotel lobby and a snack bar situated in a shopping center are examples of parasites. Their customers are not drawn to the trading area because of them but patronize these stores while they are in the area.

The kinds of merchandise a store sells also influence the size of its trading area. In a regional shopping center, department stores have the largest trading areas. Apparel stores are second, and supermarkets and other local convenience stores have comparatively small trading areas.

The size of a store's trading area is affected by the size of the store. As the store gets larger, its trading area increases. This relationship exists because the size of a store usually reflects the assortment and variety of goods and services that can be provided for customers. However, trading area size does not increase proportionally with increasing store size.

The location of a retailer's competitors determines their impact on the size of the trading area. Whenever potential customers are situated between two stores, the size of the trading area is reduced for each. The size of each store's trading area will increase as the distance between them increases (then the target markets do not overlap).

[9]"Selecting a Store Site, The Computer Way," *Chain Store Age Executive* (March 1981), p. 47.
[10]For example, see William K. West, "Computerized Site Selection: Are Other Methods Obsolete?" *Progressive Grocer* (September 1979), p. 79.
[11]Franklin S. Houston and John Stanton, "Evaluating Retail Trade Areas for Convenience Stores," *Journal of Retailing*, Vol. 60 (Spring 1984), pp. 124–136.

The Segments of a Trading Area

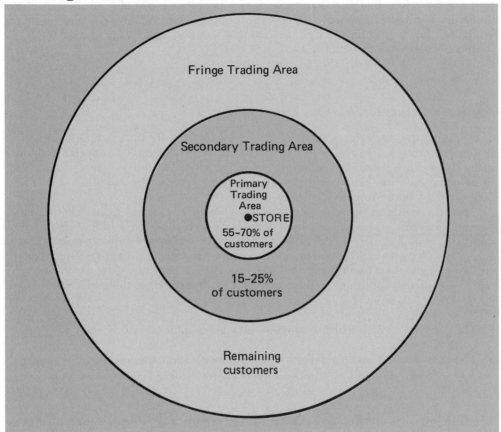

Fringe Trading Area

Secondary Trading Area

Primary
Trading
Area
●STORE
55–70% of
customers

15–25%
of customers

Remaining
customers

Figure 7-2

On the other hand, when stores are located right next to each other, the size of the trading area may not be reduced because of competition. The grouping of stores (within a common merchandise category) may actually increase the size of the trading area for each store. Customers are attracted by the variety of products. However, it is important to recognize that a store's market penetration (percentage of total retail sales) may decline with this type of competition. Also, the entry of a new store may change the shape and/or create gaps in the trading areas of existing stores.

Travel or driving time has an influence on the size of a trading area that is not clear from study of the geographic distribution of the population. Physical barriers (such as toll bridges, tunnels, poor roads, rivers, railroad tracks, and one-way streets) usually reduce trading areas and contribute to their odd shapes. Economic barriers (such as differences in sales taxes between two towns) also affect the size and shape of trading areas. If one town has significantly lower taxes than another, it may entice consumers to travel longer and save more.

As was mentioned previously, the size of a trading area can be expanded with proper promotion. In areas where newspapers and other forms of local advertising are available, a retailer can easily expand the trading area. When local media are not available, the retailer must weigh the cost and waste of advertising against the possibilities of increasing the trading area.

Delineating the Trading Area of an Existing Store

The size, shape, and characteristics of the trading area for an existing store can be delineated quite accurately. Store records (secondary data) and/or a special study (primary data) can be used to measure the trading area. In addition, many specialized firms offer computer-generated data and maps based on census and other data. These data can be tailored to individual retailers' needs.[12]

Store records can reveal the addresses of both credit and cash customers. Addresses of credit customers can be obtained through the store's billing department; addresses of cash customers can be acquired from an analysis of delivery tickets or cash sales slips. Because many large stores have computerized credit-card systems, they can easily estimate their trading areas by studying the addresses of these customers. Primary, secondary, and fringe trading areas can be described on the basis of

1. The frequency with which customers in a geographic area buy merchandise at a particular store.
2. The average purchase (in dollars) by a customer within a given geographic area.
3. The concentration of a store's credit-card holders within a given area.

Although it is usually easy to obtain data on credit-card customers, the conclusions drawn from these data may not be valid if cash customers are excluded from the analysis. The use of credit may vary among different geographic areas, especially if the characteristics of the consumers in each area are different. Therefore, an evaluation of only credit customers may overstate or understate the total number of customers in an area. This bias is eliminated if data are also collected for cash customers.

Other sources of data on the location of credit and cash customers are store contests (sweepstakes) and check-cashing operations. For both of these, the analysis of addresses is inexpensive and quick because the data are collected for other purposes (secondary data).

A retailer can also collect primary data to determine the size of the trading area. License plate numbers can be recorded (observation) and addresses obtained through

---

[12]See Robert R. Bell and Noel B. Zabriskie, "Assisting Marketing Decisions by Computer Mapping: A Branch Banking Application," *Journal of Marketing Research*, Vol. 15 (February 1978), pp. 122–128; Bernie Whalen, " 'Cheap and Friendly' Software Lets 'Little Guys' Have In-House Mapping," *Marketing News* (March 16, 1984), Section 1, pp. 1, 4–5; and "Developers Track the Data," *Chain Store Age Executive* (March 1984), pp. 80–81.

the county treasurer's office or through R. L. Polk, a marketing research firm.[13] As in the case of credit-card analysis, nondrivers must not be omitted. Customers who walk to a store or use public transportation should be included in the investigation. To collect data on these customers, questions usually must be asked (survey).

Regardless of the type of analysis, the retailer should be aware that a time bias may exist. For example, a downtown business district is patronized by different types of customers during the week than on weekends. Or "grand openings" may attract customers from great distances for only brief periods of time. After the store is open a while, the size of the trading area may decline. Therefore, an accurate estimate of the limits of a store's trading area can be obtained only through complete and continuous investigation.[14]

After the trading area is delineated, a retailer should map out the locations and densities of customers. This may be done in either of two ways. First, a geographic map may be drawn. Different colors of dots or pins are placed on this map to represent densities, incomes, size of purchases, cash and credit customers, and other factors. Second, customer addresses may be placed in zip code order. The primary, secondary, and fringe trading areas are defined by zip codes. Customers can then be reached by promotions aimed at particular zip codes.

Delineating the Trading Area of a New Store[15]

The trading area for a new store must often be estimated by an assessment of market opportunities rather than current traffic (pedestrian and vehicular) patterns. Because the techniques already described for delineating the trading area of an established store are not sufficient, additional tools must be utilized.

Trend analysis and/or surveys can be conducted. Trend analysis (estimating the future based on the past) involves the examination of government data concerning predictions about population location, automobile registrations, new housing starts, mass transportation, highways, zoning, and so on. Consumer surveys can be used to gather information about the time and distance people are willing to travel to a retail location, the features that would attract people to a new retail location, the location of the people most likely to visit a new area, and so on. Either or both of these techniques may provide a basis for delineating a new trading area.

The traditional means of trading-area delineation was developed by William J. Reilly in 1929,[16] and it is called **Reilly's law of retail gravitation.** The law's purpose is to establish a **point of indifference** between two cities, so that the trading area of each can be determined. The point of indifference is the geographic breaking point between

---

[13]See Steve Raddock, "Follow That Car!" *Marketing & Media Decisions* (January 1981), pp. 70–71ff.; "License-Plate Surveys Reveal Customer Data," *Marketing News* (September 16, 1983), Section 2, p. 9; and Larry D. Crabtree and James A. Paris, "Survey Car License Plates to Define Retail Trade Area," *Marketing News* (January 4, 1985), p. 12.

[14]Edward Blair; "Sampling Issues in Trade Area Maps Drawn from Shopper Surveys," *Journal of Marketing*, Vol. 47 (Winter 1984), pp. 98–106.

[15]A new store opening in an established trading area can use the techniques detailed in the prior section. This section refers to a newer trading area with ill-defined traffic patterns.

[16]William J. Reilly, *Method for the Study of Retail Relationships*, Research Monograph No. 4 (Austin: University of Texas Press, 1929), University of Texas Bulletin No. 2944.

two cities (at which shoppers would be indifferent to shopping at either city). The law may be expressed algebraically as[17]

$$Dab = \frac{d}{1 + \sqrt{\dfrac{Pb}{Pa}}}$$

where d = distance in miles along a major roadway between cities (towns) A and B
Pa = population of city A
Pb = population of city B
Dab = limit of city A's trading area, measured in miles along the road to city B

Based on this formula, a city with a population of 90,000 (A) would draw people from three times the distance as a city with 10,000 (B). If the cities are 20 miles apart, the point of indifference for the larger city is 15 miles, and for the smaller city, it is five miles:

$$Dab = \frac{20}{1 + \sqrt{\dfrac{10,000}{90,000}}} = \frac{20}{1 + \sqrt{\dfrac{1}{9}}} = \frac{20}{1 + \dfrac{1}{3}} = \frac{20}{\dfrac{4}{3}} = 15 \text{ miles}$$

City
A 90,000 ← 15 miles → Point of indifference → 5 miles → City B 10,000

Reilly's law rests on two major assumptions:(1) the two competing areas are equally accessible from the major road; and (2) merchants in the two areas are equally effective. Other factors are held constant or ignored. Consumers are attracted to the larger population center because a greater amount of store facilities (assortment) exists, making the increased travel time worthwhile.

The law of retail gravitation is an important contribution to trading-area analysis because of its ease of calculation and the research that has been conducted on it. Reilly's law is most useful when other data are not available or when the costs of compiling other data are too great. By combining this technique with others, a merchant can determine if the most appropriate trading area is being considered.

Despite its usefulness, Reilly's law does have limitations. First, distance measurement is confined to major thoroughfares and does not involve cross streets; yet people will travel shorter distances along these slower cross streets. A better measure might be travel time. Second, actual distance may not correspond with the consumer's perception of distance. A store that offers few consumer conveniences, few services, and crowded aisles is a greater perceived distance from the customer than a store with a more pleasant environment.

[17]Richard L. Nelson, *The Selection of Retail Locations* (New York: F. W. Dodge Corporation, 1959), p. 149.

David Huff tried to improve Reilly's law by isolating several variables and relating them to trading-area size. Huff delineates trading areas on the basis of

1. The number of items (of the types desired by the consumer) carried in the area.
2. Travel times from the customer's home to alternative shopping areas.
3. The sensitivity of the kind of shopping to distance.[18]

The size of the trading area depends on a combination of these variables. The assortment variable is measured by the square feet of selling space allocated to different items. The travel-time variable includes the costs of transportation, the effort involved in making the trip, and other opportunities that must be foregone. Sensitivity to the kind of shopping trip involves the purpose of the trip (restocking versus shopping) and the type of product sought (such as clothing versus furniture versus groceries).

Although Huff's approach is a refinement of Reilly's law (it includes traffic congestion and transportation costs, as well as driving distance), it presents some problems. Most important are the difficulties in measuring travel costs and using the approach to examine several competing retail areas.

In recent years, a number of researchers have examined trading-area size in a variety of settings, and have introduced other factors and sophisticated statistical techniques to explain the consumer's choice of shopping location.[19] For example, Gautschi added to Huff's analysis by including shopping-center descriptors (such as center design and hours of operation) and transportation conditions (such as cost, performance, and safety) in his model.[20] Weisbrod, Parcells, and Kern studied the attractiveness of shopping centers on the basis of expected population changes, expected store characteristics, and the evolving transportation network.[21]

In general, expected sales in an area can be calculated through this formula:

Expected annual sales = (number of consumers in the area)
× (percentage of consumers shopping in the area
× (annual expected purchase per consumer)

Characteristics of Trading Areas

After a trading area, existing or proposed, has been delineated, the retailer should examine the characteristics of the area. Of special interest are the attributes of the residents and how well they match with the retailer's definition of the target market. Thus an automobile repair franchisee may estimate the opportunities available in an area by examining the number of automobile registrations; a hearing-aid retailer may evaluate the percentage of the population sixty-five years of age or older; and a bookstore retailer may be concerned with the educational level of the residents.

---

[18]David L. Huff and Larry Blue, *A Programmed Solution for Estimating Retail Sales Potential* (Lawrence: University of Kansas, 1966).

[19]A good synopsis of this research is C. Samuel Craig, Avijit Ghosh, and Sara McLafferty, "Models of the Retail Location Process: A Review," *Journal of Retailing*, Vol. 60 (Spring 1984), pp. 5–36.

[20]David A. Gautschi, "Specification of Patronage Models for Retail Center Choice," *Journal of Marketing Research*, Vol. 18 (May 1981), pp. 162–174.

[21]Glen E. Weisbrod, Robert J. Parcells, and Clifford Kern, "A Disaggregate Model for Predicting Shopping Area Market Attraction," *Journal of Retailing*, Vol. 60 (Spring 1984), pp. 65–83.

Among the trading-area characteristics that must be studied by most retailers are population size and features, availability of labor, closeness to supply, promotion facilities, economic base, competition, availability of locations, and regulations. The **economic base** refers to an area's industrial and commercial structure, the companies and industries that residents depend on to earn a living. The dominant industry (company) in an area is very important because a drastic decline in the industry may have adverse effects on a large proportion of the area's residents. An area with a diverse economic base, where residents work for a variety of nonrelated industries, is more secure than an area dependent on one major industry.

Figure 7-3 summarizes some of the major factors to be considered in the evaluation of a retail area. Many of the data necessary to describe an area can be obtained from the Bureau of the Census, the *Survey of Buying Power, Editor & Publisher Market Guide, Rand McNally Commercial Atlas & Market Guide, American Demographics, Standard Rate & Data Service*, regional planning boards, public utilities, chambers of commerce, shopping-center owners, and renting agents.

Although each of the criteria in Figure 7-3 is not equally important in all retail location decisions, each should be considered (to avoid an oversight). The most important criteria should be viewed as "knockout" factors; if a location does not meet minimum standards on key criteria, it is immediately knocked out.

The following are examples of the use of detailed trading-area descriptions, as developed by some fast-food franchisors, off-price chains, and department stores:

Franchisors

1. The community meets specific population-size requirements.
2. Property at a good site is already owned or can be acquired.
3. A good franchisee is available in the community.
4. An adequate supply of labor is available.
5. The income level in the community is sufficient for an active market.
6. There is little competition.[22]

Off-price chains

1. There are stores with compatible offerings.
2. Many households have incomes over $30,000.
3. Good roads exist.
4. The population base is growing.[23]

Department stores

Each area must have a
1. Favorable economic forecast.
2. Favorable population growth for the target market.
3. Stability of payroll sources.
4. Community awareness of the parent store's existence.
5. Minimal transfer of customers from other company-owned stores.
6. Presence of the proper level of dominant retailers.[24]

[22]Ronald F. Bush, Ronald L. Tatham, and Joseph F. Hair, Jr., "Community Location Decisions by Franchisors: A Comparative Analysis," *Journal of Retailing*, Vol. 50 (Fall 1974), pp. 13–22ff.
[23]"Seeking the Elusive Dame," *Chain Store Age Executive* (January 1984), pp. 93, 95.
[24]Lewis A. Spalding, "New Store Locations," *Stores* (October 1980), pp. 30–35.

Major Factors to Consider in Evaluating a Retail Area

Population Size and Characteristics

1. total size and density
2. age distribution
3. average educational level
4. per cent of residents owning homes
5. total disposable income
6. per capita disposable income
7. occupation distribution
8. trends

Availability of Labor

1. management
2. management trainee
3. clerical

> analysis of:

a. high school and college graduates
b. outmigration of graduates
c. average wages in the area vs. average wages in the U.S.

Closeness to Source of Supply

1. delivery costs
2. time
3. number of manufacturers and wholesalers
4. availability and reliability

Promotion

1. availability and frequency of media
2. costs
3. waste

Economic Base

1. dominant industry
2. extent of diversification
3. growth projections
4. freedom from economic and seasonal fluctuations
5. availability of credit and financial facilities

Competitive Situation

1. number and size of existing competitors
2. evaluation of strengths and weaknesses for all competitors
3. short-run and long-run outlook
4. level of saturation

Availability of Store Locations

1. number and type of locations
2. access to transportation
3. owning versus leasing opportunities
4. zoning restrictions
5. costs

Regulations

1. taxes
2. licensing
3. operations
4. minimum wages
5. zoning

Figure 7-3

The entire process involved in the analysis of a retail area is shown by the flowchart in Figure 7-4. This chart incorporates not only the characteristics of residents but also the characteristics of competition. By studying both of these factors, a retailer can determine how saturated an area is for his or her type of business.

In the following sections, three factors in trading area selection will be discussed: population characteristics, economic base characteristics, and the nature of competition and the level of saturation.

Characteristics of the Population

As mentioned previously, a great deal of information on population characteristics is available from secondary data sources. These sources provide information about population size, number of households, income distribution, education levels, and age distributions. Because the *Census of Population*, the *Survey of Buying Power*, and *Editor & Publisher Market Guide* are such valuable sources, each will be briefly described.

Census of Population

The *Census of Population* supplies a wide range of population data for cities and surrounding areas. Data are organized on a geographic basis, starting with blocks (groups of about 200 households) and continuing to census tracts (which average 1,200 households), cities, counties, states, and regions. As a rule, there are less data available for blocks and census tracts than for larger units, because of concerns over individuals' privacy.

After a retailer has defined the trading area, he or she can use census data by combining the geographic units contained in that area. A major breakthrough for retailers occurred with the 1970 census, when the Census Bureau created a computer file for the storage and retrieval of population data by geographic area. A number of private marketing research firms have developed computer-based site-evaluation systems, based in part on census data.[25]

The 1980 census added data categories that are useful for retailers interested in market segmentation. These include racial and ethnic data, small-area income data, and commuting patterns. An on-line computer system also makes 1980 census data available.

The major drawback of census data is that they are gathered only once every ten years. Thus, the material can be quite out of date and inaccurate. Supplementary sources, such as municipal building departments or utilities, must be used to update census data during the later years.

The value of census tract data can be demonstrated through an illustration of Long Beach, New York, a city of more than 34,000 residents located 30 miles east of New York City on the south shore of Long Island. Long Beach is composed of six census tracts, numbers 4164, 4165, 4166, 4167.01, 4167.02, and 4168. See Figure 7-5. Al-

[25]Jacob Weissman, "Computer Graphics of Census Data Aid Market Researchers," *Marketing News* (March 6, 1981), p. 8; Peter K. Francese, "Bargain-Priced Census a Boon to Consumers, Market Researchers," *Marketing News* (May 15, 1981), Section 1, p. 11; Brian T. Becker, "On-Line Computerization of Census Data to Increase Demand for Demographic Services," *Marketing News* (April 17, 1981), pp. 8–9; and Diane Haggblom, "DemoScan," *American Demographics* (September 1984), pp. 42–44.

Analyzing a Retail Area

Source of Initial Data	Delivery and Billing Analysis	Credit Analysis	License Plate Analysis	Zip Code Analysis	Trend Analysis	Survey

Content of Initial Data
Frequency of Shopping
Average Size ($) Purchase
Concentration of Customers
(by geographic area)

Delineation of Trading Area
Primary
Secondary
Fringe

Source of Data for Characteristics of Residents
Bureau of Census
Survey of Buying Power
Editor & Publisher
Rand McNally
American
Demographics

Standard Rate & Data Service
Regional Planning Boards
Public Utilities
Chambers of Commerce
Renting Agents

Characteristics of Residents
Total Size
Age Distribution
Average Educational Level
Per Cent of Residents
Owning Homes

Total Disposable and Per
Capita Income
Occupation Distributions
Trends

Characteristics of Competitors & Level of Saturation
Number & Size of Competitors
Square Feet of Retail Space
Front Feet of Retail Space

Saturation of Area
Sales Per Square Foot
Persons Per Retail Establishment
Persons Per Store Front Foot
Store Sales Per Capita
Index of Saturation

Decision
Approve Area
Reject Area

Figure 7-4

Census Tracts: Long Beach, New York

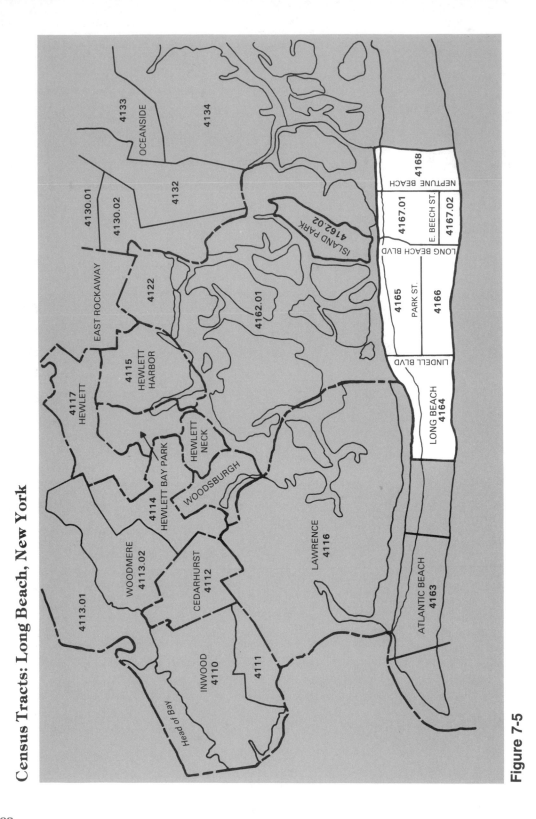

Figure 7-5

though census tract 4163 is contiguous with Long Beach, it represents Atlantic Beach, another community.

Table 7-1 contains a variety of population statistics for each of the census tracts in Long Beach. The characteristics of the residents in each tract differ markedly; a retailer who is successful in one tract may not be successful in another.

For example, the Bookends bookstore chain is evaluating two proposed areas. Area A corresponds roughly with census tracts 4165 and 4166. Area B is similar to census tracts 4167.01, 4167.02, and 4168. The population data for these two areas have been extracted from Table 7-1 and are presented in Table 7-2. Some interesting comparisons can be made.

Area A is substantially different from area B, despite their geographic proximity and similar size:

1. The population in area B is 35 per cent larger than the population in area A.
2. Area B had some population growth during 1970–80; whereas the population of area A had declined during this time period.
3. The number of area B residents age 25 and older with college degrees is more than two times greater than that of area A, while median income is over 60 per cent higher.
4. The percentage of area B workers who are managers or are in professional specialty occupations is greater in area B than in area A.

Table 7-1

Selected Characteristics of Long Beach, New York Residents by Census Tract, 1970 and 1980

	Tract Number					
	4164	4165	4166	4167.01	4167.02	4168
Total population:						
1970	6,352	5,229	6,499	4,062	4,769	6,216
1980	6,921	5,480	6,059	4,299	5,008	6,308
1980 population 25 and older	4,442	2,828	4,344	2,900	4,042	4,682
Number of Households:						
1970	1,993	1,709	2,426	1,355	2,210	2,412
1980	2,582	1,791	2,183	1,559	2,526	2,976
Education:						
College graduates (% of population 25 and older, 1980)	13.7	9.9	18.7	22.6	17.2	27.7
Income:						
Median household income, 1970	$ 8,500	$ 8,100	$ 3,100	$ 9,600	$ 5,400	$13,200
Median household income, 1980	$16,651	$14,089	$11,883	$21,955	$12,606	$21,341
Selected occupations:						
Managerial and professional specialty occupations (% of employed persons 16 and older, 1980)	24.0	14.8	26.4	28.7	27.1	35.5

Source: 1980 Census of Population and Housing, Census Tracts Nassau–Suffolk New York Standard Metropolitan Statistical Area *(Washington, D.C.: U.S. Department of Commerce, Bureau of the Census); and authors' estimates and computations.*

Table 7-2
Selected Population Statistics for Long Beach Trading Areas A and B

	Area A (Tracts 4165 and 4166)	Area B (Tracts 4167.01, 4167.02, and 4168)
Total population, 1980	11,539	15,615
Population change, 1970–80	−1.6%	+3.8%
Number college graduates, 25 and older, 1980	1,093	2,646
Median household income	$12,877	$18,352
Managerial and professional specialty occupations (% of employed persons 16 and older), 1980	21.8	30.9

The management of Bookends will probably select area B because its residents have the characteristics desired of the target market. Area A will probably be rejected because its residents do not possess the characteristics required by Bookends.

Survey of Buying Power

The *Survey of Buying Power* is published annually by *Sales & Marketing Management* magazine. This survey reports current data on metropolitan areas, cities, and state bases. It provides some data not available from census tracts, such as retail sales by specific merchandise categories, effective buying income, total retail sales by area, population projections, and retail sales projections.

The most important disadvantage of the *Survey* is its use of broad geographic territories. These territories may not correspond with a store's trading area and cannot be broken down easily.

The value of the *Survey of Buying Power* can be shown through an example of site selection by a new-car dealer. This dealer is investigating three counties near Chicago: Du Page, Kane, and Lake. A location for a new outlet is sought.

Table 7-3 lists important population data for the three Illinois counties under investigation. The statistics are updated annually (Table 7-3 is based on the year that ended on December 31, 1983), and five-year projections are made (1988 projections are made in Table 7-3).

In order for one to analyze Table 7-3, two of the terms used by *Sales & Marketing Management* must be defined. Effective buying income is personal income (wages, salaries, interest, dividends, profits, and property revenues) minus federal, state, and local taxes and nontax payments (such as personal contributions for social security insurance). Effective buying income is commonly known as disposable personal income. The **buying power index** (**BPI**) is a single weighted measure combining effective buying income, retail sales, and population size into an overall indicator of an area's sales potential, expressed as a percentage of total U.S. sales.[26]

The buying power index (BPI) is expressed as

Buying power index = 0.5 (the area's percentage of U.S. effective buying income)
+ 0.3 (the area's percentage of U.S. retail sales)
+ 0.2 (the area's percentage of U.S. population)

[26]"Definitions of Terms Used in the Survey," *1984 Survey of Buying Power: Sales & Marketing Management* (July 23, 1984), pp. C-3–C-6.

Table 7-3
Selected Data from Survey of Buying Power *Relating to the Automobile Market in Three Illinois Counties, 1983*

	County		
	Du Page	Kane	Lake
December 31, 1983			
Total population	719,700	289,100	467,100
Number of people 18 and over	520,343	203,526	334,443
Percentage of population 18 and over	72.3	70.4	71.6
Number of households	258,200	101,400	154,100
Total effective buying income (EBI)	$10,484,740,000	$3,282,957,000	$6,152,657,000
Median household EBI	$38,047	$30,084	$34,428
Per capita EBI	$14,568	$11,356	$13,172
Percentage of households with $35,000–$49,999 EBI	30.1	24.7	24.9
Percentage of households with $50,000+ EBI	26.7	13.9	23.9
Total retail sales	$5,040,580,000	$1,749,007,000	$2,374,692,000
Buying power index	0.4136	0.1392	0.2318
Percentage of U.S. EBI	0.4501	0.1409	0.2642
Percentage of U.S. retail sales	0.4249	0.1474	0.2002
Percentage of U.S. population	0.3056	0.1228	0.1984
Automobile retail sales, 1983	$771,315,000	$258,841,000	$470,108,000
Projections for December 31, 1988			
Total population	804,600	303,200	499,600
Percentage of change in population, 1983–88	11.8	4.9	7.0
Total EBI	$19,190,957,000	$5,370,355,000	$10,616,925,000
Percentage change in total EBI, 1983–88	83.0	63.6	72.6
Total retail sales	$8,881,980,000	$2,793,433,000	$3,939,151,000
Percentage change in total retail sales, 1983–88	76.2	59.7	65.9
Buying power index (%)	0.4643	0.1410	0.2457

Source: Adapted from 1984 Survey of Buying Power: Sales & Marketing Management *(July 23, 1984), pp. B-5, B-7, C-61, C-64, C-68, C-69; and* 1984 Survey of Buying Power, Part II: Sales & Marketing Management *(October 29, 1984), p. 64. Reprinted by permission of Sales & Marketing Management Inc. © 1984 S&MM Survey of Buying Power.*

Each of the three criteria in the index is assigned a weight, based on its importance. The buying power indexes for Du Page, Kane, and Lake counties are computed in Table 7-4.

The buying power index of Du Page is about three times that of Kane and over 78 per cent greater than Lake. Du Page has a larger population and more people 18 and older than either Kane and Lake. This is a vital statistic for an auto dealer. In addition, 56.8 per cent of Du Page's residents have effective buying incomes of $35,000 or better compared to 38.6 per cent of Kane's residents and 48.8 per cent of Lake's residents. In 1983, automobile sales were $771,315,000 in Du Page, compared to $258,841,000 in Kane and $470,108,000 in Lake.

Therefore, a Cadillac dealer using *Survey of Buying Power* data might select Du

Table 7-4
Computations of Buying Power Indexes: Du Page, Kane, and Lake Counties, 1983*

Du Page County

Buying power index = 0.5 (0.4501%) + 0.3 (0.4249%) + 0.2 (0.3056%)
= 0.4136%

Kane County

Buying power index = 0.5 (0.1409%) + 0.3 (0.1474%) + 0.2 (0.1228%)
= 0.1392%

Lake County

Buying power index = 0.5 (0.2642%) + 0.3 (0.2002%) + 0.2 (0.1984%)
= 0.2318%

*BPI = 0.5 (area's % of U.S. effective buying income) + 0.3 (area's % of U.S. retail sales) + 0.2 (area's % of U.S. population).

Page and a Chevrolet dealer might select Kane. It must again be noted that the *Survey* is broad in nature. Several subsections of Kane may be quite superior choices to subsections in Du Page (based on census data) for the Cadillac dealer.

Editor & Publisher Market Guide

Editor & Publisher Market Guide provides a variety of city data on a yearly basis, including principal sources of employment, transportation networks, bank deposits, automobile registrations, number of gas and electric meters, newspaper circulations, and major shopping centers. *Editor & Publisher*, like other sources, also contains statistics on population size and total households.

As with the *Survey of Buying Power*, *Editor & Publisher Market Guide* has one serious drawback for retailers. The data cover broad geographic areas and are difficult to disaggregate.

The value of *Editor & Publisher* can be described through an illustration of Sacramento, California. See Figure 7-6. Sacramento is the capital of California. It has a large transportation system involving several railroads, motor freight carriers, interstate bus routes, and airlines. The population of several hundred thousand uses 49 commercial banks, 27 savings and loan associations, 470,919 passenger autos, 562,615 electric and gas meters, and two newspapers. Among Sacramento's major industries are U.S. aircraft repair, farming, manufacturing, aerospace, food processing, and lumber products. There are a number of major shopping centers and retail outlets.

The Bookends bookstore chain may not obtain adequate consumer information from this source, but the information on shopping centers and retailers should be quite helpful. The auto dealer may also find that *Editor & Publisher* offers limited but useful data. The extent of the transportation network and the number of passenger cars are vital information. *Editor & Publisher Market Guide* is best used as a supplement to census and *Sales & Marketing Management* statistics.

It should be realized that different retailers require different kinds of information about the population characteristics of an area. The location decision for a bookstore

Editor & Publisher's Description of Sacramento, California

SACRAMENTO

1 - LOCATION: Sacramento County (MSA), E&P Map B-4, State Capital and County Seat. State Gov't; U.S. aircraft repair & modification; farming; manufacturing; aerospace; food processing; lumber products; mobile home manufacturing and wholesale center. Army depot and technical training center; electronics; Calif. Expo. 89 mi. E. of San Francisco.

2 - TRANSPORTATION: Railroads-Southern Pacific; Santa Fe; Western Pacific; Sacramento Northern; Central California Traction; overnight freight service on Sacramento R.R. between S.F. Bay and Sacramento; Sea Port (deepwater channel to San Francisco Bay; and Pacific Ocean; River Container Barge System).
Motor Freight Carriers-16 interstate common carriers with local terminals; 542 total carriers (the majority of which have p.u.c. permits).
Intercity Bus Lines-Greyhound; Continental Trailways.
Airlines-United; Western; P.S.A.; Air California; Frontier; West Air; Republic; American; PacificCal; Wings West; Pacific Coast; Pacific Express; Golden West.

3 - POPULATION:
Corp. City 80 Cen. 275,741; Loc. Est. 308,474
PMA-ABC: (80) 1,059,461; (84) 1,179,500
County 80 Cen. 783,381; Loc. Est. 854,974
MSA 80 Cen. 1,099,814; Loc. Est. 1,206,733
Demographic information available from Newspaper. See paragraph 14.

4 - HOUSEHOLDS:
Corp. City 80 Cen. 112,859; Loc. Est. 130,074
PMA-ABC: (80) 400,151; (84) 449,200
County 80 Cen. 299,805; Loc. Est. 335,044
MSA 80 Cen. 416,356; Loc. Est. 467,827

5 - BANKS	**NUMBER**	**DEPOSITS**
Commercial	49	$4,675,252,000
Savings & Loan	27	$2,679,868,000

6 - PASSENGER AUTOS: County 470,919

7 - ELECTRIC METERS: County 317,120

8 - GAS METERS: County 245,495

9 - PRINCIPAL INDUSTRIES: Industry, No. of Wage Earners-Retail Trade 76,300; Wholesale Trade 18,400; All Mfg. 25,400; Nondurable Goods 11,800; Durables 13,600; Food Products 5,500; Fed. Govt. 26,700; State & Local Govt. 118,300; Construction 14,400; Transportation & Public Utilities 21,400; Fin., Insurance & Real Estate 22,600; Services 80,800.

10 - CLIMATE: Min. & Max. Temp.-Winter 39-53; Spring 48-71; Summer 59-93; Fall 52-77.

11 - TAP WATER: Varies, soft to hard, not fluoridated.

12 - RETAILING: Principal Shopping Centers-Sunrise Mall (109 stores) 5900-6100 Sunrise Blvd.; Florin Mall (94 stores) 5901 Florin Road; Country Club Plaza (50 stores) 2300 Watt Avenue; Country Club Centre (68 stores) 3300 El Camino; Arden Fair Mall (74 stores) 1601 Arden Way; Downtown Plaza (43 stores) Downtown Plaza; Birdcage Walk (65 stores) 5901-6197 Sunrise Blvd.

Nearby Shopping Centers

Name (No. of stores)	Miles from Downtown	Principal Stores
Arcade Square(18)	NA	Raley's Mkt.
Arden Fair(74)	NA	Woolworth, Sears, Thrifty Drug, Weinstock's
Arden Plaza(74)	NA	Lucky Mkt., Manor Drug, Valley Hardware
Arden Town(16)	NA	Holiday Mkt.
Birdcage Walk(65)	NA	Long's, Wards, Corti Bros., Macy's
Camellia City(9)	NA	Lucky Mkt., TG&Y
College Greens(8)	NA	Raley's Mkt.
Country Club Center(68)	NA	Wards
Country Club Plaza(50)	NA	Weinstock's, JCPenney
Cordova(30)	NA	Lucky Mkt., Thrifty
Crestview(27)	NA	Lucky Mkt., Thrifty, Ross
Crossroads(10)	NA	Corti Bros.
Downtown Plaza(43)	NA	Macy's, Weinstock's
Florin Plaza	NA	Jumbo Mkt.
Florin Square(23)	NA	
Florin Mall(94)	NA	Weinstock's, Sears, JCPenney, Wards
Fort Sutter(11)	NA	Raley's
Fruitridge(29)	NA	Holiday Mkt., Manor Drug
Grand Oaks(23)	NA	Lucky Mkt., Hancock Fabrics
Grant Plaza (Citrus) (Heights)	NA	Thrifty, Alpha Beta
Hollywood Plaza(6)	NA	Raley's
Lanai(38)	NA	
Madison Mall(35)	NA	Raley's
Midway (El Camino)(14)	12	Jumbo Mkt.
Mills(18)	NA	Raley's Mkt.
Northridge(17)	NA	Raley's Mkt.
N. Sacramento(4)	NA	Safeway
Point West(20)	NA	Mervyn's, Consumers Distributing
River Park(13)	NA	Pantry
Roseville Sq.(37)	NA	Thrifty, Safeway, McDonalds
Southgate(27)	NA	Lucky Mkt., Hancock Fabrics, Thrifty Drug
South Hills(31)	NA	Sprouse Reitz, Jumbo
Sunrise Mall(109)	NA	Weinstock's, Sears, JCPenney
Sunrise Oaks(21)	NA	Thrifty, Alpha Beta
Tallac Vlg.(14)	NA	Vans
Taylor's(23)	NA	Lucky Mkt.
Town & Country(55)	NA	William Glen
University Vlg.(23)	NA	Safeway
Almond Orchard(20)	NA	
Country West(15)	NA	Big R
Elkhorn/Watt(11)	NA	Thrifty, Albertson's, K mart
Manzanita/ Madison(12)	NA	Cloth World, Raley's

Principal Shopping Days-Department Stores-Thur., Fri., Sat. Grocery Stores-Wed., Thur., Fri., Sat. & Sun.
Store Open Evenings-Department Stores-Mon. thru Fri. Food every night.
Stores Open Sunday-Grocery; Super Drugs; Discount; Dept.; Automotive.

13 - RETAIL OUTLETS: Department Stores-Weinstock's 5; Macy's 2; Sears 3; Montgomery Wards 3; JCPenney 3; Mervyn's 5.
Discount Stores-K mart 6; Gemco 4; Best Products 3; Consumer Dist. 3.
Variety Stores-Woolworth 5; Ben Franklin 2; Sprouse Reitz 6; TG&Y.
Chain Drug Stores-Payless 8; Manor 3; Rexall 9; Raley's 11; Thrifty 18; Long's 7.
Chain Supermarkets-Century 3; Safeway 17; Prairie 2; 7-Eleven 42; Corti Bros. 4; Bel Air 6; Lucky 24; Jumbo 9; Raley's 14; Van's 8; Albertson's 7; Alpha Beta 8; Circle K 43; Big Boy 3; Comptons/Holiday 5.
Other Chain Stores-Firestone; Goodyear; Goodrich; See's; Zale's Jewelry; Fuller Paints; Mary Carter Paints; Pittsburgh Paints; Sherwin-Williams Paints; Thom McAn; Gallenkamps; Kirby's; Chandler's; Florsheim; Leeds; Lerner; Sherman Clay; Breuners; Grodins; Kinney Shoes; Dalton Books; J. Magnin; Ransohoff's; Smith's Men's Wear; Singer Co.; Lane Bryant; Mode O'Day; Baskin Robbins; Levitz Furniture; Oshman's; Walden Books; Merribee Needlearts and Crafts; Big 5; United Sporting Goods; Furrow Bldg.; Pay N Pak; Athletic Shoe Factory; Knapp Shoes; Fleet Feet; Cousins; The Gap; Wherehouse Records; Pacific Stereo; Fashion Conspiracy; College-Hi; Lumberjack; Granat Bros.; Rogers Jewelers; Gran Tree; Mother-to-Be; Merle Norman; Radio Shack; McCurry's; Fotomat; Bedazzled; Groths Shoes; Huston Shoes; Hickory Farms; Marlenes; Devon Jewelers; Richman Bros.; Foxy Lady; Kinder-Foto; Marshalls; Pic-A-Dilly; Toys R Us; Handyman; Fox Photo; Cost Plus Imports; Pier 1 Imports; Tower Records; Tower Books; Tower of Shoes & Clothing; Ross.

14 - NEWSPAPERS: BEE (m) 224,589; (S) 259,069; Mar. 31, 1984 ABC.
Local Contact for Advertising and Merchandising Data: Clifford Chapman, Nat'l Adv. Mgr., BEE, 21st and Q Sts.; PO Box 15779, Sacramento, CA 95852; Tel. (916) 446-9354.
National Representative: Cresmer, Woodward, O'Mara & Ormsbee.
UNION (m) 98,037; (S) 97,131; Mar. 31, 1984 ABC.
Local Contact for Advertising and Merchandising: Larry Murray, Nat'l Adv. Mgr., UNION, 301 Capital Mall, Sacramento, CA 95812; Tel. (916) 442-7811.
National Representative: Landon Associates.

Source: *Editor & Publisher Market Guide*, 1985 Edition, II-40. Reprinted with permission.

Figure 7-6

or an automobile dealer usually requires more data than needed for a fast-food franchise. For a fast-food franchise location, income and education are not significant factors. The prime criterion in area evaluation is population density. Many fast-food franchises seek communities having a large number of people living within a three- or four-mile radius of their stores. On the other hand, bookstore owners and automobile dealers cannot locate merely on the basis of population density. They must consider a more complex combination of population attributes in evaluating areas and should look at the sources of data described in this section.

Economic Base Characteristics

It is important to study the characteristics of an area's economic base. This base indicates the sources of income for a community's residents. A retailer seeking stability will normally prefer an area with a diversified economic base (a large number of non-related industries) to one with an economic base consisting of one major industry. The latter area is more affected by a strike, declining demand for one product line, and cyclical fluctuations.

In evaluating a trading area, a retailer should investigate the percentage of the labor force in each industry or trade grouping, the impact of economic fluctuations on the area and particular industries, and the future of individual industries (companies). These data can be obtained from *Editor & Publisher Market Guide*, studies by regional planning commissions, regional industrial development organizations, and chambers of commerce.

The Nature of Competition and the Level of Saturation

The retail opportunity in an area cannot be accurately assessed unless the competitive structure is studied. Although an area may have residents that match the retailer's desired market and may have a strong economic base, it may be a poor location for a new store if competition is extensive. Similarly, an area with a small population and a narrow economic base may be a good location if competition is minimal.

When examining competition, several factors should be analyzed: the number of existing stores, the size distribution of existing stores, the rate of new-store openings, the strengths and weaknesses of all stores, short-run and long-run trends, and the level of saturation. These factors must be evaluated in relation to an area's population size and growth, not just in absolute terms.

For example, many retailers have recently opened new stores in Southeastern and Southwestern states with growing populations. Tiffany, Saks Fifth Avenue, Gumps, Marshall Field, Lord & Taylor, and Macy's are among the retailers that have recently begun operations in New Orleans and/or Dallas in order to locate stores in areas with expanding populations.[27] However, there is concern that locations such as these will become quickly saturated because of the influx of new stores. In fact, although the population in the Northeast is declining relative to the Southeast and Southwest, one of its major strengths—population density—should not be overlooked by retailers. The states in the Northeast have a population density of 281 persons per square mile compared with a density of less than 100 persons per square mile in Southeastern and Southwestern states.[28]

An area can be understored, overstored, or saturated. An **understored area** has too few stores selling a specified good or service to satisfy the needs of its population. An **overstored area** has so many stores selling a specified good or service that each retailer is unable to earn an adequate return on investment. A **saturated area** has just enough retail facilities to satisfy the needs of its population for a specified good or service.

[27]Jeffrey A. Trachtenberg, "The Second Battle of New Orleans," *Forbes* (July 2, 1984), pp. 65–66; and Isadore Barmash, "Battle of Retailers in Dallas," *New York Times* (September 5, 1983), pp. 31–32.
[28]Eugene Carlson, "Population Density Remains Primary Factor for Retailers," *Wall Street Journal* (November 6, 1984), p. 31; and "Developers Track the Data," *Chain Store Age Executive* (March 1984), pp. 80–81.

Measures of saturation are based on the premise that an area cannot support more than a fixed number of stores. The ratios mentioned in this section attempt to quantify store saturation. These ratios are meaningful only if norms are established; then the level of saturation in an area can be measured against a standard set by the retailer, or, it can be compared with the store saturation index of another community.

The ratios most often used to calculate an area's level of saturation are: the number of persons per retail establishment; average sales per retail store; store sales per capita; the number of persons per storefront foot; and sales per square foot of selling area. These figures enable an analyst to compare trading areas in terms of their levels of saturation.

The statistics necessary to compute a saturation index can be obtained from city and state license and tax records, telephone directories, personal visits, *Dun & Bradstreet* reference books, and *County Business Patterns*. Retail sales by product category can be found in the *Survey of Buying Power.*

In the investigation of an area's level of saturation for a specific good or service, a retailer must interpret the saturation ratios carefully. Sometimes the variations between areas may not be true indicators of differences in saturation. For example, automobile sales per capita will be different for a suburban than an urban area because suburban residents have a much greater need for automobiles. Therefore, each area's level of saturation should be evaluated against different standards—based on the optimum per capital sales figures in each area.

Table 7-5 compares the level of saturation for full-line discount stores in three metropolitan markets: Atlanta, Houston, and Milwaukee. While Houston has the greatest total full-line discount store sales, it also has the greatest number of these stores. Of the markets studied, Houston and Milwaukee have a considerably fewer number of

Table 7-5
Store Saturation Data for Full-Line Discount Stores in Three Metropolitan Markets, 1984 (Estimated)

	Metropolitan Market		
	Atlanta	Houston	Milwaukee
Total full-line discount store sales	$451,000,000	$813,000,000	$363,000,000
Total population	2,320,000	3,150,800	1,389,200
Total number of households (EBI)	839,700	1,143,100	516,000
Effective buying income per metropolitan market (thousands)	$21,667,618	$32,678,942	$13,974,086
Number of full-line discount stores	46	83	37
Square footage full-line discount stores	3,424,000	6,179,000	2,754,000
Full-line discount store sales per capita	$194.40	$258.03	$261.30
Number of persons per full-line discount store	50,435	37,961	37,546
Number of households per full-line discount store	18,254	13,772	13,946
Full-line discount store sales per $1 of EBI	$0.021	$0.025	$0.026
Average sales per store	$9,804,347	$9,795,180	$9,810,811
Average sales per square foot	$131.72	$131.57	$131.81

Source: "Census '84/'85: Discount Industry by Metro Market," Discount Store News (July 23, 1984), p. 26; and authors' computations. Reprinted by permission.

both persons per full-line discount store and households per full-line discount store than Atlanta. Full-line discount store sales per $1 of effective buying income are also less in Atlanta than in both Houston and Milwaukee. These data suggest that Atlanta is understored relative to Houston and Milwaukee.

One general ratio has been developed to measure store saturation in an area: the **index of saturation.** This index examines the number of customers, the retail expenditures, and the size of retail facilities for a specified good or service in each trading area under consideration:[29]

$$IRS_i = \frac{C_i \cdot RE_i}{RF_i}$$

where IRS_i = index of saturation for trading area i for the good (service)
C_i = number of customers in area i for the good (service)
RE_i = expenditures (dollars) per customer in area i for the good (service)
RF_i = total square feet in area i allocated to the good (service)

The use of the index of saturation can be illustrated through an example involving three alternative areas available to a retailer. See Table 7-6. The retailer has determined that sales must be at least $20 per square foot of store space in order to be profitable, and the area chosen will be the one that yields the highest index of saturation (sales per square foot). In this case, the retailer selects area 1, which has an index of saturation of $30.

When calculating this index, the retailer must remember to include the proposed store. If the proposed store is not included, the relative value of each area may be distorted. If the proposed store is excluded in Table 7-6, area 3 has the best level of sales per square foot ($60); however, this area is not desirable after the prospective store is added to the computation. It should be noted that sales per foot decline the most when new outlets are added to a small area.

Table 7-6
Using the Index of Saturation

	Area		
	1	2	3
Number of customers for the product	60,000	30,000	10,000
Average purchase per customer	$10	$12	$15
Total store footage allocated to the product	20,000	15,000	7,500
Index of retail saturation	$30	$24	$20
Total store footage allocated to the product (excluding the proposed store)	15,000	10,000	2,500
Index of saturation (excluding the proposed store)	$40	$36	$60

---

[29]Adapted from Bernard J. LaLonde, "New Frontiers in Store Location," *Supermarket Merchandising* (February 1963), p. 110.

The retailer should also examine whether a new store will expand the total consumer market for a specific good (service) or increase the firm's market share in the area without expanding the total market. This is particularly important when the retailer has either high levels of service or carries an unusually wide assortment of products.[30]

Choosing A Store Location—Trading-Area Analysis: A Summary

The store location decision is important because of its long-term nature, its investment requirements, and its effect on other elements of the retail mix. A retailer must constantly monitor changes in the population and the competitors surrounding his or her store and adapt to these changes. Location planning does not end with the opening of a store.

The choice of a store location involves four steps: (1) evaluation of alternative trading areas; (2) determination of type of location; (3) selection of a general location; and (4) choice of a site within the location. This chapter has concentrated on step 1.

A trading area is the geographic area from which a store draws its customers. An area contains primary, secondary, and fringe segments. Its size and shape depend on a variety of factors, including store type, store size, location of competitors, travel time and traffic barriers, and availability of media.

One can determine the limits of a trading area by examining store records, sponsoring contests, checking on license plate numbers, questioning customers, and/or using retail gravitation theories (for new areas).

After the area has been delineated, its characteristics should be defined. Among the most important characteristics are population features, availability of labor, closeness to supply, promotion facilities, economic base, competition, availability of locations, and regulations. The *Census of Population*, the *Survey of Buying Power*, and *Editor & Publisher Market Guide* are good sources of data for these characteristics.

Store saturation for a trading area may be computed in several ways, such as number of persons per retail establishment, number of persons per storefront footage, sales per square foot of selling space, and index of saturation. By using one or more of these ratios, the retailer can ascertain whether an area is understored, overstored, or saturated.

Questions for Discussion

1. If a retailer has a new 20-year lease, does this mean that the next time he or she studies the characteristics of the trading area should be 20 years from now? Explain your answer.
2. Illustrate how a retailer's promotion policy is influenced by location.

---

[30]Charles A. Ingene and Robert F. Lusch, "Market Selection Decisions for Department Stores," *Journal of Retailing*, Vol. 56 (Fall 1980), p. 39.

3. Explain the value of a retailer's knowing the primary, secondary, and fringe trading areas for his or her store.
4. Why do few trading areas look like concentric circles?
5. Explain the value of trading-area analysis for a chain store contemplating a new branch outlet.
6. Explain Reilly's law. What are its advantages and disadvantages?
7. Discuss Huff's and other recent contributions to trading-area analysis.
8. What are the major advantages and disadvantages of *Census of Population* data in delineating trading areas.
9. Describe the kinds of retail information contained in the *Survey of Buying Power*. What is its most critical disadvantage?
10. Define the buying power index. How may it be used?
11. Evaluate the economic base of Sacramento, California. Refer to Figure 7-6.
12. If a retail area is acknowledged to be "saturated," what does this signify for existing retailers? For prospective retailers considering this area?
13. Describe the criteria each of the following retailers should utilize in evaluating the level of competition in an area:
    a. Sporting goods store
    b. Restaurant
    c. Drugstore
14. Calculate store saturation, given the following data:

Annual sales per customer	$300
Number of customers	120,000
Existing store footage	20,000 square feet
Proposed store footage	8,000 square feet

CASES

1. Very Competitive Rentals, Inc.: Trading-Area Analysis to Determine the Feasibility of a Branch Store

Very Competitive Rentals, Inc. (VCR) is a videocassette tape rental operation started by Jonathan Smith as a supplement to his television and radio repair business. Jon realized that the decreasing prices of new color television sets was leading to fewer of his upscale customers repairing their older sets: "It's tough to convince someone to spend $100 to fix a television when a new model could be purchased for $299."

Because he had a lot of unused space in his store and videocassette recorders were becoming more popular, Jon rapidly expanded his involvement in the rental of prerecorded videocassette tapes. He now has over 1,200 families as members, who choose from VCR's selection of 1,000 tapes. Family membership costs $20 per year or $50 for a lifetime plan. Membership entitles participants to rent any movie, concert, and so on, in stock for $2 per day.

Table 1
Trading-Area Analysis for VCR, Current Location

Number of current members	1,227
Number of members living within 2.5 miles of store	860
Number of members living between 2.5 and 5 miles of store	300
Number of members living between 5 and 10 miles of store	67
Average annual rental volume per member	$50
Average annual family income of those living within 2.5 miles of store	$30,000
Number of families living within 2.5 miles of store	20,000
Number of families living within 5 miles of store	43,000
Number of families living within 10 miles of store	75,000

Trading-Area Analysis Map for VCR, Current and Potential Locations

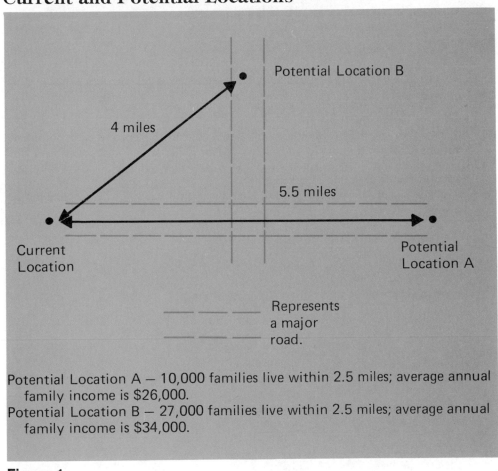

Potential Location B

4 miles

5.5 miles

Current Location

Potential Location A

— — — Represents a major road.

Potential Location A — 10,000 families live within 2.5 miles; average annual family income is $26,000.

Potential Location B — 27,000 families live within 2.5 miles; average annual family income is $34,000.

Figure 1

VCR has proven to be a very lucrative business for Jon. He annually generates $25,000 in membership fees, $60,000 in daily rentals fees, and a gross profit of $20,000 for blank tapes, videocassette recorder cleaners, and accessories. In addition, Jon repairs videocassette recorders, but does not sell them. His overall investment in prerecorded tapes is about $45,000.

Jon is seriously considering adding a second store for tape rentals. Among the benefits of this strategy are quantity discounts in buying tapes from vendors, greater leverage in securing early releases of important films, advertising economies (two stores mentioned in one ad), greater market coverage, and increased emphasis on a profitable line of business. As a first step, Jon has decided to conduct a trading-area analysis to find the optimal location.

Smith's excellent records have given him the ability to delineate his current store's trading area in terms of two key criteria: the location and density of members, and their average movie rental volume. He also has access to local population records, such as income level by section of town. Jon has compiled these data in Table 1.

After assessing eight potential locations, Jon has narrowed his choices down to the two sites shown in Figure 1. He estimates that the current and proposed stores will each have a primary trading area (accounting for 70 per cent of customers) of 2.5 miles.

Questions

1. Evaluate the data in Table 1.
2. What is the extent of trading-area overlap between the current and potential locations shown in Figure 1?
3. Under which circumstances is trading-area overlap between the current and potential locations desirable? Undesirable?
4. What additional information should Jonathan Smith examine before making a decision?

2. Abernathy's: Assessing Store Saturation Data

Abernathy's, a full-line discount store chain, has hired Location Consultants Inc. (a site-location specialist) to study the degree of market saturation by full-line discounters in three states: Connecticut, New Jersey, and New York. For now, Abernathy's is interested in learning which of these states provides the greatest overall opportunities for it to expand operations. At a later point, Location Consultants Inc. will be asked to assemble and compute store saturation data on a county-by-county basis to help Abernathy's focus on specific trading areas.

Among the sources of data being analyzed by Location Consultants Inc. are the "Census '84/'85: Discount Industry Breakdown by State" from *Discount Store News* and *Sales & Marketing Management's Survey of Buying Power* issues. Its preliminary findings are shown in Tables 1 and 2.

Table 1
Full-Line Discount Store Saturation Data

	Connecticut	New Jersey	New York
Projected full-line discounters sales, 1984 (millions)	$1,578	$1,950	$4,223
Total retail sales, 1984 (millions)	$18,925	$40,473	$81,562
Total population, 12/31/83 (thousands)	3,133.1	7,484.6	17,740.7
Number of stores, full-line discounters, 1984	161	199	431
Square footage, full-line discounters, 1984 (thousands)	12,393	19,701	40,028
Total effective buying income, 12/31/83 (millions)	$39,180.9	$87,142.8	$192,224.7
Area's percentage of U.S. total retail sales, 12/31/83	1.60	3.41	6.8
Area's percentage of U.S. total population, 12/31/83	1.33	3.17	7.5
Area's percentage of U.S. effective buying income, 12/31/83	1.68	3.74	8.2
Projections for December 31, 1988			
Total annual retail sales (millions)	$29,542	$63,051	$123,607
Total population (thousands)	3,170.2	7,661.9	18,100.9
Total annual effective buying income (millions)	$60,892.3	$136,341.2	$288,491.2

Sources: *"Census '84/'85: Discount Industry Breakdown by State,"* Discount Store News *(July 23, 1984), p. 31;* 1984 Survey of Buying Power: Sales & Marketing Management *(July 23, 1984), pp. C-39, C-41, C-128, C-129, C-135, C-138; and* 1984 Survey of Buying Power, Part II: Sales & Marketing Management *(October 29, 1984), pp. 60, 83, 85.*

Table 2
Ratios Used To Estimate Retail Store Saturation

	Connecticut	New Jersey	New York
Full-line discount sales as percentage of total retail sales	8.3	4.8	5.2
Full-line discount sales per capita	$503.67	$260.53	$238.04
Full-line discount sales as percentage of effective buying income	4.0	2.2	2.2
Average sales per year per full-line discount store (thousands)	$9,801.2	$9,799.0	$9,798.1
Average sales per square foot per full-line discount store	$127.33	$98.98	$105.50

Questions

1. Compute the buying power index for each state. Explain your answer.
2. Interpret Tables 1 and 2. Which state is the most saturated? The least saturated? Explain your answer.
3. What factors are *not* taken into account in Tables 1 and 2?
4. What sources of county-based data exist? Comment on their accuracy.

8

Choosing a Store Location: Site Selection

Chapter Objectives

1. To explain the various locational forms available to a retailer: the isolated store, the unplanned business district, and the planned shopping center
2. To study criteria for evaluating store sites
3. To examine the alternatives of building, leasing, and purchasing store facilities

For many years, the Fell's Point section of Baltimore, Maryland (a redeveloped community), had no supermarket for its residents. This was stifling the revitalization of the area: "The people who had moved into the neighborhood were tired of going to a butcher shop for meat, a fruit and vegetable stand for produce, a baker for bread, and so on. They wanted the convenience of a supermarket."

However, chains such as Safeway, Giant, and A&P showed no interest when contacted by Fell's Point community groups. They objected to the lack of available space, and would not locate in a 10,000-square-foot building. At that point, a community group began meeting with independent grocers and soon reached agreement with Paul Santoni.

This is how Fell's Point attracted Santoni's supermarket:

- The community group obtained special financing at low interest rates and paid $738,000 to construct the store.
- Paul Santoni was given a reasonable monthly lease covering 20 years. Once the lease is completed, Santoni will own the store.
- Santoni has complete control over operations.

- The 10,000-square-foot store is located on a side street between two main thorough-fares. The size is appropriate for Santoni.
- Both lower- and upper-income consumers are in the trading area, enabling Santoni to offer a good product mix.[1]

By being flexible in his selection of a store site, Paul Santoni has done well for himself—and for Fell's Point.

Overview

After a retailer investigates alternative trading areas (step 1), he or she must determine what type of location is desirable (step 2), select the general location (step 3), and choose a particular store site (step 4). Steps 2, 3, and 4 are discussed in this chapter.

Types of Locations

There are three basic types of locations that a retailer must distinguish among: the isolated store, the unplanned business district, and the planned shopping center. Each of these types of location has its own characteristics relating to the composition of competing stores, parking facilities, nearness to nonretail institutions (such as office buildings), and other factors.

Step 2 in the location process is a determination of which type of location to use.

The Isolated Store

An **isolated store** is a free-standing retail outlet located on either a highway or a side street. There are no adjacent retailers with which this type of store shares traffic.

The advantages of this type of retail structure are many:

1. There is no competition.
2. Rental costs are low.
3. There is flexibility.
   a. No group rules must be abided by in operation.
   b. Larger space may be attained.
   c. Location is by choice.
4. Isolation is good for stores involved in one-stop shopping.
5. Better road and traffic visibility is possible.
6. Facilities can be adapted to individual specifications.
7. Easy parking can be arranged.
8. Cost reductions are possible, leading to lower prices.

---

[1]Ronald Tanner, "Urban Revival: New Life for City Supers," *Progressive Grocer* (February 1985), pp. 22, 24.

There are also various disadvantages to this retail structure:

1. Initial consumers are difficult to attract.
2. Many consumers like variety in shopping.
3. Many consumers will not travel to one store.
4. Advertising costs are high.
5. Operating costs cannot be shared, such as outside lighting, security, maintenance of grounds, and garbage collection.
6. Zoning laws may restrict access to desirable locations.
7. In most cases, the store must be built rather than rented.

The difficulty of drawing and holding a target market is the reason that large retailers are usually those best suited to isolated locations. Smaller stores may be unable to develop a customer following because customers may be unwilling to travel to or shop at isolated stores that do not have a wide assortment of products (width and/or depth) and a local or national reputation.

Years ago, when discount operations were frowned on by traditional retailers, shopping centers forbade the entry of discounters. This forced the discounters to become isolated stores or to build their own centers, and they have been successful.

Today various retailers operate in isolated locations as well as at business district and shopping center sites. Examples of retailers using this location strategy are K mart, Kinney Shoes, McDonald's, Carvel, and Sears. Some retailers, such as many gasoline stations and convenience stores, continue to operate only in isolated spots.

The Unplanned Business District

An **unplanned business district** is a retail location where two or more stores are situated together or in a close proximity that is not the result of prior planning. Stores situate on the basis of what is best for them, not for the district. Accordingly four shoe stores may exist in an area that has no pharmacy.

There are four types of unplanned business districts: the central business district, the secondary business district, the neighborhood business district, and the string. A brief description of each of these follows.

The **central business district (CBD)** is the hub of retailing in a city. It is the largest shopping area in a city and is synonymous with the term "downtown." The CBD exists in that part of a town or city that has the greatest concentration of office buildings and retail stores. Vehicular and pedestrian traffic are highly concentrated. The core of the CBD usually does not exceed a square mile. Cultural and entertainment facilities surround it. Consumers are drawn from the whole urban area and include all ethnic groups and all classes of people.

The CBD has at least one major department store and a broad grouping of specialty and convenience stores. The arrangement of these stores follows no format but depends on history (first come, first located), retail trends, and luck.

The CBD has several strengths and weaknesses. Some of the strengths are excellent product assortment, access to public transportation, variety of store images within one area, variety of prices, variety of services, location of chain headquarters, and nearness to commercial and social facilities. Some of the weaknesses are inadequate parking, failure to improve old stores, high rents and taxes, discontinuity of offerings (e.g., four shoe stores and no pharmacy), traffic and delivery congestion, travel time for those living in the suburbs, high theft rates, and the declining condition of some central cities.

Much of the decline in CBDs can be explained by the increasing suburbanization of urban populations. In the beginning of the twentieth century, central cities had a well-balanced mixture of income, racial, and cultural groups, but gradually many middle-class and well-to-do people have moved to the suburbs. During the last three decades, the CBD has diminished relative to the planned shopping center.

Although many CBDs have declined, their share of retail sales is still substantial, and a number of downtown areas have been growing. Innovations have begun, such as closing off streets to vehicular traffic, modernizing storefronts and equipment, developing strong cooperative merchants' associations, planting trees to create "atmosphere," improving transportation, and integrating a commercial and residential environment. There are signs of a turnaround in many cities.

One of the best examples of a turnaround of a CBD is Minneapolis, Minnesota. Its Downtown Council has worked hard to strengthen the downtown area to make it more competitive with suburban shopping centers and to stimulate office construction. The Nicollet Mall, the hub of the Minneapolis downtown renewal area, received a $38 million investment. Most of the financing was raised through property assessments on "benefit zones" around the mall. The assessment formula included two kinds of benefit zones: on the mall and off the mall, with each zone subdivided into sectors so that properties closest to the center would bear the greatest proportion of both construction and maintenance expenses.

The mall is a totally reconstructed twelve-block section, with redesigned streets shared by pedestrians and public transit. Cars can cross the mall at through streets but are not allowed on the mall itself. Sidewalks are wide. Aboveground "skyways" connect buildings for pedestrians. There are benches for relaxing and resting. Shade trees, flowers, and fountains add to the atmosphere. Frequent activities such as boat shows, symphony orchestra performances, and antique car exhibits sustain a sense of excitement.[2]

Faneuil Hall in Boston is a different type of successful CBD renovation. When developer James Rouse took over the 6½-acre site containing three 150-year-old, block-long former food warehouses, the site had been abandoned for almost 10 years. Rouse creatively used landscaping, fountains, banners, courts, and graphics to enable Faneuil Hall to capture a "spirit of festival." Faneuil Hall has combined shopping, eating, and watching activities and made them fun. Today, Faneuil Hall attracts around 10 million visitors annually, about as many as Disneyland in California.[3]

Other major CBD projects include Omni Center (Miami), Water Tower Place

[2]Shawn Mitchell, "Downtown Renewal? Minneapolis Really Did It," *Stores* (September 1974), pp. 10–12; and "The Internationally Famous Nicollet Mall," Minneapolis Convention and Tourism Commission, n.d.
[3]Gurney Breckenfeld, "Jim Rouse Shows How to Give Downtown Retailing New Life," *Fortune* (April 10, 1978) pp. 84–91; Stanley H. Slom, "Boston's Faneuil Hall: A Rouse-ing Success," *Chain Store Age Executive* (March 1982), pp. 58, 63; and Howard Rudnitsky, "Make Room, Disney World, Federated and Gimbels," *Forbes* (May 9, 1983), pp. 100–104.

(Chicago), The Gallery (Philadelphia), City Center Square (St. Louis), the Market at Citicorp Center (New York), and Grand Avenue (Milwaukee).[4]

The **secondary business district (SBD)** is a shopping area in a city or town that is usually bounded by the intersection of two major streets. Cities generally have several SBDs, each having at least a junior department store, a variety store, and several small service shops. The SBD has grown in importance as cities have increased in population and "sprawled" over larger geographic areas.

The types of goods and services sold in the SBD are similar to those in the central business district. However, the SBD has smaller stores, less width and depth of assortment, a smaller trading area (consumers will not travel very far), and sells many convenience items.

The strengths and weaknesses of the SBD are similar to those of the CBD. The major strengths are good product assortment, access to public transportation or thoroughfares, less crowding, more personalized service, and location near residential areas. The major weaknesses are discontinuity of offerings, high rent and taxes (not as high as the CBD), congestion of traffic and deliveries, deteriorating conditions, parking difficulties, and fewer chain stores.[5] In general, these weaknesses have not affected the SBD to the extent that they have affected the CBD, and parking problems, travel time, and congestion are less for the SBD.

The **neighborhood business district (NBD)** is a shopping area that emerges to satisfy the convenience-shopping needs of a neighborhood. The NBD contains several small stores, with the major retailer being either a supermarket or a variety store, and it is located on the major street(s) of a residential area.

This business district offers a good location, long store hours, good parking, and a less hectic atmosphere than either the CBD or the SBD. On the other hand, there is a limited selection of goods and services, and prices (on the average) tend to be higher because competition is less than in the CBD or the SBD.

The **string** is composed of a group of retail stores, often with similar or compatible product lines, that has located along a street or highway. A string may start as an isolated store, success then breeding competitors. Car dealers, antique stores, and clothing stores are examples of the types of stores that locate in a string. There is little extension of the shopping area onto streets perpendicular to the string street.

The string store possesses many of the advantages associated with the isolated store (low rent, flexibility, road visibility, parking, lower operating costs), along with some of its disadvantages (limited variety of products, travel time, high advertising costs, zoning, building of premises). Unlike the isolated store, the string store has competition. This causes more traffic and allows for some sharing of common costs. It also leads to less control over prices and lower store loyalty. But the increase in traffic flow may exceed the losses caused by competition. This may explain why four gasoline service stations will locate on opposing corners.

---

[4]See Cara S. Trager, "Malls Breathe New Lives into Cities," *Advertising Age* (August 9, 1984), p. 13; Claudia Ricci, "Centers of Some Cities Bloom Anew as Havens of Boutique Shopping," *Wall Street Journal* (May 2, 1983), pp. 1, 26; G. Bruce Knecht, "Renaissance Center: Ford's Costly and Failing Bid to Revive Detroit," *New York Times* (July 3, 1983), Section 3, pp. 4–5; Barbara Bryan, "Urban Renewal," *Stores* (July 1984), pp. 47–49; and Joseph B. Clithero and Lawrence A. Levenson, "Urban Renewal Projects Pull Up Short of Revitalizing Downtown Retailing When They Only Entail Brick & Mortar," *Marketing News* (February 1, 1985), p. 23.

[5]See Barry Berman (Editor), *An Evaluation of Selected Business Districts in Nassau, Suffolk and Queens Counties* (Hempstead, N.Y.: Hofstra University Press, 1980).

Figure 8-1 shows a map depicting the various forms of unplanned business districts and isolated locations.

The Planned Shopping Center

A **planned shopping center** is centrally owned or managed, is planned as a unit, is based on balanced tenancy (the group of stores complement each other in the quality and variety of their merchandise offerings), and is surrounded by parking facilities. **Balanced tenancy** means that the type and number of stores within any planned center are related to the overall needs of the surrounding population. To ensure that balance exists, a planned shopping center often specifies the proportion of total space that can be occupied by each type of retailer. In addition, the center places limits on the merchandise lines that can be stocked by each of the various retailers.

The planned center has one or more anchor, or generator, stores and a variety of smaller stores. In most cases, a unified and cooperative retailing strategy is followed.

The planned shopping center has grown to the point where annual sales in the nation's shopping centers comprised 42 per cent of total retail store sales in 1980.[6] As the CBD has declined, the planned shopping center has grown.

There are several reasons for the success of the planned shopping center. Here are some of them:

1. Well-rounded product and service offerings because of long-range planning.
2. Growing suburban population.
3. Interest in one-stop, family shopping.
4. Cooperative planning and sharing of common costs.
5. Creation of a distinctive shopping center image.
6. Maximization of pedestrian traffic through the location of the center and individual stores.
7. Access to highways and availability of parking.
8. Declining appeal of city shopping.
9. Lower rent and taxes than central district stores.
10. Lower theft rates.
11. Popularity of malls.
    a. Open (shopping area closed to vehicular traffic).
    b. Closed (shopping area closed to vehicular traffic and all stores under one temperature-controlled roof). See Figure 8-2.
12. Growth of discount malls.

Despite this overwhelming list of reasons for locating in a planned shopping center, there are some limitations to this retail form:

1. Inflexible operations, such as store hours.
2. Rent higher than for an isolated store.
3. Restrictions as to merchandise that can be sold.
4. Competitive environment.

[6]"A Life Raft for Malls When a Tenant Sinks," *Business Week* (August 30, 1982), p. 30.

Unplanned Business Districts and Isolated Locations

LEGEND:

A Central Business District
B Secondary Business District
C Neighborhood Business District
D String
E Isolated Location

Figure 8-1
Courtesy Kenneth Cooperman.

Figure 8-2 A Closed Shopping Mall

The Courtyard shopping center (near Los Angeles) features two department stores, over 90 specialty stores, an ice-skating facility, and a community theater. Courtesy Ernest W. Hahn, Inc.

5. Payment for items that may be of no value to the individual store, such as forced membership in a merchants' association.
6. Overexpansion.
7. Domination of the large anchor store.

The success and growth of planned shopping centers has gone on for many years and is expected to continue. In 1956, there were 940 centers that accounted for 7 per cent of store sales; by 1960, there were 4,500 centers; and during 1983, there were 23,300. The International Council of Shopping Centers estimates that 50 per cent of U.S. retail store sales will be in shopping centers by 1990.[7]

The importance of shopping centers can also be seen by examining factors aside from the number of units. First, individual retail chains have large stakes in shopping

[7]Ibid., p. 10; and Robert Guenther, "Real Estate: Shopping Habits . . . Screening Tenants . . . Top U.S. Buildings," *Wall Street Journal* (April 21, 1982), p. 31.

centers. For example, Federated Stores, Allied Stores, The Limited, B. Dalton Bookseller, and J. C. Penney are among the chains that derive substantial sales and profits from outlets in shopping centers. Second, over the last several years, a number of big retailers have become involved in shopping-center development. Typically, these companies buy a desirable site of their choosing, years in advance, and contact another major retailer (depending on the size of the center). They then bring in a developer who will build, own, and lease the center and connect it to anchor stores. For instance, Sears has participated in the construction of dozens of shopping centers; and Publix Supermarkets operates a number of shopping centers with hundreds of small-store tenants. Third, about 60 per cent of total new retail square footage and 88 per cent of new department stores currently being constructed are in shopping centers.[8]

To sustain long-term sales growth, shopping centers are engaging in a variety of practices:

- Several older centers have been or are being renovated, expanded, repositioned, and so on. The Mall at 163rd Street (Miami) and The Mall at Short Hills (New Jersey) are examples of 25-year-old centers that have been revitalized.[9]
- The mix of retailers has been broadened at many centers to attract greater customers to one-stop shopping. The centers are now more likely to include banks, stock brokers, dentists, beauty salons, theaters, television repair services, and car-leasing offices.[10]
- Off-price shopping centers are being located in suburban areas; unlike traditional factory outlets, these centers feature new stores and balanced tenancy. One such off-price shopping center is the Washington Outlet Mall in Dale City, Virginia. This center will eventually contain 1.25 million square feet of space, large anchor stores, and 100 smaller stores. It expects to draw customers from as far as 250 miles away, with a regular trading area of 60 to 90 miles.[11]

There are three major types of planned shopping centers: regional, community, and neighborhood. The characteristics of these centers are displayed in Table 8-1, and described next.

The **regional shopping center** is a planned shopping area that sells predominantly shopping goods to a geographically dispersed market. The regional center has at least one or two large department stores and as many as 100 or more small retailers, as illustrated in Figure 8-3. The market for the average regional center is over 100,000 people, who live up to 30 minutes' driving time from the center. Some large regional shopping centers have as many as six major retailers and 2 million or more square feet of space.

The regional center is the result of a planned effort to re-create the shopping services of a central city in suburbia. Some experts even credit the regional shopping center with becoming the social, cultural, and vocational focal point of an entire community. Frequently, a regional shopping center is used as a town plaza, a community meeting place, and a concert hall. A *U.S. News & World Report* survey found that

[8]"A Life Raft for Malls When a Tenant Sinks," p. 30.
[9]Robert Guenther, "Old Shopping Mall Reverses Decline with Major Facelift," *Wall Street Journal* (July 20, 1983), p. 29; and Eric C. Peterson, "Short Hills," *Stores* (January 1984), pp. 99–103.
[10]Eric Peterson, "New Neighbors," *Stores* (September 1984), pp. 36ff.
[11]"Washington Outlet: Developing a Capital Idea," *Chain Store Age Executive* (September 1984), pp. 68–74. See also "Whatever the Name, Value Is the Game," *Chain Store Age Executive* (February 1985), pp. 47–48ff.

Table 8-1
Characteristics of Neighborhood, Community, and Regional Types of Planned Shopping Centers

Features	Type of Center		
	Neighborhood	Community	Regional
Floor area (sq ft)	30,000–100,000	100,000–300,000	300,000 to over 2,000,000
Average gross floor area (sq ft)	40,000	200,000	750,000
Average site area (acres)	3–10	10–30	30–100+
Number of families and people needed to support center	1,000 families; 7,000–70,000 people	5,000–10,000 families; 20,000–100,000 people	70,000–300,000 families; over 100,000 people
Principal tenant	Supermarket or drugstore	Variety or junior department store	One, two, or more department stores
Number of stores	5–15	15–25	50–125 or more
Types of goods sold	Emphasis on convenience goods	Mostly convenience goods, some shopping goods	Emphasis on shopping goods, large assortment
Trading area in driving time	Fewer than 15 minutes	Up to 20 minutes	Up to 30 minutes
Location	Along a major thoroughfare	Close to populated suburbs	Outside central city, on arterial highway or expressway
Layout	Strip	Strip or L shape	Mall, often enclosed with anchor stores at either end

Americans spend more time in shopping centers than anywhere else outside their home and workplace.

The first regional shopping center was established in 1950 in Seattle, Washington, anchored by a branch of Bon Marche, a large downtown department store. Southdale Center (outside Minneapolis), built in 1956 for the Dayton Hudson Corporation was the first fully enclosed, climate-controlled mall.

The **community shopping center** is a planned shopping area that sells both convenience and shopping items to city and suburban dwellers. The community shopping center has a variety store and/or a small department store in addition to the outlets found in the neighborhood shopping center. A greater assortment of products is available than in the neighborhood center. From 20,000 to 100,000 people, who live within 20 minutes of the center, are serviced by this type of retail arrangement.

Greater and more long-range planning is used for the community shopping center than for the neighborhood shopping center. For example, balanced tenancy is usually enforced strictly. A barbershop owner would have to sell to someone interested in continuing the business. The store could not be sold to a dry cleaner.

The Collin Creek Mall, Dallas, Texas

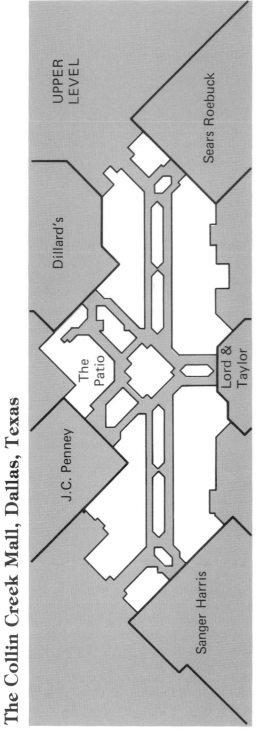

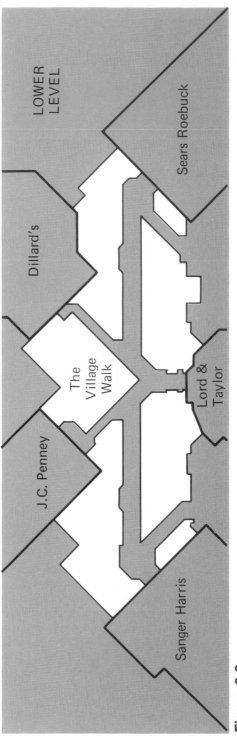

Figure 8-3

The Collin Creek Mall is anchored by the five department stores shown above. The mall also contains more than 160 other shops and restaurants (which are situated in the white spaces adjacent to the anchor stores). Over 250,000 people live within 10 miles of Collin Creek. Courtesy Collin Creek Mall.

The **neighborhood shopping center** is a planned shopping area that sells mostly convenience items. The largest store is a supermarket and/or a drugstore. Other retailers in the center may include a hardware store, a barbershop and/or a beauty parlor, a bakery, a laundry–dry cleaner, and a gasoline station. The neighborhood shopping center caters to 7,000 to 70,000 people who live within 15 minutes' driving time.

The neighborhood shopping center usually is arranged in a strip. When first developed, it is carefully planned, and tenants are balanced. Over time, the planned aspects of this center diminish as newcomers face fewer restrictions. For example, a barbershop could be replaced by a second dry cleaner. In this case, there would be no barbershop and two cleaners. The ability of the center to maintain balance depends on its continuing attractiveness to potential tenants.

The difference between the neighborhood shopping center and the string is that the former plans to satisfy a wide range of consumer needs and the latter concentrates on individual store planning and success.

Choice of a General Location

The last part of step 2 requires the retailer to choose one of the three types of locations: isolated, unplanned district, or planned center. The choice would depend on the retailer's strategy and a careful evaluation of the advantages and disadvantages of each type of location.

As an illustration, Lamston (a Northeastern variety store chain) avoids planned shopping centers and concentrates on unplanned business districts:[12]

> One reason why variety stores have not done well in malls is because that's where people go when they have a lot of time to shop. In a mall, unlike a downtown location, a customer is offered a specialty store in every line we carry. If she wants to buy a greeting card, she goes to a greeting card store or whatever.
>
> We need heavily trafficked areas where the customers have to shop in a hurry. [Then customers] want to find that variety of merchandise at one store. We benefit from offering a convenience that stands us in good stead in our locations.

Once the type of location is determined, the retailer must select a broadly defined store site, step 3. Two decisions are necessary. First the specific type of isolated store, unplanned business district, or planned shopping center location must be picked. If the retailer wants an isolated store he or she must decide whether to locate on a highway or a side street. Should the retailer desire an unplanned business area, he or she must opt for a location in a CBD, a SBD, an NBD, or a string. The retailer seeking a planned area must choose either a regional, community, or neighborhood shopping center.

Second, the retailer must define the general location. For an isolated store, a specific highway or side street is selected. For an unplanned district or planned center the specific district (e.g., downtown Los Angeles or a Pittsburgh suburb) or center (e.g., Southdale) is designated.

In step 3, the retailer narrows down the decisions made in the first two steps and selects a general location. Step 4 requires the retailer to select the exact site, including

[12]Jacquelyn Bivins, "F.W. Woolworth: Turning Back the Clock?" *Chain Store Age Executive* (October 1983), p. 32; and Isadore Barmash, "Lamston Still Small and Local," *New York Times* (November 22, 1983), pp. D1, D23.

position on block, side of street, terms of tenancy, and so on. The evaluations of a general location and a specific site within that location are described together in the next section because many strategic decisions are similar for these two steps.

Location and Site Evaluation

The evaluation of a general location and of the specific site contained within this location requires extensive analysis. Site selection is as crucial as the choice of a retail area, especially for stores that rely on customer traffic patterns to generate business.

In any area, the optimum site for a particular store is called the **one-hundred per cent location.** Because different kinds of retailers need different types of locations, a location classified as 100 per cent for one retailer may be less than optimal for another retailer.

For example, a ladies' specialty shop may seek a location with different strengths than those desired by an optical store. The specialty shop would benefit from heavy pedestrian traffic, closeness to major department stores, and proximity to other specialty stores. The optometrist would rather locate in an area with ample parking. Her customers normally do not mix shopping activities when buying eyewear, and much of the heavy traffic in a crowded area would be wasteful.

Figure 8-4 contains a checklist for location and site evaluation. When choosing a location, the retailer would rate each alternative location (and specific site) on all of the criteria and develop an overall rating for each alternative. It should be pointed out again that two stores may rate the same location quite differently, depending on the requirements of the stores. Also, this figure should be used in conjunction with the area charts shown in Chapter 7, not instead of them.

Pedestrian Traffic

Probably the single most important measure of a location's and site's value is the number and type of people passing by it. Other things being equal, the site with the highest pedestrian traffic is best.

Because everyone passing by a store site is not a good prospect for all types of stores, many retailers employ selective counting procedures, such as counting only females carrying shopping bags. Otherwise, pedestrian traffic totals will include nonshoppers. As an example, it would be incorrect for a department store to count people who pass the store on the way to work. In fact, much of the traffic in a downtown location may be people who are in the area for specific nonretailing activities.

A proper pedestrian traffic count should include these four elements:

- A separation of the count by age and gender (children under a certain age should not be counted).
- A division of the count by time (this allows the study of peaks, low points, and changes in the gender of people passing by the hour).
- Pedestrian interviews (these enable the researchers to verify the proportion of potential shoppers).
- Spot analysis of shopping trips (these interviews verify stores visited or planned to be visited).

A Location/Site Evaluation Checklist

Rate each of the following criteria on a scale of 1 to 10, with 1 being excellent and 10 being poor.

Pedestrian Traffic	Number of people	_____
	Type of people	_____
Vehicular Traffic	Number of vehicles	_____
	Type of vehicles	_____
	Traffic congestion	_____
Parking Facilities	Number and quality of parking spots	_____
	Distance to store	_____
	Availability of employee parking	_____
Transportation	Availability of mass transit	_____
	Access from major highways	_____
	Ease of deliveries	_____
Store Composition	Number and size of stores	_____
	Affinity	_____
	Retail balance	_____
Specific Site	Visibility	_____
	Placement in the location	_____
	Size and shape of the lot	_____
	Size and shape of the building	_____
	Condition and age of the lot and building	_____
Terms of Occupancy	Ownership or leasing terms	_____
	Operations and maintenance costs	_____
	Taxes	_____
	Zoning	_____
	Voluntary regulations	_____
Overall Rating	General location	_____
	Site	_____

Figure 8-4

Vehicular Traffic

The quantity and characteristics of vehicular traffic must be examined, especially by retailers who appeal to driving customers. Stores in regional shopping centers, fast-food franchises, gasoline stations, and convenience food stores are examples of drive-in retailers that depend on heavy vehicular traffic. Automotive traffic studies are particularly important in suburban areas, where pedestrian traffic is often limited.

As in the analysis of pedestrian traffic, some adjustments to the raw count of vehicular traffic should be made. Some retailers count only homeward-bound traffic. Some exclude vehicles passing on the other side of a divided highway. Many retailers omit out-of-state license plates in their counts.

Data pertaining to traffic patterns are usually available from the state highway department, the county engineer, or the regional planning commission.

In addition to traffic counts, the retailer should study the extent and timing of congestion (caused by heavy traffic, detours, narrow and poor roads, and so on). Vehicular customers will normally avoid heavily congested areas and shop in areas where driving time and driving difficulties are minimized.

Parking Facilities

The importance of good parking facilities must not be overlooked in an evaluation of a location and a specific site within it. The vast majority of all retail stores built in the United States since the end of World War II include some provision for off-street parking. In several central business districts, parking facilities are provided by individual stores, cooperative arrangements among stores, and municipal governments. The number and quality of parking spots, their distances from the store site, and the availability of employee parking should all be evaluated.

It is difficult to generalize about the parking needs of a location. However, shopping centers normally require about four to five parking spaces per 1,000 square feet of gross floor area. Other types of retailers vary significantly, depending on the length of an average shopping trip and the variation of shoppers during a day or season. A supermarket may require 10 to 15 parking spaces per 1,000 square feet of gross floor area, whereas a furniture store needs only three or four parking spaces per 1,000 square feet. With more compact cars on the road, the Urban Land Institute recommends that retailers restripe their parking lots. This would increase the number of parking spaces by 15 to 30 per cent.[13]

Sometimes free parking in shopping locations close to downtown areas creates problems. Commuters and employees of nearby businesses park in these facilities, reducing the spaces available for shoppers. This problem can be lessened by the validation of shoppers' parking stubs and requiring payment from nonshoppers.

Another problem occurs when the number of stores in a location expands. The increase in stores can be the result of a growing population in the trading area or a reaction to increased competition from another shopping location. Whatever the reason, parking facilities suffer because space that was formerly allocated to parking is

[13]Guenther, "Real Estate . . . Screening Tenants . . . Top U.S. Buildings," p. 31.

used for new store sites, and parking needs rise to accommodate new employees, new shoppers, and longer shopping trips.

Double-deck parking or parking tiers are possible solutions to this problem. In addition to saving land, these types of parking shorten the distance from a parked car to a store. This is important when one considers that a customer of a regional shopping center does not like to walk more than 500 feet from his or her car to the center.

Having too large a parking facility may also create a problem. If the facility is not full, the store's image may suffer. An illusion of emptiness is created, and customers wonder why. A parking lot may contain 150 cars, but if the capacity of the lot is 500 cars, it appears that the lot is empty and the store unpopular.

Parking adequacy, as mentioned, is difficult to determine. It depends on factors such as the trading area of the store, the type of store, the portion of shoppers using an automobile, the existence of other parking facilities, the turnover of spaces, parking by nonshoppers, and fluctuations in parking demand.

Transportation

The availability of mass transportation, access from major highways, and ease of deliveries must be examined in the evaluation of a location and a specific site.

In downtown areas, closeness to public transportation is important, particularly to customers who do not own cars or customers who would not drive into an area with heavy traffic congestion and poor parking. The availability of buses, taxicabs, subways, trains, or other kinds of public transportation must be investigated for locations not catering to vehicular traffic. Most downtown shopping areas are at the hub of a transportation network, allowing customers from all over a city to shop there.

Locations depending on vehicular traffic should be rated on the basis of their access to major thoroughfares. As mentioned in the previous chapter, driving time is an important consideration for many customers. In addition, drivers heading eastbound on a highway often do not like to make a U-turn to get to a store on the westbound side of the highway.

The transportation network should also be examined for its ability to convey heavy delivery trucks to and from the store. Many thoroughfares are excellent for customer traffic but ban truck traffic or are unable to bear its weight.

Store Composition

The store composition in the area should be studied. How many stores are there? How large are they? The number and size of stores should be consistent with the kind of location selected. For example, a retailer interested in an isolated store would want no stores nearby; a retailer interested in a neighborhood business district would want to locate in an area with ten or fewer small stores; and a retailer interested in a regional shopping center would desire a location with more than fifty stores, including at least two large ones.

A store's compatibility with adjacent or nearby retailers should be weighed. **Affinity** occurs when a store is attracted to an area because of its ability to blend in and cooperate with the other stores in that area. If stores located together have a strong level of affinity, the sales of each store are greater than they would be if the stores were situated apart from each other.

The practice of similar or complementary stores locating near each other is based on two major premises: (1) customers like to compare the offerings of similar stores as to price, style, selection, and service; and (2) customers like the concept of one-stop shopping. A variety of products are often purchased from different stores (complementary) on the same shopping trip. Thus, affinities can exist among competitive stores as well as complementary stores, because increased traffic in a location creates higher sales for all.

One measure of compatibility is the degree to which stores exchange customers. The stores within the following categories are very compatible with each other and have a high level of customer interchange:

- Drugstore, supermarket, bakery, grocery store, meat store.
- Department store, apparel store, hosiery store, lingerie shop, shoe store, variety store, jewelry store, dry goods store, knitting store.

For example, Publix Supermarkets are frequently located in neighborhood shopping centers with Eckerd drugstores; Publix does not locate in regional centers, because of the different nature of the shopping trip and the low turnover of parking spaces. Radio Shack likes its stores to be near hardware or menswear outlets; it views beauty salons negatively. Walgreen rates small centers with laundromats highly: "People in laundromats have nothing to do while waiting for their clothes to go around."[14]

A location's retail balance should also be considered. **Retail balance** refers to the mix of stores within a district or shopping center. Proper balance occurs when the number of store facilities for each merchandise or service classification is equal to the location's market potential; a wide range of product or service classifications is provided to assure one-stop shopping; there is an adequate assortment within any product or service classification; and there is a proper mix of store types (tenant balance).

Specific Site

In addition to the criteria already detailed, the specific site should be evaluated on the basis of visibility, placement in the location, size and shape of the lot, size of the building, and condition and age of the lot and building.

Visibility is a site's ability to be seen by pedestrian and vehicular traffic. A site that is on a side street or at the end of a shopping center does not achieve the same visibility as a site on a major road or at the entrance of a shopping center. High visibility makes passersby aware that a store exists and is open. Furthermore, some shoppers feel uncomfortable going down a side street or to the end of a center.

Placement in the location refers to a site's relative position in the district or center. A corner location is often desirable because it is situated at the intersection of two streets and therefore results in "corner influence." A corner site is usually more expensive to own or lease because it offers these advantages: increased show-window display area, greater pedestrian traffic due to converging traffic flows from two streets,

---

[14]"A Sixth Sense for Site Selection," *Progressive Grocer* (September 1980), p. 68; and John R. Dorfman, "Sense of Site," *Forbes* (February 14, 1983), pp. 122–123.

and easing of traffic congestion through the use of two or more entrances. Corner influence is greatest in high-volume retail locations. As an example, in 1980, 75 to 80 per cent of the new 7-Eleven stores opened were on corner lots. Of the 271 stores closed, 20 to 25 per cent were shut down simply so new outlets could be placed on nearby corners.[15]

Some of the advantages of a corner location are reduced in a shopping center. For example, traffic on the streets perpendicular to a mall is usually sparse. Accordingly little additional traffic accrues to a corner store. Also, because many stores have two entrances (one in the mall and one in the parking area), shoppers can go from parking spots to the main mall without using the designated walkways, window display space is greater, and traffic flows are eased.

Placement decisions should be keyed to retailer needs. For example, a convenience store, such as a stationery store, would have much different needs than a shopping store, such as a furniture store. The stationery store would be concerned about the side of the street, the location relative to other stores, nearness to parking, access to a bus stop, and distance from homes. The furniture store would be interested in roominess, the accessibility of its pickup platform to consumers, the ease of deliveries to the store, the use of a corner site to increase window display space, and proximity to wallpaper and other related retailers.

The size and shape of the lot should be evaluated. As an example, a department store requires significantly larger space than a boutique; and a department store may desire a square site, whereas the boutique seeks a rectangular site. Any site should be assessed in terms of total space needed: parking, walkways, selling, nonselling, and so on.

When one is buying or renting an existing building, its size and shape should be examined. In addition, the condition and age of the lot and the building should be investigated. These site characteristics are then measured against the needs of the retailer.

Several retailers have developed computer models to aid in site selection. One firm, Victory Markets (a large supermarket chain operating out of Norwich, New York), has constructed a model to predict the weekly retail sales of a potential site. Safeway has used computerized site-selection models since 1973. A number of department store chains use computer models in selecting regional shopping center sites.

There are three types of computer site-selection models: analog, regression, and gravity.[16] The analog model is the most simple and popular model. Potential sales are estimated on the basis of competition, market shares, and primary trading area. The regression model develops a series of mathematical equations that show the association between sales and a variety of independent variables at each location under consideration. As an illustration, Victory Markets analyzes population, number of households, the existence of rivers and railroad tracks, and traffic patterns. The gravity model is an adaptation of Reilly's law which is based on the theory that consumers gravitate to stores that are closer and more attractive than competitors'. Variables such as the

---

[15]Steve Frazier, "Southland's Deft Response to Troubles in '80 Puts It Back in Analysts' Favor," *Wall Street Journal* (February 3, 1981), p. 18.

[16]"Selecting a Store Site, The Computer Way," *Chain Store Age Executive* (March 1981), pp. 45–48; Saul Sands and Peter Moore, "Store Site Selection by Discriminant Analysis," *Journal of Market Research Society*, Vol. 23 (1981), pp. 40–51; "Why Site Selection," *Chain Store Age Executive* (January 1983), pp. 30, 32; and C. Samuel Craig, Avijit Ghosh, and Sara McLafferty, "Models of the Retail Location Process: A Review," *Journal of Retailing*, Vol. 60 (Spring 1984), pp. 5–36.

distance between consumers and competitors, the distance between consumers and the site, and store image are contained in a gravity model.

Computer site-selection models offer several benefits to retailers. They are more objective and systematic than nonquantitative evaluation methods. They offer insights about the weight of each locational attribute. They are useful in screening a large number of locations. They can be used to assess management performance by comparing forecasts with actual results.

Terms of Occupancy

Terms of occupancy must be evaluated. They include ownership or leasing terms, operations and maintenance costs, taxes, zoning restrictions, and voluntary regulations.

A retailer with adequate financial resources can either own or lease premises. Ownership is more common in small stores, in small communities, and/or at inexpensive locations. Ownership has several advantages over leasing, the most important being the absence of the risk that an outside property owner will not renew a lease or will double or triple rental payments when a lease expires. Many retailers are hesitant to invest in significant store renovation when they are unsure about long-run occupancy. Retailers also fear that rental increases or the possibilities of nonrenewal would substantially lower the salability of their businesses.

A second benefit of ownership is the flexibility of operations. Retail leases often stipulate that storekeepers must restrict themselves to the sale of specified merchandise and/or cannot break down walls or alter fixtures and so on. One long-range effect of inflexibility of operations in leasing may be that the retailer is unable to take advantage of scrambled merchandising.

If a retailer chooses to own its store premises, it must be determined whether a new facility is to be constructed or an existing building is to be purchased. In weighing these alternatives, the retailer would consider the age and condition of the building, the adaptability of the building to the new retailer's needs, location availability, purchase price and maintenance costs, zoning restrictions, and construction time. To encourage building rehabilitation in small towns (5,000 to 50,000 people), Congress enacted the Main Street program of the National Trust for Historic Preservation, which has invested well over $130 million in many small towns throughout the United States since 1981. Retailers benefit by participating in this program because they receive tax credits and low-interest loans.[17]

Despite the benefits of ownership, leasing has become popular. Leasing requires a lower capital investment and less financial risk than property ownership. Often retailers do not have the funds to buy properties or feel that these funds could be better spent opening new locations or investing in expanded inventories. In addition, short-run leasing allows a retailer to reappraise market conditions and relocate if necessary without incurring any financial losses.

Some large retailers build their new stores and then sell them to real-estate investors who lease the buildings back to the retailers on a long-term basis. This practice is known as a **sale-leaseback.** The retailers using sale-leasebacks are able to build stores to their own specifications, have bargaining control in leasing terms, and reduce their capital expenditures.

---

[17]"Investors Find a New Home: Small-Town Main Streets," *Business Week* (August 6, 1984), pp. 71–72.

The Major Characteristics of Ownership and Leasing Alternatives

Alternative	Advantages	Disadvantages
A. Buying a lot and building a facility on it	1. Ownership 2. Flexibility in operations 3. New facility 4. Constant mortgage payments 5. Appreciation of land value	1. High initial costs 2. Construction time 3. Lack of good available sites 4. Long-run commitment 5. Zoning problems
B. Buying an existing facility	1. Ownership 2. Flexibility in operations 3. Quick occupancy 4. Good locations 5. Limited zoning problems 6. Constant mortgage payments 7. Appreciation of land value	1. High initial costs 2. Long-run commitment 3. Adaptability of fixtures, etc. 4. Age of facility
C. Leasing	1. Low initial costs 2. Quick occupancy 3. Good locations 4. Reduced long-run commitment 5. Limited zoning problems	1. Nonrenewal problems 2. Increases in leasing terms 3. Inflexibility of operations 4. Age of facility 5. Difficulties in resale of business

Figure 8-5

Recently, tax-exempt industrial revenue bonds have also been used to finance retail stores and warehouses. A state or municipality uses the bond proceeds to build a store or warehouse and gives the retailer a long lease with the lease payments pledged to pay principal and interest. This practice reduces borrowing costs for private companies.

Figure 8-5 highlights the general advantages and disadvantages of buying a lot and building upon it, buying an existing building, and leasing.[18] Because most retailers lease their facilities, the following discussion centers on leasing terms.

[18]See "Retailers' Question: Is It Better to Lease or to Own?" *Chain Store Age Executive* (March 1980), pp. 34–35; *Retailer's Guide to Understanding Leases* (New York: National Retail Merchants Association, 1980); and Eric Peterson, "Conversions," *Stores* (July 1984), pp. 35–36ff.

It is quite important to understand lease terms, because they often involve commitments of 10, 15, 25, or even 99 years. Property owners no longer rely only on constant rentals, partly because of the inflation levels of recent years, and terms can therefore become quite complicated. The simplest, most straightforward lease is the **straight lease.** With this type of agreement, the retailer pays a fixed dollar amount per month over the life of the lease. Rent usually ranges from $1 to $50 annually per square foot, depending on the desirability of the location, store traffic, and so on. In some sites, rents can be much higher (up to $400 per square foot and more). There are four other types of rental provisions that are popular (and may be combined with each other or the straight lease): percentage lease, graduated lease, maintenance increase recoupment, and net lease.

A **percentage lease** stipulates that rent is related to the retailer's sales or profits. In contrast, a straight rental lease provides for constant payments each month, regardless of volume. For example, a drugstore may pay 4 per cent of sales, a toy store 6 per cent, and a camera store 12 per cent (these figures are keyed to space occupied and inventory turnover).[19] This type of arrangement allows the property owner to cover inflation or maintenance cost increases, and the tenant finds that the lease is a variable cost, which means that low sales for a new store will result in low rental payments. The rate varies by type of shopping district or center as well as by type of store.

Percentage leases have some variations. In one variation, a minimum or maximum rental is noted:

- Percentage lease with specified minimum—this recognizes that low sales are partly the retailer's responsibility and that the property owner should receive some minimum payments to pay taxes and maintain the property.
- Percentage lease with specified maximum—this recognizes that a very successful retailer should not pay more than a maximum rental charge. Superior merchandising, promotion, and pricing result in rewards to the retailer.

A second variation of the percentage lease is the sliding scale. In this agreement, the ratio of rent to sales changes as sales increase. The sliding-down scale requires the retailer to pay a lower percentage of sales as sales go up; 5 per cent of the first $100,000 in sales and 3 per cent of all sales over $100,000 is an example. The sliding-down scale gives an incentive to the effective retailer, while benefiting the property owner.

Another type of lease is the **graduated lease.** A graduated lease calls for rent increases over a specified period of time. Thus, rent may be $2,000 per month for the first five years, $2,400 per month for the next five years, and $2,800 per month for the last five years of a lease. The rental payments are known in advance by both the retailer and the property owner and are based on anticipated increases in sales and costs. There is no problem in auditing sales figures, as there is for percentage leases. The graduated lease is often used with small retailers, whose financial statements and controls are weak.

A lease with a provision for **maintenance increase recoupment** provides for increases in rent if the property owner's taxes, heating bills, insurance, and expenses go beyond a certain point. This provision is usually associated with a straight rental lease.

The **net lease** mandates that all maintenance expenses, such as heat, insurance, and interior repair, are to be paid by the retailer, who is responsible for the satisfactory

[19]Lewis A. Spalding, "Good Sites," *Stores* (January 1982), pp. 55–56ff.

quality of these items. A net lease allows a property owner to be freed from management of the facility and enables a retailer to have control over the maintenance items that affect the store.

Leases within shopping centers have often included restrictive clauses that usually protect the anchor tenants (large department stores) from too much competition—especially from discounters. These restrictive clauses may involve limits on merchandise lines, restrictions on employee parking, prohibitions of discounting, mandatory membership in a merchants' group, payments for common services, and control of stores' operations. Department stores have been given these protective clauses because developers need their long-term commitments to finance the building of their centers.

Some shopping-center practices have been investigated by the Federal Trade Commission (FTC). In a case involving Tyson's Corners in Virginia (one of the largest shopping centers in the United States), the center's developers and their key tenants were prohibited from using leases that allowed them to approve tenants, determine the amount of floor space available to tenants, exclude particular types of tenants, approve the types or brands of merchandise sold by tenants, specify the price range of products, control advertising content, and prohibit price advertising.[20]

Tyson's Corners was permitted to enter into leasing agreements with tenants that maintain a balanced tenancy; prohibit the occupancy of an objectionable tenant (such as an adult bookstore); do not force them to occupy space adjacent to other tenants who create undue noise, litter, or odor; require reasonable appearance standards; and establish a shopping center layout that designates stores, locations, and size and height of buildings.[21]

The FTC's actions in the Tyson's Corners and other cases have reduced the power of large tenants in shopping centers.[22] These cases represent the first major antitrust litigation against the centers.

After assessing ownership or leasing opportunities, a retailer must determine the costs of operations and maintenance. Mortgage or rental payments are only one part of a site's costs. The age and condition of a facility may cause a retailer to have high total monthly costs, even though the mortgage or rent is low. Furthermore, the costs of extensive renovations should be calculated.

Taxes must be evaluated, especially in an ownership situation. Long-run projections, as well as current taxes, must be examined. Differences in sales taxes (those that customers pay) and business taxes (those that the retailer pays) among alternative sites must be weighed.

Zoning restrictions should be analyzed. These are legal prohibitions pertaining to store location, store size, building height, type of merchandise carried, and so on. For example, San Francisco recently passed a law requiring "mandatory sunlight access" onto Union Square. As a result, new building height and size are severely restricted in this district to allow sunshine to reach sidewalks.[23] Voluntary regulations should also be examined. These are voluntary restrictions on business (which are most prevalent in planned shopping centers) and include membership in merchants' groups, uniform store hours, and cooperative security forces.

[20]Joseph Barry Mason, "Power and Channel Conflict in Shopping Center Development," *Journal of Marketing*, Vol. 39 (April 1975), p. 29.
[21]Ibid., p. 34.
[22]For example, see "Chains Protest the FTC's New Lease Probe," *Chain Store Age Executive* (August 1979), p. 15; and "FTC Opens Up Malls to Discounters," *Chain Store Age Executive* (March 1979), p. 21.
[23]Carrie Dolan, "San Francisco Keeps Stores in Sunlight," *Wall Street Journal* (November 16, 1984), p. 33.

Overall Rating

The last step in the selection of a general location, and a specific site within it, is the computation of an overall rating. First, a location is given an overall rating based on its performance on each of the criteria displayed in Figure 8-4. The overall ratings of alternative locations are then compared, and the best location is chosen. Second, the same procedure is used to evaluate the alternative sites within the location.

It is often difficult to develop and compare composite evaluations, because some attributes may be positive while others are negative. For example, the general location may be a good shopping center, but the site in the center may be poor; or an area may have excellent potential, but take two years to build a store. Therefore, the attributes in Figure 8-4 need to be weighted to reflect their importance. An overall rating should also include certain knockout factors that would preclude consideration of a site. Possible knockout factors are a short duration lease (fewer than three years), no evening or weekend pedestrian traffic, and a poor maintenance record by the landlord.

Choosing a Store Location—Site Selection: A Summary

Three types of locations for retailers were described in this chapter: the isolated store, the unplanned business district, and the planned shopping center.

The isolated store is a free-standing retail establishment, not adjacent to any other store. This type of location has several advantages: no competition, low rent, flexibility, road visibility, easy parking, and lower property costs. There are also several disadvantages: difficulty in attracting traffic, no variety for shoppers, no shared costs, and zoning restrictions.

The unplanned business district is a shopping area where two or more stores are located together or in close proximity. Store composition is not based on long-range planning. Unplanned business districts can be broken down into four categories: the central business district, the secondary business district, the neighborhood business district, and the string.

The unplanned business district has several points in its favor: variety of products, prices, and services; access to public transportation; nearness to commercial and social facilities; and the location of chain headquarters. However, the many shortcomings of this type of location have led to the growth of the planned shopping center: inadequate parking, old and decaying stores, high rents and taxes, discontinuity of offerings, delivery congestion, long travel time, high theft rates, and a declining central city.

The planned shopping center is a centrally owned or managed, well-balanced shopping area. A center usually has one or more large (anchor) stores and many smaller stores. During the past several years, the growth of the planned shopping center has been great. This growth is the result of extensive product and service offerings, growth of the suburbs, shared strategy planning and costs, location, parking, low rent and taxes, low theft rate, popularity of malls, and the declining appeal of inner-city shopping. The negative aspects of the planned shopping center include inflexible operations and domination by anchor stores. There are three forms of planned shopping centers: neighborhood, community, and regional.

After the basic type of location is chosen, the general site is determined. This choice involves the selection of a specific type of location and a broadly defined site. Then the exact site is designated. A rating system based on the following criteria can be used to evaluate locations and sites: pedestrian traffic, vehicular traffic, parking facilities, transportation, store composition, specific site characteristics, and terms of occupancy. The latter requires a decision about building a new store, buying an existing facility, or leasing.

Questions for Discussion

1. What are the characteristics of each of the major types of location discussed in this chapter?
2. What are the advantages and disadvantages of each major type of location?
3. Why do supermarkets often locate in shopping centers or business districts, whereas convenience stores like 7-Eleven often locate in isolated sites?
4. Why do you think that retailers like Sears locate in more than one type of location?
5. Differentiate among the central business district, the secondary business district, the neighborhood business district, and the string.
6. Develop a brief plan to revitalize a secondary business district near your campus.
7. Distinguish among the regional shopping center, the community shopping center, and the neighborhood shopping center.
8. Will planned shopping centers face any problems in the future? Explain your answer.
9. What criteria should a small retailer use in selecting a type of location? A large retailer?
10. Show how a 100 per cent location for a college cafeteria may not be a 100 per cent location for another type of restaurant.
11. What problems are there in using a rating scale like that shown in Figure 8-4? What are the benefits?
12. Explain how the parking needs for a supermarket and a furniture store differ.
13. What are the primary benefits of building ownership versus leasing? Explain your answer.
14. Why are leases in shopping centers so elaborate?
15. Explain the four steps used in location planning.

CASES

1. McDonald's: Expanding Through Nontraditional Store Sites*

McDonald's 1984 systemwide sales were $8.7 billion. It currently accounts for 45 per cent of the domestic fast-food burger market. On an average day, 17 million

*This material is drawn from Daniel F. Cuff, "What's New at McDonald's," *New York Times* (August 19, 1984), Section 3, p. 15; Marci Jo Williams, "McDonald's Refuses to Plateau," *Fortune* (November 12, 1984), pp. 34–36ff.; and "Where Mac Meets Mack," *Time* (September 3, 1984), p. 65.

people worldwide visit a McDonald's outlet. Nonetheless, McDonald's is concerned about maintaining its strong growth rate and its level of profitability. Over the 20 years McDonald's has been a public corporation, it has never reported quarterly earnings that were less than the comparable period the preceding year.

McDonald's recognizes that it has pretty well saturated most major U.S. urban and suburban markets. It must protect existing franchise territories, not diminish productivity per outlet, and find locations that do not require exorbitant terms. Accordingly, McDonald's is interested in capitalizing on nontraditional locations in the United States and broadening its foreign operations.

The company is actively pursuing sites in hospitals, high schools, parks, and similar locations where it can be the sole provider of food services. These are three examples of McDonald's commitment to these types of sites:

- It recently signed a 10-year contract to operate as many as 300 outlets in naval installations in the United States and overseas. Some of the outlets are or will be free-standing, others are or will fit into existing PX areas. While prices at the naval installations are set 5 per cent below civilian prices, the same menu items are being served. McDonald's has noted that annual sales at its Camp Pendleton (Oceanside, California) unit are twice those of a typical outlet.
- It secured a contract to erect ten units at state tollways on the Connecticut Turnpike. McDonald's won the contract by presenting a bid which was more than twice those offered by Howard Johnson and Marriott. It expects the sales at these sites to be about one-third greater than at traditional locations. With McDonald's permission, restaurants not operated by it are situated next to McDonald's outlets at four of the ten turnpike locales.
- It is experimenting with an office building site, using a 5,300-square-foot outlet in a midtown Manhattan building. A major problem that McDonald's must overcome is the property manager's anxiety about its impact on the building's image.

McDonald's has also developed two new store formats for nontraditional sites: McStop and McSnack. McStop outlets are designed to be placed on major thoroughfares for families and as truck stops. Each McStop has double-width lanes and extra-large parking spaces for semitrailers and recreational vehicles. They are located with a gas station, motel, convenience store, and small shopping center. McDonald's operates only the McStop units. A real-estate developer signs up the other retailers.

McSnack outlets are scaled-down McDonald's units intended for restricted-space sites in shopping malls. They concentrate on Chicken McNuggets, hamburgers, french fries, and drinks.

About half of all new McDonald's restaurants are now being built outside the United States. The company has over 1,500 foreign stores, which contribute 22 per cent of total revenues and 16 per cent of pretax profit. By 1990, new foreign units will account for as much as 80 per cent of yearly store additions. However, there are some limits on foreign growth potential. First, most countries do not have the manufacturing, distribution, and transportation systems required for a fast-food chain. Second, McDonald's needs countries with a large middle class that can afford to eat out. For these reasons, McDonald's plans to concentrate on Canada, Japan, England, Germany, France, and Australia.

Questions

1. In general, how would site selection for a McDonald's outlet differ from that for an expensive restaurant?
2. Evaluate each of McDonald's site-selection strategies.
3. Develop a ten-item checklist for McDonald's to use when analyzing a site.

2. Burnside Furniture and Appliance Centers: Adding a New Store*

Thomas and James Burnside are confronted with a major operating decision that would affect the future development of their furniture and appliance business. The decision centers on whether to add a fourth store in the southern section of Des Moines, Iowa. Thomas is reluctant to open a new store, although James thinks the time has come for an additional Burnside Furniture and Appliance Center.

The first Burnside store was opened by Tom and Jim's father, Alexander, in eastern Des Moines in 1948. It initially carried furniture only. A second store was opened in northern Des Moines in 1959. At this time, Mr. Burnside decided to broaden his product mix to include appliances.

During the 1960s, the two Burnside stores were very successful. In the 1962 to 1965 period, Tom and Jim entered the business on a full-time basis. Both were college graduates, with degrees in finance and marketing respectively.

Des Moines grew in the 1960s because of the expansion of insurance, publishing, and state government. The major growth was in the western part of the city. In a joint decision, the Burnsides agreed to open a third store in western Des Moines. This was done in 1969.

In 1973, Alexander Burnside turned the company over to his two sons. At this point, the Burnside Stores continued to do well. But after a number of years, the Burnsides realized that the population boom of the 1950s and 1960s was not being maintained in the 1970s in the parts of Des Moines where their stores were situated.

The greatest population increases were taking place in southern Des Moines, where the Burnsides did not have a store. This area was attracting young families with children. The new residents were above average in terms of education, income, and type of employment. James Burnside felt a new store should be opened in the southern part of Des Moines to capitalize on the rising population. Thomas Burnside believed that major attention should be directed at furthering the development of the three existing stores, particularly the northern and eastern stores, where sales were beginning to level off. The brothers concurred that an informal marketing analysis of southern Des Moines was in order.

Figure 1 shows the boundaries of the southern area, levels of income and population growth within the area, and existing retail conditions within the area.

The northern boundary is the railroad. The east boundary is the Des Moines River. The west and south sides are marked by Interstate 80 and State Highway 28, respectively.

*This case was prepared and written by Professor William A. Staples, University of Houston at Clear Lake City, Texas, and Professor Robert A. Swerdlow, Lamar University, Beaumont, Texas.

Characteristics of Southern Des Moines

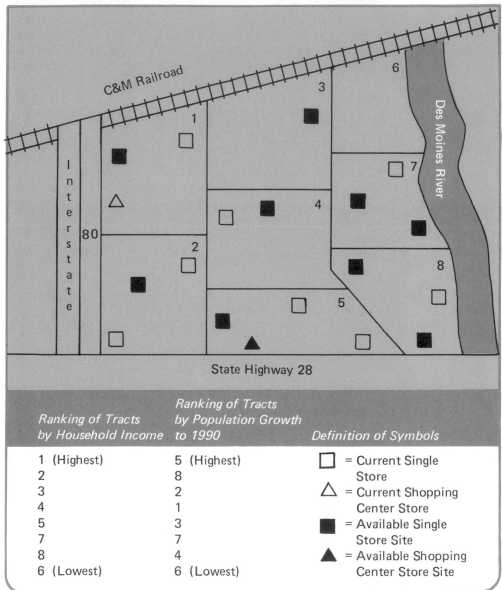

Ranking of Tracts by Household Income	Ranking of Tracts by Population Growth to 1990	Definition of Symbols
1 (Highest)	5 (Highest)	□ = Current Single Store
2	8	△ = Current Shopping Center Store
3	2	■ = Available Single Store Site
4	1	▲ = Available Shopping Center Store Site
5	3	
7	7	
8	4	
6 (Lowest)	6 (Lowest)	

Figure 1

Median household incomes and population growth through the year 1990 were obtained for the eight southern census tracts. The data came from the Des Moines Chamber of Commerce and the Planning and Zoning Commission. All the southern census tracts were either upper or middle income in comparison with the rest of Des Moines; and solid population growth was forecast for each of the southern tracts.

The competition on the south side was diverse in that there were appliance stores, furniture stores, and combination furniture and appliance outlets. In addition, a large department-store chain, Adler's, which carried furniture and appliances, had an outlet in the shopping center off Interstate 80. Another major competitor would be Odom Appliances, which had two stores in southern Des Moines. There were at least nine other furniture or appliance stores that could provide strong competition for a new store in the area under consideration.

Questions

1. Discuss the positions taken by Thomas and James Burnside.
2. Evaluate Figure 1 in terms of
   a. Boundaries.
   b. Population data.
   c. Competition.
3. What store sites appear to be most promising?
4. Should a new store be opened on the south side of Des Moines?
5. What additional information would be helpful in making a decision?

9

Retail Organization and Human Resource Management

Chapter Objectives

1. To study the steps involved in organizing a retail firm
2. To explain the various organizational forms utilized in retailing
3. To examine the principles and practices of retail human resource management

There is now a trend toward younger senior executives in retailing. For example, J. C. Penney, Dayton Hudson, Associated Dry Goods, and Best Products were all firms that had chief executive officers or presidents who were 50 years old or younger in 1985. As one retail analyst observed:

> The pace of business has become so demanding that the executive takes a lot of wear and tear. An executive can be very experienced, but it also takes a great deal of energy to run a company like Sears. Things change so rapidly today that the executive has to have not only an understanding of what is happening, but also the energy and stamina to see it through.

In selecting senior executives, retailers also look for several traits besides energy and stamina. These include a

- Strong work ethic.
- Fair amount of charm or charisma.
- Broad background.
- Good education.
- Combination of people and task orientation.
- Strategic orientation.[1]

Well-managed retail companies are those who have clear career paths for all their full-time employees and seek to manage human resources as effectively as possible. Although most employees will never reach a senior management position, each needs to be encouraged to meet his or her potential.

Overview

An **organization** is a system for achieving behavioral objectives among employees so that they work together efficiently, achieve agreed-on goals, and gain satisfaction in performing the selected and required tasks.[2]

In retailing, the objectives of an organization are to ensure that the needs of the target market, employees, and management are effectively and efficiently achieved. Figure 9-1 lists these organizational requirements.

A retail organization cannot survive unless the needs of the target market are satisfied, regardless of how successfully employee and/or management needs are met. For example, an organization plan that reduces costs through centralized buying, but results in the retailer's insensitivity to geographic differences in consumer preferences, is not a good plan.

Setting Up a Retail Organization

Although many retail firms carry out similar functions (e.g., buying, pricing, displaying, wrapping), there are many ways of organizing to perform these functions and meet the needs of customers, employees, and management. The process of developing a retail organization can be broken down into five stages as shown in Figure 9-2:

1. Outlining the specific tasks to be performed in the retail exchange process.
2. Dividing the tasks among channel members and customers.
3. Grouping tasks into jobs.
4. Classifying jobs.
5. Integrating positions through the establishment of an organization chart.

---

[1]Jacquelyn Bivins, "Executive Succession: A New Generation Arrives," *Chain Store Age Executive* (January 1985), pp. 83ff.
[2]George R. Terry, *Supervision* (Homewood, Ill.: Richard D. Irwin, 1978), p. 43. See also "Teamwork Pays Off at Penney's," *Business Week* (April 12, 1982), pp. 107–108.

Retail Organization Requirements

TARGET MARKET NEEDS

Are the desired services provided at appropriate levels (i.e., delivery, sales personnel, cashiers, credit)?
Are the specific needs of branch store customers met?
Is the store adaptive to changes in customer needs?

EMPLOYEE NEEDS

Are positions challenging enough?
Is there an orderly promotion program?
Is the employee able to participate in decision-making?
Are the channels of communication clear and open?
Are jobs satisfying?
Is the authority-responsibility relationship clear?
Does the firm promote from within?
Does each employee get treated fairly?
Is good performance rewarded?

MANAGEMENT NEEDS

Is the organization flexible enough to adapt to changes in customer preferences and/or regional growth patterns?
Does the organization provide continuity so that personnel can be replaced in an orderly manner?
Does each worker report to only one supervisor?
Can each manager properly supervise and control the number of workers reporting to him (her)?
Is it relatively easy to obtain and retain competent personnel?
Are personnel procedures clearly defined?
Do operating departments have adequate staff support (i.e., computerized reports, market research, and advertising)?
Are the levels of organization properly developed?
Are the organization's plans well-integrated?
Are employees motivated?
Is absenteeism low?

Figure 9-1

Specifying Tasks to Be Performed

The general tasks to be performed must be enumerated. Among the tasks are

- Buying merchandise.
- Shipping merchandise.
- Receiving merchandise.
- Checking incoming shipments.
- Marking merchandise.

The Steps in Organizing a Retail Firm

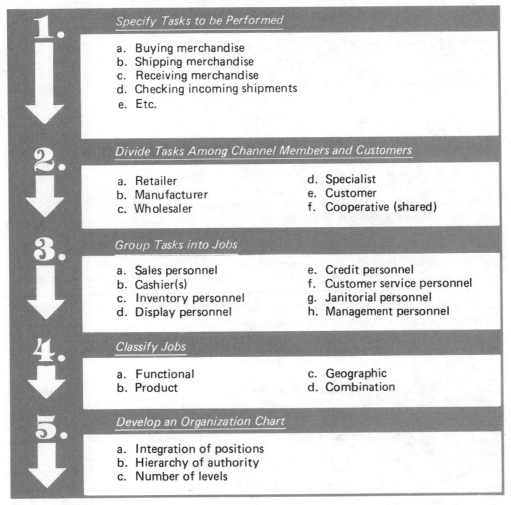

1. *Specify Tasks to be Performed*

a. Buying merchandise
b. Shipping merchandise
c. Receiving merchandise
d. Checking incoming shipments
e. Etc.

2. *Divide Tasks Among Channel Members and Customers*

a. Retailer
b. Manufacturer
c. Wholesaler
d. Specialist
e. Customer
f. Cooperative (shared)

3. *Group Tasks into Jobs*

a. Sales personnel
b. Cashier(s)
c. Inventory personnel
d. Display personnel
e. Credit personnel
f. Customer service personnel
g. Janitorial personnel
h. Management personnel

4. *Classify Jobs*

a. Functional
b. Product
c. Geographic
d. Combination

5. *Develop an Organization Chart*

a. Integration of positions
b. Hierarchy of authority
c. Number of levels

Figure 9-2

- Inventory storage and control.
- Preparation of merchandise and window displays.
- Store operations (e.g., cleanliness, maintenance).
- Customer research.
- Customer contact (e.g., advertising, personal selling).
- Customer follow-up and complaint handling.
- Personnel management.
- Repairs and alterations of merchandise.
- Billing customers.
- Handling receipts and financial records.

- Credit operations.
- Gift wrapping.
- Delivery.
- Return of merchandise to vendors.
- Sales forecasting and budgeting.
- Coordination.

The performance of these activities is necessary for an efficient retail transaction to occur.

Dividing Tasks Among Channel Members and Customers

Although the tasks mentioned are performed in retailing, they do not necessarily have to be performed by a retailer. Some can be assumed by a manufacturer, a wholesaler, a specialist, or the consumer. Figure 9-3 shows the types of functions that can be carried out by each channel member and the consumer. The following example describes some of the criteria considered in the allocation of retail tasks (with consumer credit used as the basic function).

A retail task should be carried out only if desired by the target market. An appliance dealer would offer cash-only sales if a survey of the target market proves this acceptable, not for convenience. For some retailers, liberal credit policies may provide significant advantages over competitors. For others, a cash-only policy reduces the firms' overhead and leads to lower prices.

A retail task should be performed by the party who has special competence and/or equipment. Credit collection may require a legal staff and a computer-based book-

The Division of Retail Tasks

Performer	Tasks
Retailer	Can perform all or some of the tasks listed in the preceding section, from buying merchandise to coordination.
Manufacturer or Wholesaler	Can perform few or many functions, such as: shipping, marking merchandise, inventory storage and control, display preparation, research, sales forecasting, etc.
Specialist(s)	Can include the following types: buying office, delivery firm, warehouse, marketing research firm, advertising agency, accountant, credit bureau, computer service firm. Each specializes in the performance of a particular task.
Consumer	Can assume responsibility for delivery, credit (cash-only sales), sales effort (self-service or direct marketing), product alterations (do-it-yourselfers).

Figure 9-3

keeping system. These are usually affordable only by medium-sized or large retailers. Smaller retailers would rely on bank credit cards to overcome the lack of necessary resources.

The retailer should consider the loss of control over an activity when it is allocated to another party. Delegation of a task involves the loss of some control by the retailer. A credit collection firm, pressing hard to collect on a past-due account, may antagonize a customer to the point of losing future sales for the retailer.

The institutional framework of the retailer can have an impact on the allocation of tasks. A cooperative credit bureau may be possible only in the franchise form of retailing. Independents cannot do this task as readily.

Task allocation should take into consideration cost savings achieved by the sharing or shifting of tasks. The credit function can be better performed by a credit bureau if its personnel are not unionized, WATS (long-distance phone lines) calls are used, and lower rent is paid (because of an out-of-the-way location). Many retailers cannot gain these savings themselves.

Grouping Tasks into Jobs

After the retailer decides which functions to perform, these tasks are grouped into jobs. These jobs must be clearly defined and structured. Some examples of grouping tasks into jobs are:

Tasks	Jobs
Displaying merchandise, customer contact, gift wrapping, customer follow-up	Sales personnel
Billing customers, handling cash receipts, gift wrapping, inventory control	Cashier(s)
Receiving merchandise, checking incoming shipments, marking merchandise, inventory storage and control, returning merchandise to vendors	Inventory personnel
Window dressing, interior display setups, use of mobiles	Display personnel
Billing customers, credit operations, customer research	Credit personnel
Repairs and alterations of merchandise, customer complaints, customer research	Customer service personnel
Cleaning store, replacing old fixtures	Janitorial personnel
Personnel management, sales forecasting, budgeting, coordination of tasks	Management personnel

When grouping tasks into jobs, the retailer must consider the use of specialization. Under specialization, each employee is responsible for limited functions (as opposed to each employee's performing many or all functions). Specialization has the advantages of clearly defined tasks, greater expertise, reduced training costs and time, and hiring personnel with narrow education and experience. Problems can result through extreme specialization: poor morale (boredom), personnel not being aware of the importance of their jobs, and the need for an increased number of employees.

The proper use of specialization involves assigning specific duties and responsibilities to individuals, so that a position encompasses a relatively homogeneous cluster

A Job Description for a Store Manager

JOB TITLE: Store Manager for 34th Street Branch of Pombo's Department Store

POSITION REPORTS TO: Senior Vice President

POSITIONS REPORTING TO STORE MANAGER: All personnel working in the 34th Street store

OBJECTIVES: To properly staff and operate the 34th Street store

DUTIES AND RESPONSIBILITIES:

1. Personnel recruitment, selection, training, motivation, and evaluation
2. Merchandise display
3. Inventory storage and control
4. Approving orders for merchandise
5. Transferring merchandise among stores
6. Sales forecasting
7. Budgeting
8. Handling store receipts
9. Preparing bank transactions
10. Locking and unlocking store
11. Reviewing customer complaints
12. Reviewing computer data forms
13. Semi-annual review of overall operations
14. Forwarding reports to top management

COMMITTEES AND MEETINGS:

1. Store Managers' Review Committee
2. Attendance at monthly meetings with Senior Vice President
3. Supervision of weekly meetings with department managers

Figure 9-4

of work tasks. These work tasks should have an essential and enduring purpose within the retail organization.

After tasks are grouped to form a job, a job description is constructed. A job description is a detailed outline of the job title, objectives, duties, and responsibilities for each position. It is used as a hiring, supervision, and evaluation tool. Figure 9-4 contains a job description for a store manager.

Classifying Jobs

Jobs can then be broadly categorized through a functional, product, geographic, or combination classification system. In a **functional classification,** jobs are divided among functional areas such as sales promotion, buying, and store operations. Expert knowledge is utilized.

Product classification divides jobs on a product or service basis. For example, a department store can hire personnel for clothing, furniture, giftware, appliances, and so on. Product classification recognizes that differences exist in the personnel requirements for different products. Tighter control and responsibility are also possible.

Geographic classification is useful for multiunit stores operating in different areas. Personnel are adapted to local conditions. Job descriptions and qualifications are under the control of individual branch managers.

For larger retailers, combinations of these three classifications are often used. As an example, a branch unit of a department store may hire and supervise its own selling staff, while buying personnel for each product line are centrally hired and controlled by the headquarters' store. Thus, the functional, product, and geographic forms of organization are combined.

Developing an Organization Chart

When planning the organization, the retailer must not look at jobs as individual units but as parts of the whole. Accordingly the organization must be planned in an integrated, coordinated format. Jobs must be clearly delineated and separated, and the relations among positions must be stated.

The **hierarchy of authority** outlines the job relationships within the company by describing the reporting relationships among employees (from the lowest level to the store manager or board of directors). Coordination and control are provided through this hierarchy.

The number of levels in the organization are the number of positions separating the top official from the lowest employee. An organization with a large number of subordinates reporting to one supervisor is called a **flat organization.** Some benefits of the flat organization are good communication, quicker handling of problems, and better employee identification with the job. The major problem tends to be too many employees reporting to one boss.

A **tall organization** has several levels of supervision. This arrangement leads to close supervision and fewer employees reporting to each manager. The problems are long channel of communication, impersonal impression given to employees, and inflexible rules.

With all these factors in mind, the retailer can develop an organization chart, which graphically displays the hierarchal relationships within the firm. Figure 9-5 lists the principles to be considered in the setting up of an organization chart. Figure 9-6 contains functional, product, geographic, and combination organization charts.

Organizational Patterns in Retailing

Retail organizations differ by institutional type. For example, an independent retailer has a much simpler organization than a department or chain store. The independent does not have to manage units that may be distant from the central location, the owner-manager usually personally supervises all employees, and workers have ready access to the owner-manager in the event of any personal or work-related problems. In contrast,

Principles for Organizing a Retail Firm

1. An organization should be concerned about its employees. Job rotation, promotion from within, participatory management, recognition, job enrichment, etc., improve worker morale.

2. Employee turnover, lateness, and absenteeism should be monitored, as they may indicate personnel problems.

3. The line of authority should be traceable from the highest to the lowest positions. In this way, employees know whom to report to and who reports to them (chain of command).

4. A subordinate should only report to one supervisor. This avoids the problem of workers' receiving conflicting orders (unity of command).

5. Responsibility should be associated with adequate authority. A person responsible for a given objective needs the power to achieve it.

6. While a supervisor can delegate authority, he/she retains responsibility for the acts of subordinates. The delegation of authority cannot be an excuse for a manager's failing to achieve a goal. This concept requires that a manager actively evaluate the performance of subordinates while they are working to reach a goal.

7. There is a limit to the number of employees a manager can directly supervise (span of control).

8. The firm should strive to limit the number of organization levels. The greater the number of levels, the longer the time for communication to travel and the greater the coordination problems.

9. An organization has an informal structure aside from the formal organization chart. Informal relationships exercise power in the organization and may bypass formal relationships and procedures.

Figure 9-5

the chain or department store must specify how tasks are to be delegated, must coordinate many store operations, and must establish common policies for all employees.

Even though an independent retailer requires a simple organization, it should still be structured so that all functions and employees are coordinated. A discussion of retail organizations for independents, department stores, chain stores, and conglomerchants follows.

Different Forms of Retail Organization

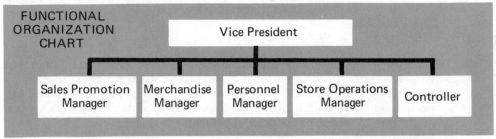

FUNCTIONAL ORGANIZATION CHART

Vice President

- Sales Promotion Manager
- Merchandise Manager
- Personnel Manager
- Store Operations Manager
- Controller

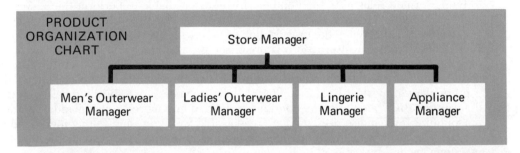

PRODUCT ORGANIZATION CHART

Store Manager

- Men's Outerwear Manager
- Ladies' Outerwear Manager
- Lingerie Manager
- Appliance Manager

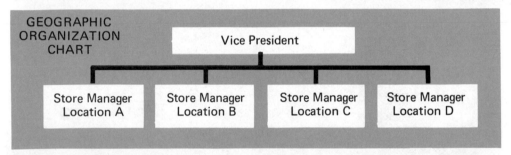

GEOGRAPHIC ORGANIZATION CHART

Vice President

- Store Manager Location A
- Store Manager Location B
- Store Manager Location C
- Store Manager Location D

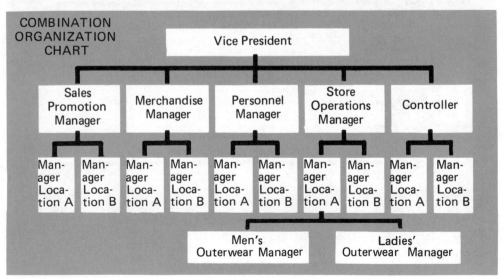

COMBINATION ORGANIZATION CHART

Vice President

- Sales Promotion Manager
  - Manager Location A
  - Manager Location B
- Merchandise Manager
  - Manager Location A
  - Manager Location B
- Personnel Manager
  - Manager Location A
  - Manager Location B
- Store Operations Manager
  - Manager Location A
  - Manager Location B
- Controller
  - Manager Location A
  - Manager Location B

Men's Outerwear Manager   Ladies' Outerwear Manager

Figure 9-6

Organizational Patterns in Small Independent Stores

The organization used by a small, independent store is usually a simple one because it contains only two or three levels (the owner-manager and employees), and the owner-manager personally operates and supervises. There are few personnel. Little departmentalization (specialization) is used. There are no branch units. These factors cause a simple organization, not the performance of fewer activities.

The small retailer has little specialization of functions because there are many tasks to be performed relative to the number of workers available to perform them. Accordingly each employee must allocate a portion of his or her time to several activities.

Figure 9-7 illustrates the organization structures of two small independent stores. In Example A, the furniture store is organized on a product-oriented basis, with the personnel in each category responsible for selected activities. Each division gets the appropriate attention, and some product expertise is developed. This special knowledge is particularly important because different skills are necessary to buy and sell each type of furniture. In Example B, the boutique is divided into merchandising and operations personnel. Merchandise personnel are responsible for buying and selling merchandise, assortment, displays, and advertising. Operations personnel are responsible for store maintenance and operations.

Organization Structures for Small Independents

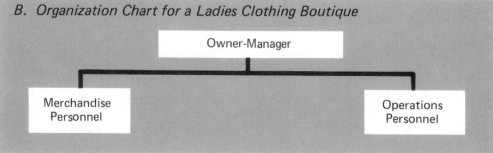

Figure 9-7

Organizational Patterns in Department Stores

Many medium-sized and large department stores use organization structures that are a modification of the Mazur plan, first presented in 1927. The **Mazur plan** divides all retail activities into four functional areas: merchandising, publicity, store management, and accounting and control.[3] These functional areas include the following activities:

1. Merchandising—buying, selling, stock planning and control, planning of promotional events.
2. Publicity—window and interior display, advertising, planning and executing promotional events (in cooperation with the merchandising department), advertising research, public relations.
3. Store management—merchandise care, customer services (such as adjustment bureaus), purchasing store supplies and equipment, store maintenance, operating activities (such as receiving, checking, marking, and delivering merchandise; maintenance of warehouse operations), store and merchandise protection such as insurance, security guard, personnel (training, compensation, and so on), workroom operations.
4. Accounting and control—credit and collection, expense budgeting and control, inventory planning and control, record-keeping.

These four areas are organized with the use of line (direct authority and responsibility) and staff (advisory or support) components. For example, the controller and the publicity manager provide staff services to the merchandising divisions, but within these staff areas, personnel are organized on a line basis. This principle can be more clearly understood from an examination of Figure 9-8, which illustrates the Mazur plan.

As can be seen in Figure 9-8, the merchandising division is responsible for buying and selling activities and is headed by a merchandising manager. This executive is often regarded as the most important area executive in the store and is responsible for supervising buyers, developing a financial control system for each department, coordinating department merchandise plans and policies (so that a store has a consistent image among departments), and interpreting economic data and their effect on the store. In stores with many departments (some stores have more than 100 departments), a divisional merchandise manager's position is utilized, so that the number of buyers reporting to a single manager does not become unwieldy.

The buyer, under the Mazur plan, has complete responsibility for controlling expenses and reaching profit goals within his or her department. The duties of the buyer include preparing preliminary budgets, studying fashion trends, bargaining with vendors over price, planning the number of salespeople needed, and informing sales personnel about merchandise purchased and fashion trends. The grouping of buying and selling activities into one job (buyer) does present a major problem. Because buyers are not constantly on the selling floor, control of personnel (training, scheduling, and discipline) suffers.

[3]Paul M. Mazur, *Principles of Organization Applied to Modern Retailing* (New York: Harper & Brothers, 1927).

The Mazur Plan for Department Stores

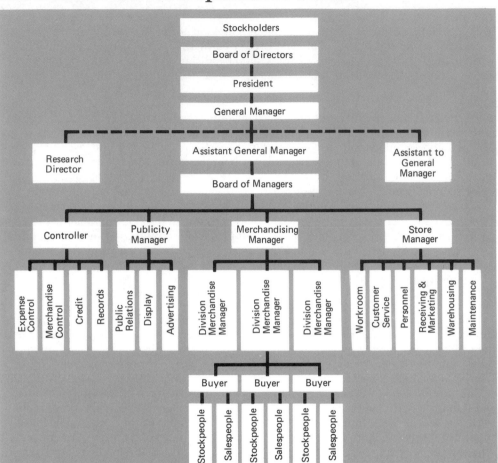

Source: Adapted from Paul Mazur, *Principles of Organization Applied to Modern Retailing* (New York: Harper & Brothers, 1927), frontispiece. Reprinted with permission.

Figure 9-8

The growth of branch stores has caused three alternative forms of the original Mazur plan to emerge:

1. The parent organization operates the branch (known as a **mother hen with branch store chickens**).
2. Each branch is treated as a separate store with its own buying responsibilities (known as **separate store**).
3. Selling responsibilities are separate from buying responsibilities. Buying is centralized, and branches become sales units with equal organization status (known as **equal store**).

Each of these forms is displayed in Figure 9-9.

Organizational Forms for Department Stores with Branches

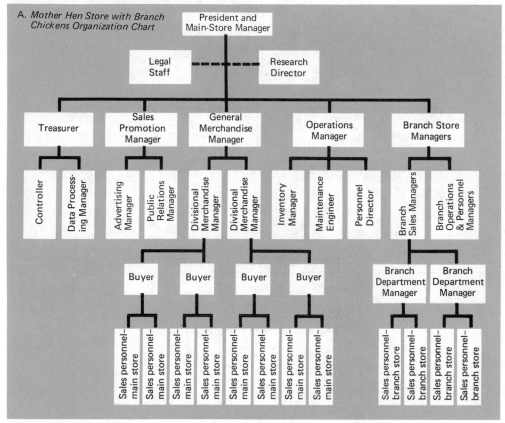

A. *Mother Hen Store with Branch Chickens Organization Chart*

Figure 9-9

In the "mother hen" organization, most authority remains with managers at the headquarters store. Merchandise planning and buying activities, advertising, financial controls, store hours, and many other areas are centrally managed. To a great extent, this organization standardizes the performance of the main store and its branches. Branch store managers hire and supervise the employees in their stores and are responsible for making sure that day-to-day operations conform to company policies. This organization works well when there are few branches and the buying preferences of branch customers are similar to those of the main store's customers. However, as the branch stores increase in number, the buyers, the advertising director, the controller, and so on become overworked and give too little attention to the branches. In addition, because the main store's personnel are physically removed from the branches, differences in customer preferences can easily be overlooked.

The "separate store" organization places merchandise managers directly in the branch stores. Each branch store has autonomy for merchandising and operations decisions. Customer needs are quickly identified, but duplication by managers in the

Organizational Forms for Department Stores with Branches (continued)

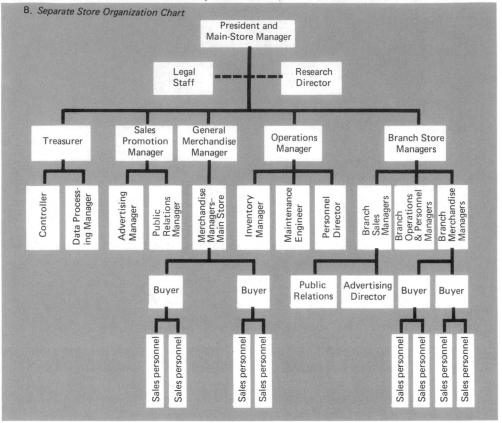

B. *Separate Store Organization Chart*

main store and the branches is possible. Coordination can also be a problem (e.g., maintenance of a consistent overall store image). Transferring stock between branches becomes more complex and more costly. This organization is best when individual branches are large, branches are geographically separated, and/or local customer tastes vary widely.

With the "equal store" organization, department stores try to accomplish the benefits of both centralization and decentralization. Buying functions such as forecasting, planning, buying, pricing, merchandise distribution to branches, and promotion are centrally managed. Selling functions such as presenting merchandise, selling, customer services, and store hours are managed in each outlet. All outlets, including the main store, are treated equally; and buyers are freed from supervising personnel in the main store. Data gathering is critical because buyers have less customer and store contact, and responsibility is more widely dispersed (and hard to pin down—buyer versus sales manager).

A recent study of fifty medium-sized and large department stores in Indiana,

Organizational Forms for Department Stores with Branches (continued)

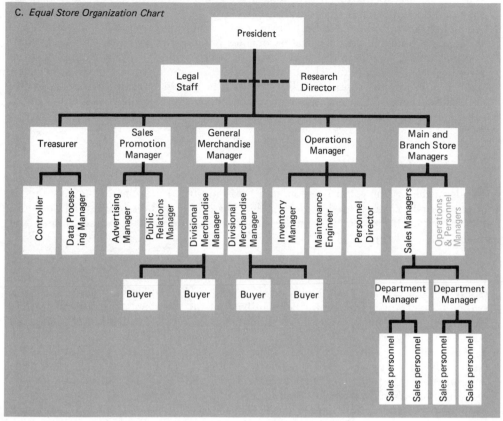

C. *Equal Store Organization Chart*

Illinois, and Kentucky showed the popularity of the "equal store" organization. Seventy-eight per cent of the respondents indicated centralized buying and decentralized selling.[4]

Organizational Patterns in Chain Stores

Chain stores often follow the equal-store organization form shown in Figure 9-9C. Although chain-store organization structures may differ, they typically have these characteristics:

1. There are a large number of functional divisions, such as sales promotion, store operations, real estate, personnel, and merchandise management.

[4]Clarence E. Vincent and John S. Berens, "Changes in Department Store Organization: Implications for Curriculum Requirements for Management Trainees," *Journal of Marketing Education*, Vol. 3 (Spring 1981), p. 21.

2. Authority and responsibility are centralized, with individual store managers responsible for sales.
3. Operations are standardized (fixtures, store layout, building design, merchandise lines, credit policy, and store service).
4. An elaborate control system keeps management informed.
5. A limited amount of decentralization enables branch stores to adapt better to local conditions and increases the store manager's responsibilities. For example, while 80 per cent of K mart's merchandise is standardized on a national basis, store managers are free to fine tune 10 to 20 per cent of the mix in an effort to appeal directly to local markets—be they rural or urban, black or Hispanic, high or low income.[5]

Organizational Patterns for Conglomerchants

A **conglomerchant,** or retail conglomerate, is a multiline merchandising firm under central ownership.[6] The conglomerchant, like the chain, contains more than one unit; however, unlike the chain, it combines diverse retail operations. Some examples of conglomerchants follow:

- F. W. Woolworth owns a variety store chain (Woolworth), the Kinney shoe division (Kinney, Foot Locker, Lady Foot Locker, Fredelle, Frugal Frank's, and Final Cut), two men's clothing store chains (Richman Brothers and Anderson-Little), an off-price clothing chain (J. Brannam), and two children's clothing chains (Little Folk Shop and Kids Mart).
- K mart operates a discount department store chain (K mart), a bookstore chain (WaldenBooks), a home-improvement chain (Home Centers of America), an off-price apparel chain (Designer Depot), cafeterias (Furr's and Bishop's), a discount gift chain (Accent), and a drugstore chain (Pay Less).
- Melville operates two shoe-store chains (Thom McAn and Open Country), four clothing chains (Chess King, Foxmoor, Wilson Suede and Leather, and Marshalls), an off-price linens chain (Linens 'n things), a drugstore chain (CVS), and a toy/hobby chain (Kay-Bee).

Because of its diverse product and/or service offerings, the conglomerchant faces several special considerations. First, interdivision control is necessary. Operating procedures and united goals must be communicated among divisions. Second, interdivision competition must be coordinated (e.g., department store and discount store carrying the same item). Third, costs must be allocated among different units. Fourth, image and advertising conflicts must be resolved. Fifth, management skills must be adapted to radically different operations. Accordingly the conglomerchant needs to develop a

[5]Molly Brauer, "K mart Assumes New Posture," *Chain Store Age Executive* (August 1984), pp. 25–26, 29.
[6]Rollie Tillman, "Rise of the Conglomerchant," *Harvard Business Review*, Vol. 49 (November–December 1971), p. 45; and Jacquelyn Bivins, "Diversification: Retailers Reach Out," *Chain Store Age Executive* (March 1984), pp. 25ff.

Figure 9-10 Federated Department Stores: A Portrait of a Conglomerchant

Each of the logos represents a division of Federated Department Stores, which operates department stores, mass merchandising (discount) stores, and supermarkets throughout the United States. Reprinted by permission.

distinctive organization chart. Figure 9-10 shows the logos of the diverse units comprising the three major areas of business of Federated Department Stores.

Human Resource Management in Retailing

Human resource management is required for all retailers, with decisions and policies dependent on the retailer's size, the number of employees, the location of outlets, store organization, and so on. Because good personnel are needed to develop and carry out retail strategies, and salaries and fringe benefits can amount to 50 per cent or more of a retailer's expenses, the need for effective human resource management is clear.

The importance of human resource management is further illustrated through the following:

- K mart recently realigned its corporate structure in order to promote younger employees to higher-level positions. This is part of an overall program to expand and upgrade the chain and assure an "orderly transition during the years immediately ahead."[7]
- Nankin Express, a Chinese fast-food chain based in Minneapolis, has reduced labor costs from 50 per cent to 5 per cent of total operating expenses by developing a four-step process for food preparation and standardizing labor tasks.[8]
- Shoney coffee shops operate in Missouri, Kansas, Oklahoma, and many Southeastern states. The chain is very profitable and expanding nicely. Experts credit "close restaurant supervision" as a key to this success. For example, each coffee shop has seven managers, two to three more than most competitors.[9]
- An Arthur D. Little consulting report predicts that "store managers of the future will be analytical, pin-stripe suit types with college degrees." They will supervise outlets with "more customers, higher sales volume, greater product diversity, and more capital investment."[10]
- The *Journal of Retailing* devoted its entire Fall 1984 issue to articles dealing with the issue of productivity. Most of these articles concentrate on labor productivity and how to improve it.

The Special Human Resource Environment of Retailing

Retailers face a special human resource environment, which is characterized by a large number of inexperienced workers, long hours, highly visible employees, many part-time workers, and variations in demand.

Perhaps the greatest difficulty with retail personnel is their inexperience. Workers are attracted to retailing because it is localized. Many retail positions do not require much education, special training, or special skills (e.g., checkout clerks, wrappers, stock clerks, and sales personnel). Also, the low wages paid for these positions necessitate the hiring of inexperienced people. These factors lead to high turnover, lateness, and absenteeism.

The long hours frequently encountered in retailing, including Saturdays and Sundays in various localities, turn off some prospective employees; and there is a strong trend toward longer store hours. Family shoppers and working-women shoppers look for stores with evening and weekend hours.

In retailing, employees are highly visible to the customer. Therefore, when a retailer is selecting and training employees, special care must be taken with regard to their manners and appearance. Unfortunately, some small retailers do not recognize the importance of employee appearance (e.g., clean-shaven, appropriately attired, neatly groomed).

Because of the long hours of store operations, retailers often have to hire part-

---

[7]"K mart Corp. Realigns Structure, Promotes Younger Employees," *Wall Street Journal* (December 20, 1984), p. 18.
[8]"Assembly-Line Chinese Food," *New York Times* (June 8, 1984), p. D22.
[9]"At Shoney's, Details Count," *New York Times* (June 8, 1984), pp. D1, D5.
[10]"Megastores Need Strategic, Not Hands-On, Managers," *Marketing News* (September 14, 1984), p. 45.

time employees. For example, in many supermarkets over half of the employees are part-time. Problems can arise. Part-time workers may be lackadaisical, late, or absent and have a high turnover rate. Accordingly, these workers must be closely monitored.

Last, variations in customer demand by time, day, or season create personnel planning problems. For example, a typical supermarket sells over 75 per cent of its volume on Thursday, Friday, and Saturday. How many employees should be used Monday through Wednesday, and how many should be used Thursday through Saturday? Demand differences during the day (morning, afternoon, evening) and by season (fall, Christmas) also affect personnel planning.

In general, retailers face these special considerations:

- Employee selection procedures must be able to screen large quantities of applicants efficiently.
- Training must be intensive and short in duration because many workers are inexperienced and temporary.
- Career paths must be available to employees who look at retailing as a career.
- Appearance and work habits must be explained and reviewed.
- Morale problems are related to turnover and part-time employees.
- Full-time and part-time employees may have conflicts, especially when part-time personnel are used to minimize overtime for full-time workers.

The Human Resource Management Process in Retailing

Retail human resource management consists of several interrelated activities: recruitment, selection, training, compensation, and supervision. This procedure is concerned with the activities of obtaining, developing, and retaining employees. In the following sections, each of these activities is discussed for retail sales clerk and middle-management positions.

Recruitment of Retail Personnel

Recruitment is the activity whereby a retailer generates a list of job applicants. Sources of potential employees are educational institutions, other channel members (such as wholesalers and manufacturers), competitors, advertisements, employment agencies, and unsolicited applicants. In addition, the retailer may have employees who are looking for promotions (transfers) or who recommend friends. Figure 9-11 lists recruiting sources and their characteristics.

For entry-level sales personnel, retailers are likely to rely on walk-ins (or write-ins), employee recommendations, educational institutions, and advertising. For middle-management positions, retailers utilize employment agencies, competitors, and advertisements.

During recruitment, the retailer's goal is to develop a large list of names, which will be sharply reduced during selection. Retailers who list applicants only if they meet minimum background standards (e.g., education, experience) can save a lot of time and money during selection.[11]

---

[11]For insights into college recruitment by retailers, see Marjorie Axelrad Lake, "Recruiting," *Stores* (April 1982), pp. 63–71.

Recruitment Sources and Their Characteristics

Sources	Characteristics

I. Sources Outside the Company

Educational Institutions	1. High schools, business schools, community colleges, universities, graduate schools 2. Good for training positions; assures minimum educational requirements are fulfilled; especially useful when long-term contacts with instructors are developed
Other Channel Members, Competitors	1. Employees of vendors, wholesalers, manufacturers, advertising agencies, competitors; leads from each of the preceding 2. Reduces extent of training; can evaluate performance with prior company (ies); must instruct in company policy; some negative morale if current employees feel bypassed for promotions
Advertisements	1. Newspapers, trade publications, professional journals 2. Large quantity of applicants; average applicant quality may not be high; cost/applicant is low; additional responsibility placed on screening; can reduce number of unacceptable applicants by noting job qualifications in the advertisement
Employment Agencies	1. Private organizations, professional organizations, government, executive search firms 2. Must be carefully selected; must be determined who pays fee; good for screening applicants; specialists in personnel
Unsolicited Applicants	1. Walk-ins, write-ins 2. Wide variance in quality; must be carefully screened; file should be kept for future positions

II. Sources Within the Company

Current and Former Employees	1. Promotion or transfer of existing full-time employees, part-time employees, laid-off employees 2. Knowledge of company policies and personnel; good for morale; honest appraisal from in-store supervisor
Employee Recommendations	1. Friends, acquaintances, relatives 2. Value of recommendation depends upon honesty and judgment of current employee

Figure 9-11

A Job Description for a Sales Clerk

JOB TITLE: Sales Clerk, Women's Jewelry Department, 34th Street Branch of Pombo's Department Store

POSITION REPORTS TO: Department Manager

POSITIONS REPORTING TO SALES CLERK: None

OBJECTIVES: To satisfy customer requests and maintain well-stocked displays

DUTIES AND RESPONSIBILITIES:

1. Customer contact
2. Stocking displays
3. Setting up displays
4. Handling cash and credit sales
5. Noting understocked merchandise

COMMITTEES AND MEETINGS:

1. No committees
2. Attendance at weekly department meeting

Figure 9-12

Selection of Retail Personnel

The major objective in a selection procedure is to match the characteristics of potential employees with the requirements of the jobs to be filled. The selection procedure includes job analysis and description, an application blank, the interview, testing, references, and a physical examination. These steps should be followed in an integrated manner.

Job analysis is the gathering of information about the functions and requirements of a job: duties, responsibilities, aptitude, interest, education, experience, and physical condition. It is used for the selection of personnel, the establishment of job performance standards, and salary administration.

Job analysis results in a written job description. The **job description** contains the job's title, the supervisory relationships (superior and subordinate), the committee responsibilities, and the specific functions, tasks, and duties to be performed on an ongoing basis. Figure 9-4 showed a job description for a store manager, and Figure 9-12 is a job description for a sales clerk.

The traditional job description has been criticized on the grounds that:

- It may limit the scope of a job, as well as its authority, responsibility, and decision-making power.
- It is static and may not allow a person to grow.
- It can limit a worker's activities to those listed.

- It does not discuss position objectives or evaluation.
- It does not describe coordination among organization levels or positions.[12]

In place of the traditional job description, some personnel authorities are advocating a **goal-oriented job description,** which enumerates basic functions, the relation of the job to overall goals, the interdependence of positions, and information flows.[13] Figure 9-13 contains a goal-oriented job description.

The **application blank** is usually the first step in screening applicants. It is short, requires little interpretation, and can be used as the basis for probing during an interview. An application blank provides data on education, experience, health, reasons for leaving previous jobs, organizational memberships, hobbies, and references.

A refinement of the basic application blank is the **weighted application blank.** Retailers using a weighted application blank can analyze the performance of current and past employees and determine which items (education, experience, and so on) correlate with job success (which can be measured by longer tenure, higher sales volume, and less absenteeism). Items that have a high relationship to success can be given more weight than others, and a certain number of points can be assigned to each step or gradient within each trait. After the weighted scores have been totaled for each application blank, a total score can be determined to use as a cutoff point for hiring. An effective weighted application blank should aid a retailer in predicting job turnover, job performance, and security risks.

The application blank should be used in conjunction with the job description. Those meeting the minimum requirements of a job are processed further (interview). Those not meeting the minimum requirements of a job are immediately rejected. In this way, the application blank provides a quick and inexpensive method of screening.

The interview seeks to obtain information that can be amassed only through personal observation and questioning. An interview enables the prospective employer to determine the oral ability of the candidate, note his or her appearance, ask questions based on the application blank, and probe into career objectives.

Several decisions about the interviewing process must be made: level of formality, number of interviews, length of each interview, physical location of interviews, the person to do the interviewing, relaxed or tense atmosphere, and the degree to which the interview is structured. These decisions depend on the ability of the interviewer and the requirements of the job.

Many, particularly smaller, retailers hire an applicant if he or she performs well during the interview. Other, usually larger, retailers use an additional selection device: testing. In this case, a candidate who does well during the interview is asked to complete psychological (personality, intelligence, interest, and leadership skills) tests and/ or achievement tests (which measure learned knowledge). The Ghiselli Self-Description Inventory is an example of a psychological test that has been used in the evaluation of store managers. It tests intelligence, supervisory ability, initiative, self-assurance, perceived occupational level, decision-making approach, and sociometric popularity.

Among the other psychological tests available to retailers are the Strong Vocational Interest Blank, Minnesota Multiphasic Personality Inventory, Edwards Personal Preference Scale, Wonderlic Personnel Test, and the Kuder Preference Record. These tests should be administered and interpreted by professionals. It is important that

---

[12]Dennis J. Sutherland, "Managing by Objectives in Retailing," *Journal of Retailing*, Vol. 47 (Fall 1971), p. 15.
[13]See George Odiorne, *Management by Objectives II: A System of Managerial Leadership* (Belmont, Calif.: Pitman Learning, 1979).

A Goal-Oriented Job Description for a Management Trainee

Attributes Required	ability	desire	In the Retailing Environment
ANALYTICAL SKILLS: ability to solve problems; strong numerical ability for analysis of facts and data for planning, managing and controlling.			Retail executives are problem solvers. Knowledge and understanding of past performance and present circumstances form the basis for action and planning.
CREATIVITY: ability to generate and recognize imaginative ideas and solutions; ability to recognize the need for and to be responsive to change.			Retail executives are idea people. Successful buying results from sensitive, aware decisions, while merchandising requires imaginative, innovative techniques.
DECISIVENESS: ability to make quick decisions and render judgments, take action and commit oneself to completion.			Retail executives are action people. Whether it's new fashion trends or customer desires, decisions must be made quickly and confidently in this ever-changing environment.
FLEXIBILITY: ability to adjust to the ever-changing needs of the situation; ability to adapt to different people, places and things; willingness to do whatever is necessary to get the task done.			Retail executives are flexible. Surprises in retailing never cease. Plans must be altered quickly to accommodate changes in trends, styles and attitudes, while numerous ongoing activities cannot be ignored.
INITIATIVE: ability to originate action rather than wait to be told what to do and ability to act based on conviction.			Retail executives are doers. Sales volumes, trends and buying opportunities mean continual action. Opportunities for action must be seized.
LEADERSHIP: ability to inspire others to trust and respect your judgment; ability to delegate and to guide and persuade others.			Retail executives are managers. Running a business means depending on others to get the work done. One person cannot do it all.
ORGANIZATION: ability to establish priorities and courses of action for self and/or others; skill in planning and following up to achieve results.			Retail executives are jugglers. A variety of issues, functions and projects are constantly in motion. To reach your goals, priorities must be set, work must be delegated to others.
RISK-TAKING: willingness to take calculated risks based on thorough analysis and sound judgment and to accept responsibility for the results.			Retail executives are courageous. Success in retailing often comes from taking calculated risks and having the confidence to try something new before someone else does.
STRESS TOLERANCE: ability to perform consistently under pressure, to thrive on constant change and challenge.			Retail executives are resilient. As the above descriptions should suggest, retailing is fast-paced and demanding.

Source: *Rate Yourself as a Retail Executive* (New York: Abraham & Straus), p. 1. Abraham & Straus is a division of Federated Stores. Reprinted with permission.

Figure 9-13

standardized examinations not be used unless they are proved effective as predictors of job performance.

Achievement tests deal with specific skills or knowledge, such as industry knowledge, ability to make a sales presentation, and insights into principles of retailing. These tests are much easier to administer and interpret than psychological tests, and direct relationships between knowledge and ability can be determined.

In conjunction with interviewing and testing, retailers gather references from the applicants. References can be checked either before or after the interview stage. The purposes of a reference check are to determine the honesty of the applicant, to ascertain the employer's reasons for the applicant's leaving a prior job, and to review the types

Table 9-1
Employee Selection Tools Used by Department and Specialty Stores

Selection Tool	Firms Using Selection Tool by Type of Employees (%)		
	Exempt Employees*	Full-Time Nonexempt Employees†	Part-Time Nonexempt Employees‡
Interview	82.3	95.2	93.4
Application blank	77.8	92.3	90.2
Business references	70.4	74.9	66.4
Personal references	55.6	62.4	58.5
Credit report	33.3	27.0	19.6
Police check	19.0	21.7	19.8
Physical examination	13.8	14.0	9.5
Testing	9.0	16.4	13.5
Polygraph (lie detector)	4.5	7.1	5.8
Specialized assessment center	3.4	1.3	0.3
Handwriting analysis	0.0	1.1	1.1

*Exempt employees are not covered by the minimum wage and overtime provisions of the Federal Labor Standards Act. They include store managers, lawyers, and merchandise managers.

†Full-time nonexempt employees are covered by the minimum wage and overtime provisions of the Federal Labor Standards Act. They include full-time sales clerks, store clerks, and office workers.

‡Part-time nonexempt employees are covered by the minimum wage and overtime provisions of the Federal Labor Standards Act. They include part-time sales clerks, store clerks, and office workers.

Source: Charles J. Hollon and Myron Gable, "Information Sources in Retail Employment Decision Making Process," Journal of Retailing, Vol. 55 (Fall 1979), p. 62. Reprinted with permission.

of people who will vouch for the applicant. Mail and telephone reference checks are inexpensive, fast, and easy to do.

If a candidate successfully completes the interview, testing, and reference check steps, many retailers require a physical examination before giving a job. This is especially important because of the physical activity, long hours, and tensions involved in retailing. A clean bill of health means that the candidate is accepted as an employee.

Each of the steps in the selection process complements the others, and they give the retailer a total package of information upon which to base personnel decisions. In general, retailers should use a job description, an application blank, an interview, and a reference check. The use of additional interviews, psychological and achievement tests, and a physical examination depends on the nature of the retailer and the open position.

Inexpensive tools (such as application blanks) should be used in the early screening stages, whereas more expensive, in-depth tools (such as personal interviews) should be used after the number of applicants has been reduced substantially. Table 9-1 shows the selection tools used by a sample of department and specialty stores with annual sales volume greater than $250,000.

Federal regulations require that only questions that are directly linked to job performance may be asked in the selection process.[14]

[14]"Uniform Guidelines on Employee Selection Procedures," *Federal Register*, Vol. 43 (August 25, 1978); and Duane E. Thompson and Toni A. Thompson, "Court Standards for Job Analysis in Test Validation," *Personnel Psychology* (Winter 1982), pp. 865–874.

Training Retail Personnel

When a new employee first joins the company, he or she should be exposed to a pretraining session. **Pretraining** is an indoctrination on the history and policies of a store and a job orientation on the hours, compensation, chain of command, and job duties. In addition, the new employee should be introduced to his or her co-workers.

Training programs are used to teach new (and old) employees how best to perform their jobs or how to improve themselves. Training can range from one- or two-day sessions on writing sales checks, operating a cash register, personal selling techniques, or compliance with affirmative action programs to two-year programs for buyers and merchandise managers on all aspects of the store and its operations. Figure 9-14 provides an outline of the initial executive training program at Emporium-Capwell.

Effective retailers realize that training is an ongoing activity. New equipment, changes in laws, and new product lines, as well as employee turnover, necessitate not only training but retraining as well. For example, Scandinavian Design, a Massachusetts-based furniture retailer, operates a major training program for employees at all levels. It has established its own Scandinavian Design University with courses in sales

Emporium-Capwell's Initial Executive Training Program

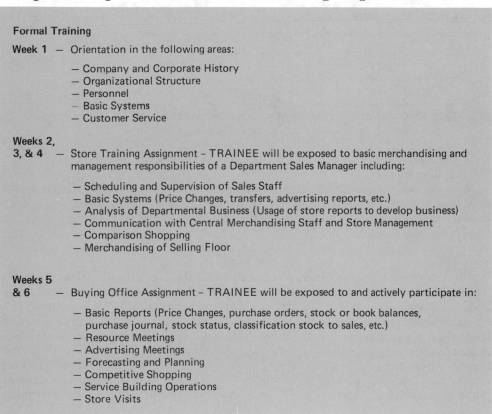

Formal Training

Week 1 — Orientation in the following areas:

        — Company and Corporate History
        — Organizational Structure
        — Personnel
        — Basic Systems
        — Customer Service

Weeks 2,
3, & 4 — Store Training Assignment – TRAINEE will be exposed to basic merchandising and management responsibilities of a Department Sales Manager including:

        — Scheduling and Supervision of Sales Staff
        — Basic Systems (Price Changes, transfers, advertising reports, etc.)
        — Analysis of Departmental Business (Usage of store reports to develop business)
        — Communication with Central Merchandising Staff and Store Management
        — Comparison Shopping
        — Merchandising of Selling Floor

Weeks 5
& 6 — Buying Office Assignment – TRAINEE will be exposed to and actively participate in:

        — Basic Reports (Price Changes, purchase orders, stock or book balances, purchase journal, stock status, classification stock to sales, etc.)
        — Resource Meetings
        — Advertising Meetings
        — Forecasting and Planning
        — Competitive Shopping
        — Service Building Operations
        — Store Visits

Figure 9-14

Emporium-Capwell's Initial Executive Training Program (continued)

Seminar Training

Seminars are held two times per week during the six weeks of formal training. All sessions are taught by EXECUTIVES in the Company and TRAINEES are expected to prepare for and actively participate in each seminar. Topics covered include:

- Merchandise Presentation
- Floor Merchandising Disciplines
- Merchandise Math/Gross Margin
- Trend and Item Merchandising
- Merchandise Traffic and Transportation
- Time Management

- Sales Staffing
- Labor Relations
- Analyzing Your Business
- Supervision of Sales Performance
- Retail Selling Skills
- Advertising

Evaluation

The TRAINER will complete a performance evaluation on the TRAINEE at the end of each on-the-job assignment. Additionally, an exam will follow the six week program to assess the TRAINEES' understanding of basic retailing concepts taught in the seminars. TRAINEES will also be asked to evaluate their training at the conclusion of the six weeks, as well as evaluate their TRAINERS.

Placement

TRAINEES will competitively interview for Department Sales Managers positions.

Source: Emporium-Capwell (a division of Carter Hawley Hale Stores). Reprinted with permission.

training, time management, leadership skills, product training, and so on. Overall, the firm allots $500,000 (about 1 per cent of sales) to employee development annually.[15]

Several training decisions must be made. Among them are

1. When does training occur? (At time of hiring or after being on the floor?)
2. How long should it be?
3. Who should conduct the training? (Supervisor, co-worker, or training department?)
4. Where should training take place? (On the floor or in a training room?)
5. What material (content) should be learned? How should it be taught?
6. Should audiovisuals be used?
7. How can the effectiveness of training be measured?

In setting up a training program, one can divide the preceding decisions into three basic categories: identifying needs, devising appropriate training methods, and evaluation.

By measuring the gap between employee skills and job skills, one can identify immediate training needs. Furthermore, training should prepare an employee for a promotion. A five-year plan for manpower development will enable the retailer to identify future needs and train employees accordingly. Short-run and long-run training needs can be identified through informal observations, requests from management, group discussions, employee requests, employee performance, and analysis of reports.

[15]Ellen Wojahn, "A Touch of Class, *Inc.* (September 1983), pp. 79–86.

After needs are identified, the best training method(s) for satisfying these needs must be uncovered from among lectures, demonstrations, films, programmed instruction, conferences, sensitivity training, case study, role playing, behavior modeling, and competency-based instruction.[16] The characteristics of these training methods are shown in Figure 9-15. Often retailers use two or more techniques during the training period to reduce boredom and cover the material better.

For training to be successful, an environment conducive to learning must be created. The essential principles of a good learning environment are

- All people can learn if taught properly.
- A person learns better when motivated; intelligence alone is not sufficient.
- Learning should be goal oriented.
- A trainee learns more when he or she participates and is not a passive listener.
- The teacher must provide guidance.
- Learning is viewed as a process of steps rather than a one-time occurrence.
- Learning is spread out over a reasonable period of time rather than compressed.
- The learner is encouraged to do homework or otherwise practice.
- Different methods of learning are combined.
- Performance standards are set, and good performance is recognized.
- The learner feels a sense of achievement.
- The teacher adapts to the learner and the situation.

A training program must be systematically evaluated for effectiveness. Comparisons may be made between the performances of those who have received training and those who have not. Comparisons may also be made among employees receiving different types of training for the same job. When one is measuring the success of a training program, evaluations should always be made in relation to stated training objectives. In addition, the effects of training should be measured over several time intervals (e.g., immediately, 30 days later, six months later), and appropriate files should be maintained.

Compensation of Retail Personnel

Compensation includes direct monetary payments (such as salary, commission, and bonus) and indirect payments (such as paid vacations, benefits, and retirement plan). Larger retailers often have profit-sharing plans that help better motivate employees. To be effective, total compensation should be fair to both the retailer and the employee.

For many retailers, compensation is determined through collective-bargaining contracts. As an example, in 1983, 52 per cent of supermarket chain companies had unionized personnel.[17] Union contracts also affect nonunion personnel, who ask for similar compensation.

Small retailers often pay employees salary and/or commission, with little emphasis on fringe benefits. Large retailers pay employees salary and/or commission plus fringe benefits.

[16]For example, see "Retailers Discover an Old Sales Tool: Sales Training," *Business Week* (December 22, 1980), pp. 51–52; "Training Films That Work: Behavior Modeling," *Progressive Grocer* (May 1981), pp. 77–78; Lance Ringel, "Buyer Training," *Stores* (April 1981), pp. 47–48; and Carolyn Lochhead, "Well Trained Personnel Can Whip Up Sales Totals," *Chain Store Age Executive* (November 1983), pp. 15–17.

[17]"51st Annual Report of the Grocery Industry," *Progressive Grocer* (April 1984), p. 94.

The Characteristics of Retail Training Methods

Method	Characteristics
Lecture	Factual, uninterrupted presentation of material; can use professional educator and/or expert in the field; no active participation by trainees
Demonstration	Good for showing equipment or sales presentation; shows relevance of training; active participation by trainees
Film	Animated; good for demonstration; can be used many times; no active participation by trainees
Programmed Instruction	Presents information in a structured manner; requires response from trainees; provides performance feedback; adjustable to trainees' pace; high initial investment
Conference	Useful for supervisory training; conference leader must encourage participation; reinforces training
Sensitivity Training	Extensive interaction; good for supervisors as a tool for understanding employees
Case Study	Actual or hypothetical problem presented including circumstances, pertinent information, and questions; learning by doing; exposure to a wide variety of problems
Role Playing	Trainees placed into real-life situations and act out conflicts
Behavior Modeling	Trainees taught to imitate models shown on videotape or in role-playing sessions
Competency-Based Instruction	Trainees given a list of tasks or exercises that are developed in a self-paced format

Figure 9-15

Under a straight-salary plan, an employee is paid a fixed amount per hour, week, month, or year. Earnings are not directly related to productivity. The advantages of a straight-salary plan are control, security for employees, and known expenses. The disadvantages are inflexibility, limited incentive to increase productivity, and fixed costs. Lower-level retail personnel are almost always paid salaries (e.g., clerks, cashiers).

With a straight-commission plan, the earnings of an employee are directly related to productivity (e.g., sales volume or customer returns). A fixed amount is not paid out. The advantages of straight commission are flexibility, the tie to productivity, no fixed costs, and incentive. The disadvantages are lack of control over employees, risk to employees, instability, and lack of limits placed on earnings. Sales personnel for automobiles, real estate, insurance, jewelry, furniture, and other expensive items are sometimes paid on straight commission. Direct-to-home sales personnel are also paid this way.

To combine the attributes of salary and commission, some retailers pay their employees a salary plus commission. Shoe salespeople, clothing salespeople, and some management personnel are among the employees paid in this manner. Sometimes bonuses are awarded as supplements to salary and/or commission. These are normally given for outstanding company or individual performance.

In some instances, top retail management is paid via a compensation cafeteria, where the executive can choose his or her own combination of salary, bonus, deferred bonus, fringe benefits, life insurance, stock options, and deferred retirement benefits.

Supervision of Retail Personnel

Supervision is the manner of providing a job environment that encourages accomplishment. The objectives of supervision are to control personnel, achieve good performance, maintain employee morale and motivation, decrease expenses, decrease redundancies, communicate company policies, and solve problems. Supervision is provided through personal contact, meetings, and written reports.

An important element of supervision is the motivation of employees. **Motivation** is the drive within people to achieve goals. The role of supervision is to motivate employees to achieve company goals, or to harness human energy to the retailer's needs. Several theories of motivation have been developed, two of which are McGregor's Theory X and Theory Y and Herzberg's theory of satisfiers and dissatisfiers.

Theory X is the traditional view of motivation and applies to lower-level retail positions:

1. Management is responsible for organizing money, materials, equipment, and people resources.
2. Personnel are directed, motivated, controlled, and modified in accordance with the needs of the organization.
3. Management must actively intervene with personnel; otherwise, people are passive and resistant to organizational needs.
4. The average worker lacks ambition, dislikes responsibility, and prefers to be led.
5. The average worker is self-centered and resistant to change.[18]

Theory Y is a more modern view of motivation and applies to all levels of retail personnel:

1. Management is responsible for organizing money, materials, equipment, and people resources.
2. People are not by nature passive or resistant to organizational needs.

[18]Douglas McGregor, "The Human Side of Enterprise," in Warren G. Bennis and Edgar Schein (Editors), *Leadership and Motivation: Essays of Douglas McGregor* (Cambridge, Mass.: MIT Press, 1966).

3. Motivation, potential for development, capacity for assuming responsibility, and readiness to achieve company goals are all present in people. Management must make it possible for people to recognize and develop their abilities.
4. The essential task of management is to arrange the organizational environment so that employees can achieve their own goals by directing their efforts toward company objectives.[19]

Theory X assumes that employees must be closely supervised and controlled. Economic inducements provide motivation. Theory Y assumes that employees can use self-management and can be delegated authority. Motivation is social and psychological. Management is decentralized and participatory.

In retailing, the recent turnaround of A&P represents a good illustration of Theory Y in action. When A&P said that it would close eighty Philadelphia stores in 1981, employees negotiated wage reductions in exchange for active participation in management decisions (e.g., store hours, product mix) and a share of gross sales if they improved labor productivity. As a result, over fifty stores remain open under the Super Fresh name, sales are better than expected, and expenses are down. Two other stores are now owned by former employees.[20]

Herzberg's theory offers another perspective on motivation. The factors involved in producing job satisfaction and motivation (satisfiers) are distinct from the factors that lead to job dissatisfaction (dissatisfiers). Satisfiers are achievement, recognition for achievement, the job itself, responsibility, and growth or advancement. Dissatisfiers are company policy and administration, supervision, interpersonal relationships, work conditions, salary, and security.[21]

It is the supervisor's role to motivate employees in a manner that yields job satisfaction, low turnover, low absenteeism, and high productivity.[22]

Retail Organization and Human Resource Management: A Summary

A retail organization outlines an orderly pattern of human relationships. The organization must satisfy the needs of the target market, employees, and management. Five steps are involved in setting up the retail organization: outlining the specific tasks to

---

[19]Ibid.

[20]David I. Diamond, "A&P's Worker-Managers," *New York Times* (May 21, 1983), pp. 37, 46; Paul A. Engelmayer, "Worker Owned and Operated Supermarket Yields Financial Success, Personal Rewards," *Wall Street Journal* (August 18, 1983), p. 25; and John Merwin, "A Piece of the Action," *Forbes* (September 24, 1984), pp. 146–148ff.

[21]Frederick Herzberg, "One More Time: How Do You Motivate Employees?" *Harvard Business Review*, Vol. 46 (January–February 1968), pp. 53–62.

[22]See, for example, Bobby J. Calder, "Improving Productivity: Are You Doing It All Wrong?" *Progressive Grocer* (June 1981), pp. 58ff.; Dan Shannon, "Productivity: Quality Circles for Supermarkets," *New York Times* (April 18, 1982), Section 3, p. 19; Penny Gill, "Families Matter," *Stores* (March 1982), pp. 37–40; R. Kenneth Teas, "Performance–Reward Instrumentalities and the Motivation of Retail Salespeople," *Journal of Retailing*, Vol. 58 (Fall 1982), pp. 4–26; and Alan J. Dubinsky and Steven J. Skinner, "Impact of Job Characteristics on Retail Salespeople's Reactions to Their Jobs," *Journal of Retailing*, Vol. 60 (Summer 1984), pp. 35–62.

be performed, dividing the tasks among channel members and customers, grouping tasks into jobs, classifying jobs, and integrating through an organization chart.

Specific tasks include buying, shipping, receiving, checking, and marking merchandise; inventory control; display preparation; operations; research; customer contact and follow-up; management; finances; gift wrapping; delivery; returns; forecasting; and coordination. These tasks are divided among retailers, manufacturers, wholesalers, specialists, and customers.

After the retailer determines which functions to perform, the functions are grouped into jobs, such as salesperson, cashier, inventory personnel, display personnel, credit personnel, customer service personnel, janitorial personnel, and management. Jobs can be categorized according to functional, product, geographic, or combination classifications. The organization chart graphically displays the hierarchy of authority and the relationship among jobs, and it coordinates the personnel of the store. Small independents, department stores, chain stores, and conglomerchants each utilize different organizational forms.

Retail human resource management is composed of several interrelated activities: recruitment, selection, training, compensation, and supervision. Special human resource considerations for retailers are inexperienced workers, long hours, visible employees, part-time workers, and variations in customer demand.

Recruitment is the solicitation of job applicants. Sources are educational institutions, channel members, competitors, advertisements, employment agencies, current and former employees, and unsolicited applications.

The selection of retail personnel requires a thorough job analysis, the creation of a job description, the use of an application blank, interview(s), testing (optional), the checking of references, and the completion of a physical examination. After personnel are selected, employees go through pretraining (job orientation) and job training. An effective training program revolves around identifying needs, devising appropriate training methods, and evaluating the results.

Employees can be compensated on a straight-salary, straight-commission, salary-plus commission, or salary-plus bonus basis. Also to be considered are fringe benefits, such as paid vacations, health benefits, and retirement plans.

Supervision and motivation are necessary to obtain good employee performance. Supervision can be provided through personal contact, meetings, and written reports. Motivation theories include McGregor's Theory X–Theory Y and Herzberg's satisfiers–dissatisfiers.

Questions for Discussion

1. List at least five objectives retailers should take into consideration when setting up their organizational structures.
2. Are the steps involved in setting up a retail organization the same for small and large retailers? Explain your answer.
3. Why are target-market needs important in developing a retail organization?
4. Give an example of how a specialist can perform the delivery function better and more economically than a retailer.
5. What is the purpose of an organization chart?
6. Would you rather work for a retailer using a tall or a flat organization chart? Explain your answer.

7. Differentiate among these department store organizations.
   a. Mother hen with branch chickens
   b. Separate store
   c. Equal store
8. What is a conglomerchant? Describe its organizational needs.
9. Distinguish between small and large retailer strategies for each of the following.
   a. Recruitment
   b. Selection
   c. Training
   d. Compensation
   e. Supervision
10. Why are the job analysis and the job description so important in selection?
11. What problems can occur during the interviewing and testing of prospective employees?
12. How may training needs be determined?
13. Describe the goals of a compensation plan in a retail setting.
14. Under what circumstances should Theory X be used? Theory Y?
15. Comment on Herzberg's theory of satisfiers.

CASES

1. Murphy's Department Store: Implementing a Training Program*

Murphy's is a five-unit department store chain located in central Pennsylvania. The main store is in a city of 75,000 persons, and each branch store is in a town of between 25,000 and 40,000 persons. All branch stores are within a 100-mile radius of the main store. Murphy's handles mainly softgoods, and would be called a "junior department store" by many. The main store is 50,000 square feet; the branch stores average 25,000 square feet. Total annual sales are about $15,000,000.

Ezra Murphy, founder, president, chairman, and CEO, recently read a *Wall Street Journal* article on the importance of training in increasing productivity. Training activities at Murphy's are of a basic nature and take place mainly on the job. Training covers such necessary tasks as receiving procedures, operating the point-of-sale terminals, and so on. Although the companywide *Operations Manual* (known to employees as "the Bible") states that "It is each store manager's responsibility to make sure that all store personnel are properly trained in *all* aspects of their jobs," there are no formal training programs.

A man of action, Murphy quicky appointed a task force to evaluate training needs and make recommendations (including a proposed budget) for implementation. The task force is made up of:

Barbara Gold (chairperson)	Store manager
Doug Babson	Girls' clothing buyer
Jane Paulson	Store manager
Jeff Rogers	Assistant store manager
Pat Coley	Comptroller

*This case was prepared and written by Dr. Franklin D. Rubenstein, retail management consultant.

As preparation for the first meeting of the task force, Barbara asked each of the members to talk extensively with the people with whom they work in order to find out what employees perceive their needs are in the way of training. Below is an excerpt from the first official task force meeting.

Barbara: Jane, let's start with you. What did you find out?

Jane: Well, you know, as store manager I get all the real tough customer complaints. So I tried to remember the situations. It turns out that most of these customers could have been satisfied by one of our salespeople, if only they knew how to deal effectively with the customers. Things like:

- How to say "no" on a return without insulting the customer.
- How to acknowledge a waiting customer and tell her when you'll get to her.
- How to suggest a substitute for an out-of-stock sale item.
- Paying attention to a customer instead of completing a stocking task while the customer waits.

We need to train our salespeople . . . they are the ones who have 90% of the customer contact. It's the customers' experiences with the salespeople that determine whether they'll return to our store or go across the street to O'Malley's.

Doug: I agree, but it's not just customer service. Selling is a lost art around here. How many customers buy a skirt for their daughter, and nobody even *suggests* a blouse to go with it . . . not to mention socks, a belt, or a second blouse! If our salespeople could sell better, our sales and profits would jump dramatically. I could do 30% more volume if our salespeople knew how to approach customers, close, and build the sale (like that blouse I mentioned).

Jeff: Selling and customer service are important, but salespeople are only as good as their managers. If we knew how to better motivate the salespeople, they'd be more productive in all their tasks. We, the managers, know retailing, but none of us are experts in managing . . . some less so than others. Let me give you an example. If a salesperson doesn't handle a job right, I need to be able to tell her what she did wrong, help her learn what to do next time instead, and all this without making her angry, defensive, or demotivated! I think that if we can train the managers, assistant managers, and department heads, then all employees would be more productive.

Jane: The other thing I thought of is that we often just don't hire the right people. If we could have a training program to teach us how to interview better, we could avoid a lot of costly mistakes. If you get the right people in there in the first place, you've got the battle half won . . . maybe three-quarters!

Doug: So far, all we're addressing are the store operations aspects of the business. For one thing, store managers and assistants could learn a lot more about merchandising. I don't think that they, as a group, understand concepts that are the heart of our business . . . concepts such as open-to-buy, markdown timing, gross margin calculations, and so on. They could make better decisions if they were more knowledgeable.

Also, the buyers and DMMs are constantly negotiating for the best prices and terms. We might be able to improve our gross margin by at least two points if we were better negotiators. In fact, the buying and merchandising functions are probably the best place to start.

Jane: Doug, merchandising is important, but the key to our business is customer service. Let's face it; we sell pretty much the same brands and styles as our competition. It's the service that can induce the customer to come to Murphy's instead of buying the same item at one of the new off-price chains for less!

Jeff: Jane's right, but without proper supervision and encouragement, training the salespeople will be a wasted effort. We've got to train the managers first. Then *they* can train the salespeople.

Pat: All this would be nice, but we're missing an area of big bucks. The paperwork around here stinks. Our shortages are higher than our profits . . . and a lot of it comes from sloppy paperwork. Let's start with the basics, and then go on to the fancy stuff. The store people (and the buyers) need to know their paperwork. The savings would be enormous.

Barbara: We're getting a lot of good ideas here, but now it's five of ten, and I know that some of you have other commitments now and that we'll have to wind this meeting up. I must confess, though. E.M. wants recommendations, and he'll think I'm crazy if I suggest even half of what we've discussed today . . . not to mention the budgetary implications. At the next meeting we'll have to talk about priorities.

Questions

1. Would Barbara Gold really be "crazy" to suggest all or most of the training ideas discussed? Why?
2. What would your implementation plan look like? (Be specific.)
3. What are some of the organizational factors affecting what can be accomplished?
4. What should be the role of Mr. Murphy and other top management?

2. London's: Evaluating Employees*

Two weeks ago you were hired for the position of Department Manager of the Housewares Department at London's, a full-line department store.

Three months before you were hired, the previous manager of this department was promoted and transferred to another store. Since the managerial structure of

*This case was prepared and written by John Roman, Director of Stores, Rochester Institute of Technology, Rochester, New York.

the store was being reorganized, management decided not to fill the vacancy in housewares until the new organization was in place. Thus, for three months prior to your arrival, your department did not have a manager.

The Divisional Merchandise Manager (DMM), your boss, oversaw the operation, but could not give the department the attention it needed. Therefore, the head salespeople, Jack Mason and Mary South, were acting as assistants to the DMM in managing the department. In addition to their selling responsibilities, they were given authority to schedule the sales personnel, authorize customers' bank checks and employee discounts, and enter daily sales and markdowns in the department's records.

Jack and Mary are both recent graduates from a local junior college who worked their way through college as salespersons in London's. London's normally requires a person to have a bachelor's degree to enter the executive training program. However, your DMM was so impressed by Jack and Mary, that upon graduation, they were offered positions as head salespeople for the department, and are soon to begin the executive training program.

On your first day at London's two weeks ago, your DMM told you that Jack and Mary were of great assistance, assumed responsibility well, and credited them for the smooth operation of the department for the past three months. Frankly, you felt glad to have them in your department, especially since you were new at London's.

This morning you were reviewing your department records to prepare for the planning meeting for next season with the DMM. You noted that this season's sales were ahead of plan, the stock turnover had increased, and that there was little "outdated" or "shopworn" merchandise on-hand. This did not surprise you, as London's has always held a strong position in the housewares market. You then remembered how your DMM praised Jack and Mary your first day on the job. You thought, "I guess the DMM was right." Then you noticed that the department records reflected an unusually high amount of markdowns. This did not seem appropriate. The increased sales volume and stock turnover should have reduced markdowns, not increased them. Upon further investigation, you found that a large number of markdowns were recorded during the past two months, most of them were for only one or two pieces of merchandise at a time, and always by the same two people—Jack and Mary.

Questions

1. Evaluate the Divisional Merchandise Manager's decision to make Jack Mason and Mary South assistants in managing the Housewares Department. Why would Mason and South allow markdowns to be so high?
2. How should you respond to the discovery of unusually high markdowns?
3. What roles would you give Jack and Mary until they begin the executive training program?
4. Develop a plan for approaching the DMM and telling her what was wrong in the department.

10

Merchandise Planning and Management: Buying and Handling

Chapter Objectives

1. To describe the major aspects of nonfinancial merchandise planning and management
2. To explain the merchandise buying and handling process and each of its elements: organization, merchandise plans, customer information, merchandise sources, evaluation methods, negotiations, concluding the purchase, merchandise handling, reordering, and re-evaluation
3. To consider merchandise quality, innovativeness, assortment, timing, and storage
4. To examine the functions performed when handling merchandise, with special emphasis on inventory shrinkage

Phil Cosentino, co-owner of the 25,000-square-foot Cosentino's supermarket in San Jose, California, has a unique merchandise buying and handling approach for produce (fruit and vegetables). Cosentino's carries 600 different produce items, about double the amount stocked by chain supermarkets, and they account for 23 per cent of the store's $400,000 weekly sales volume.

To obtain merchandise, Phil travels to produce terminals twice a week; he begins each Tuesday and Thursday workday at 1:00 A.M. Phil regularly shops at one terminal in Oakland and two in San Francisco. He periodically goes to Salinas, Watsonville, and other agricultural areas, where he buys directly from small farmers. Phil also encourages local San Jose gardeners to bring him products—some he buys for cash, others are obtained on consignment. Sometimes, produce is imported from New Zealand, Greece, and Italy. Among the unusual produce sold at Cosentino's are Persian vegetables, gourmet wild mushrooms, fifteen fresh herbs, and croppolini from Italy.

All fruit and vegetables are sold from bulk displays. After selecting merchandise, customers have the produce processed at the four weighing stations near the displays. Full-time employees weigh the merchandise and adhere UPC labels. Then, when the customer finishes a shopping trip, he or she has the produce electronically scanned at the checkout counter. Few supermarkets use UPC labels for produce; they prefer to handle it by hand marking or by processing it at the checkout counter (Cosentino says that his system is more efficient and avoids long lines of people waiting for a cashier).[1]

Overview

The development and implementation of a merchandise plan is an important component of the retail strategy. To be successful, a retailer must have the proper assortments of products when they are in demand and must sell them in a manner consistent with the overall strategy.

Merchandising is defined as:

> The planning and supervision involved in marketing the particular merchandise or service at the places, times, and prices and in quantities which will best serve to realize the marketing objectives of the business.[2]

In this chapter, the buying and handling aspects of merchandise planning and management will be discussed. The financial side of merchandising will be described in Chapter 11. Planning for a service retailer will be examined in Chapter 15.

The Merchandise Buying and Handling Process

Figure 10-1 shows the stages involved in an integrated merchandise buying and handling process. It is important that each of the stages be utilized when buying and handling merchandise. In addition, a systematic approach to merchandising should be followed.

Establishing a Formal or Informal Buying Organization

The first step in the merchandise buying and handling process is the establishment of a buying organization. Merchandising cannot be conducted in a thorough, systematic manner unless the buying organization is well defined. This organization specifies who is responsible for merchandise decisions, the activities of these people, the authority to make decisions, and the relationship of merchandising to overall store operations. Figure 10-2 highlights the attributes of buying organizations.

[1]Lee Dyer, "How Cosentino's Produce Produces $100,000 a Week," *Progressive Grocer* (February 1985), pp. 71–73.
[2]Ralph S. Alexander (Chairman), *Marketing Definitions: A Glossary of Marketing Terms* (Chicago: American Marketing Association, 1960), p. 17.

The Merchandise Buying and Handling Process

1. Establish a Formal or Informal Buying Organization
- A.   Formal-informal
- B.   Centralized-decentralized
- C.   General-specialized
- D.   Inside-outside
- E.   Cooperative
- F.   Merchandising-buying
- G.   Staffing

2. Outline Merchandise Plans
- A.   What to stock
- B.   How much to stock
- C.   When to stock
- D.   Where to store

3. Gather Information about Customer Demand
- A.   Customers
- B.   Sources of supply
- C.   Personnel
- D.   Competitors
- E.   Others

4. Determine Merchandise Sources
- A.   Company-owned
- B.   Outside, regularly-used
- C.   Outside, new

5. Evaluate merchandise
- A.   Inspection
- B.   Sampling
- C.   Description

6. Negotiate the Purchase
- A.   Negotiated contract
- B.   Uniform order
- C.   Terms

7. Conclude the Purchase
- A.   Automatic-manual
- B.   Central-regional-local approval
- C.   Transfer of title (billing cycle)
- D.   Consignment-memorandum

8. Handle the Merchandise
- A.   Receiving
- B.   Marking
- C.   Displays
- D.   On-floor assortments
- E.   Customer transactions
- F.   Delivery or pick-up
- G.   Returns and damaged goods
- H.   Inventory shrinkage
- I.   Control

9. Reorder Merchandise
- A.   Order and delivery time
- B.   Turnover
- C.   Outlay
- D.   Inventory vs. order costs

10. Re-evaluate on a Regular Basis
- A.   Overall procedure
- B.   Individual products

Figure 10-1

The Attributes of Buying Organizations

Factor	Attributes
LEVEL OF FORMALITY	
Formal	Well-defined responsibilities and authority, use of full-time specialists; costly
Informal	Low costs, flexible; poorly-defined responsibilities and authority, de-emphasis on merchandise planning
DEGREE OF CENTRALIZATION	
Centralized	Integrated effort, strict controls, consistent image, nearness to management, staff support, volume discounts; inflexible, time delays, poor morale at branch stores, excessive uniformity
Decentralized	Adaptable, quick, improved morale; disjointed planning, inconsistent image, limited controls and staff support, loss of volume discounts
BREADTH	
General	Better for small stores or few products
Specialized	Improved knowledge, well-defined responsibility; high costs, extra personnel
SOURCE OF PERSONNEL	
Internal	Staffed by store personnel, who make all merchandise decisions
External	Outside personnel hired (usually at a fee), used by small retailers or those far from supply sources
Resident buying office	Located in important merchandise centers, staffed by internal or external personnel
Cooperative buying	Independent retailers involved with shared purchases
PHILOSOPHY	
Merchandising	All stages in the buying and selling of products, smooth flow of command through an integrated effort, buyer's expertise used in selling, clear responsibility and authority, proper displays, reduced costs, closeness to consumer
Buying	Separation of buying and selling functions, recognizes dissimilar skills required for each function, higher morale of in-store personnel, selling not treated as subordinate, greater closeness to consumers, specialization, buyers not required to be good supervisors
STAFFING	
Buyer	Aggressive, travel oriented, customer oriented, creative
Sales manager	Planner and supervisor, detail oriented, customer oriented
Merchandising buyer	Attributes of buyer and sales manager

Figure 10-2

A **formal buying organization** exists when the merchandising function is viewed as a distinct retail task and a separate department is set up. All merchandising operations (Figure 10-1, steps 2 through 10) are under the control of this department. A formal organization usually occurs among larger retailers and involves distinct buying personnel. In an **informal buying organization,** the merchandising function is not viewed as a distinct task. Existing personnel handle merchandising and other retail functions. Responsibility and authority are not always clear cut. Informal buying generally occurs among smaller retailers.

The major advantages of a formal buying organization are well-defined responsibilities and authority and the use of full-time, specialized merchandisers. The major disadvantage is the cost of operation. The important advantages of an informal buying organization are low costs and flexibility. The important disadvantages are poorly defined responsibilities and authority, and the de-emphasis on merchandise planning.

Both structures exist in great numbers. It is not crucial that a retailer use a formal buying organization. However, it is crucial that the retailer realize the role of merchandising and ensure that responsibility, activities, authority, and the interrelationship with store operations are systematically defined and enacted.

Multiunit retailers must also determine whether to create a centralized buying organization or a decentralized one. In a **centralized buying organization,** all purchase decisions emanate from one office. For example, a chain may have fourteen stores, and all merchandise decisions are made in the headquarters store. In a **decentralized buying organization,** purchase decisions are made locally or regionally. As an example, a chain with eight stores may allow each outlet to select its own merchandise, or a chain with twelve stores may divide the branches into geographic territories (four per territory) and have regional decisions made by the headquarters store in each territory.

Among the advantages of a centralized buying organization are integration of effort, strict controls, consistent image, nearness to top management, staff support, and discounts through volume purchases. Among the disadvantages of centralized buying are inflexibility, time delays, poor morale at local stores, and excessive uniformity.

Decentralized buying offers the following advantages: adaptability to local market conditions, quick order process, and improved morale because branches have autonomy. The disadvantages are disjointed planning, inconsistent image, limited management controls, little staff support, and loss of volume discounts.

Many chains have combined the benefits of both systems. A centralized buying organization is used, but local store managers are given substantial power to revise merchandise orders or place their own orders (if substantiated).

A choice must be made between a general buying organization and a specialized buying organization. In the general buying organization, one or several people buy all the store's merchandise. For example, the owner of a small hardware store may buy all merchandise for his store. In a specialized buying organization, each buyer is responsible for a product category. As an example, a department store may have separate buyers for girls', misses', and women's clothing.

The general approach is better when the store is small or there are few products. The specialized approach is better when the store is large or many products are handled. With specialization, knowledge is improved and responsibility well defined; however, costs are high and usually extra personnel are required.

The retailer can choose between an inside buying organization and an outside one. An **inside buying organization** is one that is staffed by store personnel. All merchandise

Figure 10-3 An Inside Buying Organization

Buyers at J.C. Penney examining important merchandising reports that assist them in making decisions and assessing product line success. Courtesy J.C. Penney.

decisions are made by employees of the store. See Figure 10-3. With an **outside buying organization,** personnel external to the company are hired, usually on a fee basis.

An outside organization is most often used by small or medium-sized retailers or by those that are far from their sources of supply. In these cases, it is cheaper and more efficient for the retailers to hire an outside buyer than to use company personnel. An outside organization has clout in dealing with suppliers (due to the volume of purchases), usually services noncompeting retailers, offers marketing research expertise, and sometimes sponsors private-label merchandise. Outside buying organizations may be paid by retailers who subscribe to their services, or by manufacturers, which give commissions. Sometimes individual retailers decide to set up their own internal organizations if they believe their outside group is dealing with direct competitors or the retailers find that they can buy merchandise more efficiently. This situation recently occurred when Federated Department Stores announced that it would phase out its relationship with the Associated Merchandising Corporation.[3]

Resident buying offices are used to allow buyers to keep in close touch with the market. These offices operate in important merchandise centers (sources of supply) and provide valuable information and contacts. A resident buying office can be an inside or outside organization. In 1983, there were more than 300 such offices in New York City, about 40 in California, and 30 in other U.S. cities. These offices served approximately 7,500 retailers.[4]

[3]Isadore Barmash, "Shakeout in Retail Buying," *New York Times* (January 20, 1983), pp. D1, D13.
[4]Lewis A. Spalding, "Buying Offices: A Changing Business," *Stores* (April 1983), pp. 18–21.

Smaller, independent retailers are now using cooperative buying to a greater degree than ever before (in an attempt to compete successfully with larger chains). Under **cooperative buying,** a group of independent retailers gets together to make a large single purchase from a supplier. Volume discounts are then achieved. Cooperative buying is most popular among food and hardware retailers. In some cases, the retailers initiate the cooperative; in others, the wholesaler or manufacturer may initiate the cooperative as an attempt to cut costs.

Another decision involves the retailer's determination of whether the buying organization is concerned with merchandising or buying. As stated at the beginning of the chapter, merchandising includes all the steps in the buying and selling of products, such as purchase, pricing, storage, display, and delivery. Buying includes only the purchasing of products and not the sale of them. Many retailers consider merchandising as the key to their success and buyers (or merchandise managers) are involved with buying and selling. Other retailers consider their buyers as highly skilled specialists who should not be active in the selling process. This function is assumed by skilled selling specialists.

The advantages of a merchandising philosophy are that a smooth flow of command is caused by an integrated effort; the expertise of the buyer is used in selling; responsibility and authority are clear (the buyer does not blame sales personnel for poor sales efforts, and vice versa); the buyer ensures that the merchandise is properly displayed; costs are reduced (few staff specialists); and the buyer is close to the consumer through his or her interaction with the sales function.

The advantages of separate buying and selling functions are that similar skills are not required for each function; the morale of in-store personnel increases as authority is granted; selling is not treated as a subordinate function; salespeople are closer to customers than buyers; specialists can develop in each area; and buyers may not be good supervisors because of their time away from the store and differences in the management of buying and selling personnel.

Both approaches are used, and the advantages of merchandising or buying are still disputed. The individual retailer must evaluate which procedure is better for his or her store.

The last decision in this stage of buying and handling merchandise centers on the staffing of the buying organization. What positions must be filled, and what qualifications should the retailer require? Retailers who take a merchandising perspective are most concerned with hiring good buyers. Retailers who take a buying and selling perspective are concerned with hiring buyers and sales managers.

Many large retailers hire college graduates whom they place in extensive training programs and promote internally to positions as buyers and sales managers (women have historically done well in this field). The buyer must be aggressive to be successful in bargaining sessions with suppliers. The buyer will also have to travel to major marketplaces, making extensive use of trip buying plans (detailed shopping lists that completely outline purchases). The sales manager must be a good planner and supervisor. The merchandising buyer must possess the attributes of both.

More and more retailers are realizing that the most important qualification for good buying personnel is the ability to relate to customers and anticipate their future needs. To an extent, buyers are involved with each of the remaining activities described in the balance of this chapter and many of those detailed in Chapter 11.

For some students of retailing, the job of buyer (in either a merchandising or buying structure) is the most glamorous in retailing. It is viewed as high-paying, prestigious, interesting, exciting, and powerful. However, two important points should be made. First, there are other positions in retailing that offer these rewards; buying is not the only worthwhile position. Second, the buyer's job can sometimes be viewed as pressure-packed, hectic, time-consuming, and thankless. This discussion is intended not to criticize buyers but to balance the perspectives of some readers.[5]

Outlining Merchandise Plans

Merchandise planning centers on four basic decisions: what merchandise to stock, how much merchandise to stock, when to stock merchandise, and where to store merchandise.

What Merchandise Is Stocked

First, the retailer must determine what quality of merchandise to carry. Should the store carry top-line, expensive items and sell to the upper class? Should the store carry middle-of-the-line, moderately priced items and cater to the middle class? Should the store stock bottom-line, cheap products and attract the lower class? Or should the retailer try to draw more than one market segment by offering a variety in quality, such as middle- and top-line merchandise for the middle and upper classes? And should promotional merchandise (low prices on closeout merchandise or special buys that are used to generate store traffic) be offered?

In considering the quality of merchandise to be carried, the retailer should evaluate several factors: the desired target market(s), competition, store image, store location, turnover of stock, profitability, national versus private brands, services that must be offered, type of personnel needed, the perceived benefits of the product, and constrained decision making. Table 10-1 shows how each of these factors affects the planning of the quality of merchandise.

For example, Caldor is a Northeastern chain of almost 100 full-line discount stores. It has a very consistent merchandising strategy that stresses these factors:

- Only first-quality items are carried. No irregulars or closeouts are ever stocked.
- No sales are final. Goods may be returned.
- Store are clean, neat, and bright.
- Very competitive prices are offered.
- Upscale customers are sought.

Caldor is so successful that 1983 sales exceeded $1 billion.[6]

---

[5]See, for example, Glenn H. Snyder, "The Buyers: Straight Shooters with Fast Answers," *Progressive Grocer* (October 1980), pp. 55–58; Brian F. Harris and Michael K. Mills, "Evaluating the Retail Buyer: An Exploratory Study," in Kenneth Bernhardt et al. (Editors), *The Changing Marketing Environment: New Theories and Applications* (Chicago: American Marketing Association, 1981), pp. 43–46; Enid Nemy, "For a Buyer, a Hectic City Pace," *New York Times* (August 28, 1983), p. 62; Jeffrey H. Birnbaum, "A Menswear Buyer for Discount Stores Haunts Lofts, Cutting Rooms to Find Bargains in Volume," *Wall Street Journal* (March 31, 1982), p. 54; Isadore Barmash, "Buying for Bloomingdale's," *New York Times* (November 29, 1983), pp. D1, D5; *Business Basics: Retail Buying Function*, self-instructional booklet 1010 (Washington, D.C.: Small Business Administration, 1980); Hank Gilman, "Bribery of Retail Buyers Is Called Pervasive," *Wall Street Journal* (April 1, 1985), p. 6; and Steve Weiner, "K mart Apparel Buyers Hopscotch the Orient to Find Quality Goods," *Wall Street Journal* (March 19, 1985), pp. 1, 22.

[6]*Associated Dry Goods Corporation 1983 Annual Report*, p. 8.

Table 10-1
The Factors to Be Considered in the Planning of Merchandise Quality

Factor	Relevance for Merchandise Quality Planning
Target market	Quality must be matched to the wishes of the desired target market.
Competition	A retailer can choose to sell similar quality (follow competition) or different quality (carry different merchandise and appeal to a different market than competitors).
Store image	The quality of merchandise is directly related to the image customers have of the store.
Store location	A location affects store image and the number of competitors, which, in turn, relate to quality.
Stock turnover	High quality and high prices usually yield a lower turnover than low quality and low prices.
Profitability	High-quality merchandise generally brings higher profit per unit than low-quality merchandise; however, turnover may cause total profits to be higher for low-quality merchandise.
National versus private brands	For many consumers, national (manufacturer) brands connote higher quality than private (dealer) brands.
Services to be offered	High-quality merchandise requires personal selling, alterations, delivery, and so on. Low-quality merchandise may not.
Personnel	Skilled, knowledgeable personnel are necessary for quality merchandise. Limited personnel are needed for low-quality merchandise.
Perceived product benefits	Low-quality merchandise attracts customers who desire functional product benefits (e.g., warmth, comfort). High-quality merchandise attracts customers who desire extended product benefits (e.g., status, services, style).
Constrained decision making	a. Franchise or chain operators have limited or no control over product quality. They either buy directly from the franchisor (chain) or must abide by quality standards. b. Independent retailers who buy from a few large wholesalers will be limited to the range of quality offered by the wholesalers.

The second major decision a retailer makes concerning what merchandise to handle involves determining how innovative (new) the store should be. Several factors should be examined before the retailer plans the level of innovativeness: the target market, product growth potential, fashion trends and theories (where applicable), store image, competition, market segmentation, responsiveness to consumers, investment costs, profitability, risk, constrained decision making, and dropping of old products. These factors are summarized in Table 10-2.

An innovative store, one that carries new products and plans for upcoming trends, faces great opportunity (a monopoly position in the market) and great risk (misreading the market and being stuck with large inventories). By evaluating each of the factors in Table 10-2 and developing a thorough plan for handling new products, the retailer should be able to maximize opportunity and minimize risk.

These are illustrations of innovative merchandising strategies by retailers:

- In 1984, Wendy's introduced a special light menu of entrée items with less than 400 calories. Included are taco salad (390 calories), tuna salad with tomato (260 calories), and cottage cheese salad (130 calories). Said a Wendy's vice-president, "All you have

Table 10-2
The Factors to Be Considered in Planning Innovativeness

Factor	Relevance to Innovativeness Planning
Target market	Evaluate whether the target market is conservative or progressive.
Product growth potential	Consider each new product on the basis of rapidity of initial sales, maximum sales potential per time period, and length of sales life.
Fashion trends and theories	Understand the "trickle-down" and "trickle-across" theories (explained in the text), if selling fashion merchandise.
Store image	The kinds of products a store carries are influenced by its image. The level of innovativeness should be consistent with this image.
Competition	Lead or follow competition in the selection of new products.
Market segmentation	The market can be segmented by the division of merchandise into established-product displays and new-product displays.
Responsiveness to consumers	New products should be handled when they are requested by the target market.
Amount of investment	These types of investment are possible for each new product: product costs, new fixtures, and additional personnel (or additional training for old personnel).
Profitability	Each new product should be assessed for potential profits (on the product and additions to the profits of the overall store).
Risk	The major risks are damages to image, investment costs, and opportunity costs.
Constrained decision making	Franchise and chain operators may be restricted in the new products they can order.
Dropping old products	Old products should be deleted when sales and/or profits are low.

to do is look at the boom in low-calorie frozen foods like Stouffer's Lean Cuisine to know consumers are interested in eating light. . . . Restaurants have to react."[7]

- Sears was the first major retailer to open full-service, full-product-line computer centers in its stores. Sears decided on its strategy after evaluating its strengths: an existing service network, good facilities, seasoned personnel, an existing credit operation, good distribution networks, and a trusted company name. By the end of 1984, Sears had 100 computer centers in major markets throughout the country.[8]
- Bamberger's, a department store chain based in New Jersey, has been adding buyers so that it can concentrate on emerging opportunities in several of its departments. For example, in 1975, the higher-priced women's sportswear division had one buyer; today, it has a vice-president, a merchandise counselor, and six buyers. As a result, sales have increased twelvefold.[9]

The retailer should evaluate the growth potential for each new product. Three elements of growth are of special interest: rapidity of initial sales, maximum sales potential per period, and length of sales life. How fast will the product generate sales?

[7]Scott Hume, "Fast-Food Marketers Lighten Their Menus," *Advertising Age* (May 24, 1984), p. 3.
[8]Donald A. Hughes, "Case History: New Product Development by Retailers: Type I and Type II," *Marketing Review* (September–October 1984), pp. 16–17.
[9]Isadore Barmash, "Macy's Profits by Going Its Own Way," *New York Times* (May 15, 1983), Section 3, pp. 1, 12–13.

What are the most sales (dollars and units) that can be achieved in a season or a year? Over what time period will the product continue to sell?

A useful tool for estimating product potential is the **product life cycle.** This cycle shows the sales behavior of a product over its life. The traditional product life cycle contains four stages: introduction, growth, maturity, and decline. Figure 10-4 shows the shape of the basic product life cycle and describes each of the four stages. An understanding of this tool is quite helpful in strategy planning.

During the introductory stage of the cycle, the retailer should anticipate a limited target market, consisting of high-income and innovative consumers. The product will be produced in one basic model, not a choice of alternatives. The manufacturer may limit the distribution of the product to "finer" stores. However, convenience items are normally mass distributed. Food and houseware products fit into this pattern. Items that are initially distributed selectively utilize a skimming (high) price strategy. Merchandise that is mass distributed uses penetration (low) pricing to encourage fast acceptance by consumers. In either case, introductory promotion must be explanatory in nature, geared to informing hesitant consumers.

As innovative consumers buy a new product and recommend it to their friends, sales increase rapidly and the product life cycle enters the growth stage. The target market expands to include middle-income consumers who are somewhat more innovative than the average. Variations of the basic product appear; width and depth of assortment expand. The number of retailers carrying the product increases. Price discounting is not widely employed, but a wide variety of retailers offer a large range of prices, services, and quality. Retail promotion is more persuasive and is aimed at acquainting consumers with product availability and extended services.

In the maturity stage of the life cycle, product sales reach their maximum. The largest portion of the target market is reached during this period. Lower-, middle-, and upper-class consumers select from a very wide variety of products and options. All types of retailers (discount to finer stores) carry the product in some form. Although the upper-class stores continue to emphasize brand names and services, other stores enter into active price competition. Price is prominently mentioned in promotional activities. For manufacturers and retailers, the maturity stage is the most competitive.

A product then enters the decline stage, usually brought on by two factors: the target market shrinks (saturation and product obsolescence) and price cutting minimizes profit margins. In the decline stage, the target market becomes the lowest-income consumer and laggards. Product variety is cut back to a few basic models. Many retailers drop the product for image and profit reasons. Low prices are offered, and promotion is reduced and geared to price.

It should be noted that all new products do not conform to the life cycle displayed in Figure 10-4. Some derivatives of the basic product life cycle are shown in Figure 10-5. In a boom sales pattern, sales rise quickly and maintain a high level for a long period of time. Many cosmetics and pharmaceutical products can be placed in this category.

A fad curve occurs when a product generates a lot of sales, but only for a short time. The retailer must be careful not to overorder because of enthusiasm over high sales. Hand-held electronic games did very well for a short time until Atari introduced its first video-game console (which is now being replaced by inexpensive computers). An extended fad is like a fad, except that residual sales continue for a long period at a fraction of earlier sales. The hula hoop had very high sales in the 1950s and still maintains a sizable, but much smaller market. Clothing with designer insignias is another example of a product that can be classified as an extended fad.

The Product Life Cycle

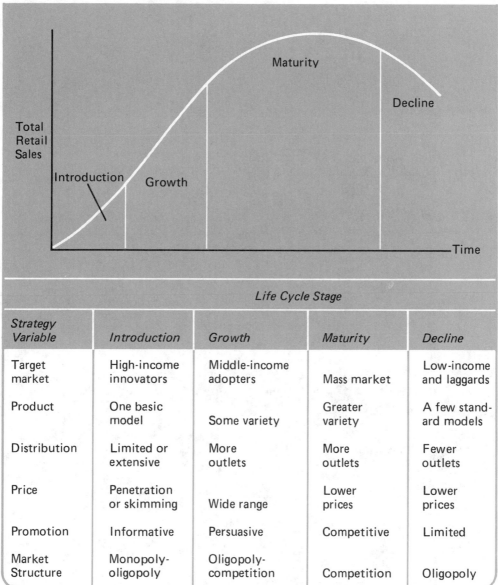

| Strategy Variable | Life Cycle Stage | | | |
	Introduction	Growth	Maturity	Decline
Target market	High-income innovators	Middle-income adopters	Mass market	Low-income and laggards
Product	One basic model	Some variety	Greater variety	A few stand-ard models
Distribution	Limited or extensive	More outlets	More outlets	Fewer outlets
Price	Penetration or skimming	Wide range	Lower prices	Lower prices
Promotion	Informative	Persuasive	Competitive	Limited
Market Structure	Monopoly-oligopoly	Oligopoly-competition	Competition	Oligopoly

Figure 10-4

Selected Product Life Cycles

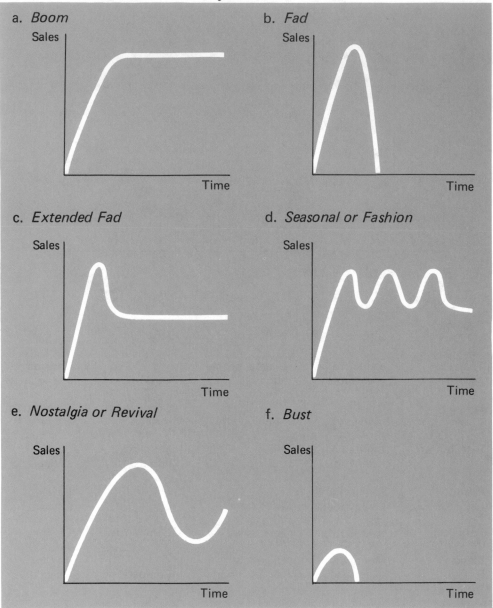

Figure 10-5

A seasonal or fashion curve results when a product sells well during nonconsecutive time periods. Seasonal products, such as camping equipment or snow tires, have good sales during one season each year. Usually, the sales of seasonal products occur during the same season each year, and retail planning is simple. A fashion product is much less predictable. Sales of products like bow ties or maxiskirts are often sizable for a number of years, become unpopular for a number of years, and then become popular again. For these products, retail planning is quite risky.

The nostalgia or revival curve happens when a seemingly obsolete product is revived. The innovative retailer will recognize the potential in this area and merchandise accordingly. For example, direct marketers frequently use television advertising to sell records emphasizing music or artists that were previously successful. They heavily promote "greatest hits albums" featuring a combination of artists.

The bust product life cycle is one in which the product is not successful at all (unlike the fad), and the retailer loses money and status. This occurred with the videodisc recorder developed by RCA. Despite a strong push by the manufacturer, the product never did well and was removed from the market in 1984. As a result, retailers had to slash prices drastically and they were stuck with a huge amount of excess inventory.

The retailer who sells fashion merchandise must be familiar with fashion trends and theories. Fashion trends are both vertical and horizontal. Fashions may go through one or a combination of these trends. A vertical trend occurs when a fashion is accepted by one market segment and undergoes changes in its basic form as it is accepted by the general public. The **trickle-down theory** states that a fashion is passed from the upper to the lower classes, through three vertical stages: distinctive (original designs, designer dress shops, custom-made, worn by high society), emulation (modification of original designs, finer department stores, alterations, worn by the middle class); and economic emulation (simple copy of original, discount and bargain stores, mass-produced, mass-marketed). Under this theory, Paris has usually been considered the fashion capital of the world.

In recent years, the importance of horizontal fashion trends has also been recognized. A horizontal trend occurs when a fashion is accepted by the general public while retaining its basic form. According to the **trickle-across theory,** within any social class there are innovative customers who act as opinion leaders. Fashion must be accepted by these leaders, who then convince other members of the same social class (who are more conservative) to buy the item. Merchandise is sold across the class and not from one class down to another.

By understanding both theories and determining which one is more appropriate for a specific fashion, the retailer is better able to predict fashion successes and the types of customers fashions will appeal to during each stage of their product life cycle. Figure 10-6 contains a checklist for predicting fashion adoption.

In planning innovativeness, the retailer's emphasis is too often on new-product additions. Equally important are the decisions involved in dropping existing products. Because of limited resources and shelf space, some products have to be dropped when others are added. Instead of intuitively removing old products, the retailer should use structured guidelines:

1. Select products for possible elimination on the basis of declining sales, prices, and profits; the appearance of substitutes; the loss of usefulness; and excessive demands on executives' time.
2. Gather and analyze information about these products, including profits, financial considerations, employee relations, and marketing factors.

A Checklist for Predicting Fashion Adoption

1.	Does the fashion satisfy a consumer need?
2.	Is the fashion compatible with emerging consumer life-styles?
3.	Is the fashion oriented towards the mass market or a market segment?
4.	Is the fashion radically new or a reintroduction of a previous success?
5.	What are the reputation of the designer(s) and the retailers carrying the fashion?
6.	Are several designers marketing some version of the fashion?
7.	What is the price range for the fashion?
8.	Will extensive advertising be used?
9.	How will the fashion change over time?
10.	Will consumers view the fashion as a fad or a long-term trend?

Figure 10-6

3. Consider nondeletion strategies such as cutting costs, revising marketing efforts, adjusting prices, and cooperating with other retailers.
4. After a deletion decision is made, consider timing, parts and replacements, inventory, and holdover demand.[10]

As an illustration, J. C. Penney stopped selling home computers in early 1984. At that time, less than 1 per cent of Penney sales were in home computers. Price cuts by manufacturers had reduced profit margins; and competition from toy stores and discounters was quite heavy. Penney also concluded that home computers did not fit in with its changing product mix, which placed greater emphasis on clothing.[11]

How Much Merchandise Is Stocked

After the retailer decides what merchandise to carry, he or she must determine how much merchandise to stock.[12] Width and depth of assortment should be planned. With how many product categories should the firm be involved, and how many varieties should be stocked in any product category? As described in Chapter 4, product assortment can range from wide and deep (a department store) to narrow and shallow (a

---

[10]Adapted from the classic article by Ralph S. Alexander, "The Death and Burial of 'Sick' Products," *Journal of Marketing*, Vol. 28 (April 1964), pp. 1–7.
[11]Bob Davis, "Penney Stores Won't Sell Home Computers After Feb 1; Price Cuts and Supplies Cited," *Wall Street Journal* (December 16, 1983), p. 6.
[12]For a good discussion, see Edgar A. Pessemier, *Retail Assortments—Some Theoretical and Applied Problems* (Cambridge, Mass.: Marketing Science Institute, 1980).

Table 10-3
Retail Assortment Strategies

Advantages	Disadvantages
Wide and Deep (many product categories and a large assortment within each category)	
Broad market	High inventory investment
Full stocking of products	General image
High level of traffic	Many items have low turnover
Customer loyalty	Obsolete merchandise
One-stop shopping	
No disappointed customers	
Wide and Shallow (many product categories and a limited assortment in each category)	
Broad market	Limited variety
High level of traffic	Disappointed customers
Emphasis on convenience customers	Weak image
Less costly than wide and deep	Many items have low turnover
One-stop shopping	Reduced loyalty
Narrow and Deep (few product categories and a large assortment in each category)	
Specialist image	Limited variety
Full stock in the product category(ies)	Limited market
Specialized personnel	Limited traffic
Customer loyalty	
No disappointed customers	
Less costly than wide and deep	
Narrow and Shallow (few product categories and a limited assortment in each category)	
Aimed at convenience customers	Limited variety and traffic
Least costly	Disappointed customers
High turnover of items	Weak image
	Reduced loyalty

box store). Some of the advantages and disadvantages of each type of assortment strategy are shown in Table 10-3.

Assortment strategies vary widely, as these two examples show. Kentucky Fried Chicken emphasizes "We do chicken right" and specializes in chicken products. Tandy (Radio Shack) sells products in several categories: radios, tape recorders, and phonographs; citizen band radios; stereo receivers, speakers, and turntables; microphones and headphones; electronic parts, tapes, and batteries; telephones and intercoms; and microcomputers.

Several factors should be considered in the planning of how much merchandise (width and depth of assortment) to carry. Sales should be evaluated. If product variety is increased, will overall sales go up? Will overall profits rise? Carrying ten varieties of cat food will not necessarily produce greater sales or profits than stocking four varieties. The retailer should also look at the investment costs that occur with a large variety.

Space requirements should be examined in the planning for products. How much space is required for each product category? How much space is available? Because available selling space is limited, it should be allocated to those products generating the greatest customer traffic and sales. Turnover should also be considered in the assigning of shelf space.

A careful distinction should be made between scrambled merchandising, complementary goods, and substitute goods. With scrambled merchandising, the retailer adds unrelated items to generate greater store traffic and improve profit margins (e.g., a florist adding greeting cards). Handling complementary goods enables the retailer to sell basic items and related products (e.g., stereo and records, automobile and tires, shoes and shoe polish). Both scrambled merchandising and the stocking of complementary goods are intended to raise sales. However, the handling of many substitute products (e.g., competing brands of toothpaste) may shift sales from one brand to another but have little impact on overall store sales.

For some retailers, particularly supermarkets, the proliferation of substitute products has created a difficult problem—how to offer consumers an adequate choice without tying up too much investment and floor space in one product category. At Ralph's supermarkets, a California-based chain, shelves are stocked with fifteen varieties of green peas, seventeen kinds of chicken noodle soup, and over a dozen brands of frozen pizza.[13]

In some instances, the retailer has no choice about stocking a full product line. The manufacturer may insist that the retailer carry the entire product line or else the product will not be distributed through the retailer. However, more and more, retailers are standing up to manufacturers, and in many cases, retailers stock their own brands next to the manufacturers' brands. As retail chains grow larger, this phenomenon increases. When retailers and manufacturers compete for the shelf space allocated to various brands and for control over the location of displays, this is known as the battle of the brands.

The retailer needs to consider the proper mix of manufacturer (national), dealer (private), and generic brands that should be carried. **Manufacturer brands** are produced and controlled by manufacturers. These brands are usually well known, supported by manufacturer advertising, somewhat presold to consumers, require limited retailer investment, and represent maximum product quality to consumers. Manufacturer brands dominate retail sales for most product categories.

Dealer brands contain the retailer's name, are more profitable to retailers, are controlled by retailers, are less expensive for consumers, and generate store (rather than manufacturer) loyalty. However, with private-label goods, retailers must line up suppliers, arrange for physical distribution and warehousing, sponsor advertising, create in-store displays, and absorb losses from unsold items. Retailers' interest in expanding the sales of their own brands can be shown through the following examples:

- ComputerLand, the world's largest computer store chain, sells computer monitors, disk drives, modems, and other items under its Sysdyne label. Its products have gross margins of 50 per cent or higher, and are expected to provide 10 per cent of chain sales by 1989.[14]
- Carter Hawley Hale sells fourteen different dealer brands in its six department store divisions. These brands account for almost 12 per cent of the firm's apparel sales.[15]

---

[13]Betsy Morris, "Food Items Proliferate, Making Grocery Aisles a Corporate Battlefield," *Wall Street Journal* (April 17, 1984), pp. 1, 5.
[14]Brian Moran, "ComputerLand Sells Labeled Line," *Advertising Age* (September 6, 1984), pp. 3, 34.
[15]Hank Gilman, "Retailers Bet Their Designer Wear Can Lure You Past Calvin Klein," *Wall Street Journal* (February 1, 1985), p. 25.

- At Lucky Stores, a large supermarket chain, private-label and generic brands represent about 19 per cent of total food sales. Lucky carries dealer brands when they are of good quality, can be sold at low prices, yield good profit margins, and require a moderate advertising effort.[16]

As one merchandising executive noted:

> Because of the frequency of margin erosion in national brands, stores find it necessary to have their own private brands to gain exclusivity and to achieve satisfactory profit margins. Since no other store in the same market has the same private brands, the retailer can be realistic in his initial markup and merchandise his own labels without being compelled to meet the national brands head-on in price.[17]

Generics are items that are unbranded, no-frills goods stocked by some retailers. These goods receive secondary shelf locations, obtain little or no advertising support, are sometimes of less overall quality than other brands, are stocked in limited assortments, and have plain packages. Generics are controlled by retailers and are priced well below other brands. In the 80 per cent of U.S. supermarkets carrying them, generics have stabilized at about 4 per cent of food sales. However, in the prescription drug industry, where the product quality of manufacturer brands and generics is virtually identical, generics' share of retail sales rose from 12 per cent in 1978 to 20 per cent in 1983.[18]

There are several other considerations that take on added importance as the retailer moves toward a wide and deep strategy:

1. Risks expand. Merchandise investments rise, and damages and obsolescence increase.
2. Personnel are spread too thinly, sometimes over dissimilar products.
3. Scrambled merchandising and its attendant risks increase.
4. Inventory control procedures become much more difficult. Merchandise turnover slows down.

Merchandise assortment planning is conducted with the use of a basic stock list (for staples), a model stock plan (for fashion merchandise), and a never-out list (for best-sellers). Staple merchandise includes such items as luggage, cameras, housewares, glassware, and china. Because these items have relatively stable sales (sometimes seasonal) and the basic nature of the merchandise does not change drastically, a retailer can clearly specify the requirements for each stock item. The **basic stock list** specifies the inventory level, color, brand, style category, size, package, and so on for every staple item carried by the store.

Assortment planning for fashion merchandise is more difficult than for staples because of variations in demand, changes in styles, and the number of sizes and colors

---

[16]*Lucky Stores Corporate Profile 1984*, p. 14.

[17]Isadore Barmash, "Talking Business with Lawson of Frederick Atkins Inc.," *New York Times* (July 17, 1984), p. D2. See also Lewis A. Spalding, "Private Label," *Stores* (September 1983), pp. 16–21; and Lewis A. Spalding, "A Tricky Business!" *Stores* (September 1984), pp. 24–29.

[18]"No-Frills Products Decline in Popularity," *Wall Street Journal* (November 15, 1984), p. 34; Linda Savage Ruhe, "Sun May Be Setting on Generic Products," *Advertising Age* (May 3, 1984), p. 47; Pamela G. Hollie, "Generic Drugs in Bigger Role," *New York Times* (July 23, 1984), pp. D1, D5; and Martha R. McEnally and Jon M. Hawes, "The Market for Generic Brand Grocery Products: A Review and Extension," *Journal of Marketing*, Vol. 48 (Winter 1984), pp. 75–83.

that must be carried. Fashion planning involves two stages. First, product lines, styles, designs, and colors are selected. Second, a **model stock plan** is used to order items by size and color. With a model stock plan, many items of popular sizes and colors are ordered; nonetheless, small amounts of less-popular sizes and colors are ordered to fill out the assortment. For example, a dress store may stock one size 14 dress and six size 10 dresses for each style.

Never-out lists are utilized when one is planning the stock for best-sellers. Items that account for large sales volume are stocked in a manner to ensure that they are always available. Items are added to and deleted from this list as their popularity and their importance to the store vary. For example, when a new Stephen King or Robert Ludlum book is released, bookstores order a large quantity to be sure that they can meet anticipated sales. After the book disappears from newspaper best-seller lists, smaller quantities are maintained.

When Merchandise Is Stocked

Next the retailer should ascertain when each type of merchandise will be stocked. For new products, the retailer must decide when the product will first be displayed. For established products, the retailer must plan the regular merchandise flow during the year.[19]

To order merchandise properly, the retailer should forecast sales during the year, and take into account various other factors: peak seasons, order time, delivery time, routine versus special orders, turnover, discounts, and improved inventory procedures.

As mentioned earlier in the chapter, some products have peak seasons during the year. For these products (e.g., winter coats and bathing suits), the retailer should plan large inventories during the peak periods and minimal stock during the off-season. Because some customers like to shop during the off-season, the retailer should not eliminate the items.

The retailer should plan merchandise purchases based on order time and delivery time. How long does it take the retailer to process a merchandise order? After the order is sent to the supplier, how long does it take to receive delivery of the merchandise? By adding these two time periods together, the retailer can get a good idea of the lead time necessary to restock his or her shelves. For example, if it takes the retailer seven days to process an order and the supplier an additional 14 days to deliver the products, the retailer should begin to order new merchandise 21 days before the old inventory runs out.

Planning differs for routine versus special orders. A routine order involves the restocking of convenience or other regularly sold items. Deliveries are received weekly, monthly, and so on. Accordingly planning and problems are minimized. A special order involves the purchase of merchandise that is not sold regularly. This order involves a lot of planning and close cooperation between retailer and supplier. A special delivery date is usually arranged. Custom furniture is an example of this type of product.

Turnover (how quickly merchandise sells) greatly influences how often products must be ordered. Convenience items like milk and bread (which are also highly perishable) have a high turnover rate and must be restocked quite often. Shopping items like refrigerators and color televisions have a lower turnover rate and must be restocked less often.

In deciding when and how often to purchase merchandise, the retailer should consider quantity discounts. Large purchases may result in lower per unit costs. Also, the use of improved inventory procedures, such as computers and the Universal Product Code (UPC), decreases costs and order times while increasing merchandise efficiency.

Where Merchandise Is Stored

The last basic merchandise planning decision involves where products are handled. A single-unit retailer usually must determine how much merchandise to place on the selling floor, how much to place in the stockroom, and the use of a warehouse. A multiunit retailer must also allocate merchandise among stores.

Many retailers use warehouses as central distribution centers. Merchandise is shipped from the supplier to the warehouses. Products are then allotted and shipped to individual stores. Some retailers do not use central warehouses. Instead products are shipped directly to each store. The advantages of central warehousing include reduced transportation and handling costs, the mechanized processing of goods, improved security, the efficient marking of merchandise, the ease of returns, and the smooth flow of merchandise. The major disadvantages of central warehousing are excessive centralized control and order-processing time delays.[20]

In allocating merchandise among store outlets, the retailer should consider the target market and store size. Products should be carried by a branch store only if the tastes and the needs of the customers served by that branch are satisfied. The more geographically dispersed a retailer is, the more important it is to pinpoint the differences in store product assortments.

Store size should also be considered in the allocation of products among branch stores. When the target markets are similar, the allocation should be based on sales. If Store A has sales of $1 million and Store B has sales of $2 million, Store B should receive twice as many items as A. Refinements must be made when the target markets are different. Woolworth learned this after placing the wrong merchandise into some of its stores:

> Oh let's say a lady's skirt was selling well in the larger stores where we carried eight different varieties. The theory was take the two best-selling skirts and put them in the smaller stores. Well, it doesn't work that way. There are different customer profiles. Different traffic patterns.[21]

Gathering Information About Consumer Demand

After overall merchandising plans are established, information about the target market is needed. The retailer should gather information about consumer demand before purchasing any merchandise.

---

[20]For information on warehousing versus direct deliveries, see Howard Way, Jr., and Edward W. Smykay, "Who's Minding the Storage," *Management Review*, Vol. 69 (August 1980), pp. 14–22; Mary Johnson and Mary Ann Linsen, "DSD Keeps on Truckin'," *Progressive Grocer* (August 1983), pp. 81–83; and Warren Strugatch, "Traffic Update," *Stores* (August 1984), pp. 60–66.

[21]Geoffrey Smith, "We're Moving! We're Alive!" *Forbes* (November 21, 1983), pp. 66ff.

The marketing research process, as related to retailing, was detailed in Chapter 6. A good merchandising plan depends on the retailer's ability to generate an accurate sales forecast. After all, the most important functions performed by the retailer are the anticipation and the satisfaction of demand.

In gathering data for merchandising decisions, the retailer has several important sources of information. The most important source is the consumer. By researching the target market's demographics, life-styles, and stated purchase plans, the retailer is able to study consumer demand directly.

Other sources of information can be used when direct consumer data are unavailable or insufficient. Suppliers (manufacturers, and/or wholesalers) usually do their own sales forecasts and market research (e.g., test marketing). They also know how much outside promotional support the retailer will get, and this has an important impact on sales. When closing a deal with the retailer, the supplier may present charts and graphs,

A Competition Shopping Report

COMPETITION SHOPPING REPORT

STORE # _____   DATE _____

DEPT. # _____

QUALIFIED COMPETITION SHOPPED:

1. _____

2. _____

I.B.M. STYLE NO.	MFR. MODEL OR STYLE	DESCRIPTION	OUR PRICE	1st COMPET. PRICE	2nd COMPET. PRICE	STORE'S RECOM. PRICE	BUYER'S RECOM. PRICE

ITEM SEEN AT OUR COMPETITOR'S STORE WHICH WE SHOULD CARRY:

MANUFACTURER	MFR. MODEL OR STYLE	DESCRIPTION	REG. OR LIST PRICE	SALE PRICE	BUYER'S COMMENTS

Signature of Shopper   Store Manager

Figure 10-7

showing sales forecasts and promotional support. However, the retailer should remember one significant point: it is the retailer who has direct access to the target market and its needs.

Retail personnel can provide information about consumer demand. Sales personnel have direct contact with customers and can pass their observations along to management. The retailer can maintain a **want book** or a **want slip** system. These are tools for recording consumer requests on unstocked or out-of-stock merchandise. The want book is used in smaller stores; and want slips are requests for individual items that are used in larger stores. These tools are very helpful to a retailer's buyers.

Personnel should be encouraged to offer feedback and not be shut off from making comments based on interaction with consumers. Outside of the customer, sales personnel may provide the most useful information for merchandising decisions. Buying personnel learn a lot about consumer demand by visiting suppliers, talking with sales personnel, and observing customer behavior. Usually, buyers are responsible for complete sales forecasts and merchandise plans. Top management combines the forecasts and plans to obtain overall company projections.

Competitors are another source of information. A conservative retailer may not stock an item until the competition does so. Therefore, comparison shoppers (who look at product assortments and prices of competitors) are employed. In addition, trade publications report on trends in each area of retailing and provide a legal way of gathering information from competitors. See Figure 10-7 for an example of a competition shopping report.

Other sources may offer useful pieces of information: government sources can show unemployment, inflation, and product safety data; independent news sources conduct their own consumer polls and do investigative reporting; and commercial data can be purchased.

Information should be considered from each of these sources. One type of data is usually insufficient. Whatever the amount of information acquired, the retailer should feel comfortable that it will enable him or her to make an accurate decision. For routine merchandising decisions (e.g., milk and bread), limited information may be sufficient. On the other hand, new-car sales can fluctuate widely and require extensive data for sales forecasts.

Determining Merchandise Sources

The next step in merchandise buying and handling is to determine the sources of merchandise. Three major sources exist: company-owned; outside, regularly-used; and outside, new.

With the company-owned supplier, a large retailer owns a manufacturing and/or wholesaling facility. The company-owned supplier handles whatever merchandise the retailer requests.

An outside, regularly-used supplier is one that is not owned by the retailer but is used regularly by the retailer. The retailer knows the quality of the goods and the reliability of the supplier through experience.

An outside, new supplier is one that is not owned by the retailer and has not been dealt with before by that retailer. Therefore, the retailer may be unfamiliar with the quality of the merchandise and the reliability of this supplier. The basic types of outside suppliers (regularly used and new) are shown in Figure 10-8.

Outside Sources of Supply

Source	Characteristics
1) Manufacturer	Physically produces goods, may provide shipping and credit
2) Full-Service Merchant Wholesaler	Buys product from manufacturer, performs many services for retailer (shipping, storing, credit, information, etc.)
a. General Merchandise	Carries a very wide assortment of goods
b. Specialty Merchandise	Carries a very deep assortment of goods
c. Rack Jobber	Brings and sets up own displays, usually deals with nonfood items in supermarkets and foodstores, paid in cash after merchandise is sold, convenient for store
3) Limited-Service Merchant Wholesaler	Same as full service, except that fewer services are provided and costs are lower
a. Drop Shipper	Buys and sells via the telephone (never physically touches merchandise), major task is connecting buyer and seller
b. Mail Order	Catalog sales to small retailers
c. Cash-and-Carry	Store where small retailers buy and take merchandise
4) Agents and Brokers	Do not take title to goods (ownership remains with manufacturer), provide a variety of functions for a fee or commission. Included are auction companies, salespeople, and selling agents.

Figure 10-8

These two examples show the complexity involved with choosing suppliers. Sears purchases goods from approximately 9,800 suppliers in the United States alone; this means constantly evaluating potential vendors and the performance of existing suppliers.[22] The annual Southern Furniture Market in High Point, North Carolina, is the world's largest wholesale furniture fair. The fair lasts nine days, takes place in ninety

[22]*Sears, Roebuck and Company Form 10K,* for the fiscal year ended December 31, 1983, p. 4.

locations, involves 1,300 showrooms, draws 40,000 people (over half of whom are retail buyers), and results in purchases of several hundred million dollars.[23]

In selecting a merchandise source, the retailer should consider several criteria:

- Reliability—Will the supplier fulfill all promises?
- Price–quality—Who provides the best merchandise at the lowest price?
- Order-processing time—How fast will a delivery be made?
- Exclusive rights—Will the supplier give exclusive selling rights?
- Functions provided—Will the supplier provide shipping, storing, and other functions, if needed?
- Information—Will the supplier pass along any important product information?
- Ethics—Will the supplier sell at lower prices to a competitor?
- Guarantee—Does the supplier stand behind the products?
- Credit—Can a credit purchase be made?
- Long-run relations—Will the supplier be available over an extended period of time?
- Reorders—Can suppliers fill reorders?
- Markup—Will markup be adequate?
- Innovativeness—Is the supplier's line innovative or conservative?
- Local advertising—Does the supplier advertise in local media?
- Risk—How much risk is involved in dealing with the supplier?
- Investment—How large are total investment costs?

Evaluating Merchandise

Whatever source is chosen, the retailer should develop a procedure for evaluating the merchandise that is under consideration for purchase. Should each individual unit be examined, or can an item be bought by description?

Three types of evaluation are possible. The choice of technique depends on the cost of an item and its regularity of purchase. Inspection occurs when each product unit is examined before purchase and after delivery. Jewelry and art are two examples of expensive, one-time purchases where the retailer would carefully examine each item.

Sampling takes place when a large quantity of breakable, perishable, or expensive items is regularly purchased. It becomes inefficient to inspect each piece of merchandise in this situation. Therefore, items are sampled for quality and condition. For example, a retailer purchasing several hundred tomatoes or bananas would not inspect each tomato or banana. Instead a number of units (a sample) would be examined. The entire selection would be purchased if the sample is satisfactory. An unsatisfactory sample can cause a whole shipment to be rejected. Sampling also occurs on receipt of the merchandise.

Description buying takes place when the retailer purchases standardized, unbreakable products. The items are not inspected or sampled; they are ordered in quantity from a verbal or pictorial description. For example, an office supply retailer can order paper clips, pads, typing paper, and so on from a catalog or order form. When the order is received, only a count of items is conducted.

[23]James A. Revson, "The Furniture Connoisseurs Go to Market," *Newsday* (October 15, 1984), At Home Section, pp. 12–13.

Negotiating the Purchase

After the merchandise sources have been investigated and the merchandise has been evaluated, the retailer has to negotiate the purchase and its terms. A new or special order will usually result in a negotiated contract. In this case, the retailer and the supplier carefully negotiate all aspects of the purchase. On the other hand, a regular order usually results in a uniform contract. In this instance, terms have already been agreed on, and the order is handled in a routine manner.

Many purchase terms must be taken into consideration, including

- Date of delivery.
- Quantity purchased.
- Price.
- Discounts.
- Form of delivery.
- Point of transfer of title.

The date of delivery and the quantity purchased should be clearly stated. A retailer can cancel the order if either provision is not carried out. The selling price and the stipulations for discounts are also important. In many cases, the selling price will be discounted for early payments (e.g., 2/10/net 30 means that a 2 per cent discount will be given if the full bill is paid in ten days; the full bill is due in 30 days), trade activities (such as setting up displays), and quantity purchases. Specifications are necessary for the form of delivery (water, air, truck, rail, and so on) and the party responsible for shipping charges (FOB—free on board—means that the supplier places the merchandise with the shipper, but the retailer pays the freight). Finally, the point of transfer of title—when ownership changes from supplier to buyer—should be stipulated.

Concluding the Purchase

For large retailers, purchases are concluded automatically. Computers are used to complete and process orders. Each purchase is fed into the computer's data file.[24] Smaller retailers must conclude their purchases manually. Orders are written up and processed manually, and purchases are added to the store's book inventory in the same manner.

Multiunit retailers must determine whether to use central, regional, or local approval for purchases. Should central or regional management have the final authority in purchase decisions, or should the local manager have strong input? This question was discussed in detail in the buying organization part of this chapter. Advantages and disadvantages accrue to each approval technique.

As mentioned in the previous section, **transfer of title** should be carefully noted. Several alternatives are possible:

1. The buyer takes title immediately upon purchase.
2. The buyer assumes ownership after the merchandise is loaded onto the mode of transportation.

[24]See Jules Abend, "Computer Links," *Stores* (June 1984), pp. 75–80.

3. The buyer takes title when the shipment is received.
4. The buyer does not take title until the end of the billing cycle, when the supplier receives payment.
5. The retailer accepts the merchandise on consignment and does not own the items.

It is important that the retailer understand the differences among these alternatives, because his or her responsibilities and rights differ in each case.

Consignment or **memorandum purchases** are made when the supplier is in a weak position and wants to get the retailer to carry merchandise. In both instances, the retailer does not pay for the items until they are sold and has the right to return merchandise. With a consignment deal, the retailer runs no risk because title is not taken until after the merchandise is sold. With a memorandum deal, risk is still low, but the retailer takes title on delivery and is responsible for damages.

Handling the Merchandise

During this phase, the retailer is concerned with the physical handling of merchandise, which involves a variety of functions: receiving merchandise; marking prices; setting up displays; determining on-floor quantities and assortments; completing customer transactions; arranging for customer delivery or pickup; processing returns and damaged goods; monitoring pilferage; and controlling merchandise.[25]

First, items are shipped from the supplier to the retailer, who warehouses them or stocks them in the store. For example, traditional supermarkets receive an average of three deliveries per week from primary warehouses and about 100 deliveries per week directly from vendors.[26] On the other hand, Loehmann's (an off-price retailer of high-quality women's apparel) picks up merchandise from its manufacturers, ships items to a central warehouse, and then delivers them to its stores—all within 48 hours.[27] Figure 10-9 shows one of the four automated distribution centers operated by Southland for its 7-Eleven stores.

Next, prices and inventory information are marked on merchandise. Supermarkets estimate that price marking on individual items costs them an amount equal to annual profits, and look forward to the time when shelf prices will be sufficient.

Price marking can be conducted in several ways. Small retailers often handpost prices. Some larger retailers rely on UPC information on packages. Others rely on batch tags, which usually have price and inventory data that are computer and human readable; Kimball Systems makes a variety of product tags that contain this information. The Dennison Manufacturng Company produces a system for receiving, marking, and routing merchandise to sales floors. The more information that labels or tags possess, the more efficient the inventory control system. For example, Figure 10-10 shows the Pathfinder printer developed by Monarch Marking Systems. This hand-held device can print OCR-A or UPC-based labels. It can also be connected to a store's computer system.

Store displays and on-floor quantities and assortments depend on the type of store and merchandise involved. Supermarkets usually utilize rack displays and place most

[25]For a comprehensive report on merchandise handling, see *Receiving, Marking and Merchandise Handling* (New York: National Retail Merchants Association, 1981).
[26]"50th Annual Report of the Grocery Industry," *Progressive Grocer* (April 1983), p. 118.
[27]*1983 Associated Dry Goods Corporation Annual Report*, p. 10.

Figure 10-9 A Southland Distribution Center

This highly automated distribution center is designed to maintain 7-Eleven stores' well-stocked position through frequent deliveries of small quantities of goods—usually in less than case lots. This enables the stores to offer a wider selection of products, increase inventory turnover, and ensure product freshness. Courtesy Southland Corporation.

inventory on the sales floor. Department stores have all kinds of interior displays and place a lot of inventory in the back room, off the sales floor. Displays and on-floor merchandising are discussed more fully in Chapter 12.

Merchandise handling is not completed until the customer purchases and receives it from the retailer. This involves order taking, credit or cash transactions, packaging, and delivery or pickup. Automation has improved retailer performance in each of these areas.

Next, a procedure for processing returns and damaged goods must be developed. In particular, the retailer needs to determine who is responsible for returns (the manufacturer or the retailer) and under what provisions damaged goods would be accepted for refund (such as the length of time under which a warranty is honored).

Monitoring and reducing inventory shrinkage is an aspect of merchandise handling that has rapidly grown in importance. **Inventory shrinkage** can be broken down into three distinct categories: customer shoplifting, employee theft, and inventory record-keeping errors. For many stores, shoplifting and employee theft alone represent up to

each new employee. The test costs $9 to $12 per employee, but has reduced inventory shrinkage by 28 per cent.[30]

- Employee training programs on the impact of inventory shrinkage and incentives for reducing it are being offered by more retailers. Neiman-Marcus shows employees a film containing interviews with convicted shoplifters in prison to demonstrate the seriousness of the problem. Woodward & Lothrop, another department store chain, offers employees $500 in cash plus half the value of the merchandise in question for turning in fellow employees involved in theft.[31]

- Many retailers have toughened their attitudes and are now prosecuting offenders; and courts are imposing stiffer penalties. In most areas, store detectives are empowered by local police to make arrests.[32]

- Retailers are increasingly using new technologies, including antishoplifting merchandise tags and sophisticated alarm systems, to limit shrinkage. General-merchandise retailers are utilizing plastic tags which are clipped to items and must be removed mechanically. Supermarkets are utilizing paper labels which are adhered to high-shrinkage goods and desensitized by electronic scanning equipment. In both cases, a failure to have an item processed by a cashier will result in an alarm going off.[33] See Figure 10-12.

- Obvious protection tools are being employed. These include uniformed security guards, television cameras positioned in the middle of a store, and store signs. See Figure 10-13.

Figure 10-14 presents a comprehensive list of the ways various retailers are combatting shopper, employee, and delivery person theft.

Unfortunately, some antishoplifting strategies such as closing off multiple entrances and exits, chaining expensive wearing apparel together, or putting small but expensive merchandise behind locked displays, may adversely affect retail sales.

Merchandise control includes evaluating sales, profits, turnover, shrinkage, seasonality, costs, and other factors for each product category and item carried by the retailer.[34] Control is achieved by the development and maintenance of a book (perpetual) inventory. A physical inventory is conducted periodically to check the accuracy of the book figures. The latter must be adjusted because of damages, pilferage, and store returns. An in-depth discussion of this topic appears in Chapter 11.

Reordering Merchandise

A plan for reordering merchandise must be developed for those items that are purchased more than once. As shown in Figure 10-1, four factors are most important for generating such a plan.

[30]"Prehire Tests Cut Chain's Theft by 28%," *Chain Store Age Executive* (June 1983), p. 25.

[31]Jules Abend, "Back to Basics," *Stores* (June 1983), p. 54; and "Security Report: Retailers on the Defensive," p. 16.

[32]Claudia Ricci, "If You're Primping in This Window, Say Hello to Bernard," *Wall Street Journal* (March 8, 1983), p. 19.

[33]"EAS Thwarts Shoplifters at Las Vegas Diamonds," *Chain Store Age Executive* (September 1984), pp. 149ff.; and Robert E. O'Neill, "Giant to Shoplifters: Gotcha!" *Progressive Grocer* (April 1984), pp. 129–135.

[34]See Marian Burk Rothman, "Expanding the Concept of Inventory Management," *Stores* (June 1979), pp. 30–32ff; Jules Abend, "Automated Inventory Management: New Aim," *Stores* (March 1982), pp. 54–59; and "Inventory Management: Sanger Harris," *Stores* (June 1983), pp. 27–28.

MicroLabel™
How it works.

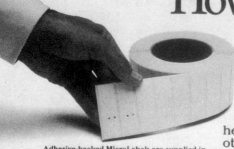

Adhesive-backed MicroLabels are supplied in convenient 1,000 label rolls.

Just ¾″ wide by 2½″ long, MicroLabel™ tags set the world's standard for small, disposable electronic article surveillance labels. Now it's possible to effectively protect a variety of hard goods and prepackaged soft goods that could never be protected before. Like cosmetics, audio and video tapes, fashion accessories, health and beauty aids, blister packages and many other items. MicroLabel combines the advantages of an incredibly micro-thin electronic label and a super strong adhesive. This makes MicroLabel the economical solution to protect products found in drug stores, discount stores, home centers, etc. Anywhere packaged items need protection.

MicroLabel works under the same principle as Sensormatic tags for the soft goods industry. Therefore, MicroLabel may be used with most existing Sensormatic surveillance systems to protect both hard goods and soft goods with the same system.

Here's how MicroLabel works.

First, all items to be protected are labelled either by hand or with a MicroLabel applicator. When customers purchase labelled merchandise, MicroLabel is electronically deactivated with a hand held "wand" at the point-of-sale. MicroLabels which have not been deactivated and pass through the Sensormatic

System at the exit will trigger an alarm, alerting personnel in time to prevent the unauthorized removal of merchandise.

Additionally, MicroLabel offers the flexibility of a specially designed hand held applicator, as well as custom-imprinting, using standard compatible price marking equipment.

The MicroLabel deactivator utilizes a special lightweight wand that is easy to use and effective. It provides both a visible and audible signal to cashiers as it deactivates each MicroLabel in 2 milliseconds, for fast, sure processing at the point-of-sale.

MicroLabels can be applied quickly and easily by hand or with this special hand held applicator.

Figure 10-12   An Antishoplifting Label System

Courtesy Sensormatic Electronics Corporation.

Figure 10-13 Anti-shoplifting Warning Sign

Courtesy Checkpoint Systems, Inc.

Order and delivery time should be calculated. How long does it take for the retailer to process an order and the supplier to deliver this order? It is possible that delivery time is so lengthy that the retailer must reorder while a full inventory still exists. On the other hand, overnight delivery is available for some items.

The turnover rate for the merchandise should be calculated. How long does it take for the retailer to sell out his or her inventory? A fast-selling product allows the retailer to have two choices: order a surplus of items and spread out reorder periods, or keep a low inventory and order frequently (short order periods). A slow-selling item allows the retailer to reduce his or her inventory and spread out the reorder period.

The financial outlay that must be made under various purchase plans should be considered. A large order, which provides discounts, may involve a large cash outlay. On the other hand, a small order, although more expensive per item, may result in lower total costs at any one time (because less inventory is maintained).

Ways to Deter Shopper, Employee, and Delivery Person Theft

1. Using in-store detectives or uniformed guards.

2. Prosecuting all individuals charged with theft.

3. Using electronic article surveillance wafers, electro magnets, or stick-ons for high-value and theft-prone goods.

4. Developing comprehensive employee training programs.

5. Providing employee bonuses based upon overall reduction in shortages or based on value of recovered merchandise.

6. Inspecting all packages brought into store.

7. Utilizing self-closing/self-locking showcases for high-value items such as jewelry.

8. Chaining down expensive samples, such as high-fidelity equipment, to fixtures.

9. Placing goods with high value/small size in locked showcases.

10. Attaching expensive clothing together.

11. Alternating the direction of hangers on clothing near doors.

12. Limiting the dollar value and quantity of merchandise displayed near exits.

13. Limiting the number of entrances and exits to the store.

14. Utilizing cameras and mirrors to increase visibility, especially in low traffic areas.

15. Using two-way mirrors where appropriate.

Shopper Theft While Store Is Closed

1. Conducting thorough check of the building at night to make sure no one is left in store.

2. Locking all exits, even fire exits, at night.

3. Utilizing ultrasonic/infrared detectors, burglar alarm traps, or guards with dogs when store is closed.

4. Placing valuables in safe.

Figure 10-14

Ways to Deter Shopper, Employee, and Delivery Person Theft (continued)

5. Using shatterproof glass and/or iron gates on display windows to prevent break-ins.

6. Making sure exterior lighting is adequate when store is closed.

7. Periodically testing burglar alarms.

Employee Theft

1. Utilizing undercover personnel to control theft.

2. Using polygraph tests, voice stress analysis, and psychological tests as employee screening devices.

3. Developing a system of locking up trash to prevent merchandise from being thrown out and then retrieved.

4. Verifying through use of undercover personnel whether all sales are rung up.

5. Utilizing cameras, mirrors.

6. Implementing central control of all exterior doors to monitor opening and closing.

7. Sealing all trucks after they are loaded with goods.

8. Inspecting worker packages, tool boxes, lunch boxes.

9. Dividing responsibilities (e.g., having one employee record sales; another making deposits).

10. Vigorously investigating all known losses.

11. Firing offenders immediately.

Delivery People

1. Properly identifying delivery people.

2. Verifying receipts and goods taken out.

3. Utilizing cameras, mirrors.

4. Implementing central control of all exterior doors to monitor opening and closing.

Finally, inventory holding versus order costs must be measured. The advantages of maintaining a large inventory are customer satisfaction, discounts, low transportation charges, and ease of control and handling. The disadvantages are high investment costs, obsolescence, deterioration, damages, storage costs, insurance costs, and opportunity costs. The advantages of placing many orders and keeping a low inventory are low investment, low opportunity costs, low storage costs, and limited damages and obsolescence. The disadvantages are disappointed customers, higher per unit costs, time delays, partial shipments, service charges, and complex control and handling. Retailers normally try to trade off these two costs by maintaining a large enough inventory to satisfy customers while not keeping a high surplus inventory. This is examined further in Chapter 11.

By studying these four factors, the retailer can develop a consistent plan for the timing and processing of recurrent orders.

Re-evaluating on a Regular Basis

Once a well-integrated buying and handling plan is established, the retailer should not ignore this area. Re-evaluation should take place on a regular basis. Management should review the buying organization (step 1 in Figure 10-1), and the buying organization should review the buying and handling process (steps 2 through 9). The overall procedure, as well as the handling of individual products, should be constantly monitored.

Merchandise Planning and Management— Buying and Handling: A Summary

A key element in a successful retail strategy is the development and implementation of a merchandise plan. Merchandising includes all the activities involved in the buying and selling of products by a retailer. A merchandise buying and handling plan is an integrated, systematic procedure for acquiring and processing merchandise. Ten steps are involved:

1. Establish a formal or informal buying organization.
2. Outline merchandise plans.
3. Gather information about consumer demand.
4. Determine merchandise sources.
5. Evaluate merchandise.
6. Negotiate the purchase.
7. Conclude the purchase.
8. Handle the purchase.
9. Reorder merchandise.
10. Re-evaluate on a regular basis.

Buying-organization decisions include the level of formality, degree of centralization, amount of specialization, inside–outside, cooperative efforts, buying versus merchandising, and staffing. Buying includes only the purchasing of products and not the sale of them, whereas merchandising entails both activities. Some retailers separate buying and selling functions.

Merchandise plans involve four basic decisions. In determining what merchandise to handle, the retailer must decide on the quality of merchandise (bottom, top, or middle) to stock and how innovative (progressive or conservative) to be. The product life cycle is a useful tool for estimating the sales of a product over its lifetime and the types of customers who purchase during different time periods.

How much merchandise is handled is a decision involving width and depth of assortment. A product assortment can range from wide and deep to narrow and shallow. When one is planning an assortment, many factors should be examined: sales, profits, investment costs, complementary and substitute products, space requirements, turnover, and manufacturer insistence.

A third decision required is when merchandise is to be handled. An accurate sales forecast is necessary for efficient planning. Among the points to be considered are peak seasons, order time, delivery time, routine versus special orders, turnover, discounts, and improved inventory procedures.

A fourth decision must be made concerning where merchandise is handled. The retailer must determine whether to use warehouses or a central distribution center, and merchandise has to be allocated among store branches.

Information from customers, sources of supply, personnel, competitors, and others must be collected to help the retailer forecast and adapt to demand.

A retailer must choose among sources of supply: company-owned; outside, regularly-used; and outside, new. Inspection, sampling and/or description techniques of merchandise evaluation must be planned.

The terms of the purchase have to be negotiated in their entirety, and the purchase must be concluded (automatic–manual, management approval, transfer of title).

Merchandise handling must be outlined, including receiving, marking, displays, on-floor assortments, customer transactions, delivery or pickup, returns and damaged goods, inventory shrinkage, and control.

Reorder procedures are necessary and depend on order and delivery time, turnover, outlay, and efficiency.

Finally, the overall procedure and specific products are regularly reviewed.

Questions for Discussion

1. Describe the merchandise buying and handling process.
2. What are the advantages and disadvantages of centralized buying?
3. Distinguish between merchandising and buying. Why does a controversy exist?
4. Under what circumstances can a retailer carry a wide range of quality merchandise without hurting his or her image? When should the quality of merchandise carried be quite narrow?
5. Should the following retailers plan for innovativeness in the same way? Why or why not?
   a. Department store
   b. Supermarket
   c. Small grocer
   d. Dress boutique
6. How may a retailer use the product life-cycle concept?
7. What risks does a retailer incur by not innovating?

8. If you were a franchise operator, how would you react to constrained decision making?
9. Why do retailers spend little time deleting old products?
10. Give several examples of stores that would fit into each of the following product assortment plans.
    a. Narrow-deep
    b. Wide-deep
    c. Wide-shallow
11. What problems can occur if a retailer mistimes purchases?
12. What types of information are necessary for merchandise buying and handling?
13. Name some advantages and disadvantages for each merchandise source.
    a. Company-owned
    b. Outside, regularly-used
    c. Outside, new
14. Under what circumstances should inspection, description, and sampling be used?
15. If you apprehended a shoplifter leaving your store, what action would you take? Why?
16. Which is more difficult to do, merchandise planning for a superstore or a clothing store? Explain your answer.

CASES

1. Lamm's Department Stores: Reappraising a Merchandising Strategy for Consumer Electronics

Lamm's is a high-fashion apparel-oriented department store chain of four outlets which began carrying consumer electronics (televisions, VCRs, stereos, etc.) about three years ago. However, the department's sales volume has consistently not met the projections set by senior management. Both the buyer and divisional merchandise manager are anxious to turn the situation around. Accordingly, they have requested that the new assistant buyer for consumer electronics (Angie Laube) do some preliminary research and offer some basic recommendations, specifically for VCRs (videocassette recorders).

Angie is a 1984 graduate of a major state university with a degree in retail management. She has been with Lamm's for a year and just completed the training program for assistant buyer. Angie was assigned to the consumer electronics department, her first choice, because she had performed well in the training program and had previous experience in electronics. She had worked as an electronics salesperson for a large, very successful, discount-oriented specialty chain while at college.

Angie began by noting some of the differences between Lamm's and her former employer:

- The specialty chain uses centralized buying for twenty-five stores and purchases large quantities from vendors to secure optimal quantity discounts. Lamm's allows the department managers at each of its four units to place orders. This results in smaller, uncoordinated purchases.
- The specialty chain aggressively seeks discontinued models, closeouts, canceled orders, and so on and offers merchandise at low prices to its customers. Lamm's

stocks only current first-quality models of leading brands and sets prices that are close to the manufacturers' suggested list prices.
- The specialty chain has a much greater selection than Lamm's.
- The specialty chain emphasizes self-service, leaves items in their packages, and keeps a full inventory in each store. Lamm's emphasizes personal selling, has attractive displays, and keeps a limited amount of inventory on hand; it runs out of stock periodically.

Next, Angie turned her attention to a study of the department's VCR products. At present, Lamm's handles three brands of VCRs: Panasonic, Sharp, and Sony. Each of these is stocked in basic, intermediate, and top-of-the-line models. While all the models of a particular brand have the same picture quality, the intermediate and top-of-the-line models have additional features (e.g., wireless remote control, greater recording options, cable compatibility, stereo sound). The models of the three brands are priced within $50 of one another (e.g., Panasonic's basic model is $10 higher than Sharp's basic model and $40 lower than Sony's basic model). The Panasonic and Sharp models are carried in the VHS format; Sony machines are in the Beta format. The tapes used in VHS and Beta formats are different.

After observing consumers' in-store behavior, undertaking a number of visits to competitors (both department stores and specialty stores), reading trade publications, and monitoring sales (total and by brand), Angie has reached these important conclusions about VCR products:

- Lamm's should add a lower-priced brand, such as Sanyo, to increase customer traffic into the VCR department. Sanyo's basic model can be sold for $150 less than Sony's basic model.
- Lamm's should drop the Sharp and Panasonic brands and add Fisher, which advertises extensively and has a high level of consumer preference. Also, Fisher is not as readily available in discount stores as Sharp and Panasonic.
- Sony Beta-format VCRs should be kept. Although sales of VHS-format VCRs are much higher and many retailers renting and selling prerecorded tapes (e.g., movies) handle mostly VHS-format tapes, Angie believes the Beta-format will continue to have a loyal market. Sony is a well-liked brand, and a recent consumer survey by *Chain Store Age* revealed that 63 per cent of consumers had no preference about VCR format.
- Extended product warranties should be provided to further differentiate Lamm's from discounters.

Questions

1. What are the pros and cons of having Angie conduct this research?
2. Comment on the differences Angie noted between the merchandising of consumer electronics at Lamm's and at a discount specialty chain. Make several recommendations for Lamm's.
3. Evaluate Angie's conclusions about VCR products.
4. Develop a checklist for Lamm's to use when evaluating vendors and physically handling merchandise.

2. Flemington Fur: 5,000 Garments Under One Roof*

The Flemington Fur Company of New Jersey operates the largest retail fur store under one roof in the United States, and probably the entire world. On an annual basis, Flemington sells more than $20 million in a single, one-level outlet containing 60,000 square feet. During peak seasons, as many as 5,000 cloth, suede, and fur garments may be kept at the store—with half on the selling floor and half in the stockroom. Flemington employs over one hundred people, including sales personnel, designers, craftspeople, buyers, and other personnel. Customers come from as far as 60 miles away and more, with 50 to 60 per cent of sales on weekends.

Despite its size and merchandise availability, Flemington does not emphasize low-end prices. It stresses assortment, quality products, and good value. For example, ready-made furs are stocked in sizes from 2 to 44; yet $99 rabbit jackets are not carried. Fur jacket prices range from $450 to $60,000 with an average of $2,500. Flemington does very little customized work.

To encourage shopping trips by customers, Flemington has a large storage facility. Each season, 30,000 furs are maintained in temperature-controlled vaults. The storage program has increased the sales of cloth coats to 12 per cent of total store volume; customers like to shop when dropping off or picking up their furs. The cloth coat business is important to Flemington, which realizes that furs are bought only once every four or five years.

Flemington has a Seventh Avenue (Manhattan garment district) buying office. In addition, Flemington's chief executive officer buys skins abroad through fur brokers. He personally selects pelts, styles, and sizes and oversees manufacturing.

Interestingly, all the garments Flemington sells are under its own brand name. While designer patterns are purchased, they are modified and sold under the Flemington label. Most other fur retailers rely on designer labels.

Flemington's merchandising is in sharp contrast with Evans, Inc., the largest fur retailer in the United States with annual sales of over $100 million. Evans owns about thirty fur and apparel stores and operates more than 100 licensed fur salons[1] in several different department store chains. About 35 per cent of sales are through the fur salons. Average inventory on hand is $50 to $60 million at retail.

With the salons, Evans selects the locations, provides the managers, performs merchandising functions, and is responsible for sales support functions. The department managers act as both buyers and merchandise managers for their individual salons. They report to their department stores' general merchandise managers as well as to Evans. The managers participate in frequent merchandising seminars in New York and go on buying trips in groups. The best salons depend on their stores' internal management for leadership.

In persuading department stores to include an Evans fur salon, two other features are noted. First, Evans is using a videocassette training program for its managers. The cassettes deal with fur types and how furs are made, selling techniques, and fur care. Evans' management visits salon locations and presents the training material. Second, inventory can be readily transferred between stores, based upon demand, due to Evans' size and dispersed operations.

*The material in this case is drawn from "Two Approaches to Selling Fur," *Stores* (March 1982), pp. 17–28.
[1]These are leased departments.

Evans' chairman sums up the firm's store selection strategy:

We want to be in the finest stores interested in the best merchandise. We're still heavily into department stores, but lately we've been going into more specialty stores, and find they are more aggressive in helping us promote.

Questions

1. What are the benefits and risks of Flemington's merchandising strategy of having up to 5,000 garments sold in one large outlet?
2. Develop a merchandise handling plan for Flemington.
3. How do Flemington's and Evans' merchandising philosphies differ?
4. For a fur retailer, enumerate each of the following:
   a. Merchandise sources and how to analyze them.
   b. How to obtain information about customer demand (sales forecasts).
   c. How to determine inventory to be maintained.
   d. Reorder procedures.
   e. A typical one-week itinerary for a buyer.
   f. Inventory shrinkage control.

11

Merchandise Planning and Management: Financial

Chapter Objectives

1. To describe the major aspects of financial merchandise planning and management
2. To explain the cost and retail methods of accounting
3. To study the inventory investment planning and control process
4. To examine alternative methods of physical inventory unit control
5. To integrate dollar and unit control concepts

Financial merchandise planning and management is difficult, even for highly skilled retailers. During 1984, Macy's, K mart, and Federated Department Stores were among the many firms that were caught with inventory levels that were too high. By year's end, these retailers were heavily discounting prices to clear out old merchandise and make room for new items.

Macy's optimistically began 1984 with an inventory level which was 35 per cent higher than the previous year. This was consistent with Macy's policy of "overloading inventories to maximize potential." But Macy's sales forecasts were much too high, and the chain "took heavy markdown money" to reduce inventory. For 1985, Macy's was much more conservative in its inventory planning.

K mart also overstocked merchandise in 1984. In addition, its evolution toward higher-priced product lines meant discounting the lines the chain no longer planned to carry; and the amount of inventory in the latter situation was much greater than anticipated by K mart: "Our own aggressive inventory reduction and promotional programs resulted in much heavier markdowns than expected."

Federated acknowledged carrying too many products that were not geared to its customers and subject to price cutting. To remedy this, the chain planned to improve buying and marketing practices: "Shoppers will buy clothes that appeal to them, regardless of price, and the trick will be to make sure we have that merchandise when the customer wants it. [This] should help to improve our inventory-to-sales ratio, cut our markdowns, and improve our profits."[1]

Overview

A **financial merchandise plan** specifies which products are purchased, when products are purchased, and how many products are purchased. Both dollar and unit controls are employed in a merchandise plan.

    Dollar control refers to the planning and monitoring of the total inventory investment a retailer makes during a stated period of time. **Unit control** relates to the quantities of merchandise handled during a stated period of time. Dollar controls usually precede unit controls, as the retailer must plan his or her total dollar investment before making assortment decisions.

    The establishment of a financial merchandise plan has several advantages for a retailer:

- It controls the amount and value of inventory in each department or store unit during a given period of time. Stock is balanced, and few markdowns are necessary.
- It stipulates the amount of merchandise (in terms of investment) that a buyer can purchase during a given period of time. This gives the buyer direction.
- It enables the buyer to determine the level of stock shortages, giving an estimate of pilferage.
- It allows the buyer to balance total inventory investment with planned and actual sales. This improves the return on investment.
- It helps determine storage space requirements by estimating beginning-of-month and end-of-month inventory levels.
- It can be used to evaluate the performance of buyers. Stock reductions, purchases, markups, and gross margins may be used as performance standards.
- It classifies slow-moving items, which allows increased sales efforts or markdowns to be made.
- It maintains a proper balance between inventory level and out-of-stock conditions.

    This chapter divides financial planning into four main sections: methods of accounting, merchandise forecasting and budgeting, unit control systems, and financial inventory control.

Inventory Valuation: The Cost and Retail Methods of Accounting

Retail inventory accounting systems are often quite complex. The retailer's dollar control system must provide information such as sales, additional purchases allowed during

[1]Isadore Barmash, "For Retailers, a Winter of Discontent," *New York Times* (January 13, 1985), Section 3, pp. 1, 8–9; and Damon Darlin, "K mart Expects Profit Was Flat for Fiscal 1985," *Wall Street Journal* (February 8, 1985), p. 5.

a budget period, the extent of markups and markdowns, merchandise shortages, and the value of stock on hand.

Two inventory accounting systems are available to a retailer: the cost and retail methods of accounting. The cost accounting system values merchandise at cost plus inbound freight. The retail accounting system values merchandise at current retail prices.

Retailers have substantially different information needs than manufacturers. Retail assortments are larger; costs cannot be printed on cartons unless coded (because of customer inspection). Stock shortages are greater; sales are more frequent; and retailers require monthly, not quarterly, profit data.

The cost and retail inventory methods are described and analyzed here on the basis of the frequency with which merchandise information is received, difficulties in completing a physical inventory, difficulties in maintaining records, the ease of settling insurance claims (in case of inventory damage), the extent to which stock shortages can be calculated, and the complexities of the systems.

The Cost Method

In the **cost method of accounting,** the cost of each item is recorded on an accounting sheet or is coded on a price tag or merchandise container. When a physical inventory is conducted, the costs of each item must be ascertained, the quantity of each item in stock counted, and the total inventory value at cost calculated.

One method of coding the cost of merchandise is to use a ten-letter equivalency system, such as $M = 0$, $N = 1$, $O = 2$, $P = 3$, $Q = 4$, $R = 5$, $S = 6$, $T = 7$, $U = 8$, $V = 9$. A product coded with the letters $STOP$ has a cost value of $67.23. This is useful as an accounting tool and also for retailers who allow price bargaining by customers (profit per item is easy to calculate).

The cost method can be used when one is conducting physical or book inventories. A physical inventory involves an actual count of merchandise, whereas a book inventory depends on bookkeeping entries.

A Physical Inventory System Using the Cost Method

Table 11-1 shows a profit-and-loss statement for a furniture dealer for the period of January 1, 1985 through June 30, 1985. The sales amount is from the total store's receipts during this time period. Beginning inventory is calculated by a count of the merchandise in stock on January 1, 1985, which is recorded at cost. Purchases (at cost) are derived by the addition of the invoice slips for all merchandise bought by the store during this time period. Ending inventory is determined by a count of the merchandise in stock on June 30, 1985, which is recorded at cost.

Gross profits cannot be computed until after the ending inventory is valued. Thus, a retailer using the cost method and relying on a **physical inventory system** can determine gross profits only as often as he or she conducts a complete physical inventory. Because most retailers undertake physical inventories just once or twice a year, the physical method imposes severe limitations on retailers' merchandise planning.

The physical inventory method also prevents a retailer from calculating inventory shortages (resulting from pilferage, unrecorded breakage, and so on) because the ending inventory is determined by adding the costs of all items in stock. What the ending inventory level should be is not computed.

Table 11-1
G&L Furniture Corporation Profit-and-Loss Statement, January 1, 1985–June 30, 1985

Sales		$600,000
Less cost of goods sold:		
Beginning inventory (at cost)	$450,000	
Purchases (at cost)	120,000	
Merchandise available for sale	$570,000	
Ending inventory	180,000	
Cost of goods sold		390,000
Gross profit		$210,000
Less operating expenses:		
Salaries	$ 60,000	
Advertising	15,000	
Rental and other expenses	25,000	
Total operating expenses		100,000
Net profit before tax		$110,000

A Book Inventory System Using the Cost Method

A **book inventory system** (commonly called a perpetual inventory system) avoids the problem of infrequent financial statements by keeping a running total of the value of all inventory on hand at cost at a given time. In addition, it allows a retailer to ascertain the level of shortages. One maintains a perpetual system by adding purchases to current inventory value and then subtracting sales to arrive at the new current inventory value (all at cost). Table 11-2 shows a book (perpetual) inventory system for the G&L Furniture Corporation.

The data contained in Table 11-2 for beginning inventory, total purchases, total costs of merchandise sold, and ending inventory are the same as those in Table 11-1. One can construct the profit-and-loss statement from Table 11-2 by including store sales, rearranging the figures (as in Table 11-1), and deducting operating expenses.

Table 11-2
G&L Furniture Corporation Perpetual Inventory System

Date	Beginning-of-Month Inventory (at Cost)	+	Monthly Purchases (at Cost)	−	Monthly Sales (at Cost)	=	End-of-Month Inventory (at Cost)
1/1/85	$450,000		$ 30,000		$ 90,000		$390,000
2/1/85	390,000		30,000		90,000		330,000
3/1/85	330,000		30,000		90,000		270,000
4/1/85	270,000		30,000		60,000		240,000
5/1/85	240,000		0		30,000		210,000
6/1/85	210,000		0		30,000		180,000
		Total	$120,000		$390,000		(as of 6/30/85)

As mentioned earlier, the perpetual method is superior to the physical inventory system for two major reasons. First, end-of-month inventory values can be computed without a physical inventory, and frequent financial statements can be developed. Second, a book inventory value is available for comparison with a physical inventory to determine shortages.

Table 11-2 assumes that merchandise costs are constant and that monthly sales at cost are easily computed. However, suppose that merchandise costs are rising. How, then, should inventory be valued?

Two methods of costing inventory are **LIFO** (last-in–first-out) and **FIFO** (first-in–first-out). Under the LIFO method, it is assumed that new stock is sold first and that old stock remains on the shelves. Under the FIFO method, it is assumed that old stock is sold first and that new stock remains on the shelves. LIFO matches current sales with the current cost structure. FIFO matches inventory value with the current cost structure.[2] According to a study by the accounting firm of Peat, Marwick, Mitchell & Co., the overwhelming majority of large retailers use the LIFO method. During periods of rising inventory values, LIFO gives retailers a tax advantage.[3]

Disadvantages of Cost-Based Inventory Systems

The cost-based physical and perpetual systems have significant disadvantages. First, both cost techniques require the retailer to ascribe costs to each item in stock (and to each item sold). Therefore, cost-based inventory valuation systems are useful only for those retailers who have low inventory turnover, limited variety and assortments, and high average sales price. Examples of retailers with these characteristics are car dealers, furriers, furniture stores, large-appliance dealers, and jewelry stores.

Second, neither cost method provides for adjusting inventory values to reflect style changes, end-of-season markdowns, or sudden surges of demand, which may increase prices. Thus, the ending value of inventory, based on the cost of the merchandise, may not reflect its actual worth. This discrepancy is particularly troublesome when the ending inventory valuation is used in the calculation of required insurance coverage or the filing of insurance claims for losses.

Despite these disadvantages, some retailers—such as bakeries, restaurants, and furniture workrooms—must keep their records on a cost basis. A department store with these departments (or others involving manufacturing) uses the cost method for them and the retail method for other departments.

The Retail Method

With the **retail method of accounting,** the closing inventory value is determined by calculating the average relationship between the cost and retail value of goods available for sale during the period. While the retail method overcomes the disadvantages of the cost method, it requires a detailed bookkeeping system. The complexity of the retail method is due to the fact that inventory is valued in retail dollars and must be converted to cost if one is to compute gross margin (gross profit).

[2]The retail method of inventory, which combines LIFO and FIFO techniques, is explained later in this chapter. LIFO and FIFO calculations may be found in any basic accounting text.
[3]Isadore Barmash, "LIFO Inventory Helps Retailers," *New York Times* (June 16, 1981), p. D2. See also "LIFO Survey Shows It's Here to Stay," *Chain Store Age Executive* (January 1984), pp. 32–33.

Table 11-3
Handy Hardware Store Calculation of Merchandise Available for Sale, 7/1/85–12/31/85

	At Cost	At Retail
Beginning inventory	$225,000	$300,000
Net purchases (purchases less returns)	70,000	100,000
Additional markups	—	12,500
Freight-in	125	—
Total merchandise available for sale	$295,125	$412,500

There are three basic steps in computing an ending inventory value, using the retail method:

1. Calculation of the cost complement.
2. Calculation of deductions from retail value.
3. Conversion of retail inventory value to cost.

Calculation of the Cost Complement

Under the retail method, beginning inventory and purchase figures are kept at both cost and retail levels. Table 11-3 shows a six-month inventory statement for the Handy Hardware Store.

The beginning inventory is valued at cost and retail. Net purchases, which are the total purchases less returns by the store, are valued at cost and retail. Additional markups are the total increases in the merchandise's selling price during the six-month period (due to inflation or demand). Freight-in is the cost to the retailer for the transportation of the merchandise that is purchased.

Based on the figures in Table 11-3, the average relationship of cost to retail value for all merchandise available for sale during the six-month period can be calculated. This concept is called the **cost complement**:

$$\text{Cost complement} = \frac{\text{Total cost valuation}}{\text{Total retail valuation}} = \frac{\$295,125}{\$412,500} = 0.7155$$

Because the cost complement is 0.7155, or 71.55 per cent, an average of 71.55 cents of every retail sales dollar is comprised of merchandise cost.

Calculation of Deductions from Retail Value

The retail valuation process must reflect any deductions from inventory. In addition to sales, deductions include: markdowns (special sales, reduced prices on discontinued merchandise, reduced prices on end-of-season and shopworn merchandise), employee discounts, and stock shortages (pilferage, unrecorded breakage). Markdowns and employee discounts can be recorded throughout an accounting period, but a physical inventory is required to compute stock shortages.

From Table 11-3, it was determined that Handy Hardware has a retail value of merchandise available for sale of $412,500. This amount must be reduced by sales of

Table 11-4
Handy Hardware Store Computation of Ending Retail Book Value, as of December 31, 1985

Merchandise available for sale (at retail)		$412,500
Less deductions:		
Sales	$100,000	
Markdowns	10,000	
Employee discounts	2,000	
Total deductions		112,000
Ending retail book value of inventory		$300,500

$100,000 and recorded markdowns and employee discounts of $12,000. The ending book value of inventory at retail equals $300,500. See Table 11-4.

Actual **stock shortages** can now be computed from a physical inventory. This is much simpler with the retail than with the cost method, because inventory is measured at actual retail prices. The retail book value is compared to the actual physical inventory value; if the book value is greater than the physical inventory, shortages exist. Table 11-5 shows the results of a physical inventory by the Handy Hardware Store. Shortages of $12,500 are revealed, and the book value is adjusted accordingly. The shortages are due to pilferage (by customers and/or employees); bookkeeping errors (not recording markdowns, employee discounts, and breakage); and overshipments not billed to customers. The proportions of each of these factors cannot be determined.

In contrast to a stock shortage, a **stock overage** is an excess of physical inventory value over book value. This overage generally occurs when there are errors in the taking of a physical inventory or in the compilation of a book inventory.

Because a retailer must conduct a physical inventory to compute shortages (overages), and a physical inventory is taken only once or twice a year, shortages (overages) are often estimated for monthly merchandise budgets.

Conversion of Retail Inventory Value to Cost

One must convert to cost the adjusted retail book value in order to compute dollar gross margin (gross profit); the closing inventory at cost equals the adjusted retail book value multiplied by the cost complement:

$$
\begin{aligned}
\text{Closing inventory at cost} &= \text{Adjusted retail book value} \\
&\quad \times \text{ Cost complement} \\
&= \$288,000 \times 0.7155 \\
&= \$206,064
\end{aligned}
$$

Table 11-5
Handy Hardware Store Computation of Stock Shortages, as of December 31, 1985

Ending retail book value of inventory	$300,500
Physical inventory (at retail)	288,000
Stock shortages	$ 12,500
Adjusted ending retail book value of inventory	$288,000

Table 11-6
Handy Hardware Store Profit-and-Loss Statement,
7/1/85–12/31/85

Sales		$100,000
Less cost of goods sold:		
Total merchandise available for sale (at cost)	$295,125	
Adjusted ending inventory (at cost)	206,064	
Cost of goods sold		89,061
Gross profit		$ 10,939
Less operating expenses:		
Promotion	$ 2,000	
Rent and other expenses	3,000	
Utilities	500	
Total operating expenses		5,500
Net profit before tax		$ 5,439

This equation does not yield the actual closing inventory at cost for Handy Hardware but approximates this value based on the average relationship between cost and retail selling price for all merchandise available for sale. The adjusted ending inventory at cost can then be used to find gross profit. See Table 11-6. The cost of goods sold is $89,061; gross profit is $10,939. By deducting operating expenses of $5,500, it is determined that net profit before tax equals $5,439.

Advantages of the Retail Method

In a comparison of the cost and the retail accounting methods, several strengths of the retail method are evident:

1. The retail method is easy to use when taking a physical inventory. Therefore, the chances of error in the valuation of merchandise are reduced because the physical inventory is recorded at retail value, and costs do not have to be decoded.
2. Because the task of taking a physical inventory is simplified, physical inventories can be completed more frequently. This frequency enables the retailer to be aware of slow-moving items and stock shortages and to take appropriate corrective actions.
3. The physical inventory method at cost requires a physical inventory for the preparation of an operating statement. In contrast, the retail method allows a retailer to prepare an operating statement on the basis of book inventory figures. These figures can be adjusted to account for stock shortages between physical inventory periods. Because frequent operating statements are necessary if one is to examine profit trends by department, a book inventory system is superior to a physical system at cost.
4. A complete record of ending book values is extremely important in the determination of the appropriate level of insurance coverage and in the settling of insurance claims. The retail book method gives the retailer an estimate of inventory value throughout the year. Because physical inventories are usually taken when inventory levels are low, the book value at retail allows retailers to plan insurance coverage during peak periods and shows the values of the goods on hand (in case of a claim adjustment). The retail method is accepted in insurance claims.

Limitations of the Retail Method

The greatest limitation of the retail method is the bookkeeping burden of recording price changes. The ending book inventory figures can be correctly computed only if the following are accurately noted: purchases, freight-in, markups, markdowns, employee discounts, transfers from other departments or stores, returns, and sales. Although store personnel are freed from the burden of taking many physical inventories, the ending book value at retail may be a meaningless figure unless these required data are precisely recorded. With computerization, this is not a problem.

A second limitation of the retail method is that the cost complement is an average figure based upon the total cost of merchandise and its total retail value. Therefore it is possible that the resultant ending inventory only approximates the true cost of the merchandise on hand. This is especially true if fast-selling merchandise has different markups than slow-selling merchandise and/or if there are wide variations among the markups of goods within a single department.

Familiarity with the retail and cost methods of inventory is essential for an understanding of the financial merchandise-planning material described in the balance of the chapter.

Merchandise Forecasting and Budgeting: Dollar Control

Dollar control refers to the process of planning and controlling the total inventory investment during a specified time period. Figure 11-1 illustrates the dollar control process. As can be seen, the process is broken down into six successive stages: designating control units, forecasting sales, inventory-level planning, retail-reduction planning, planning purchases, and profit-margin planning.

It is important that the sequential nature of this process be comprehended. A change in a variable affects the elements below it. For example, assume that a store using the retail method underestimates its markdowns by $20,000 during a monthly period. The firm must revise planned purchases (up $20,000) and planned profit margins to reflect the markdowns.

Designating Control Units

Merchandise forecasting and budgeting require the selection of **control units;** these are the merchandise categories for which data are gathered. It is important that control unit classifications be narrow enough to isolate opportunities and problems with specific lines of merchandise. A store wishing to control merchandise within departments must separately record data relating to dollar allotments for each category.

As an example, knowing that total markdowns in a department are 20 per cent above last year's level is less valuable than knowing the specific merchandise lines in which large markdowns are taken. It should be noted that a retailer can broaden his or her control system by summarizing the categories that comprise a department. However, a broad category cannot be broken down into components. Therefore, it is better to err on the side of too much information than too little.

It is also helpful to select control units that are consistent with other store data

The Merchandise Forecasting and Budgeting Process: Dollar Control

Designation of Control Units

↓

Sales Forecasting

↓

Inventory-Level Planning

↓

Reduction Planning

↓

Planning Purchases

↓

Planning Profit Margins

Figure 11-1

and trade association data, wherever possible. Intrastore comparisons are meaningful only when the classification method is stable over time. A classification system that shifts over time because of fashions or fads does not allow comparisons between time periods. External comparisons can be made if the control systems are similar (e.g., company and trade associations).

Inventory may be categorized on the basis of departments, classifications within a department, standard merchandise classifications, and price line classifications.

Adequate information may be obtained by specifying departmental categories. Thus, even a small specialty shop that sells ladies' sportswear should acquire data on a departmental basis for buying, inventory control, and markdown decisions. The broadest practical division of control is the department unit, in that this unit allows the retailer to evaluate the performance of each buyer.

Classification merchandising divides each department into related types of merchandise. For example, a houseware department needs data not only on overall performance but also on the performance of electric appliances–food preparation, electric appliances–fans, knives–gourmet, knives–regular, kitchen gadgets, and so on in order to plan merchandise activities.

In 1969, the National Retail Merchants Association (NRMA) developed a **Standard Merchandise Classification,** useful for a wide range of stores and products. The NRMA Financial Executives Division annually publishes a summary of merchandising statistics for U.S. department stores by merchandising category.[4]

---

[4]See *Department and Specialty Store Merchandising and Operating Results* (New York: National Retail Merchants Association, annual).

Price line classifications involve the analysis of retail sales, inventories, and purchases by retail price category. This analysis has special utility when different prices of the same product type are offered to different customers (e.g., $8 and $20 transistor radios). Retailers with wide assortments are involved with price line control. As a case in point, a men's clothing department, for merchandise budgeting purposes, may want to differentiate between sports jackets selling in the $79 to $99 price range and those selling in the $139 to $179 price range. Such diverse categories of sports jackets are usually sold to different customers or to the same customers for different purposes.

After the appropriate dollar control unit is determined, all transactions—such as sales, purchases, transfers, markdowns, and employee discounts—must be recorded under the proper classification number. For instance, if stationery is Department 25 and pens are 25-1, all transactions must carry these category designations.

Sales Forecasting

Storewide sales and departmentwide sales are often forecast by the use of statistical techniques such as trend analysis, time series analysis, and multiple regression analysis. A discussion of these techniques is beyond the scope of this text. It should be noted that few small retailers use these procedures; they rely on "guesstimates," projections based on past experience.

Sales forecasting for classifications within departments, for standard merchandise classifications, and for price line classifications generally relies on more qualitative techniques, even for larger retailers. One way of forecasting these narrower categories is to forecast sales on a storewide basis and then break down the overall figure judgmentally into component classifications, based on external and internal store factors.

Perhaps the most important element of any budgetary process is an accurate sales forecast. An incorrect estimate of future sales throws off the entire budgeting process. The sales forecast must carefully incorporate external variables that influence sales, internal store factors that can influence sales, and seasonal trends.

External factors affecting future sales include population size, changes in disposable income, changes in the age distribution of the population, mobility of the population, the number and size of competitors, the economy, and changes in the life-style of the target market.

Internal store factors affecting future sales include additions and deletions of merchandise lines, changes in promotion and credit policies, changes in store hours, the opening of new stores, and the enlargement of existing stores. Seasonal variations must also be taken into account in the development of a sales forecast. For example, yearly toy sales should not be estimated from December sales alone.

A retailer can make an estimate of future store sales by examining past trends and determining future growth (based on external and internal factors). See Table 11-7. However, the forecast should be regarded only as an estimate, subject to revisions. The merchandise plan should be a flexible buying tool.

A retailer should be aware that some factors are difficult to incorporate in a sales forecast, such as merchandise shortages, major shifts in consumer purchasing habits, strikes of store personnel, strikes affecting the earnings of customers, and enactment of new government legislation.

After an annual sales forecast is made, it is broken down into planning periods (i.e., quarterly or monthly). In retailing, monthly sales forecasts are usually required.

Table 11-7
A Simple Sales Forecast for Harley's Clothing Store by Product Control Unit

Product Control Units	Actual Sales 1985	Projected Growth/ Decline (%)	Sales Forecast 1986
Suits	$200,000	+12.5	$225,000
Sports jackets	140,000	+7.1	150,000
Shirts	120,000	+25.0	150,000
Slacks	120,000	+8.3	130,000
Sweaters	80,000	+10.0	88,000
T-shirts	30,000	−12.5	26,250
Undershorts	25,000	−20.0	20,000
Cuff links	5,000	+10.0	5,500
Handkerchiefs	3,000	0.0	3,000
Belts	5,000	0.0	5,000
Hosiery	5,000	+10.0	5,500
Ties	20,000	+16.7	23,340
Total year	$753,000	+10.4	$831,590

To acquire these estimates, a retailer uses a **monthly sales index,**[5] which he or she calculates by dividing each month's actual sales by average monthly sales and multiplying the results by 100.

For example, Table 11-8 shows actual monthly sales and monthly sales-index calculations for a camera store in 1985. The data reveal that the store is highly seasonal, with peaks occurring at the beginning of summer (as children are outfitted for camp and people stock up on film for vacations) and during the Christmas season.

Table 11-8
Beth's Camera Store, 1985 Sales by Month

Month	Actual Sales	Monthly Sales Index $= \left(\dfrac{\text{Monthly Sales}}{\text{Average Monthly Sales}} \times 100 \right)$
January	$ 77,000	68
February	71,500	63
March	66,000	58
April	68,200	60
May	93,500	82
June	165,000	146
July	121,000	107
August	143,000	126
September	77,000	68
October	66,000	58
November	165,000	146
December	247,500	218
Total yearly sales	$1,360,700	
Average monthly sales	$ 113,392	
Average monthly index		100

[5]See Penny Gill, "The ABC's of Selling Basic Toys," *Stores* (February 1982), pp. 29–36.

In Table 11-8, the average monthly sales for the year are $113,392 ($1,360,700/ 12). As the table shows, the monthly sales index for January is 68 [($77,000/$113,392) × 100]; other monthly indexes are calculated similarly. The sales indexes show the percentage deviations of each month's sales from average monthly sales. Therefore, the November index of 146 means that sales in November are 46 per cent higher than average monthly sales. The October index of 58 means that sales in October are 42 per cent below the average.

Once monthly sales indexes are determined, a retailer can forecast monthly sales, given a yearly sales estimate. Table 11-9 demonstrates how the camera store's monthly sales can be forecast if next year's average monthly sales are expected to be $125,000. November sales are projected to be $182,500 ($125,000 × 1.46). October sales would be $72,500 ($125,000 × 0.58).

Inventory-Level Planning

After a retailer forecasts sales for a specified time period, he or she must plan the inventory levels for this period. Inventory must be sufficient to meet sales expectations, allowing a margin for error. Among the techniques used to plan inventory requirements are the basic stock method, the percentage variation method, the weeks' supply method, and the stock-to-sales ratio method.

The **basic stock method** dictates that a retailer carry more items in stock than can be sold during the specified time period. In the basic stock plan, a retail buyer purchases an amount equal to planned sales plus a basic stock:

$$\text{Basic stock} = \begin{array}{l} \text{Average monthly stock at retail} \\ - \text{ Average monthly sales} \end{array}$$

$$\begin{array}{l} \text{Beginning-of-month} \\ \text{planned inventory level} = \begin{array}{l} \text{Planned monthly sales} \\ + \text{ Basic stock} \end{array} \\ \text{(at retail)} \end{array}$$

For example, if a store with average monthly sales of $100,000 wants to have excess stock equal 10 per cent of average monthly sales (or $10,000), and estimates January sales to be $120,000:

$$\text{Basic stock} = \$110,000 - \$100,000 - \$10,000$$

$$\begin{array}{l} \text{Beginning-of-January} \\ \text{planned inventory level} = \$120,000 + \$10,000 = \$130,000 \\ \text{(at retail)} \end{array}$$

The basic stock method gives a retailer a cushion in case sales are higher than anticipated, merchandise shipments are delayed, and customers want to select from a variety of items. This method is recommended when inventory turnover is low.

The **percentage variation method** is recommended when stock turnover is more than six times a year. With this method, the actual stock on hand during any month

Table 11-9
Beth's Camera Store, 1986 Sales Forecast by Month

Month	Actual Sales 1985	Monthly Sales Index	Monthly Sales Forecast 1986 =	(Average Monthly Forecast × Monthly Index)
January	$ 77,000	68	$125,000 × .68 = $	85,000
February	71,500	63	125,000 × .63 =	78,750
March	66,000	58	125,000 × .58 =	72,500
April	68,200	60	125,000 × .60 =	75,000
May	93,500	82	125,000 × .82 =	102,500
June	165,000	146	125,000 × 1.46 =	182,500
July	121,000	107	125,000 × 1.07 =	133,750
August	143,000	126	125,000 × 1.26 =	157,500
September	77,000	68	125,000 × .68 =	85,000
October	66,000	58	125,000 × .58 =	72,500
November	165,000	146	125,000 × 1.46 =	182,500
December	247,500	218	125,000 × 2.18 =	272,500
Total sales	$1,360,700		Total sales forecast	$1,500,000
Average monthly sales	$113,392		Average monthly forecast	$125,000

varies from average planned monthly stock by only half of the month's variation from average estimated monthly sales:

Beginning-of-month
planned inventory level = Planned average monthly stock at retail
(at retail)

$$\times \frac{1}{2} \left(1 + \frac{\text{Estimated monthly sales}}{\text{Estimated average monthly sales}} \right)$$

If a store plans average monthly stock of $105,000 and October sales are estimated as 30 per cent more than average monthly sales of $90,000, the store's planned inventory level at the beginning of October is:

Beginning-of-October
planned inventory level (at retail) $= \$105,000 \times \frac{1}{2} \left(1 + \frac{117,000}{90,000} \right)$

$$= \$105,000 \times \frac{1}{2} (2.3)$$

$$= \$120,750$$

For stores with high inventory turnover, the percentage variation method provides less stock fluctuation than the basic stock method.

The **weeks' supply method** involves the planning of sales on a weekly basis, so that stock on hand is equal to several weeks' sales. This method assumes that the stock carried is in direct proportion to sales. Accordingly too much merchandise may be stocked in peak selling periods (when turnover is high) and too little during slow selling periods:

$$\text{Beginning-of-month planned inventory level (at retail)} = \text{Average weekly sales} \times \text{Number of weeks to be stocked}$$

If average weekly sales are $20,000, and a store wants to stock seven weeks of merchandise (based on turnover), beginning inventory is $140,000:

$$\text{Beginning inventory level (at retail)} = \$20,000 \times 7 = \$140,000$$

The **stock-to-sales ratio** assumes that a retailer wants to maintain a specified ratio of goods-on-hand to sales. A stock-to-sales ratio of 3 means that a retailer planning sales of $10,000 per month must have $30,000 worth of merchandise available during the month. Like the weeks' supply method, the stock-to-sales ratio tends to adjust inventory levels more drastically than changes in sales require. Stock-to-sales ratios are available from several trade sources, among them *Departmental Merchandising and Operating Results of Department and Specialty Stores* (New York: National Retail Merchants Association, annual), *Industry Norms and Key Business Ratios* (New York: Dun and Bradstreet, annual), and *Annual Statement Studies* (Philadelphia: Robert Morris Associates). Thus a retailer can compare his or her ratios with other stores.

Planning Retail Reductions

The difference between planned purchases and planned inventory levels, when beginning and ending inventories remain constant, is planned reductions. In addition to sales, **retail reductions** include markdowns, employee and other discounts, and stock shortages:

$$\text{End-of-month inventory} = \text{Beginning inventory} + \text{Purchases} - \text{Retail reductions (including sales)}$$

Markdowns are reductions in price to stimulate merchandise sales; employee and other discounts are reductions in price given to employees, senior citizens, clergy, and nonprofit organizations; and stock shortages are caused by pilferage, breakage, and receipt of shortweighted merchandise.

Reduction planning for a retailer involves two specific factors: determining the total retail reductions for the budget period and distributing total reductions by month. The retailer should study the following in planning total reductions for the budget period:

- Past experience with reductions.
- Markdown data for similar stores.
- Changes in store policies.

- Carryover of merchandise from one budget period to another.
- Price trends.
- Stock shortages.

Past experience is a good starting point in reduction planning. This information can be compared with that of similar stores. A retailer having more markdowns than competitors should investigate and correct this situation by adjusting buying practices and price levels or training sales personnel better. The *Financial and Operating Results of Department and Specialty Stores* published annually by the National Retail Merchants Association shows retail reduction data for department and specialty stores of various sizes. In 1983 for department stores having annual sales of over $1 million, markdowns were 13.8 per cent of sales and stock shortages were 1.7 per cent of sales. Specialty stores with annual sales over $1 million had markdowns of 16.1 per cent of sales and stock shortages of 2.0 per cent of sales.[6]

In evaluating past reductions, a retailer must consider his or her store policies. Changes in policy during a budget period often affect the quantity and timing of markdowns. For example, a retailer's expanding the selection of seasonal and fashion merchandise would lead to an increase in markdowns.

Merchandise carryover, price trends, and stock shortages also affect merchandise planning. When items such as gloves and antifreeze are held in stock during off-seasons, markdowns are not used to clean out inventory. In other cases, the carryover of fad merchandise merely postpones reductions. Price trends of product categories influence retail reductions. For example, digital watches are now available for $9.99, down substantially from the introductory prices. This means that the higher-priced watches must be marked down. On the other hand, inflation (leading to higher costs) may make large purchases by retailers attractive.

Stock-shortage planning means estimating these reductions. As described in the retail accounting section, one computes stock shortages by taking a physical inventory and comparing the closing book inventory value at retail with the physical inventory at retail. Figure 11-2 contains a checklist that retailers could use to reduce inventory shortages.

On a divisional basis, department stores with annual sales over $1 million have stock shortages ranging from 0.9 per cent of sales for shoes to 2.5 per cent for women's apparel. In specialty stores with annual sales over $1 million, stock shortages range from 0.7 per cent of sales for shoes to 3.6 per cent for hobby, recreation, and transportation products.[7] The Food Marketing Institute estimates supermarket shortages at between 1.0 and 3.0 per cent of sales.[8] Some individual items have much higher stock shortage rates. For example, in department stores, stock shortages for small leather goods, women's and misses' suits, costume jewelry, junior dresses, men's accessories, and sporting goods are all 5 per cent or more of their sales.[9]

After total reductions are determined, they must be distributed by month because reductions as a percentage of sales are not the same during each month. For example, they may be much higher during busy periods when stores are more crowded and transactions happen more quickly.

[6]David P. Schulz, "FOR: Financial and Operating Results," *Stores* (November 1984), p. 5.
[7]David P. Schulz, "NRMA'S New MOR," *Stores* (October 1984), pp. 22–23.
[8]Andrew Pollack, "A New Assault on Shoplifters," *Wall Street Journal* (January 28, 1982), p. 2.
[9]Isadore Barmash, "Retailers Losing Theft Battle," *New York Times* (May 27, 1981), p. D1.

A Checklist to Reduce Inventory Shortage Errors
Answer yes or no to each of the following questions. A no answer to any question means corrective measures must be taken.

Buying

1. Is the exact quantity of merchandise purchased always specified in the contract?
2. Are purchase quantities recorded by size, color, model, etc.?
3. Are special purchase terms clearly noted?
4. Are returns to the vendor recorded properly?

Marking

5. Are retail prices clearly marked on merchandise?
6. Are the prices marked on merchandise checked for correctness?
7. Are markdowns and additional markups recorded by item number and quantity?
8. Does a cashier check with a manager if a price is not marked on an item?
9. Are the prices shown on display shelves checked for consistency with those marked on the items themselves?
10. Are old price tags removed when an item's price is changed?

Handling

11. After receipt, are purchase quantities checked against contract specifications?
12. Is merchandise handled in a systematic manner?
13. Are goods separated by merchandise classification?
14. Are all handling operations monitored properly (e.g., receiving, storing, distribution)?
15. Is enough merchandise kept on the selling floor (to reduce excessive handling)?
16. Are items sold in bulk (such as produce, sugar, candy) measured accurately?
17. Are damaged, soiled, returned, or other special goods handled separately?
18. Are employees monitored to prevent pilferage?

Figure 11-2

A Checklist to Reduce Inventory Shortage Errors (continued)

Selling

19. Do sales personnel know correct prices or have easy access to them?
20. Are markdowns, additional markups, etc. communicated to sales personnel?
21. Are misrings by cashiers made on a very small percentage of sales?
22. Are special terms noted on sales receipts?
23. Do sales personnel confirm that all items are rung up by cashiers?
24. Are employee discounts noted?
25. Is the addition on sales receipts done mechanically or double checked if computed by hand?
26. Are sales receipts numbered and later checked for missing invoices?

Inventory Planning

27. Is a physical inventory conducted at least annually?
28. Is a book inventory maintained throughout the year?
29. Are the differences between physical inventory counts and book inventory always accounted for?
30. Are sales and inventory records reviewed regularly?

Accounting

31. Are permanent records on all transactions kept?
32. Are both retail and cost data maintained?
33. Are all types of records monitored for accuracy?
34. Are inventory shortages compared with industry averages to determine acceptability of performance?

Planning Purchases

The formula for calculating planned purchases for a period is:

Planned purchases at retail = Planned sales for the month + Planned reductions for the month + Planned end-of-month stock − Beginning-of-month stock

If a retailer estimates monthly sales to be $200,000 and planned reductions to be 10 per cent of sales, plans ending inventory to be $50,000, and has a beginning inventory of $50,000, planned purchases are:

Planned purchases = $200,000 + $20,000 + $50,000 − $50,000
at retail   = $220,000

Since the retailer expects merchandise costs to be 70 per cent of retail selling price, it is planning to purchase $154,000 of goods at cost:

$$\text{Planned purchases at cost} = \begin{array}{l}\text{Planned purchases at retail} \\ \times \text{ Merchandise costs as a per cent of selling price}\end{array}$$

$$= \$220,000 \times 0.70$$

$$= \$154,000$$

Open-to-buy is the difference between planned purchases and purchase commitments made by a buyer during the month. The open-to-buy is the amount the buyer has left to spend during any point in the month, and it is reduced each time a purchase is made. Open-to-buy is recorded at cost.

As an illustration of the open-to-buy, a jeweler plans to sell $80,000 in watches during the month of December. He has a December 1 inventory of $100,000 and plans a December 31 inventory of $40,000. Planned reductions (markdowns, discounts, and shortages) for the month are $6,000. Planned purchases at retail for December = $80,000 + $6,000 + $40,000 − $100,000 = $26,000. By December 7, the jeweler has ordered $9,000 in merchandise. His open-to-buy at retail for the rest of the month is $17,000:

Open-to-buy for
December 7–31 = Planned purchases − Purchase commitments
(at retail)
               = $26,000 − $9,000
               = $17,000

To obtain the open-to-buy at cost, $17,000 is multiplied by the jeweler's merchandise costs as a percentage of selling price. If the jeweler plans merchandise costs to be 70 per cent of the retail price then his open-to-buy for the rest of December is $11,900:

$$\begin{array}{l}\text{Open-to-buy for} \\ \text{December 7–31} \\ \text{(at cost)}\end{array} = \begin{array}{l}(\text{Planned purchases − Purchase commitments}) \\ \times \text{ Merchandise costs as a per cent of selling price}\end{array}$$

$$= \$17,000 \times 0.70$$

$$= \$11,900$$

The open-to-buy concept has two significant strengths. First, it assures the retailer that a specified relationship between stock on hand and planned sales is maintained, which avoids overbuying and underbuying. Second, it shows a retailer how to adjust merchandise purchases to reflect changes in sales, markdowns, and so on. For instance, if the jeweler cited as an example revises his sales estimate to $70,000 for December, he will automatically decrease his planned purchases and open-to-buy by $10,000 at retail and $7,000 at cost.[10]

From a strategic perspective it is advisable for a buyer to leave himself or herself with an open-to-buy figure. This allows the buyer to take advantage of special deals, to purchase new items, and to fill in merchandise that sells out. Sometimes the open-to-buy limit must be exceeded because of underestimations of demand (low sales forecasts).

Planning Profit Margins

When developing a merchandise budget, the retailer is quite interested in profitability and must price merchandise on the basis of sales, retail expenses, profits, and retail reductions:

$$\text{Required initial markup percentage} = \frac{\text{Retail expenses} + \text{Profit} + \text{Reductions}}{\text{Net sales} + \text{Reductions}}$$

The required markup figure is an overall store average; individual items may be priced according to demand and other factors, as long as the store average is maintained. A more complete discussion of markup is contained in Chapter 14. Initial markup is introduced at this point for continuity in the description of merchandise budgeting.

As an example of markup planning, a dress department has $40,000 in monthly operating expenses and planned monthly sales of $330,000. Reductions are anticipated to be $30,000. A profit goal of $50,000 is established. Therefore, the required initial markup is 33.3 per cent:

$$\text{Required initial markup percentage} = \frac{\$40,000 + \$50,000 + \$30,000}{\$330,000 + \$30,000} = 33.3\%$$

$$\text{Required initial markup percentage (all factors expressed as a percentage of net sales)} = \frac{12.1\% + 15.2\% + 9.1\%}{100\% + 9.1\%} = 33.3\%$$

Figure 11-3 summarizes the merchandise forecasting and budgeting process. It expands on Figure 11-1 by including the bases for each decision point.

---

[10]At the beginning of the month, planned purchases and open-to-buy are equal if no purchases are committed to being received in that month.

The Merchandise Forecasting and Budgeting Process: Dollar Control

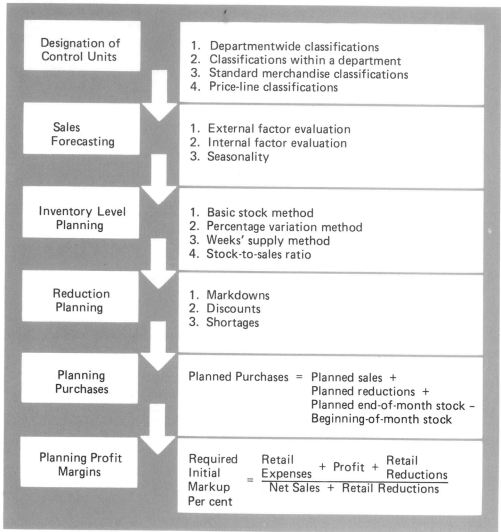

Figure 11-3

Unit Control Systems

Unit control systems regulate quantities of merchandise in units rather than in dollars. Information typically contained in unit control systems includes

- The identification of items that are selling well and those that are selling poorly.
- A focus on opportunities and problem areas for buyers in terms of price, color, style, size, and so on.

- The computation (where a perpetual inventory system is used) of the quantity of goods on hand. This minimizes overstocking and understocking.
- An indication of the age of the inventory, highlighting those items that are candidates for markdowns or special promotions.
- A determination of the optimal time to reorder merchandise.
- An examination of experiences with alternative sources (vendors) when problems arise.
- The level of inventory and sales for each item in each store branch. This improves the flow of goods transfer between branches and alerts sales personnel as to which branches have desired products. Also, less stock can be maintained in each store, reducing costs.

Physical Inventory Systems

A physical-inventory unit-control system is similar to a physical-inventory dollar-control system. Whereas the dollar control system is concerned with the dollar value of inventory, the unit control system examines the number of units by item classification. In the unit control system, someone within the retail firm is assigned the responsibility for monitoring inventory levels of merchandise, either by visual inspection or by actual count.

An example of a **visual inspection system** is the use of stock cards in the houseware and hardware displays of many discount, department, and variety stores. Merchandise is placed on pegboard displays, with each item numbered on the back of its package on a stock card. Minimum stock quantities are clearly noted on the item, and sales personnel are responsible for reordering when the items reach minimum inventory levels. Accuracy occurs only if the merchandise is placed in numerical order on the displays.

Although this concept is easy to maintain and inexpensive, it has two shortcomings. First, it does not provide information on the rate of sales of individual items. Second, minimum stock quantities may be arbitrarily defined and not drawn from in-depth analysis.

The other physical inventory system, actual counting, relies on the tabulation of the number of units on hand at regular intervals. A **stock-counting system** records inventory on hand, purchases, sales volume, and shortages during specified periods. For example:

	Number of Items, for the Period 2/1/85–4/30/85
Beginning inventory, February 1, 1985	200
Total purchases for period	150
Total units available for sale	350
Closing inventory, April 30, 1985	120
Sales and shortages for period	230

The stock-counting system requires more clerical work than the visual inspection system, but it enables a retailer to obtain sales data for given periods and stock-to-sales relationships as of the time of each count. A physical system is not as sophisticated as a perpetual inventory system, and its use is more justified with low-value items having predictable sales rates.

Perpetual Inventory Systems

Perpetual (book) inventory systems can be maintained manually, can use merchandise tags that are processed by computers, or can employ point-of-sale information tools such as optical scanning devices. Technological advances have greatly improved retailers' abilities to develop strong perpetual inventory systems and to utilize computers.

A **perpetual inventory system** keeps a running total of the number of units handled by a retailer by adjusting for sales, returns, transfers to other departments or stores, receipt of merchandise shipments, and so on. All additions and subtractions from beginning inventory are recorded.

A manual system requires employees to gather information by examining sales checks, merchandise receipts, transfer requests, and other merchandise documents. This information is then coded and tabulated.

A merchandise-tagging system relies on preprinted tags attached to each item in stock. These tags include data on department, classification, vendor, style number, date of receipt, color, and material. When an item is sold, one copy of the merchandise tag is removed and sent to a tabulating facility, where the coded information is transferred to tapes or data cards that can be summed by computer. Because preprinted merchandise tags are processed in batches, they can be used by small and medium-sized retailers (who subscribe to independent service bureaus) and by branches of chains (with data being processed at a central location).

Point-of-sale systems, developed and sold by companies such as IBM and NCR, feed information from merchandise tags or product labels directly into computers for immediate processing. The newest point-of-sale system involves an optical scanner, which transfers information from merchandise to a computer via a wand or a stationary device that interacts with a sensitized strip on the merchandise. See Figure 11-4 for an example of a wand-based system.

As noted in Chapter 6, the **Universal Product Code (UPC)** used in the food industry and **Optical Character Recognition (OCR-A)** used in nonfood stores are industrywide classification systems for coding information onto merchandise. The UPC requires that manufacturers premark packages with a series of thick and thin vertical lines. Product and inventory data are contained in the UPC but are not readable by employees or customers. OCR-A is readable by both machines and humans and can handle greater information than the UPC. With the UPC, prices must still be marked on the merchandise, but OCR-A is slower to process. See Figure 11-5 for an example of a UPC system.

Computer-based systems are quicker, more accurate, and of higher quality than manual systems. And because of the availability of service bureaus, computer costs are reduced for smaller retailers.

A retailer does not have to use a perpetual system for all of his or her inventory. Many retailers combine perpetual and physical systems. Key items, accounting for a large proportion of sales, are controlled through a perpetual system, and other items are controlled through a physical inventory system. In this way, attention is properly placed on the firm's most important products.

Figure 11-4   A Wand-Based Point-of-Sale System

This hand-held "wand" can help a department store improve customer service by enabling the NCR 2152 point-of-sale terminal to read merchandise information directly from encoded price tags. While speeding consumer transactions, the device also can help a store insure that accurate, comprehensive sales data are captured at the point of sale. Courtesy NCR.

Financial Inventory Control: Integration of Dollar and Unit Concepts

Until this point, dollar and unit control concepts have been discussed as separate entities. However, in practice, dollar and unit controls are directly linked. For example, the decision on how many units to buy at a given time affects and is affected by dollar investment, inventory turnover, quantity discounts, warehousing and insurance costs, and so on.

Three financial inventory controls are described in this section: stock turnover and gross margin return on investment, when to reorder, and how much to reorder.

How Does the UPC Scanner System Work?

When the checker passes an item with the UPC symbol over a scanning device, the symbol is read by a low-energy laser.

The UPC symbol is found on many supermarket products and looks like this.

Each product has its own unique identification number. For example, the first five digits, 11146, represent the manufacturer, Giant in this case. The second five digits represent the specific items; 01345 identifies 24 ounce iced tea mix.

Note that the price is not in the symbol. The symbol identifies the product, not the price.

11146 01345

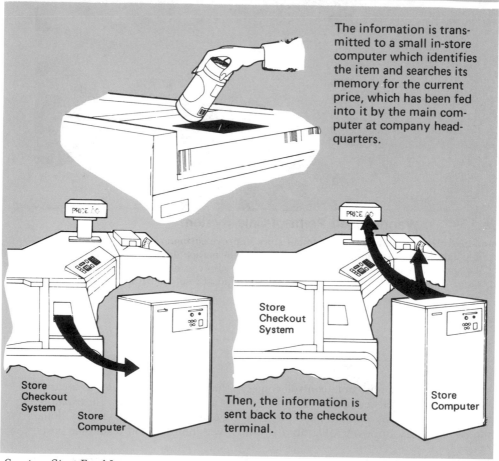

The information is transmitted to a small in-store computer which identifies the item and searches its memory for the current price, which has been fed into it by the main computer at company headquarters.

Store Checkout System

Store Checkout System

Store Computer

Store Checkout System

Then, the information is sent back to the checkout terminal.

Store Computer

Courtesy Giant Food Inc.

Figure 11-5

Stock Turnover and Gross Margin Return on Investment

Stock turnover is defined as the number of times during a specific period, usually one year, that the average inventory on hand is sold. A high level of stock turnover has several virtues:

- Inventory investments are productive on a per dollar basis.
- Merchandise on the shelves is fresh.
- Losses due to changes in styles and fashion are reduced.
- Costs associated with maintaining inventory—such as interest, insurance, breakage, and warehousing—are lessened.

Stock turnover can be calculated in units or in dollars (at retail or at cost):

$$\text{Annual rate of stock turnover (units)} = \frac{\text{Number of units sold during year}}{\text{Average inventory on hand (in units)}}$$

$$\text{Annual rate of stock turnover (retail dollars)} = \frac{\text{Net yearly sales (in retail dollars)}}{\text{Average inventory on hand (in retail dollars)}}$$

$$\text{Annual rate of stock turnover (cost)} = \frac{\text{Cost of goods sold during the year}}{\text{Average inventory on hand (at cost)}}$$

The choice of a stock turnover formula depends on the accounting system used by the retailer.

The computation of stock turnover should reflect the average inventory level for the entire time period covered in the analysis. Computations will be incorrect if the true average inventory is not used, as occurs when a retailer mistakenly uses the inventory level of a peak or slow month as the yearly average.

Table 11-10 shows stock turnover rates for a variety of retail stores. Gasoline service stations and grocery stores have very high turnover rates. These retailers rely on high sales volume for their success. Jewelry, family clothing, hardware, and shoe stores have very low turnover rates. They rely on large profits for each item they sell and must maintain a sizable assortment for their customers.

A retailer can increase stock turnover through a number of different strategies, including reductions in assortment, elimination of slow-selling items, maintenance of minimal inventory for slow-sellers, efficient and timely buying, and transactions with reliable distributors.

Despite the advantages of high stock turnover, there are instances in which it can adversely affect profits. First, purchasing units in small quantities can increase merchandise costs because quantity discounts may be lost and transportation charges may rise. Second, a high turnover rate can result in low width and/or depth of assortment. Lost sales must be measured against high turnover. Third, a high stock turnover may result in low profits if prices are reduced to move inventory quickly. A retailer's return on investment is composed of both turnover and profit per unit.

Table 11-10
*Annual Median Stock Turnover Rates for Selected Retail
Institutions (1984)*

Type of Retailer	Annual Median Stock Turnover Rate
Auto and home supply stores	5.8 times
Clothing: men's and boys' stores	3.6
Department stores	4.7
Family clothing stores	3.3
Furniture stores	4.6
Gasoline service stations	31.4
Grocery stores	17.2
Hardware stores	3.4
Household appliance stores	5.4
Jewelry stores	2.5
Lumber and other building materials dealers	5.8
New and used car dealers	6.8
Shoe stores	3.4
Women's accessory and specialty stores	3.8

Source: 1984–1985 Industry Norms and Key Business Ratios *(New York: Dun
& Bradstreet Credit Services, 1984).*

Gross margin return on investment (GMROI) shows the relationship between total dollar operating profits and the average investment in inventory by combining profitability and sales-to-stock measures:

$$\text{Gross margin return on investment (GMROI)} = \frac{\text{Gross margin in dollars}}{\text{Net sales}} \times \frac{\text{Net sales}}{\text{Average inventory at cost}}$$

$$= \frac{\text{Gross margin in dollars}}{\text{Average inventory at cost}}$$

In this formula, gross margin in dollars (total dollar operating profits) is defined as net sales minus the cost of goods sold. Gross margin in dollars divided by net sales is the gross margin percentage. Net sales divided by average inventory at cost provides a sales-to-stock ratio. [*Note:* This ratio may be converted to stock turnover by multiplying by (100 − Gross margin percentage)/100.]

GMROI is a useful concept for several reasons:

• It shows how different retail institutions can prosper despite different gross margins and sales-to-stock ratios. For example, a conventional supermarket may have a gross margin percentage of 20 and a sales-to-stock ratio of 22, resulting in a GMROI of 440 per cent (20% × 22). A department store may have a gross margin percentage of 44 and a sales-to-stock ratio of 10, resulting in a GMROI of 440 per cent (44% × 10). The GMROIs of the two stores are the same because of the trade-off between profitability per item and turnover.

- It is a good indicator of a manager's performance, since it focuses on factors controlled by the manager. Interdepartmental comparisons can also be made.[11]
- It is simple to plan and understand, and data collection is easy.
- The retailer can determine if GMROI performance is consistent with other company goals, such as store image and cash flow.

Recently, some retailing analysts have suggested that the basic GMROI formula shown in this section be expanded to include accounts receivables, accounts payable, and inventory carrying costs.[12]

When to Reorder

One means of controlling inventory investment is to establish stock levels at which new orders must be placed. These stock levels are called **reorder points.** The determination of reorder points depends on three factors: order lead time, usage rate, and safety stock. **Order lead time** is the time span from the date an order is placed to the date merchandise is ready for sale (received, price marked, and put on the selling floor). The **usage rate** refers to average sales per day, in units, of merchandise. **Safety stock** is the extra inventory kept on hand to protect against out-of-stock conditions due to unexpected demand and delays in delivery. Safety stock is planned in accordance with the retailer's policy toward running out of merchandise (service level).

The formula for when to reorder is

Reorder point = Usage rate × Lead time

In this case, no safety stock is planned. Thus, a firm that sells ten pairs of socks a day and needs eight days to order, receive, and display merchandise has a reorder point of eighty pairs of socks. This means that the retailer reorders socks once his or her inventory on hand reaches eighty. By the time the new order is completed (eight days later), stock on hand will be zero, and the new stock will replenish the inventory.

This strategy is correct only if the retailer has a perfectly steady customer demand of ten pairs of socks per day and it takes exactly eight days to process all orders. However, this does not normally occur. For example, should consumers buy fifteen pairs of socks per day, the retailer will run out of merchandise in 5⅓ days and be without socks for 2⅔ days. Similarly, should an order take 10 days to process, the retailer will have no merchandise for two full days, despite correctly estimating demand. Figure 11-6 graphically demonstrates how these stockouts may occur if safety stock is not planned.

---

[11]Daniel J. Sweeney, "Improving the Profitability of Retail Merchandising Decisions," *Journal of Marketing*, Vol. 37 (January 1973), pp. 30–38.

[12]See Ray R. Serpkenci and Robert L. Lusch, "New Model Offers Retailers a Realistic Estimate of Gross Margin Return from Merchandise Lines," *Marketing News* (February 18, 1983), p. 6; Charles A. Ingene and Michael Levy, "GMROI: A New View of Planning and Measuring Merchandising Performance," in Bruce J. Walker et al. (Editors), *An Assessment of Marketing Thought & Practice* (Chicago: American Marketing Association, 1982), pp. 216–219; and Michael Levy and Charles A. Ingene, "Residual Income Analysis: A Method of Inventory Investment Allocation and Evaluation," *Journal of Marketing*, Vol. 48 (Summer 1984), pp. 93–104.

How Stockouts Occur

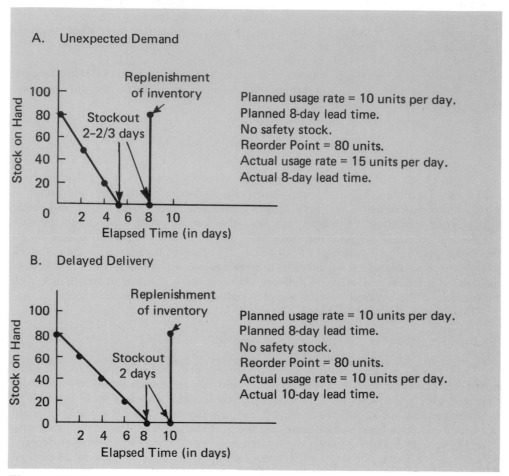

A. Unexpected Demand

Replenishment of inventory

Stockout 2-2/3 days

Stock on Hand

Elapsed Time (in days)

Planned usage rate = 10 units per day.
Planned 8-day lead time.
No safety stock.
Reorder Point = 80 units.
Actual usage rate = 15 units per day.
Actual 8-day lead time.

B. Delayed Delivery

Replenishment of inventory

Stockout 2 days

Stock on Hand

Elapsed Time (in days)

Planned usage rate = 10 units per day.
Planned 8-day lead time.
No safety stock.
Reorder Point = 80 units.
Actual usage rate = 10 units per day.
Actual 10-day lead time.

Figure 11-6

When the firm plans to incorporate safety stock into its planning, the reorder formula becomes

Reorder point = (Usage rate × Lead time) + Safety stock

As previously indicated, safety stock should be included because demand is not completely static and deliveries can be delayed. Suppose the retailer mentioned wants to maintain a safety stock of 30 per cent; then the reorder point is

Reorder point = (80) + 30%(80) = 80 + 24 = 104

Table 11-11
Safety Stock Levels Required to Obtain Various Probabilities of Not Running Out of Staples

Estimated Reorder Point	Retail Stock Policy Chance of Not Running Out of Stock (%)	Safety Stock Needed to Achieve Stock Policy	Required Reorder Point $=\left(\begin{array}{c}\text{Estimated Reorder Point}\end{array}+\begin{array}{c}\text{Safety Stock}\end{array}\right)$
25	99	$2.3\sqrt{\text{Estimated reorder point}}$ $= 2.3\sqrt{25} = 12$	37
40	99	$2.3\sqrt{40} = 15$	55
100	99	$2.3\sqrt{100} = 23$	123
200	99	$2.3\sqrt{200} = 33$	233
400	99	$2.3\sqrt{400} = 46$	446
25	95	$1.6\sqrt{\text{Estimated reorder point}}$ $= 1.6\sqrt{25} = 8$	33
40	95	$1.6\sqrt{40} = 10$	50
100	95	$1.6\sqrt{100} = 16$	116
200	95	$1.6\sqrt{200} = 23$	223
400	95	$1.6\sqrt{400} = 32$	432
25	80	$\sqrt{\text{Estimated reorder point}}$ $= \sqrt{25} = 5$	30
40	80	$\sqrt{40} = 6$	46
100	80	$\sqrt{100} = 10$	110
200	80	$\sqrt{200} = 14$	214
400	80	$\sqrt{400} = 20$	420

In this case, the retailer still expects to sell an average of ten pairs of socks per day and receive orders in an average of eight days. A safety stock of twenty-four extra pairs of socks is kept on hand to protect against unexpected demand or a late shipment.

For retailers who deal with staples (products with small sales variations throughout the year), a procedure is available for estimating safety stock. This procedure is based on the Poisson probability distribution and is shown in Table 11-11. In the sock example cited, the retailer should have a safety stock of nine if he or she wants an 80 per cent probability of not running out of stock; fourteen if he or she wants a 95 per cent probability of not running out of stock; and twenty-one if he or she wants a 99 per cent probability of not running out of stock. Therefore, the retailer takes a 20 per cent chance of being out of stock should he or she plan a reorder point of eighty-nine.

Table 11-11 shows that the level of safety stock is proportionately greater for low-turnover items than for high-turnover items. For example, at the 99 per cent level, safety stock for a retailer having a reorder point of forty is 37.5 per cent (15/40) of estimated reorder point. Safety stock for a retailer having a reorder point of four hundred is 11.5 per cent (46/400) of estimated reorder point.

The combination of a perpetual inventory system and a reorder point means that merchandise orders can be programmed into a computer and reorders can take place automatically when stock on hand reaches the reorder point. This is referred to as an **automatic reordering system.** Intervention by a store manager or buyer must be possible, especially in cases where monthly sales fluctuate greatly.

How Much to Reorder

The decision about how much to order affects how often a retailer must order merchandise. A retailer who places large orders reduces ordering costs but increases inventory-holding costs. A retailer who places small orders minimizes inventory-holding costs while maximizing ordering costs.

The **economic order quantity (EOQ)** is the order quantity that minimizes the total costs of processing orders and holding inventory. Order-processing costs include computer time, order forms, labor, and handling new merchandise. Holding costs include warehousing, inventory investment, insurance, taxes, depreciation, deterioration, and pilferage. EOQ can be utilized by both large and small firms.[13]

As can be seen in Figure 11-7, order-processing costs drop as order quantity goes up because fewer orders are needed to purchase the same total annual quantity, and inventory holding costs increase as order quantity goes up because more units must be maintained in inventory and they are kept for longer periods. The two costs are summed into a total cost curve.

Economic Order Quantity

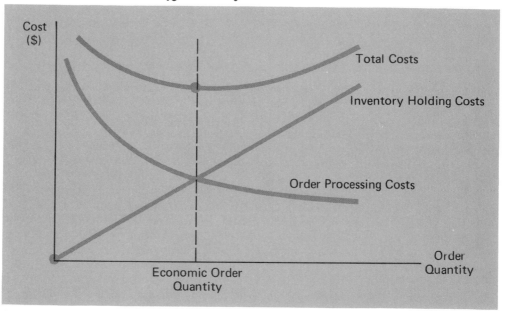

Figure 11-7

[13]See Larry H. Beard, Al L. Hartgraves, and Fred A. Jacobs, "Managing Inventories in a Small Business," *Business,* Vol. 33 (April–June 1983), pp. 45–49.

Mathematically, the economic order quantity (EOQ) is

$$EOQ = \sqrt{\frac{2DS}{IC}}$$

where EOQ = order quantity, in units

D = annual demand, in units

S = costs to place an order

I = percentage of annual carrying cost to unit cost

C = unit cost of an item

For example, a retailer estimates that he can sell 500 dish sets per year. These sets cost $150 each. Breakage, insurance, tied-up capital, and pilferage equal 20 per cent of the costs of the sets (or $30 each). Order costs are $5 per order. The economic order quantity is

$$EOQ = \sqrt{\frac{2(500)(\$5)}{(0.20)(\$150)}} = \sqrt{\frac{\$5,000}{\$30}} = \sqrt{166.67} = 13$$

The EOQ formula must often be modified to take into account changes in demand, quantity discounts, variable order costs, and variable holding costs.

Merchandise Planning and Management—Financial: A Summary

Financial merchandise planning stipulates which products are purchased, when products are purchased, and how many products are purchased. Financial planning consists of methods of accounting, merchandise forecasting and budgeting, unit control systems, and financial inventory control.

The two accounting systems available to retailers are the cost and the retail methods of inventory valuation. Physical and book (perpetual) procedures are possible with each. The cost method is simple to use, but the retail method more accurately reflects market conditions. Physical inventory involves the actual counting of merchandise at prescribed intervals. Book inventory relies on accurate bookkeeping and a smooth flow of information.

Merchandise forecasting and budgeting is a dollar control system that incorporates designation of control units, sales forecasting, inventory-level planning, retail-reduction planning, planning purchases, and profit-margin planning. Adjustments at any stage of the process require that all later stages be modified accordingly.

A unit control system specifies the quantities of merchandise to be handled, in terms of physical units. Unit control information includes sales this month, sales last month, merchandise on hand, markups and markdowns, rate of stock turnover, price per unit, merchandise classification, vendor, and style designation. Physical inventory and book (perpetual) inventory procedures are available. Manual systems, merchandise tagging, and point-of-sale systems are used.

Financial inventory control integrates dollar and unit control concepts. Three financial controls are stock turnover and gross margin return on investment, when to reorder, and how much to reorder.

Throughout the chapter, a number of merchandising equations have been introduced, including the cost complement in the retail method, closing inventory at cost, the basic stock method, the percentage variation method, the weeks' supply method, the stock-to-sales ratio, planned purchases, open-to-buy, initial markup, stock turnover, gross margin return on investment, reorder point, and economic order quantity.

Questions for Discussion

1. Show how a buyer can determine the level of stock shortages by using a financial merchandise plan.
2. Why is the retail method of inventory valuation more desirable than the cost method to most retailers?
3. What kind of retailers can best use a perpetual inventory system that involves the cost method?
4. Explain the cost complement concept in the retail method.
5. Differentiate between the basic stock method and the stock-to-sales method of merchandise planning.
6. Illustrate two situations in which it would be advisable to carry over merchandise from one budget period to another, instead of taking a markdown.
7. What are the disadvantages of a high stock turnover?
8. How does an automatic reordering system work? What are its shortcomings?
9. Why is the formula for the economic order quantity shown in this chapter an oversimplification?
10. A retailer has yearly sales of $1.5 million. Inventory on January 1 is $600,000 (at cost). During the year, $1.5 million of merchandise (at cost) is purchased. The ending inventory is $880,000 (at cost). Operating costs are $100,000. Calculate the cost of goods sold and net profit, and set up a profit-and-loss statement. There are no retail reductions in this problem.
11. A retailer has a beginning inventory valued at $300,000 at retail and $210,000 at cost. Net purchases during the month are $100,000 at retail and $60,000 at cost. Freight charges are $2,000. Sales are $200,000. Markdowns and discounts equal $14,000. A physical inventory at the end of the year shows merchandise valued at $185,000 (at retail) on hand. Calculate the following.
    a. Total merchandise available for sale—at cost and at retail
    b. Cost complement
    c. Ending retail book value of inventory
    d. Stock shortages
    e. Adjusted ending retail book value
    f. Gross profit

12. The monthly sales of a clothing store are listed here. Calculate the monthly sales indexes. What do they mean?

January	$20,000	July	$ 80,000
February	15,000	August	50,000
March	15,000	September	50,000
April	30,000	October	60,000
May	40,000	November	80,000
June	60,000	December	100,000

13. If the planned average monthly stock for the clothing store named in Question 1 is $150,000, how much inventory should be planned for December if the retailer uses the percentage variation method?

14. As of December 10, the clothier in Question 14 purchased $40,000 of merchandise. What is the open-to-buy for the rest of December?

15. A retailer sells an average of ten standard touch-tone telephones per day and desires a safety stock of ten phones. If it takes 12 days for an order to be placed and received by the retailer, what is its reorder point? Explain your answer.

CASES

1. Appliances Plus: Financial Merchandise Planning

Appliances Plus is a 5,000-square-foot retail store situated in downtown Portland, Oregon. The store, which opened in January 1985, sells a full complement of major appliances, including refrigerators, freezers, stoves, ovens, dishwashers, clothes washers and driers, and trash compactors. Among the brands carried by Appliances Plus are White-Westinghouse, General Electric, Whirlpool, Frigidaire, and Roper.

Within each of its product categories, Appliances Plus stocks a wide variety of merchandise. For example, the store carries regular refrigerators, refrigerators with

Table 1
Appliances Plus—Physical Inventory, as of 12/31/85

Product Categories	Value of Inventory (at Retail)
Refrigerators/freezers	$ 75,000
Stoves/ovens	63,000
Dishwashers	40,000
Clothes washers/driers	60,000
Trash compactors	20,000
Accessories	10,000
	$268,000

Table 2
Appliances Plus—Perpetual Inventory System, for the Period 1/1/85–12/31/85

Date	Beginning-of-Month Inventory (at Cost)	Monthly Purchases (at Cost)	Monthly Sales (at Cost)	End-of-Month Inventory (at Cost)
1/1/85	$155,000	$ 60,000	$ 60,000	$155,000
2/1/85	155,000	60,000	60,000	155,000
3/1/85	155,000	40,000	50,000	145,000
4/1/85	145,000	30,000	40,000	135,000
5/1/85	135,000	40,000	40,000	135,000
6/1/85	135,000	40,000	40,000	135,000
7/1/85	135,000	40,000	40,000	135,000
8/1/85	135,000	40,000	40,000	135,000
9/1/85	135,000	60,000	50,000	145,000
10/1/85	145,000	70,000	60,000	155,000
11/1/85	155,000	110,000	85,000	180,000
12/1/85	180,000	105,000	95,000	190,000
		$695,000	$660,000	(as of 12/31/85)

Table 3
Appliances Plus—Merchandise Available for Sale, for the Period 1/1/85–12/31/85

	Cost Method	Retail Method
Beginning inventory	$155,000	$ 220,000
Net purchases	695,000	980,000
Additional markups	—	—
Freight-in	10,000	—
	$860,000	$1,200,000

Table 4
Appliances Plus—Ending Retail Book Value, as of 12/31/85

Merchandise available for sale		$1,200,000
Less deductions:		
Sales	$900,000	
Markdowns	25,000	
Total deductions		925,000
Ending retail book value of inventory		$ 275,000

freezers, refrigerators with freezers and extra features (such as ice makers), and freezers. It handles traditional ovens, microwave ovens, and newer "space-saver" ovens. Portable and full-size models are sold.

Recently, Appliances Plus completed its first annual physical and book inventory for the period January 1, 1985 through December 31, 1985. The results are shown in Tables 1 to 4.

Questions

1. Compute the following for Appliances Plus during 1985:
   a. Stock shortages (at retail).
   b. Adjusted ending retail book value of inventory.
   c. Cost complement.
   d. Closing inventory (at cost).
   e. Gross profit.
   f. Monthly sales index.
2. What was the annual rate of stock turnover in retail dollars for Appliances Plus during 1985 if the average inventory on hand (in retail dollars) was $195,000? Is this good or bad?
3. Which inventory-level planning methods should Appliances Plus employ? Why?

2. The Sporting Life: Analyzing a Financial Merchandising Plan

The Sporting Life is a moderate-sized sporting goods store located in a regional shopping mall in a suburb of Pittsburgh. The store has been open since 1977 and offers a broad assortment of warm-up suits, athletic shoes (for tennis, jogging, skiing, etc.), athletic equipment (tennis rackets, skis, baseball gloves, etc.), and accessories (socks, T-shirts, wristbands, etc.). It stresses a full-service, personal approach and sets prices accordingly. The Sporting Life is well respected in the community and consumers particularly like the advice provided by its experienced sales force.

The store has a clear merchandising plan:

- It concentrates on seven key sports and maintains a good product depth in these categories: baseball, basketball, football, golf, jogging (running), skiing, and tennis. The Sporting Life does not carry bowling, physical fitness, and other equipment, nor does it offer bicycles or bicycle accessories.
- Prices are similar to those in department stores and 20 per cent higher than in discount stores.
- Inventory is limited to national brands that are heavily advertised by manufacturers. Private-label brands are not stocked.
- All merchandise is coded with date of purchase and cost information that cannot be read by consumers.
- A physical inventory is conducted once every two months. A book inventory is maintained using the LIFO method. The Sporting Life does not use the retail method of inventory.
- Sales forecasts are made annually by sports category; the forecasts are broken down by month.

Table 1
Selected Financial Data

Factor	The Sporting Life	Sporting Goods Stores— Industry Average
Annual sales	$500,000	$350,000
Annual sales per square foot	$145	$150
Markdowns, discounts, and stock shortages (% of sales)	9.0	7.5
Initial markup percentage	40.4	36.7
Gross margin percentage (maintained markup)	35.0	32.0
GMROI (%)	110	120
Net profit before taxes (% of sales)	7.0	5.0
Stock turnover (times per year)	3.0	3.5

- Regular prices are maintained throughout the year. A special clearance sale is conducted once a year (in February); then the prices of all merchandise are reduced by 30 per cent.
- Merchandise is reordered when stock levels for an item are low; safety stock is not kept.

Recently, the manager of The Sporting Life completed an analysis of the firm's merchandising plan. He focused on financial measures and compared The Sporting Life with average industry data found in Dun & Bradstreet and Robert Morris Associates. See Table 1.

Questions

1. Evaluate The Sporting Life's merchandising plan.
2. What conclusions can be reached from Table 1?
3. What other financial merchandising factors discussed in this chapter should The Sporting Life consider? Why?
4. Offer several suggestions for The Sporting Life to improve its financial merchandising plan.

12

Communicating with the Customer: Establishing and Maintaining a Store Image

Chapter Objectives

1. To show the importance of communicating with customers
2. To describe the components of store image
3. To examine how store image is established through the use of atmosphere, storefronts, store layouts, displays, customer services, and community relations
4. To consider the complexities involved in maintaining a store image

L. L. Bean, a leading mail-order firm, operates a 60,000-square-foot, multilevel store in its home town of Freeport, Maine. The store is open 24 hours a day and attracts more than 2 million shoppers annually. Average sales per square foot of selling space are five to six times greater than those for successful department stores.

However, the amount of customer traffic did cause some problems. Floors wore out quickly. Aisles were not wide enough. Customer space in various departments was too tight. There was not enough nearby storage room for inventory. As a result, L. L. Bean hired Retail Planning Associates to improve the atmosphere of its store.

Today, the store has a "sense of the outdoors, but it's really a very theatrical presentation of the outdoors." There are exciting custom-made fixtures; walls, ceilings, beams, and posts are all made of laminated layers of pine. Special wood and acrylic coverings enable floors to last longer. A trout pond surrounds the stairway connecting the old and new areas of the store. Some merchandise is suspended in air. Rust-colored carpeting is used in women's and and children's clothing departments; this separates these departments from those with men's apparel. There are large windows and skylights in various places. The other problems noted above have also been resolved.

Like other retailers, L. L. Bean realizes that its image is greatly affected by the atmosphere it creates. The renovations undertaken by Retail Planning Associates have retained its long-standing image while better serving consumers.[1]

Overview

Communicating with the customer is necessary to convey a firm's philosophy of business, objectives, and strategy. The retailer has information to present to his or her customers, and this information must be interpreted as intended if sales are to be made. A variety of physical and symbolic forms are used to transmit this information from the retailer to the customer.

In Chapter 12, the establishment of a store image is described. The use of atmosphere, storefronts, store layouts, displays, customer services, and community relations are enumerated, as they relate to communicating with the customer. Chapter 13 concentrates on the standard promotional tools available to retailers in reaching their customers. Advertising, publicity, personal selling, and sales promotion are detailed.

The Significance of Store Image

To be successful, a retailer must create a distinctive, clear, and consistent image. Once established, this image permeates all product and service offerings. In the consumer's mind, the store is placed in a niche relative to its competitors, based on a perceived image. It is extremely difficult to break out of this niche once it is firmly implanted in consumers' minds.[2] **Store image** can be defined as:

> the way in which the store is defined in the shopper's mind, partly by its functional qualities and partly by an aura of psychological attributes.[3]

> It is *not* simply someone's impersonal observations of a store's characteristics. Thus I consider image a combination of factual and emotional material. The customer reacts to the store's characteristics, as he views them, in an emotional way.[4]

Common to these definitions are the concepts that image is comprised of functional (physical) and emotional attributes, that these attributes are organized into perceptual frameworks by shoppers, and that the frameworks determine shoppers' expectations about a store's overall policies and practices.

---

[1]"Design Lends Sense of Theater to Mail Order Firm's Home Town Store," *Marketing News* (February 1, 1985), p. 26.
[2]See Paula Silbey, "Working for an Image Change," *Stores* (March 1982), pp. 60–62.
[3]Pierre Martineau, "The Personality of the Retail Store," *Harvard Business Review*, Vol. 36 (January–February 1958), p. 47.
[4]Alfred R. Oxenfeldt, "Developing a Favorable Price-Quality Image," *Journal of Retailing*, Vol. 50 (Winter 1974–75), p. 9.

Components of Store Image

There are numerous components in a store's image. The total package of variables determines the overall image. In different settings, it has been stated that store image is composed of

- Quality, price, and assortment.[5]
- Fashionability, salesmanship, outside attractiveness, and advertising.[6]
- Clientele mix, institutional maturity, merchandise offerings, locational convenience, shopping pleasure, transaction convenience, promotional emphasis, integrity, and image strength and clarity.[7]

From these lists, the following is offered as a detailed summary of the components of store image:

1. Characteristics of the target market.
2. Store positioning.
3. Store location.
4. Product assortment.
5. Level of prices.
6. Physical attributes of the store (atmosphere).
7. Availability of credit and other services.
8. Civic responsibility.
9. Mass advertising and publicity.
10. Type and extent of personal selling.
11. Sales promotions.

Items 1 through 5 and their relation to image are examined elsewhere in the text. Items 6 through 11 are the focal points for the discussion involving communications with the consumer in this and the next chapter. Table 12-1 contains a detailed breakdown of all the elements of store image (incorporating items 1 through 11).[8]

The Dynamics of Creating and Maintaining a Store Image

Creating and maintaining a store image is not a simple task for retailers, as these examples show. Bloomingdale's prides itself on an image as "the country's trendiest department store." To preserve this image, Bloomingdale's must constantly introduce merchandise before competitors and display it in an exciting manner. When adding

---

[5]Don L. James, Richard M. Durand, and Robert A. Dreves, "The Use of a Multi-Attribute Attitude Model in a Store Image Study," *Journal of Retailing*, Vol. 52 (Summer 1976), p. 30.
[6]Ronald B. Marks, "Operationalizing the Concept of Store Image," *Journal of Retailing*, Vol. 52 (Fall 1976), p. 44.
[7]Edgar A. Pessemier, "Store Image and Positioning," *Journal of Retailing*, Vol. 56 (Spring 1980), pp. 96–97.
[8]See Figures 6-5 and 6-6 for examples of how to measure store image.

Table 12-1
The Elements of Store Image

1. General attributes
   a. How long store has been operating
   b. How well store is known
   c. Extent of geographic coverage (i.e., spread of branches)
   d. Target market sought
   e. Positioning of store

2. Physical attributes
   a. Storefront, marquees, entrances, display windows
   b. Visibility of storefront
   c. Uniqueness of storefront
   d. Surrounding stores and area
   e. Parking and congestion, access from highways, etc.
   f. Flooring, colors, lighting, scents, sounds
   g. Fixtures
   h. Width of aisles
   i. Dressing facilities, vertical transportation
   j. Technology
   k. Cleanliness
   l. Layout of merchandise, display of merchandise
   m. Traffic flow in store
   n. Information

3. Personnel attributes
   a. Knowledge of personnel
   b. Friendliness of personnel
   c. Amount of personnel
   d. Neatness of personnel

4. Product attributes
   a. Assortment
   b. Quality
   c. Availability
   d. Use of brand names
   e. Dependability
   f. Innovativeness

5. Price attributes
   a. Level
   b. Range
   c. Comparison with competitors
   d. Number of sales

6. Customer service attributes
   a. Number
   b. Level
   c. Manner of payment
   d. Responsiveness to consumers

7. Communications attributes
   a. Media used
   b. Amount of communication
   c. Content
   d. Believability

8. Community service attributes
   a. Amount
   b. Level
   c. Perception by consumers

boutique departments, Bloomingdale's evaluates the merchandise itself, salability, freshness, innovativeness, uniqueness, and customer appeal.[9]

Between 1984 and 1988, Sears, J. C. Penney, and K mart are expected to spend a total of at least $5.4 billion to remodel their stores and strengthen their images. Sears wants its image to be that of a full-line general merchandiser which is the leading source for major appliances and other hard goods in the United States. J. C. Penney wants to be viewed as the leading national fashion and soft goods department store. K mart wants customers to envision it as the leading national low-priced, improved-quality discounter. All three retailers are planning "to offer more merchandise of better quality in clean, attractive stores, coaxing regular customers to spend more and luring new ones."[10]

"From the dawn of bookselling history until the early 1980s, a bookstore was a bookstore—known for its books, not its innovative marketing techniques." As a result, bookstore sales stagnated as competition from other retailers (book clubs, stationery stores, supermarkets, etc.) grew. In response, bookstores are now working hard to revitalize their image. At WaldenBooks, a chain of 800 stores, these strategies are being enacted: the first 20 to 25 feet of store space displays best-sellers, magazines, computer software, and cassettes; storefront themes are changed every two weeks; phone and mail orders, major credit cards, and gift certificates are accepted; each store has a book club; special discount offers are used; and communications are aided by a monthly newsletter and a national radio show.[11]

Of particular concern to chain retailers and franchisers is maintaining a uniform image among all branches and units. However, despite the best planning, a number of factors may vary widely and have an effect on image. These factors include management and employee performance, consumer profiles, competitors, convenience in reaching the store, parking, safety, the ease of finding merchandise, and the quality of the surrounding area.

Sometimes retailers with good images receive negative publicity. This must be countered in order for the company to maintain its desired image. A few years ago, McDonald's had problems with a promotion it was using, called Glasses to Go. On the outside of these glasses were lead paint decals. An uproar arose when the lead content was disclosed, and although it was not proven harmful (the decals were on the outside of the glasses), parents were quite alarmed. But McDonald's voluntarily removed the glasses from its stores and thereby blunted the negative publicity. Because of its quick actions, McDonald's sales did not suffer.

There have been many other investigations of store image. Retailers should look at these studies as they develop and maintain their own store images.[12]

---

[9]Joan Bergmann, "How Bloomingdale's Evaluates Boutiques," *Stores* (April 1981), pp. 38–39; and Sandra Salmans, "The Sweet Smell of Success at Bloomingdale's," *New York Times* (December 21, 1984), pp. D1, D4.

[10]Steve Weiner, "Large Retailers Are Changing Strategy, Image by Remodeling Stores, Upgrading Product Lines," *Wall Street Journal* (July 10, 1984), p. 2; and "Penney, Sears Invest Billions to Update Retail Images," *Chain Store Age Executive* (February 1984), pp. 27–29.

[11]Bonnie K. Predd, "Marketing Writes New Chapter in Bookselling History," *Marketing News* (September 14, 1984), p. 51.

[12]A cross-section of these studies are Dennis Menezes and Norbert F. Elbert, "Alternative Semantic Scaling Formats for Measuring Store Image: An Evaluation," *Journal of Marketing Research*, Vol. 16 (February 1979), pp. 80–87; Robert N. Zelnio and Jean P. Gagnon, "The Construction and Testing of an Image Questionnaire," *Journal of the Academy of Marketing Science*, Vol. 9 (Summer 1981), pp. 288–298; and Jacob Jacoby and David Mazursky, "Linking Brand and Retailer Images—Do the Potential Risks Outweigh the Potential Benefits?" *Journal of Retailing*, Vol. 60 (Summer 1984), pp. 105–122.

Atmosphere

The creation of an image depends heavily on the atmosphere that the store develops. **Atmosphere** refers to the physical characteristics of the store that are used to develop an image and to draw customers. It is a major component of image.

The smells, sounds, sights, and so on of a store contribute greatly to the image that is projected to consumers. It is important that atmosphere be understood as the psychological feeling a customer gets when visiting a store or as the personality of the store.

Many consumers form impressions of a store before entering (because of store location, storefront, and so on) or upon entering (because of type of floors, width of aisles, and so on). These customers judge the store prior to closely examining products and prices. One study on store atmosphere found that it influences the enjoyment of the shopping experience, the time spent browsing and examining the store's offerings, the willingness to converse with store personnel, the tendency to spend more money than originally planned, and the likelihood of future patronage.[13]

Atmosphere can be divided into several elements: exterior, general interior, store layout, and displays. Table 12-2 contains a detailed breakdown of these elements.

Exterior

The exterior characteristics of a store have a strong impact on its image and should be planned accordingly.

The **storefront** is the total physical exterior of the store itself. It includes marquees, entrances, windows, lighting, and construction materials. Through the storefront, a retailer can present a conservative, progressive, lavish, discount, or other image to the consumer. A retailer should not underestimate the importance of the storefront as a major determinant of image, particularly for new customers. When passing through an unfamiliar business district or shopping center, consumers often judge a store by its exterior. Figure 12-1 shows an open storefront in a college department store. Figures 12-2 and 12-3 contain pictures of two attractively designed outside storefronts.

There are various alternatives that the retailer can consider when planning the basic storefront:

1. A modular structure can be used. In this instance, the building is a one-piece rectangle or square and sometimes attached to several stores.
2. A prefabricated (prefab) structure utilizes a store frame that is built in a factory and assembled at the store site.
3. A prototype store is used by franchisors and chains. Because a uniform image is sought, uniform storefronts are constructed.
4. A recessed storefront can be built. In this case, the store is located among several others. To lure customers, the storefront is recessed from the level of the other stores. Customers have to walk in a number of feet to examine the storefront.
5. A unique building design can be developed. For example, round structures are quite distinctive.

[13]Robert J. Donovan and John R. Rossiter, "Store Atmosphere: An Environmental Psychology Approach," *Journal of Retailing*, Vol. 58 (Spring 1982), pp. 34–57.

Table 12-2
The Elements of Atmosphere

1. Exterior
   a. Storefront
   b. Marquee
   c. Entrances
   d. Display windows
   e. Height of building
   f. Size of building
   g. Visibility
   h. Uniqueness
   i. Surrounding stores
   j. Surrounding area
   k. Parking
   l. Congestion

2. General interior
   a. Flooring
   b. Colors
   c. Lighting
   d. Scents, sounds
   e. Fixtures
   f. Wall textures
   g. Temperature
   h. Width of aisles
   i. Dressing facilities
   j. Vertical transportation
   k. Dead areas
   l. Personnel
   m. Self-service
   n. Products
   o. Prices (level and manner of displays)
   p. Placement of cash registers
   q. Modernization
   r. Cleanliness

3. Store layout
   a. Allocation of floor space for selling, merchandise, personnel, and customers
   b. Product groupings
   c. Traffic flow
   d. Space/product category
   e. Department locations
   f. Arrangements within departments

4. Interior (point-of-purchase) displays
   a. Assortment
   b. Theme-setting
   c. Ensemble
   d. Racks and cases
   e. Cut cases and dump bins
   f. Posters, signs, and cards
   g. Mobiles
   h. Wall decorations

In addition to the actual storefront, atmosphere can be created by trees, fountains, and benches placed in front of the store. These enhance the consumer's feelings about shopping and the store by establishing a relaxed environment.

A **marquee** is a sign that is used to display the store's name. The marquee can be painted or a neon light, printed or script, and alone or mixed with a slogan (trademark) and other information. To be effective, the marquee should stand out and attract attention. Image is influenced because a marquee can be gaudy and flashy or subdued and subtle. Probably the most widely known marquee in the world is the McDonald's golden arch, which some communities consider an environmental eyesore.

The entrances to the store should be designed well; and three major decisions must be made. First, the number of entrances is determined. Many smaller stores have only one entrance. Larger department stores may have four to eight or more entrances. A store hoping to draw vehicular and pedestrian traffic should have at least two entrances (one in the front of the store to lure pedestrians, another in the rear of the store adjacent to the parking lot). Because front and back entrances serve different purposes, they should be designed separately. A factor limiting the number of entrances is the problem of pilferage. Some urban stores have closed off entrances to reduce the size of their security forces.

Figure 12-1   An Open Storefront

A distinctive open storefront for Campus Connections at the RIT on-campus department store. Courtesy of Rochester Institute of Technology Communications Department.

Figure 12-2   The Store Exterior of Youth Centre in Bloomfield, Connecticut

Courtesy Selame Design.

Figure 12-3   The Integrated Exterior and Interior of Store 24, a convenience store in Waltham, Massachusetts

Courtesy Selame Design.

Second, the type of entrance is planned from among many options. The doorway is selected: revolving; electric, self-opening; regular, push-pull; or climate-controlled open entry. The climate-controlled entry is an open entrance with a curtain of warm or cold air, set at the same temperature as inside the store. This entry makes the store inviting, reduces pedestrian traffic congestion, and enables customers to see inside the store. The outside flooring is chosen: cement, tile, or carpeting. Lighting is ascertained: direct, fluorescent, white–colors, and/or flashing–constant.

Third, the walkways are considered. A wide, lavish walkway creates a very different image and mood from a narrow, constrained one. In the construction of the storefront, ample room must be provided for the walkways. Large window displays may be very attractive, but customers are unhappy when there is insufficient space for a comfortable entry into the store.

Display windows serve two main purposes: to identify the store and its offerings, and to induce customers to enter. Display windows give a wide variety of information about a store. By showing a representative sample of its product offering, the store can create an overall image. By showing fashion or seasonal merchandise, the store can show that it is contemporary. By showing sale merchandise, the store can lure price-conscious consumers. By showing eye-catching displays that have little to do with its product offering, the store can attract the attention of pedestrians. By showing public service messages, the store can show its concern for the community (e.g., a window display for the Jerry Lewis Telethon).

Considerable planning is necessary to develop good display windows. More and more, larger stores are employing specialists to set up their displays properly. Window decisions include number, size, shape, color, theme, and changes per year. Some stores, particularly in shopping centers, are turning away from display windows and constructing solid buildings. These stores feel that vehicular patrons are not lured by expensive, time-consuming outside display windows.

The height and the size of the exterior building also contribute to a store's image. The height of a building can be disguised or nondisguised. Disguised building height occurs when part of the store is beneath ground level. As a result, the building is not so intimidating to consumers who are turned off by a large, impersonal structure. Nondisguised building height is when the entire store can be seen by pedestrians (all floors are ground level or higher). This is most often true of small stores. The overall size of a building cannot really be disguised; the target market should be researched for a correlation of store size and patronage. An intimate boutique image cannot be generated with a block-long building. Neither can a department store image be linked to a quarter-block site.

Few retailers are able to succeed without good exterior visibility. This means that pedestrian and/or vehicular traffic can clearly see the storefront or marquee. For this reason, a store located behind a bus stop has poor visibility for vehicular traffic and pedestrians across the street. Many retailers who operate near highways must use billboards for visibility because drivers quickly pass by.

Visibility is developed through a combination of storefront characteristics. The objective is to make the store appear unique, to make it stand out somehow, and catch the consumer's eye. A distinctive store design; an elaborate marquee; recessed, open-air entrances; decorative windows; and different building height and building size are one grouping of storefront features that can attract consumers through uniqueness. In the process, a store image is fostered. Figure 12-4 shows a unique storefront.

Uniqueness, although it provides excellent visibility, is not without its problems. An example is Macy's in Elmhurst, Queens, New York, which is a "store-in-the-round."

Figure 12-4   A Unique Storefront
Ivey's Florida store in the Pinellas Square Mall, Pinellas Park, Florida. Reprinted by permission.

The department store, located on a square city block, is round-shaped. Parking is provided on each level of the store, making the walking distances of customers very short. The problems with the store-in-the-round are that a rectangular store provides greater floor space on a lot of the same size; convenient on-floor parking may minimize customer shopping on other floors; added entrances increase chances for pilferage; customers dislike inclined and circular driving; and architectural costs are high for unique buildings.

When the retailer is planning a store's exterior, the surrounding stores and the surrounding area should be examined. Each contributes to the store's image, regardless of the retailer's distinctive storefront and building. The surrounding stores present an image to consumers. The image may be progressive, conservative, high price, personal service, and so on. This overall area image rubs off on the individual retailer because consumers tend to have a general image of a shopping center or a business district. Therefore, the individual storefront should be distinctive but not contradictory to the image of the area chosen by the retailer to do business.

The surrounding area includes the demographics and the life-styles of people living near the store. Store image is affected by the type of neighborhood in which it is located. An unfavorable atmosphere exists if vandalism and crime are high, the citizens living near the store are not part of the target market, and the area is rundown.

Parking facilities can add to or detract from a store's atmosphere. Plentiful, free, nearby parking (with large parking spaces) creates a much more positive atmosphere than scarce, costly, distant parking (with tiny parking spaces). Countless potential shoppers may never enter the store if they drive around looking for on-street parking spaces, and not finding them, they go elsewhere or return home disgruntled. Other customers may run in and out of the store so that they can complete their shopping before the parking meters expire. In assessing parking facilities, retailers should also be aware that some customers may have a limit to the distance they will walk from a parking space to the most distant stores, and many customers dislike multilevel garages (because of discomfort in driving or a concern for safety).

Allied with the parking problem is that of congestion. The store's atmosphere is diminished when its parking lot, sidewalks, and entrances are jammed. Consumers who feel crushed in the crowd spend less time shopping and are in poorer moods than those who feel comfortable.

General Interior

Once the customer is inside the store, there are numerous elements that affect his or her perception of it. Figure 12-5 contains an example of a well-integrated store interior. The general interior elements of atmosphere are described here and shown in Table 12-2.

Flooring can be made of cement, wood, linoleum, carpet, earth, and so on. A plush, thick carpet creates one kind of image, and a cement floor causes another.[14] Because customers use cues to develop their store perceptions, the materials used in floors are important. As an example, a high-quality shoe store uses thick carpeting; a discount, pick-a-shoe store often uses linoleum.

[14]See "Flooring Functions as a Funnel as Well as a Fashion Feature," *Chain Store Age Executive* (February 1985), p. 30; and "Shiny Floors Can Reflect Badly on Retailers' Safety Record," *Chain Store Age Executive* (February 1985), pp. 35, 38.

Figure 12-5   A Well-Integrated Store Interior
A store interior photo of the main floor of Neiman-Marcus, Dallas, Texas, as it appeared for the "Britain: Then and Now" theme. Courtesy Neiman-Marcus.

Colors and lighting affect the store's image.[15] Bright, vibrant colors contribute to a different atmosphere than light pastels or plain white walls. Lighting can be direct–indirect, white–colors, constant–flashing. For instance, a jeans boutique uses bright colors and bright, flashing lights to establish one atmosphere, and a maternity dress shop utilizes pastel colors and indirect lighting to foster a different atmosphere. Recently, Carson, Pirie, Scott & Co. (a Chicago-based department-store chain) replaced the light-and-dark-brown interior colors it had used for almost 50 years with a gray-and-white color scheme. It noted that the change was "part of a total plan to convey an image that is coordinated, contemporary, sophisticated, and fashionable."[16]

Scents and sounds are used to influence the customer's mood. A pet store wants

[15]See Joseph A. Bellizzi, Ayn E. Crowley, and Ronald W. Hasty, "The Effects of Color in Store Design," *Journal of Retailing*, Vol. 59 (Spring 1983), pp. 21–45; and "Resourceful Lighting Can Transform a Store into Theater," *Chain Store Age Executive* (February 1985), p. 32.
[16]Lynn Reiling, " 'Video Shock' Gives Retailer Low-Cost Promotional Boost," *Marketing News* (February 1, 1985), pp. 22, 24.

the natural scents and sounds of its animals to woo customers. A cosmetics store hopes that its array of perfume scents will result in sales. A record store plays its top sellers. A beauty salon plays soft music or rock, depending on its target market. A restaurant uses the scents from the kitchen to increase customers' appetites. Slow-tempo music in supermarkets encourages consumers to move more slowly (and purchase more) than fast-tempo music, which speeds behavior.[17] In each case, a favorable atmosphere is sought.

Store fixtures should not be planned only on the basis of their utility but also because of their aesthetics. Pipes, plumbing, vents, beams, doors, storage rooms, and display racks and tables should be considered in the interior decorating. A store seeking a high-price, high-quality image should disguise and decorate the fixtures. A store seeking a low-price, low-quality image should leave the fixtures exposed. Because the latter choice is inexpensive, it reinforces the desired image.

Wall textures can enhance or diminish a store's image. Prestigious stores often employ fancy wallpaper. Department stores use flat wallpaper. Discount stores have barren walls. Prestige stores might also have elaborate chandeliers while discount stores have simple lighting fixtures.

The customer's mood is affected by the temperature of the store and its manner of achieving it. A customer is uncomfortable if there is insufficient heat in the winter and coolness in the summer. This can hasten his or her trip through the store. In another vein, the store's image is influenced by the use of central air-conditioning, unit air-conditioning, fans, or open windows.

The width of the aisles has an impact on store image. Wide, uncrowded aisles create a better atmosphere than narrow, crowded aisles. Customers shop longer and spend more when they are not pushed and shoved while walking or looking at merchandise. In Boston, Filene's basement has many items at bargain prices; however, overcrowding keeps some customers away.

Dressing facilities may be elaborate, plain, or nonexistent. A prestige store has carpeted, private dressing facilities. An average store has linoleum, semiprivate facilities. A discount store has small, linoleum, semiprivate stalls or no dressing facilities at all. For a number of customers, a store's dressing facilities (and their maintenance) is a major factor in store selection. Atmosphere and type of dressing facility are closely intertwined.

Multilevel stores must have some form of vertical transportation. The choices are elevator, escalator, and/or stairs. Larger stores may have a combination of all three. Traditionally the operator-run elevator has appeared in finer stores, and stairs have appeared in discount stores. Today escalators are quite popular and are gaining in stature. They provide consumers with a quiet ride and a panoramic view of the store. Finer stores decorate their escalators with fountains, shrubs, and trees. The placement and design of vertical transportation determine its contribution to atmosphere. Stairs remain important for discount and smaller stores.

Lights, beams, doors, rest rooms, dressing facilities, vertical transportation, and so on leave dead areas for the retailer. **Dead areas** are awkward spaces where normal displays cannot be set up. In many instances, it is not possible for these areas to be used profitably or attractively. However, retailers are learning to improve their dead

---

[17]Ronald E. Milliman, "Using Background Music to Affect the Behavior of Supermarket Shoppers," *Journal of Marketing*, Vol. 46 (Summer 1982), pp. 86–91.

areas. For example, mirrors are attached to exit doors. Vending machines are located near rest rooms. Advertisements are placed in dressing rooms.

The most creative use of a dead area involves the escalator. For a long time, retailers viewed it as an ugly fixture in the middle of the store. Now it is evaluated differently. The escalator enables the consumer to view the whole floor of the store, and sales of impulse items go up when placed at the entrance or exit of the escalator. In addition, most retailers build their escalators so that customers must get off at each floor and pass by attractive displays.

The number, manner, and appearance of store personnel reflect the store's atmosphere. Polite, well-groomed, knowledgeable personnel generate a positive atmosphere. Ill-mannered, poorly groomed, unknowing personnel establish a negative one. In general, research findings show that customers like to deal with personnel having demographics similar to themselves; therefore, store personnel should resemble the target market as closely as possible. The store that uses self-service minimizes its personnel and creates a discount, impersonal image. A store cannot develop a prestige image if it is set up for self-service.

The products that a retailer sells influence his or her image. Top-of-the-line merchandise yields one kind of image, and bottom-of-the-line merchandise yields another. The mood of the customer is affected accordingly.

Store prices contribute to image in two ways. First, the level of prices yields a perception of store image in the consumer's mind. Second, the way that prices are displayed is a vital part of atmosphere. Prestige stores have few or no price displays and rely upon hidden price tags. Sales are de-emphasized. Discount stores accentuate price displays and show prices in large numbers. The placement of cash registers is associated with the type of price displays a store uses. A prestige store hides its cash registers behind posts or in employee rooms. Discount stores locate their cash registers centrally and have large signs to point them out.

The technology of the store and the modernization of its building and fixtures also have an impact on image. A store that employs current technology, such as computerized cash registers and automated inventory-movement procedures, impresses customers with its efficiency and speed of operations. A store that uses slower, older techniques can have long lines and impatient customers. A store with a modernized building (new storefront, marquee, and so on) and new fixtures (lights, floors, walls, and so on) fosters a more favorable atmosphere than one with older facilities.

A 1984 survey of 120 large discount chains, department-store chains, supermarket chains, and drugstore chains yielded these findings about store remodeling:

- Renovations are easier, faster, and less costly than building or opening new stores.
- Improving store appearance, updating facilities, expansion, and the need to reallocate space are the main reasons for remodeling.
- On average, remodeling costs $16.43 per square foot and results in strong sales and profit increases after completion. Supermarkets spend the most per foot on remodeling, drugstores the least.
- The average life span for fixtures is 9.5 years; it is 13.5 years for ceilings.
- Ninety-seven per cent of stores are kept open during a renovation.[18]

---

[18]"Store Remodeling: How Profitable Can It Be?" *Chain Store Age Executive* (April 1984), pp. 17–20. See also "Store of the Future: On a Hot Streak at Sears," *Chain Store Age Executive* (September 1984), p. 48.

Last, but certainly not least, the retailer must plan for the cleanliness of the store. No matter how impressive the store exterior and interior, an unkempt store will be received negatively by customers. Noted a Filene's (a Boston department store) manager about cleanliness:

> I think it's the most important thing in a store. It sets the tone. Housekeeping is many things; keeping showcases clean; keeping bases clean where they are rapped by the vacuum cleaner. Everybody thinks of a department store as the place where the merchandise is. But are your toilet facilities taken care of properly? Are the trash baskets empty? It's not merely going through with a vacuum cleaner. It's the cleaning of the doors, of the countertops, of dust on top of seven foot units.[19]

Store Layout

Next the specifics of store layout are planned and set up.

Allocation of Floor Space

Floor space is allocated among selling, merchandise, personnel, and customers. Each store has a total square footage available and must divide it among these components. **Selling space** is the area set aside for displays of merchandise, interactions between sales personnel and customers, demonstrations, and so on. A retailer such as a supermarket or other self-service business usually has selling space as a large portion of total store space.

Merchandise space is the area where nondisplayed items are kept in stock or inventory. A shoe store is a good example of a retailer whose merchandise space takes up a large percentage of total store space.

Store personnel require space for changing clothes, lunch and coffee breaks, and rest room facilities. Retailers try to minimize **personnel space** by insisting on off-the-job clothes changing and other tactics. Because floor space is so valuable, that part allotted to personnel is strictly controlled. However, when planning personnel space, the retailer should consider employee morale and personal appearance.

Customers also require space, and this space contributes greatly to a store's image. **Customer space** can include a lounge, benches and/or chairs, dressing facilities, rest room facilities, a restaurant, vertical transportation, smoking areas, a nursery, parking, and wide aisles. Low-image retailers skimp on or omit many of these areas; retailers with consumer-oriented images provide their customers with adequate amounts of space for all or most of these factors.

The retailer cannot go any further in his or her store-layout planning until floor space is properly allocated among selling, merchandise, personnel, and customers. Without this allocation, the retailer has no conception of the space available for displays, signs, rest rooms, and so on.

Classification of Store Offerings

The store's offerings are then classified into product groupings. Four types of groupings and their combinations can be employed: functional, purchase motivation, market seg-

---

[19]Jules Abend, "Neat and Clean," *Stores* (November 1983), p. 15.

ment, and storability. In **functional product groupings**, the store's merchandise is categorized and displayed by common end uses. For example, a men's clothing store might carry these functional groups: shirt–tie–cuff links–tie pins; shoes–laces–shoe polish; T-shirts–undershorts–socks; suits; and sports jackets–slacks.

Purchase motivation product groupings appeal to the consumer's urge to buy a product and the amount of time he or she is willing to spend in shopping. A committed customer with time to shop will visit the upper floors and extremities of a store; a browsing customer with little time to spend will gravitate to displays on the first floor, near the exit. A retailer can capitalize on this fact by grouping his or her products by purchase motivation. Examine the first floor of any department store. The items located there are impulse products and other quick purchases. On the third floor of the department store are items that encourage and require thoughtful shopping.

Market segment product groupings can be used. In this instance, all products appealing to a given target market are grouped together. Some examples are a clothing store dividing its products into juniors', misses', and ladies' clothing categories; a record store separating its merchandise into rock, jazz, classical, rhythm and blues, country and western, and popular music sections; an art gallery placing its paintings in different price groups; and a toy store setting up two distinct displays for children and adult games.

For products requiring special handling, **storability product groupings** are employed. A supermarket has freezer, refrigerator, and room-temperature sections. A florist keeps some flowers in a refrigerator and others at room temperature. The same is true for a bakery or a fruit store.

Progressive retailers often use a combination of product groupings and plan their store layouts accordingly. In addition to the considerations already covered, provisions must be made for minimizing shoplifting and pilferage. This means positioning product groups away from corners and doors.

Determination of a Traffic-Flow Pattern

The traffic-flow pattern of the store is determined next. There are two basic traffic-flow alternatives available to a retailer: straight (gridiron) and curving (free flow). A **straight traffic flow** means that displays and aisles are constructed in a rectangular or gridiron pattern, as shown in Figure 12-6. A **curving traffic flow** means that displays and aisles are constructed in a free-flowing pattern, as shown in Figure 12-7.

The straight traffic pattern is most often used by supermarkets, discount stores, hardware stores, and other convenience stores. This layout has several advantages:

- An austere, efficient atmosphere is created.
- Customers can shop quickly; regular customers particularly desire clearly marked, distinct aisles and develop a routine pattern through the store.
- All available floor space is utilized.
- Inventory control and security are simplified.
- Self-service is possible, thereby reducing labor costs.

The disadvantages of the gridiron are a cold atmosphere, limited browsing, and rushed shopping behavior.

An Example of a Straight (Gridiron) Traffic Pattern
in Big "B" Food Warehouse (Baltimore, Maryland)

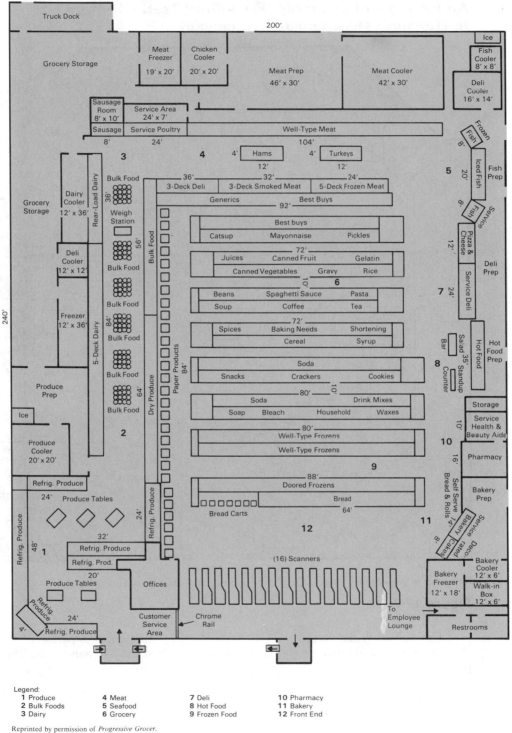

Reprinted by permission of *Progressive Grocer*.

Figure 12-6

Legend:
1 Produce   4 Meat   7 Deli   10 Pharmacy
2 Bulk Foods 5 Seafood   8 Hot Food   11 Bakery
3 Dairy   6 Grocery   9 Frozen Food 12 Front End

An Example of a Curving (Free-Flow) Traffic Pattern in Hudson's (East Lansing, Michigan)

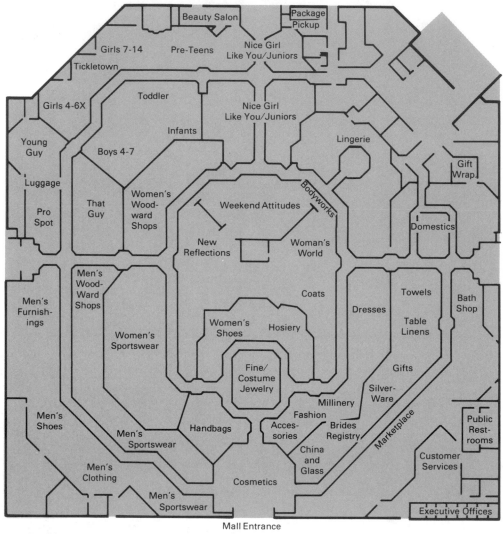

Mall Entrance

Reprinted by permission of Stores. Copyright National Retail Merchants Association.

Figure 12-7

The curved traffic pattern is most often used by boutiques, department stores, clothing stores, and other shopping stores. There are several benefits from this approach:

- A friendly atmosphere is developed.
- Shoppers do not feel rushed and will browse around.

- Customers are encouraged to walk through the store in any direction or pattern they desire.
- Impulse or unplanned purchases are increased.

The disadvantages of the free flow are the encouragement of loitering, potential customer confusion, wasted floor space, difficulties in inventory control and security, and high labor-intensiveness. In addition, free-flow displays are often more expensive than standardized gridiron displays.

Determination of Space Needs

The space for each product category is then ascertained. Selling as well as nonselling space must be considered in any calculations. Two approaches are possible, the model stock method or the space-productivity ratio. Under the **model stock approach**, the retailer tabulates the amount of floor space necessary to carry a proper assortment of merchandise. Clothing stores and shoe stores are examples of retailers who use the model stock method. With the **sales-productivity ratio**, the retailer assigns floor space on the basis of sales or profits per foot. Highly profitable product categories receive large chunks of space; marginally profitable categories receive limited space. Food stores and bookstores are examples of retailers who use space-productivity ratios in planning floor space.

Mapping Out Locations

Department locations are mapped out at this point. For multilevel stores, this procedure includes allocating departments to floors and laying out the individual floors. What product categories should be placed on each floor? What should the layout of each floor be? The single-level store is concerned with only the second issue. Generally speaking, the following questions have to be considered:

- Which products should be placed in the basement and on the first floor, the second floor, and so on?
- On a given floor, how should the groupings be placed in relation to doors, vertical transportation, and so on?
- Where should impulse or unplanned product categories be located in relation to categories that consumers preplan to buy?
- Where should convenience products be situated?
- How should associated product categories be aligned?
- Where should seasonal and off-season products be placed?
- Where should space-consuming categories like furniture be located?
- How close should product displays and stored inventory be to each other?
- What travel patterns do consumers follow once they enter the store?
- How can lines be avoided near the cash register, and how can the overall appearance of store crowding be averted?

Arrangement of Individual Products

Individual products are then arranged within departments. A number of criteria may be used in the positioning of individual items. The most profitable items and brands receive favorable locations where consumer traffic is heavy. Products may also be arranged by package size, price, color, brand, level of personal service required, and/ or customer interest.

End-aisle display positions, eye-level positions, and checkout counter positions are most likely to increase sales for individual items. Continuity of locations is also important; shifts in store layout may decrease sales. The least desirable display position is knee or ankle level, because consumers do not like to bend down.

Individual retailers should conduct their own research and experiments to measure the effects of different product positions on sales. It must also be remembered that the objectives of the manufacturer and the retailer are quite dissimilar. The manufacturer wants the sales of his or her brand to be maximized and therefore pushes for eye-level, wide, end-aisle locations. On the other hand, the retailer is concerned with maximizing total store sales.

Retailers who utilize self-service have special considerations to make. The gridiron layout is normally used to minimize customer confusion. Similarly, aisles, displays, and merchandise must be clearly marked. A large selling space, with on-floor assortments, is necessary. Cash registers must be plentiful and accessible. It is difficult to sell complex and/or expensive items through self-service.

Interior (Point-of-Purchase) Displays

After the store layout is fully detailed, the retailer devises interior displays. These **point-of-purchase displays** provide consumers with information, add to store atmosphere, and serve a substantial promotional role.[20] In this section, several types and forms of displays are described. Most retailers use combinations of several or all of these kinds of displays.

An **assortment display** is one in which the retailer exhibits a wide range of merchandise for the customer. With an open assortment, the customer is encouraged to feel and/or try on a number of products. Pocketbooks, greeting cards, and magazines are the kinds of products for which retailers use open assortments. Recently, a number of supermarkets have returned to a practice that they had all but abandoned—selling items such as candy in open, bulk displays.[21] With a closed assortment, the customer is encouraged to look at a variety of merchandise but not touch it or try it on. Shirts, games, and records are prepackaged items that the customer is not allowed to open before buying.

A **theme-setting display** positions the product offering in a thematic environment or setting. A theme enables the retailer to generate a specific atmosphere or mood. A store like Neiman-Marcus annually re-creates a foreign country in the store. Other stores often change their displays to reflect seasons or special events; some have their employees dress to fit the occasion. All or part of a store may be adapted to a theme, such as Washington's Birthday, Columbus Day, Valentine's Day, Independence Day,

---

[20]See John A. Quelch and Kristina Cannon-Bonventre, "Better Marketing at the Point of Purchase," *Harvard Business Review*, Vol. 61 (November–December 1983), pp. 162–169; "Panelists Comment on Drugstore Merchandising Efforts," *Marketing News* (December 7, 1984), pp. 17–18; Glenn Snyder, "Special Fixturing Helps Non-Foods Win Attention," *Progressive Grocer* (October 1984), pp. 91–96; and Gary Vineberg, "Self-Service Shoe Stores Rack in Bigger Profits," *Chain Store Age Executive* (January 1985), pp. 37–39.
[21]Dave Galanti, "Grocers Stock Super Candy Selection," *Advertising Age* (September 27, 1984), pp. 47–49; and "Good News/Bad News About Bulk Foods," *Progressive Grocer* (February 1985), pp. 43–46.

Figure 12-8   An Ensemble Display

Coordinated male mannequins surrounded by related clothing displays at J. C. Penney. Courtesy J. C. Penney.

Lunch with a Star, or other concept. Each special theme is enacted to attract customers' attention and make shopping enjoyable, not a chore. For example, Marshall Field (a Chicago-based chain) invested two years and more than $5 million for the personnel, events, displays, advertising, and supplies involved with Christmas 1984. It planned for 30 per cent of annual sales and 70 per cent of annual profits during the six weeks before Christmas.[22]

Ensemble displays have become very popular in recent years. Instead of grouping and displaying merchandise in separate categories (e.g., shoe department, sock department, pants department, shirt department, sports jacket department), complete ensembles are displayed. For example, a mannequin could be dressed in a matching combination of shoes, socks, pants, shirt, and sports jacket, and these items would be readily available in one department. Customers are pleased with the ease of a purchase and like being able to envision an entire outfit. See Figure 12-8.

Rack displays are heavily used by clothing retailers, houseware retailers, and others. These racks have a primarily functional use: to neatly hang or present the products. The major problems are rusty pipes and cluttering. Current technology allows retailers to use sliding, disconnecting, contracting, attractive rack displays. **Case displays** are employed to exhibit heavier, bulkier items than racks hold. Records, books, prepackaged goods, and sweaters are contained in case displays. See Figure 12-9.

[22]Steve Weiner, "Marshall Field's Does Christmas in a Big Way with an Eye on Profits," *Wall Street Journal* (November 29, 1984), pp. 1, 31.

Figure 12-9   Rack Displays

These are some of the very attractive rack displays used by K mart to display clothing in its stores. Reprinted by permission.

Cut cases are inexpensive displays, in which the merchandise is left in its original cartons. Supermarkets and discount houses frequently set up cut-case displays. These cases do not create a warm atmosphere. Neither do **dump bins**, which are cases that house piles of sale clothing, marked-down books, and so on. Instead of neat, precise

Figure 12-10   Dump Bin Displays
These dump bin displays utilize copper clad surfaces. D. H. Holmes Suburban Department Store, New Orleans, Louisiana. Courtesy Copper Development Association Inc.

displays, dump bins contain open assortments of roughly handled items. The advantages of cut cases and dump bins are reduced display costs and a low-price image. Figure 12-10 shows a dump bin display.

Posters, signs, and cards can be used to dress up all types of displays, including cut cases and dump bins. These tools provide information about in-store product locations and stimulate customers to shop. **Mobiles**, a type of hanging display with parts that move, especially in response to air currents, serve the same purpose—but are more appealing to the eye and stand out. Wall decorations also enhance a store's atmosphere and add to displays. Wall decorations are particularly useful with thematic displays and ensemble displays.

Customer Services

The number and variety of customer services that a store provides have a strong impact on and contribute to the image that is created. To use customer services successfully, a retailer should first outline an overall service strategy and then plan individual services.[23]

Developing a Service Strategy

In developing a customer-service strategy, a retailer has to make decisions involving the range, level, choice, price, measurement, and retention of services.

What services are primary and ancillary for the retailer? **Primary customer services** are those that are considered basic ingredients in the retail offering and must be provided. Examples are credit for a furniture retailer, new car preparation for an automobile dealer, and a liberal return policy for a gift shop. These services form an essential part of the retailer's offering, and a store could not stay in business without them.

Ancillary customer services are extra ingredients that add to the retail offering. A retailer can adequately cater to a target market without these services. Examples are delivery for a supermarket, an extra warranty for an automobile dealer, gift wrapping for a toy dealer, and credit for a discounter.

It is vital that the retailer determine which customer services are primary and which are ancillary for his or her particular store. Primary services for one retailer, such as delivery, may be ancillary for another. Remember that primary services have to be used; ancillary services enhance a store's competitive advantage but are not required.

What level of services is necessary to complement the store's image? A prestige store has more services defined as primary than a discount store, because consumers expect a prestige store to supply a wide range of services as part of the store's basic retail offering. This is not true of the discount store. In addition, the performance of services is different. As an example, the customers of a prestige store may expect elaborate gift-wrapping facilities, valet parking, a restaurant, and a ladies' room attendant, whereas the customers of a discount store may expect cardboard gift boxes, self-service parking, a lunch counter, and an unattended ladies' room. In these instances, the generic services are the same; however, the level of the services is quite dissimilar.

Should a choice of customer services be furnished? Some retailers allow their customers to choose among levels of service; others provide one level of service. For instance, a store may honor several credit cards or only its own. Trade-ins may be allowed on some items or all. Television warranties may have optional extensions or fixed lengths. A store may supply one-month, three-month, and six-month payment plans or may insist on a one-month payment period.

Should services be free? Two factors are causing a number of retailers to charge

---

[23]See, for example, Jules Abend, "Aiming to Please," *Stores* (October 1984), pp. 50–54 ff.; Bernie Whalen, "Retail Customer Service: Marketing's Last Frontier," *Marketing News* (March 15, 1985), pp. 10, 18; and Albert D. Bates and Jamie G. Didion, "Special Services Can Personalize Retail Environment," *Marketing News* (April 12, 1985), p. 13.

for customer services: rapidly increasing costs and consumer behavior. Delivery, gift wrapping, and other services are labor-intensive, and their costs are rapidly rising. Also it has been found that customers are more likely to remain at home for a delivery or a service call if a fee is imposed. Without a fee, retailers may have to deliver an item two or three times to find someone at home. In settling on a free or fee service strategy, the retailer must determine which services are primary (these are usually free) and which are ancillary (these are provided for a fee). Furthermore, competitors and profit margins should be watched closely, and the target market should be surveyed. When setting service fees, the retailer must also decide whether his or her objective is to break even or to make a profit on the services.

How can the benefits of services be measured against their costs? Retailers provide services that attract and retain consumers. Their goal is to increase store sales and profits. Ancillary services that do not increase sales and profits should not be offered. Unfortunately, little investigation of the benefit-cost ratios of various services has been undertaken. Therefore, the retailer must plan ancillary services on the basis of experience, competitive actions, and customer comments. When the retailer's costs of providing these services increase, this increase should be passed on to the consumer.

How can services be terminated? Once a store achieves an established image, consumers react poorly to any reduction of services. Nonetheless, inefficient and costly ancillary services might be discontinued. In discontinuing services, the retailer's best strategy is to go on the offensive and explain why the service is being terminated and how the customer will benefit through low prices and so on. Many times the retailer chooses a middle ground, charging for previously free services and allowing the customers who want the services to continue to receive them.

Planning Individual Services

After a broad customer-service strategy is outlined, individual services are planned. A recent study found that the most popular services provided by department stores include gift wrapping (89 per cent), layaway plans (73 per cent), pay telephones (72 per cent), bridal registry (68 per cent), car parking (68 per cent), restaurant (50 per cent), women's beauty salon (47 per cent), carpet installation (41 per cent), baby strollers available (39 per cent), and fur storage (37 per cent).[24] The range of customer services described in this section is shown in Table 12-3.

Today, the vast majority of retailers allow their customers to make credit purchases. The last major holdouts, supermarkets and discount stores, now usually accept personal checks with proper identification. Whereas smaller and medium-sized retailers rely on bank cards and companies such as American Express to process purchases made on credit, larger retailers generally have their own credit systems and credit cards. In greater numbers, larger retailers have begun to accept outside credit cards in addition to their own.

The role of credit in retail purchases can be seen through the following:

• Visa, MasterCard, American Express, Carte Blanche, and Diners Club are just some of the national credit cards accepted by various retailers.
• Well over half of department store and specialty store purchases are made on credit.

[24]Marian Burk Rothman, "Hot New Services? Health Care!" *Stores* (June 1980), p. 52.

Table 12-3
Typical Customer Services

1. Credit
2. Delivery
3. Alterations and installations
4. Packaging (gift wrapping)
5. Complaints and returns
6. Gift certificates
7. Trade-ins
8. Trial purchases
9. Special sales for regular customers
10. Extended store hours
11. Mail and telephone orders
12. Miscellaneous
    a. Bridal registry
    b. Interior designers
    c. Personal shoppers
    d. Ticket outlets
    e. Parking
    f. Water fountains
    g. Rest rooms
    h. Restaurant
    i. Baby sitting
    j. Fitting rooms
    k. Shopping bags
    l. Information

- Together, Sears and J. C. Penney have about 65 million holders of their credit cards. In early 1985, Sears also announced plans to distribute a general-purpose credit card to compete with bank cards.[25]
- Computerization has eased the credit process and made it more efficient, thus encouraging more retailers to accept some form of credit system. See Figure 12-11.

Retailer-generated credit cards have four advantages. The retailer saves the 3 to 6 per cent of sales that it would have to pay for outside card sales. The customer is encouraged to shop at a given store because the card is not recognized elsewhere. Contact can be maintained with customers, and information learned about them. Card design contributes to overall store image. There are also disadvantages to retailer cards: startup costs are high; the retailer must worry about unpaid bills and slow cash flow; credit checks and follow-up tasks must be performed; and customers without the retailer's card may be discouraged from making purchases.

Bank and commercial credit cards enable small and medium-sized retailers to offer credit, generate increased business for all types of retailers, appeal to tourists and mobile consumers, provide advertising support from the sponsor, reduce bad debts, eliminate startup costs for the retailer, and provide information. However, these cards do charge a service fee for each transaction (based on the purchase amount) and do not engender store loyalty.

[25]Steve Weiner and Jeff Bailey, "Sears Roebuck Plans to Issue New Credit Card," *Wall Street Journal* (February 21, 1985), p. 12.

Figure 12-11   A Credit-Authorization System

Courtesy Omron Business Systems, Inc.

As noted, both types of credit cards enhance retailer's information capabilities. They provide data on sales, customers, and branch store performance. For example, Buffums, a 15-unit California-based department store chain, has its own credit card. The card plan is compatible with the company's computer system, enables 1,000 credit applications to be processed at one location in a week (and provides customers with

Table 12-4
Credit Payment Plans

Example 1: Option Account

Purchases in June	$100.00	
End-of-month bill		$100.00
Payment		$100.00
Balance due		$ 0.00

Example 2: Revolving Account

Purchases in June	$100.00	
End-of-month bill		$100.00
Payment		$ 50.00
Balance Due		$ 50.00
Purchases in July	$ 0.00	
Balance from June	$ 50.00	
One month's interest	$ .75	
(at 1½% per month)		
Total end-of-month bill		$ 50.75
Payment		$ 50.75
Balance due		$ 0.00

Example 3: Revolving Account

Purchases in June	$400.00	
End-of-month bill		$400.00
Payment		$100.00
Balance due		$300.00
Purchases in July	$400.00	
Balance from June	$300.00	
Interest on balance	$ 4.50	
Total end-of-month bill		$704.50
Payment		$200.00
Balance due		$504.50
Purchases in August	$ 0.00	
Balance from July	$504.50	
Interest on balance	$ 7.57	
Total end-of-month bill		$512.07
Payment		$512.07
Balance due		$ 0.00

instant credit), can be used with OCR-A product tags, and can be read by a wand rather than punched into a cash register.[26]

All bank credit cards and some retailer credit cards are based on "revolving accounts." With a **revolving credit account**, a customer charges items during the month and is billed at the end of the month on the basis of the outstanding balance. An **option credit account** is a form of the revolving account; no interest is assessed if the consumer pays the bill in full when it is due. See Table 12-4, Example 1. However, should the customer make a partial payment, he or she will be assessed interest monthly on the unpaid amount. See Table 12-4, Examples 2 and 3.

The customer receives a credit limit with a revolving account, and his or her total balance cannot exceed this limit. Because of the recent high costs of money, many states have allowed retailer and bank credit cards to raise their interest rates, some to 2 or more per cent per month (an annual rate of 24 per cent or more) on unpaid balances.

Some retailers use **open credit accounts**. In this arrangement, the consumer must pay his or her bill in full when it comes due. Partial, revolving payments are not permitted. A consumer operating with an open account is also given a credit limit.

Under a **monthly payment credit account**, the consumer pays for a product in equal monthly installments. Interest is usually charged. As an illustration, a consumer buys a $300 camera and pays for it over 12 months. Equal monthly payments of $27.50 ($25 principal and $2.50 interest) yield a total cost of $330 for the camera. The true interest rate is 18.46 per cent on the average monthly balance.[27]

Deferred billing enables regular charge customers to buy merchandise and not pay for it for several months, with no interest charge. Deferred billing is frequently used as a Christmas promotional tool. Customers are encouraged to buy in November and December and not pay until March.

A **layaway plan** allows any customer to give the store a deposit to hold a product. When the customer completes payment, he or she takes home the item. In the meantime, the consumer does not have to worry about the store's running out of stock.

COD (collect on delivery) lets the customer receive a product before paying for it. Payment in full must be made when the merchandise is delivered. Direct marketers frequently use COD.

It should be apparent that retailers have a wide flexibility in choosing a credit strategy. The strategy that best fits the store's image, customers, and needs should be selected.

While the trend toward credit-card usage continues, some retailers have moved in the opposite direction. For example, Arco recently terminated its service-station credit cards in order to reduce costs and lower gasoline prices.[28] In some settings, discounts for cash payments also seem feasible.[29]

A retailer has three considerations in setting up delivery service: the method of transportation, ownership versus rental of equipment, and timing. The method of trans-

---

[26]"New Charge Card Cuts Costs, Adds Convenience," *Chain Store Age Executive* (January 1981), p. 131.

[27]The computation for this = ($30 interest)/[(½) ($300 initial principal + $25 last month principal)] = ($30)/[(½) ($325)] = ($30)/($162.50) = 18.46 per cent.

[28]Liz Murphy, "Pumping Up for the Great California Gasoline War," *Sales & Marketing Management* (April 2, 1984), pp. 51–54.

[29]Michael Levy and Charles A. Ingene, "Retailers: Head Off Credit Cards with Cash Discounts?" *Harvard Business Review*, Vol. 61 (May–June 1983), pp. 18–22.

portation can be car, van, truck, train, boat, mail, or plane. The costs and appropriateness of these methods depend on the product.

Large retailers find it economical to own their own trucks. Ownership also enables retailers to advertise their company names, have control over delivery time, and have company employees handle deliveries. Small retailers may operate out of their own cars. However, many small, moderate-sized, and even large retailers use United Parcel Service or utilize commercial truckers, when consumers reside away from the delivery area, transportation is used sporadically, and shipments are not efficient (less than full truckloads are shipped).

Last, the timing of deliveries is planned. The retailer must decide how quickly orders are to be processed and how often deliveries are to be made to different geographic areas. For example, will customers in a Baton Rouge, Louisiana, suburb receive deliveries daily, once a week, or monthly?

For some retailers, alterations and installations are primary services and are treated accordingly, although more of these stores charge fees. Many discount stores have discontinued giving alterations of clothing and installations of heavy appliances on both a free and a fee basis. These stores have concluded that the services are too ancillary to their business and not worth the expense. Other retailers offer only basic alterations: shortening pants, taking in the waist, and lengthening the jacket sleeves. They do not adjust jacket shoulders or width and so on. Appliance retailers may hook up a washing machine but will will not do plumbing work. Some clothing store chains have set up centralized alteration systems to reduce costs.

Packaging and complaints and returns can be centrally located or decentralized. Centralized packaging counters and complaints and returns departments have several advantages: they may be located in otherwise dead spaces; the main selling areas are not cluttered; specialized personnel can be used; and a common store policy is implemented. The advantages of decentralized facilities are that consumers are not inconvenienced; customers are kept in the selling area, where a salesperson may resolve any problems or offer different products; and extra personnel are not required. A clearly established store policy regarding the handling of complaints and returns must be stated. The axiom "The customer is always right" should be followed whenever possible. Unfortunately customers are often not convinced this policy is used.

Gift certificates encourage new customers to shop at a store. Many retailers require the gift certificates to be spent and not redeemed for cash. As a result, new consumers come into contact with the store's atmosphere while shopping. Trade-ins induce regular and new customers to patronize a store. Customers get a feeling of a bargain and an accommodation. Trial purchases enable shoppers to try out products before purchases become final, thereby reducing risks. If the customers like the merchandise, it is kept and paid for; should the customer dislike the merchandise, it is simply returned. Trial purchases are often given by mail-order retailers.

Increasingly, stores are offering special services to regular customers.[30] Special sales, not open to the general public, are run to increase customer loyalty. Extended hours, such as evenings and weekends, are provided. This policy extends in-store shopping time and decreases rushing. Mail and telephone orders placed by regular

[30]See "Frequent Shopper Programs Help Deal with Retailing's 'Four Revolutions'," *Marketing News* (July 6, 1984), p. 6; Katherine Joyce, "Personal," *Stores* (December 1983), pp. 20–21ff.; and Joanne Lipman, "Personal Advisors Save Shoppers Money, but Beware of Their Expensive Tastes," *Wall Street Journal* (April 1, 1985), p. 25.

customers are handled for convenience. All of these tactics give a store an atmosphere of warmth for its most important customers.

Other useful customer services, some of them discussed previously, include bridal registry, interior designers, personal shoppers, ticket outlets, free (or low-cost) and plentiful parking, in-store fountains, rest rooms, a restaurant, baby sitting, fitting rooms, shopping bags, and in-store information. The latter should not be underestimated; confused customers are less likely to be satisfied and/or to complete their shopping trips. The store's willingness to offer some or all of these services indicates to its customers its concern for them and is a strong contribution to image.

In particular, stores need to be attentive to consumer needs and consider the impact of excessive self-service. As these marketing consultants have pointed out, customers do not have a high opinion of sales service:[31]

> You can hardly find anyone to wait on you, or if you do, they usually know less about what you want to buy than you do (Maxwell Sroge).
>
> Americans have developed an utter contempt for the retail clerk. When the choice is between bad service and no service, the American will always choose no service (Leo J. Shapiro).

Community Relations

The manner in which retailers relate to the communities around them also has an impact on store image. Stores can enhance their images by actions such as:

* Showing a concern for ecology, such as clean streets.
* Employing area residents.
* Running special sales for senior citizens and other groups.
* Sponsoring little league and other youth activities.
* Cooperating with neighborhood planning groups.
* Supporting charities.

For example, McDonald's sponsors Ronald McDonald Houses, where terminally ill children and their families can live. Montgomery Ward has educational programs on energy conservation and other topics. Act Now Real Estate Inc. (a Florida realtor) raises money for the Muscular Dystrophy Association by running a garage sale.[32]

Communicating with the Customer—Establishing and Maintaining a Store Image: A Summary

Creating the proper store image is an essential aspect of the retailing mix. Store image refers to the way a store is perceived by its customers. Atmosphere is defined as the physical attributes of the store utilized to develop an image and is composed of exterior, general interior, store layout, and displays.

[31]Steve Weiner, "Find It Yourself," *Wall Street Journal* (March 16, 1981), p. 1.
[32]David A. Aaker, "Developing Effective Corporate Consumer Information Programs," *Business Horizons*, Vol. 25 (January–February 1982), p. 35; and Sara Delano, "Give and You Shall Receive," *Inc.* (February 1983), p. 128.

The exterior of the store is planned in terms of storefront, marquee, entrances, display windows, building height and size, visibility, uniqueness, surrounding stores and area, parking, and congestion.

The general interior of the store incorporates flooring, colors, lighting, scents, sounds, fixtures, wall textures, temperature, width of aisles, dressing facilities, vertical transportation, dead areas, personnel, self-service, products, price displays, cash register placements, technology, modernization, and cleanliness.

In laying out the store's interior, six steps are followed. Floor space is allocated among selling, merchandise, personnel, and customers. Product groupings are determined. Traffic flows are planned. The space per product is calculated. Departments are located. Products are arranged within departments.

Interior display possibilities include assortment, theme, ensemble, racks and cases, cut cases and dump bins, posters, mobiles, and wall decorations.

The customer services that a retailer offers affect his or her image. When the retailer is developing a services strategy, several decisions must be made: What services are primary and ancillary? What level is necessary to complement the store's image? Should a variety be presented? Should fees be charged? How can service effectiveness be measured? How can unprofitable services be terminated? Customer services include credit, delivery, alterations, installations, packaging, returns, gift certificates, trade-ins, and so on.

Customers react favorably to stores that show community interest and involvement in such activities as trash cleanups, special sales, and charity collections.

Questions for Discussion

1. Why is it sometimes difficult for a retailer to convey his or her image to the consumer?
2. Can a store change its image? Explain why or why not.
3. Define the concept of *atmosphere*. How does this differ from that of *store image*?
4. Which aspects of the store's exterior are controllable? Which are uncontrollable?
5. How would the following be different for a prestige than for a discount store?
   a. Flooring
   b. Lighting
   c. Fixtures
   d. Width of aisles
   e. Dressing facilities
   f. Vertical transportation
   g. Personnel
   h. Level of self-service
   i. Placement of cash registers
6. Must all clothing stores offer dressing facilities? Explain your answer.
7. What are the disadvantages of self-service?
8. What are meant by selling, merchandise, personnel, and customer space?
9. Develop a market-segmentation product grouping.
10. What questions should a retailer ask himself or herself when positioning products in the store?
11. Which stores should not use a free-flowing layout? Why?
12. How can thematic and ensemble displays be combined?

13. For the following services, give examples of retailers who would consider them primary and retailers who would consider them ancillary.
    a. Delivery
    b. Credit
    c. Alterations
    d. Packaging
    e. Gift certificates
    f. Trade-ins
    g. Mail order
14. Develop a checklist of questions a retailer should consider when determining whether to use a bank credit card plan.
15. Distinquish among revolving, open, and monthly credit accounts.
16. What kinds of complaints do you have about the retailers with whom you deal? How do the retailers usually react to them?
17. Why should a retailer pay to sponsor a little league team?

CASES

1. The Woman's Place: Designing an Interior for a New Specialty Store*

Donald Warren recently leased a 4,000-square-foot store in a regional shopping center. Warren plans to renovate the store (which sold women's blouses and sweaters) into The Woman's Place, a specialty store featuring moderately priced women's clothing such as skirts, blouses, dresses, sweaters, sportswear, lingerie, and outerwear. The store will appeal to middle-income, price-conscious working women between the ages of 25 and 45. The shopping center has three other women's clothing stores, one similar to The Woman's Place.

At present, Warren is outlining plans for a distinctive interior store design. Based on an analysis of specialty clothing stores in the shopping center and elsewhere, he has learned several facts about store design.

Specialty stores have design strategies that are quite different than those used by department stores. Specialty stores use simpler designs, use more permanent displays, emphasize total area design, and hire career sales personnel and tailors. Department stores are more flexible, plan more tentatively, have large seasonal variations, encourage customer self-selection, and hire less-experienced personnel. On average, specialty stores invest 20 per cent more per square foot than department stores on store interiors. These expenditures go for improved flooring and wallcoverings, more furniture and fitting-room space, greater reliance on incandescent lighting, and "privileged" access to stock space (better shelving, carpeted aisles, and subtle security).

Specialty stores are following these general trends. Nonselling space has been cut from 18 to 20 per cent to 10 to 12 per cent of total space. Nonselling space has been used for stock, merchandise held for customer pick-ups, offices, and employees; but this has changed. As one store manager found out, "Your desk is to be two feet of the cash wrap register, under which there will be a three-drawer steel cabinet and

*The material in this case is drawn from Lewis A. Spalding's, "How They're Striving to Be Unique," *Stores* (March 1981), pp. 30–37; and "Specialty Chains," *Stores* (March 1980), pp. 23–25ff.

your phone." The manager asked where confidential meetings could be held. "On shoe leather in a quiet corner of the store, or on two stools at Friendly's restaurant."

Redecorations occur more frequently. For example, lighting and carpeting are now frequently replaced every three or four years, instead of every eight to ten years. This is the result of customer abuse and decorating trends. In addition, stores have modified fixtures to accommodate handicapped shoppers.

Merchandise is exposed more fully. Instead of edgewise displays, garments are shown in breadth. "Waterfall" displays have rods extending from walls and floor fixtures, arranged to contain single hangers so that garments face out. Ensemble and other coordinated displays are popular. Complementary items are placed near each other.

Stock turnover is important. Waterfall displays have reduced the number of garments that can be shown; therefore, each garment must be sold more quickly. Similarly, stores are working hard to minimize pilferage. Product tags and anchoring merchandise to fixtures are most commonly used. In addition, the use of two-way mirrors and trained salespeople is increasing.

Finally, although it is difficult to plan, stores are striving to become more energy efficient. One tactic that has not worked well is to lower lighting levels. This has resulted in poorly lit displays and a more austere atmosphere. Similarly, low temperatures discourage clothing shoppers from trying on garments.

With this information, Warren is ready to develop his store interior.

Questions

1. Evaluate the facts uncovered by Warren.
2. How can Warren develop a distinctive interior?
3. What are some "don'ts" that Warren should consider?
4. Develop a store interior for The Woman's Place. Include lighting, ceilings and wallcoverings, fixtures, space allocations, product groupings, displays, traffic flow, department locations, dressing facilities, and placement of registers.

---

2. Zales Diamond Card: Offering Credit to Underserved Target Markets*

Zales, and its various subsidiaries, is the largest retailer of fine jewelry in the world. In 1984, it operated 767 jewelry stores (in forty-eight states and Puerto Rico) and 122 leased jewelry departments in discount and department stores. Zales' main product lines are diamond jewelry, other jewelry, and watches. Basic prices range from $10 to over $10,000. Annually, Zales' total sales are about $1 billion.

As part of an overall strategy to increase sales, the firm recently decided to develop a campaign to reach new market segments. Specifically, Zales wanted to focus on groups that are often reluctant to purchase diamond jewelry because of high prices. These groups include college students, recent college graduates, newlyweds, young families, teachers, nurses, technical school students, and military personnel.

Zales' plan was to offer credit to these groups through a "Diamond Card," entailing very simplified application procedures. The Diamond Card was promoted through

*This case was prepared and written by Professor Elaine Sherman, Hofstra University, Hempstead, New York.

ZALES

3000 Diamond Park, Dallas, Texas 75247

Dear Mr. or Ms. _____ ,

You've been working hard to build your career. Every week, day after day, you devote to learning the ins and outs of your trade. And that's terrific preparation — for your future. But have you done anything special for yourself for now? Like buying a glorious gift just for yourself or someone you love? Some fine jewelry perhaps?

Now you can — with the ZALES Diamond Card.

In view of your excellent credit rating, we've waived our usual application procedures. The ZALES Diamond Card is yours when you complete the brief Acceptance Form below. Bring it to your nearest ZALES store or mail it to us in the enclosed postage-paid envelope.

Not everyone is invited to accept the Diamond Card on a pre-approved basis. Designed to put a sparkle into your gift-giving moments, the Diamond Card reserves a $XXX line of credit for you at over 750 ZALES jewelry and gift stores nationwide. Generous credit makes buying a little treasure or a beautiful bauble what it should be — a delight.

The Diamond Card opens the door to ZALES. Established about 60 years ago, we are the world's largest jeweler. You can buy with confidence because we buy from the source — and control the quality from rough cut stone to polished gem.

Yes, please send me the ZALES Diamond Card

Mr. or Ms. _____

_____

(For your personal protection, please provide the following information.)

Date of Birth _____ Telephone Number _____

Social Security Number _____

Employer _____

Position _____ City, State _____

X _____
Applicant's Signature _____ Date

Number of Credit Cards _____
☐ I would like an Individual Account
☐ I would like a Joint Account with:

Co-Applicant's Name (please print) _____

CO-APPLICANT INFORMATION (if joint account is desired):

Social Security Number _____

Employer _____

Position _____ City, State _____

X _____
Co-Applicant's Signature _____ Date

Please provide name of nearest relative if Applicant is under 25 years of age.

Name _____ City, State _____

Acceptance forms received after _____ , subject to additional credit approval.

Courtesy Zales.

Figure 1

posters and counter-card displays in college stores, point-of-purchase displays in Zales jewelry stores, and so on. In addition, 500,000 direct-mail pieces were sent to potential consumers.

The direct-mail letters were personalized (e.g., Dear Ms. Connors) and targeted specifically for each market segment. For example, the letters to military personnel opened with this paragraph:

> You're a member of the most prestigious military in the world. You devote each week, day after day, to serving your country. And work hard to insure that American values will never be compromised. But you don't always receive the credit you deserve—especially from the civilian world.

All the direct mail letters also mentioned the consumer's excellent credit rating, the waiving of Zales' usual credit application procedures, and the consumer's preapproved credit status (along with a credit limit). At the bottom of each letter, the consumer was provided with a brief "Acceptance Form" to complete. Among the information requested were date of birth, telephone number, social security number, employer, position at work, number of credit cards desired, and co-applicant's name (if a joint account was desired). The name of the nearest relative was required if the applicant was under 25 years old.

Figure 1 shows the type of letter and acceptance form sent to nurses, teachers, and recent college graduates.

Questions

1. Would you consider credit to be a primary or ancillary service for Zales? Explain your answer.
2. What are the benefits and potential problems of Zales' efforts to offer credit to the groups noted in this case?
3. Evaluate Zales' letter and simplified credit application shown in Figure 1.
4. What criteria should Zales use to evaluate the success or failure of this campaign?

13

Communicating with the Customer: Promotional Strategy

Chapter Objectives

1. To examine retail promotion, specifically how a retailer can inform, persuade, and remind the target market
2. To study the elements of retail promotion: advertising, publicity, personal selling, and sales promotion
3. To explain the strategic aspects of retail promotion: objectives, budget, mix of forms, implementation of mix, and review and revision of the plan

When Jordan Marsh opened its first Connecticut store in New London's Crystal Mall, a careful promotion plan was enacted. The plan was conceived several months before the store actually opened, and the first news release was distributed eight weeks before the opening:

> We began publicity build-up eight weeks out, with releases on store construction progress; store management appointments; departmental listings mentioning JM's brand and designer names; gala party bulletins to the charity organizations; and ribbon cutting details. Ten mail-outs in all.
>
> More than 85 press clips resulted in Connecticut and Boston papers. More than half were re-handles by newspaper staff writers, with 14 of these getting front page position.

The gala store opening was an invitational $25 per person charity ball, which raised several thousand dollars. "For ribbon cutting, we had TV coverage on three stations, twenty live radio interviews with JM executives, and personal appearances of about fifteen local, regional, and state VIPs."

To complement these efforts, Jordan Marsh ran a number of thematic newspaper ads and outdoor (billboard) signs within a 20-mile radius of the store. Many of the ads featured area landmarks, such as the U.S. Coast Guard Academy and the Eugene O'Neill Theater Center. A large advertising push was made throughout the first week the store opened, using the slogan "This is the place!"[1]

Overview

Retail promotion is broadly defined as any communication by a retailer that informs, persuades, and/or reminds the target market. This chapter deals with the development of a retail promotional strategy. In the first part of the chapter, the elements of promotion (advertising, publicity, personal selling, and sales promotion) are detailed. The second part centers on the strategic aspects of promotion: objectives, budget, mix of forms, implementation of mix, and review and revision of the plan.

Elements of the Retail Promotional Mix

Advertising, publicity, personal selling, and sales promotion are the four elements of promotion. Each is discussed here in terms of objectives, advantages and disadvantages, and basic forms. Although these elements are described individually, a good promotional plan normally integrates them—based on the overall strategy of the retailer. A movie theater concentrates more on advertising and sales promotion (point-of-purchase displays to prompt food and beverage sales), with less emphasis on personal selling and publicity. An upscale independent specialty store stresses personal selling, with less emphasis on advertising, publicity, and personal selling.

Retailers spend significant sums on their promotion efforts. For example, in a typical department store, about 3.1 per cent of sales is spent on advertising, 7.5 per cent on personal selling, and 3.0 per cent on sales promotion.[2] In addition, most department store chains employ inside or outside public relations offices to generate favorable publicity and respond to media requests for information.

Advertising

Advertising is "any paid form of nonpersonal presentation and promotion of ideas, goods, and services by an identified sponsor."[3] Three aspects of this definition merit further clarification:

---

[1]Lewis A. Spalding, "Ribbon-Cutting Time," *Stores* (January 1985), pp. 72–77.
[2]David P. Schulz, "NRMA's New MOR," *Stores* (October 1984), p. 22; and Schonfeld & Associates, Inc.," Advertising-to-Sales Ratios, 1983," *Advertising Age* (August 13, 1984), p. 44.
[3]Ralph S. Alexander (Chairman), *Marketing Definitions: A Glossary of Marketing Terms* (Chicago: American Marketing Association, 1960), p. 9.

1. Paid form—This distinguishes advertising from publicity, for which no payment is made by the retailer for the time or space to convey a message.
2. Nonpersonal presentation—In advertising, a set format is delivered to the entire audience, and it cannot be adapted to individual customers. Mass media rather than personal contacts are used.
3. Identified sponsor—Advertising clearly divulges the name of the sponsor, unlike publicity.

In 1983, the three largest U.S. retailers also had the highest dollar expenditures for advertising: Sears—$733 million, 2.2 per cent of sales; K mart—$400 million, 2.2 per cent of sales; and J. C. Penney—$292 million, 2.5 per cent of sales. By comparison, many other retailers had much higher advertising-as-a-percentage-of-sales ratios, despite lower dollar expenditures; these included McDonald's (4.4 per cent) and Tandy, the operator of Radio Shack (6.7 per cent).[4] Table 13-1 shows 1983 advertising-to-sales ratios for a number of retailing categories.

Table 13-1
Selected Advertising-to-Sales Ratios, 1983, by Type of Retailer

Type of Retailer	Advertising Dollars as Per Cent of Sales
Amusement and recreation	4.4
Apparel and accessories	2.4
Automobile dealers and gasoline stations	1.4
Automobile repair and service	3.0
Computer	2.8
Department store	3.1
Drug and proprietary	1.8
Eating	3.2
Fuel and ice	0.8
Furniture	6.8
Grocery	1.3
Hotel/motel	2.6
Household appliance	5.4
Jewelry	5.8
Lumber and building material	2.3
Mail order	17.1
Mobile home	2.0
Motion-picture theater	4.7
Personal services	5.7
Sewing and needlework	4.4
Shoe	1.6
Variety store	2.1

Source: Schonfeld & Associates Inc., "Advertising-to-Sales Ratios, 1983," Advertising Age (August 13, 1984), p. 44. Reprinted by permission. Copyright Crain Communications Inc., 1984.

[4]"Advertising Expenditures as a Percentage of U.S. Sales in 1983 ($000)," *Advertising Age* (September 14, 1984), p. 8.

Differences Between Retailer and Manufacturer Advertising Strategies

Although the definition given applies to all advertising, it is important to examine the differences between retailer and manufacturer advertising strategies. First, retailers usually have more geographically concentrated target markets than manufacturers. This means that a retailer can better adapt to local needs, habits, and preferences than can a manufacturer. However, a retailer is not able to utilize national media as readily as a manufacturer. For example, only large retail chains and franchises can advertise on national television programs. An exception to this is direct marketing because trading areas for these firms are geographically dispersed.

Second, retail advertising emphasizes immediacy. Individual items are placed for sale and advertised during specific, short time periods. Immediate purchases are sought. On the other hand, a manufacturer is often concerned with developing a favorable attitude toward a product or the company and not with short-run sales increases.

Third, retailers generally stress price in advertisements, whereas manufacturers usually emphasize several attributes of a product. In addition, retailers display a number of different products in one advertisement, whereas manufacturers minimize the number of products mentioned in one advertisement.

Fourth, media charges are often lower for retailers than for manufacturers. Because of this factor and the desire of many manufacturers and wholesalers for wide distribution, the costs of retail advertising are frequently shared by a manufacturer or wholesaler and a retailer. Two or more retailers may also share costs. This is known as **cooperative advertising.**

Objectives

Retail advertising is based on a wide number of specific objectives, including

- Short-term sales increases.
- Increases in store traffic.
- Developing and/or reinforcing a store image.
- Informing customers about product and/or store attributes.
- Easing the job for sales personnel.
- Developing demand for private brands.

A retailer selects one or more of these objectives and bases advertising on it (them).

Advantages and Disadvantages

The major advantages of advertising are that

1. A large audience is attracted. Also, for print media, circulation is supplemented by the passing of a copy from one reader to another.
2. The costs per viewer or reader or listener are low.
3. A large number of alternative media are available. Therefore, the retailer can match the medium to the target market.
4. The retailer has control over message content, graphics, times, and size (or length), so that a standardized message in an ideal format is delivered to the entire audience.
5. In print media, the message can be studied and restudied.

6. Editorial content (a television show, a news story, and so on) often surrounds an advertisement. This may increase the credibility of an advertisement or may increase the probability that it will be read.
7. Because the customer becomes aware of the store and its products or services before shopping, self-service or reduced-service operations are possible.

The major disadvantages of advertising are that

1. Because the message is standardized, it is inflexible. The retailer is unable to focus on the needs of individuals.
2. Some types of advertising require high levels of investment. This may eliminate the access of small retailers to certain media (e.g., television).
3. Many media appeal to large geographic areas, and for retailers, waste occurs. For instance, a small supermarket chain may find that only 40 per cent of a newspaper's readers reside within its trading area.
4. Some media require an extremely long lead time for the placing of advertisements. This reduces a retailer's ability to advertise fad items or to react to some current events themes.
5. Some media have a high throwaway rate. For instance, circulars and mail advertisements are often thrown away without being read.
6. Advertisements must be brief. For example, a thirty-second television commercial or a one-eighth-of-a-page newspaper advertisement cannot contain much information.

These are broad conclusions about the entire field of advertising. Generalities have been made. The pros and cons for specific media are described in the following section.

Media

The retailer can choose from among newspapers, telephone directories, direct mail, radio, television, transit, outdoor, magazines, and flyers/circulars. A summary of the attributes of these media appears in Table 13-2.

Newspapers can be classified as dailies, weeklies, and shoppers. Among retailers, the newspaper is the most preferred medium, having the advantages of market coverage, reasonable costs, flexibility, longevity, graphics, and editorial association (ads next to columns or articles). Disadvantages are waste (circulation to a wider geographic area than that containing the target market), black-and-white format, and appeal to fewer senses than television. To maintain their dominant position with retailers, many newspapers have redesigned their graphics and some have begun running a limited amount of color ads.[5] Free-distribution shopper newspapers (also known as "penny savers") that are delivered to all consumer households in a geographic area are growing strongly, sometimes at the expense of other types of newspapers.[6] Figure 13-1 shows a creative newspaper ad used by Neiman-Marcus.

Telephone directories (the White and Yellow Pages) are important advertising media. In the White Pages, the retailer receives a free alphabetical listing along with

[5]David P. Schulz, "Color," *Stores* (February 1983), pp. 38–40.
[6]Gregory Stricharchuk, "Free-Distribution 'Shoppers' Are Posing Serious Threat to Local Daily Newspapers," *Wall Street Journal* (June 19, 1984), p. 31.

Table 13-2
Advertising Media Comparison Chart

Medium	Market Coverage	Type of Audience	Sample Time/Space Costs*	Particular Suitability	Major Advantage	Major Disadvantage
Daily newspaper	Simple community or entire metro area; zoned editions sometimes available.	General; tends more toward men, older age group, slightly higher income and education.	Per agate line, weekday; open rate: Circ: 7,800:$0.25 16,500:$0.35 21,300:$0.60 219,200:$2.10	All general retailers.	Wide circulation.	Nonselective audience.
Weekly newspaper	Single community usually; sometimes a metro area.	General; usually residents of a smaller community.	Per agate line, open rate: Circ: 5,400:$0.35 20,900:$0.55 40,000:$1.20	Retailers who service a strictly local market.	Local identification.	Limited readership.
Shopper	Most households in a single community; chain shoppers can cover a metro area.	Consumer households.	Per one-quarter page, black-and-white; open rate: Circ: 13,000:$45.00 22,500:$185.00 183,400:$760.00	Neighborhood retailers and service businesses.	Consumer orientation.	A giveaway and not always read.
Telephone directories	Geographic area or occupational field served by the directory.	Active shoppers for goods or serices.	Yellow Pages, per double half column, per month: Pop: 10,000– 49,000:$35.00 100,000– 249,000:$63.00 500,000– 999,000:$152.00	Services, retailers of brand-name items, highly specialized retailers.	Users are in the market for goods or services.	Limited to active shoppers.
Direct mail	Controlled by the advertiser through use of demographic lists.	Controlled by the advertiser.	Production and mailing of 8½" × 11" two-color, 4-page letter; order card and reply envelope; label addressed; third-class mail: $.35 each in quantities of 50,000	New and expanding businesses; those using coupon returns or catalogs.	Personalized approach to an audience of good prospects.	High CPM (cost per thousand).

Medium	Market coverage	Type of audience	Sample costs	Particular suitability	Special advantages	Major disadvantage
Radio	Definable market area surrounding the station's location.	Selected audiences provided by stations with distinct programming formats.	Per 60-second morning-drive time spot, one time: Pop: 400,000:$ 45.00 1,100,000:$115.00 3,500,000:$200.00 13,000,000:$385.00	Business catering to identifiable groups: teens, commuters, housewives.	Market selectivity, wide market coverage.	Must be bought consistently to be of value.
Television	Definable market area surrounding the station's location.	Varies with the time of day; tends toward younger age group, less print oriented.	Per 30-second daytime spot; one time; nonpreemptible status: Pop: 400,000:$125.00 1,100,000:$370.00 3,500,000:$615.00 13,000,000:$740.00	Sellers of products or services with wide appeal.	Dramatic impact, wide market coverage.	High cost of time and production.
Transit	Urban or metro community served by transit system; may be limited to a few transit routes.	Transit riders, especially wage earners and shoppers; pedestrians.	Inside 11″ × 28″ cards; per month: 1 bus:$5.00 500 buses:$2,500.00 Outside 30″ × 144″ posters; per month: 1 bus:$85.00 170 buses:$14,110.00	Businesses along transit routes, especially those appealing to wage earners.	Repetition and length of exposure.	Limited audience.
Outdoor	Entire metro area or single neighborhood.	General, especially auto drivers.	Per 12′ × 25′ poster; 100 GRP per month: Pop: 17,900:$130.00 484,900:$180.00 10,529,300:$325.00	Amusement, tourist businesses, brand-name retailers.	Dominant size, frequency of exposure.	Clutter of many signs reduces effectiveness of each one.
Local magazine	Entire metro area or region; zoned editions sometimes available.	General; tends toward better-educated, more affluent.	Per one-sixth page, black-and-white; open rate: Circ: 30,000:$285.00 43,750:$435.00 163,460:$770.00	Restaurants, entertainment, specialty shops, mail-order businesses.	Delivery of a loyal, special-interest audience.	Limited audience.
Flyers/Circulars	Single neighborhood.	Consumer households.	$.10 to $.20 per plus minimum hourly wage for delivery.	Restaurants, dry cleaners, service stations, and other neighborhood retailers.	Caters to specific audience.	Not always read.

*Agate line—the column inch of a newspaper (1 inch deep by 2 inches wide) contains fourteen agate lines. GRP—gross rating points, a percentage figure used to measure market coverage and frequency.

Source: This table (with the exception of "flyers") is from Advertising Small Business (*Bank of America, 1982*), *pp. 10–11. Reprinted with permission from Bank of America, NT & SA, "Advertising Small Business," Vol. 15, No. 2, Small Business Reporter, Copyright 1976, 1978, 1981, 1982.*

Figure 13-1 A Thematic 1985 Newspaper Advertisement

Courtesy Neiman-Marcus.

all other telephone subscribers, commercial and noncommercial. The major advantage of the White over the Yellow Pages is that a customer who is familiar with the retailer's name is not distracted by seeing other names. The major disadvantage as contrasted with the Yellow Pages is the alphabetical rather than type-of-business listing. A customer unfamiliar with repair services in his or her area will usually look in the Yellow Pages under "Repair" and choose a firm that is listed.

In the Yellow Pages, the retailer pays for an alphabetical listing (and a larger display ad, if desired) within a business category. The overwhelming majority of retailers advertise in the Yellow Pages. The advantages are widespread customer usage and long life (one year or more). The disadvantages are limited flexibility and long lead time for new ads. As a result of the breakup of AT&T, retailers now have many Yellow Pages companies vying for their business—at lower rates.[7]

Direct mail is the medium whereby the retailer sends customers catalogs or advertisements via the U.S. mail. Some of its advantages are low total costs, targeted audience, tailor-made format, quick feedback, and tie-in (for example, a retailer with his or her own credit card can send advertisements with the monthly billing statements). Computer advances have greatly improved the efficiency of direct-mail adver-

---

[7]Steven Flax, "Whirlwinds Hit the Yellow Pages," *Fortune* (October 1, 1984), pp. 113–114.

tising.[8] Some disadvantages of direct mail are a low response rate, high throwaway rate ("junk mail"), and obsolete mailing lists (addresses have moved).

Radio is utilized by a variety of retailers. Its major advantages are short lead time, importance as a medium for car drivers and riders, market segmentation, and wide reach. Major disadvantages are no visual impact, a need for brevity, a need for repetition, and waste. The use of radio by retailers has gone up in recent years.[9]

Television, although increasing in importance because of the rise of national and regional retailers, is far behind newspapers in retail advertising expenditures. Advantages of television are video messages (impact), large market, creativity, and program affiliation (for regular sponsors). Disadvantages of television are high minimum costs, waste, need for brevity, need for repetition, and limited availability of time slots for nonregular sponsors.

Transit advertising is utilized by retailers in urban areas that have mass-transit systems. Advertisements are displayed on buses and in subway cars and taxis. Nationwide, $100 million is spent annually on transit ads.[10] Transit advertising has the advantages of a captive audience, mass market, high level of repetitiveness, and geographically defined market. Disadvantages include lack of availability in smaller cities, restricted travel paths, and graffiti. In addition to the transit advertising already mentioned, retailers often advertise on their delivery trucks.

Outdoor or billboard advertising is sometimes used by retailers. Posters and signs are displayed in public places, on buildings, and alongside highways.[11] Advantages are high exposure, economy, and informativeness. Disadvantages are limited information, clutter, high-speed travel (missing the message), and some legislation against pollution caused by signs.

Magazines are growing in importance because of three factors: the increase in national and regional retailers, the creation of regional editions, and use by mail-order retailers. Advantages of magazines are tailoring to a specific market, editorial association, longevity of a single message, and color. Among the disadvantages are long lead time, costs, and waste.

Flyers/circulars are an important advertising tool. Single-page (flyers) or multiple-page (circulars) ads are distributed in parking lots or door-to-door. Advantages include low costs, flexibility, speed, and targeted audience. Disadvantages are the high level of throwaways, poor quality of paper, and clutter. Flyers are good for smaller retailers, while circulars are used by larger ones.

Types

Advertisements can be classified by content and by manner of payment. An advertisement may be pioneering, competitive, reminder, or institutional in nature. A **pioneer advertisement** has awareness as its objective and provides information (usually about a new store or location). A **competitive advertisement** has persuasion as its objective. A **reminder advertisement** is geared to the loyal customer and emphasizes the attributes that have made the store successful. An **institutional advertisement** strives to keep the retailer's name before the public without emphasizing product sales. Public

[8]Jeffrey L. Seglin, "The Direct Approach," *Inc.* (September 1984), pp. 149–154.
[9]Sara Delano, "Tuning in to Radio," *Inc.* (December 1983), pp. 156–159.
[10]"The Growing Appeal of Transit Advertising," *New York Times* (April 16, 1984), pp. D1, D5.
[11]"Selling in the Great Outdoors: How Four Retailers Went by the Boards," *Advertising Age* (March 29, 1982), pp. M–58 to M–60.

service messages (such as sponsorship of a telethon or a little league team) are institutional in nature.

When using advertisements, the retailer may pay his or her own way and/or seek cooperative ventures. For the retailer who pays his or her own way, the major advantages are control and flexibility. The major disadvantages are costs and time requirements. A cooperative venture is one where two or more parties share the costs and the decision making. Annually, about $8 billion to $10 billion is spent on cooperative advertising, most through vertical agreements. Newspapers are much preferred over any other medium for cooperative ads.[12]

In a **vertical cooperative-advertising agreement,** a manufacturer and a retailer or a wholesaler and a retailer share an advertisement. The duties and responsibilities of each party are usually specified contractually. Retailers are not reimbursed until after advertisements are run and invoices are provided to the manufacturer or the wholesaler.[13] The advantages of a vertical agreement are reduced costs, assistance in the preparation of advertisements, greater coverage of the market, and less expenditure of the retailer's time. Disadvantages include less control, flexibility, and distinctiveness. Some retailers are particularly bothered about the requirements they must satisfy to be eligible for supplier support and the emphasis on the supplier's name in ads. Manufacturers are responding to this by becoming more flexible and understanding of retailer concerns.[14]

Under a **horizontal cooperative-advertising agreement,** two or more retailers (usually small) share an advertisement. The advantages and disadvantages are similar to those in a vertical agreement. An additional benefit is the increased bargaining power of retailers in dealing with the media.

When planning a cooperative advertising strategy, the retailer must consider these questions:

- What advertising qualifies, in terms of products and special requirements?
- What percentage is paid by each party?
- When can advertisements be run?
- What media can be used?
- Are there special provisions regarding message content?
- What documentation is required for reimbursement?
- How does each party benefit?
- Do cooperative advertisements obscure the image of the individual retailer?[15]

---

[12]Crimmins Co-Op Marketing, 1984 study.

[13]Vertical cooperative advertisements are regulated by the Robinson-Patman Act. Manufacturers and wholesalers must offer similar arrangements to all retailers on a proportional basis. See Carroll Shelton, "Watching Out for the Regulations," *Advertising Age* (August 17, 1981), pp. S–14 to S–15.

[14]Renee Blakkan, "Savory Deals Tempt Hungry Retailers," *Advertising Age* (March 7, 1983), pp. M–9 to M–11; Martin Everett, "Minding the Stores," *Sales & Marketing Management* (May 14, 1984), pp. 72–77; and "To Succeed in Co-Op, Forget the Clerical Side and Spend More Time on Marketing," *Sales & Marketing Management* (June 6, 1983), pp. 88–92.

[15]See Robert D. Wilcox, "Tracking the Road to Better Co-Op Use," *Advertising Age* (August 17, 1981), pp. S–4, S–6; "Strengthening the Link Between Manufacturer and Retailer," *Sales & Marketing Management* (July 6, 1981), pp. 46–53; Janet Berg, "More Creative Ways to Use Co-Op," *Stores* (June 1981), pp. 58–60; Sara Delano, "How to Get a Fix on Free Ad Dollars," *Inc.* (July 1983), pp. 94–96; and Robert F. Young and Stephen A. Greyser, "Guidelines for Getting the Most Out of Co-Op," *Sales & Marketing Management* (May 16, 1983), pp. 92, 94.

Publicity

Publicity is the:

> nonpersonal stimulation of demand for a product, service, or business unit by planting commercially significant news about it in a published medium or obtaining favorable presentation of it upon radio, television, or stage that is not paid for by the sponsor.[16]

The basic distinction between advertising and publicity is the nonpaid nature of the latter. Because of this difference, publicity messages are not controllable. For example, a story about a new store opening may not appear at all, may appear after the fact, or may not appear in the form desired. On the other hand, publicity is usually considered to be more credible and important than an advertisement. Accordingly advertising and publicity should be viewed as complements and not as substitutes for each other. In many cases, publicity precedes advertising.

Objectives

Retail publicity seeks to accomplish one or more objectives:

- To maintain or improve store image.
- To show the retailer as a contributor to the quality of life.
- To demonstrate innovativeness.
- To present a favorable message in a highly believable manner.
- To increase awareness of the store and its products or services.
- To minimize total promotion costs.

Advantages and Disadvantages

The major advantages of publicity are that

1. A store image can be presented or enhanced.
2. An objective source presents the message for the retailer, providing credibility (e.g., a good review of a restaurant).
3. There are no costs for the message time or space.
4. A mass audience is addressed.
5. Carryover effects are possible (e.g., the store is community oriented; therefore, the products it carries are good).
6. People pay more attention to news stories than to clearly identified advertisements.

The major disadvantages of publicity are that

1. There is no control over the message, its timing, its placement, and its coverage by a given medium.
2. It is difficult to plan in advance and is more suitable in short-run rather than long-run planning.
3. Although there are no media costs, there are costs for a public relations staff, planning activities, and the activities themselves (e.g., parades and store openings).

[16]Alexander, *Marketing Definitions: A Glossary of Marketing Terms*, p. 19.

Types

Community services, such as donations and special sales, are often reported in the media. Parades are sponsored on holidays. Macy's Thanksgiving Day Parade receives tremendous media coverage. The sales of new products and services are presented in the media. Local news programs and others many times show new items and mention where they are sold. The opening of a new store can receive media coverage if the store location or design is particularly newsworthy.[17] Television and newspaper reporters visit restaurants and other retailers and rate their performance and quality.

Each of these forms of publicity enhances a store's image and provides the other advantages already mentioned. However, there may be difficulties. For example, Macy's parade, although it receives free television time, is not inexpensive. The publicity for McDonald's muscular dystrophy contributions is free, but the costs of the donation run into seven figures. In addition, how long do people remember the contribution, which is once-a-year occurrence?

In the case of a store opening, the media may describe the location in less than glowing terms and may criticize the store's effects on the environment and so on. The retailer has no control over the message. Also, the media may not cover this or any other publicity event.

Finally, some publicity events can be planned in advance (parades, donations), but others cannot (the appearance of a newspaper reporter, interest by a local television station, and so on). Publicity must be viewed as a component of the promotion mix, not as the whole mix.

Personal Selling

Personal selling involves an "oral presentation in a conversation with one or more prospective purchasers for the purpose of making sales."[18]

Objectives

Among the objectives of personal selling are to

* Persuade the customer to consummate a purchase, because the customer often enters a store after acquiring some information through advertising.
* Create awareness of direct-to-home sales products.
* Feed back information to the retailer.
* Provide adequate levels of service.
* Improve and maintain customer satisfaction.

---

[17]Lauranne Gray Berliner, "What They Do When They Open a Store." *Stores* (January 1982), pp. 83–89; and Robert R. Robichaud, "How to Milk a Store Opening for All It's Worth," *Marketing News* (March 16, 1984), Section 2, p. 8.

[18]Alexander, *Marketing Definitions: A Glossary of Marketing Terms*, p. 18.

Advantages and Disadvantages

The major advantages of personal selling are related to the nature of personal contact:

1. Immediate feedback is provided.
2. A salesperson is able to alter his or her message to the needs of the individual customer.
3. A salesperson can be flexible in analyzing alternative solutions to a customer's needs.
4. The attention span of the customer is high.
5. There is little or no waste; most people who walk into a store are potential customers.
6. Customers respond more often to personal selling than to advertisements.

The major disadvantages of personal selling are that

1. Only a small audience is reached at a given time.
2. The costs of interacting with each customer are high.
3. Customers are not lured into a store through personal selling.
4. Self-service is discouraged.

Types

Most types of retail selling can be categorized as either order taking or order getting. An **order-taking** position is one in which the salesperson is involved with routine clerical and sales functions, such as setting up displays, placing inventory on the shelves, filling reorders, answering simple questions, and ringing up the sale. This type of selling most often occurs in stores that have a strong mix of self-service with some personnel on the floor.

Order-getting personnel are more involved with informing and persuading customers. These are the true "sales" employees. Order getters usually sell high-priced or complex items like real estate, automobiles, and refrigerators. On the average, they are more skilled and better paid than order takers.

In some instances, a manufacturer helps finance the personal selling function by providing **PMs** (defined as promotional money, push money, or prize money) for retail salespeople who sell the manufacturer's brand. PMs are additions to the compensation received from the retailer. Retailers are concerned about this practice because it encourages retail personnel to be loyal to the manufacturer, and salespersons may be less responsive to actual customer desires (if customers desire brands not yielding PMs).

Functions

Sales personnel are responsible for many functions: greeting customers, determining customer wants, showing merchandise, giving a sales presentation, demonstrating products, answering objections, and closing the sale.

Upon entering a store or a department within the store, the customer is greeted by the salesperson. Typical greetings are:

"Hello, may I help you?"

"Good morning [afternoon], if you need any help please call upon me."

"Hi, is there anything in particular you are looking for?"

With any greeting, the salesperson seeks to put the customer at ease and build a rapport.

Next the salesperson determines what the customer wants, such as:

* Is the customer just looking, or is there a specific product in mind?
* For what purpose is the item to be used (gift or personal)?
* Does the customer have a price range in mind?
* What additional information can the customer provide?

From a marketing perspective, the salesperson cannot be successful without first ascertaining the consumer's wants.

At this point, the salesperson shows or presents the merchandise. Based on a determination of customer wants, the salesperson selects the product that is most likely to be satisfactory and shows it to the customer. The salesperson may decide to trade up (show a more expensive version of the product) or present a substitute (particularly if the store does not carry or is out of the requested item).

Now the salesperson makes a sales presentation to influence the customer to buy the product. Two kinds of presentations are most common: the **canned sales presentation** and the **need-satisfaction approach.** The canned sales presentation is a memorized, repetitive speech given to all customers interested in a particular item. The need-satisfaction approach is based upon the principle that each customer has a different set of wants and that the sales presentation should be geared to the demands of the individual customer. This approach is being utilized more and more in retailing.

During the sales presentation, a demonstration may be helpful. The demonstration shows the customer the actual utility of the item and allows customer participation. Demonstrations are often used to sell stereos, automobiles, televisions, dishwashers, television games, and watches.

The customer may raise questions during the sales presentation, and the salesperson must answer these objections. After the questions are answered, the salesperson closes the sale. This involves getting the customer to conclude his or her purchase. Typical closing lines are:

"Will you take it with you or have it delivered?"

"Cash or charge?"

"Would you like this gift-wrapped?"

"Have you decided on the color, red or blue?"

In order for the personal selling function to be completed effectively, sales personnel must be enthusiastic, knowledgeable about the store and its offerings, interested

Table 13-3
Reasons Why Sales Are Lost

1. *Poor qualification of the customer:* Information should be obtained from the customer that would enable a salesperson to tailor his or her presentation to the prospective buyer.
2. *Salesperson does not demonstrate the product:* A good sales presentation should be built around the item shown in use; product benefits can be easily visualized.
3. *Failure to put feeling into presentation:* The salesperson should be sincere and consumer oriented in his or her presentation.
4. *Poor product knowledge:* The salesperson should know the major advantages and disadvantages of his or her products as well as those of competitors and be able to answer questions.
5. *Arguing with a customer:* A good salesperson should avoid arguments in handling customer objections, even if the customer is completely wrong.
6. *No suggestion selling:* A salesperson should attempt to sell related items (such as service contracts, product supplies, and installation) along with the basic product.
7. *Giving up too early:* If an attempt at closing a sale is unsuccessful, it should be tried again.
8. *Inflexibility:* A salesperson should be flexible in analyzing alternative solutions to a customer's needs as well as in altering his or her message to the requirements of the individual consumer.
9. *Poor follow-up:* A salesperson should be sure that the order is correctly written, that merchandise arrives at the agreed on time, and that the customer is satisfied.

in their consumers, and able to communicate effectively. For example, at Nordstrom (a Western specialty clothing store chain), salespeople keep notebooks on the shoe and apparel sizes of regular customers, their favorite styles and colors, their hobbies, and so on. They assemble coordinated outfits from various store departments while customers wait or do errands. They even call customers when new items are stocked or to discreetly suggest that it is time to replace last year's wardrobe.[19]

Table 13-3 contains a list of reasons how retail sales can be lost through poor personal selling, and how to correct these problems.[20]

Sales Promotion

Sales promotion consists of

> those marketing activities, other than personal selling, advertising, and publicity, that stimulate consumer purchasing and dealer effectiveness, such as displays, shows and exhibitions, demonstrations, and various nonrecurring selling efforts not in the ordinary routine.[21]

[19]Patricia A. Bellow, "Nordstrom Strategy of Coddling Shoppers Facing Challenge in California Expansion," *Wall Street Journal* (May 10, 1984), p. 37.
[20]See also Isadore Barmash, "Selling, Retailing's Lost Art," *New York Times* (May 15, 1983), pp. D1, D4; Jules Abend, "Gimbels to Sales Staff: Function Is Selling," *Stores* (October 1984) pp. 50–51; and "Unctuous Auto Salespeople May Be a Thing of the Past, Study Suggests," *Marketing News* (April 27, 1984), pp. 1, 9.
[21]Alexander, *Marketing Definitions: A Glossary of Marketing Terms*, p. 20.

Objectives

Sales promotion objectives include

- Supplementing other promotion tools.
- Increasing short-run sales.
- Maintaining customer loyalty.
- Emphasizing novelty.

Advantages and Disadvantages

The major advantages of sales promotion are that

1. It has eye-catching appeal.
2. The themes and tools are unique.
3. The consumer may receive something of value, such as coupons, stamps, calendars, and so on.
4. It helps draw customer traffic and maintain store loyalty.
5. Impulse purchases are increased.
6. Customers have fun, particularly with contests and demonstrations.

The major disadvantages of sales promotion are that

1. It is difficult to terminate special promotions without adverse customer reactions.
2. Store image may be hurt if low-status promotions are used.
3. Sometimes frivolous selling points are emphasized, as opposed to product assortment and prices.
4. Many sales promotions are short run.
5. It can only be used as a supplement to other promotional forms.

Types

Table 13-4 contains a listing of the major types of sales promotions. Point-of-purchase promotion consists of in-store displays, which are designed to increase sales. The effect of point-of-purchase displays on store image was discussed in Chapter 13. From a promotional perspective, point-of-purchase displays remind customers, stimulate impulse behavior, allow self-service to be used, and reduce promotion costs because of manufacturers' supplying these displays.[22] The long-run effects of point-of-purchase promotions must be carefully studied. It may be that total sales do not rise; customers may stockpile when displays are used and purchase less when they are not.

Following are several examples of the value of point-of-purchase displays:

- Actmedia, a promotional firm, provides ads that appear on 2 million shopping carts in 4,900 stores, reaching 40 per cent of U.S. households.[23]

---

[22]Lee W. Dyer, "Retailers POP with Enthusiasm for P.O.P.," *Progressive Grocer* (January 1982), pp. 112–116; and John A. Quelch and Kristina Cannon-Bonventre, "Better Marketing at the Point of Purchase," *Harvard Business Review*, Vol. 61 (November–December 1983), pp. 162–169.

[23]"Supermarket Aisle Ads Provide Manufacturers a Cheap Medium," *Marketing News* (January 18, 1985), p. 4.

Table 13-4
Types of Sales Promotion

Type	Features
Point-of-purchase	Window, floor, and counter displays that allow a retailer to remind customers and stimulate impulse purchases. Sometimes the materials are supplied by manufacturers.
Contests	Customers compete for prizes by completing a contest (game), such as a crossword puzzle, a slogan, or a football lottery. Winning is at least partially based on a correct answer (skill).
Sweepstakes	Similar to a contest, except that participants merely fill out application forms and the winner is picked at random (chance). No skill is involved. Direct-mail retailers use this tool quite often.
Coupons	Stores advertise special discounts for customers who redeem advertised coupons. Customers clip coupons from newspapers and redeem them in the store.
Trading Stamps	Customers are given free trading stamps based on the dollar amounts of their purchases. These stamps are accumulated and are used to acquire products.
Prizes	Similar to stamps, except that the store gives prizes immediately, like glasses, silverware, and others. Usually, one piece of a set is obtained with each purchase.
Samples	Free tastes or smells of items are given to customers.
Demonstrations	Products are regularly shown cleaning floors, mixing foods, and so on. Services are also demonstrated (e.g., Evelyn Woods Reading Dynamics).
Referral gifts	Presents or gifts are given to current customers when they bring in new customers.
Matchbooks, pens, calendars, shopping bags, etc.	Items that contain the store's name are given to customers.
Special events	Include fashion shows, autograph sessions with book authors, art exhibits, and holiday activities (such as rides for children).
Skywriting	Attention-getting messages are printed in the sky.

- Surveys of supermarket and drugstore consumers find that most purchase decisions are finalized in the store.[24]
- To obtain preferred shelf locations and encourage retailers to use their special displays, many manufacturers (such as Coke and Pepsi) offer retailers price breaks and promotional allowances.[25]
- Point-of-purchase displays greatly increase sales for such items as hand and body lotions, shampoo, salad dressings, and canned fruit drinks.[26]
- The Point-of-Purchase Advertising Institute estimated that manufacturers and retailers spent almost $8 billion on in-store displays in 1984.[27]

[24]Kevin Higgins, "In-Store Merchandising Is Attracting More Marketing Dollars with Last Word in Sales," *Marketing News* (August 19, 1983), pp. 1, 16; and "Rx for Drugstores: More Pizzazz," *Sales & Marketing Management* (May 14, 1984), p. 28.
[25]Ford S. Worthy, "Coke and Pepsi Stomp on the Little Guys," *Fortune* (January 7, 1985), pp. 67–68.
[26]"Display Effectiveness: An Evaluation," *Nielsen Researcher* (Number 2, 1983), p. 8.
[27]"Point-of-Purchase Advertising Institute, In-Store Merchandising Spending," *Marketing News* (December 7, 1984), p. 18.

Contests and sweepstakes are similar in nature; they seek to attract and retain customers through participation in events that can lead to substantial prizes. A contest requires a customer to demonstrate some skill in return for a reward. A sweepstakes requires only participation, with the lucky winner chosen at random. The disadvantages of contests and sweepstakes are their costs, the customers' reliance on these tools as the reason for continued retailer patronage, and entries by nonshoppers. Together, manufacturers and retailers spend about $200 million each year on contests and sweepstakes.[28]

Coupons are used to offer discounts in the selling prices of store and manufacturer brands. During 1983, about 143 billion coupons were distributed. Daily newspaper coupons represented about 40 per cent of the total. Sunday newspaper magazines, free-standing inserts in Sunday newspapers, regular magazines, direct mail, and in–on packages accounted for the rest of distribution. Consumers saved $1.7 billion through coupons, while retailers received $390 million for handling redeemed coupons. The average face value of a coupon reached $0.24 in 1983.[29]

There are four important advantages of coupons. First, in many cases, manufacturers pay for the advertising and the redemption of coupons. Second, coupons are very helpful to an ongoing advertising campaign and increase store traffic. Coupons are redeemed at least once a year by 76 per cent of U.S. households; and 46 per cent of food shoppers define themselves as regular or frequent coupon users.[30] Third, the use of coupons increases the consumer's perception that a retailer offers good value. Fourth, the effectiveness of advertisements can be measured by a count of the redeemed coupons. The disadvantages of coupons include their effect on store image, consumers shopping only when coupons are available, low redemption rates, the clutter of coupons (largely due to the expanding number of coupons distributed), retailer and consumer fraud, and handling costs. For example, only about 4 per cent of all coupons are redeemed by consumers; about 20 per cent of coupons are misredeemed; and handling costs average 8 to 10 cents per coupon.[31]

Trading stamps were very popular in the 1950s and early 1960s; however, they had a significant decline during the late 1960s and early 1970s. From a peak of over $800 million in trading stamps during 1969, the industry bottomed out at less than $300 million in 1975. Since then, a moderate revival has taken place; in 1983, stamp volume was about $550 million.[32]

The advantages of trading stamps are store loyalty (accumulation is made possible only through patronage at one or a few stores), the "free" nature of stamps to many

---

[28]Franklynn Peterson and Judi Kesselman-Turkel, "Catching Consumers with Sweepstakes," *Fortune* (February 18, 1982), pp. 84–88; Alan Radding, "Filene's Catalog Makes Game of Holiday Shopping," *Advertising Age* (November 26, 1984), p. 60; and Incentive Marketing, "Liquidators Lead the Pack," *Advertising Age* (May 10, 1984), p. M–16.

[29]Lisa Belkin, "Hunting Buyers with Coupon Promotions," *New York Times* (January 26, 1985), p. 44; and "Coupons," *Progressive Grocer* (September 1984), pp. 186, 188.

[30]Robert D. Hisrich and Michael P. Peters, "Coupon Mania Presents Opportunities and Problems for Manufacturers, Users," *Marketing News* (October 12, 1984), p. 34; and "Incentives Serenade Supermarket Shoppers," *Chain Store Age Executive* (May 1984), p. 35.

[31]"Coupons," p. 186; "Bonus Couponing Strikes Out as Supermarket Traffic Builder," *Marketing News* (May 11, 1984), pp. 7, 9; and Kevin Higgins, "Couponing's Growth Is Easy to Understand: It Works," *Marketing News* (September 28, 1984), pp. 12–13.

[32]Betsy Gilbert, "Retailers Stamp Out Loyalty Problems," *Advertising Age* (May 10, 1984), pp. M–34 to M–35; "Trading Stamps Aren't Licked Yet," *Newsday* (September 19, 1984), p. 41; and Incentive Marketing, "Liquidators Lead the Pack," p. M–16.

consumers, and a competitive edge for a store that is similar to others. On the other hand, a number of consumers realize that stamps are not free and therefore shop at lower-priced, nonstamp stores. In addition, profit margins may be small if trading-stamp stores try to price competitively with nonstamp stores.

Prizes are similar in concept to stamps. Instead of stamps, prizes are given. Prize giveaways are most effective when sets of glasses, silverware, dishes, place mats, and so on are distributed. These encourage store loyalty. The problems are costs, difficulty of termination, and impact on image.

As a supplement to personal selling, free samples (e.g., taste of cake, smell of perfume) and/or demonstrations (e.g., cooking lessons) are used. These are effective because the customer becomes involved, and impulse purchases increase. Loitering and costs are problems.

Referral gifts are used to encourage existing customers to bring in new customers. Direct marketers, such as book and record clubs, often use this tool. It is a technique that has no important shortcomings and recognizes the value of friends in influencing purchasing decisions.

Items such as pens, matchbooks, calendars, and shopping bags are often given to customers. They differ from prizes in that they advertise the store's name and are usually not part of a set. These items should be used as supplements. Their advantage is longevity. There is no real disadvantage.

Retailers often use special events to generate consumer enthusiasm. The special events can range from fashion shows to art exhibits. For example, Marshall Field holds lectures by celebrities that attract 500+ consumers. Manufacturers Hanover Bank is a co-sponsor of the New York City Marathon. In 1984, Carson, Pirie, Scott & Co., the Chicago department store retailer, invited 2,000 men to a two-hour shopping party featuring women's clothing.[33] The increase in consumer awareness and store traffic need to be weighed against an event's costs.

Skywriting is used by restaurants, hotels, and others as an attention getter. It can be helpful in creating awareness or reminding customers. However, store image can be affected, and costs can be high.

Planning the Retail Promotional Strategy

In order to communicate successfully with the consumer, the retailer must carefully plan his or her overall promotion and publicity strategy. A systematic five-step approach to an overall promotion plan is contained in Figure 13-2 and explained in the following sections.

Determining Promotional Objectives

Broad promotional objectives include increasing sales, stimulating impulse and re-minder buying, increasing store traffic, producing leads for sales personnel, developing and reinforcing a store image, informing customers about product attributes, establish-

---

[33]Jules Abend, "Special Events," *Stores* (May 1984), pp. 18–24; Kurt Hoffman, "Banks Earn Dividends from Special Events," *Advertising Age* (October 25, 1984), pp. 26, 30; and "Retailer's Hope Last-Minute Gimmicks Will Lure Shoppers into Spending More," *Wall Street Journal* (December 21, 1984), p. 6.

Planning the Retail Promotional Strategy

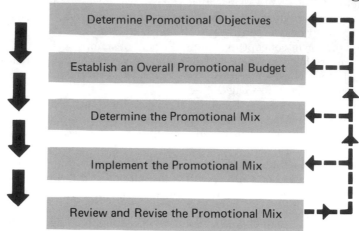

Figure 13-2

ing a new store location, capitalizing on manufacturer support, offering customer service and improving customer relations, and maintaining customer loyalty.

In developing a promotional strategy, a retailer must determine which of these objectives are most important. It is necessary for the retailer to state his or her goals clearly in order to give direction to the selection of promotional types, media, and messages.

Objectives must be stated as specifically as possible. For example, increasing store sales is not a specific enough goal. However, increasing sales by 20 per cent is directional, quantitative, and measurable. With this objective, a retailer is able to develop a thorough promotional plan and evaluate its success.

Establishing an Overall Promotional Budget

There are several procedures available for ascertaining the size of the promotion budget. Five alternative budgeting techniques are discussed in this section.

The **all-you-can-afford** procedure is probably the weakest of the budgeting methods. In this procedure, the retailer first allocates funds for every element of the retailing mix except promotion. Whatever funds are left over are placed in a promotional budget. The shortcomings of this method are that little importance is placed on promotion as a crucial retail-mix variable; expenditures are not linked to objectives; and if no funds are left over, there is no promotion budget. This method is used predominantly by small, conservative retailers.

The **incremental method** of promotion budgeting relies on previous budgets in the allocation of funds. A percentage is either added to or subtracted from this year's budget to determine next year's budget. For instance, if this year's promotion budget is $10,000, next year's budget is calculated by the addition or subtraction of a percentage. A 10 per cent increase means that next year's budget will be $11,000. This technique is useful for a small retailer. A reference point is used. The budget is adjusted based on the retailer's feelings about past successes and future trends. It is an easy method to calculate. However, important disadvantages do exist. The size of the budget is rarely tied to specific objectives. Intuition or "gut feelings" are used. Evaluation is also difficult.

The **competitive parity method** has utility for small and large retailers. In this procedure, a retailer's budget is raised or lowered according to the actions of competitors. For example, if the leading retailer in an area raises the promotion budget by 8 per cent, competitors in the area will follow suit. The advantages of competitive parity are that it utilizes a point of comparison and is market-oriented and conservative. The disadvantages are the following, not leading philosophy; the difficulty of obtaining data; and the assumption of a similarity in firms (years in business, size, type of location, products, prices, and so on). The last point is particularly important.

With the **percentage-of-sales technique,** the retailer bases the promotion budget on sales revenue. In the first year, the retailer develops a promotion-to-sales ratio. During succeeding years, the percentage of promotion dollars to sales dollars remains constant, although the value may vary. For example, a retailer determines that promotion costs should be 10 per cent of sales. First-year sales are estimated at $100,000, and a $10,000 promotion budget is planned. Second-year sales are estimated at $140,000 and a $14,000 promotion budget is planned. The benefits of this procedure are the use of sales as a base, adaptability, and the correlation of promotion with sales. Shortcomings are that there is no relation to objectives (e.g., for an established retailer, an increase in sales may not require an increase in promotion); promotion is not utilized as a leader of sales, but a follower; and promotion decreases during poor sales periods when increases could be beneficial. This technique provides too many promotional funds in periods of high sales and too few funds in periods of low sales.

The **objective-and-task method** is probably the best of the budgeting methods. Under this procedure, the retailer clearly defines his or her promotional objectives and then determines the size of the budget necessary to satisfy these objectives. For example, a retailer may decide that he or she would like to have 90 per cent of the people in the trading area know the store's name (objective). He or she then calculates what tasks and costs are required to achieve this objective:

Objective	Task	Cost
1. Gain awareness of housewives	Use four quarter-page ads in four successive Sunday editions of local newspapers.	$2,000
2. Gain awareness of motorists	Use ten 30-second spot radio commercials during prime time on two local radio stations at $50 each.	500
3. Gain awareness of pedestrians	Give away shopping bags—1,000 bags at $.30 each.	300
	Total budget	$2,800

The advantages of the objective-and-task technique are that objectives are clearly stated; expenditures are related to the completion of goal-oriented tasks; it is adaptable; and success (or failure) can be evaluated. The major shortcoming is the complexity in setting goals and specific tasks, especially for small retailers.

Table 13-5
Advertising as Practiced by Selected Small Businesses

Type of Business	Average Ad Budget (% of Sales)	Favorite Media	Other Media	Special Considerations	Promotional Opportunities
Apparel stores	2.5–3.0	Weekly or suburban newspapers; direct mail.	Radio; Yellow Pages; exterior signs.	Cooperative advertising available from manufacturers.	Fashion shows for community organizations or charities.
Auto supply stores	0.5–2.0	Local newspapers; Yellow Pages.	Point-of-purchase displays; exterior signs.	Cooperative advertising available from manufacturers.	For specialty stores, direct mail is a popular medium.
Bars and cocktail lounges	1.0–2.0	Yellow Pages; local newspapers (entertainment section).	Tourist publications; radio; specialties; exterior signs.	Manufacturers do all product advertising.	Unusual drinks at "happy hour" rates; hosting postevent parties.
Bookstores	1.5–1.7	Newspapers; shoppers; Yellow Pages; local magazines.	Radio; exterior signs.	Cooperative advertising available from publisher.	Autograph parties.
Coin-op laundries	0.6–2.0	Yellow Pages; flyers distributed in area; local newspapers.	Direct mail; exterior signs.		Coupons in newspaper ads for "free trial."
General job printing	0.4–1.0	Yellow Pages; trade journals.	Local newspapers; direct mail; exterior signs.		Samples of work can be used as promotional tools.
Gift stores	1.5–2.5	Weekly newspapers; Yellow Pages.	Radio; direct mail; consumer magazines; exterior signs.		Open houses; in-store demonstrations of products such as cookware.
Hairgrooming/ beauty salons	2.5–3.0	Yellow Pages.	Newspapers; name credits for styles in feature articles; exterior signs.	Word-of-mouth advertising is very important to a salon's success.	Styling for community fashion shows; conducting free beauty clinics and demonstrations.
Health food stores	1.1–2.8	Local newspapers; shoppers; college newspapers.	Direct mail; point-of-purchase displays; exterior signs.		Educational displays and services.
Restaurants	0.8–3.0	Newspapers; radio; Yellow Pages; transit; outdoor.	Local entertainment guides or tourist publications; theater programs; TV for chain or franchise restaurants; exterior signs.	Word-of-mouth advertising is relied upon heavily by independently owned restaurants.	"Free" advertising in critics' columns; specialties; birthday cakes or parties for customers.

Source: Advertising Small Business *(Bank of America, 1982), p. 16. Reprinted with permission from Bank of America, NT & SA, "Advertising Small Business,"* Vol. 15, No. 2, Small Business Reporter, *Copyright 1976, 1978, 1981, 1982.*

In selecting a method for planning the promotion budget, a retailer should weigh the strengths and weaknesses of each technique in relation to his or her individual requirements and constraints.

Table 13-5 shows the advertising expenditures of selected small businesses, expressed as a percentage of sales. These expenditures vary from 0.4 to 1 per cent of sales for general printers to 2.5 to 3.0 per cent of sales for apparel stores and beauty salons.

Determining the Promotional Mix

After a budget is determined, the retailer must determine his or her promotional mix: the combination of advertising, publicity, personal selling, and sales promotion. A firm with a relatively small budget may rely on in-store displays, flyers, and publicity to generate store traffic, whereas a firm with a large promotion budget may rely heavily on newspaper advertising.

The type of retailer often affects the choice of promotional mix. For example, Table 13-5 shows that coin-operated laundries emphasize Yellow Page directories, whereas health food stores emphasize local newspapers as well as point-of-purchase displays. Table 13-6 shows the usage of selected promotional forms by supermarkets. Newspapers and flyers/circulars are used most often in advertising. Merchandise prizes and bonus coupons are the sales promotion techniques used most.

Frequently, retailers use a variety of promotional forms that reinforce one another.

Table 13-6
The Usage of Selected Promotional Tools by Supermarkets, 1983

Advertising		
Media	Per Cent Using	Per Cent of Total Advertising Budget
Newspapers	88	58
Flyers/circulars	69	31
Radio	55	7
Television	23	3
Outdoor	15	1

Sales Promotion	
Technique	Per Cent Using
Merchandise prizes	55
Bonus coupons	40
Games	30
Trading stamps	12
Sweepstakes	10

Source: "51st Annual Report of the Grocery Industry," Progressive Grocer *(April 1984), p. 80. Reprinted by permission.*

Table 13-7
Promotion and the Hierarchy of Effects

Hierarchy of Effects	Behavioral Objective of Promotion	Selected Promotional Types Relevant to Each Step
Awareness ↓ Knowledge	Provide information	Advertising (classified, use of slogans, jingles, descriptive copy), publicity, premiums, point-of-purchase, window displays
Liking ↓ Preference	Change attitudes and feelings	Combination of media advertising (competitive advertisements, argumentative copy, "image advertisements," status appeals), sales force (use depending on complexity of product or service, store image, extent of manufacturer advertising), demonstrations, publicity
Conviction ↓ Purchase	Stimulate desires	Point-of-purchase, advertising (deals, last-chance offers, price appeal, testimonials), direct mail, demonstrations, sales force

Source: Adapted from Robert Lavidge and Gary A. Steiner, "A Model for Predictive Measurements of Advertising Effectiveness," Journal of Marketing, *Vol. 25 (October 1961), p. 61. Reprinted with permission of the American Marketing Association.*

For example, one study concluded that a combination of media advertising and point-of-purchase displays is more effective in getting across a message than one form alone.[34]

When reacting to promotion, a consumer goes through a series of steps called the **hierarchy of effects,** leading from awareness to purchase. The steps are awareness, knowledge, liking, preference, conviction, and purchase.[35] Different promotional mixes are required during each step; these are listed in Table 13-7. In general, advertising and publicity are most effective in developing awareness, and personal selling is most effective in changing attitudes and stimulating desires. This is especially true for expensive and complex products or services.

Implementing the Promotional Mix

Implementation of the promotional mix involves determining which specific media to use (Newspaper A versus Newspaper B), the timing of promotion, the content of the messages, the makeup of the sales force, specific sales promotion tools, and the responsibility for coordination.

Media Decisions

The choice of specific media is based on a wide variety of elements, including overall costs, efficiency (cost to reach a member of the target market), lead time, and editorial content. Overall costs are important because the extensive use of an expensive medium

[34]"Display Effectiveness: An Evaluation," p. 8.
[35]Robert Lavidge and Gary A. Steiner, "A Model for Predictive Measurements of Advertising Effectiveness," *Journal of Marketing*, Vol. 25 (October 1961), pp. 59–62.

may preclude the implementation of a balanced promotional mix. In addition, a retailer may not be able to repeat a message in a costly medium, and advertisements are rarely effective when shown only once.

The efficiency of a medium relates to the cost of reaching a given number of target customers. Newspaper efficiency is measured by the milline rate which reflects both the cost per **agate line** (there are 14 agate lines to an inch of space, one column wide) and the newspaper's circulation:

$$\text{Milline rate (newspaper efficiency)} = \frac{\text{Cost per agate line} \times 1,000,000}{\text{Circulation}}$$

The **milline rate** represents the cost to a retailer of one agate line per million circulation. A newspaper with a circulation of 400,000 and an agate-line rate of $5.50 has a milline rate of $13.75.

Magazine efficiency is based on cost per thousand (rather than a milline rate):

$$\text{Cost per thousand (magazine efficiency)} = \frac{\text{Cost per page} \times 1,000}{\text{Circulation}}$$

A magazine with a circulation of two million and a per-page rate of $23,000 has a cost per thousand of $11.50.

In both of these calculations, total circulation is used to obtain efficiency. However, because a retailer appeals to a limited target market, only the relevant portion of circulation should be considered. Thus, if 70 per cent of the magazine's readers are target customers, the real cost per thousand is

$$\text{Cost per thousand (target market)} = \frac{\text{Cost per page} \times 1,000}{\text{Circulation} \times \dfrac{\text{Target market}}{\text{Circulation}}}$$

$$= \frac{\$23,000 \times 1,000}{2,000,000 \times 0.70}$$

$$= \frac{\$23,000,000}{1,400,000} = \$16.43$$

Different media require different lead times. For instance, a newspaper advertisement can be placed shortly before publication, whereas a magazine advertisement must be placed months in advance. In addition, the retailer must decide what editorial content he or she wants to be near the advertisement (e.g., sports story, comics, personal care column, or feature story).

Timing of the Promotional Mix

Advertising decisions involve the concepts of reach and frequency. **Reach** refers to the number of distinct people who are exposed to an advertisement during a specified time period. **Frequency** measures the average number of times each person who is reached is exposed to an advertisement during a given time period.

Table 13-8
When Customers Shop and Supermarkets Advertise

Day of Week	Per Cent of Customers Shopping on Given Day*	Per Cent of Independent Supermarkets Placing Newspaper Advertisement*
Sunday	4	15
Monday	5	17
Tuesday	10	15
Wednesday	16	62
Thursday	27	21
Friday	25	3
Saturday	19	6

*Includes multiple answers.

Source: "Wednesday: Best Food Day for Advertising," Progressive Grocer (April 1983), pp. 80, 130. Reprinted by permission.

A retailer can advertise extensively or intensively. **Extensive coverage** means that the advertisement reaches many people but with relatively low frequency. **Intensive coverage** means that the advertisement is placed in selected media and is repeated frequently. Repetition is important, particularly for a store seeking to develop an image or selling new products or services.

In implementing the promotional mix, a retailer must consider peak seasons and whether to mass or distribute the effort.[36] When peak seasons occur, all of the elements of the mix are usually utilized; during slow periods, promotional efforts are usually reduced. A **massed advertising effort** is used by retailers like Avon, who promote mostly during one or two seasons. A **distributed advertising effort** is employed by retailers like McDonald's, who promote constantly throughout the year.

Peak advertising is practiced by supermarkets. As can be seen in Table 13-8, the majority of independently owned supermarkets (62 per cent) named Wednesday as the day when a major weekly newspaper advertisement was placed. This placement takes advantage of the fact that a heavy proportion of consumers conduct their major shopping trip on Thursday, Friday, and Saturday.

Sales-force size can vary by time (morning versus evening), day (weekdays versus weekends), and month (December versus January). Sales promotions also vary in their timing. Store openings and holidays are especially good times for sales promotions.

Content of Messages

Whether written or spoken, personally or impersonally delivered, message content is important. In advertising, themes, wording, headlines, use of color, size, layout, and placement must be decided on. Publicity releases need to be written. In personal selling, the greeting, the sales presentation, the manner of demonstration, and the closing must be implemented. In sales promotion, the firm's message must be composed and placed on the promotional device.

[36]See Jesse E. Teel and William O. Bearden, "A Media Planning Algorithm for Retail Advertisers," *Journal of Retailing*, Vol. 56 (Winter 1980), pp. 23–30.

To a large extent, the characteristics of the promotional form determine the message. A shopping bag usually contains no more than a store's name; a billboard (seen at 55 miles per hour) is good for pictures but can hold limited written material; and a salesperson can maintain a customer's attention for a while, thus expanding the content of the message that is conveyed. Franchisors can develop national campaigns and slogans.[37]

In advertising, distinctiveness is an aid to the retailer because of the proliferation of messages. For example, cluttered advertisements displaying many products suggest a discounter's orientation, and fine pencil drawings and limited product displays suggest a specialty store orientation.

Recently, more retailers have become involved with **comparative advertising,** whereby messages compare their offerings with those of competitors. Comparative advertising is used to help position a retailer in relation to competitors, increase awareness of the retailer, maximize the efficiency of a limited budget, and provide credibility. However, comparative ads provide visibility for competitors, may confuse consumers, and may lead to legal action by competitors. Fast-food and off-price retailers are among those now utilizing comparative advertising.[38]

Makeup of Sales Force

Qualifications for sales personnel are detailed, and personnel are recruited, selected, trained, compensated, supervised, and controlled. Personnel are also classified (order takers versus order getters) and assigned to the appropriate departments. An in-depth discussion regarding the personal sales force was provided in Chapter 9.

Sales Promotion Tools

The specific sales promotion tools are chosen from among those listed in Table 13-4. The combination of sales promotion tools depends on short-run (and changing) objectives and the other components of the promotion mix. Wherever possible, cooperative ventures with manufacturers or wholesalers are sought, and tools inconsistent with store image are not used.

Responsibility for Coordination

Regardless of a store's size or organizational form, someone within the retail organization must have authority over and responsibility for the promotion function. Larger retailers normally assign this job to a vice-president of promotion, who is in charge of display personnel, works with the firm's advertising agency, supervises the store's own advertising department, and supplies branch stores with necessary supplementary (in-store) materials. Personal selling is usually under the jurisdiction of the store manager in a large retail setting.

[37]Ronald Alsop, "Ad Agencies Press Franchises to Join National Campaigns," *Wall Street Journal* (January 17, 1985), p. 29.
[38]Scott Hume, "Fast-Food's Favorites Fire Fast, Furious Flurries," *Advertising Age* (October 29, 1984), pp. 10, 82; and Katherine Joyce, "Name Names?" *Stores* (September 1983), pp. 22ff.

The Eaton Centre 1984/85 Promotion Schedule

Week of Monday	NOV 29	NOV 5	NOV 12	NOV 19	NOV 26	DEC 3	DEC 10	DEC 17	DEC 24	JAN 31	JAN 7	JAN 14	JAN 21	FEB 28	FEB 4	FEB 11	FEB 18	FEB 25	MAR 4	MAR 11	MAR 18	MAR 25	APR 1	APR 8	APR 15	APR 22	MAY 29	MAY 6	MAY 13	MAY 20	JUNE 27	JUNE 3	JUNE 10	JUNE 17	JUNE 24	JULY 1	JULY 8	JULY 15	JULY 22	AUG 29	AUG 5	AUG 12	AUG 19	SEPT 26	SEPT 2	SEPT 9	SEPT 16	SEPT 23	OCT 30	OCT 7	OCT 14	OCT 21
Television: 30's (52 Weeks)	X	X	X	X	X	X	X	X	X	X	X	X	X	X	X	X	X	X	X	X	X	X	X	X	X	X	X	X	X	X	X	X	X	X	X	X	X	X	X	X	X	X	X	X	X	X	X	X	X	X	X	X
Subway Door Cards (200)	X	X	X	X	X	X	X	X	X	X	X	X	X	X	X	X	X	X	X	X	X	X	X	X	X	X	X	X	X	X	X	X	X	X	X	X	X	X	X	X	X	X	X	X	X	X	X	X	X	X	X	X
Queen Street Sign	X	X	X	X	X	X	X	X	X	X	X	X	X	X	X	X	X	X	X	X	X	X	X	X	X	X	X	X	X	X	X	X	X	X	X	X	X	X	X	X	X	X	X	X	X	X	X	X	X	X	X	X
Information Centres	X	X	X	X	X	X	X	X	X	X	X	X	X	X	X	X	X	X	X	X	X	X	X	X	X	X	X	X	X	X	X	X	X	X	X	X	X	X	X	X	X	X	X	X	X	X	X	X	X	X	X	X
Newspaper																																																				
Star (SUN) B&W			X			X								X						X							X							X							X						X		X			
(M-F) B+1 Color								X				X																						X				X														
(M-F) B+1 Color									X				X																										X													
Sun (SUN) B+W			X			X								X						X							X							X							X						X					
(M-F) B+1 Color								X				X																						X				X														
(M-F) B+1 Color									X				X																										X													
Magazines																																																				
Toronto Life Fashion 4 Color	X																									X															X				X							
Toronto Life 4 Color																X													X				X				X									X						
Key to Toronto 4 Color																													X			X				X																
Transit Shelters																																X	X	X	X	X	X	X	X				X									X
Special Events and Promotions	X	X			X	X		X			X	X		X	X	X	X	X		X							X		X			X		X		X		X		X	X		X			X	X		X			X

Courtesy Eaton Centre, Toronto, Canada.

Figure 13-3

For promotional strategy to be successful, its components have to be coordinated with other elements of the retail mix. As an example, sales personnel must be informed of a special sale and must know product characteristics; sales items must be received, marked, and properly displayed; and the bookkeeping entries must be made.

Often a shopping center or a shopping district runs a theme promotion, such as "Back-to-School," and someone has to be charged with the responsibility of coordinating the activities of all the stores participating in the event. Figure 13-3 shows the promotion plan of a shopping center over a full year.

Reviewing and Revising the Promotional Plan

An analysis of the success of a promotion plan depends on the objectives of the plan, and analysis is simplified if promotional objectives are clearly stated in advance (as suggested in this chapter). Modifications would be made for promotional tools not achieving their preset goals.

Table 13-9 lists a number of research approaches for testing the effectiveness of a promotional effort. Although difficulties exist in reviewing promotion (e.g., increased

Table 13-9
Measuring Promotional Effectiveness

Behaviorally Oriented Promotion Objectives	Selected Retail Promotion Objectives	Research Approaches for Evaluating Promotion Effectiveness
Cognitive: the realm of thoughts; promotion designed to provide information and facts	Inform current customers about new credit plans; acquaint potential customers with new products	Study store and product awareness before and after promotion; evaluate extent of promotion readership by number of people and degree of readership
Affective: the realm of emotions; promotion designed to change attitudes and feelings	Develop and reinforce high-fashion image; maintain customer loyalty	Study image via semantic differential, projective techniques, rank-order preference for stores, and rating scales before and after promotion
Conative: the realm of motives; promotion designed to stimulate or direct desires	Increase store traffic; produce leads for salespeople; increase sales over last year; reduce customer returns from last year	Evaluate sales performance and number of inquiries; study consumers' intentions to buy before and after promotion; study customer trading areas and average purchases; study coupon redemption

Source: Adapted from Robert Lavidge and Gary A. Steiner, "A Model for Predictive Measurement of Advertising Effectiveness," Journal of Marketing, Vol. 25 (October 1961), p. 61. Reprinted with permission of the American Marketing Association.

sales may be due to a variety of factors, not just promotion), it is still necessary for a retailer to systematically study and adjust the promotional mix.[39]

Communicating with the Customer— Promotional Strategy: A Summary

Retail promotion involves informing, persuading, and/or reminding customers through advertising, publicity, personal selling, and sales promotion. Advertising is nonpersonal and has the advantages of a large audience, low costs per person, many alternative media, and so on. The disadvantages of advertising include an inflexible message, high absolute costs, and a wasted portion of audience. The major advertising media are newspapers, telephone directories, direct mail, radio, television, transit, outdoor, magazines, and flyers/circulars. Of particular importance are cooperative ads, for which the retailer shares the costs and message with manufacturers, wholesalers, or other retailers.

Publicity is nonpersonal, nonpaid communication. Advantages include enhancing image, objective source, and no costs for message. Disadvantages include actual costs, short-run nature, and lack of control over message. Types of publicity are community service, parades, new-product introductions, store openings, and media visits (gourmet reporter).

Personal selling involves personal contact with customers and is important in closing sales. Some advantages are personalization, flexibility, and immediate feedback. Some disadvantages are small audience, high costs per customer, and inability to lure customers into the store. Order-taking (routine) and order-getting (creative) selling personnel are employed. Sales functions include greeting the customer, determining wants, showing merchandise, making a sales presentation, demonstrating merchandise, answering objections, and closing the sale.

Sales promotion is a supplement to advertising and personal selling. Among the advantages are that it is eye catching, unique, and valuable to the customer. Among the disadvantages are that it is difficult to terminate, may have a negative effect on image, and relies on frivolous selling points. Examples of sales promotion are contests, sweepstakes, coupons, trading stamps, prizes, samples, demonstrations, referral gifts, matchbooks, pens, calendars, shopping bags, special events, and skywriting.

Planning a retail promotional strategy consists of five steps: determining promotion objectives, establishing a promotion budget, determining the promotion mix, implementing the mix, and reviewing and revising the promotion plan.

First, objectives need to be stated in specific and measurable terms. Second, an overall promotion budget is set with the selection of one technique from among the all-you-can-afford, incremental, competitive-parity, percentage-of-sales, and objective-and-task methods. Third, the promotional mix is outlined, based on the size of the budget, the type of retailing, the coverage of the media, and the stage in the hierarchy-of-effects model.

Fourth, the promotional mix is implemented. Included are decisions involving

---

[39]See also Lawrence C. Soley and William L. James, "Estimating the Readership of Retail Newspaper Advertising," *Journal of Retailing*, Vol. 58 (Fall 1982), pp. 59–75; Mark Moriarity, "Feature Advertising-Price Interaction Effects in the Retail Environment," *Journal of Retailing*, Vol. 59 (Summer 1983), pp. 80–98; and Dale H. Stern, "Account Analysis Yields Better Promotion Tactics," *Marketing News* (January 4, 1985), p. 58.

specific media, timing of promotion, content of messages, makeup of the sales force, specific sales promotion tools, and responsibility for coordination. Last, the retailer systematically reviews and revises the promotional plan, consistent with the preset objectives.

Questions for Discussion

1. Are there any retailers who should not use advertising? Explain your answer.
2. How would an advertising plan for a small retailer differ from that of a large retail chain?
3. How do manufacturers' and retailers' cooperative advertising goals overlap? How do they differ?
4. Why is publicity difficult to plan?
5. How should a store react to negative publicity?
6. Develop a plan for a small retailer to generate positive publicity for his or her store.
7. Give three examples of order takers and order getters. Under which circumstances should each type of salesperson be used?
8. How do advertising and personal selling complement each other for a retailer?
9. Are there any retailers who should not use sales promotion? Explain your answer.
10. Develop sales promotions for each of the following.
    a. A new music hall in a major metropolitan area
    b. An existing restaurant now open on Sunday for the first time
    c. An existing newspaper stand
    d. A new supermarket in a moderate-sized suburb
11. Which method of promotional budgeting should a small retailer use? Why? A large retailer? Why?
12. Explain the hierarchy-of-effects model from a retail perspective.
13. Describe the difference between frequency and reach in retail advertising.
14. Develop a checklist for coordinating a promotional plan.
15. For each of the following promotional objectives, explain how to evaluate promotional effectiveness.
    a. Increase store traffic by 10 per cent
    b. Develop a high-fashion image
    c. Maintain customer loyalty

CASES

1. Long John Silver's: A National Promotion Plan*

Long John Silver's Seafood Shoppes is a large fast-food restaurant chain, with 1,350 outlets and annual sales of several hundred million dollars. The company accounts for about 60 per cent of fast-food seafood sales in the United States. It

*The material in this case is drawn from Richard Kreisman, "Jerrico Taking Slow Approach to Fast Growth," *Advertising Age* (December 14, 1981), pp. 4, 77; Television Bureau of Advertising, "Fast-Food Chains' TV Spending," *Advertising Age* (March 19, 1984), p. 1, and (December 10, 1984), p. 2; and Scott Hume, "Silver Sets Sail for Showdown," *Advertising Age* (February 11, 1985), p. 62.

contains both company-owned and franchised outlets; new company-owned units are totally financed from internal funds.

Most of Long John Silver's success and growth are relatively recent. In the mid-1970s, operations were ineffective and quality control was poor. By 1977, the chain had to close stores in a number of cities, including Boston and New York. The company's revival began in 1978 as a modified strategy stressed food quality, increased portion sizes, incentives for managers, and a product-centered advertising campaign. One agency, Abbott Advertising, began developing plans for the entire chain.

These are the highlights of Long John Silver's current promotion plan:

- About $25 million is spent annually on advertising, most for television and print media. Unlike many other chains, Long John Silver's total television budget is used for commercials running in specific markets (in comparison, about two-thirds of McDonald's television ads are presented nationally). The firm runs television ads in about 130 of 200 major markets.
- Sales promotions do not include chainwide games and sweepstakes, which are sometimes used by fast-food restaurants such as Burger King. Instead, special offers and coupons are often featured, together with local tie-ins.
- With the assistance of its advertising agency, Long John Silver's has divided its markets and promotional efforts into four groups. See Table 1. As shown, each market type has different characteristics and a different media mix.

The future plans of Long John Silver's will be affected by three factors. One, competition from McDonald's and Burger King and others is increasing as these firms add fish products. In response, Long John Silver's is diversifying its product line. Two, further market expansion in California is being actively considered; in addition, Long John Silver's plans to strengthen already solid markets. Three, the

Table 1
Market Analysis by Long John Silver's

Market Group	Characteristics*
Mature markets	Large density of Long John Silver's stores. Rely on a large television effort. Account for about 40 per cent of outlets. High average annual sales for outlets.
Emerging markets	Growing density of Long John Silver's stores. Depend on a moderate television effort. Contain about 38 per cent of outlets.
Underdeveloped markets	Low number of Long John Silver's. Can use limited amount of television. Newspaper ads more important. Good growth potential. Possess about 15 per cent of outlets.
Pioneer markets	Only one or a few scattered Long John Silver's. Cannot utilize television. Newspaper ads essential. Some markets with strong growth potential, others with limited potential. Contain about 7 per cent of outlets. Lowest average annual sales for outlets.

*The percentage of outlets in each type of market is estimated by the authors.

feasibility of cable television advertising, which pinpoints key markets, is under investigation.

Questions

1. Evaluate Long John Silver's strategy not to use sweepstakes.
2. Analyze the information in Table 1. What conclusions should Long John Silver's reach?
3. As a Long John Silver's franchisee, what types of cooperative promotional efforts would you expect?
4. Develop a retail promotional strategy to be used by outlets in pioneer markets as they become underdeveloped, emerging, and mature markets. Include the hierarchy-of-effects model in your discussion.

---

2. Ellie's Leather Goods: Modifying a Promotion Strategy

Ellie Farmer owns two leather goods stores that feature luggage, women's bags, attaché cases, and wallets. One of the stores is over 20 years old, the other was opened just two years ago. While the stores are located within 7 miles of each other, there is little overlap in the outlets' target markets, location strategy, and image.

The older store is situated on a major street in a working-class area, surrounded by neighborhood-oriented shops (such as a dry cleaner, fruit store, and bakery). It has old, blond-color cabinets and dated fixtures. In comparison with the newer store, its customers are less concerned with style (fashion), less likely to comparison shop, more influenced by sales personnel recommendations, and more likely to buy an item as a gift. Fewer high-priced goods are carried in the older store.

In contrast, the newer store is situated in a community shopping center anchored by a junior department store in an affluent neighborhood. Its fixtures are chrome and glass, and it utilizes plush carpeting and silver/black stripes on the walls. This outlet's customers are more knowledgeable, less susceptible to sales presentations, value conscious, style (fashion) conscious, more likely to comparison shop, and less likely to buy an item as a gift. Many unique, high-priced goods are carried in the newer store.

Each store has a separate name and a distinctive retailing mix; however, Ellie does not hide the fact that she owns both stores. Furthermore, she frequently transfers merchandise between stores, recommends that shoppers in the older store who are interested in more expensive goods visit the newer store, and stocks 80 per cent of the same merchandise in the two stores. She does feel somewhat apprehensive about customers of the newer store traveling to the older store.

Until now, Ellie has relied on personal selling, in-store displays, special mailings to loyal customers, and word-of-mouth communication in her promotion strategy. But for three reasons, Ellie believes the time is right to begin advertising. One, the older store has a new competitor. Advertising will help reinforce the store's image in the community. Two, the existence of two stores may allow Ellie to use advertising more efficiently than would the ownership of one leather goods store. Three, area department stores have increased their advertising expenditures for leather goods. Ellie needs to make sure customers are aware of her stores.

In developing her advertising plan, Ellie has identified the following as key factors to be considered:

- Both stores are based on a full-service, fair-profit-margin concept—personal service, a generous return policy, and repair services are provided.
- First-quality, popular brands are carried. All products are genuine leather. No synthetics are sold.
- Ads should not be dominated by price. A "classy" look is necessary.
- While flyers and penny-saver newspapers have excellent geographic fit for both stores, garage sales, used furniture vendors, car washes, and others are advertising in these media.
- Customer demand is seasonal, and it varies by product category. For example, attaché cases are good gift items and have high holiday sales. Luggage is popular during May and June, as consumers prepare for vacations.
- One advertising message can be used for both stores or separate messages can be developed.
- Between $10,000 and $15,000 is available for yearly advertising.

Questions

1. What are the advantages and disadvantages of using one advertising message for both stores? Would you recommend this approach? Why or why not?
2. Develop a yearly media plan for Ellie Farmer. Explain your answer.
3. Which types of sales promotion should Ellie use at each store? Explain your answer.
4. How could Ellie determine the effectiveness of her new promotion plan?

Pricing in Retailing

Chapter Objectives

1. To describe the role of pricing in a retail strategy
2. To evaluate the effects of the consumer, the government, manufacturers, wholesalers, suppliers, and current and potential competitors on pricing decisions
3. To integrate a retailer's pricing objectives with organizational objectives
4. To examine demand, cost, and competitive pricing strategies and their implementation
5. To study the price-adjustment process

American TV & Appliance is a discount retailer that sells televisions, cameras, computers, stereo equipment, appliances, and furniture in extremely large, warehouse-type stores. It operates outlets in Madison, Appleton, and Milwaukee, Wisconsin, and Marquette, Michigan. The most distinctive aspect of American's strategy is its flexible pricing policy. Except for sales, American has no fixed prices; customers come in and bargain with salespeople.

American's sales force is paid on a straight commission basis, keyed to the markup received on each item sold—the higher the markup, the higher the commission. Accordingly, a salesperson can make different commissions by selling the identical product to two customers at different prices.

The company's pricing policy is simple:

> The rule of thumb says you tie your prices to your costs . . . But we try to tie ours as close as we can to just how much the customers are willing to pop. We don't ask ourselves, 'Gee, what did this product cost us?' We ask, 'What will this particular customer be willing to pay for this particular product at this particular moment?' How do you establish that? Well, we give every customer a shot at setting their own price.

To the displeasure of competitors, American's customers are doing their best to be prepared for its sales personnel. Before going to American, they visit small full-service stores, where they learn about product features. Next, they comparison shop at other discounters. Finally, they ask American to beat the lowest price.[1]

Overview

A retailer must price merchandise in a manner that achieves profitability for the store and satisfies customers, while adapting to a variety of constraints.

Pricing is a crucial strategic variable for a retailer because of its direct relationship with a firm's objectives and its interaction with other retailing-mix elements. A retailer's pricing strategy must be consistent with his or her overall sales, profit, and return-on-investment objectives. For example, a retailer interested in an early recovery of a cash investment, because of expansion plans, might enact a mass-marketing strategy. This approach utilizes low prices.

The interaction of price with other retail elements can be shown through the following illustration. Tie Town is a proposed tie shop whose two partners are evolving a broad strategy consisting of

* A target market of price-conscious men.
* Selling inexpensive ties in the $7.00 to $10.00 range.
* A limited range of merchandise quality.
* Self-service.
* A downtown location.
* Depth of assortment.
* Quantity purchases at discount.
* An image of efficiency and variety.

This chapter divides retail pricing into two major sections, factors affecting price strategy and the development of a price strategy.

Factors Affecting Retail Price Strategy

Before detailing the development of a pricing strategy, it is necessary to discuss the factors that affect price decision making. Consumers, government, manufacturers and wholesalers, and competitors each have an impact on the pricing strategy of a retailer, as shown in Figure 14-1. In some cases, these factors severely restrict a retailer's options in setting prices; in other cases, the factors have only a minor effect.

The Consumer and Retail Pricing

A retailer must understand the relationship between price and consumers' purchases and perceptions. Two economic principles explain this relationship: the law of demand and the price elasticity of demand.

The **law of demand** states that consumers usually purchase more units at low prices than at high prices. The **price elasticity of demand** relates to the sensitivity of buyers

---

[1]Ralph Whitehead, Jr., "Name Your Price," *Inc.* (December 1984), pp. 214, 216.

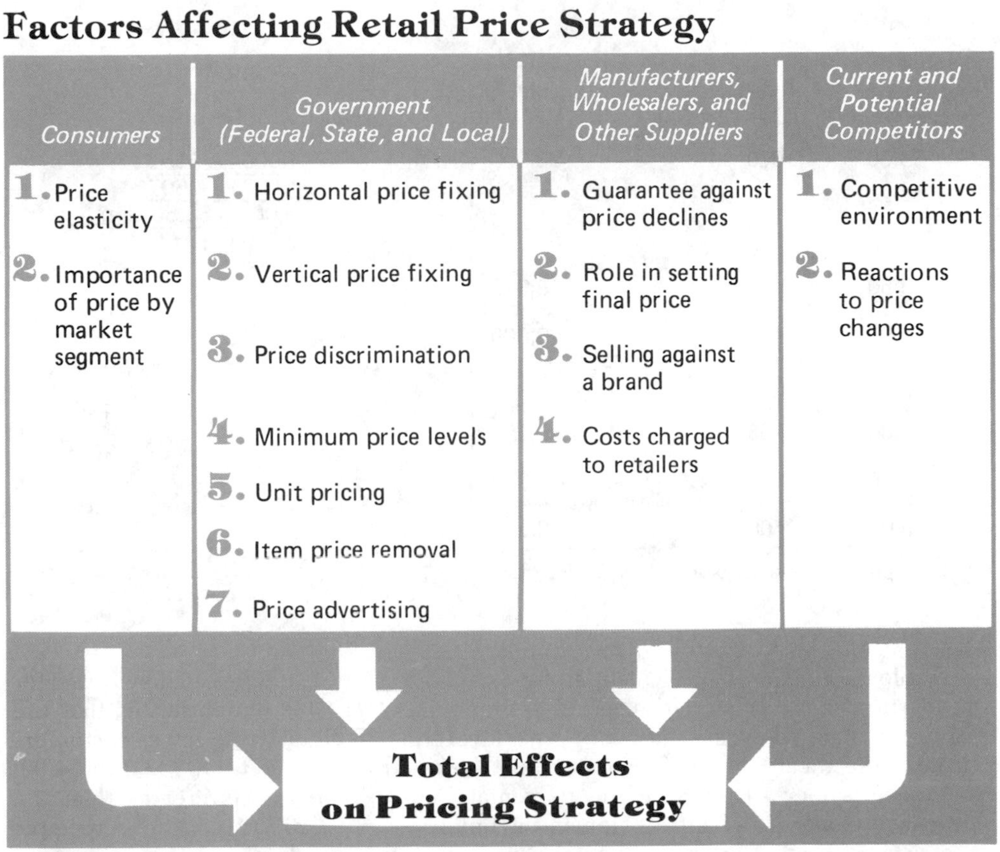

Factors Affecting Retail Price Strategy

Consumers	Government (Federal, State, and Local)	Manufacturers, Wholesalers, and Other Suppliers	Current and Potential Competitors
1. Price elasticity	1. Horizontal price fixing	1. Guarantee against price declines	1. Competitive environment
2. Importance of price by market segment	2. Vertical price fixing	2. Role in setting final price	2. Reactions to price changes
	3. Price discrimination	3. Selling against a brand	
	4. Minimum price levels	4. Costs charged to retailers	
	5. Unit pricing		
	6. Item price removal		
	7. Price advertising		

Total Effects on Pricing Strategy

Figure 14-1

to price changes in terms of the quantities they will purchase. If relatively small percentage changes in price result in substantial percentage changes in the number of units purchased, then price elasticity is high. This occurs when the urgency of a purchase is low or acceptable substitutes exist. However, when large percentage changes in price have small percentage changes in the number of units purchased, demand is considered to be inelastic. This occurs when the urgency of purchase is high or there are no acceptable substitutes (as takes place with store loyalty). Unitary elasticity occurs in the cases where percentage changes in price are directly offset by percentage changes in quantity.

Price elasticity is computed by dividing the percentage change in quantity demanded by the percentage change in the price charged:

$$\text{Elasticity} = \frac{\dfrac{\text{Quantity 1} - \text{Quantity 2}}{\text{Quantity 1} + \text{Quantity 2}}}{\dfrac{\text{Price 1} - \text{Price 2}}{\text{Price 1} + \text{Price 2}}}$$

Because the law of demand shows that quantities purchased decline as prices go up, elasticity is usually a negative number.

Table 14-1
A Movie Theater's Elasticity of Demand

Price	Tickets Sold (Saturday Night)	Total Ticket Receipts	Elasticity of Demand*	
$3.00	1000	$3,000	$E = \dfrac{\dfrac{1{,}000 - 950}{1{,}000 + 950}}{\dfrac{\$3.00 - \$3.50}{\$3.00 + \$3.50}} = 0.33$	
3.50	950	3,325	$E =$	0.41
4.00	900	3,600	$E =$	1.00
4.50	800	3,600	$E =$	1.27
5.00	700	3,500	$E =$	1.62
5.50	600	3,300	$E =$	2.09
6.00	500	3,000		

*Expressed as a positive number.

Table 14-1 shows the calculation of price elasticity for a 1,200-seat movie theater (the elasticities are converted to positive numbers). The table demonstrates that the quantity demanded declines at every price level from $3.00 to $6.00; fewer customers patronize the theater at $6.00 than at $3.00. Demand is inelastic from $3.00 to $4.00; total receipts increase because the percentage change in price is greater than the percentage change in quantity. Demand is unitary from $4.00 to $4.50; total receipts are constant because the percentage change in quantity exactly offsets the percentage change in price. Demand is elastic from $4.50 to $6.00; total receipts decline because the percentage change in quantity is greater than the percentage change in price.

For this example, total ticket receipts are highest at $4.00 or at $4.50. But what about the total revenues for the theater? If patrons spend an average of $2 each at the concession stand, the best price would be $4.00 (total overall revenues of $5,400). The movie theater is interested only in revenues, because costs would be the same whether there would be 900 or 800 patrons. Other retailers would evaluate profit as well as sales.

In retailing, the computation of price elasticity is often difficult for two reasons. First, as in the case of the movie theater, demand for individual events or items may be hard to predict. One week the theater may attract 1,000 patrons to a movie and the following week it may attract 400 patrons to a different movie. Second, retailers such as supermarkets and department stores sell thousands of items and could not possibly compute elasticities for each. Accordingly, many retailers rely on average markup pricing, competition, tradition, and industrywide data as indicators of price elasticity.

Consumer sensitivity to price varies by market segment. On the basis of a classic study, consumers can be divided into four categories, depending on their shopping orientations:

1. Economic—interested primarily in shopping for values and extremely sensitive to price, quality, and merchandise assortment.

2. Personalizing—shops where he or she is known, strong personal attachment with store personnel and the store itself.
3. Ethical—willing to sacrifice lower prices and better assortment of goods in larger stores or chains to help the smaller store stay in business.
4. Apathetic—shops only because he or she must, wants to finish as quickly as possible, and places emphasis on convenience.[2]

The Government and Retail Pricing

When examining the impact of government on planning a pricing strategy, it must be remembered that three levels of government exist: federal, state, and local. Although many of the key laws are federal, these laws apply only to interstate commerce. Therefore a retailer who operates exclusively within the boundaries of one state may not be restricted by federal legislation.

Legislation focuses on seven major areas: horizontal price fixing, vertical price fixing, price discrimination, minimum price levels, unit pricing, item price removal, and price advertising.

Horizontal Price Fixing

Horizontal price fixing involves an agreement among manufacturers, among wholesalers, or among retailers to set certain prices. Such agreements are illegal according to the Sherman Antitrust Act and the Federal Trade Commission Act, regardless of how "reasonable" the resultant prices may be. It is also illegal for retailers to reach agreements with one another regarding the use of coupons, rebates, or other price-oriented tactics.

Following are two recent examples of horizontal price fixing and the legal ramifications:

- The managers of three supermarkets (First National, Fisher Foods, and Stop-&-Shop) met weekly in parking lots late at night and jointly decided what "specials" each would offer and at what prices. These managers knew their actions were not legal and worked hard to keep them secret. As a result, the supermarkets were fined a total of $1.7 million and four executives were fined $100,000 each. The executives also received suspended jail sentences and were placed on five years' probation.[3]
- Four supermarket chains (Waldbaum, Supermarkets General–Pathmark, King Kullen, and LAMM) had an agreement that limited the use of double and triple coupons. With these coupons, the retailers would match or exceed the coupon value offered by the manufacturer with store discounts. However, it was charged that the chains conspired to stop double and triple couponing during certain periods. The chains were ordered to pay fines totaling $830,000.[4]

---

[2]Gregory P. Stone, "City Shoppers and Urban Identification: Observation on the Social Psychology of City Life," *American Journal of Sociology*, Vol. 60 (July 1954), pp. 36–45.
[3]Michael A. Duggan, "United States v. First National Supermarkets," *Journal of Marketing*, Vol. 47 (Fall 1983), pp. 127–128.
[4]"Four Supermarket Concerns Are Fined Total of $830,000," *Wall Street Journal* (November 27, 1984), p. 64.

Vertical Price Fixing

Vertical price fixing occurs when manufacturers or wholesalers are able to control the retail prices of their goods and services. Until 1975, this practice was allowed because of the belief that manufacturers and wholesalers had the right to protect the reputations of their brands and that these reputations could be diluted through indiscriminant price cutting by retailers. In addition, vertical price fixing was viewed as providing **fair trade** protection for smaller and full-service retailers in competition with discounters. Manufacturers enforced fair trade legislation by setting uniform retail prices for their items and then refusing to sell to those retailers utilizing price cutting or by seeking government intervention.

Fair trade laws were criticized by consumer groups and many manufacturers, wholesalers, and retailers as being anticompetitive, keeping prices artificially high, and allowing inefficient retailers to stay in business. As a result, the Consumer Goods Pricing Act of 1975, which terminated the interstate use of fair trade practices and resale price maintenance, was enacted. At present, retailers cannot be required to adhere to list prices developed by manufacturers and wholesalers.

Today, manufacturers and wholesalers can control retail prices only through one of these methods. One, they can own retail facilities. Two, they can use consignment selling, whereby the supplier owns items until they are sold and assumes all costs normally associated with the retailer. Three, they can carefully screen retailers. Four, they can set realistic list prices. Five, they can preprint prices on products. Six, they can establish regular prices that are accepted by consumers (such as $0.25 for a newspaper.)[5]

The continuing legal struggle among manufacturers, wholesalers, and retailers for control of selling prices can be seen through the following:

- In 1984, the U.S. Supreme Court upheld a $10.5 million judgment against Monsanto. The Supreme Court found that Monsanto and its distributors agreed to fix the resale prices of herbicides in order to drive price cutters out of business. However, the court also ruled that a manufacturer could terminate agreements with individual distributors as long as there was no collusive action.[6]
- Fortunoff, a four-store discount chain, recently filed suit against North American Watch Corporation (the wholesaler for Piaget, Corum, Concord, and Movado watches) and Tiffany & Co. (a prestige jewelry store chain). Fortunoff accused North American and Tiffany with conspiring to fix prices by refusing to sell premium watches to it and other discounters.[7]
- As of June 1983, Pioneer Electronics cut off distribution to all retail catalog showrooms. Pioneer stated that it wanted to reduce the number of retailers it was using. Its president noted: "Our product was overdistributed. When you have product in too many places, it doesn't have much value to anybody." To this, a catalog showroom dealer responded: "The end result is that consumers pay more."[8]

---

[5]Joel R. Evans and Barry Berman, *Marketing*, Second Edition (New York: Macmillan, 1985), pp. 544–545.
[6]Pravat K. Choudhury, "Antitrust Decision Provides Succor for Price-Cutters and Manufacturers," *Marketing News* (November 23, 1984), p. 18.
[7]"Fortunoff Files Suit Against Watch Firms, Charging Price Fixing," *Wall Street Journal* (May 3, 1984), p. 14.
[8]Claudia Ricci, "Discounters, Alleging Price-Fixing, Are Fighting Cuts in Their Supplies," *Wall Street Journal* (June 21, 1983), p. 37.

- The FTC has been besieged by advocates representing both sides of the vertical pricing issue. Discounters want it to enforce the laws against price setting. High-fashion retailers want it to restore resale price maintenance; they argue that consumers gather information at full-service stores and then buy at no-frills discount stores.[9]

Price Discrimination

The **Robinson–Patman Act** prohibits manufacturers from discriminating in price or terms of sale among retailers purchasing products of "like quality" if the effect of such discrimination is to injure competition.

Supporters of the Robinson–Patman Act seek to prevent large retailers from using their power to obtain discounts that are not justified by the cost savings achieved through sizable orders. It is feared that smaller retailers will be driven out of business because of noncompetitive final prices if the Robinson–Patman Act is not enforced.

There are exceptions to the Robinson–Patman Act, that allow some forms of price discrimination when

1. Products are physically different.
2. Buyers are not competitors.
3. Competition is not injured.
4. Price differences can be justified by differences in costs.
5. Market conditions change.
   a. Manufacturing costs and so on increase or decrease.
   b. Competitive manufacturers change their prices.

Discounts are not illegal, provided that the manufacturer demonstrates that they are cost-justified, available to all competitive retailers on an equal basis, and sufficiently graduated so that small, as well as large, retailers can qualify. Discounts for cumulative purchases (total orders during the year) and for multistore purchases by chains are extremely difficult to justify.

Although the Robinson–Patman Act seems to restrict sellers more than buyers, retailers do have specific liabilities under Section 2(F) of the Act, which states:

> it shall be unlawful for any person engaged in commerce, in the course of such commerce, knowingly to induce or receive a discrimination in price which is prohibited in this section.

From a strategic perspective, a retail buyer must attempt to receive the lowest prices charged to any competitor of his or her class; yet, he or she must also be careful not to bargain so hard that the discounts received cannot be justified by one of the acceptable exceptions.[10]

[9]Tamar Lewin, "The Noisy War Over Discounting," *New York Times* (September 25, 1983), Section 3, pp. 1, 28; and Stanley E. Cohen, "FTC Re-examines Fair Trade Pricing Laws," *Advertising Age* (April 23, 1984), p. 52.
[10]James C. Johnson and Kenneth C. Schneider, "The Robinson-Patman Act: Potential Pitfalls for Retailers," *Business*, Vol. 34 (January–March 1984), pp. 34–42.

Minimum-Price Laws

Several states have enacted **minimum-price laws** that prevent retailers from selling merchandise for less than the cost of the product plus a fixed percentage that covers overhead. Merchandise costs are defined in various ways; typically, they are the acquisition or replacement costs, whichever are lower.

Minimum-price laws are intended to protect small retailers from predatory pricing by larger competitors. In **predatory pricing,** big retailers attempt to destroy competition by selling goods at extremely low prices, which causes small retailers to go out of business.

Loss leaders—items priced below cost to draw customer traffic into the store—are restricted by minimum-price laws. Retailers such as supermarkets frequently use loss leaders to increase overall sales and profits under the assumption that consumers will buy more than one item once drawn into the store. Because loss leaders are usually consumer oriented, minimum-price laws are rarely applied in these cases.

In addition to general laws, a number of states have acts that set minimum prices for specific products. For instance, in New Jersey and Connecticut, state laws require that the retail price of liquor be not less than the wholesale cost (including taxes and delivery charges).[11]

Unit Pricing

The proliferation of different-sized packages has led to the enactment of **unit-pricing** legislation. The aim of this legislation is to enable consumers to compare prices of products that come in many sizes (e.g., small, medium, and large).

Food stores are most affected by unit price regulations, and in many cases, these stores must express price per unit of measure and total package size. For example, a 6.5-ounce can of tuna fish priced at 89 cents must also be marked as $2.19 per pound. Therefore, a consumer can determine that a 12-ounce can of soda selling for 27 cents (2.25 cents per ounce) is actually cheaper than a 28-ounce bottle of soda selling for 80 cents (2.86 cents per ounce).

Unit-pricing laws are intended to give necessary information to consumers who feel price is an important decision variable and to provide additional information for those customers who consider brand-name or other product variables as most important. Although early research studies questioned the effectiveness of unit pricing, later findings indicated that unit pricing is advantageous to retailers as well as consumers.[12]

Not all stores must comply with unit pricing. There are generally exemptions for retailers with low-volume sales or for those operating only one outlet. In addition, grocery items are much more heavily regulated than nongrocery items.

The costs of unit pricing to retailers include calculations of per unit prices, printing of product labels, printing of shelf labels, and computer records. These costs are affected by the way prices are adhered (manually versus machine), the number of items in a store subject to unit pricing, the frequency of price changes, sales volume, and the number of stores in a chain. A number of supermarket chains have reported that the costs of unit pricing are not excessive, whereas smaller food stores report that the costs are quite high.

[11]Joseph P. Fried, "Court Upsets New York's Minimum Liquor Pricing," *New York Times* (June 12, 1984), p. B4.
[12]See David A. Aaker and Gary T. Ford, "Unit Pricing Ten Years Later: A Replication," *Journal of Marketing,* Vol. 47 (Winter 1983), pp. 118–122.

Unit pricing is an advantageous strategy for consumer-oriented retailers to follow, even when not required to by law. As an illustration, Giant Food found that its unit-pricing system more than paid for itself through decreases in price-marking errors, better inventory control, and improved space management.

Item Price Removal

The expansion of computerized checkout systems has led many retailers, particularly supermarkets, to advocate **item price removal.** With item price removal, prices are marked only on shelves or signs and not on individual items. This practice is banned in several states and local communities.

Supermarkets advocate that item price removal would significantly reduce their labor costs and enable them to offer lower prices to consumers. Opponents argue that item price removal would lead to more checkout errors against consumers and make it virtually impossible for consumers to verify prices as they are rung up.[13]

Nationwide, over 1,200 food retailers had stopped item pricing by 1982. These stores save from 0.2 to 0.5 per cent of sales annually by eliminating the costs associated with item pricing. Giant Food practices item price removal in all its supermarkets, and there has been little consumer resistance and considerable cost savings. Giant carefully maintains accurate, highly visible shelf prices and gives items free to consumers if the prices processed by its electronic cash registers (equipped with scanners) are higher than those posted on shelves.[14]

Price Advertising

Both the Federal Trade Commission (FTC) and the Better Business Bureau (BBB) have guidelines with regard to the advertising of retail prices. These guidelines deal with the advertising of price reductions, the advertising of a retail price in relation to its list price or a competitor's price, and bait-and-switch advertising.

In general, the FTC guidelines state that a merchant cannot claim or imply that a price has been reduced from some former level unless the former price was an actual, bona fide one at which the merchant offered a product to the public on a regular basis during a reasonably substantial, recent period of time.

When the retailer claims that his or her price is lower than the manufacturer's list or suggested list price or lower than the price in other stores, the FTC guidelines state that the retailer must make certain that the price comparisons pertain to competitive stores selling large quantities in the same trading area. For example, in 1981, the FTC issued a consent order against Kroger. The supermarket chain was prohibited from advertising itself as the "price leader" on the basis of a comparison of its prices with those of competitors for just 100 to 150 items (out of the thousands stocked).[15] The consent order ended in 1984.

[13]See Brian F. Harris and Michael K. Mills, "The Impact of Item Price Removal in Scanner Supermarkets. A Survey of Los Angeles Shoppers," *Journal of Consumer Affairs*, Vol. 16 (Winter 1982), pp. 362–383; Frederick W. Langrehr and Virginia Blansett Langrehr, "Consumer Acceptance of Item Price Removal: A Survey Study of Milwaukee Shoppers," *Journal of Consumer Affairs*, Vol. 17 (Summer 1983), pp. 149–171; and Valarie A. Zeithaml, "Consumer Response to In-Store Price Information Environments," *Journal of Consumer Research*, Vol. 8 (March 1982), pp. 357–368.
[14]Charlene C. Price and Charles Handy, "The Electronic Scanner Checkout and Item Price Removal, *USDA National Food Review* (Winter 1982), pp. 15–17.
[15]Louis W. Stern and Thomas L. Eovaldi, *Legal Aspects of Marketing Strategy* (Englewood Cliffs, N.J.: Prentice-Hall, 1984), p. 394.

Bait advertising or **bait-and-switch advertising** is an illegal procedure whereby the retailer lures a customer into the store by advertising products at exceptionally low prices and then telling the customer that the item is out of stock or of inferior quality. The salesperson attempts to convince the customer that a better, more expensive substitute is available. In bait advertising, the retailer has no intention of selling the advertised item.

Although bait advertising is usually associated with unreliable and unethical retailers, sometimes reputable retailers have troubles in this area. As an illustration, a number of automobile dealers have been accused of bait-and-switch practices. These dealers advertise models in "stripped-down" versions at very low prices. Customers place deposits on these models and agree to accept delivery six to eight weeks later. Then, when higher-priced models equipped with factory-installed options are received by the dealers, the customers are given the choice of a refund (after eight weeks of waiting for the car) or purchasing the model in stock at the dealer's price. Many consumers buy the higher-priced autos to avoid going through the process again.[16]

Manufacturers, Wholesalers, and Other Supplies—and Retail Pricing

Manufacturers, wholesalers, and other suppliers have an impact on the retailer's pricing strategy. In cases where suppliers are unknown or products are new, retailers seek price guarantees to ensure that inventory values and profits will be maintained. **Price guarantees** protect retailers against price declines. For example, a new manufacturer sells a retailer radios that have a final selling price of $20. The manufacturer guarantees this price to the retailer; if the retailer is unable to sell the radios at this price, the manufacturer pays the difference. Should the retailer have to sell the radios at $15, the manufacturer gives a rebate of $5 per radio. The relative power of the retailer and his or her suppliers determines whether a guarantee is provided.[17]

As noted earlier in the chapter, there are often conflicts between manufacturers and retailers in setting final prices. Manufacturers and retailers would each like to control the final selling price of merchandise. The manufacturer wants to achieve and retain a certain image and to allow all retailers, even those who are inefficient, to make profits. In contrast, the retailer would rather set prices based upon his or her store image, objectives, and so on.

The manufacturer can control prices by utilizing an exclusive distribution system and refusing to sell to price-cutting retailers. A strong manufacturer can even open his or her own retail outlets. The retailer can gain control through importance to the manufacturer as a customer, threats to discontinue carrying the manufacturer's line, and private branding.

In many instances, manufacturers derive their selling prices by ascertaining the final selling price and subtracting from this the retailer and wholesaler profit margins. For example, in the men's haberdashery industry, the common retail markup (gross profit) is 50 per cent of selling price. A man's shirt that retails at $18.00 can be sold to the retailer for no more than $9.00. If a wholesaler is involved in the transaction, the manufacturer's price must be substantially less than $9.00.

[16]Crain News Service, "NJ Consumer Group Investigates Bait-and-Switch Automobile Ads," *Advertising Age* (December 5, 1983), p. 94.

[17]Another type of price guarantee is one where the supplier guarantees the retailer that no other retailer will buy the product for a lower price. If anyone does, the retailer gets a rebate.

Sometimes retailers carry merchandise and place very high prices on it. When they do this, rival brands (such as store brands) can be sold more easily. This is called **selling against the brand** and is disliked by manufacturers because sales of their brands decline.

A retailer has suppliers other than manufacturers and wholesalers. These include employees, store fixtures manufacturers, landlords, and outside agents (e.g., advertising firms). Each of these has an impact on price because of their costs to the retailer.

Competition and Retail Pricing

The degree of control a firm has over prices often depends on the competitive environment in which it operates. In a market-pricing situation, there is a lot of competition, and consumers can seek out the lowest prices. Retailers price similarly to each other and have little control over price. Supermarkets, fast-food retailers, and gas stations are all in highly competitive industries and sell similar products or services; therefore retailers in these categories utilize **market pricing.** Demand for these retailers is weak enough so that a number of customers will switch to a competitor if prices are raised.

Under **administered pricing,** retailers attempt to attain consumer loyalty on the basis of a distinctive retailing mix. If strong store differentiation is possible, the retailer can have control over the prices it charges. This occurs when consumers consider image, assortment, personal service, and so on more important than price and will pay a high price for products when shopping at desirable stores (under the assumption that undesirable stores do not offer a good image, a good assortment, personal service, and so on). Department stores, clothing stores, and restaurants are retailers that are able to create distinctive offerings and have some control over their prices.

Because most price strategies can be easily copied in a short time, the reaction of competition is predictable if the leading firm is successful. Accordingly a retailer may have to view price strategy from short-run as well as long-run perspectives.

In some cases, competitive reactions to price changes result in **price wars** whereby various retailers continually lower prices below regular amounts and sometimes below merchandise costs to attract consumers. Price wars frequently result in low profits, losses, or even bankruptcy for competitors. These are three examples of recent price wars:

- As a result of disjointed responses to deregulation, U.S. airlines have often engaged in large-scale price wars. In 1982, the airlines brought one-way New York-to-Florida ticket prices down to $77, a fare that required almost 100 per cent capacity to break even; the price rose to $135 after two months when the Civil Aeronautics Board (CAB) became involved. In 1984–85, the traditional airlines lowered fares by 25 to 40 per cent to compete with discounters.[18]
- Cub Foods, a Chicago warehouse store, offers prices that are 20 per cent lower than the regular prices at traditional stores; its annual sales exceed $50 million. In response to Cub's success, supermarket chains such as Jewel and Dominick have been forced to cut prices by up to 10 per cent.[19]

[18]"UAL Chairman Sees Airline Fare Battles Continuing in 1985," *Wall Street Journal* (November 29, 1984), p. 25.
[19]Richard Gibson, "Cub Foods Throws Curve at Chicago's Top Grocery Chains," *Wall Street Journal* (March 23, 1984), p. 44.

- When gasoline was scarce in the 1970s, prices rose sharply and consumers cut back on their driving mileage. But with the currently large supply of gasoline, some service stations have returned to the price wars that plagued the industry in the 1950s and 1960s. In Houston, some service stations were buying gasoline for 99.3 cents per gallon and selling it for 99.9 cents during late 1984.[20]

Development of a Retail Price Strategy

Development of a retail price strategy is broken down into five components (objectives, policy, strategy, implementation, and adjustments) as depicted in Figure 14-2. First, it is important to note that all aspects of the process are affected by the external factors already discussed. Second, like any other strategic activity, pricing begins with a clear statement of objectives and ends with an adaptive or corrective mechanism. Third, pricing policies must be integrated with the firm's total retail mix. This occurs in the second step of price planning. Fourth, price planning is complex because of the often erratic nature of demand and the number of items carried by many retailers.

Retail Objectives and Pricing

A retailer's pricing strategy must be consistent with and reflect overall objectives. As discussed in Chapter 2, retail objectives can be stated in terms of sales, profits, and return on investment. In addition to these broad objectives, a retailer needs to develop more specific pricing objectives to avoid potential problems such as

- The company being viewed as exploitive of customers.
- Price differences among items being objectionable or unintelligible.
- Too-frequent price changes.
- Prices reflecting negatively on the retailer or products.
- The availability of too many confusing price choices.
- Attracting customers without store loyalty.
- Unduly price-sensitive customers.[21]

Overall Objectives and Pricing

A sales goal is usually stated in terms of dollar revenues or unit volume. An example of a sales goal and a resultant pricing strategy is a car dealer's desire to capture large dollar revenues by setting low prices and selling a high unit volume. This strategy is called **market penetration.** A penetration strategy is proper when customers are highly sensitive to price, low prices discourage actual and potential competition, and total retail costs do not increase as much as sales volume increases.[22]

---

[20]George Getschow, "Pressure on Gasoline Prices Ignites Marketing Battle Among Retailers," *Wall Street Journal* (November 16, 1984), p. 33.

[21]Alfred R. Oxenfeldt, "A Decision-Making Structure for Price Decisions," *Journal of Marketing*, Vol. 37 (January 1973), p. 51.

[22]See "Is 'Everyday Low Pricing' a Viable Concept for Your Brand?" *Nielsen Researcher* (Number 1, 1983), pp. 14–16.

A Framework for Developing a Retail Price Strategy

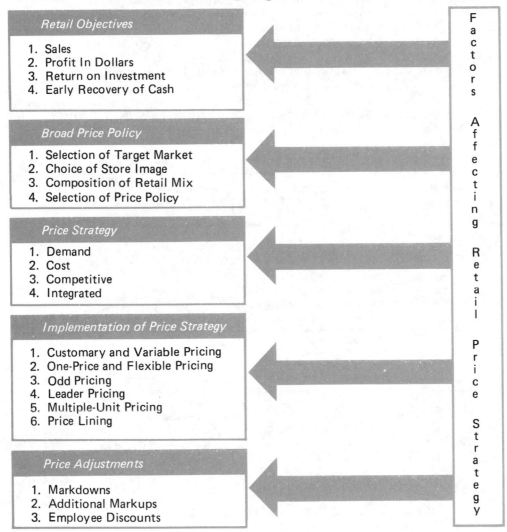

Retail Objectives

1. Sales
2. Profit In Dollars
3. Return on Investment
4. Early Recovery of Cash

Broad Price Policy

1. Selection of Target Market
2. Choice of Store Image
3. Composition of Retail Mix
4. Selection of Price Policy

Price Strategy

1. Demand
2. Cost
3. Competitive
4. Integrated

Implementation of Price Strategy

1. Customary and Variable Pricing
2. One-Price and Flexible Pricing
3. Odd Pricing
4. Leader Pricing
5. Multiple-Unit Pricing
6. Price Lining

Price Adjustments

1. Markdowns
2. Additional Markups
3. Employee Discounts

Factors Affecting Retail Price Strategy

Figure 14-2

A profit-in-dollars objective is sought when the retailer concentrates on total profits or profits per unit. With a **market skimming** strategy, the retailer charges premium prices and attracts those customers who are less concerned with price than with service, assortment, and status. Although this approach does not maximize sales, it does achieve high profits per unit. This strategy is appropriate when the market segment that the retailer defines as the target market is insensitive to price, new competitors will not enter the market, and additional sales will greatly increase total retail costs.

A return-on-investment objective is sought when the retailer stipulates that profits must be a certain percentage of his or her investment, such as profits being 20 per cent of inventory investment. Early recovery of cash is a goal set up by retailers who are short on cash, wish to expand, or are uncertain about the future. A market skimming strategy is often used by retailers with return on investment or early recovery of cash as an objective.

Tie Town, the proposed tie shop mentioned in the beginning of the chapter, offers a good illustration of a retailer examining sales, profit, and return-on-investment objectives. Tie Town wants to sell inexpensive ties (avoiding competition from department and haberdashery stores), use a single selling price (between $7.00 and $10.00), minimize operating costs, maximize self-service, and carry extensive selections to generate traffic.

Table 14-2 contains data gathered by Tie Town pertaining to demand, costs, profit, and return-on-inventory investment at various prices between $7.00 and $10.00. Table 14-3 shows the methods used to arrive at the figures in Table 14-2.

Table 14-2
Tie Town: Demand, Costs, Profits, and Return on Investment*

Selling Price (in $)	Quantity Demanded (in units)	Total Sales Revenue (in $)	Average Cost of Merchandise† (in $)	Total Cost of Merchandise (in $)	Total Nonmerchandise Costs‡ (in $)	Total Costs (in $)
7.00	57,000	399,000	5.60	319,200	52,000	371,200
8.00	50,000	400,000	5.85	292,500	47,000	339,500
9.00	40,000	360,000	6.25	250,000	44.000	294,000
10.00	30,000	300,000	6.75	202,500	40,000	242,500

Selling Price (in $)	Average Total Costs (in $)	Total Profit (in $)	Profit/Unit (in $)	Markup at Retail (in %)	Profit/Sales (in %)	Average Inventory on Hand (in units)
7.00	6.51	27,800	0.49	20	7	6,000
8.00	6.79	60,500	1.21	27	15	6,500
9.00	7.35	66,000	1.65	31	18	7,000
10.00	8.08	57,500	1.92	33	19	8,000

Selling Price (in $)	Inventory Turnover (units)	Average Investment in Inventory at Cost (in $)	Inventory Turnover (in $)	Return on Investment (in %)
7.00	9.5	33,600	9.5	83
8.00	7.7	38,025	7.7	159
9.00	5.7	43,750	5.7	151
10.00	3.8	54,000	3.8	106

*Numbers have been rounded off.
†Reflects quantity discounts.
‡Includes all retail operating expenses.

From Table 14-2, several conclusions concerning price strategy for Tie Town can be drawn:

- A sales objective will lead the store to a selling price of $8.00. At this price, total sales are highest ($400,000).
- A dollar profit objective will lead the store to a selling price of $9.00. At this price, total profits are highest ($66,000).
- A return-on-investment objective will also lead the store to a selling price of $8.00. At this price, return on inventory investment is 159 per cent.
- Although a large quantity can be sold at $7.00, this selling price will lead to the lowest profit ($27,800).
- Although a selling price of $10.00 will yield the highest profit per unit and as a per cent of sales, total dollar profits are not maximized at this price.
- High inventory turnover will not necessarily lead to high profits.

Table 14-3
Derivation of Tie Town Data

Column in Table 14-2	Source of Information or Method of Computation
Selling price	Trade data, comparison shopping, experience
Quantity demanded (in units) at each price level	Consumer surveys, trade data, experience
Total sales revenue	Selling price × quantity demanded
Average cost of merchandise	Contacts with suppliers, quantity discount structure, estimates of order sizes
Total cost of merchandise	Average cost of merchandise × quantity demanded
Total nonmerchandise costs	Experience, trade data, estimation of individual retail operating expenses
Total costs	Total cost of merchandise + total nonmerchandise costs
Average total costs	Total costs ÷ quantity demanded
Total profit	Total sales revenue − total costs
Profit per unit	Total profit ÷ quantity demanded
Markup (at retail)	(Selling price − average cost of merchandise) ÷ selling price
Profit as a percentage of sales	Total profit ÷ total sales revenue
Average inventory on hand (in units)	Trade data, merchandise turnover data, experience
Inventory turnover (in units)	Quantity demanded ÷ average inventory on hand (in units)
Average investment in inventory (at cost)	Average cost of merchandise × average inventory on hand (in units)
Inventory turnover (in $)	Total cost of merchandise ÷ average investment in inventory (at cost)
Return on inventory investment	Total profit ÷ average investment in inventory (at cost)

Specific Pricing Objectives

1.	Desensitize customers to price.
2.	Discourage competitive entrants.
3.	Speed exit of marginal firms.
4.	Avoid government investigation and control.
5.	Avoid demand for 'more' from suppliers—labor in particular.
6.	Enhance image of firm and its offerings.
7.	Be regarded as fair by customers.
8.	Help in the sale of weak items in the line.
9.	Discourage others from cutting prices.
10.	"Spoil Market" to obtain high price for sale of business.
11.	Build traffic.

Source: Adapted from Alfred R. Oxenfeldt, "A Decision-Making Structure for Price Decisions," *Journal of Marketing*, Vol. 37 (January 1973), p. 50.

Figure 14-3

Specific Pricing Objectives

Figure 14-3 provides a list of specific pricing objectives other than sales, profits, return on investment, and early recovery of cash. Although a number of pricing objectives are enumerated, each retailer must determine the relative importance of goals in his or her situation and plan accordingly.

Broad Price Policy

A broad price policy helps a retailer generate a coordinated series of actions, a consistent image (especially important for chain and franchise units), and a strategy that incorporates short- and long-run considerations (where the retailer balances immediate and long-term goals). A popular technique for planning a broad price policy is the **multistage approach.**

This approach divides the major elements of pricing into six successive steps, with each step placing limits on the following steps: selection of a target market, choice of a store image, composition of the retail mix, selection of a broad price policy, selection of a price strategy, and choice of specific prices.[23] The first four steps concentrate on

[23]Alfred R. Oxenfeldt, "Multi-Stage Approach to Pricing," *Harvard Business Review*, Vol. 38 (July–August 1960), pp. 125–133.

the evolution of a broad policy; the last two steps center on specific decisions and their implementation (which are discussed later in this chapter).

The starting point in the development of any price policy is the selection of a target market. Once the market is selected, an appropriate store image is created that will establish the relevant associations in the minds of the target market. Thus, the selection of a target market limits the retailer's choice of a store image. In composing its retail mix, the firm must assign a role to price, such as appealing to customers via extensive price cutting or generating store traffic through convenience, quality of service, and so on, rather than price.

Next, the retailer determines his or her broad price policy. This translates price decisions into an integrated framework. For example, the retailer must decide whether prices should be established for individual items, interrelated for a group of products, or based on the extensive use of special sales.

Some of the price policies from which a retailer can choose follow:

- No retailers will sell products for lower prices; no retailers will sell products for higher prices; or prices will be consistent with competitors' prices.
- All items will be priced independently, depending on the demand for each; or the prices for all items will be interrelated to maintain an image and ensure proper markups.
- Price leadership will be exerted; no other firm will adjust prices earlier; or other retailers will be price leaders and set prices first.
- Prices will be constant throughout the year or season; or prices will change if merchandise costs change.

Price Strategy

A price strategy can be either demand, cost, or competitive in orientation. In demand-oriented pricing, the retailer sets prices based on consumer desires. He or she determines the range of prices acceptable to the target market. The top of this range is called the demand ceiling, the maximum consumers will pay for a product.

Cost-oriented pricing sets a price floor, the minimum price acceptable to a retailer so that he or she can obtain a specified profit goal. Usually, the retailer computes merchandise and retail operating costs and adds to these figures a profit margin.

With competitive-oriented pricing, the retailer sets prices in accordance with competitors. In this technique, the price levels of key competitors and how they affect the retailer's sales are studied.

All three approaches should be considered when one is setting a price strategy. They do not operate independently of one another.

Demand-Oriented Pricing

Demand-oriented pricing is often used by retailers whose goals are listed in terms of sales or market share. It seeks to estimate the quantities demanded at various price levels and concentrates on the price associated with the stated sales goals. Whereas a cost-oriented pricing strategy examines costs, a demand-oriented approach looks at demand irrespective of costs.

When one is using a demand-oriented approach, it is necessary to understand the psychological implications of pricing. The term **psychological pricing** refers to the consumers' perceptions of retail prices. Two aspects of psychological pricing are the price–quality association and prestige pricing.

The **price–quality association** is the concept that consumers believe that high prices connote high quality and that low prices connote low quality. This is particularly true in cases where product quality is difficult to judge on bases other than price, buyers perceive large differences in quality among brands, buyers have little experience or confidence in judging quality (as in the case of a new product), and brand names are an insignificant factor in product choice.

Although a number of studies document the price–quality relationship, research indicates that when other quality cues, like product features and a well-known brand name, are introduced, these factors may be more important than price in the consumer's judgment of overall product quality.

Prestige pricing is drawn from the price-quality association. In **prestige pricing,** it is assumed that consumers do not buy products at prices that are considered too low. Consumers actually set price floors and do not buy certain products if priced below these floors. The feeling is that too low a price means that product quality and status are also low. In addition, some consumers use prestige pricing in the selection of retail stores and do not shop at stores that have prices that are too low. For example, Saks Fifth Avenue and Neiman-Marcus do not carry inexpensive versions of items because their customers may perceive them to be inferior.

It should be noted that prestige pricing does not apply to all customers. That is why the target market must be defined before the retailer reaches this stage. Some customers may be economizers and may always shop for bargains. For these consumers, neither aspect of psychological pricing—price–quality and prestige—may be applicable.

Cost-Oriented Pricing

The **cost-oriented approach,** markup pricing, is the most widely practiced retail-pricing technique. In the cost-oriented method, a retailer sets prices by adding per-unit merchandise costs, retail operating expenses, and desired profits. The difference between merchandise costs and selling price is the retailer's **markup.** For example, a retailer buys an office desk for $200 and wants to sell it for $300. The extra $100 is needed for retail operating expenses and profit. The markup is 33⅓ per cent on retail price, or 50 per cent on cost.

The markup percentage depends upon a wide variety of factors, such as the product's traditional markup, the manufacturer's suggested list price, the product's turnover, the competition, the extent to which the product must be altered or otherwise serviced, and the effort required to sell the product.

Although markups can be computed on the basis of retail selling price or cost, they have generally been calculated in terms of retail selling price. Several reasons explain why retail selling price is used as the base. First, retail expenses, markdowns, and profits are always computed as a percentage of sales. Therefore, when markups are expressed as a percentage of sales, these percentages are quite meaningful. Second, manufacturers quote their selling price to retailers and trade discounts as percentage reductions from retail list prices. Third, retail selling-price information is more readily available than cost information. Fourth, profitability statistics appear to be smaller if expressed on the basis of retail price instead of cost; this can be useful when dealing with the government, employees, and consumers.

Markup percentages are calculated as

$$\text{Markup percentage (at retail)} = \frac{\text{Retail selling price} - \text{Merchandise cost}}{\text{Retail selling price}}$$

$$\text{Markup percentage (at cost)} = \frac{\text{Retail selling price} - \text{Merchandise cost}}{\text{Merchandise cost}}$$

As shown in these equations, the difference is in the denominator used. In both formulas, merchandise cost is the per unit invoice and freight cost to the retailer, less per unit trade or quantity discounts.[24]

Table 14-4 contains markups at retail and at cost for a wide range of percentages. As the markup increases, the disparity between retail and cost percentages grows. For example, a watch retailer buys a watch for $20 and is undecided as to whether to sell it for $25, $40, or $80. In evaluating markup, it is determined that the $25 price yields a markup of 20 per cent (at retail) or 25 per cent (at cost), the $40 price yields a markup of 50 per cent (at retail) or 100 per cent (at cost), and the $80 price yields a markup of 75 per cent (at retail) or 300 per cent (at cost).

Table 14-4
Markup Equivalents

Per Cent at Retail	Per Cent at Cost
5.0	5.3
10.0	11.1
15.0	17.7
20.0	25.0
25.0	33.3
30.0	42.9
35.0	53.9
40.0	66.7
45.0	81.8
50.0	100.0
60.0	150.0
75.0	300.0
80.0	400.0
90.0	900.0

[24]Markup calculations are explained in depth in Marvin A. Jolson, "Markup Calculations—Still a Fuzzy Area?" *Journal of Retailing*, Vol. 49 (Winter 1973–74), pp. 77–80ff.; and Marvin A. Jolson, "A Diagrammatic Model for Merchandising Calculations," *Journal of Retailing*, Vol 51. (Summer 1975), pp. 3–9ff.

The markup concept has various applications in pricing and purchase planning. The following illustrations of markups detail the usefulness of the concept:

- A discount clothing store can purchase a shipment of men's jeans at $10 each and wants to obtain a 40 per cent markup at retail. What retail price should the store charge to achieve this markup?

$$\frac{\text{Markup percentage}}{\text{(at retail)}} = \frac{\text{Retail selling price} - \text{Merchandise cost}}{\text{Retail selling price}}$$

$$0.40 = \frac{\text{Retail selling price} - \$10.00}{\text{Retail selling price}}$$

$$0.40 \text{ (Retail selling price)} = \text{Retail selling price} - \$10.00$$
$$0.60 \text{ (Retail selling price)} = \$10.00$$
$$\text{Retail selling price} = \$16.67$$

The retailer should charge $16.67 to achieve the 40 per cent markup at retail.[25]
- A stationery store store desires a minimum 30 per cent markup at retail for legal-sized envelopes. If the retailer feels that the envelopes should retail at 59 cents per box, what is the maximum price the retailer can pay for the envelopes?

$$\frac{\text{Markup percentage}}{\text{(at retail)}} = \frac{\text{Retail selling price} - \text{Merchandise cost}}{\text{Retail selling price}}$$

$$0.30 = \frac{\$0.59 - \text{Merchandise cost}}{\$0.59}$$

$$\$0.59 - \text{Merchandise cost} = (0.30)(\$0.59)$$
$$\$0.59 - \text{Merchandise cost} = \$0.177$$
$$\text{Merchandise cost} = \$0.59 - \$0.177$$
$$\text{Merchandise cost} = \$0.413$$

To achieve at least a 30 per cent markup, the retailer cannot pay more than 41.3 cents per box of legal-sized envelopes.[26]
- A bicycle store has been offered a closeout purchase on an imported line of bicycles. The per-unit cost of each bicycle is $80, and the bikes should retail for $120 each.

---

[25]One may also calculate selling price by transposing the markup formula into

$$\text{Retail selling price} = \frac{\text{Merchandise cost}}{1 - \text{Markup}}$$

$$\text{Retail selling price} = \frac{\$10.00}{1 - 0.4} = \frac{\$10.00}{0.6} = \$16.67$$

[26]One may also compute merchandise cost by transposing the markup formula into

$$\text{Merchandise cost} = (\text{Retail selling price}) (1 - \text{Markup})$$
$$\text{Merchandise cost} = (\$0.59) (1 - 0.3) = (\$0.59) (0.7) = \$0.413$$

What markup at retail will the store obtain?

$$\text{Markup percentage (at retail)} = \frac{\text{Retail selling price} - \text{Merchandise cost}}{\text{Retail selling price}}$$

$$\text{Markup percentage} = \frac{\$120.00 - \$80.00}{\$120.00}$$

$$\text{Markup percentage} = \frac{\$40.00}{\$120.00}$$

$$\text{Markup percentage} = 33.3$$

The store will receive a markup of 33.3 per cent on these bikes.

Markup may also be determined by examining planned retail operating expenses, profits, and net sales:

$$\text{Markup percentage (at retail)} = \frac{\text{Planned retail operating expenses} + \text{Planned profits}}{\text{Planned net sales}}$$

As an example, a florist estimates retail operating expenses (rent, salaries, electricity, cleaning, bookkeeping, and so on) to be $45,000 per year. The desired profit is $35,000 per year, including the owner's salary. Net sales are forecast to be $200,000. The planned markup is

$$\text{Markup percentage (at retail)} = \frac{\$45,000 + \$35,000}{\$200,000} = 40$$

Because flowers cost the florist an average of $8.00 a dozen, the retailer's selling price per dozen is

$$\text{Retail selling price} = \frac{\text{Merchandise cost}}{1 - \text{Markup}}$$

$$\text{Retail selling price} = \frac{\$8.00}{1 - 0.40} = \$13.33$$

The florist will need to sell approximately 15,000 dozen flowers at $13.33 per dozen to achieve sales and profit goals. In order to achieve goals, all flowers must be sold at the $13.33 price.

Because it is highly unusual for a retailer to be able to sell all items in stock at their original prices, it is necessary to compute initial markup, maintained markup, and gross margin. **Initial markup** is based on the original retail value assigned to merchandise less the costs of the merchandise. **Maintained markup** is based on the actual prices received for merchandise sold during a time period less merchandise cost. Because maintained markups are related to actual prices received, it is difficult to estimate them in advance. The difference between initial and maintained markups is that the latter reflect adjustments from original retail values caused by markdowns, markups, shortages, and discounts.

The initial markup percentage depends on planned retail operating expenses and profits plus planned reductions:

$$\text{Initial markup percentage (at retail)} = \frac{\text{Planned retail operating expenses} + \text{Planned profit} + \text{Planned retail reductions}}{\text{Planned net sales} + \text{Planned retail reductions}}$$

If retail reductions are zero, the markup is equal to retail operating expenses plus profit, which results in the markup formula explained earlier in this section.

To return to the florist example, suppose that the retailer projects that retail reductions will be 20 per cent of estimated sales, or $40,000. The initial markup will have to be

$$\text{Initial markup percentage (at retail)} = \frac{\$45,000 + \$35,000 + \$40,000}{\$200,000 + \$40,000} = 50$$

and the original selling price will be

$$\text{Retail selling price} = \frac{\text{Merchandise cost}}{1 - \text{Markup}} = \frac{\$8.00}{1 - 0.50} = \$16.00$$

This means that the original retail value of 15,000 dozen flowers will be about $240,000. Retail reductions of $40,000 will result in net sales of $200,000. Therefore, the retailer must begin selling flowers at $16.00 per dozen if the objective is to have an average selling price of $13.33 per dozen and a maintained markup of 40 per cent.[27]

Maintained markup percentages can be viewed as

$$\text{Maintained markup percentage (at retail)} = \frac{\text{Actual retail operating expenses} + \text{Actual profit}}{\text{Actual net sales}}$$

or

$$\text{Maintained markup percentage (at retail)} = \frac{\text{Average selling price} - \text{Merchandise cost}}{\text{Average selling price}}$$

Gross margin is the difference between net sales and the total cost of goods sold. The total cost figure, as opposed to the gross cost figure, adjusts for cash discounts and additional expenses:

$$\text{Gross margin (in \$)} = \text{Net sales} - \text{Total cost of goods}$$

[27]There are small rounding errors in these calculations.

For the florist, gross margin (which is the dollar equivalent of the maintained markup) is $200,000 − $120,000 = $80,000. The total costs are merchandise cost times the number of units purchased.[28]

Although a retailer must set an overall store markup goal, the markups for categories of merchandise or even individual products may differ. In fact, markups may vary significantly. In department stores, maintained markup as a percentage of sales averaged 41.9 per cent in 1983 for the total upstairs portion of stores with over $1 million in sales and 43.6 per cent for the total upstairs portion of specialty stores with sales in excess of $1 million.[29]

The utilization of a **variable markup policy** achieves three major purposes. First, variable markup recognizes that costs associated with separate product categories may fluctuate widely. Some items require extensive alterations (such as clothing) or installation (such as carpeting). Even within a product line like women's clothing, expensive fashion items require greater end-of-year markdowns than inexpensive items. Therefore, the more expensive line must receive a higher initial markup.

Second, variable markup allows for differences in product investments. For instance, in a large appliance department where the retailer orders regularly from a wholesaler, lower markups are required than in a fine jewelry department where the retailer must maintain a complete stock of merchandise.

Third, a variable policy accounts for differences in selling efforts and merchandise skills. The selling of a food processor may necessitate substantial sales effort, whereas a blender may involve significantly less effort and skill.

The use of a variable markup policy on a systematic basis is referred to as **merchandise-management accounting.** The essence of merchandise-management accounting is that markups are planned in accordance with relevant cost information for individual items. Instead of determining costs for each item, merchandise-management accounting sets standards that are applicable to given categories of items. As examples, the costs of charge transactions can be standardized for all items, and delivery costs can be standardized for items of specified physical dimensions and weights.

From an individual-item perspective, this accounting technique helps to distinguish between variable and fixed costs. Variable costs are incurred because particular units are stocked and sold; fixed costs are incurred whether or not particular items are stocked and sold. Variable costs include costs of merchandise and commissions for sales personnel. Fixed costs included rent and salaries.

Before making a price decision under the merchandise-management accounting (MMA) system, the retailer has to

1. Determine the activities necessary in the purchase, sale, delivery, and service of an item.
2. Compute variable costs for services.
3. Estimate sales volumes over a wide range of possible prices.
4. Ascertain controllable profit (sales less variable costs) at each price level.
5. Find out whether to stock an item and the appropriate price level for it.

Although the MMA system is conceptually sound in that it establishes a good framework for variable markup pricing, it has not been widely adopted. There are

---

[28]There are small rounding errors in these calculations.
[29]David P. Schulz, "NRMA's New MOR," *Stores* (October 1984), pp. 22–23.

several reasons for this. First, the system has high installation and operation costs. Second, the standard cost percentages used in MMA often cannot be accurately applied across broad categories of merchandise. Third, the system focuses more on costs than on demand. Fourth, a rigid markup system used intelligently by a buyer is helpful in negotiating with vendors because it prespecifies acceptable prices.

Despite its problems, cost-oriented (markup) pricing remains popular for many retailers. It is fairly simple, especially as a retailer can apply a standard markup for a category of products much more easily than he or she can estimate demand at various price levels; the retailer can also adjust prices according to changes in demand or segment a market. Markup pricing has an inherent sense of equity in that the retailer earns a fair profit. In addition, when all retailers adhere to similar markups, price competition is significantly reduced. Lastly, markup pricing is quite efficient if it takes into account competition, seasonal factors, and difficulties in selling specific merchandise categories.

Competitive-Oriented Pricing

In a **competitive-oriented pricing** approach, the retailer uses competitors' prices as guideposts, rather than demand or cost considerations. Thus, a competitive-oriented retailer does not alter prices to react to changes in demand or costs unless competitors alter their prices. Similarly, a competitive-oriented retailer alters prices when competitors do, even if demand or cost factors remain the same.

A competitive-oriented retailer can price below the market, at the market, or above the market. Table 14-5 outlines the conditions that enable the retailer to set his or her prices at one of these levels. It is clear from this table that pricing strategy must be integrated with the retail mix. A retailer with a strong location, a high level of services, broad product assortments, a favorable image, and exclusive brands can price above the market. This strategy is inappropriate for a retailer who has an inconvenient location, relies on self-service, concentrates on best-selling items, is a fashion follower, and stocks private-label merchandise.

Competitive-oriented pricing is utilized for several reasons:

1. It is simple. There are no calculations of demand curves or concern with price elasticity.
2. The ongoing market price is assumed to be fair for both the consumer and the retailer.
3. Pricing at the market level does not disrupt competition and therefore does not lead to retaliation.

Integration of Approaches to Price Strategy

The three approaches to setting retail price strategy must be integrated because each has strengths and weaknesses. Before completing a price strategy, the retailer must answer the following series of questions:

- Will a given price level allow me to attain the traditional markup? (Cost orientation)
- If I reduce a price, will sales increase greatly? (Demand orientation)
- Should I charge different prices for a product, based on negotiations with customers, seasonality, and so on? (Demand orientation)

Table 14-5
Competitive-Oriented Pricing Alternatives

Retail Mix Variable	Alternative Price Strategies		
	Pricing Below the Market	Pricing At the Market	Pricing Above the Market
Location	Poor, inconvenient site	Close to competitors, no locational advantage	Absence of strong competitors, convenient to consumers
Personal service	Self-service, little product knowledge on part of salespeople, no displays	Moderate assistance by sales personnel	High levels of personal selling, delivery, exchanges, etc.
Product assortments	Concentration on best-sellers	Medium assortment	Broad assortment
Atmosphere	Inexpensive fixtures, little or no carpeting or paneling, racks for merchandise	Moderate atmosphere	Attractive, pleasant decor with many displays
Role of fashion in assortment	Fashion follower, conservative	Concentration on accepted best-sellers	Fashion leader
Special services	Cash and carry	Not available or extra charge to customers	Included in price
Merchandise lines carried	Private labels, name-brand closeouts, small manufacturers	Name brands	Exclusive brands

- What price levels are competitors setting? (Competitive orientation)
- Can I charge higher prices than competitors because of my reputation and image? (Competitive orientation)
- What price level is necessary for a product that requires special costs in purchasing, selling, or delivery? (Cost orientation)

By no means is this list complete, but it should give some idea as to how a retailer can apply the demand, cost, and competitive orientations to pricing.

Implementation of Price Strategy

The implementation of a price strategy involves a wide variety of separate but interrelated specific decisions in addition to those broad concepts discussed previously. Examples of these decisions are listed in Table 14-6. In this section, many of the specifics of pricing strategy are detailed.

Customary and Variable Pricing

Customary pricing exists when a retailer sets prices for products or services and seeks to maintain them over an extended period of time. Prices are not altered during this time period. Examples of products or services with customary prices are newspapers,

Table 14-6
Selected Specific Elements of Retail Pricing

1. What to charge different types of customers (use of discounts and bargaining)
2. Whether to vary prices systematically over time (as in special sales)
3. Whether to price all items separately or as part of a team
4. How many different price offerings to have for each item (including varying prices by day and time)
5. What timing and level of markdowns to use for slowselling merchandise
6. If lower prices of competitors should be met and how
7. Whether merchandise prices should be advertised
8. Whether a limit should be placed on sale merchandise
9. If employees should receive discounts
10. How services should be priced—separately or as a part of the overall price
11. How to react to manufacturers' suggested list prices
12. If prices should be the same or different in branches of a chain

Source: From Alfred R. Oxenfeldt, Pricing for Marketing Executives *(Belmont, Calif.: Wadsworth Publishing Company, 1961), pp. 19–20.*

candy, mass transit, telephone booths, pinball machines, cigarettes, vending machine items, and foods on restaurant menus. In each of these cases, the retailer seeks to establish a customary price and have consumers take it for granted.

However, in many instances, a retailer cannot or should not use customary pricing. The retailer cannot maintain constant prices if his or her costs are rising. The retailer should not maintain constant prices if consumer demand varies. Under **variable pricing,** the retailer alters prices to coincide with fluctuations in cost or consumer demand.

Cost fluctuations can be seasonal or trend. Seasonal fluctuations affect retailers who sell items whose production is limited to certain times during the year. For example, prices in supermarkets and floral shops vary during the year because of the seasonal nature of many agricultural and floral products. When items are scarce, their costs to the retailer go up. Trend fluctuations, which are common to almost all retailers today, refer to the constant upward (or downward) spiral of costs to the retailer. As costs increase, the retailer must raise prices permanently (unlike seasonal fluctuations, which cause temporary changes).

Demand fluctuations can be place- or time-based. Place fluctuations exist for retailers who sell seat locations, such as concert theaters and athletic stadiums. Different prices can be charged for different seat locations; tickets close to the stage or the field command higher prices. If variable pricing is not followed, seat location is based on first-come, first-served. Time fluctuations occur when consumer demand differs by hour, day, or season. For example, demand for a movie theater is greater on Saturday than on Wednesday; demand for an airline is greater during December than during February. Accordingly prices should be lower during periods of low demand.

It is possible to combine customary and variable pricing. For instance, a theater can charge $2 every Wednesday night and $4 every Saturday. An airline can lower prices by 20 per cent during off-seasons.

One-Price Policy and Flexible Pricing

Under a **one-price policy,** the retailer charges the same price for all customers who seek to purchase an item under similar conditions. A one-price policy may be used in conjunction with customary pricing or variable pricing. In the latter case, all customers interested in a particular section of seats or arriving at the same time pay the same price.

The one-price policy was begun by John Wanamaker, who was the first major merchant to mark prices clearly on each item in stock. This marking system did away with price bargaining, found favor with consumers, and was quickly copied by others. Throughout the United States, one-price policies are the rule for most retailers, and bargaining over price is usually not permitted.

In contrast, **flexible pricing** allows consumers to bargain over selling price, and those consumers who are good at bargaining obtain lower prices than those who are not. Jewelry stores, automobile dealers, house painters, flea markets, health spas, and appliance stores are examples of retailers that use flexible pricing. Retailers using flexible pricing do not clearly post prices; consumers must have prior knowledge in order to bargain successfully.[30]

The one-price policy speeds up transactions, reduces labor costs, and permits self-service, catalogs, and vending machine sales. Flexible pricing requires high initial prices and qualified sales personnel.

Odd Pricing

An **odd-pricing strategy** occurs when retail prices are set at levels below even dollar values, such as $0.49, $4.95, and $199. The assumption is that consumers feel that these prices represent bargains or that the amounts are beneath the consumers' price ceilings. For example, realtors hope that consumers who set a price ceiling of under $80,000 will be attracted to houses selling for $79,500. From this perspective, odd pricing is a form of psychological pricing (which was discussed earlier in the chapter).

Originally, odd prices were imposed to force sales clerks to give change on each purchase, thus preventing the clerks from pocketing receipts without ringing up sales. Now odd prices are accepted as part of the American system of retailing and are used more for psychological reasons.

Odd prices that are one cent or two cents below the next highest even price (e.g., $0.29, $0.99, $2.98) are most common up to the $4 level. Beyond that point and up to $50, five-cent reductions from the highest even price (e.g., $19.95, $49.95) are more usual. For higher-priced merchandise, odd endings are in dollars (e.g., $399, $4,995).

Despite the importance of odd pricing in retailing, there have been extremely few studies on its psychological effects. Although the findings are not conclusive, one research study showed that perceptions of bargains caused by consumers' rounding odd numbers to the next lowest price take place under certain circumstances for some products but not for all products under all circumstances.[31]

Leader Pricing

In **leader pricing**, a retailer advertises and sells key items in the product assortment at less than their usual profit margins. The objective of leader pricing is to increase customer traffic into the store in the hopes of selling regularly priced merchandise in

---

[30]See Whitehead, "Name Your Price," pp. 214, 216.
[31]Zarrell V. Lambert, "Perceived Prices As Related to Odd and Even Price Endings," *Journal of Retailing*, Vol. 51 (Fall 1975), pp. 13–22. See also Bernard F. Whalen, "Strategic Mix of Odd, Even Prices Can Lead to Increased Retail Profits," *Marketing News* (March 7, 1980), p. 24.

addition to the specially priced items. It is different from bait-and-switch, in which the sale items are not sold.

Leader pricing is generally associated with the sale of frequently purchased, nationally branded, high-turnover products. The use of these goods is explained by the customer's ease in detecting low prices and the high traffic they generate.

There are two kinds of leader pricing: loss leaders and sales at lower than regular prices (but higher than costs). As described earlier in the chapter, loss leaders are regulated on a statewide basis under sales-below-cost laws.

In drugstores, the best-selling item in terms of dollar sales is film. To stimulate consumer traffic, drugstores price film at low markups, sometimes close to cost. Film is an excellent item for leader pricing, because consumers know a good value and are likely to add a shopping trip to make a purchase.

Multiple-Unit Pricing

Multiple-unit pricing is a strategy whereby the retailer offers customers discounts for buying in quantity. By selling items at two for $0.79 or six for $2.19, the retailer attempts to sell more products than at $0.40 each.

There are two reasons for utilizing multiple-unit pricing. First, the retailer seeks to have customers increase their total purchases of an item. However, if customers buy multiple units and stockpile them, instead of consuming more, the sales of the retailer do not increase. Second, multiple-unit pricing enables the retailer to clear out slow-moving and end-of-season merchandise.

Price Lining

Instead of stocking merchandise at all different price levels, retailers usually use **price lining** and sell merchandise at a limited range of prices, with each price representing a distinct level of quality. First, retailers determine the price floors and ceilings for their offerings. Then they set a limited number of prices (price points) within the range. For example, department stores generally carry good, better, and best versions of merchandise consistent with their overall price policy and set individual prices accordingly.

Price lining benefits both consumers and retailers. For the consumer, price lining minimizes confusion in shopping. If a price range for personalized stationery is $6 to $12 and the price points are $6, $9, and $12, the consumer knows that distinct product qualities exist. However, should the retailer have prices of $6, $7, $8, $9, $10, $11, and $12, the consumer is usually confused about product qualities and differences.

For the retailer, price lining greatly aids the purchase process. A retail buyer seeks out only suppliers who carry products at appropriate prices; and he or she can use final selling price as a starting point in negotiations with suppliers. The retailer automatically disregards products that do not fit within the price line and thereby reduces inventory investment. Also, stock turnover is greatly increased by limiting the models carried.

Four difficulties do exist with price lining. First, depending on the specific price points selected, a price-lining strategy may have gaps between prices that are perceived as too large by the consumer. Thus, a mother shopping for a graduation gift for her son might find a $100 typewriter to be too inexpensive and a $220 typewriter to be too expensive. Second, inflation makes it difficult to maintain price points and the price range. When costs rise, retailers can either eliminate lower prices or reduce markups. Third, markdowns or special sales may disrupt the balance in a price line, unless all

GIMBELS EAST PRICE CHANGE AUTHORIZATION 418651

MARK THE BLANK BOX TO THE LEFT OF EACH STORE AFFECTED WITH AN "X"

33	86	WE	PA	VS	RF	BS	ST	CO	WH

ALL (SOUTH ONLY)	ME	CH	UD	NE	MO	KP	EC	LA	OX	GR

TYPE OF PRICE CHANGE: MARK "X" NEXT TO TYPE

MARKDOWN 1 | MARKDOWN CANCELLATION 2 | MARKUP 3 | MARKUP CANCELLATION 4 | ACTION DATE MM DD YY | DEPT

MARKING INSTRUCTIONS: NEW TICKET 1 PEN 2 CHANGE SIGNS 3

POS FROM BEFORE AND AFTER COUNTS 2 POS FROM SALESCHECKS 3

SOUTHERN REGION ONLY ☐ PERMANENT ☐ TEMPORARY | DIVISION

REASON FOR PRICE CHANGE/ ORIGINAL AUTHORIZATION NO. | AD MERCHANDISE ☐ NO ☐ YES | DATES OF SALE FROM / TO /

STOCK STATUS DEPARTMENTS: CIRCLE ONE CODE ONLY FOR ALL STYLES: 1 TO BE REPORTED IN REGULAR SECTION OF STOCK STATUS 3 TO BE REPORTED IN MARKDOWN SECTION OF STOCK STATUS

SPECIAL INSTRUCTIONS

	% OFF	MERCHANDISE DESCRIPTION (CC 1-31)	CLASS	SKU NUMBER VENDOR	SKU NUMBER STYLE	UNIT RETAIL OLD	UNIT RETAIL NEW	CHANGE PER UNIT	EST COUNT (ALL STORES)	TOTAL DOLLARS
01			0							
02			0							
03			0							
04			0							
05			0							
06			0							
07			0							
08			0							
09			0							
										MEMO TOTAL

REASON (CIRCLE)	LEAD TIME	REASON (CIRCLE)	LEAD TIME
1. COMPETITION	2 DAYS	5. NORMAL CLEARANCE	5 DAYS
2. STORE WIDE EVENTS DIV/DEPT SALE	5 DAYS	6. SLOW SELLING LIQUIDATION	5 DAYS
3. EQUALIZATION	5 DAYS	7. CURRENT RECEIPTS NOT SELLING	4 DAYS
4. MARKOUT/SALVAGE BREAKAGE	5 DAYS		

BUYER | DATE | BUYER EXT | DIV. MDSE. MGR. | DATE | GEN. MDSE. MGR. | DATE | PRICE CHANGE CONTROL | DATE

F3774 (7-83) PRICE CHANGE CONTROL COPY

Figure 14-4 A Price Change Authorization Form

Courtesy Gimbels.

items in the line are reduced proportionally. Fourth, price lines must be coordinated for complementary product categories such as blazers, skirts, and shoes.[32]

Price Adjustments

Price adjustments allow retailers to use price as an adaptive mechanism.[33] Markdowns and additional markups are necessary in adjusting to factors such as competition, seasonality, style preferences, and pilferage. For example, a **markdown** from the original retail price of an item may be used to meet the lower price of another store, to adapt to errors in overstocking fashions, to clear shopworn merchandise, to deplete assort-

[32]"Information System Helps Retailers to Mine Overlooked 'Acres of Diamonds'," *Marketing News* (May 11, 1984), p. 4.

[33]See Phillip G. Carlson, "Fashion Retailing: The Sensitivity of Rate of Sale to Markdown," *Journal of Retailing*, Vol. 59 (Spring 1983), pp. 67–76; William Burston, "A Checklist of 38 Ways of Controlling Markdowns," (New York: National Retail Merchants Association, n.d.); Steve Weiner, "Marshall Field's Does Christmas in a Big Way with an Eye on Profits," *Wall Street Journal* (November 29, 1984), p. 31; and Robert E. O'Neill, "2-Way Radio Eases Price Maintenance," *Progressive Grocer* (November 1983), pp. 95–100.

ments of odds and ends, and to increase store traffic. Figure 14-4 shows a price-change authorization form.

Consumers sometimes perceive and interpret markdowns in the following ways:

- The item is about to be superseded by a later model.
- The item is relatively unwanted; the retailer is left with excess inventories.
- The peak season for the product has passed.
- The retailer is in financial difficulty. Consequently, product guarantees may not be honored and repair parts may not be provided.[34]

These interpretations may adversely affect the sales of marked-down products and hurt a store's image.

Additional markups are increases in retail prices after and in addition to original markups that are used when demand is unexpectedly high or when costs are rising.

A third type of price adjustment, discounts to employees, is mentioned here because discounts influence the computation of markdown percentages. In addition, although employee discounts are not an adaptive mechanism, they affect employee morale. Some retailers give employee discounts on all merchandise and also let employees buy sale merchandise before it is made available to the general public.

Computation of Markdowns and Additional Markups

Markdowns and additional markups can be calculated in dollars (total dollar markdown or markup) or percentages. Two ways of calculating a markdown are the markdown percentage and the off-retail percentage. The **markdown percentage** is computed as

$$\text{Markdown percentage} = \frac{\text{Total dollar markdown}}{\text{Net sales (in \$)}}$$

A difficulty with this formula is that additional markups and employee discounts must be included in net sales (along with dollar markdowns). Furthermore, this formula does not enable a retailer to determine the percentage of items that are marked down as compared to those sold at the original price.

A complementary measure is the **off-retail markdown percentage**:

$$\text{Off-retail markdown percentage} = \frac{\text{Original price} - \text{New price}}{\text{Original price}}$$

With this formula the percentage of markdown for each item can be computed, as well as the percentage of each item marked down.

For example, a gas barbecue grill sells for \$100 at the beginning of the summer and is reduced to \$70 at the end of the summer. The off-retail markdown is 30 per cent [(\$100 − \$70)/\$100]. If 100 grills are sold at the original price and 20 are sold at the sale price, the percentage of items marked down is 17 per cent, and the total dollar markdown is \$600.

---

[34]Alfred R. Oxenfeldt, *Pricing for Marketing Executives* (San Francisco: Wadsworth, 1961), p. 28.

Additional markup percentages and **additions to retail percentages** are computed by

$$\text{Additional markup percentage} = \frac{\text{Total dollar additional markups}}{\text{Net sales (in \$)}}$$

$$\text{Addition to retail percentage} = \frac{\text{New price} - \text{Original price}}{\text{Original price}}$$

Table 14-7 shows markdown performance for several departments in department and specialty stores with sales of $1 million or more per year. Markdowns averaged 14.9 per cent and 17.3 per cent of sales for the department and specialty store groups, respectively. Note the higher-than-average markdowns on women's apparel and the lower-than-average markdowns on personal needs, small wares, food, and tobacco items.

Markdown Control

Markdown control evaluates the number of markdowns, their proportion of sales, and their causes. It must be such that reductions can be evaluated and buying plans altered in later periods to reflect the markdowns. A good technique for evaluating the causes

Table 14-7
Markdowns as a Percentage of Sales for Department and Specialty Stores, by Division, in 1983 (for All Stores with Annual Sales over $1 Million)

Division	Department Stores	Specialty Stores
All shoes	20.3	18.6
Women's apparel	22.5	22.1
Women's accessories and intimate apparel	10.4	13.2
Men's apparel	15.5	15.9
Infants', boys', and girls' clothing and accessories	17.5	18.1
Personal needs, small wares, food, and tobacco	3.2	3.2
Hobby, recreation, transportation	9.8	14.6
Home furnishings: furniture and decorative accessories	12.4	17.8
Home furnishings: appliances and equipment	9.5	—
Domestics, draperies, home goods	11.6	14.7
Total upstairs store	14.9	17.3

Source: David P. Schulz, "NRMA's New MOR," Stores (October 1984), pp. 22–23. Reprinted from STORES magazine: National Retail Merchants Association © 1984.

of markdowns is to have a buyer record the reasons for each markdown he or she uses and to examine these reasons on a regular basis. Examples of buyer notations are end of season, to match the price of a competitor, worn merchandise, and obsolete style.

Markdown control enables a retailer to monitor store policies, such as the way merchandise is stored and late acceptance of fashion shipments. In addition, careful planning may allow a retailer to avoid some markdowns by increasing advertising, training and compensating employees better, shipping goods more efficiently among branch units, and returning items to vendors.

However, the need for markdown control should not be interpreted as meaning that all markdowns can be minimized or eliminated. In fact, too low a markdown percentage may be an indication that a store buyer has not assumed enough risk in purchasing goods.

Timing of Markdowns

Although there is some disagreement among merchants as to the best timing sequence for markdowns, much can be said about the benefits of implementing an early markdown policy. First, this policy offers merchandise at reduced prices when demand is still fairly active. Second, an early markdown policy requires lower markdowns to sell products than markdowns late in the selling season. Third, early markdowns free selling space for new merchandise. Fourth, a retailer's cash flow position is improved.

The main advantage of a late markdown policy is that the retailer has every opportunity to sell merchandise at the original prices. However, the advantages cited for an early policy are disadvantages under a late markdown policy.

Retailers can also use a staggered markdown policy, where prices are marked down throughout the selling season. A staggered markdown policy of reducing prices throughout the selling season is often associated with an **automatic markdown plan.** In such a plan, the amount and timing of markdowns are controlled by the length of time merchandise remains in stock.[35] For example, Filene's basement in Boston operates markdowns under the following timetable:

Length of Time in Stock	Per Cent of Markdown (from Original Price)
12 selling days	25
18 selling days	50
24 selling days	75
30 selling days	Given to charity

Such a plan ensures fresh stock and early markdowns.

A storewide clearance, usually conducted once or twice a year, is another way of timing markdowns. Often a storewide clearance takes place after peak selling periods like Christmas and the Fourth of July. The objective is to clean out merchandise before taking a physical inventory and beginning the next season. The advantages of a storewide clearance over an automatic (staggered) markdown policy are that

[35]Deborah Blumenthal, "Boston's Favorite Bargain Store," *New York Times* (April 18, 1982), p. 12; and Isadore Barmash, "Discounting Comes to Wanamaker," *New York Times* (August 18, 1984), p. 31.

- A larger period is provided for selling merchandise at original prices.
- Frequent markdowns can destroy a consumer's confidence in the store's regular pricing policy: "Why buy now, when it will be on sale next week?"
- An automatic policy encourages a steady stream of bargain hunters who may not be potential customers for the store's regular products. Clearance sales limit bargain hunting to once or twice a year.

Pricing in Retailing: A Summary

Pricing is important to a retailer because of its interrelationship with overall objectives and the other components of the retail mix. Before developing a price strategy, the retailer must study the factors that affect pricing. These include consumers, government, manufacturers, wholesalers, other suppliers, and competitors. In some instances, these factors severely limit a retailer's pricing discretion; in others, they have only a minor effect.

A framework for planning retail prices consists of five stages: objectives, broad price policy, price strategy, implementation of price strategy, and price adjustments.

Retail-pricing objectives are chosen from among sales, dollar profits, return on investment, and/or early recovery of cash. After the objectives are chosen, broad policy is set. A coordinated series of actions is outlined, consistent with the store's image and oriented to the short and long run. In setting policy, the retailer uses the multistage approach to pricing.

The price strategy integrates demand, cost, and competitive concepts. Each of these orientations must be understood separately and jointly. Psychological pricing, markup, gross margin, merchandise-management accounting, and pricing below, at, or above the market are key aspects of strategy planning.

When implementing a price strategy, the retailer uses several specific tools to supplement the broad base of strategy. Retailers must be familiar with and know when to use customary and variable pricing, one-price policies and flexible pricing, odd pricing, leader pricing, multiple-unit pricing, and price lining.

Price adjustments are necessary if one is to adapt to a variety of internal and external conditions. Adjustments include markdowns, additional markups, and employee discounts. It is important that adjustments be controlled by a budget, that the causes of markdowns be noted, and that future store buying reflect earlier errors or adaptations.

Questions for Discussion

1. Why is it important for retailers to understand the concept of price elasticity even if they cannot compute it?
2. Comment on each of the following.
   a. Horizontal price fixing
   b. Vertical price fixing
   c. Price discrimination
   d. Minimum-price law
   e. Item price removal

3. How can a manufacturer control retail prices now that fair trade has been abolished?
4. What is a buyer's liability under the Robinson–Patman Act? How can a buyer avoid prosecution?
5. Why do retailers sometimes seek price guarantees?
6. Differentiate among demand, cost, and competitive approaches to pricing.
7. Give an example of a price strategy that integrates demand, cost, and competitive criteria.
8. Explain why markups are usually computed as a percentage of selling price rather than of cost.
9. A floor tiles retailer wants to receive a 40 per cent markup (at retail) for all merchandise. If one style of tile retails for $4.00 per tile, what is the maximum the retailer can pay for a tile?
10. A car dealer purchases CB radios for $40 each, and desires a 35 per cent markup (at retail). What retail price must be charged?
11. A photo store charges $5.00 to process a roll of slides; its cost is $3.20. What is the markup percentage (at retail)?
12. Differentiate between initial and maintained markup.
13. What are the advantages of a variable markup policy?
14. Describe merchandise-management accounting. Why isn't it widely used?
15. How would price lining differ for a discount store and a specialty shop?
16. What is the difference between markdown percentage and off-retail percentage?
17. What are the advantages of an early markdown policy? A late markdown policy?

CASES

1. Higbee: Marketing Housewares at "Fair" Prices*

In the six-county Cleveland market, the twelfth largest in the United States, the leading department store chain is Higbee. Its annual sales are over $275 million. An important, growing product category for Higbee is housewares, which generates $6 million in yearly sales.

To maintain its strength in housewares, Higbee follows this approach:

- Items are grouped into three main categories: cookware (e.g., pots, pans), tabletop (e.g., dishes, silverware), and electrics (e.g., coffeemakers, blenders). In addition, there are "gray" products, those that can be placed into two of the three categories (e.g., copper can be cookware and tabletop); these are displayed in ways that provide transitions between the categories. Until recently, Higbee had nine housewares departments, making it difficult for customers to shop.
- Upscale customers are targeted. "Our customer is interested in quality merchandise. Although most customers are not loyal, we do have our own group of customers. This Higbee's customer doesn't enter the May Co. across the street to compare prices."

*The material in this case is drawn from "Housewares Stirring in Cleveland," *Chain Store Age, General Merchandise Trends* (January 1985), pp. 77–78.

- A select number of brands is carried in each housewares category, but there is a deep assortment within those brands. Both popular brands and imports are stocked. "The name brands bring in traffic while imports help margins."
- Fair prices are offered, but a discount strategy is not used. "We won't be the lowest guy on the block but we definitely offer value for our basics [name brands]."

Higbee faces intense competition for housewares sales in Cleveland. Among its competitors are J. C. Penney, Joseph Horne, May Co., Gold Circle, and K mart. May Co. is its toughest competitor, with $5 to $5.5 million in annual housewares' sales. Table 1 shows the results of a recent survey on the models of coffeemakers and the prices charged by various Cleveland stores.

Table 1
Coffeemaker Comparisons in Cleveland

	Store					
Coffeemaker Model	Higbee	J. C. Penney	Joseph Horne	May Co.	Gold Circle	K mart
Krups 268	$ 89.99	—	$95.00	$ 79.99	—	—
Krups 259	139.99	—	—	139.99	—	—
Krups 261	59.99	—	75.00	59.99	—	—
Krups 260	39.99	—	—	34.99	—	—
Oster 666–06	64.99	$89.99	69.95	—	—	$49.88
Oster 656–06	49.99	—	—	—	—	—
Proctor Silex A416	27.99	—	—	—	—	—
Salton MC–12	69.99	—	—	—	—	—
Bunn	49.99	—	—	—	$39.88	44.88
Melitta ACM–10A	38.99	—	—	—	—	—
Melitta Aroma Plus	39.99	—	—	—	—	—
Melitta MA 8040	49.99	—	—	—	—	—
Hamilton Beach 803	39.99	—	46.95	—	—	—
Braun KF 35	79.99	—	—	69.99	—	—
Braun KF 30	59.99	—	—	59.99	—	—
GE DCM9B	27.99	—	—	—	—	—
GE SDC-2	69.99	74.99	—	69.99	59.99	59.88
Krups 267	—	—	49.95	49.99	—	—
Farberware 265D	—	—	42.99	39.99	—	—
Mr. Coffee MC 101A	—	—	—	34.99	32.99	—
Mr. Coffee US001	—	—	—	29.99	—	29.96
Mr. Coffee US002	—	—	—	49.99	44.99	46.88
Regal K7560BW	—	—	—	21.99	—	—
Toshiba HCD850	—	—	—	119.99	—	—
Proctor Silex A-506	—	—	—	29.99	—	—
Krups 247	—	—	—	79.99	—	—
Sunbeam Coffeemaster 15306	49.99	—	49.95	49.99	—	—

Source: Reprinted by permission from Chain Store Age, General Merchandise Trends, *January 1985. Copyright Lebhar-Friedman, Inc. 425 Park Avenue. New York, NY. 10022.*

Questions

1. Evaluate Higbee's pricing strategy for housewares.
2. Comment on Higbee's decision not to carry Mr. Coffee while stocking other less-known coffeemaker brands, such as Krups, Bunn, and Melitta. (See Table 1.)
3. Would you categorize Higbee's pricing strategy as demand-, cost-, or competition-oriented? Why?
4. From Table 1, would you conclude that Higbee's is using price lining? Explain your answer.

2. Thomas Teaberry's, Inc.: Evaluating the Pricing Abilities of Employees*

Tom Teaberry, Jr., executive vice-president of the $60 million (annual sales) department store chain bearing his family's name, winced as he studied the results of a report prepared by the Retail Consulting Services Division of Touche, Ross, and Company. The report presented the results of an examination given to key merchandising personnel—divisional merchandise managers (DMMs), buyers, and assistant buyers—of a major East Coast department store chain. The exam consisted of five sections: (1) knowledge of basic terms associated with pricing, merchandise planning, and inventory management and control, (2) understanding of basic merchandising arithmetic and profitability, (3) invoice mathematics and terms of sale, (4) pricing and repricing, and (5) dollar planning and control.

Teaberry was particularly disturbed with the following highlights of the test results that Touche, Ross analysts seemed to think were representative of the results that would emerge if the same test were given to other groups of retailing executives:

- On the average, the group tested (99 participants) answered only 19 per cent of the questions correctly—even though they dealt with basic merchandising procedures.
- The highest overall score was 52 per cent.
- DMMs answered an average of 30 per cent of questions correctly; buyers averaged 25 per cent and assistants 13 per cent.
- Merchandising arithmetic and profitability questions was correctly answered by 43 per cent of those tested; 8 per cent correctly answered dollar planning and control questions. Only 9 per cent defined "gross margin" correctly.
- Buyers and DMMs with 3 to 10 years' experience scored higher than those who worked fewer than 3 years or more than 10 years.
- The group had very little understanding of overall store operations and their role in them; they did not know how the store determined profitability.
- Despite the respected positions held by those who took the examinations, the results reveal a lack of understanding of such basic concepts as markups and markdowns.

*This case was prepared and written by Professor Marvin A. Jolson, University of Maryland, College Park, Maryland.

Teaberry's mini-exam (time allowed, 30 minutes)

1. The buyer for the home entertainment department is determined to have an overall gross margin of 40.0 per cent on 9-inch color television sets after all markdowns have been taken. One hundred sets are purchased for $240 each, and an initial price of $425 is set for each. After selling 80 sets, the buyer decides to clear out the remaining unit at a reduced price. What should the per unit price of the 20 units be to reach the maintained markup objective?

(Answer: $300.00)

2. A suit is priced at $150 and subsequently reduced and sold for $100 What is the store´s markdown percentage (using net sales as a base on this item?

(Answer: 50 per cent)

3. In a channel of distribution for ladies' sweaters, wholesalers earn a 30 per cent markup and retailers earn 40 per cent (all markups are on selling price). If, for cashmere turtlenecks, the producer's selling price is $25.20, what should be the suggested retail price of the item?

(Answer: $60.00)

4. A new buyer has just taken over the appliance department at Teaberry's. One of the best sellers has been a deluxe vacuum cleaner the store previously purchased for $130 and has retailed for $299.50. At the present time, 200 units are in stock. The buyer wishes to buy 1,000 additional units, but the vendor's price on this item is now $160. The profit target for the month on this item is $20,000, and operating expenses for the month (allocated to this product), including vigorous advertising, are planned at $62,000. The buyer feels that at the end of the month all units will be sold, but plans total reductions including markdowns at 10 per cent of net sales. How should the store price these items, initially assuming that merchandise on hand and new merchandise will be priced the same? What initial markup percentage will the department realize on this item?

(Answer: Price   = $245.67
Markup = 36.9 per cent)

NOTE: Answers were not made available to Teaberry employees taking the exam.

Figure 1

Teaberry discussed the test findings with Angela Ott, director of training, for his own company. Ms. Ott commented, "I shudder to think of how our own executives would perform if given a similar test." Teaberry responded, "There's no better time to find out than right now. But I have no intention of asking a bunch of elementary questions such as 'Compare the terms *initial markup* and *maintained markup.*' Frankly, if my sophisticated executives are unable to answer questions related to basic merchandising tools that are used every day of the week, they shouldn't be working for Teaberry's. I'm going to ask three or four thought-provoking questions and the answers will tell me whether my merchandising people are prepared to plan, analyze, and execute their responsibilities profitably."

Figure 1 contains the test devised by Teaberry. Of his 27 merchandising executives, only one answered all the questions correctly. This made Teaberry furious. He proposed to his father, the store's president, that all the merchandising executives undergo an intensive 40-hour training program (on their own time) and then take a similar test again. Those still answering any questions incorrectly would be placed on probation until they could answer all of these types of questions.

Questions

1. How do you explain the dismal showing on both the Touche, Ross and the Teaberry tests?
2. Take the Teaberry exam yourself, within the 30-minute time limit.
3. What parts of the exam are most difficult? Why?
4. Do you agree that poor performance on this exam would be an indicator that one is ill prepared to plan, analyze, and execute responsibilities profitably? Explain your answer.

15

Planning by a
Service Retailer

Chapter Objectives

1. To examine the scope of service retailing and show how it differs from product retailing
2. To describe the special considerations facing service retailers
3. To demonstrate how retail strategy elements apply to service retailing: situation analysis, objectives, target marketing, overall strategy, implementation, and re-evaluation
4. To evaluate controllable and uncontrollable factors as they pertain to service retailers

Century 21 Real Estate Corp. is the leading residential realtor in the United States. In total, its 6,400 offices are staffed by 75,000 full- and part-time sales associates who annually generate $30 billion in transactions and earn more than $1.4 billion in commissions. Each year, Century 21 is involved with the sales of an average of 3 million houses.

Since its inception, Century 21 has followed a clear retailing strategy. Most of its offices are franchised (at a current purchase price of $12,000 to the franchisee). Every office contributes about 2 per cent of revenues to a national advertising fund (over $20 million per year). A distinctive image is portrayed through the firm's logo and the gold coats worn by its sales associates. Service standards are high and maintained uniformly throughout the United States.

However, Century 21 has also discovered that service retailing can be volatile. Because of high interest rates on mortgages, the housing market was very depressed in the early 1980s. As a result, Century 21's unit sales fell from 4 million in 1979 to about 2 million in 1982, before rebounding in 1983 and 1984. In addition, Sears' Coldwell Banker is upgrading its efforts rapidly and has increased market share from 1 per cent in 1981 to approximately 6 per cent now.

Like other good service retailers, Century 21 is responding to its environment. Its current five-year plan calls for an increase in market share, a doubling of the sales force, establishment of a mortgage brokerage program to aid buyers, creation of an insurance program, and extensive employee training.[1]

Overview

Service retailing is increasing steadily and represents a very large portion of overall retail trade. Consumers now spend about half of their aftertax income on services such as travel, recreation, credit, product rentals, personal care, education, medicine, and shelter.

As defined in Chapter 4, there are three general categories of service retailing: rented goods, owned goods, and nongoods. With rented–goods services, consumers lease physical products for a specified period of time. With owned–goods services, consumers have products that they own repaired or altered. With nongoods services, consumers receive the personal expertise of the service provider; products are not involved.

The size of service retailing and the differences in strategic planning for a service retailer make this a part of retailing that should be thoroughly examined. In the future, the service sector will continue to expand in importance. Opportunities will be plentiful for those who know how to react to them.

Strategy Concepts Applied to Service Retailing

The unique aspects of services, which influence the retail strategy, are that (1) the intangible nature of services makes a consumer's choice of competitive offerings more difficult than with products; (2) the producer and his or her services are inseparable (this localizes marketing and gives consumers a more limited choice of alternatives); (3) the perishability of services prevents storage and increases risks; and (4) the human nature of services makes them more variable. The intangible (and sometimes abstract) nature of services makes it difficult to outline a successful, consumer-oriented strategy, particularly as many retailers (e.g., carpenter, repairperson, landscaper) start businesses on the basis of product expertise. The inseparability of the producer and his or her services means that the owner-operator is often indispensable and good customer relations are necessary. Perishability presents a risk that in many instances cannot be overcome. For example, the revenues from an unrented hotel room are forever lost. Variability means that service quality may differ for each shopping experience, store, or service provider.

Although a service retailer is quite different from the goods (product) retailer, strategy planning is conducted by use of the same overall procedure:

1. The situation is analyzed, including a definition of the service category.
2. The objectives of the firm are enumerated and ranked.
3. Consumer characteristics and needs are identified.
4. The overall strategy is outlined.
5. The strategy is implemented.
6. The strategy is constantly re-evaluated and adjusted.

[1]Ruth Stroud, "Century 21 Cultivates a Changing Estate," *Advertising Age* (September 10, 1984), pp. 4, 95.

A Classification System for Service Retailers

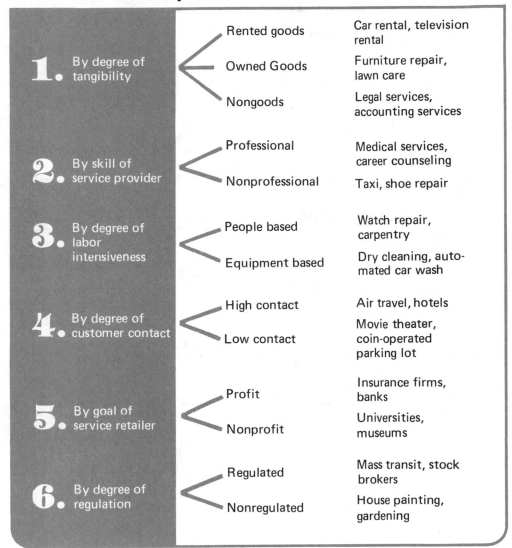

1. By degree of tangibility	Rented goods	Car rental, television rental
	Owned Goods	Furniture repair, lawn care
	Nongoods	Legal services, accounting services
2. By skill of service provider	Professional	Medical services, career counseling
	Nonprofessional	Taxi, shoe repair
3. By degree of labor intensiveness	People based	Watch repair, carpentry
	Equipment based	Dry cleaning, automated car wash
4. By degree of customer contact	High contact	Air travel, hotels
	Low contact	Movie theater, coin-operated parking lot
5. By goal of service retailer	Profit	Insurance firms, banks
	Nonprofit	Universities, museums
6. By degree of regulation	Regulated	Mass transit, stock brokers
	Nonregulated	House painting, gardening

Source: Adapted from Joel R. Evans and Barry Berman, *Marketing,* Second Edition
(New York: Macmillan, 1985), p. 648.

Figure 15-1

In particular, service retailers must understand their business, set clear objectives, efficiently select service opportunities, cater to consumer needs, become cost effective, plan for competition, present a distinctive offering, and determine how to set prices. Figure 15-1 shows a classification system for service retailers, who should precisely identify the combination of attributes in this figure that they possess and act accord-

Table 15-1
Implications for Service Retailing in Seven Managerial Areas

Services as Compared with Products	Managerial Changes Needed for Service Retailing
a. *Measuring performance*	
Capital expenditures vary widely for different services	Return on net worth may not be the most important measurement of the value of a service to the retailer.
Little or no inventories are required to offer services	Turnover, markdown controls, and other goods-related controls are not appropriate.
Higher labor costs	Profit after labor costs replaces the gross margin of goods retailing.
Some services support the sale of products	Sales-supporting services should be evaluated differently from revenue-producing services.
Cost accounting is more important	Job-specific records will be required to assess the profitability of each sale.
b. *Store organization*	
More specialized supervision	Separate management for service areas will be required.
More specific search for service employees	Nontraditional sources for identification of employees must be used.
Lower employee turnover	Frequent salary and performance reviews must be carried out.
Higher pay for skilled craftspeople than for merchandising personnel	Pay levels will need to be adjusted upward over periods of longevity for service employees.
c. *Service production*	
More involvement in manufacturing of the service	Production skills will need to be obtained by supervisors.
More emphasis on quality control	Supervisors must be able to assess the quality of a service performed for a customer.
More need to monitor consumer satisfaction	Need for research with prior customers to measure their satisfaction with the service.
More need to refine scheduling of employees	Maximizing the service employees' time requires matching consumer purchasing to ability to produce the service.
Quality must be consistent among all outlets	Standards for consistency of the service must be established and continually evaluated; central training may be required for craftworkers in multiple branch operations.
d. *Pricing*	
Services vary in cost; therefore, pricing is more difficult	Prices may be quoted within a range instead of an exact figure before the purchase.
More difficulty in price competition or promotion based on price	Services should be promoted on the basis of criteria other than price.

Table 15-1 (continued)
Implications for Service Retailing in Seven Managerial Areas

Services as Compared with Products	Managerial Changes Needed for Service Retailing
e. *Promotion*	
Value is more difficult for consumers to determine	Consumers need to be convinced of value through personal selling.
Difficult to display within store	In-store signing or a service center are required to notify customers of services availability.
Visual presentation is more important	Photographs of before-and-after may be possible with some services. Testimonials may be possible with other services.
Cross-selling with products is important	A quota or bonus for product salepersons who suggest services will lead to increased service selling.
More difficult to advertise in catalogs	Conditions for the sale and away-from-the-store performance must be specified.
f. *Complaints*	
More difficult to return a service	Policies must be established on adjusting the service purchased with a dissatisfied customer.
A customer is more sensitive about services involving the person	Specific guarantees and policies about adjustments must be established; new types of insurance must be added to cover liabilities.
g. *Controls*	
Greater opportunity to steal customers	Employee assurance of loyalty must be established. Protection of store loyalty must be obtained.

Source: J. Patrick Kelly and William R. George, "Strategic Management Issues for the Retailing of Services," Journal of Retailing, Vol. 58 (Summer 1982), pp. 40–42. Reprinted by permission.

ingly. Table 15-1 points out how companies can plan for the differences between service and product retailing.

Situation Analysis

When developing a service strategy, a retailer must determine whether rented-goods, owned-goods, or nongoods services are involved, because planning is different for each type of service. Then the service category must be more narrowly defined, as the following illustrations show:

- Is the retailer interested in opening a barber shop and giving haircuts? Or is he interested in opening a men's personal-care salon, where services include haircutting, manicure, facial massage, hair coloring, and facial care advice?

- Is the retailer going to start a resort hotel centering on couples, singles, or families? Or can it offer different features aimed at each?
- A new college is opening. Should it offer classes in liberal arts and sciences, education, premedicine, and/or business administration?
- A dry cleaner is undecided between consumer dry cleaning and commercial dry cleaning. She knows that one or the other must be chosen. The two cannot be combined.

These illustrations indicate the range of options available to a prospective service retailer and demonstrate the necessity of defining the service category.

The retailer should decide on the broad service category before making any other strategic decisions. A narrow definition of the service category (e.g., liberal arts college) runs the risk of attracting a small target market and ignoring related services that are vital to customer satisfaction. For example, a retailer that repairs typewriters may be flooded with requests from existing customers to repair printing calculators. If the firm defines its offering too narrowly, it takes a chance of losing typewriter repair business from these customers. On the other hand, a broad definition of the service category (e.g., equipment repair) may result in a nonspecialist image and may require a larger operation and greater investment.

In determining the service category, personal abilities, financial resources, and time resources should be matched to the requirements of the business. The personal abilities required of a service retailer are usually quite different from those of a product retailer:

1. In service retailing, the major value provided to the customer is some type of service, not a physical product.
2. Many specific skills are required; these skills may not be transferable from one type of service to another. For example, a television repairperson, a beautician, and an accountant cannot easily change positions or transfer skills. However, an appliance retailer, a grocery retailer, and a toy retailer would have a much easier time in changing and transferring their skills to another area.
3. Many service retailers must possess licenses or certification in order to operate their businesses. Barbers, real-estate brokers, medical personnel, attorneys, plumbers, and others must pass examinations in their chosen fields.
4. A service retailer really needs to enjoy his or her profession and have an aptitude for it. Because of the close personal contact with customers, these elements are essential and difficult to fake.

The financial resources necessary for a service retailer may differ significantly from those of a product retailer. The major ongoing cost for many service retailers is labor. Whereas the opening of a service station demands a high capital investment, the compensation for mechanics is the largest ongoing cost of doing business. For a product retailer, the major ongoing investment is inventory.

Therefore, many service retailers can operate on lower overall investments and require less yearly revenue than product retailers. A new service station can function with one gas attendant and one skilled mechanic. A tax preparation firm can succeed with one accountant. A watch repair business needs only one repairperson. In each case, the owner may be the only skilled laborer. Accordingly, costs can be held down.

In contrast, a product retailer must have an adequate assortment and supply of inventory, which imposes financial obligations, requires storage facilities, and is costly.[2]

It must be pointed out that some service retailing requires not only an initial capital investment but also other ongoing (nonlabor) costs. For instance, an amusement park, a car wash, and a laundromat all have expensive electrical and maintenance costs.

In the selection of a service category, it is crucial that all costs be calculated. The owner's labor should not be viewed as cost-free because he or she could earn wages as someone else's employee (and the owner needs a steady income to maintain a given life-style).

The time resources of the prospective retailer should be weighed in terms of the time requirements of alternative business opportunities. Some businesses, like a self-service laundromat or a movie theater, require low time investments. Other businesses, like house painting or a travel agency, require large time investments because personal service is the key to profits. More service retailers fall into the high time-investment than the low time-investment category.

Setting Objectives

In addition to the sales, profit, and image objectives sought by product retailers, service retailers set other objectives because of their unique characteristics. These include increasing service tangibility, matching demand and supply, standardizing services, and making services more efficient.

Service tangibility can be increased by stressing service-provider reliability, promoting a continuous slogan (e.g., "At Eastern Airlines, we work harder to serve you better"), describing specific service accomplishments (such as an automobile tune-up improving gasoline consumption by one mile per gallon), and offering warranties. In 1985, H&R Block began a promotion campaign that promised free tax returns if it did not secure the largest IRS refunds possible for its customers.[3]

Demand and supply can be better matched by marketing similar services to market segments having different demand patterns, marketing new services having demand patterns that are countercyclical from existing services, marketing new services that complement existing services, marketing "extras" during nonpeak times, and marketing new services not subject to existing capacity constraints (e.g., a restaurant starting a catering service).[4]

Standardizing services reduces variability, makes it easier to set prices, and improves efficiency. Services can be standardized by clearly defining each of the tasks involved, determining the minimum and maximum time necessary to complete each task, selecting the best order for tasks to be completed, and specifying the optimum time and quality of the entire service. Figure 15-2 shows how a corner shoeshine operator can standardize services.

In addition to standardizing services, retailers may be able to make services more efficient by automating them, thereby substituting machinery for labor. Among the service retailers that have automated most are car washes, banks, supermarkets, telephone companies, movie theaters, and hotels.

---

[2]This difference is not as great as might be expected, because manufacturers and wholesalers may allow product retailers to receive inventory on consignment or offer good credit terms.

[3]Gary Levin, "Chip Off the Old Block?" *Advertising Age* (January 7, 1985), pp. 1, 64.

[4]Leonard L. Berry, A. Parasuraman, and Valarie A. Zeithaml, "Synchronizing Demand and Supply in Service Businesses," *Business*, Vol. 34 (October–December 1984), pp. 35–36.

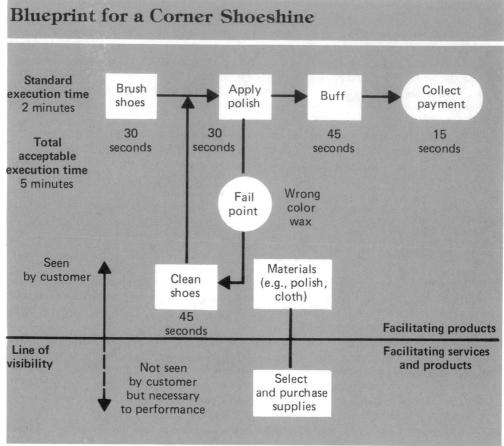

Blueprint for a Corner Shoeshine

Source: G. Lynn Shostack, "Designing Services That Deliver," *Harvard Business Review*, Vol. 62 (January-February 1984), p. 134. Copyright © 1984 by The President and Fellows of Harvard College; all rights reserved.

Figure 15-2

Defining and Examining the Target Market

The target market must be defined and examined, and the consumer and the service offering carefully matched. Consumer demographics, life-styles, and decision making should all be studied. In this way, the retailer can develop a strategy in a logical and consistent manner. To illustrate with an earlier example, a barber shop attracts customers who are more conservative, less affluent, less mobile, and more convenience oriented than those drawn to a personal-care salon.

Service retailers can use segmentation and/or mass-marketing approaches. These examples show the variety of target market alternatives available to service firms:

- Rent-A-Center leases appliances and household goods through its 140+ stores nationwide. Its major target market consists of 18- to 35-year-old blue-collar workers with an annual household income of $20,000 or less. These consumers have no opportunity to own in the traditional way and have limited access to credit or savings.[5]

- The Marriott Corporation has identified four key market segments in its quest for long-term growth: the medium-priced business travel market, the upscale hotel market, the elderly interested in life-care communities, and vacationers attracted to time-sharing condominiums.[6]

- Hyatt Legal Services (not affiliated with the hotel chain) aims its offerings at the "middle 70 per cent of the market" not served by traditional lawyers or legal clinics. To attract clients, Hyatt has low prices, convenient locations and hours, internal training programs for its lawyers, speedy service, and respect for consumers. Television is heavily used in promotion.[7]

- To attract and satisfy a mass market, General Motors has developed a national "Mr. Goodwrench" service program with its automobile dealers. The program requires participating dealers to satisfy ten specific quality standards. In return, General Motors sponsors mass advertising and encourages standardized performance among dealers.[8]

Outlining Overall Strategy

In planning the overall strategy for operating a service business, the full range of controllable (store location and operations, service offering, store image and promotion, and pricing) and uncontrollable (consumer, competition, technology, economic conditions, seasonality, and legal restrictions) factors must be examined. Figure 15-3 contains a list of the special considerations and problems facing a service retailer in each of these areas. They are detailed in the following sections.

Controllable Factors: Store Location and Operations

The store location and operations aspect of strategy must be thoroughly outlined. The importance of store location to service retailers varies greatly. In some service categories, such as repairs, house painting, and lawn care, the service is "delivered" to the appropriate site. The retailer's location becomes the client's home or office, and the actual office of the retailer is unimportant. Many clients never even see the retailer's office and maintain contact by telephone or personal visits by the retailer.

Other retailers are visited on "specific-intent" shopping trips. Although the customer is concerned about the convenience of a location, he or she usually does not select a skilled practitioner such as a doctor or a lawyer on the basis of location. It is common for doctors and attorneys to locate offices in their homes or near hospitals and courts, respectively.

For some service retailers who are visited by customers, location is quite important. Car washes, travel agencies, and airline reservation offices are examples of retailers who must be concerned about the convenience of their locations. In fact, car rental agencies pay premium rents to be situated in airports.

---

[5]Tom Bayer, "Rental Outlets Assure Folks Renting is OK," *Advertising Age* (October 25, 1984), p. 5.
[6]"Bill Marriott's Grand Design for Growth: Upscale and Down in the Lodging Market," *Business Week* (October 1, 1984), p. 62.
[7]"Hyatt Targets Legal Market with Five Benefits," *Marketing News* (October 26, 1984), p. 6.
[8]Gregory D. Upah, "Mass Marketing in Service Retailing: A Review and Synthesis of Major Methods," *Journal of Retailing*, Vol. 56 (Fall 1980), pp. 59–76.

Special Strategy Considerations and Problems Faced by a Service Retailer

I. Controllable Factors

A. Store Location and Operations

1. Location
2. Store size
3. Level of investment
4. Fixtures and maintenance
5. Personnel management
6. Store hours
7. Franchising

B. Service Offering

1. Intangibility
2. Quality
3. Uniformity
4. Assortment
5. Combining service and product retailing
6. Level of innovativeness
7. Forecasting and budgeting
8. Control

C. Store Image and Promotion

1. Image creation
2. Atmosphere
3. Customer service
4. Promotion
5. Word-of-mouth

D. Pricing

1. Cost-plus
2. Fixed
3. Competitive
4. Value
5. Negotiated
6. Contingency
7. Price lining
8. Diversionary

II. Uncontrollable Factors

A. Consumer

1. Decision process
2. Loyalty and trust
3. "Do-it-yourselfer"

B. Competition

1. Ease of entry
2. Level of competition

C. Technology

1. Costs
2. Efficiency

D. Economy

1. Luxuries
2. Necessities

E. Seasonality

1. Inability to stockpile
2. Peak vs. nonpeak periods

F. Legal Restrictions

1. Federal
2. State
3. Local

Figure 15-3

The store size and level of investment are considerably lower for many service retailers. A small store can often be utilized, because little or no room is needed for displaying merchandise. As an example, a travel agency may have twelve salespeople and book several million dollars in trips; yet it may fit into a store with less than 500 square feet. The investment factor relates to the absence of inventory, as discussed in the previous section. In addition, telephone business can further reduce the importance of store size and fixtures.

Some fixtures and maintenance are more important to a service retailer than to a products retailer. Because tangible, branded products (which can be compared among different stores) are not sold, the customer may base part of his or her opinion of the store on its visible fixtures and appearance. To use the travel agency example again, the desks, carpeting, light fixtures, typewriters, and so on are used by the customer in developing an image of the store—even though these items are not part of the promotion mix.

Some aspects of personnel management can be difficult and frustrating for a service retailer:

- When should the store be staffed? Are there peak business hours?
- How can customer waiting time be minimized?
- What should the permanent employees do during the time when no customers appear?
- How can an employee's performance be measured?
- How can productivity be increased?
- How should employees be paid (salary, commission, and so on)?
- If an employee is fired, will the customers follow him or her?

Because of the personal nature of many service businesses, these and other questions must be considered before a strategy is implemented.[9]

The decision on store hours should be made in conjunction with personnel management decisions. Store hours must be planned on the basis of customer, not employee, convenience. For example, a shoe repair store should be open mornings, and a savings bank should have evening and/or Saturday hours. Although the shoe repair store can have one worker open the store in the morning just to receive broken or worn shoes, as the work will be done later, the savings bank must plan to have enough employees during the evening and/or weekend hours to handle all customer services while they wait.

Franchised services are expanding. Dentahealth, Holiday Inn, Budget Rent a Car, Arthur Murray Dance Studios, and Century 21 Real Estate are some examples of franchises involved in service retailing. The greatest potential problem facing each of these companies is the lack of uniformity in services provided by different franchisees. Dentahealth must ensure that its dentists provide similar services at similar prices. Holiday Inn must provide uniform sleeping and eating accommodations. Budget Rent a Car must have economy car rentals available at all locations. Arthur Murray must have professional, knowledgeable instructors at each studio. Century 21 must weed out unethical brokers and insist on certain performance standards.[10]

---

[9]See John Helyar, "Banks Training Workers to Market a New Wave of Financial Services," *Wall Street Journal* (July 20, 1983), pp. 29, 53.

[10]See Julie Liesse Erickson, "Franchises Biting into Dental Business," *Advertising Age* (November 8, 1984), pp. 28–29; and Stroud, "Century 21 Cultivates a Changing Estate," pp. 4, 95.

If any unit in the franchise fails, the whole franchise suffers. Because service is such an intangible, extra care should be given to generating and maintaining a company image. Training and supervision take on added importance.

Controllable Factors: Service Offering

A product retailer, carrying items such as perfume or automobiles or televisions, has tangible products to offer. The merchandise can be seen, smelled, touched, heard, and in some cases, tasted. A service retailer who handles rentals and/or repair services also deals with tangible products. It is the service retailer offering nongoods services who has intangible items to sell, and these present a special problem.

For example, how can the Evelyn Woods Reading Dynamics Course be described? How should a customer choose between a vacation in Rome and Madrid; and why should he or she use a travel agent? What exactly is a college education? What makes H&R Block different from other tax preparers? How can a customer choose an efficient, honest service station? Why patronize Jack LaLanne?

Each of the preceding retailers offers an intangible service. The attributes and benefits of the service, as well as its differential advantages, are difficult to convey. However, these service retailers are successful. Here is why.

Evelyn Woods advertises extensively; and because the concept of speed reading is hard to get across, Evelyn Woods offers a free lesson in its ads. Prospective customers are invited to a session where a sampling of the course is shown and their reading speed is increased. In this way, people participate in the course and see the results. An advertisement alone cannot be as effective as this approach.

Foreign countries and the fifty states are always promoting tourism. Each country and state has an office of tourism. The goals of this office are to attract new vacationers, to woo conventioners, and to get people to switch from their usual vacation spots. Lavish brochures and extensive newspaper advertising are used. Magazines like *Travel and Leisure* (the publication of American Express) are good places for advertisements. The selling points are culture, sightseeing, shopping, weather, gambling, entertainment, price and so on.

The travel agent tries to sell his or her expertise. The agent knows all the available packages and options for a variety of vacation spots. The agent also has connections with airlines and hotels and provides a one-stop service. The customer uses an agent when he or she is convinced that time is saved, the price is right, and the arrangements are better than could otherwise be secured.

Defining and promoting a college education is extremely difficult. First, a college education must be defined as more than forty courses leading to an undergraduate degree. The contents of many courses are certainly intangible. For instance, how can an art course be described, as it reaches so many levels? Second, the benefits of a college education are sometimes hard to convey. Knowledge, insight, sociability, and aesthetics are harder to explain than a good job. Third, ethics and good taste limit the range of "puffery" that can be used to sell a student on a university. Given these constraints, many colleges are following sound retail strategies. Advertisements are put in newspapers and magazines and on radio and even television, extolling the virtues of a college education. Recruiters actively seek out potential students. Finally, the most interesting development in recent college planning is the establishment of more contemporary courses and nondegree programs (geared to non 18- to 21-year-olds).

H&R Block sells tax preparation services. The great success of this company can be attributed to three factors. First, the service category has been properly defined. Many people do not like to do their own taxes, are afraid of them, or feel they consume too much time. Second, Block tries to make the service more tangible by presenting a detailed list of reasons that the company should be used. Third, convenience is provided through hundreds of locations and a consistent and reputable image is produced.

The service station operator, in the absence of meaningful licensing regulations, relies on word-of-mouth promotion. Because efficiency, reliability, and honesty are almost impossible for the consumer to measure, personal contact with other customers is important. A profitable service station need not advertise. In fact, advertising does little to convince customers that the station is good.

Jack LaLanne health studios are in the personal care business. Through extensive advertising, LaLanne emphasizes two points: a healthy body makes a person more attractive; and this attractiveness can be achieved through a carefully prepared regimen involving exercise and diet. LaLanne is extremely successful because of the public's desire to feel younger and look better. But again, this is an intangible and difficult concept to market.

The nongoods retailer who follows a good planning format, clearly specifying the service and its market, will usually be successful. The examples given should be helpful in tying strategy to an intangible offering. This should be under the retailer's control.

Like the product retailer, the service retailer must consider the quality of the offering. Airlines are always competing on the basis of "no frills" versus "extra service," trying to satisfy different market segments. For instance, students look for no-frills flights, whereas businesspeople are more concerned about time of departure and direct flights, and tourists desire inflight services.

Quality is also difficult to plan because of different customer perceptions of the same service. As an example, a tax preparation service may be purchased because of accurate mathematical computation, opportunity for financial savings, convenience, or freedom from responsibility. Different market segments are lured by each of these perceived benefits.[11]

Limousines and taxis provide the same type of service, but the quality is significantly different. A country club may have two golf courses, locker room facilities, a pool, a dining room, eight tennis courts, and exclusive membership, or it may have one golf course, a fast-food restaurant, no locker room, two tennis courts, and open membership. A car rental agency can handle Lincoln Continentals and Cadillacs or Chevrolet Cavaliers and Plymouth Horizons.

In the selection of a level of quality, the target market, competition, image, store location, turnover, profitability, national versus private brands, services to be offered, personnel, perceived customer benefits, and constrained decision making should each be considered. An additional factor (of greater importance than to a product retailer), the uniformity of the offering provided by the same service firm, must be thoroughly planned. This is even more critical than the variability among units for a service franchise.

The customer is interested in receiving the same service each time a particular retailer is patronized. For example, employees' appearance, skills, attitude, and performance must be consistent. Customer loyalty is predicated on uniform service. If a

---

[11]G. Lynn Shostack, "Breaking Free from Product Marketing," *Journal of Marketing*, Vol. 41 (April 1977), p. 77.

person eats at a restaurant where it usually takes one hour to complete dinner, this person will be very dissatisfied with a wait of two hours to finish dinner. On the other hand, when a restaurant normally has two-hour service, its regular customers will not be unhappy with the wait.

Service assortment needs to be determined. Width and depth of assortment, although different from that of a product retailer, must be planned. Two illustrations will demonstrate this point. The width of assortment for a car rental agency may consist of cars, trucks, vans, and camper-trailers. The depth of assortment consists of the various models within any line (e.g., cars) and the range of services (e.g., daily, weekly, and monthly rentals; automatic and manual transmissions; air-conditioned and non-air-conditioned). In Florida, many car rental agencies concentrate on one product line (cars) and offer small, economy cars only. This is a narrow-shallow service assortment that has proved very popular with the budget-oriented vacationer.

Sports arenas must also make assortment decisions involving the events they will exhibit. Madison Square Garden, owned by Gulf & Western, utilizes a wide–deep strategy. The assortment is wide because all types of sports and nonsports events are exhibited, including basketball, hockey, tennis, boxing, wrestling, rodeo, circus, dog show, Ice Capades, political conventions, rock concerts, and trade shows. There is depth of assortment because numerous basketball teams, hockey teams, tennis stars, and others play there. In addition, tickets are priced over a wide range and are available on a daily, seasonal (one sport), and all-events basis.

Every service retailer, small or large, must define the limits of the offering in terms of the width and the depth of assortment. This decision is not restricted to product retailers.

Because of the growth of service retailing, many traditional retailers are now combining service and product retailing. Among the traditional retailers operating a retail service in the same stores they sell products are the following:

- Sears owns and operates insurance, real estate, stock brokerage, and other services.
- Record stores rent videocassettes.
- Many larger department stores own and operate restaurant facilities.
- Woolworth operates a shoe repair service in some stores.
- Many larger supermarkets sell film processing and contain automatic banking windows.

Other traditional retailers lease sections of their stores to service operators, such as banks, opticians, beauty parlors, jewelry appraisers, and professionals, such as dentists and lawyers. In some instances, traditional retailers have working arrangements with finance companies (automobile dealers) and repairpeople (television appliance stores) and receive commissions for performing the sales function for them.

The retailer who combines goods and services into one offering must follow a consistent strategy. The goods and services should complement each other, be a logical extension for the store, and not adversely affect the store's image. The combinations already listed follow these guidelines. Combination retailing will continue to grow rapidly in the future.

Planning for innovation by a service retailer is significantly different from product retailing and is sometimes unpredictable. The rented-goods retailer must anticipate which models or styles will be popular. For example, which movies will be the most desirable videocassettes to be rented in 1986? Which car models will customers prefer to rent?

The service retailer who handles repairs and improvements is faced with two types of planning for innovation. First, techniques for repairing or improving new products must be learned. There is normally sufficient time to prepare for these products (e.g., the modular transistor television to replace the tube television) because the products often have factory warranties for ninety days up to one year or longer. Second, new techniques must be developed and marketed for servicing existing products (e.g., a new way to paint a car or treat the lawn). Customers must be sold on the technique, which requires overcoming resistance to the new method.

The nongoods retailer has the toughest job in planning new services because he or she deals with intangibles. For example, an accountant has to determine which financial planning services to offer clients. A university must decide which courses and programs to add and which to delete.

Forecasting and budgeting are central to any retailer's plans. The service retailer must forecast daily, weekly, monthly, and yearly sales. For established retailers, past sales estimates often provide good estimates for the future, when combined with an analysis of competition, the target market, and the economy. Strong customer loyalty means that repeat sales can be predicted. The new retailer must look at demographics and so on but will rely essentially on estimates that are subject to large errors. The budget must be constructed on the basis of projected sales and must allow for an acceptable profit margin.

A specified control mechanism is necessary to the evaluation and the revision of the service retailer's strategy. As compared to the product retailer, the service retailer has one problem reduced and another magnified. Inventory control, including pilferage, is not a problem for nongoods retailers. For repair and rental retailers, the problem of inventory is less than for product retailers, although the rental retailer is sometimes confronted with sloppy or malicious customers. However, the nongoods retailer is hard-pressed to measure productivity. After all, a fast worker may be a messy worker. To overcome this difficulty, performance standards must be set, and, equally important, employees must be compared with one another on their overall performances.

Controllable Factors: Store Image and Promotion

Proper image creation is crucial to the service retailer's success. People patronize the retailer because a unique and desirable image is created and reinforced. Every restaurant presents an image, whether it be clean and efficient, rustic, romantic, or a gourmet's delight. Each movie theater constructs an image by virtue of prices, selection of movies, cleanliness, parking, and waiting lines. Dry cleaners develop their images through quality of cleaning, speed, and prices.

The most important element in a service retailer's image is the customer's perception of how well the basic service is performed. A clear image can be relatively easily established by a rental retailer because tangible products are involved; the consumer perceives a well-defined offering, which can be compared with that of other retailers. The repair or nongoods retailer finds it more difficult to carve out a distinct place in the market because of the intangibility of the offering (which makes it hard for people to comparison shop). To succeed, the repair or nongoods retailer must generate an image based on a stated set of criteria, as in the H&R Block illustration mentioned earlier.

In the creation of an image, the proper atmosphere must be established. A clean and efficient restaurant image is aided by waxed floors, regularly washed windows, functional booths and tables, and counter service. A rustic image is fostered by early American furniture, lanterns, wooden fixtures, and pioneer attire for the waiters and waitresses. The romantic restaurant has secluded booths, candlelight, and soft background music. The gourmet's delight has the local newspaper critic's comments in the window, a lavish dessert display near the front door, and freshly cooked meals.

The movie theater affects its image by having extra cashiers on busy nights, separating smokers and nonsmokers, cleaning popcorn and other debris from the floors, and projecting a clear picture and sound. The dry cleaner can influence store image by providing an easy-opening front door, having a clean countertop, displaying prices and cleaning data, and arranging clean clothes neatly on hangers.

An important part of atmosphere is the store's design. This includes the storefront, the store layout, and the displays. The design must be constructed in a manner that is consistent with and adds to the store's image and atmosphere. For example, a recent consumer survey found that the major factor (after quality of care) in attracting and retaining dental patients was the reception area. Cleanliness, lighting, roominess, and reading materials all contribute to patient perceptions.[12]

The level of customer services has a strong impact on image. Personal care, parking, delivery, credit, and telephone sales are some of the supplemental services for the service retailer to consider. A self-service laundromat is perceived much differently from a laundry service that picks up, cleans, and returns clothes. A restaurant that has metered, on-street parking is viewed as distinct from a restaurant that has valet parking. A university that provides deferred tuition has an image unlike one that insists on full payment before the semester begins. A taxi service that operates via the telephone is not the same as one that requires the patron to stand in the middle of a crowded street and wave.

At many banks, several of the services once provided free to all customers are now provided free only to their most affluent customers. These banks charge fees for "excessive" withdrawals from savings accounts, cashing social security checks, using live tellers, and balancing checkbooks. The banks believe that the charges are necessary for them to survive in today's highly competitive environment.[13]

Some service retailers are rarely involved with extensive mass promotion. Seldom do barber shops, dry cleaners, repair retailers, house painters, laundromats, taxis, parking lots, or interior decorators advertise in any media other than Yellow Pages. They are small and localized and rely on loyal customers and/or convenient locations. Other service retailers do rely heavily on promotion. These include hotels, motels, health spas, insurance companies, banks, and travel agents. These retailers are usually larger and have a wider geographic market. In addition, multiple outlets are common.[14]

Until the late 1970s many professional associations did not allow their members to advertise. However, the courts and the Federal Trade Commission have ruled that doctors, pharmacists, optometrists, opticians, attorneys, accountants, and others may advertise. Through their advertising, professionals must exhibit high standards of ethics and concern for clients, explain when services should be sought, outline the attributes

[12]Randall E. Wade, "Study Suggests 10 Critical Areas for Dentists' Attention," *Marketing News* (December 9, 1983), p. 8.

[13]Daniel Hertzberg, "Smaller Customers Get Less Service at Banks and Pay More Charges," *Wall Street Journal* (October 18, 1983), pp. 1, 18.

[14]See Dan T. Dunn, Jr., Claude A. Thomas, and Robert F. Young, "Banking: The Marketing Battle Heats Up," *Business*, Vol. 34 (January–March 1984), pp. 3–12.

clients should consider when evaluating professionals, describe how clients can communicate with professionals, and state what they can realistically provide to clients.[15]

With the exception of self-service businesses, all types of service retailers stress personal selling in their promotion mix. The barber, the dry-cleaning attendant, the repairperson, the painter, the taxi driver, and the parking-lot attendant all provide an important selling function as well as their primary service. So do hotel and motel personnel, health spa employees, insurance agents, bank tellers, and travel agents. Again it must be mentioned that it is the personal attention that wins customers for service retailers.

Sometimes, service retailers supplement their communication effort with sales promotions. A credit-card company may offer a free month's trial for a new credit-card protection program. An airline may offer extra discounts for frequent passengers. A cruise ship may run coupon offers in newspapers. Premiums or prizes can be given by banks, insurance companies, movie theaters, and car-rental firms.[16]

As a result of good performance, the service retailer hopes to attain positive word-of-mouth communication. This occurs when a satisfied customer tells his or her friends to use the retailer, and this builds into a chain of customers. No service retailer can succeed if he or she is receiving extensive negative word-of-mouth communication. These negative comments will cause the retailer to lose business:

"The food at the restaurant was lousy, and it was overpriced."

"After I took my car through the car wash, it had black streaks on the sides."

"The hotel advertised that everything was included in the price. Yet it cost me twenty dollars to play golf."

"I paid five hundred dollars to take a course and the instructor missed five classes. What a rip-off!"

The service retailer, much more than his or her product counterpart, must have positive word-of-mouth to attract new customers and retain the old ones. For example, health-care professionals credit word-of-mouth with generating 63 per cent of all new patients. Noted one marketing expert: "Advertising can only bring a person into an office once. If you are incompetent, don't treat patients properly, or overcharge, you're not going to get any repeat business. Word-of-mouth is still the most important source of new patients."[17]

Controllable Factors: Pricing

In setting prices, the service retailer has several alternative methods to consider: cost-plus, fixed, competitive, value, negotiated, contingency, price lining, and diversionary. Many of these methods may be combined.

Cost-plus pricing occurs when the retailer uses the cost of the service as the basis for price. He or she adds the cost to a profit margin to arrive at the selling price. This

[15]Paul N. Bloom, "Effective Marketing for Professional Services," *Harvard Business Review*, Vol. 62 (September–October 1984), pp. 102–110.
[16]Christopher H. Lovelock and John A. Quelch, "Consumer Promotions in Service Marketing," *Business Horizons*, Vol. 26 (May–June 1983), p. 70.
[17]"Experience Belies Healthcare Professionals' Ad Fear," *Marketing News* (June 8, 1984), p. 1.

is straightforward for some service retailers, such as coin-operated laundromats. Comtech, a New York laundromat chain, estimates that 60 per cent of its revenue covers leases; 17 per cent goes to repairs, service, and collections; 10 per cent goes to new washing/drying machines; 5 per cent covers operating expenses; and 8 per cent is profit.[18]

The problem is that the cost of a service may be hard to determine. For instance, how does a self-employed repairperson determine labor costs? The simplest way is to find out the wages earned by a comparable repairperson working as an employee. In addition to labor costs, materials, rent, taxes, and so on must be included in the calculation.

Cost-plus pricing has many disadvantages. It is not market-oriented; the price consumers are willing to pay for a service is not ascertained. Idle time is seldom included in this technique. Total per sale costs are difficult to compute. Cost cutting is rarely pursued actively.

Fixed pricing exists in situations where the government or professional organizations have control and retailers must conform to the stated price structure. In some cities, parking-lot rates are fixed by law. Congress sets the rates for postage stamps. Train and bus prices must, in most cases, be government approved.

Fixed pricing produces mixed results. Advantages are the elimination of price wars, the protection of small firms, and consumer protection. Disadvantages are the lack of retailer control over an important marketing factor, inflexibility, and complacency.

Competitive pricing is a marketing-oriented strategy. In this instance, the service retailer sets his or her prices on the basis of those of competitors. If a neighborhood theater charges $3 per ticket for a movie that has been in circulation for six months, a theater showing first-run movies can charge $4 to $6. Similarly, two hotels with comparable facilities and locations, catering to the same market, should have similar prices. Competitive pricing is the simplest, and probably the most effective, method for pricing services (because costs can always be adjusted to accommodate the price). As always, pricing must be consistent with the overall retail strategy.

The use of competitive pricing is easy, responsive to the marketplace, and adaptive to the environment. It is a conservative strategy because the retailer goes along with his or her competitors. In addition, the retailer assumes that his or her costs, image to consumers, and service offering are identical to competitors.

With **value pricing,** prices are set on the basis of fair value for both the service provider and the consumer. For value pricing to be effective, service retailers must be in a strong competitive situation and have relative control over prices. Value pricing is common for service professionals such as doctors and lawyers. They set fees based upon the value of their time and the services performed.

Negotiated pricing occurs when the retailer works out pricing arrangements with individual customers. A unique or complex service is desired by the customer, and a one-time price must be negotiated. Unlike cost-plus, fixed, or competitive pricing (whereby each consumer pays the same price for a standard service), each consumer may be charged a different price under negotiated pricing (depending on the nature of the unique service). For example, a moving company charges different fees, depending on the distance of the move, stairs versus elevator, access to highways, and the weight of furniture such as a piano.

[18]"A Growing Operator of Laundry Rooms," *New York Times* (January 3, 1984), p. D1.

Under negotiated pricing, the retailer can be very responsive to the consumer and develop a tailor-made proposal. It is critical that the negotiated price be competitive with those of other service retailers and include a thorough cost analysis. This technique can also be quite time consuming and expensive (because an estimate must usually be given to the consumer). Negotiated pricing is inefficient for standardized, recurrent services.

Contingency pricing is an arrangement whereby the retailer does not receive payment from the customer until after the service is performed and payment is contingent on the service's being satisfactory. A real-estate broker earns his or her fee only when a house purchaser (who is ready, willing, and able to purchase a house) is produced. Several brokers may show the house to prospective buyers, but only the broker who sells the house earns a commission. Many lawyers work on a contingency basis. They receive a percentage of the settlement if the client wins and nothing if the client loses.

In some areas, such as real estate, law, and lawn care, consumers insist on contingency payments because they want to be assured that the service will be satisfactorily performed. This pricing technique presents some risks to the retailer because considerable time and effort may be spent without payment. A real-estate broker might show a house twenty-five times, not sell it, and therefore not be paid.

A **price-lining strategy** is used by service retailers who provide a wide selection of services. A line of prices is matched to the services. A travel agent handling European vacations can use price lining by creating several packages over a price range. Vacations to Spain, France, and Italy may be priced from $900 to $2,800 per person. At each price, a different combination of travel services is offered. A country club can use price lining by creating different types of membership: golf, tennis, and pool; golf and pool; golf only; tennis and pool; tennis only; and pool only. Each membership, from pool to all three activities, is priced differently.

Price lining, as a supplement to one of the other pricing methods already mentioned, enables the retailer to expand the target market and to create a differentiated service offering. The latter point is very important because many consumers relate price to quality. Therefore, price lining helps a retailer to foster a diversified service image.

Diversionary pricing is a practice used by deceptive service retailers. In this case, a low price is stated for one or a few services (which are emphasized in promotion) to give the illusion that all of the retailer's prices are low. However, the prices of services that are not stressed are higher than the average. The intention is to attract the consumer to the low-priced service and then entice him or her to purchase the high-priced ones as well. A service station may promote an inexpensive tune-up to give the impression that all prices are low and then have high prices on repairs.

Because price and image are so closely related for the service retailer, it is imperative that a thoughtful, cohesive pricing strategy be implemented. The techniques described in this section provide good insights into the alternatives available. The difficulties lie in assessing market demand and determining service costs.

Uncontrollable Factors: The Consumer

The service retailer must understand and respond to the consumer, who goes through the decision process in the selection and purchase of services. The use of the process depends on the cost of the service, the newness of the service, the recurrence of the purchase, and so on. Because of the intangible nature of many services, it is imperative that each element in the decision process be studied: stimulus, problem awareness, information search, evaluation of alternatives, purchase, and postpurchase behavior. In addition, the relation of purchase behavior to demographics and life-style should be studied.

The successful service retailer relies upon the loyalty and trust of customers. Many customers exhibit high levels of loyalty once they have selected a barber, a dentist, a doctor, a plumber, an accountant, or a service station. This loyalty is usually much greater than for a product retailer. Customers can easily switch among retailers selling the same products, but it is not easy to switch among repair or nongoods retailers. Satisfaction with these service retailers is based upon a total offering that is hard to compare. In addition, loyal customers have a trust that is sometimes impossible for a competitor to break.

Once a service retailer is established, business should be good as long as a consumer orientation is maintained. In this situation, a new barber, dentist, doctor, plumber, accountant, or service station will find it extremely difficult to break into the market.

One type of customer is beyond the reach of some service retailers: the do-it-yourselfer. This type of person is growing, as costs and leisure time increase. The do-it-yourselfer does his or her own tune-ups, paints his or her house, landscapes the lawn, plans his or her own vacation, and sets up his or her own darkroom for developing film. Retailers of discount products do very well by selling supplies to do-it-yourselfers. However, service retailers suffer because the major service (labor) is undertaken by the customer himself or herself. Market segmentation becomes desirable and perhaps even necessary to avoid the do-it-yourself segment or to serve it by offering low prices.

Uncontrollable Factors: Competition

The ease of entry into service retailing differs for rentals and for repairs and nongoods. A rental retailer must often invest a large amount in the item to be rented, such as an automobile or an apartment. This investment limits entry into the market. On the other hand, a repair or nongoods retailer usually relies on labor (often his or her own) and tools, which minimizes investment costs. In this case, entry into the marketplace is easy. An exception occurs when extensive education and licensing provisions restrict entry.

Where easy entry exists, the level of competition will be high. In particular, small businesses will crop up, and they can be profitable if they appeal to specific target markets. Numerous small travel agencies, restaurants, and film processors flourish. Where entry is difficult, the level of competition is low. There are few airlines, amusement parks, and country clubs operating in any geographic area.

When a retailer is choosing a location, the amount of existing and potential competition should be measured. The site selected should have sufficient traffic and growth potential to justify the addition of a new service retailer. It must be pointed out that a location with one profitable car wash may result in two unprofitable car washes if a second opens up and shares business with the first. And the car wash cannot easily be moved once it is constructed.

Sometimes, new types of service retailers appear and increase competition for product retailers. For example, some video-rental firms also rent VCRs and video cameras; and many supermarkets rent carpet cleaners. About 14,000 retailers now rent videocassettes.[19]

Uncontrollable Factors: Technology

A service retailer has a wide option of investments in running his or her business. New, expensive reservation systems or older, less-expensive manual reservations can be used. An old Yellow Cab can be used, or a new, compact Renault Alliance can be bought. Cars can be washed by hand or via large machines. A gardener can use a hand mower and cutting shears or elaborate automatic tools. An airline can fly with 707s, 747s, 757s, 767s, or SSTs.

The businessperson who relies on older technology must provide good personal service and generate a loyal customer following; the firm that depends on newer methods can eventually lower costs and do a better job. New technology leads to increased efficiency, which in turn results in an improved image and lower prices than competitors.

A modern reservation system eliminates duplication, provides accurate information, and aids in strategy planning. A new, compact taxi gets good gas mileage and is inexpensive to maintain. An automatic car wash has the capacity to clean and wax 100 or more cars per hour and leaves the cars sparkling. A gardener with automatic tools handles twice as many customers and does a consistent job. A 767 jet allows an airline to schedule large, fuel-efficient flights. This cuts down on expenses.

Sometimes, improvements in product technology can have a negative impact on service retailers because they result in less frequent maintenance requirements or repair. The following shows the impact of improved automobile technology on the frequency of car servicing:[20]

Part	1970*	1980*
Points	10,000 miles	Minimal
Spark plugs	10,000 miles	15–20,000 miles
Oil	2,500 miles	7–15,000 miles
Transmission	24,000 miles	Lifetime
Tires	25,000 miles	40,000 miles
Brakes	20,000 miles	40,000 miles
Engine coolant	Two years	Three years
Filters	5,000 miles	15,000 miles

*Replacement or service intervals.

Uncontrollable Factors: The Economy

The service retailer should consider the effect of the economy on business. Because a number of services can be classified as luxuries, they are greatly affected by economic conditions. When the economy is poor, air travel, overseas vacations, restaurants, and others are adversely influenced. The laundromat, the beauty salon, the dry cleaner, and others are minimally affected because they are more necessities than luxuries.

[19]Ellen Paris, "Coming Distractions," *Forbes* (July 16, 1984), p. 46.
[20]"How ARCO Used Marketing Research to Go 'Cash-Only in a Plastic Society'," *Marketing News* (January 6, 1984), p. 26.

In adapting to economic conditions, the retailer can reduce sales fluctuations by offering a variety of services and de-emphasizing the luxury aspects of the services. It is important that business conditions be anticipated and included in strategy planning.

Uncontrollable Factors: Seasonality

Some service retailers are faced with a seasonal demand for their services. Country clubs are most popular in the late spring, the summer, and the early fall. Hotels are busiest on weekends and holidays. Landscapers work most often in the fall and spring. Local buses and trains are most crowded during the morning and evening rush hours.

The greatest problem for these service retailers is the inability to stockpile resources. If a country club has the capacity to accommodate 500 people, it cannot admit 750 people on Friday because there were only 250 on Thursday. Similarly, a hotel cannot fill 1,000 rooms with 6,000 people, even though during midweek, half the rooms were empty. A landscaper cannot handle two customers at the same time during the spring to make up for idle time in the winter. Buses and trains cannot sell 2,000 tickets for 500 seats during the rush hour to make up for the lack of passengers during the day.

Service businesses must be oriented toward satisfying peak demand periods. Employees must be deployed accordingly, and long-range planning must be based on sound forecasting (including peak and nonpeak periods). Special services and offers can be used to attract customers during nonpeak times. Country clubs can introduce indoor activities. Hotels can offer low prices and additional services (such as the free use of a golf cart or free drinks at a show) for midweek patrons. Landscapers can offer snow removal and other winter services. Buses and trains can offer fare discounts and tie-ins with restaurants and theaters for off-hour riders.

Uncontrollable Factors: Legal Restrictions

All service retailers should be familiar with the federal, state, and local restrictions under which they must operate. On the federal level, various agencies, such as the Interstate Commerce Commission, Federal Aviation Administration, and the Federal Deposit Insurance Corporation, oversee service retailers. In addition, many national self-governing bodies set guidelines for their members. These groups include the American Assembly of Collegiate Schools of Business, the American Medical Association, and the American Institute of Certified Public Accountants.

In recent years, the federal government has actively pursued a policy of deregulating transportation, banking, communications, and other service industries. This has greatly increased the flexibility of firms in developing and carrying out their strategies. It has also led to a greater use of marketing practices, such as consumer research.

On the state level, these are some illustrations of the legal restrictions facing service retailers: insurance companies and their rates are approved; licensing exams are administered and qualifications set for various professionals; utility rates are approved; and trade schools are certified.

At the local level, the retailer must be aware of zoning, operating, and other laws. Each municipality has different limitations, and this factor should be considered when one is selecting a store location.

Implementing a Service Strategy

After a general strategy is outlined, the service retailer must put it into action. The tactics followed must conform to the company's overall strategy, and an integrated plan must be carried out. In addition, the strategy should be fine-tuned whenever necessary. The following are a wide variety of examples involving the implementation of service strategies.

Retail strategies followed by service professionals vary greatly. On the one hand, there are many doctors, lawyers, dentists, and other professionals who do not practice or believe in retailing tactics. They do not accept the fact that they are service retailers, think that practices such as advertising are demeaning, deplore competitive tactics, and do not understand all the elements in strategic retail planning. These professionals believe that their services and skills market themselves.

On the other hand, there is a growing number of service professionals who are involved in retail strategies because of growing competition. For example, it is predicted that there will be a surplus of several thousand medical doctors in the United States by 1990. Accordingly, more and more doctors are building and maintaining their practices by sending flowers to patients who refer their friends, calling patients to "chat," and conducting surveys of peoples' likes and dislikes. Similarly, more lawyers and dentists are adopting business practices such as locating in retail stores or shopping centers, advertising, and/or franchising in order to compete in the marketplace.[21]

Rented-goods retailing has expanded as the costs of purchasing merchandise have risen sharply. Annually, U.S. consumers spend over $7 billion renting appliances, tools, household goods, and television sets. For example, retailers involved with television rentals emphasize product currency, no large initial payments, repair service, consumer mobility, free delivery and installation, loaner sets, and trade-ins. Some firms provide ownership at the end of the rental agreement. Although consumers make no large initial payment, total rental costs are greater than outright purchase. Typically, sets must be rented for two years before they return a profit to the firm.[22]

Club Med operates a large chain of vacation resorts throughout the world. Its unique strategy is so successful that it attracts 800,000 visitors each year; Club Med is the eleventh largest hotel chain in the world. The chain features all-inclusive, prepaid vacation packages. There is a single, simple level of accommodations at each resort, many meals are buffet style, and dress is casual. A full range of activities, from wind surfing to nightly entertainment, are offered at all locations. Statistics show that more than half of the visitors are married, with an average annual income of $54,000.[23]

The household goods moving industry is undergoing significant changes because of deregulation. Prior to the Household Goods Transportation Act of 1980, interstate shippers were limited to hauling used household goods at rates controlled by federal

[21]See Laurel Sorenson, "Hospitals and Doctors Compete for Patients, With Rising Bitterness," *Wall Street Journal* (July 19, 1983), pp. 1, 40; Myron Magnet, "Here Come McDentists," *Fortune* (February 21, 1983), pp. 135–139; and Bernie Whalen, "Legal Services Marketing Enters New Era with Ad Co-op's 'Slick,' Professional TV Commercial," *Marketing News* (March 5, 1982), pp. 1, 14.
[22]Jeff Blyskal, "An Expensive Way to Borrow," *Forbes* (July 18, 1983), pp. 126–127.
[23]"Club Med's Big Plans in U.S.," *New York Times* (February 8, 1985), pp. D1, D3.

regulators. Now, carriers can ship a wide range of goods, offer a variety of services, and control the prices they charge. As the president of Allied Van Lines noted:

> We didn't pay a whole lot of attention to what the customer wanted before. Our services were pretty well governed by what the Interstate Commerce Commission would let us do. Now we're out battling for customers like everyone else in the competitive environment. There's more emphasis on sales and market training, guarantees, and other consumer attractions. We certainly have hiked our media advertising and our marketing research as a result of deregulation.[24]

Re-evaluating the Service Strategy

Once the service strategy is in full operation, it should be continuously monitored. For example, Figure 15-4 contains a questionnaire that CPAs (certified public accountants) can use to evaluate their level of marketing orientation.

The overall strategy and its implementation should be re-evaluated on a regular basis and adjustments made when necessary. In this way, the retailer can quickly and accurately adapt to changes in the uncontrollable factors (consumer, competition, technology, economy, seasonality, and legal restrictions). The retail audit, described in Chapter 16, is as useful a tool for the service retailer as for the product retailer.

Planning by a Service Retailer: A Summary

Service retailing now represents a sizable share of total retail sales and will continue to expand in the future. Service retailing can be divided into three broad categories: rentals, repairs and improvements, and nongoods. In each category, the customer receives a service but does not obtain ownership of a physical product.

Strategy planning and implementation are the cornerstones of a profitable service business. Although the overall principles of strategy are the same whether service or product retailing is involved, there are some major differences. These differences exist because of the intangibility, inseparability, perishability, and variability associated with many services.

When conducting a situation analysis, the service category must be well defined. Personal abilities, financial resources, and time resources should be weighed in the selection of a service category. Next objectives are set to reflect service tangibility, demand and supply, standardization, and efficiency of services. Then the target market is specified and described.

The overall strategy is outlined consistent with the service category and target market. In planning the general strategy, the retailer must consider various controllable factors. Store location and operations factors include location, store size, investment, fixtures, management, hours, and type of ownership. Service-offering factors include intangibility, quality, uniformity, assortment, combinations, innovativeness, forecasting, and control. Image and promotion factors include image creation, atmosphere,

---

[24]Kevin Higgins, "Movers Grope for Marketing Orientation," *Marketing News* (May 11, 1984), p. 1.

Quiz for Assessing a CPA Firm's Marketing Orientation

		True	False
1	Marketing accounting services means selling accounting services.		
2	Concentration on servicing clients' needs is the best marketing plan to follow.		
3	Individual offices and sectors (auditing, tax, management advisory services, etc.) within the firm mainly concern themselves with expanding the firm's services in their respective areas of responsibility.		
4	Professional staff are hired on the basis of technical competence only.		
5	Developing new business is not important enough to put a senior officer in charge with firmwide responsibility.		
6	Marketing of accounting services means advertising accounting services.		
7	Most of the top officers of the firm have not attended a marketing seminar within the past two years.		
8	We do not have a written list of target customers for business expansion.		
9	Marketing, for an accounting firm, is inconsistent with professionalism.		
10	We do not have a written business expansion plan.		
11	It is best to hold business development meetings outside regular business hours so they won't interfere with ongoing operations.		
12	Less than 10 per cent of total company time is spent on planning and preparing for business development.		

Interpretation key

9-12 falses: truly marketing-oriented
5-8 falses: somewhat marketing-oriented
0-4 falses: not at all marketing-oriented

Source: John G. Keane, "How Accounting Firms Can Use Marketing Concept, Techniques to Develop Their Practices," *Marketing News* (March 6, 1981), p. 12. Reprinted from *Marketing News,* published by the American Marketing Association.

Figure 15-4

customer services, promotion, and word-of-mouth. Pricing techniques include cost-plus, fixed, competitive, value, negotiated, contingency, price lining, and diversionary. Uncontrollable factors must also be analyzed while one is developing the overall strategy. The consumer, competition, technology, economy, seasonality, and legal restrictions should each be investigated. The strategy should adapt to these variables.

After the strategy is carefully outlined, it must be implemented as prescribed. The strategy is then regularly monitored and adjusted when necessary.

Questions for Discussion

1. What are the unique aspects of service retailing? Give an example of each.
2. It has often been stated that service retailers are not consumer-oriented. Why do you think this comment is made? Is it accurate?
3. Should medical, accounting, and other services be considered a part of retailing? Why or why not?
4. In what kinds of service retailing are personal skills important? In what kinds are they unimportant?
5. For each of the following, name several alternative market segments to which they can appeal.
   a. Car-rental agency
   b. Dry cleaner
   c. Restaurant
   d. Accountant
   e. Amusement park
   f. Lawn service
6. What reasons can you give for the growth of the franchising of services?
7. Give several advantages and disadvantages for combining service and product retailing under the same roof.
8. Why is personnel management difficult in service retailing?
9. Explain the concept of atmosphere from a service-retailer perspective.
10. Explain the importance of word-of-mouth to a service retailer.
11. Present an example of each type of pricing.
    a. Cost-plus
    b. Fixed
    c. Competitive
    d. Value
    e. Negotiated
    f. Contingency
    g. Price lining
    h. Diversionary
12. Does the consumer use the decision process differently for services than for products? Explain.
13. What alternative strategies can be used to deal with the do-it-yourselfer?
14. Why can a service retailer succeed without new technology?
15. Describe the difficulties in evaluating a service-retailing strategy.

CASES

1. Bruce Larrick, D.D.S.: Using a Consumer-Oriented Strategy*

Dr. Bruce Larrick operates a dental practice in a "Dentique" outlet in the Oak Malls regional shopping center in Gainesville, Florida. Among the retailers in this shopping center are Sears, J. C. Penney, and Radio Shack.

The consumer-oriented marketing techniques used by Dr. Larrick have been so successful that they attract over 200 new patients each month for he and his associates. His innovative ideas have been presented at an annual meeting of the American Dental Association and at speaking engagements across the United States. Among Dr. Larrick's concepts for building and maintaining a successful dental practice are these:

- The cornerstone for any professional relationship is quality service. No marketing strategy will succeed in the long run unless delivered by a professional who cares.
- Mall locations draw customer traffic. For example, the Oak Malls shopping center attracts 250,000 people weekly; each is viewed as a prospective patient.
- Dental offices should be open during all mall hours, utilize distinctive storefronts, have window displays, and encourage walk-ins. The Dentique has a video unit that shows famous people eating, kissing, and smiling. Other slides and videoclips are also shown at "The Tooth Booth."
- A patient should be encouraged to feel good about his or her mouth and the practice of dentistry. Larrick uses the word "situation" instead of "problem," does not rush patients into treatment, explains treatment options (such as watchful waiting), and communicates to patients with nontechnical terms.
- A personal approach should be employed. A warm handshake lets patients know the dentist cares, and literature and appointment letters can be embossed with the patients' names (and accompanied by handwritten notes).
- Advertising messages can reinforce the dentist's philosophy of conservative treatment, the image of modern dentistry, and "hassle-free" dental health. Larrick runs a newspaper ad every three weeks (and on Saturday and Sunday during football weekends). The adds feature a special logo, a mnemonic (Dr.-Smile) to help patients remember the phone number, the mall location of the Dentique, and hours open.
- Fees should not encourage discount-oriented patients. They do not become loyal, long-run patrons; and they are less concerned with service quality than with prices.

Dr. Larrick's success is in contrast to that of many other dentists. Although the American Dental Association estimates that the typical dentist nets about $60,000 a year, the real income of dentists has been shrinking. Over a recent 10-year period, dental fees lagged behind inflation by 10 per cent. Furthermore, there are now 52 dentists per 100,000 people in the United States; 20 years ago, there were 49. It is

*The material in this case is drawn from Bruce Larrick, "Total Marketing: The Best Way to Build Your Practice," *Dental Management* (January 1985), pp. 30–32ff.; and Richard Greene, "What's Good for America Isn't Necessarily Good for the Dentists," *Forbes* (August 13, 1984), pp. 79–81ff.

projected that there will be 61 dentists per 100,000 people by 1990. At the same time, only half of the population sees a dentist regularly; and improved technology (e.g., fluoride) is reducing the level of demand for dental services.

Questions

1. Evaluate Dr. Larrick's approach to dentistry.
2. Compare Dr. Larrick's approach to that used by traditional dentists. Why do many service professionals not utilize the practices suggested in this case?
3. Would the tactics noted by Dr. Larrick be successful in attracting all types of people? Explain your answer.
4. Develop a list of factors that a dentist should consider when opening a new practice.

---

2. The Second New West Bank: Adapting to a Deregulated Environment*

The banking industry has undergone extensive changes over the past several years, in large part due to the deregulation of the industry. Deregulation has provided banks with increased flexibility in establishing branch locations, adding new services, setting interest rates, and so on. As a result, competition for customers has risen sharply and many banks have encountered tough times. Also, technological improvements (such as automatic teller machines) now enable customers to use nonbank locations, complete transactions 24 hours a day, and employ in-house banking via computers. All of these factors have led to greater importance being placed on retailing techniques such as advertising and service planning to attract and maintain customers.

Recently, the Second New West Bank hired William Smith to head its new retail banking department aimed at final consumers. Smith is a 32-year-old banker who possesses a B.B.A. in Marketing, an M.B.A. in Finance, and three years of retail banking experience with a leading competitor. Although Bill accepted the position with Second New West, he was concerned about the firm's resistance to change and its staid image. For example, the bank did not have a detailed marketing research plan, a new services plan, or any data on the feasibility of its adding automatic teller machines.

Smith's first assignment was to study the various potential retail banking segments available to Second New West. After these segments were identified, he was to develop services to attract customers. Bill was also asked to evaluate the bank's promotional efforts. A senior vice-president noted that a considerable amount of promotional attention was given to reviving dormant accounts; however, the bank considered advertising to the general public to be in poor taste. In addition, the firm did not like to advertise the rates given to depositors on various accounts (such as day of deposit/day of withdrawal, six-month certificates of deposit, one-year certificates of deposit, etc.) or to use premiums (such as watches, pen sets, toaster ovens, and bathroom scales) to attract new depositors.

After conducting a thorough marketing research project, Bill identified several

---

*This case was prepared and written by Professor Kevin F. McCrohan, George Mason University, Fairfax, Virginia.

market segments that were being poorly served by Second New West and its nearby competitors: college students, single professionals, young families with children at home, and retired individuals. To attract these consumers, Smith proposed that the bank have special services geared toward them. He suggested offering low-cost checking and easier credit terms and requirements. Bill also wanted New Second West to provide overdraft privileges (by which automatic loans would be provided to customers if they exceeded the balances in their checking accounts) and service packages (combining a checking account, charge card, savings account, and overdraft privileges). These and other services would be advertised on local radio stations that appealed to specific audiences (e.g., college-aged adults) and area newspapers.

The senior vice-president is less than enthusiastic about Bill's plans for segmenting the market, providing new services, and redirecting promotion. In particular, he does not like the use of different credit policies for different market segments. He wonders if the bank made the right decision in hiring Bill. This has gotten Bill quite upset, he believes the plans are well conceived and necessary for Second New West to survive in the turbulent deregulated environment of the 1980s.

Bill Smith and the senior vice-president will be meeting next week with the bank's president to discuss their differing viewpoints.

Questions

1. Did Second New West make the right decision in hiring Bill Smith? Explain your answer.
2. Why do you think the bank is in its current predicament?
3. Evaluate Bill's suggestions regarding market segments, services, and promotion.
4. Present a systematic group of reasons that Bill should present to the bank's president to convince him to follow the recommendations made in this case.

16

Integrating and Controlling the Retail Strategy

Chapter Objectives

1. To demonstrate the importance of integrating a retail strategy
2. To examine four key factors in the development and enactment of an integrated retail strategy: planning and opportunity analysis, performance measures, productivity, and the uses of new technology
3. To show how industrywide data can be used in strategy planning
4. To explain the principles of a retail audit, its utility in controlling a retail strategy, and the difference between horizontal and vertical audits
5. To provide examples of audit forms

A key aspect of integrating and controlling retail strategy is the use of performance measures to assess productivity. Retailers have a number of measures available to them, as these illustrations show.

At Allied Stores, sales per net square foot is the most dominant measure of productivity for its department stores. "That's because it's the easiest to measure since everybody has the information and in essence all expenses must eventually be related to sales." Sales per labor hour are also important.

For Ames Department Stores (a full-line discount store chain): "The key figure we measure is sales and general administration expenses as a percentage of sales—we try to keep it as low as possible. The spread between S&GA and gross margin percentage is where your profitability is." In addition, sales and gross profit per square foot and gross profit percentages are examined.

Begley Drug uses several measures:

> In the pharmacy we measure the number of prescriptions per shift. When it comes to the manager or assistant manager, we measure a combination of sales per week and gross margin—since they have a lot of latitude to be innovative, the margin is something they can control. The cashiers are judged according to transactions per hour at the cash register. In cosmetics, we measure productivity almost totally by sales and in liquor we measure by sales; in both departments we measure seven-day cycles and end of month sales per employee.[1]

Overview

Throughout the text, a variety of individual factors pertaining to the development of retail strategies have been examined. This chapter focuses on integrating and controlling retail strategy. Accordingly, the chapter ties together the material detailed previously, shows why it is necessary for retailers to plan and enact coordinated strategies, and describes how to assess success or failure.

Integrating the Retail Strategy

It is vital that a retailer view strategy planning as an integrated and ongoing process and not as a fragmented and one-time-only concept. One of the major objectives of this text has been to explain the interrelationships between the various stages of strategy and the need to operate in an integrated format. Figure 16-1, reproduced from Chapter 2, shows the overall development of a retail strategy and how the steps are interconnected and integrated.

In particular, four fundamental factors need to be considered in the development and enactment of any integrated retail strategy: planning procedures and opportunity analysis, performance measures, productivity, and the uses of new technology. These factors are discussed next.

Planning Procedures and Opportunity Analysis

Planning procedures can be optimized by following a series of coordinated activities. First, senior management outlines the general direction and goals of the firm. Next, written guidelines are provided to middle- and lower-level managers. Then, these managers get input from all types of internal and external sources. Fourth, middle- and lower-level managers are encouraged to offer new ideas at an early stage of planning. Fifth, top-down (generated by top management) and horizontal (generated by middle- and lower-level management) plans are combined. Finally, specific plans are presented, including checkpoints and dates.[2] By following these activities, planning is made systematic and information is acquired from all types of relevant sources.

---

[1]"Choosing a Yardstick to Measure Productivity," *Chain Store Age Executive* (September 1984), p. 26.
[2]Stanley F. Stasch and Patricia Lanktree, "Can Your Marketing Planning Be Improved?" *Journal of Marketing*, Vol. 44 (Summer 1980), pp. 88–89. See also "CEOs Give Mixed Reviews to Staffs," *Chain Store Age, General Merchandise Trends* (January 1985), pp. 20, 23.

Development of an Integrated Retail Strategy

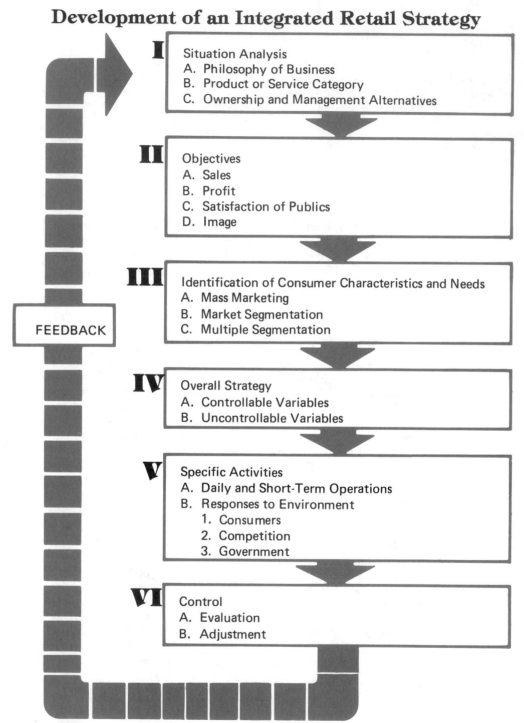

Figure 16-1

Table 16-1
Sales Opportunity Grid of a Supermarket
for Two Brands of Shoe Polish

	Brand	
Criteria	A (established)	B (new)
Retail price	$1.00/bottle	$1.00/bottle
Floor space needed	6 square feet	6 square feet
Display costs	$10.00/month	$20.00/month
Sales costs	$ 0.12/unit	$ 0.12/unit
Markup	30%	32%
Sales estimate		
During first month	$ 750	$ 300
During first six months	$3,000	$1,000
During first year	$5,000	$5,500
Gross profit estimate*		
During first month	$ 225	$ 96
During first six months	$ 900	$ 320
During first year	$1,500	$1,760
Net profit estimate†		
During first month	$ 125	$ 40
During first six months	$ 480	$ 80
During first year	$ 780	$ 860

*Gross profit estimate = Sales estimate − [(1.00 − markup per cent) × (sales estimate)].
Example: Brand A gross profit estimate during first six months = $3,000 − [(1.00 − 0.30) × ($3,000)] = $3,000 − [(0.7) × $3,000)] = $900.
†Net profit estimate = Gross profit estimate − (display costs + sales costs).
Example: Brand A net profit estimate during first six months = $900 − ($60 + $360) = $480.

Opportunities need to be systematically examined in terms of their impact on overall strategy, and not in an isolated manner. For example, Woolworth now emphasizes merchandise in which it can excel, such as health and beauty aids, candy, handbags, stationery, notions, children's wear, and hosiery. More ego-sensitive merchandise classifications (such as shoes and women's clothing) have been scaled down or eliminated.[3]

When evaluating new opportunities, retailers should develop some form of **sales opportunity grid,** which rates the promise of new products and/or store outlets across a variety of criteria.[4] In this way, opportunities are evaluated on the basis of the integrated strategies the retailers would follow if the opportunities are pursued.

Table 16-1 shows a sales opportunity grid for a large supermarket that wants to select one brand of shoe polish from among two alternatives. The supermarket's man-

[3]Jacquelyn Bivins, "F.W. Woolworth: Turning Back the Clock?" *Chain Store Age Executive* (October 1983), pp. 29–30ff.
[4]See "Developing a Sales Opportunity Grid," *Nielsen Researcher* (Number 1, 1980), pp. 10–11.

Table 16-2
Supermarket Sales by Product Category, 1983

	Performance Measure				
Product Category	Dollar Sales (millions)	Per Cent of Overall Store Sales	Dollar Gross Margin (millions)	Gross Margin Percentage*	Overall Store Dollar Gross Margin (%)
Baby foods	989.37	0.52	94.72	9.6	0.21
Bakery foods	6,583.12	3.48	1,342.96	20.4	2.95
Baking needs	4,182.55	2.22	769.14	18.4	1.69
Beer and wine	6,053.44	3.20	1,327.98	21.9	2.92
Breakfast foods	3,760.71	1.99	795.82	21.2	1.76
Candy and gum	2,226.53	1.18	720.90	32.4	1.58
Canned and dry soup	1,365.80	0.72	299.55	21.9	0.66
Canned fish	1,670.39	0.88	368.25	22.0	0.81
Canned fruit	1,076.38	0.57	249.10	23.1	0.55
Canned juice	2,497.03	1.32	560.04	22.4	1.23
Canned meat and specialty foods	1,129.37	0.60	274.37	24.3	0.60
Canned vegetables	2,381.65	1.26	538.56	22.6	1.18
Coffee	3,170.49	1.68	373.41	11.8	0.83
Cookies and crackers	3,783.40	2.00	911.61	24.1	2.00
Desserts and toppings	499.44	0.26	119.54	23.9	0.26
Diet and low-calorie	724.52	0.38	194.02	26.8	0.43
Dressings	1,188.00	0.63	226.15	19.0	0.50
Dried fruits	302.66	0.16	88.35	29.2	0.19
Dried vegetables	646.96	0.34	169.55	26.2	0.37
Nuts	735.88	0.39	209.82	28.5	0.46
Pasta products	970.46	0.51	250.73	25.8	0.55
Pickles and relishes	478.62	0.25	134.60	28.1	0.30
Olives and vinegar	384.01	0.20	114.70	29.9	0.25
Sauces	1,736.58	0.92	418.42	24.1	0.92
Snacks	2,572.71	1.36	751.88	29.2	1.65
Soft drinks and mixes	7,122.25	3.76	1,303.37	18.3	2.86
Spices and extracts	703.71	0.37	260.41	37.0	0.57
Spreads	1,006.39	0.53	237.06	23.6	0.52
Syrups	389.71	0.21	92.06	23.6	0.20
Tea	569.40	0.30	132.32	23.2	0.29
Total grocery food	**60,901.53**	**32.19**	**13,329.39**	**21.9**	**29.29**

ager has specified the integrated strategy that would be followed for each brand; Brand A is established, whereas Brand B is new. Because of its newness, the manager believes initial sales of Brand B would be lower; but total first year sales would be similar. The brands would be priced the same and occupy identical floor space. Brand B would require more display costs but would offer the store a larger markup. Brand B would return a greater total gross profit ($1,760 to $1,500) and net profit ($860 to $780) than Brand A by the end of the first year. On the basis of this grid, the store manager chooses Brand B. If the store needed an immediate profit, Brand A might have been chosen instead, because it is expected to take B much longer to be accepted by consumers.

Table 16-2 (continued)
Supermarket Sales by Product Category, 1983

Product Category	Dollar Sales (millions)	Per Cent of Overall Store Sales	Dollar Gross Margin (millions)	Gross Margin Percentage*	Overall Store Dollar Gross Margin (%)
			Performance Measure		
Cleansers	1,420.68	0.75	366.62	25.8	0.81
Laundry and ironing aids	1,019.64	0.54	220.23	21.6	0.48
Miscellaneous household supplies	410.51	0.22	127.17	31.0	0.29
Paper, plastic, film, and foil	6,996.43	3.70	1,433.24	20.5	3.15
Pet foods	4,027.41	2.13	893.52	22.2	1.96
Soaps and detergents	3,702.06	1.96	691.67	18.7	1.52
Tobacco products	7,237.66	3.83	1,030.59	14.2	2.26
Waxes and polishes	289.45	0.15	87.23	30.1	0.19
Total grocery nonfoods	**25,103.84**	**13.28**	**4,850.27**	**19.4**	**10.66**
Dairy products	18,608.66	9.84	4,519.83	24.3	9.93
Delicatessen	4,161.75	2.20	1,125.00	27.0	2.47
Frozen foods	11,728.54	6.20	3,739.48	31.9	8.21
Meat	34,277.60	18.12	7,061.19	20.6	15.51
Produce	15,511.94	8.20	5,041.38	32.5	11.07
Total perishables	**84,288.49**	**44.56**	**21,486.88**	**25.5**	**47.19**
General merchandise	**8,342.41**	**4.41**	**3,083.51**	**37.0**	**6.77**
Health and beauty aids	**7,027.00**	**3.71**	**1,884.48**	**26.8**	**4.14**
Unclassified†	**3,506.73**	**1.85**	**888.58**	**25.3**	**1.95**
Total supermarket	**189,170.00**	**100.00**	**45,523.11**	**24.1**	**100.00**

*Does not take into consideration in-store promotions or markdowns.
†Includes products and services such as pharmacy, fresh fish, catering, sit-down eating, bakery, seasonal merchandise, liquor, and money orders.
Source: "Supermarket Sales by Category," Progressive Grocer *(July 1984), p. 42. Reprinted by permission.*

Performance Measures

By determining the relevant measures of performance and setting standards (goals) for each of them, a retailer can better develop and integrate strategy. Among the **performance measures** most frequently used by retailers are sales revenues, sales increases over prior periods, gross margin percentages, markdown percentages, stock turnover, stock age, employee turnover, financial ratios, and profitability.

Retailers of varying sizes and in different product or service lines can acquire a lot of industrywide data for firms like themselves from secondary data sources such as Dun & Bradstreet, National Retail Merchants Association, *Progressive Grocer, Chain Store Age,* and Robert Morris Associates. This enables these retailers to use industry norms to set company standards. Tables 16-2 through 16-6 contain a wide variety of industry performance data for a number of retail categories, and provide a large amount of information that could be used by individual retailers to set their own performance standards.

Table 16-3
Selected Performance Data for Independent Supermarkets, 1983

Performance Measure	Annual Store Sales		
	$2–4 million	$6–8 million	$12+ million
Weekly sales/checkout	$13,265	$19,647	$28,420
Weekly sales/employee	$ 2,777	$ 3,193	$ 3,542
Sales/employee hour	$ 69.75	$ 79.97	$ 88.65
Store sales/hour	$ 657	$ 1,419	$ 2,909
Weekly sales/square foot of selling area	$ 5.64	$ 7.98	$ 10.11
Average selling area (square feet)	10,222	16,869	32,429
Average total store area (square feet)	13,589	22,507	46,111
Average number of items stocked	8,174	11,229	16,136
Average inventory value (thousands)	$ 158.7	$ 259.7	$ 600.6
Number of weekly transactions	6,000	9,535	16,571
Average customer transaction size	$ 9.64	$ 14.12	$ 19.78
Annual inventory turnover	15.8	22.6	23.5
Number of checkouts	4.4	6.9	11.6
Number of full-time employees	14.0	26.4	54.9
Number of part-time employees	13.4	31.4	76.3
Manufacturer coupons redeemed weekly	1,078	3,656	12,834
Store coupons redeemed weekly	386	1,033	3,405
Hours open per week (median)	86	89	98

Source: "51st Annual Report of the Grocery Industry," Progressive Grocer (April 1984), pp. 98, 100. Reprinted by permission.

Tables 16-2 and 16-3 present industry performance data for supermarkets. Table 16-2 shows sales and gross margins for each product category in a supermarket. For example, in a typical supermarket, perishable items account for the largest percentage of overall store sales and dollar gross margin. Sales are lowest for waxes and polishes and highest for meat. The gross margin for baby foods is only 9.6 per cent, while it is 37 per cent for general merchandise. Although general merchandise accounts for just 4.41 per cent of store sales, it contributes 6.77 per cent of overall store dollar gross margin.

Table 16-3 provides many industry performance statistics for independent supermarkets, classified by store size. In this way, industrywide performance can be compared for small, medium, and large independent supermarkets. From the table, it is clear that large supermarkets are significantly more effective than smaller ones. Several measures support this: sales per employee, sales per square foot of selling space, average customer transaction size, and inventory turnover. Smaller supermarkets must keep this in mind when designing strategy and setting performance standards. These standards should realistically reflect the impact of store size on effectiveness.

Table 16-4 provides industry performance data for department stores and specialty stores with annual sales of over $1 million. These are just a few of the conclusions that are reached by studying this table. In department stores, sales per square foot are highest for shoes and lowest for furniture; the level of sales promotion varies little by product category; the level of personal selling varies greatly by product category; stock shortages are very high for women's apparel; women's apparel yields by far the highest gross margin return on investment; annual turnover for furniture is low; and most

Table 16-4
Selected 1983 Performance Data for Department Stores and Specialty Stores with Annual Sales of over $1 Million

Performance Measures	Product Category								
	Shoes	Women's Apparel	Men's Apparel	Children's Apparel	Personal Needs	Hobby and Recreation	Furniture	Appliances	Draperies and Home Goods
Department Stores									
Annual sales/square foot	$189.9	$145.5	$182.8	$ 93.8	$180.1	$102.6	$ 59.3	$ 79.8	$ 74.7
Sales promotion costs/sales	3.3%	3.0%	3.0%	3.1%	2.4%	3.4%	4.2%	3.9%	4.1%
Sales salaries/sales	10.2%	6.7%	6.7%	7.8%	8.8%	8.2%	9.0%	7.9%	8.6%
Stock shortages/sales	0.9%	2.5%	2.1%	1.8%	1.3%	1.9%	1.1%	1.7%	1.5%
Gross margin return per dollar of inventory (GMROI)	1.84	3.29	2.36	2.21	1.58	1.30	1.33	1.01	1.61
Annual inventory turnover	2.2	3.9	2.9	3.0	2.9	2.3	1.7	2.1	1.9
Per cent of inventory 0–6 months old	71.5	86.6	77.7	76.6	84.4	79.1	69.0	72.1	81.1
Specialty Stores									
Annual sales/square foot	$119*	$143.9	$215.4	$104.3	$346.0	—	$ 79.7	—	$163.2
Sales promotion costs/sales	—	2.9%	2.2%†	3.0%	2.0%	—	—	—	4.5%†
Sales salaries/sales	—	6.9%	7.7%†	9.5%*	8.2%*	—	—	—	9.3%†
Stock shortages/sales	0.7%	1.9%	2.4%	1.7%	1.3%	3.6%	1.4%*	—	2.4%
Gross margin return per dollar of inventory (GMROI)	1.99	3.31	2.79	2.45	1.38	1.26‡	2.03	—	1.75
Annual inventory turnover	2.4	3.8	2.6	2.6	2.1	2.2	2.2	—	2.3
Per cent of inventory 0–6 months old	73.4*	88.8	79.0	80.6	87.5	71.3‡	100.0†	—	88.4%*

*1982 data.
†1981 data.
‡1980 data.

Source: David P. Schulz, "NRMA's New MOR," Stores (October 1984), pp. 21, 23. Copyright National Retail Merchants Association 1984. Reprinted by permission.

inventory is six months old or less. In specialty stores, sales per square foot are highest for personal needs and lowest for furniture; the level of sales promotion is lower and the level of personal selling is higher than in department stores; there is little theft of shoes but a great deal for hobby and recreation items; women's apparel has the highest gross margin return on investment and inventory turnover; and merchandise on hand is very fresh. Individual retailers should set separate performance standards for each category of merchandise they carry, based on the special characteristics of the product category.

Table 16-5 displays industry performance statistics for full-line discount stores. An analysis of this table reveals the following. Women's apparel is the leading product category in terms of industry sales volume, sales per store, department size, and inventory turnover. However, the largest sales per square foot are from the photo/camera category; and the highest maintained markup is for stationery. While women's apparel has the greatest initial markup, it also undergoes many markdowns, which result in a 10.8 per cent difference between initial and maintained markup.

Table 16-6 presents median key business ratios for a number of retailer categories. Each of the ratios in this table has a strong impact on the short- and long-run performance of retailers. The definitions of these ratios are as follows:

• Quick ratio—cash plus accounts receivable divided by total current liabilities, those due within one year. This ratio establishes the retailer's liquidity. A ratio greater than one to one means the firm is liquid and therefore easily able to cover short-term liabilities.

Table 16-5
Selected 1984 Performance Data for Full-Line Discount Stores

	Performance Measure						
Product Category	Industry Sales Volume (billions)	Sales per Store (thousands)	Average Dept. Size	Annual Sales per Square Foot	Annual Inventory Turnover	Initial Markup (%)	Maintained Markup (%)
Women's apparel	$14.3	$1,763	10,000	$176	4.6	48.0	37.2
Men's and boys' wear	8.2	1,011	7,690	132	3.4	44.6	36.0
Housewares	6.3	777	5,770	135	3.2	41.1	30.2
Consumer electronics	5.9	728	2,300	316	3.2	31.4	19.4
Health and beauty aids	5.6	691	3,150	219	4.5	26.0	20.5
Automotive	5.2	641	2,300	279	2.6	34.9	28.7
Hardware	4.8	592	3,210	184	2.4	41.9	32.1
Toys	4.1	506	2,500	202	3.1	36.5	28.4
Sporting goods	3.8	469	2,500	187	2.0	36.8	26.9
Photo/camera	3.3	407	675	603	3.2	24.5	16.6
Domestics	3.2	395	3,130	126	2.5	43.4	35.3
Personal care	2.9	358	850	421	3.3	30.4	20.0
Stationery	2.1	259	1,850	140	3.5	46.7	40.1
Paint	1.8	222	1,250	178	2.4	43.9	35.2
Electric housewares	1.7	210	880	238	3.4	33.2	21.4
Jewelry	1.4	166	575	290	1.8	49.9	37.7
Glassware	0.7	80	620	129	4.0	40.7	34.9

Source: "Census '84/'85: Merchandising Profiles," Discount Store News (July 23, 1984), p. 67. Copyright Lebhar-Friedman, Inc., 425 Park Avenue, New York, NY 10022. Reprinted by permission.

- Current ratio—total current assets (including cash, accounts receivable, inventories, and marketable securities) divided by total current liabilities. A ratio of two to one or more is considered good.
- Collection period—accounts receivable divided by net sales and then multiplied by 365. This ratio measures the quality of accounts receivable (the amounts due, but

Table 16-6
Median Key Business Ratios for Selected Retailer Categories, 1984

Line of Business	Quick Ratio (times)	Current Ratio (times)	Collection Period (days)	Assets to Net Sales (%)	Accounts Payable to Net Sales (%)	Return on Net Sales (%)	Return on Net Worth (%)
Lumber and other building materials dealers	1.0	2.4	34.3	43.4	5.3	2.6	9.6
Hardware stores	0.7	3.3	17.3	54.2	5.0	3.4	10.7
Department stores	1.2	3.3	25.2	49.5	4.7	2.3	8.8
Grocery stores	0.5	2.2	2.5	18.3	2.1	1.7	15.2
Motor vehicle dealers (new and used)	0.2	1.4	5.8	23.0	0.9	1.7	21.1
Auto and home supply stores	0.8	2.2	22.2	39.9	6.5	3.4	15.2
Gasoline service stations	0.9	2.1	6.2	16.9	1.9	2.2	17.5
Men's and boys' clothing and furnishing stores	0.7	3.1	14.2	49.9	5.8	4.7	13.9
Women's ready-to-wear stores	0.9	3.2	17.1	45.1	5.1	5.5	16.3
Family clothing stores	0.7	3.6	12.7	54.3	4.9	4.5	12.9
Shoe stores	0.4	3.0	6.5	47.4	6.2	5.0	15.7
Furniture stores	0.9	2.7	30.6	51.0	5.1	4.1	11.0
Radio and television stores	0.5	1.9	9.8	41.9	4.4	5.5	21.3
Eating places	0.6	1.3	4.7	32.1	2.5	4.2	19.3
Sporting goods and bicycle stores	0.5	2.8	7.3	47.1	5.9	4.5	16.6
Drug and proprietary stores	0.7	2.7	22.5	42.1	6.8	1.4	8.3
Jewelry stores	0.7	3.3	23.3	70.6	7.9	5.7	13.1
Hobby, toy, and game shops	0.6	3.5	5.1	47.9	5.0	5.5	17.3
Gift, novelty, and souvenir shops	0.7	3.7	6.5	51.4	3.5	6.0	20.9
Sewing, needlework, and piece goods stores	0.4	4.1	5.1	55.3	5.6	4.4	13.1
Mail-order houses	0.8	2.4	14.6	40.0	4.9	4.4	18.9
Vending machine operators	0.5	1.3	5.8	38.1	3.2	3.1	12.6
Direct-selling companies	1.3	2.7	41.9	45.7	3.3	7.2	15.3
Florists	1.1	2.2	24.0	37.4	3.9	5.7	25.4
Newsstands	0.5	3.3	2.9	28.9	2.8	3.8	20.2

Source: 1984–85 Industry Norms and Key Business Ratios *(New York: Dun & Bradstreet, 1985), pp. 144–159. Reprinted by permission.*

not yet paid, by customers). In general, when most sales are on credit, any collection period more than one-third over normal selling terms (e.g., 40.0 for 30-day credit arrangements) indicates slow-turning accounts receivable.

- Assets to net sales—total assets divided by annual net sales. This ratio links sales and the total investment needed to generate those sales. An excessively low number may indicate financial difficulty. A high number may indicate that the firm's policies are too conservative.
- Accounts payable to net sales—accounts payable divided by annual net sales. This compares how a retailer pays suppliers relative to volume transacted. A figure larger than the industry average may indicate that the retailer relies on suppliers to finance operations.
- Return on net sales (profit margin)—net dollar profit after taxes divided by annual net sales. This measures profitability per dollar of sales.
- Return on net worth—net dollar profit after taxes divided by net worth. This ratio is used to examine the ability of management to achieve an adequate return on the capital invested. Generally, 10 per cent is regarded as a desirable objective.[5]

From Table 16-6, a hardware store manager or owner would learn that the industry average is an extremely poor quick ratio of 0.7; liquid assets are less than current liabilities. The current ratio of 3.3 is quite good, mostly because of the value of inventory on hand. The collection period of 17.3 days is moderate, considering that many small purchases are paid for by cash. Assets to net sales are strong, 54.2 per cent, another indicator of the value of inventory. Accounts payable of 5.0 per cent of sales is good. The return on net sales of 3.4 per cent is a low-to-middle figure for retailing. The return on net worth percentage of 10.7 is barely acceptable. In sum, hardware stores require inventory and other investments and yield a low-to-medium profit.[6]

Productivity

As a result of erratic sales, mixed economic growth, rising labor costs, increasing competition, and other factors over the last several years, more and more retailers are placing priority on improving **productivity,** the efficiency with which retail functions are performed. Their goal is to make the implementation of retail strategy as efficient as possible, thereby lifting industry and company performance standards.

As an illustration, the recession of the early 1980s caused the profits of G. C. Murphy (a Midwestern and Eastern discount and variety store chain) to decline drastically. The firm was stuck with excess merchandise that it had to mark down; and inefficient store operations also led to problems. Murphy turned its profit situation around by cutting the purchases of seasonal goods, eliminating local store promotions, reducing chainwide special offers, revising merchandise assortments, dropping some

---

[5]*1984–85 Industry Norms and Key Business Ratios* (New York: Dun & Bradstreet, 1985), pp. v–vii.
[6]For further information on performance measures, see Roger A. Kerin and Richard D. Miller, "Diversity of Retail Operations and Financial Performance" in Kenneth Bernhardt et al. (Editors), *The Changing Marketing Environment: New Theories and Applications* (Chicago: American Marketing Association, 1981), pp. 24–26; Mary Ann Edwards, "How Some Are Using ROI Analysis," *Stores* (February 1982), pp. 12–16; Robert F. Lusch and Ray R. Serpkenci, "Improving Your Financial Performance in Retailing," *Business,* Vol. 33 (January–March 1983), pp. 9–18; and Bert C. McCammon, Jr., "The New Strategic Era in Retailing," Retailing Workshop, Eleventh Annual Southwestern Federation of Administrative Disciplines, 1984.

merchandise lines, redesigning some stores, and greatly upgrading inventory control and handling.[7] Table 16-7 shows some of the methods a broad cross section of retailers are using to improve their overall productivity.

In the following sections, five aspects of productivity are discussed: operations management, human resource management, energy management, inventory management, and credit management.

Operations Management

Productivity issues in operations management involve store size, store hours, space allocation, manpower needs, in-store displays, the use of self-service, product alterations, services to be offered, and related areas. For example:

- What is the optimal store size?
- What is the amount of customer traffic during each hour of the day? Are current hours too long or too short?
- What is the relation among shelf space, shelf location, and sales for each item in the store? How would total store sales change by varying allocations?
- Are personnel matched to customer traffic flows? Would increased staffing improve or reduce productivity?
- Are in-store displays easy to read? Do they facilitate consumer shopping? Do they encourage impulse purchases?
- What impact does the use of self-service versus sales personnel have on the sales of each product category?
- What impact does offering product alterations have on sales? Can the staff be reduced without drastically affecting output?
- Which services could be dropped without affecting sales?

Retailers need to constantly monitor the preceding factors and devise the best combination of them:

> Given the "best" production technology, efficient use of the firm's resources requires that management allocate resources in a mix that lowers the total cost of output as much as possible. Thus, efficiency-level decisions demand that resources be viewed as a group and not in isolation. Relative resource productivities and costs determine the most efficient mix of resources to employ.[8]

Human Resource Management

Maximizing human resource productivity is important for several reasons. First, the costs of labor are high. As an example, in the supermarket industry, the average part-time clerk is paid about $4.75 an hour, the average full-time clerk is paid about $5.75 an hour, and the average meat cutter is paid $9.25 an hour; and the latter two also receive fringe benefits.[9] Second, high employee turnover leads to increased recruiting,

---

[7]Susan Carey, "Three Regional Retailers Prosper in Hard Times by Tightening Up," *Wall Street Journal* (May 19, 1983), p. 37.

[8]Dale D. Achabal, John M. Heinke, and Shelby H. McIntyre, "Issues and Perspectives on Retail Productivity," *Journal of Retailing*, Vol. 60 (Fall 1984), p. 123.

[9]"51st Annual Report of the Grocery Industry," *Progressive Grocer* (April 1984), p. 94.

Table 16-7
Selected Methods Being Employed to Improve Retail Productivity*

Methods	Discount Stores (% using)	Drugstores (% using)	Supermarkets (% using)	Department Stores (% using)	Home Centers (% using)	Specialty Stores (% using)	Total Stores (% using)
Changing merchandise mix	70	80	53	87	77	70	73
Improving sales training	73	80	67	80	73	60	72
Redesigning stores	80	60	73	63	53	73	67
Adding/improving point-of-sale computers	60	33	73	43	53	50	52
Changing the personnel mix in departments	43	33	47	53	30	30	39
Adding/improving nonpoint-of-sale computers	30	33	40	47	17	40	34
Creating incentives for salespeople	30	30	17	33	33	47	32
Reducing existing selling space	20	13	7	27	7	17	15
Building smaller stores	20	27	3	10	7	20	14
None of the above	3	3	—	—	—	3	2

*This table is based on the results of a survey of executives at 180 retail chains, 30 for each type of store shown.

Source: "Retailers Developing Methods to Gauge Productivity," Chain Store Age Executive (September 1984), p. 25. Copyright Lebhar-Friedman, Inc., 425 Park Avenue, New York, NY 10022. Reprinted by permission.

training, and supervision costs. Third, poor personnel may mistreat customers, misring sales transactions, and make other costly errors. Fourth, productivity gains in technology have taken place much more rapidly than those in labor; yet much of retailing is labor intensive.

A number of research studies have been conducted on human resource productivity. These are the key findings of four of them:

- In the retail grocery industry, it was discovered that increased capital intensity (facilities and technology), higher retail wages, larger customer transactions, and increased population mobility lead to improved labor productivity. Larger store size, the existence of store saturation, and congestion in the retail area lead to lower labor productivity.[10]
- In the retail hardware industry, it was found that wages, store size, type of ownership, gross margin level, and location and type of store affect labor productivity. Higher wage rates are most closely associated with higher productivity.[11]
- In the fast-food industry, it was discovered that employee-hours worked per week, service capacity, and the value of restaurant facilities (technology and capital investment) influence sales. As these related factors rise, total sales volume and sales per worker increase.[12]
- In an analysis of twelve retailer categories (apparel, cafeteria, department stores, drugstores, fast-food, furniture, general merchandise, grocery, hardware, restaurant, sporting goods, and variety store), it was ascertained that capital intensity has the greatest impact on labor productivity for drugstores, grocery stores, department stores, restaurants, variety stores, general merchandise stores, and hardware stores. Store size (capacity) has the greatest positive effect on labor productivity for drugstores; for apparel stores, fast-food outlets, restaurants, and sporting goods stores, there is a decreasing return as store size (capacity) increases—e.g., a doubling of store size does not lead to a doubling of sales. Store saturation has the greatest negative effectives on productivity for grocery stores and department stores. Productivity is higher for apparel stores, department stores, furniture stores, grocery stores, and sporting goods stores situated in larger urban areas.[13]

Energy Management

Because of the rapid rise in energy costs during the 1970s and early 1980s, energy management has become a major component of strategy planning for a wide variety of retailers. In particular, retailers must resolve the following questions:

- What temperature levels are required during hours when the store is open and when it is closed?
- Do certain product categories require special energy needs? How should they be handled?

[10]Charles A. Ingene, "Labor Productivity in Retailing," *Journal of Marketing*, Vol. 46 (Fall 1982), pp. 75–90.
[11]Robert F. Lusch and Soo Young Moon, "An Exploratory Analysis of the Correlates of Labor Productivity in Retailing," *Journal of Retailing*, Vol. 60 (Fall 1984), pp. 37–61.
[12]Jeffrey T. Doutt, "Comparative Productivity Performance in Fast-Food Retail Distribution," *Journal of Retailing*, Vol. 60 (Fall 1984), pp. 98–106.
[13]Charles A. Ingene, "The Effect of Scale, Localization and Urbanization Economies on Productivity in Retailing," in Russell W. Belk et al. (Editors) *1984 AMA Educators' Proceedings* (Chicago: American Marketing Association, 1984), pp. 190–194.

- At what point should air conditioning or heating be turned on or off?
- If less energy is consumed, what will be the impact on sales?
- Will renovations allow greater energy conservation? At what cost?
- Will computerized energy systems improve energy planning? At what cost?
- How will employee and customer attitudes change if energy consumption is reduced?
- Are there pending innovations that will lower energy costs?

An electronic energy-management system is shown in Figure 16-2.

Retailers are taking various approaches to energy management, as these examples indicate. Southland is testing a computerized system that controls the energy consumed by air conditioners and heaters, while allowing its 7-Eleven managers to control refrigeration: "The entire store is one unit, a food preservation center. We don't want to

Figure 16-2   An Energy-Management System

The EMS–Z system by Energy Management Corporation performs energy management, environmental control, and data reporting functions. It is an input-driven system that gathers and analyzes analog and digital information. Based upon this information and the microprocessor's individually programmed control strategies, it then determines what configuration of equipment will most effectively meet the facility's needs. Courtesy Energy Management Corporation.

give up the control to an outsider."[14] Ivey's Florida, a department store chain, has installed UPS (uninterruptible power system) devices in selected outlets. These devices are tied into the firm's computer and equipment network and protect it against electrical disturbances and blackouts.[15] Between 1980 and 1983, Hess Department Stores, a Pennsylvania chain, was able to reduce electrical consumption by 17 per cent and save more than $1 million by employing a computerized energy-management system that could take individual store requirements into account.[16] Sloan's Supermarkets, a New York chain, substituted high-efficiency 60-watt fluorescent lamps for 75-watt lamps. The difference in lighting was negligible, but the 60-watt lamps required 20 per cent less energy.[17]

During 1983, the median costs per square foot for heating, ventilation, and air conditioning were $1.51 for supermarkets, $0.97 for drugstores, $0.93 for department stores, $0.51 for discount stores, and $0.49 for home centers. As a result, in 1983, supermarkets spent an average of $0.63 per square foot for energy management, compared with $0.62 for drugstores, $0.42 for discount stores, $0.32 for department stores, and $0.20 for home centers.[18] To aid in retail energy planning, the National Lighting Bureau has developed a manual that is applicable for a wide range of firms.[19]

Inventory Management

Retailers of various types are quite involved with improving their inventory management systems. Their goals are to increase inventory turnover, reduce breakage and pilferage, optimize order size, maintain fresh merchandise, avoid running out of stock, anticipate consumer demand, and so on. To achieve their goals, more retailers are addressing questions such as these:

- What is the proper level and assortment of merchandise for each product category? How many brands of the same product should be carried?
- How can breakage and pilferage be reduced?
- What is the trade-off between ordering costs and holding costs in determining optimal order size (EOQ) for each product category? What are the pros and cons of frequent, smaller orders?
- How should older merchandise be handled (e.g., markdowns, advertising)?
- What level of safety stock is acceptable in balancing inventory costs and the probability of running out of merchandise?
- Can peak and off-peak seasons be clearly predicted? Should new products be added before requested by consumers?

[14]"Southland Tests Demand Controllers in Denver," *Chain Store Age Executive* (April 1984), pp. 62, 64.
[15]"Ivey's Opts for Power Protection with UPS," *Chain Store Age Executive* (February 1985), pp. 61–62.
[16]Jules Abend, "Hess's: Saving $1 Million on Electricity, Oil and Gas," *Stores* (August 1983), pp. 54–55.
[17]Mark Harris, "Evaluate Lighting Systems as a Marketing Device, Not Overhead," *Marketing News* (October 26, 1984), p. 1.
[18]"Wanted: One-Step Systems," *Chain Store Age Executive* (July 1983), p. 56; and "Investments Showing Paybacks," *Chain Store Age Executive* (July 1984), p. 88.
[19]*Lighting Energy Management in Retailing* (Washington, D.C.: National Lighting Bureau, 1981).

Credit Management

As credit transactions in retailing have increased, many retailers have moved vigorously to maximize credit sales while holding the line on credit costs (such as processing applications and billing), reducing bad debts, and avoiding other problems.[20] They also constantly weigh the advantages and disadvantages of employing their own credit system versus accepting a bank or other commercial credit card. For retailers offering their own credit plans, these are some of the questions being considered:

- What is the optimal level of credit sales? What should the credit operation cost as a per cent of overall stores sales? What is the acceptable level of bad debts?
- Which criteria should be used to screen credit applicants?
- How large should credit limits be? Monthly? Cumulatively?
- What should the percentage interest charges be?
- At what point should collection procedures be implemented for past-due accounts? How aggressively should collection be pursued?
- At what point should bad debts be written off? Customers dropped?
- Which credit functions should be performed by the retailer? Which can be undertaken by outside parties (e.g., credit checks, collection procedures)?

Uses of New Technology

Throughout the text, new retail technology, such as computerized retail information systems, has been described. New technology is also discussed in Chapter 17. In this section, examples of how retailers are using technology in integrating their strategies are presented.

Day & Palin IGA is a four-store Illinois supermarket chain that recently implemented a new computer-based program to control labor, advertising, and merchandising costs as well to make department managers more knowledgeable. The chain acquired an IBM PC, an Epson printer, and relevant software programs for about $4,000. Then all types of data were keyed into the system and reviewed regularly. Said one executive: "We found out things about our sales, our merchandising abilities, our staff potential—and about our competitors—that we never knew before." As a result, Day & Palin IGA has increased gross margins by 1.4 per cent.[21]

Businessland, a California-based chain of retail computer centers, acquired a complex computerized merchandising software package costing $106,000 (and capable of handling up to ninety-six stores). This package enables the firm to use IBM PCs as point-of-sales registers and aids in distribution, basic stock replenishment, sales analysis, open-to-buy, physical inventory, management planning, and a number of other tasks.[22]

Medicare-Glaser, a St. Louis-based pharmacy chain, took seven years and spent

[20]See David P. Schulz, "Collections," *Stores* (April 1984), pp. 69–70.

[21]Robert E. O'Neill, "SLAM Adds 1.4 Points to Gross Profit," *Progressive Grocer* (February 1985), pp. 55–59.

[22]"Merchandise System Businessland Counts On," *Chain Store Age Executive* (August 1984), pp. 67–68, 71.

Table 16-8
How Retailers Use Point-of-Sales (POS) Systems

	Per Cent Using a POS System to Acquire Information			
Factors	Mass Merchandisers	Department Stores	Specialty Stores	Food Stores
Unit control	37	50	38	13
Sales reporting	61	73	59	87
Daily bank deposits	40	27	41	47
In-house credit	24	69	25	7
Outside credit	21	57	28	0
Timekeeping	8	8	13	7
Promotional-price look-up	47	19	9	60
Full-price look-up	24	4	13	87
Price changes	32	23	25	80
Replenishment/reorder	11	12	22	0
Merchandise receipt	11	12	38	13
Coupons	29	19	16	40
Inventory	16	8	31	7
Labor scheduling	8	15	0	20

Source: Arthur Young, "How Retailers Use POS," Retail Technology (January 1985), p. 3. Copyright Lebhar-Friedman, Inc., 425 Park Avenue, New York, NY 10022. Reprinted by permission.

over $1 million to develop its Medicom computerized information system. Medicom enables pharmacists to quickly determine if prescriptions would have any adverse side effects for the patients for whom they are given. It is estimated that 15 to 20 per cent of all prescriptions involve a potentially dangerous drug interaction. Medicare-Glaser expects to generate additional revenues of $1 million to $2 million annually from consumers educated about the benefits of Medicom.[23]

Table 16-8 shows how mass merchandise, department store, specialty store, and food-store chains are using computerized point-of-sales systems to better coordinate strategy.

Control: Using the Retail Audit

After a retail strategy has been developed and put into action, it must be continuously evaluated, and necessary adjustments must be made. An important tool of evaluation is the **retail audit,** which may be defined as

> a systematic, critical, and unbiased review and appraisal of the basic objectives and policies of the retail function, and of the organization, methods, procedures, and personnel employed to implement those policies and to achieve those objectives. Clearly, not every

[23]"Medicom: State-of-the-Art Rx Interaction Guardian," *Chain Store Age Executive* (May 1984), pp. 146, 151.

evaluation of retail personnel, organization, or methods is a retail audit: at best, most such evaluations can be regarded as parts of an audit.[24]

and

an independent examination of the entire retailing effort of a company, or some specific retailing activity, covering objectives, strategy, implementation, and organization, for the triple purpose of determining what is being done, appraising what is being done, and recommending what should be done in the future.[25]

An audit includes an investigation of a retailer's objectives, strategy, implementation, and organization. First, the objectives of the firm are ascertained and then evaluated for clarity, consistency, and appropriateness. Second, the firm's strategy and its methods for deriving it are examined and evaluated. Third, the implementation of the strategy is examined and evaluated. Fourth, the retail organizational structure is analyzed. Lines of command, types of organization charts, and so on are the kinds of information gathered in this phase.

A good retail audit incorporates four elements. First, it is conducted on a regular, periodic basis. Second, it is comprehensive. Third, the audit is systematic. Fourth, the audit is conducted in an independent manner.[26]

Undertaking an Audit

Several steps are completed in undertaking a retail audit:

1. Determining who does the audit.
2. Determining when and how often the audit is conducted.
3. Determining areas to be audited.
4. Developing audit form(s).
5. Conducting the audit.
6. Reporting to management.

See Figure 16-3 for a description of the retail audit process.

Determining Who Does the Audit

When a retail audit is conducted, one or a combination of three sources can be utilized: company specialists, company department managers, and outside auditors. The advantages and disadvantages of each are noted here.

Company specialists are internal personnel whose prime responsibility is the retail audit. The advantages of this source include: specialized, thorough, knowledgeable

---

[24]Adapted from A. Schuchman, "The Marketing Audit: Its Nature, Purpose, and Problems," *Analyzing and Improving Marketing Performance*, Report No. 32 (New York: American Management Association, 1959), p. 13; and Alfred R. Oxenfeldt, *Executive Action in Marketing* (Belmont, Calif.: Wadsworth, 1966), p. 746.
[25]Adapted from Philip Kotler, *Marketing Management: Analysis, Planning, and Control*, Second Edition (Englewood Cliffs, N.J.: Prentice-Hall, 1972), p. 776.
[26]Philip Kotler, *Marketing Management: Analysis, Planning, and Control*, Fifth Edition (Englewood Cliffs, N.J.: Prentice-Hall, 1984), p. 765.

The Retail Audit Process

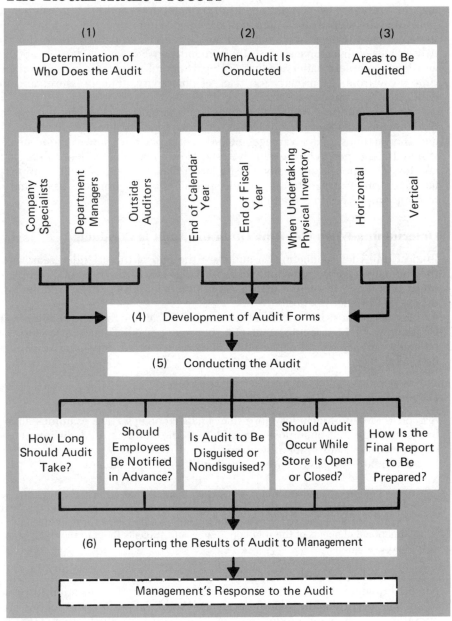

Figure 16-3

about the store, and ongoing (no time lags). Disadvantages include cost (very expensive for small retailers who do not need full-time auditors) and limited independence.

Company department managers are internal personnel whose prime responsibility is department management, but they are also asked to participate in the retail audit. Advantages of this source are that they are inexpensive, knowledgeable about the store, and have complete understanding of departmental operations. Disadvantages include time away from the primary job, lack of objectivity, time pressure, and inability to conduct a horizontal audit.

Outside auditors are people who are not permanent employees of the retailer but work as consultants (usually for fees). Advantages include broad experience, objectivity, and thoroughness. Disadvantages include costs per day (however, for small retailers, it may be cheaper to hire expensive, short-term consultants than to employ full-time auditors; the opposite is usually true for larger firms), time lags while gaining familiarity, failure of some retailers to use outside specialists on a continuous basis, and reluctance of some employees to cooperate.

Determining When and How Often the Audit Is Conducted

Logical times for conducting an audit are the end of the calendar year, at the end of the company's annual reporting year (fiscal year), or at the time of a complete physical inventory. Each of these times is appropriate for evaluating a retailer's operations during the previous period.

An audit must be enacted at least annually, although some retailers desire more frequent analysis. It is important that the same period(s), such as January-December, be analyzed each year if meaningful comparisons, projections, and adjustments are to be made.

Determining Areas to Be Audited

A good retail audit includes more than financial analysis and examines all aspects of a firm's strategy and operations. In addition, the audit is used during successful and unsuccessful periods to identify strengths and weaknesses.

There are two basic types of retail audits—horizontal and vertical:

> The horizontal audit examines all of the elements that go into the retailing whole, with particular emphasis upon the relative importance of these elements and the "mix" between them. It is often referred to as a "retailing mix" audit. The vertical audit singles out certain functional elements of the retail operations and subjects them to thorough searching study and evaluation.[27]

The **horizontal audit** is an analysis of the overall performance of the retailer, from personal qualifications to achievement of objectives to store location to personnel and so on. The **vertical audit** is an in-depth analysis of the performance of one area of retail operations, such as the credit function, store hours, product assortment, parking, or displays. The two audits should be used in conjunction with one another because the horizontal audit often reveals areas that need further investigation.

[27]Adapted from Richard D. Crisp, "Auditing the Functional Elements of a Marketing Operation," *Analyzing and Improving Marketing Performance* (New York: American Management Association, 1959), pp. 16–17.

Developing Audit Forms

In order to be systematic and thorough, the retailer should construct detailed retail audit forms. These **audit forms** list the areas to be examined and the exact information required for an evaluation of each area. Audit forms usually resemble questionnaires, and they are completed by the auditor.

Without audit forms, the analysis becomes haphazard and subjective, and it is not standardized. Important questions may be omitted or poorly worded. The biases of the auditor may show through. And most significantly, questions may differ from audit to audit, which limits the utility of comparisons.

Examples of audit forms are presented later in the chapter.

Conducting the Audit

After the auditor is selected, the timing of the audit is determined, the areas to be analyzed are chosen, and the audit forms are constructed, the audit itself is undertaken. Among the decisions to be made at this stage are

- How long should the audit take?
- Should employees be notified in advance?
- Is the audit to be disguised or nondisguised?
- Should the audit occur while the store is open or closed?
- How is the final report to be prepared?

Management should specify in advance how long the audit will take and conform to this timetable. Prior notification of employees depends on management's perception of two factors: the need to gather information in advance to increase efficiency and save time versus the desire to present a true picture and not a distorted one.

A **disguised audit** is one in which the store's employees are not aware that an audit is taking place. This is useful if the auditor is investigating an area like personal selling and wishes to act out the role of a customer to elicit employee responses. A **nondisguised audit** is one in which the store's employees are aware that an audit is being conducted. This technique is desirable when employees are asked specific operational questions and help in gathering data for the auditor.

Some audits are conducted while the store is open, such as analyses of the adequacy of the parking lot, in-store traffic flow, the adequacy of vertical transportation, and customer relations. Other audits are completed while the store is closed, such as analyses of the condition of fixtures, inventory levels and turnover, financial statements, and employee records. When the audit is undertaken depends on the type of information required.

It must be determined what form the audit report will take. The report can be formal or informal, brief or long, oral or written, and a statement of findings or a statement of findings plus recommendations. A report has a much greater chance of acceptance if it is presented in the format desired by management.

Reporting Audit Findings and Recommendations to Management

The last step in an audit is the presentation to management of the findings and recommendations. It is the responsibility of management, not the auditor, to determine what adjustments (if any) to implement. It is hoped that the audit report will be read thoroughly, each point will be considered, and the necessary changes will be made.

It is important that management regard the report seriously and react accordingly. A serious mistake is made if the report is downgraded or only lip service is paid to the findings. Long-term success is predicated on evaluating the present and adapting to the future. No matter how well an audit is performed, it is a worthless exercise if not taken seriously by management.

Responding to the Audit

After management has studied the findings of the audit, appropriate actions are taken. Areas of strength are continued and areas of weakness are revised. All actions must be consistent with the retail strategy and should be stored in the retail information system. For example, at Younkers (a Des Moines, Iowa, department store chain):

> Every department in every store comes under automatic review once a year; but also whenever our ongoing renovation program calls for any substantial floorspace revamp. In recent years such renovations have seen our elimination of white goods, fabrics, and notions from all stores; and the space reduction or elimination of art needlework, drapery, and records in some. These have generally, but not with store-by-store uniformity, been replaced with food departments, wine bars, life-style furniture, computers, and wrapit-mailit-sendit stations.[28]

Problems in Conducting a Retail Audit

There are several potential problems that may occur when one is conducting a retail audit; a retailer should be aware of them:

- The audit may be very expensive.
- The audit may be quite time-consuming.
- Performance standards may be inaccurate.
- Employees may feel threatened and not cooperate as much as desired.
- Incorrect data may be collected.
- Management may not be responsive to the findings.[29]

At the present time, a number of retailers do not understand or perform systematic retail audits. As retailing moves through the 1980s, this will have to change if companies are to analyze themselves appropriately and plan correctly for the future.

Illustrations of Retail Audit Forms

In this section, a management audit form for retailers and a retailing checklist are presented. Each of these forms demonstrates how small and large retailers can inexpensively, yet efficiently, utilize retail audits.

An auditor completes one of these forms in a systematic, periodic manner and

---

[28]Lewis A. Spalding, "Down and Out?" *Stores* (February 1984), p. 13.
[29]Adapted from Martin L. Bell, *Marketing: Concepts and Strategy*, Third Edition (Boston: Houghton Mifflin, 1979), pp. 473–474.

then discusses the findings with management. The examples described are both horizontal audits. A vertical audit consists of an in-depth analysis of any one area contained in these forms.

A Management Audit Form for Retailers

The Small Business Administration has published a booklet entitled *Management Audit for Small Retailers* (Small Business Management Series No. 31, 3rd ed.), by John W. Wingate and Elmer O. Schaller. This booklet, although written for small retailers, provides a series of questions and discussions that are applicable to all retailers; in it the components of a retail audit are comprehensively detailed.[30]

Figure 16-4 contains selected questions from each of the sixteen areas covered in the *Management Audit for Small Retailers*. "Yes" is the desired answer to every question in Figure 16-4. For those questions answered in the negative, a retailer needs to determine the causes for these responses and adjust strategy accordingly. Figure 16-4 should be viewed as a single, overall horizontal audit, not as fragmented pieces.

A Retailing Checklist

Figure 16-5 shows another type of audit form, the retailing checklist, which is used to evaluate overall strategy performance. Included are each of the components of a retail strategy. The checklist, which is a horizontal audit, can be used by small and large retailers alike.

The purpose of the checklist is to pinpoint a retailer's areas of strength and weakness, so that strategy can be adjusted accordingly. Unlike the yes–no answers in Figure 16-4, the checklist enables the retailer to rate performance in each area. This provides more in-depth information. A total score is not computed. Because each item is not equally important, a simple summation does not present a meaningful score.

Integrating and Controlling the Retail Strategy: A Summary

This chapter shows why it is necessary for retailers to plan and enact coordinated strategies, and describes how to assess success or failure. Retail strategy must be viewed as an ongoing, integrated process of interrelated steps.

The development and enactment of an integrated retail strategy must take into account planning procedures and opportunity analysis, performance measures, productivity, and the uses of new technology. Planning procedures can be optimized by following a series of coordinated activities. Opportunities need to be examined in terms of their impact on overall strategy, and not in an isolated manner. By determining the relevant measures of performance and setting standards for them, a retailer can better develop and integrate strategy.

---

[30]In addition to the information presented here, *Management Audit for Small Retailers* discusses each point of the audit in great detail and lists a number of sources of further information. The booklet is available for sale, at nominal cost, from the Superintendent of Documents, U.S. Government Printing Office, Washington, D.C.

A Management Audit Form for Retailers

Answer Yes or No to Each Question

A Look at Yourself and Your Ability to Grow

_____ 1. Do you keep abreast of changes in your field by subscribing to leading trade and general business publications?

_____ 2. Do you plan for a profit (your net income) above a reasonable salary for yourself as manager?

_____ 3. Are you an active member of a trade association?

Customer Relations

_____ 4. Do you purposely cater to selected groups of customers rather than to all groups?

_____ 5. Do you have a clear picture of the store image you seek to implant in the minds of your customers?

_____ 6. Do you evaluate your own performance by asking customers about their likes and dislikes and by shopping competitors to compare their assortments, prices, and promotion methods with your own?

Personnel Management and Supervision

_____ 7. Do employees in your firm know to whom they each report?

_____ 8. Do you delegate as much authority as you can to those immediately responsible to you, freeing yourself from unnecessary operating details?

_____ 9. Do you seek your employees' opinions of stock assortments, choice of new merchandise, layout, displays, and special promotions?

_____10. Do you apply the concept of "management by objectives," that is, do you set work goals for yourself and for each employee for the month or season ahead and at the end of each period check the actual performance against these goals?

Merchandise Inventory Control

_____11. Do you keep sales, inventory, and purchase records by types of merchandise within your departments?

_____12. Do you control your purchases in dollars by means of an open-to-buy system?

_____13. For staple and reorder items, do you prepare a checklist (never-out list) that you frequently check against the actual assortment on hand?

_____14. Do you make certain that best-sellers are reordered promptly and in sufficient volume and that slow-sellers are processed swiftly for clearance?

_____15. Are you taking adequate safeguards to reduce shoplifting and pilferage in your store?

Budgetary Control and Productivity

_____16. In controlling your operations, do you frequently compare actual results with the budget projections you have made; and do you then adjust your merchandising, promotion, and expense plans as indicated by deviation from these projections?

_____17. Do you study industry data and compare the results of your operation with them?

_____18. Do you think in terms of ratios and per cents, rather than exclusively in dollars-and-cents?

_____19. Do you use a variety of measures of performance, such as:

    _____ a. Net profit as a per cent of your net worth?

    _____ b. Stockturn (ratio of your sales to the value of your average inventory)?

    _____ c. Gross profit margin per dollar of cost investment in merchandise (dollars of gross margin divided by your average inventory at cost)?

    _____ d. Sales per square foot of space (net sales divided by total number of square feet of space)?

    _____ e. Selling cost per cent for each salesperson (remunerations of the salesperson divided by that person's sales)?

Figure 16-4

A Management Audit Form for Retailers (continued)

Buying

_____ 20. Are you continually searching the market for the most suitable merchandise, prices, and services rather than relying too much on established sources?

_____ 21. When reordering new items that have shown volume potential, do you make it a point to order a sufficient number?

_____ 22. Do you keep up assortments through important selling seasons, such as Christmas and Easter, in spite of the probability of markdowns on the remainders?

_____ 23. For goods having a short selling season (such as straw hats), do you predetermine the following dates: (a) when first orders are to be placed, (b) when retail stocks are to be complete, (c) extent of peak selling period, (d) start of clearance, and (e) final cleanup?

_____ 24. Do you take advantage of all available discounts—trade, quantity, seasonal, and cash—and do you include them on your written orders?

Pricing

_____ 25. Do you figure markup as a percentage of retail selling price rather than as a percentage of cost?

_____ 26. Do you set price lines or price zones?

_____ 27. Do the prices you set provide adequate markups within the limits of competition?

_____ 28. In retail pricing of new items and in evaluating their cost quotations, are you guided by what you think the typical customer will consider good value?

_____ 29. Before you mark down goods for clearance, do you consider alternate or supplementary ways of moving them—such as special displays, repackaging, or including them in a deal?

Advertising and Sales Promotion

_____ 30. Do you advertise consistently in at least one appropriate medium: newspapers, direct mail, handbills, local television or radio?

_____ 31. Does each of your ads specifically "sell" your store in addition to the merchandise advertised?

_____ 32. Do you regularly and systematically familiarize your salespeople with your plans for advertised merchandise and promotions?

_____ 33. Do you consult your suppliers about dealer aids helpful to the promotion of their merchandise in your store?

_____ 34. Do you use "co-op ads" with other merchants in your community?

_____ 35. Do you conduct a continuing effort to obtain free publicity in the local press or broadcast media?

Display

_____ 36. Are your window displays planned to attract attention, develop interest, create desire, and prompt a customer to enter your store for a closer inspection?

_____ 37. Do you give as much attention to your interior displays as to your windows?

Equipment and Layout

_____ 38. Are goods that the customers may not be specifically looking for but are likely to buy on sight (impulse merchandise) displayed near your store entrances and at other points that have heavy traffic?

_____ 39. Are your cash registers well located?

_____ 40. Are nonselling and office activities kept out of valuable selling space?

_____ 41. Do you receive, check, and mark incoming goods at central points rather than on the selling floor?

A Management Audit Form for Retailers (continued)

Cash and Finance

_____ 42. Does someone other than the cashier or bookkeeper open all mail and prepare a record of receipts that will be checked against deposits?

_____ 43. Do you deposit all of each day's cash receipts in the bank without delay?

_____ 44. Do you calculate your cash flow regularly (monthly, for example) and take steps to provide enough cash for each period's needs?

_____ 45. Have you established, in advance, a line of credit at your bank, not only to meet seasonal requirements but also to permit borrowing at any time for emergency needs?

Credit

_____ 46. Do you have a credit policy?

_____ 47. Are your bad-debt losses comparable with those of other similar stores?

_____ 48. Periodically, do you review your accounts to determine their status?

Insurance

_____ 49. Is your store insurance handled by a conscientious and knowledgeable agent?

_____ 50. Have you updated your insurance needs to assure adequate protection for buildings, equipment, merchandise, and other assets, as well as for public liability?

Accounting Records

_____ 51. Do you have your books balanced and accounts summarized each month?

_____ 52. Do you use a modern point-of-sale register for sales transactions and modern equipment to record accounts receivable?

_____ 53. Do you keep data on sales, purchases, inventory, and direct expenses for different types of merchandise in your store?

Taxes and Legal Obligations

_____ 54. To be sure you are not overpaying your taxes, do you retain a tax accountant to review your accounting records and prepare your more complicated tax returns?

_____ 55. Do you retain a good lawyer to confer with on day-to-day problems that have legal implications?

Planning for Growth

_____ 56. Over the past few years, have you done very much long-range planning for growth?

_____ 57. When you find that change is called for, do you act decisively and creatively?

_____ 58. Do you make most of your changes after thoughtful analysis rather than as reactions to crises?

_____ 59. Are you grooming someone to succeed you as manager in the not too distant future?

Source: This table is adapted from John W. Wingate and Elmer O. Schaller, *Management Audit for Small Retailers* (Washington, D.C.: Small Business Administration, Small Business Management Series No. 31, 3rd ed., 1977).

A Retailing Checklist

Rate the store's performance for each of the following criteria on a scale of 1 to 5, with 1 being excellent and 5 being poor.

I. Development of strategy
   1. Adherence to the philosophy of business _____
   2. Clear objectives _____
   3. Consistent objectives and image _____
   4. Well-defined product and/or service offerings _____
   5. Well-defined and ongoing budget _____
   6. Proper use of research _____
   7. Thorough short-run planning _____
   8. Thorough long-run planning _____
   9. Reactions to external environment _____
   10. Well-established evaluation criteria _____
   11. Adjustments in strategy _____

II. The consumer
   1. Well-defined target market _____
   2. Consistency with image _____
   3. Size of target market _____
   4. Knowledge of consumer needs _____

III. Store location and operations
   1. Consistency with image _____
   2. Size of trading area _____
   3. Popularity of trading area _____
   4. Access to vehicular traffic _____
   5. Access to mass transportation _____
   6. Parking facilities _____
   7. Composition of existing stores _____
   8. Affinity with existing stores _____
   9. Turnover of stores _____
   10. Visibility of store _____
   11. Condition of building _____
   12. Terms of occupancy _____
   13. Store hours _____
   14. Store facilities _____
   15. Maintenance of facilities _____

IV. Product/service offering
   1. Consistency with image _____
   2. Width of assortment _____
   3. Depth of assortment _____
   4. Level of innovativeness _____
   5. Availability of national brands _____
   6. Availability of private brands _____
   7. Well-defined buying procedures _____

V. Personnel
   1. Consistency with image _____
   2. Number of employees _____
   3. Clearly defined authority _____
   4. Level of training _____
   5. Appearance _____
   6. Manners _____
   7. Opportunities for advancement _____

Figure 16-5

A Retailing Checklist (continued)

VI. Communications: The store itself, promotion, personal selling, publicity,
and customer services
1. Consistency with image _____
2. Storefront(s) _____
3. Cleanliness of store _____
4. Traffic flow _____
5. Width of aisles _____
6. Use of dead space _____
7. Displays _____
8. Information _____
9. Amount of promotion _____
10. Quality of promotion _____
11. Diversity of promotion _____
12. Amount of personal selling _____
13. Quality of sales force _____
14. Uses of publicity _____
15. Uses of customer services _____

VII. Pricing
1. Consistency with image _____
2. Range of prices _____
3. Uses of price lining _____
4. Uses of psychological pricing _____
5. Profitability _____

To improve productivity, retailers need to make the implementation of their strategies as efficient as possible, to lift industry and company performance standards. Operations management, human resource management, energy management, inventory management, and credit management are five major contributors to the level of retail productivity. By using new technology, retailers are often able to better integrate strategies and raise performance.

The strategy needs to be constantly monitored, evaluated, and revised. The retail audit is utilized to accomplish the control function. The retail audit is a systematic, critical, and unbiased review and appraisal. Objectives, strategy, implementation, and organization are each investigated.

A retail audit consists of six steps: determining who does the audit, determining when and how often it is conducted, determining areas to be audited, developing audit forms, conducting the audit, and reporting to management. After management reads the audit report, the necessary revisions in strategy are made.

Among the problems of auditing are costs, time consuming, inaccurate performance standards, poor employee cooperation, collection of incorrect data, and unresponsive management. A number of retailers do not utilize the audit. They will have problems in evaluating their positions and planning for the future.

Two examples of audit forms have been presented here: a management audit for retailers and a retailing checklist.

Questions for Discussion

1. Why is it so important for a retailer to view strategy as an integrated and ongoing process?
2. Develop a sales opportunity grid for a department store planning to add women's gloves to its clothing line.
3. Cite five performance measures commonly used by retailers and explain what could be learned by studying each.
4. Of the aspects of productivity described in this chapter, which is the most difficult for retailers to improve? Why?
5. How would energy management plans differ for supermarkets and banks?
6. Under which circumstances should a retailer use its own credit card? What are the pros and cons of this approach?
7. Distinguish between horizontal and vertical retail audits.
8. Why must a good retail audit be periodic, comprehensive, systematic, and independent?
9. Distinguish among the following auditors.
   a. Outside auditors
   b. Company specialists
   c. Company department managers
10. Why is it advantageous to conduct an audit when a complete physical inventory is taken?
11. Under what circumstances should a disguised audit be used?
12. Should an auditor be a "yes man" for management? Explain your answer.
13. How should management respond to the findings of an audit? What may happen if the findings are ignored?
14. Why do many retailers not conduct any form of retail audit? Are these reasons valid? Explain your answer.

CASES

1. Harold's Pharmacy: Analysis of Product Lines

Diane Harold owns and operates a moderate-sized pharmacy in Birmingham, Alabama. The store has been open since 1967 and attracts a loyal, but small, clientele. While Harold continues to earn solid profits, competition from supermarkets, stationery stores, off-price chains, and others is increasing rapidly.

In response, Harold has engaged in a heavy amount of scrambled merchandising. Her store carries everything from cosmetics, stationery, and greeting cards to toys, batteries, and small electrical appliances.

Recently, Harold began an intensive evaluation of the store that focused on the merchandise lines and the individual items being sold. The analysis included operating ratios, sales, gross margin (profit), stock turnover, and floor space. Important data are shown in Table 1.

A new product line, inexpensive watches, is under consideration. In order to add this line, an existing product category must be deleted. The watches would have the characteristics represented in Table 2.

Table 1
Analysis of Harold's Pharmacy

A. *Overall Operating Ratios*

Quick ratio	1.0 times
Current ratio	3.5 times
Collection period	18 days
Assets to net sales	33.5 per cent
Accounts payable to net sales	4.5 per cent
Return on net sales	2.3 per cent
Return on net worth	10.1 per cent

B. *Selected Product Lines*

Criteria	Appliances	Batteries, Film, Etc.	Costmetics, Health Care	Stationery/ Cards	Toys/ Gifts	Total Store
Annual sales						
Past	$20,000	$35,000	$75,000	$47,000	$32,000	$320,000
Current	$20,000	$40,000	$75,000	$50,000	$28,000	$340,000
Future	$20,000	$45,000	$75,000	$50,000	$25,000	$350,000
Gross margin (per cent)	26	32	25	35	34	30
Stock turnover (per year)	3 times	15 times	7 times	4 times	4 times	4.9 times
Floor space (per cent of total selling space)	10	5	25	15	10	100.0

Table 2
Harold's Proposed Watch Line

Characteristics	
Models	Three men's and three women's—two of each to be quartz and one to be digital
Brand	Timex
Price range	$25 to $60
Estimated annual sales	$30,000
Gross profit	30 per cent
Stock turnover	6 times per year
Floor space	5 per cent of total selling space

Questions

1. Evaluate the data in Table 1. How well is Harold's performing?
2. Which product line should be dropped in order to add watches? What are the risks of this?
3. What other factors should Harold's consider before adding the watch line, aside from those shown in Table 2?
4. Using Figure 16-3 in this chapter, develop an auditing procedure for Harold's.

2. Sears, Roebuck and Company: Integrating and Controlling a Retail Strategy*

Sears, Roebuck and Company is the world's largest retailer of general merchandise. Sears' headquarters and most of its buying offices are located in Sears Tower in Chicago. Central buyers in these offices work with thousands of suppliers and negotiate product specifications, prices, and purchase terms. Items approved for sale in Sears stores are noted in a series of books called "merchandise lists."

In the past, Sears had a decentralized merchandising system, in which a store manager and his or her regional supervisor could vary product selection, pricing, and promotions to best suit local market conditions. However, Sears learned that the decentralized system had some significant problems.

While a buyer would make arrangements to purchase large quantities of a product, he or she would not know how many stores would stock it. At times, a sizable portion of Sears stores did not want to stock a particular product. A buyer at the Chicago headquarters might make arrangements to purchase hundreds of thousands of record players, only to have a sizable portion of them rejected by store managers because the profit margin was too thin.

Store managers tended to overbuy goods that received special promotions from Sears suppliers. After a sale was over, these managers would then mark up the remaining inventory. The higher gross margin would improve the manager's bonus which was based on his or her store's profitability.

A chain with 860 stores, about 2,000 catalog and telephone sales offices, 13 distribution centers, and 124 warehouses required significant coordination. This was not possible under the disjointed organization structure in effect.

In 1982, Sears instituted its present structure by reorganizing its buying and merchandising practices based on the recommendations of two major consulting firms: McKinsey and Company, and Hay Associates. McKinsey was responsible for the organizational changes, the first Sears had undertaken in 30 years. Hay designed a new compensation system for store managers.

Through the reorganization, a policy-setting body was established. This body included the chief executive officer of Sears Merchandise Group of Field Operations, who brought field managers under closer control. Store managers lost most of their pricing authority. Centralized merchandising allowed nationwide promotions to be implemented. Sears also reduced the tendency of store managers to overbuy promotional merchandise by refusing to allow them to use the lower initial cost figures to compute their bonuses after special sales were completed. A store manager's bonuses were to be based on the overall sales and profits of his or her store and the performance of all stores in the region.

A computer system now provides sales data, which are updated on a daily basis, for Sears buyers in Chicago. This system also coordinates sales and inventory information among Sears catalog offices, its warehouses, and its leading suppliers. In addition, the computer system records credit-card purchases and updates credit balances, determines salesperson commissions, compares inventory with preset minimum and maximum levels, and even prints purchase orders. All of this helps reduce credit losses and inventory shortages, speeds up checkout lines, enables store managers to have an optimum product mix on shelves, and handles accounting and personnel records which were previously processed manually.

*This case was prepared and written by Professor Steven J. Shaw, University of South Carolina, Columbia, South Carolina.

Questions

1. "A chain-store retailer must be concerned about maintaining a delicate balance between centralization and decentralization of its organization structure." Explain this statement with reference to Sears.
2. Describe the benefits in the use of external consultants instead of internal Sears personnel to examine the previous organization structure and recommend alternatives.
3. Construct an audit form for Sears to evaluate the effectiveness of its current merchandising structure on a regular basis.
4. How could Sears' computer system aid in conducting retail audits?

17

The Changing Environment of Retailing

Chapter Objectives

1. To examine demographic, life-style, consumerism, and regulatory trends and consider the impact of these factors on retailing
2. To evaluate the development of new technology in the 1980s and 1990s
3. To discuss the adaptation of retail institutions to environmental trends
4. To consider the international dimension of retailing

Throughout the 1980s and 1990s, retailers will increasingly turn to computers for assistance in planning, implementing, and controlling their strategies. The computers will be less expensive to purchase and operate, and have a broad range of applications for retailers. Today, far-sighted retailers are getting a jump on their competitors by using computers in an innovative way.

One progressive retailer is Frederick & Nelson, a Seattle department-store chain. The company has a mainframe computer system that it utilizes for basic planning and analysis. It recently added a personal computer (PC) system to improve operations in specific areas, such as the distribution center, and has designed its own computer software programs.

The distribution center is able to use a stand-alone PC system (which operates independently of the firm's mainframe computer) to determine

- When orders are received and shipped out.
- The length of time it takes to process orders.
- When "trouble" shipments occur.
- The accuracy of vendor shipments.
- Home delivery patterns of truckers.
- Inventory movement by branch.

Through this system, Frederick & Nelson is increasing the percentage of orders filled within five working days, making delivery routes more efficient, and providing executives with a great deal of information for decision making.[1]

Overview

In order to attain and maintain long-run success, a retailer must anticipate and plan for the future.[2] The retailer needs to spot and react to trends early enough to satisfy the target market, yet not so early that the target market is unready for changes or false trends are incorrectly labeled. A late response to trends means that a retailer might miss profitable opportunities but minimize risks.

Strategic planning for the future must take into account the nature of variables in terms of certainty of occurrence and magnitude of change, their effect on the retailer's business, and the time required for the retailer to react properly. Demographics, life-styles, consumerism, the regulatory environment, new technology, institutional changes, and internationalization are among the factors that will affect the long-run success of retailers.

Environmental variables range in terms of their certainty of occurrence. For example, population size can be forecast more accurately than household income because the former relies on birth rates and death rates (which can be estimated precisely), whereas the latter depends on unemployment, productivity, inflation, imports, and so on (which are difficult to predict). When forecasts are accurate, future planning is simplified; for uncertain forecasts, retailers are forced to be more hesitant in their adaptations.

A retailer must plan greater alterations in strategy if a variable's magnitude of change is large. For instance, a retailer of appliances has to develop significant changes in strategy to adjust to the large long-term increase in working women. Hardware and other retailers must react to the rise in do-it-yourselfers.

The time required for a retailer to adapt to change varies with the strategic element undergoing change. Merchandising strategy shifts—for example, the stocking of an unexpectedly popular fad item—are much more quickly consummated than adjustments in a firm's overall pricing, promotional, or locational strategy. In addition, a new store can more readily adapt to trends than existing stores with established images, ongoing leases, space limitations, and so on.

Although other years are noted, this chapter emphasizes the changes in the environment of retailing between now and 2000. Trends in demographics, life-styles, consumerism, the regulatory environment, technology, retail institutions, and the international environment of business are each discussed and related to retail strategy.

The period of the present to 2000 is emphasized because

- Relatively short forecasts are more accurate than longer ones.
- This time period is lengthy enough for one to develop long-range retail plans and react to forecast changes.
- Much research is available.

[1]Jules Abend, "How Micros Ease F&N's Distribution Ills," *Stores* (October 1984), pp. 66–67.
[2]For example, see Jagdish N. Sheth, "Emerging Trends for the Retailing Industry," *Journal of Retailing*, Vol. 59 (Fall 1983), pp. 6–18.

Table 17-1

U.S. Population by Age, 1980–2000 (thousands)

Age	1980 #	1980 %	1985 #	1985 %	1990 #	1990 %	1995 #	1995 %	2000 #	2000 %
Under 5 years	16,457	7.2	18,453	7.7	19,198	7.7	18,615	7.2	17,626	6.6
5–13	31,080	13.6	29,654	12.4	32,189	12.9	34,436	13.3	34,382	12.8
14–17	16,139	7.1	14,731	6.2	12,950	5.2	14,082	5.4	15,381	5.7
18–24	30,347	13.3	28,739	12.0	25,794	10.3	23,702	9.1	24,601	9.2
25–34	37,593	16.5	41,788	17.5	43,529	17.4	40,520	15.6	36,415	13.6
35–44	25,881	11.4	32,004	13.4	37,847	15.2	41,997	16.2	43,743	16.3
45–54	22,795	10.0	22,466	9.4	25,402	10.2	31,397	12.1	37,119	13.9
55–64	21,698	9.5	22,188	9.3	21,051	8.4	20,923	8.1	23,767	8.9
65 years and older	25,714	11.3	28,608	12.0	31,697	12.7	33,887	13.1	34,921	13.0
Total population*	227,704	100.0	238,631	100.0	249,657	100.0	259,559	100.0	267,955	100.0
Median age	30		31.5		33		34.5		36	

*Totals may not equal exactly 100.0 per cent due to rounding errors.

Source: U.S. Bureau of the Census, Current Population Reports, *Series P-25.*

Demographic Trends[3]

Trends involving population size and age distribution, the number of households, mobility, the location of population, working women, and income are detailed in this section. Individually, each of these variables has a great impact on retailing; collectively, they dominate a retailer's planning for the future.

Population Size and Age Distribution

Table 17-1 shows the growth in U.S. population size by age from 1980 to 2000. Although the rate of population growth will be less than 1 per cent per year from 1980 to the year 2000, the United States will add about 40 million people during this period. The median age of the population will rise from 30 years to 36 years.

When studying U.S. population size and age trends, retailers also need to be aware of these factors:

- The average life span of U.S. males will expand from 70 years for those born in 1980 to 73 years for those born in 2000. The corresponding figures for females are 77.5 and 80.5.
- The average annual number of births will range from 3.5 million to 3.9 million (compared with about 4 million annually during the 1960s). However, more of these will involve firstborns, requiring parents to spend several hundred dollars in "tooling up" costs for items such as baby furniture.

[3]Unless otherwise indicated, the data in this section are drawn from U.S. Bureau of the Census, *Current Population Reports* and *Census of Population.* For a good review article, see "The Year 2000: A Demographic Profile of Consumer Market," *Marketing News* (May 25, 1984), Section 1, pp. 8, 10.

- Couples will continue to get married at later ages than previously. In 1970, men were 22 years old at first marriage while women were 20. Today, men are about 26 and women about 23 at first marriage; and they are waiting to have children.
- The fastest-growing age segments will be 35 to 44, 45 to 54, and 65 and over. The under-35 segments will fall from a total of 57.7 per cent of the population in 1980 to 47.9 per cent in 2000.

Retailers must recognize that while younger markets will always represent large segments of the population, their relative importance is declining; and retailers should respond accordingly. For example, the eating, shopping, recreational, and other patterns of younger people are far different than those of their older counterparts. In addition, the approximately one-fifth of the population ages 55 and older controls one-third of all personal household income in the United States.[4]

Number of Households

Despite the slow rate of overall population growth, the number of households is forecast to rise significantly by the year 2000. From a definitional perspective, a **household** is comprised of a person or a group of persons occupying a dwelling unit, whether related or unrelated. In contrast, a **family** consists of two or more people residing together who are related.

There were almost 81 million households in 1980. This figure is expected to rise to 95 million in 1990 and 105 million by 2000. At the same time, the average size of a U.S. household will drop from about 2.8 in 1980 to about 2.5 to 2.6 in 2000. The percentage of single-person households is predicted to go from 23 per cent in 1980 to 25 per cent in 1990 to 27 to 28 per cent in 2000.[5]

The increase in the number of households is based on three major trends: the high divorce rate, the greater tendency of young singles to live apart from their parents, and the larger number of senior citizens who live apart from their grown children.

Not only the number but also the rate of divorces has increased greatly. Between 1970 and 1980, the number of divorces rose by two-thirds, and one in three marriages now ends in divorce. The high number of divorces is expected to continue while the rate per 1,000 marriages declines slightly.

Young people will live apart from their parents with much greater frequency. At present 6.7 million people aged 15 to 44 live alone, and this number is expected to rise by 1.5 million between now and the year 2000. Furthermore, about 10 to 12 per cent of all adults will never marry.

Senior citizens will increasingly live apart from their grown children. In the late 1940s, 55 per cent of those over age 65 were heads of households; by 1980, this figure grew to 65 per cent, and the percentage continues to increase. Part of the growth is the number of widows. As of 1980, 53 per cent of women aged 65 and over were widows. Forty per cent of all single-person households involve senior citizens.

These household trends will have two major impacts on retailers. First, decisions will be made by individuals functioning as both buyers and consumers; there will be

[4]Jacquelyn Bivins, "Senior Citizen Marketing: Shattering Stereotypes," *Chain Store Age Executive* (August 1984), pp. 17–20; and Peter Francese, "Myths About Elderly Fall Short of Truth," *Advertising Age* (January 24, 1985), p. 46.
[5]Paul C. Glick, "How American Families Are Changing," *American Demographics* (January 1984), pp. 21–25.

more purchasing for self-use. Second, because each separate household requires furniture, housewares, and so on, there will be opportunities for retailers in these areas.

Mobility

Each year, about 12 to 17 per cent of all Americans move, and this percentage is expected to continue. According to the Bureau of the Census, about 60 per cent of the moves are made locally, and approximately 40 per cent of the moves are out of the area, state, or country.

The rate of mobility varies widely by age group. The 20 to 24 age group has the highest mobility, followed by the 25 to 29 and 30 to 34 age groups. Older persons have below-average mobility rates.[6] Mobility is also high among military personnel, migrant or seasonal workers, and executives.

In the future, many citizens will move in greater numbers to the Sunbelt; children will leave home at earlier ages; people will be displaced by urban renewal. And the number of Americans living in condominiums and mobile homes is bound to get larger.

Some retail implications of high mobility follow:

- Well-known chains and franchises will prosper.
- National brands will sell well among mobile persons.
- Purchase levels, particularly of clothing and home products, will be high because many people discard items when moving to new environments (particularly changes in climate or long-distance moves).
- Rentals become important.
- Shopping centers will be focal points for purchases.
- A unified, nationwide credit system will be necessary.
- Large-scale advertising will be needed.

Location of Population

During the last decade, the number of people living in suburban communities has increased by over 18 per cent, or almost twice as much as the total U.S. population. In the same time period, the number of people living in big cities has remained almost constant. A similar trend is foreseen through 2000.

Many young people spend the early years of marriage in a city, but later, by the time the second child arrives and the head of household is aged 30 to 34, families move to the suburbs. Additionally, the average earnings of suburban families are higher than the average earnings of city families. It is estimated that the suburbs account for well over two-thirds of all personal income in metropolitan areas and an even higher proportion of discretionary income.

The growth of suburban markets has important implications for retailers:

- It will force chain stores and department stores to re-examine the use of central buying offices as the suburban market gets larger and more affluent.
- Retail store locations may have to shift to suburban areas or add branch stores.

[6]Steven J. Shaw, "Major Life-Style Trends and Marketing Opportunities," unpublished working paper, University of South Carolina, p. 2.

- Warehouse locations will have to be relocated to be near store locations.
- Retail opportunities will exist relating to suburban home ownership and life-styles for items such as lawn care, snow blowers, do-it-yourself projects, and home freezers.
- Planned shopping centers will maintain their strength.

Working Women

At present, about 53 per cent of all U.S. adult women are in the labor force; and the trend for more women to work outside the home is projected to continue. Table 17-2 shows the growth between 1970 and 2000. During this period, the number of women in the labor force will almost double and account for 46.6 per cent of the total adult working population by the year 2000.

In addition, the profile of the working woman is changing. Traditionally the working woman was young and unmarried (including divorced and separated) or her husband was unable to provide for the family. Now, the working woman is likely to be married (60.0 per cent) and older (mean age of 36 years) and to have one or more children under the age of 6 in the home (50 per cent).

The factor most directly related to female employment is the level of education. The higher the education achieved, the greater the probability of a female's working.

The increase in the number of females combining the roles of working woman, wife, and mother has significant implications for retailers:

- Working wives spend large amounts for major appliances and household equipment, especially when they are timesaving.
- Working wives are independent in their purchases, as they seek individualism and personal identity.
- Working wives are prone to use their leisure time for pleasure. This has a strong influence on the market for ready-made clothing, sporting goods, and rental agencies.
- Working wives may be unable to shop during regular retail hours. This has meaning for mail-order retailers and round-the-clock retailers.

Table 17-2
The U.S. Female Labor Force, 1970–2000 (thousands)

Age (in years)	1970 Number	1970 Per Cent	1980 Number	1980 Per Cent	1990* Number	1990* Per Cent	2000* Number	2000* Per Cent
16–24	8,148	25.8	11,731	25.7	11,500	22.1	12,000	20.8
25–44	11,686	37.0	20,906	45.8	25,000	48.1	26,000	45.0
45–64	10,707	33.9	11,822	25.9	14,000	26.9	18,000	31.1
65 and over	1,042	3.3	1,187	2.6	1,500	2.9	1,800	3.1
Total	31,583	100.0	45,646	100.0	52,000	100.0	57,800	100.0
Females as a percentage of total labor force		36.7		43.1		44.4		46.6

*Projections.

Sources: U.S. Bureau of Labor Statistics, Employment and Earnings; *and the authors' estimates.*

- Working wives have less time to prepare meals. Growing in importance are prepared foods, convenience foods, and fast-food restaurants. Some forecasters are predicting no growth in supermarket sales.
- Working wives require that services (e.g., repairs) be offered during evenings and weekends.
- Working wives increase family affluence, expanding the use of household help, gardeners, travel, and so on.
- Working wives will respond to advertising placed in evening time periods, particularly for television.

Income

After a decade of almost no **real income** growth during the 1970s, whereby household income after adjusting for inflation did not increase, the 1980s and 1990s are forecast to witness solid real income rises (averaging 1 to 3 per cent per year). Figure 17-1 shows the trends in real income between 1980 and 1995, assuming a 1.5 per cent annual increase. By 1995, 45 per cent of all U.S. households will have annual incomes of $25,000 and over; and the number of households with incomes of $50,000 and over will triple between 1980 and 1995.[7]

The higher incomes suggest broadened markets for luxury goods and services. It can also be anticipated that the demand for quality and specialty merchandise, better customer services, and wider assortments will increase. At the same time, retailers need to consider the effect of unemployment, inflation, and resource shortages on consumer spending patterns and plan accordingly.

Life-Style Trends

In addition to analyzing demographic trends, it is necessary for a retailer to study the life-style trends of his or her target market. As explained in Chapter 5, life-styles refer to "the patterns in which people live and spend time and money."[8] Included in an analysis of life-styles are gender roles, consumer sophistication, poverty of time, leisure, and self-fulfillment. The life-style trends described next must be interpreted by retailers and interrelated with demographics.

Gender Roles

The increasing number of working women, who may work an average of sixty to seventy hours each week between job and home responsibilities, is altering life-styles significantly.

[7]William Lazer, "How Rising Affluence Will Reshape Markets," *American Demographics* (February 1984), pp. 17–21. See also Thomas J. Stanley and George P. Moschis, "America's Affluent," *American Demographics* (March 1984), pp. 28–33.

[8]James F. Engel and Roger D. Blackwell, *Consumer Behavior*, Fourth Edition (Hinsdale, Ill.: Dryden Press, 1982), p. 188.

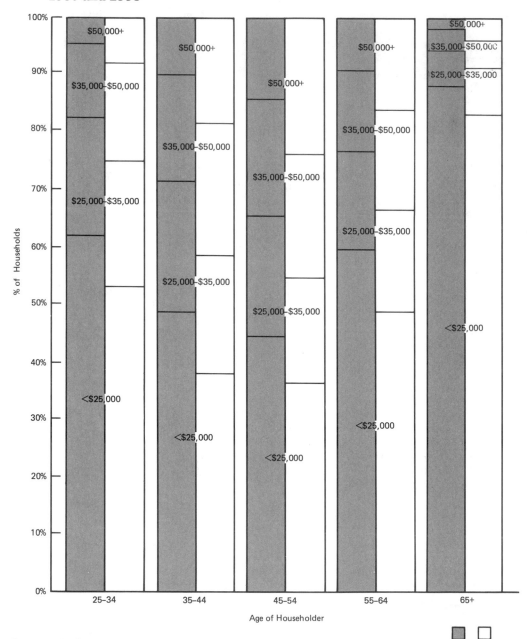

Households by Age of Householder and Household Income: 1980 and 1995

Assumes a 1.5 per cent growth in real income each year.

1980 1995

Source: William Lazer, "How Rising Affluence Will Reshape Markets," *American Demographics* (February 1984), p. 18. Reprinted by permission.

Figure 17-1

In comparison to women who have not worked, working women tend to be more[9]

- Appearance-conscious (concerned with fashion and dress).
- Interested in maintaining a youthful posture.
- Confident and individualistic.
- Adept at dealing with the external world.
- Concerned with the convenience and ease of performing household duties.
- Cosmopolitan in taste and knowledgeable and demanding as consumers.
- Interested in leisure and travel.
- Concerned with improving themselves and their educational background.
- Interested in equal rights.
- Indifferent to small price differences among stores or products.
- Disinterested in leisurely shopping trips.

As a result of the trend toward more working women, the life-styles of American males are also changing. Large numbers of men now take care of children, take out the garbage, wash the dishes, cook for the family, vacuum the house, shop for food, do the laundry, and clean the bathroom. There are four groups of husbands: progressives (13 per cent), who are young, affluent, and well educated; traditionalists (39 per cent), who are older and less educated; ambivalents (15 per cent), who possess average demographics and have internal conflicts over old and new values; and all talk, no action (33 per cent), who possess average demographics, except for greater youthfulness.[10]

The future will see still more changes in women's roles and the questioning of these roles. Furthermore, the powers and duties of husbands and wives will be shared with greater frequency.[11] Retailers need to understand and adapt to these trends.

Consumer Sophistication and Confidence

Consumer life-styles will reflect increased levels of education. For example, as of 1980 almost one third of all Americans 25 years of age and older had completed at least one year of college. This figure is expected to be almost 40 per cent by 1990; and 20 per cent will have 4-year degrees by that time. For younger adults, education levels are even higher.

Thus, the emerging consumer will be more knowledgeable and cosmopolitan; more cognizant of national and worldwide trends in tastes, styles, and products; and more sophisticated. Furthermore, nonconforming behavior will be more widely accepted

[9]John Smallwood, William Lazer, et al., *A Report on Consumer Environments and Life Styles of the Seventies* (Benton Harbor, Mich.: Whirlpool Corporation, 1971), pp. 18–31; Alladi Venkatesh, "Changing Roles of Women—A Life-Style Analysis," *Journal of Consumer Research*, Vol. 7 (September 1980), pp. 189–197; Barbara A. Price, "What the Baby Boom Believes," *American Demographics* (May 1984), pp. 31–33; and Joan Kron, "Clothes-Shopping Habits Changing As Men Seek Style, Women Service," *Wall Street Journal* (December 21, 1984), pp. 21, 28.

[10]"Large Numbers of Husbands Buy Household Products, Do Housework," *Marketing News* (October 3, 1980), pp. 1, 3.

[11]For example, see Pierre Filiatrault and J. R. Brent Ritchie, "Joint Purchasing Decisions: A Comparison of Influence Structure in Family and Couple Decision-Making Units," *Journal of Consumer Research*, Vol. 7 (September 1980), pp. 131–140; and "Changes Found in Attitudes, Shopping Behavior of U.S.'s Two-Income Couples," *Marketing News* (October 28, 1983), p. 12.

because increased education will create the self-assurance that shoppers need to reduce their need for conformity, while providing an appreciation of available choices. The confident shopper depends less on brands and labels and is more willing to experiment, but the more educated consumer also insists on detailed information about products and services.

As an example, supermarket customers are becoming much more demanding. They want "delicate and interesting blends of spices" but not a lot of sodium or monosodium glutamate. Growing numbers of consumers "perceive foods that are loaded with additives, salt, sugar, and fat as not good for them. They want foods that make them feel healthy."[12] A recent survey found that 95 per cent of supermarket shoppers are very concerned or somewhat concerned about the nutritional content of what they eat.[13]

Commented one analyst:

> Education changes career expectations, social attitudes, and consumer behavior. Once consumers start thinking, they change. They begin to ask questions, and businesses have to provide satisfactory answers.[14]

Poverty of Time

For some consumer households, the increased number of working women, the desire for personal fulfillment, longer distances between the location of work and home, and the greater amount of people working at second jobs contribute to the concept of **poverty of time.** Greater affluence may result in less rather than more free time, because the alternatives competing for consumers' time will rise significantly. Therefore, these customers are likely to place high values on products and services that minimize time expenditures.

Retailers can respond to the importance of time through a variety of activities:[15]

- Stocking prepackaged products, which can be selected through self-service.
- For example, certain items can be pre-gift-wrapped, so that they can be selected and purchased immediately.
- Speeding checkout time.
- Setting up specialized boutiques by product category within the store. For instance, retailers can place gourmet dining products in one integrated department, instead of scattering chafing dishes, serving trays, and ice buckets throughout three different departments.

---

[12]R. Gordon McGovern, "The Consumer Revolution in the Supermarket," *Journal of Business Strategy*, Vol. 5 (Fall 1984), pp. 93–95.

[13]Food Marketing Institute, "Trends: Consumer Attitudes & the Supermarket," 1984.

[14]"The Year 2000: A Demographic Profile of Consumer Market," Section 1, p. 10.

[15]Sidney Packard and Abraham Raine, *Consumer Behavior and Fashion Marketing* (Dubuque, Iowa: Kendall/ Hunt, 1977), p. 171; Marian Burk Rothman, "Personal Shopping: New Needs, New Tactics," *Stores* (November 1979), pp. 38–43; Leonard L. Berry, "The Time-Buying Consumer," *Journal of Retailing*, Vol. 55 (Winter 1979), pp. 58–69; and Ronald D. Michman, "New Directions for Life-Style Behavior Patterns," *Business Horizons*, Vol. 27 (July–August 1984), pp. 59–64.

- Reducing out-of-stock conditions.
- Describing, labeling, and identifying merchandise more clearly in advertising and displays.
- Increasing the number of store outlets to reduce travel time.
- Maintaining longer store hours, including Sunday openings.
- Adding fashion and other consultants.

In addition, growth is foreseen for retailers emphasizing convenience, such as direct selling, catalogs, telephone selling, and television selling.

Leisure Activities

While a greater proportion of days and time is spent away from the primary job, many Americans are now involved with second jobs and they and others seek leisure-oriented activities, not shopping-oriented activities on days off (as discussed under "Poverty of Time"). As a result, people are spending blocks of time on passive entertainment (e.g., television) and/or active recreation (e.g., tennis).

It is necessary for the retailer to determine whether his or her customers have a poverty of time or excess leisure time and how much of their leisure time consumers are willing to spend in shopping. The latter seems to be decreasing, as evidenced by the growth of stores and shopping centers catering to one-stop shopping.

In addition, retailers need to assess the size and growth possibilities of various types of leisure activities and plan accordingly. For example, one of the most heavily researched consumer segments is the generation of "baby boomers" born between 1946 and 1962. Overall, there are nearly 70 million baby boomers, representing a large and increasingly affluent consumer group. Table 17-3 shows how baby boomers may be categorized on the basis of their leisure activities: actives—all around (31 per cent), exercisers (16 per cent); and sedentaries and inactives—cable television viewers (9 per cent), readers (6 per cent), and inactives (38 per cent). This table also contrasts the activities of baby boomers and nonbaby boomers, based on the results of a survey of 2,000 adults aged 18 to 65.[16]

Self-Fulfillment

Of growing importance to Americans is the concept of **self-fulfillment,** whereby

> people want to express themselves by purchasing goods and services which are meaningful to them rather than symbols of conspicuous consumption.[17]

These are some of the ways in which different individuals are seeking to fulfill themselves:

- Emphasizing physical health, fitness, and exercise.
- Searching for meaningful work.

[16]Barbara I. Brown, "How the Baby Boom Lives," *American Demographics* (May 1984), pp. 35–37.
[17]Michman, "New Directions for Life-Style Behavior Patterns," p. 59.

Table 17-3
The Leisure Activities of U.S. Adults (Per Cent)

Leisure Activity	All Baby Boomers	Nonbaby Boomers	All-Around Actives	Exercisers	Cable TV Viewers	Readers	Inactives
			Actives		Sedentaries/Inactives		
Belong to a health club	17	8	6	72	14	15	2
Currently participate in exercise classes	18	9	6	72	19	17	4
Engage in on a regular basis:							
Walking (or climbing stairs)	56	56	58	57	57	54	54
Swimming	46	23	55	52	55	36	36
Dancing (e.g., aerobic, disco, ballroom)	39	18	52	58	25	26	27
Baseball/softball	30	7	47	30	32	14	17
Camping	31	20	46	28	38	31	18
Fishing	29	26	42	24	33	32	19
Regular bicycling	29	11	39	37	26	25	19
Boating	19	13	34	17	13	22	9
Jogging (running)	26	10	33	37	23	24	17
Football	18	4	31	18	25	11	7
Hiking	17	10	27	17	14	24	9
Basketball	18	3	26	21	20	18	8
Calisthenics (home or gym)	23	13	26	48	17	31	12
Hunting	14	10	24	6	17	21	8
Tennis	19	5	24	30	17	19	9
Racquetball	12	3	20	23	10	11	2
Skiing	14	3	19	26	11	11	4
Stationary bicycling	9	5	9	16	13	7	6
Attending events:							
Movies	66	35	84	74	49	63	52
Sporting events	36	29	56	50	39	25	16
Concerts	33	16	54	41	30	26	15
Plays	18	19	31	34	10	19	2
Other Activities:							
Attending parties/social gatherings	66	49	91	82	43	69	45
Eating out	68	67	80	83	57	58	55
Hobbies (outside home)	30	17	38	32	43	35	19
Work-related education	22	14	28	33	17	26	14
Nonwork-related education	16	9	23	30	7	17	7
Gambling	11	9	16	13	10	13	5
Volunteer work	12	19	15	15	13	8	9

Table 17-3 (continued)
The Leisure Activities of U.S. Adults (Per Cent)

Leisure Activity	All Baby Boomers	Nonbaby Boomers	Baby Boomer Category				
			Actives		Sedentaries/Inactives		
			All-Around Actives	Exercisers	Cable TV Viewers	Readers	Inactives
At home:							
Listening to radio	78	66	84	76	78	75	74
Playing stereo/records	71	46	80	77	65	57	65
Watching television	80	85	77	78	97	67	83
Entertaining friends	59	56	69	63	62	61	48
Reading	63	65	64	75	60	82	55
Garden and lawn work	49	61	51	50	60	56	44
Home improvements	46	48	51	50	47	53	39
Repair work on automobile	33	25	44	29	39	38	24
Entertaining relatives	44	55	44	49	45	53	41
Hobbies (at home)	36	32	41	43	31	50	28
Playing video games	25	8	29	28	37	25	17
Caring/baby-sitting for children	25	19	19	23	36	29	27
Using a home computer	4	4	7	4	1	1	1
Number of:							
Books read in past year (median)	5.2	4.3	5.7	5.6	3.9	54.4	3.7
Hours radio listened to per week (median)	11.1	7.3	14.7	9.8	19.4	10.3	10.0
Hours television watched per week (median):							
Noncable	10.4	11.5	10.3	8.0	3.7	10.1	13.5
Cable (nonpay)	0.4	0.4	0.3	0.3	14.5	0.6	0.3
Pay cable	0.3	0.3	0.3	0.3	11.8	0.3	0.3

Source: Barbara I. Brown, "How the Baby Boom Lives," *American Demographics (May 1984), pp. 36–37. Reprinted by permission.*

- De-emphasizing material possessions and status symbols.
- Becoming interested in mysticism and romanticism.
- Turning away from bigness and searching for simplicity.
- Trying for self-improvement.
- Insisting on social responsibility by business and industry.
- Improving the environment.
- Attaining individuality ("Do your own thing").

These principles have significant meanings for retailing:

- The interest in physical fitness has led to the growth of health spas, bicycle and exercise equipment sales, and health food and diet food products.

Apparel Market Segments Based on Consumer Life-Styles

A study by North Coast Research identified eight fashion life-style groups.

THREE APPAREL-SHOPPING style dimensions define fashion life-styles: investment vs. utility quality demands, novelty vs. conservative taste, and bargain vs. regular price buying. For example, the investment buyer views clothing as a necessity of his or her life-style, not a luxury, and the preference is for the most expensive apparel.

Novelty buyers value newness and high fashion and enjoy the process of shopping. Bargain buyers check prices, shop sales, and don't mind spending time to find the best buy.

Figure 17-2

Apparel Market Segments Based on Consumer Life-Styles (continued)

None of these styles is mutually exclusive. A strong investment orientation does not preclude a novelty or bargain orientation. Each person can be characterized as high or low on each style dimension, eight fashion life-style types:

1. **Clothes Horses** (regular price, investment, novelty): Men and women of all ages and occupations can belong to this group, but they are especially likely to be in sales. Apparel spending is very high.

2. **Executives** (regular price, investment, conservative): More likely to be men than women, they have high incomes, tend to be in management, professional, or technical occupations, and spend a lot on apparel.

3. **Savvy Shoppers** (bargain price, investment, novelty): Primarily women age 25 and older with incomes of $20,000+, they are likely to be housewives or clerical workers. Apparel spending is moderately high, and they are the most frequent shoppers.

4. **Sensibles** (bargain price, investment, conservative): Primarily women over age 35 with incomes under $30,000, they are likely to be housewives or clericals, but their apparel spending is very low.

5. **Daddy's Dollars** (regular price, utility, novelty): People under age 25 of all income ranges, most likely students, belong to this group. Apparel spending is moderate.

6. **Reluctants** (regular price, utility, conservative): Primarily men, they are all ages and income ranges, although they tend to be blue-collar workers or retirees. They are infrequent shoppers and are low apparel spenders.

7. **Trendy Savers** (bargain price, utility, novelty): Primarily women age 18–45, they are in all income groups and are likely to be clericals, housewives, or students. Their apparel spending is low.

8. **Make-Do Shoppers** (bargain price, utility, conservative): Middle-aged and middle-income people, they are likely to have family responsibilities. All occupations are represented, but especially the skilled trades. Apparel spending is very low.

Source: Rebecca C. Quarles, "Shopping Centers Use Fashion Lifestyle Research to Make Marketing Decisions," *Marketing News* (January 22, 1982), Section 1, p. 18. Reprinted by permission of The American Marketing Association.

- The de-emphasis of material possessions has resulted in the popularity of jeans and army jackets among the young.
- Mysticism and romanticism have caused the success of movies such as *Star Wars* and *Rocky* and the growth of specialty stores.
- The interest in self-improvement has made adult education and travel popular.
- The attainment of individuality explains the success of diverse product selections (e.g., hair styles, automobile models, watch styles, etc.).

The interest in self-fulfillment will continue to expand in the future, and the examples cited in the preceding list only touch the surface of possibilities for future-oriented retailers.

Figure 17-2 contains an illustration of life-style analysis. In this figure, apparel retailers are shown how the consumer market can be divided into eight market segments on the basis of life-style factors. A different retail strategy is required for each segment.

Consumerism and the Regulatory Environment

Consumerism is defined as the

> activities of government, business, and independent organizations that are designed to protect individuals from practices that infringe upon their rights as consumers.[18]

and as

> a social force within the environment designed to aid and protect the consumer by exerting legal, moral, and economic pressure on business.[19]

Both definitions focus on the fact that consumers have rights and that these rights should be protected by government, business, and independent organizations. As enunciated by President Kennedy in 1962, consumers have the right to safety (protection against hazardous goods), the right to be informed (protection against fraudulent, deceptive, or misleading information, advertising, and labeling), the right to choose (access to a variety of products and services), and the right to be heard (participation of consumers in the formulation of company and government policy).

There are a number of reasons why retailers need to avoid deceptive or potentially dangerous business practices, and why they should do all they can to understand and protect consumer rights:

- Since retailing is so competitive, consumers will be likely to patronize firms that are perceived as "customer-oriented" and not shop with those perceived as "greedy."
- Consumers are becoming more knowledgeable, selective, and affluent than those of the past; and this trend is continuing. Therefore, retailers must offer good value, provide detailed information, and be prepared to handle questions and complaints.

[18]George S. Day and David A. Aaker, "A Guide to Consumerism," *Journal of Marketing*, Vol. 34 (July 1970), p. 12.
[19]David W. Cravens and Gerald E. Hills, "Consumerism: A Perspective for Business," *Business Horizons*, Vol. 13 (August 1970), p. 24.

- When inflation is high, consumers become quite price conscious. The popularity of off-price retailing is also heightening consumer awareness of prices.
- Large retailers are sometimes perceived as indifferent to consumers. They may not provide enough personal attention for shoppers or have inadequate control over employees (resulting in poor practices and a lack of uniformity from one branch outlet to the next).
- The use of self-service is increasing, and it can cause confusion and frustration for consumers.
- The rise in new technology is unsettling to many consumers, who must learn new shopping behavior (e.g., automatic teller machines).
- Because retailers are in direct contact with consumers, they are frequently blamed for and asked to resolve problems actually caused by manufacturers (such as defective products and unclear operating instructions). Retailers need to be able to balance the interests of their suppliers and their customers. In addition, retailers can pass along safety, information, and other recommendations to manufacturers.

Accordingly, several retailers have developed and implemented programs to protect consumer rights without waiting for government or consumer pressure to do so. Following are examples of these actions.

J. C. Penney adopted the "Penney Idea" in 1913 and still adheres to its seven basic concepts: "to serve the public, as nearly as we can, to its complete satisfaction; to expect for the service we render a fair remuneration and not all the profit the traffic will bear; to do all in our power to pack the customer's dollar full of value, quality, and satisfaction; to continue to train ourselves and our associates so that the service we give will be more and more intelligently performed; to improve constantly the human factor in our business; to reward men and women in our organization through participation in what the business produces; and to test our every policy, method, and act in this way—'Does it square with what is right and just?'"[20]

During the 1970s, Giant Food hired Esther Peterson (formerly President Johnson's special consumer-affairs assistant) at a rank equivalent to vice-president. Mrs. Peterson headed the firm's efforts to get the management of Giant Food and consumer leaders to work together for their mutual benefit.

Giant Food then developed a consumer's bill of rights, fashioned after President Kennedy's:

1. Right to safety—The presence of phosphates in laundry products led to the development of an ecologically acceptable detergent under the Giant Food label; "hard pesticides" were removed from the store; toys unable to meet federal standards of safety were not carried; toys were age labeled.
2. Right to be informed—A better labeling system was instituted; comments on issues affecting consumers and food retailers were developed; unit pricing, open dating, and nutritional labeling were implemented.
3. Right to choose—Consumers who wanted to purchase harmful or hazardous products could do so (e.g., cigarettes, foods with additives).
4. Right to be heard—A continuing dialogue with reputable consumer groups was established.

[20]J. C. Penney.

5. Right to redress—A money-back guarantee policy on all products was implemented.
6. Right to service—Customers were to expect and receive store services.[21]

A number of retailers have voluntarily enacted product-testing programs. Products are tested for value, quality, misrepresentation of contents, and durability before they are placed on sale. Among the retailers involved in product testing are Sears, J. C. Penney, A&P, Macy's, Target Stores, Montgomery Ward, and Giant Food. See Figure 17-3.

A great many retailers now have formal consumer-affairs departments. The department usually follows one of several forms: standing committee with representatives from each retail department (T. Eaton of Canada); expert advisory committee with representatives from manufacturers, government, and consumers (Giant Food); consumer advisory board consisting of several consumer and company executives (Stop & Shop); and dialogue sessions with small groups of students, community newcomers, and others (United Banks of Colorado).[22]

Other consumerism programs undertaken by retailers relate to the handling of complaints, the provision of information (such as fact tags, labeling, and unit pricing), consumer education, reviewing of advertisements, product service, and the training of store personnel.

It should be noted that consumer-oriented programs are not limited to large retail chains; small retailers can also be involved. For example, John and Janice Shuster own one supermarket (Ideal Super Foods) in Laramie, Wyoming, a city with a population of 35,000 and Safeway and Albertson's outlets. Ideal Super Foods has a full-time, in-store home economist and uses an eighteen-member consumer panel. Each year, Ideal conducts three educational programs through its panel that involve learning about and responding to community concerns.[23]

After considerable government legislation in the 1960s and 1970s to protect consumer rights, consumerism is now in a period of maturity. Major federal consumer legislation will not be forthcoming in the near future. Congress is more interested in self-regulation by business than in new legislation; and federal agencies are encouraging greater voluntary actions on the part of business. In addition, because many firms have done a good job in responding to consumer issues, the American public will be more concerned with resource shortages, inflation, industrial productivity, and jobs than consumerism. Finally, consumer groups will be consolidating the gains made during the 1960s and 1970s rather than emphasizing new issues.[24]

Deregulation of industries will continue throughout the 1980s and 1990s. In particular, banks, communications companies, professions, transportation firms, and insurance companies will face more competitive environments. Laws affecting retail prac-

[21]Adapted from Esther Peterson, "Consumerism as a Retailer's Asset," *Harvard Business Review*, Vol. 52 (May–June 1974), pp. 91–92ff. See also "Speaking Out for Consumers," *Chain Store Age Supermarkets Edition* (December 1981), p. 54; and Mary Johnson, "A Giant Step Toward Consumer Protection," *Progressive Grocer* (August 1983), p. 21.
[22]Adapted from Leonard L. Berry, James S. Hensel, and Marion C. Burke, "Improving Retailer Capability for Effective Consumerism Response," *Journal of Retailing*, Vol. 52 (Fall 1976), pp. 3–14ff.
[23]Mary Johnson, "The New Consumer Advocate: Supermarkets," *Progressive Grocer* (January 1983), pp. 83–88.
[24]Paul N. Bloom and Stephen A. Greyser, "The Maturing of Consumerism," *Harvard Business Review*, Vol. 59 (November–December 1981), pp. 130–139.

Voluntary Product Testing at Target Stores

Target's Responsibility

At Target, toys are an important part of our business. We want the toys you buy to meet Target's and the U.S. Government's high standards of quality, value and safety. Therefore, we abide by all U.S. Consumer Product Safety Regulations. Target also utilizes an independent testing agency. They test samples of all toys we sell to help ensure your child's safe play.

All toys sold at Target are tested to be certain they are free from these dangers:

Sharp edges

Toys of brittle plastic or glass can be broken to expose cutting edges. Poorly made metal or wood toys may have sharp edges.

Small parts

Tiny toys and toys with removable parts can be swallowed or lodged in child's windpipe, ears or nose.

Loud noises

Noise making guns and other toys can produce sounds at noise levels that can damage hearing.

Sharp points

Broken toys can expose dangerous points. Stuffed toys can have barbed eyes or wired limbs that can cut.

Propelled objects

Projectiles and similar flying toys can injure eyes in particular. Arrows or darts should have protective soft tips.

Electrical Shock

Electrically operated toys that are improperly constructed can shock or cause burns. Electric toys must meet mandatory safety requirements.

Wrong toys for the wrong age

Toys that may be safe for older children can be dangerous when played with by little ones.

Courtesy Target Stores.

Figure 17-3

tices such as pricing, merchandise assortment, and store hours will also be loosened in the future.

To succeed in this deregulated environment, retailers will need to be innovative, responsive to consumer needs, flexible, and responsible. Strategies resulting in deceptive practices, price wars, or defamatory criticism of competitors will not be effective. They will motivate consumers to select the most efficient and reputable retailers.

Technology

The 1980s and 1990s will see many major technological changes. The new technology most affecting retailers will center on electronic banking, video-ordering systems, and computerization of operations.

Electronic Banking

Electronic banking involves the use of automatic teller machines (ATMs) and the instant processing of retail purchases. It provides centralized record-keeping and allows customers to complete transactions 24 hours a day, seven days a week at a variety of bank and nonbank locations (such as supermarkets).[25] In addition to bank transactions (deposits, withdrawals, and transfers), electronic banking will increasingly be used in retailing; the purchase price of a product would be automatically deducted from a customer's bank account and entered into the retailer's account without cash changing hands by using an appropriate computer terminal. See Figure 17-4.

At present, there are about 60,000 automatic teller machines in use in the United States. They are located in banks, shopping centers, department stores, airports, and a host of other sites. For example, by the end of 1986, virtually all 7,400 7-Eleven stores will have ATMs; this will enable customers to make cash payments for purchases. There are over 200 regional and national ATM networks, such as Cirrus. These networks allow consumers to make transactions at ATMs outside their local area.[26]

In the future, many banks and other retailers will rely on **debit-only transfer systems,** whereby purchase prices are immediately charged against a buyer's account. This is quite different from regular credit cards that rely on end-of-month billings (with no interest charges if payments are made promptly). With debit cards, delayed billing carries interest charges from the day of purchase. As of 1983, about 5 million Visa and MasterCard debit cards and over 50 million bank debit cards had been issued. In 1984, debit card sales volume was estimated at $4 billion, up from $2 billion during 1982.[27]

Although some retailing experts believe that individual-store credit cards and accounts will be eliminated by the year 2000 because of the implementation of a centralized, nationwide credit and banking system, consumers have been more reluctant to accept the concept of the electronic transfer of funds. Some consumers fear the loss of canceled checks; others prefer to deal with humans rather than machines; still others are concerned about the possibility of computer error or the invasion of privacy. Similarly, many retailers feel that they will lose their identities if store credit cards are used less frequently.

[25]Joel R. Evans and Barry Berman, *Marketing*, Second Edition (New York: Macmillan, 1985), p. 756. See also David P. Schulz, "EFTS Status Report," *Stores* (March 1985), pp. 61–63.

[26]Daniel Hertzberg, "If Carrots Don't Persuade People to Use ATMs, Banks Go for Sticks," *Wall Street Journal* (February 21, 1985), p. 35; Tom Bayer, "Southland Tests New Market Directions," *Advertising Age* (December 3, 1984), p. 93; Daniel Hertzberg, "Banks Linking Cash Machines Across the U.S.," *Wall Street Journal* (November 16, 1983), pp. 33, 38; and Steve Weiner and Hank Gilman, "Debate Grows on Retailers' Bank Services," *Wall Street Journal* (May 18, 1984), p. 29.

[27]Thomas P. Fitch, "Who Pays?" *Stores* (October 1983), pp. 41–54ff.

Figure 17-4   Electronic Banking

One of the hundreds of Citicard Banking Centers now in operation. These Centers can process all types of consumer transactions, from check deposits to cash withdrawals. Reprinted by permission of Citibank.

These are some of the ramifications of the growth in electronic banking:

- More stores will have to accept credit cards other than their own store cards.
- Store operating expenses will be reduced. Collection, bad debts, and so on will not be retailer problems.
- Store loyalty will be reduced because cards will be accepted in a number of stores and not just in those originally granting the cards.
- Banking operations will occur in more nonbank settings, such as supermarkets and department stores.
- Bank personnel will be decreased.
- Banking services will be available 24 hours per day, seven days a week.

Video-Ordering Systems

A substantial number of retailers believe that the spread of cable television and video catalogs will have a revolutionary effect on sales and promotional methods. Because cable television (CATV) is expected to grow from usage in 20 per cent of U.S. households in 1980 to 50 to 60 per cent by 1990, its influence will be large. Similarly, by 1990, over 25 per cent of U.S. households will own videocassette and/or videodisc players, up from 2 per cent in 1980. By 1990, up to 25 per cent of households will have interactive communications capabilities through their home computers. As a result, one study predicts that video shopping will reach $50 billion in annual sales by 1995.[28]

Many retailers will expand their use of video shopping for several reasons:

* Inventory needs are lowered (stock can be obtained as orders come in).
* Investment costs are reduced (e.g., no need for an expensive store location or displays).
* Less personnel are needed.
* The geographic trading area can be expanded.
* Efforts can be targeted to specific groups.
* Ordering can be completed 24 hours per day, seven days a week.

Video-ordering systems will open the way for nonstore selling on a massive scale. All the consumer will have to do is turn on his or her television, request to see a product or service, and immediately contact the retail store or its warehouse. Convenience and staple items will be more readily adaptable than most other types of products to a highly centralized, mechanized computer-distribution technique.

A video-ordering system will work as follows.[29] First, the consumer views a videotex service on cable television. A **videotex service** is a television channel that displays graphic and pictorial representations of products and services with accompanying text descriptions and ordering information. Second, the consumer orders by punching a product code number into a home computer console and indicating the quantity desired. Regular repeat purchases are made through a special code number, programmed especially for the consumer. Weekly specials are shown on a teleshopper screen. It is possible for a consumer to complete all purchases in 10 to 15 minutes. Third, a computer records and interprets the order, schedules delivery, and posts transactions in a checkless account. This system provides consumers with convenience because waiting lines, traffic jams, and parking problems are avoided. See Figure 17-5.

Retailers are also beginning to experiment with video catalogs, which reproduce printed shopping catalogs on videocassettes or videodiscs. In-home shoppers watch the catalogs on their television sets and then telephone orders. In-store shoppers view the catalogs on display terminals and then write orders or place them with store personnel.

[28]Watson S. "Jay" James, "The New Electronic Media: An Overview," *Journal of Advertising Research*, Vol. 23 (September 1983), pp. 33–37; "25% of Homes to Get Videotex by '90: Delphi Panel," *Marketing News* (November 9, 1984), p. 6; and Bill Abrams, "Electronic Shopping Is Called Imminent, but Doubts Persist," *Wall Street Journal* (June 23, 1983), p. 33.

[29]See "Electronic Retailing Enters the Realm of Reality," *Chain Store Age Executive* (October 1983), pp. 37–40; Joel E. Urbany and W. Wayne Talarzyk, "Videotex: Implications for Retailing," *Journal of Retailing*, Vol. 59 (Fall 1983), pp. 76–92; and Stephanie Flory, "Are Shop-at-Home Services a Friend or Foe to Retailers?" *Merchandising* (June 1984), pp. 32, 34.

Here's what you need to access Viewtron on your TV set.

Actual size—
6½" x 5⁄16" x 1¾"

Sceptre
The new videotex terminal from AT&T.

Viewtron is delivered through your current home TV set and telephone line. To access Viewtron subscription service, all you need is the Sceptre terminal from AT&T.

Connecting Sceptre to your TV and telephone line is simple and easy. You can do it yourself in just minutes.

The unit comes in two parts: a control unit and a remote control keypad. All you do is connect the control unit to your TV set and telephone jack and you're ready to sit back and begin using your keypad to request information from Viewtron.

The remote control keypad is wireless, which means you can operate the terminal from anywhere in the room.

Sceptre comes with all the quality AT&T products are known for, and provides security for banking services.

Viewtron is delivered to your Sceptre terminal and home TV set via your telephone line. By pushing a few keys on your keypad, you request information and it will be instantly transmitted and displayed in full color text and graphics on your TV screen. It's that simple.

Here's how Viewtron and Sceptre work.

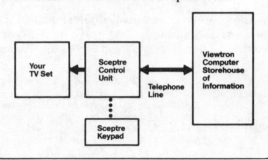

Figure 17-5 An In-Home Banking and Shopping System

Courtesy Viewdata Corporation of America, Inc.

549

Despite the long-run potential of video-shopping systems, retailers should keep these points in mind:[30]

- A relatively small percentage of the population will have both home computers and cable television by 1990.
- Access costs for consumers may limit involvement.
- Many consumers will not be interested in video shopping, preferring to go to stores.
- Expensive, complex items do not readily lend themselves to video shopping.
- Without personal selling, consumers may not trade up to higher-priced models or add options.
- Attractive in-store displays are usually more likely to generate impulse purchases.
- Image is difficult to portray through graphic representations.

Sears, WaldenBooks, American Airlines, Bloomingdale's, J. C. Penney, Saks Fifth Avenue, and Neiman-Marcus are among the retailers now participating in some type of video-ordering system.[31]

Computerization of Operations

The 1980s and 1990s will see more and more retailers computerizing their operations, as a result of improving technology, interest in productivity, and the affordability of new computer networks. In this section, computerized checkouts and electronic point-of-sale systems, computer software, and applications of computer utilization by retailers are discussed.

Computerized checkouts, used by many department stores and supermarkets, enable retailers to efficiently process transactions and maintain strict control over inventory. Generally, they are tied to an Optical Character Recognition or Universal Product Code system. Under either technique, a cashier manually rings up a sale or passes an item over or past an optical scanner. Then the computerized checkout instantly records and displays the sale, the customer is given a detailed receipt, and all inventory information is stored in the computer's memory bank.

The computerized checkout lowers costs through reductions in checkout time, employee training, misrings, and price markings on merchandise. In addition, retailers increase their efficiency because of better inventory control, reduced spoilage, and improved ordering. It is also valuable for a retailer to obtain a list of data on an item-by-item basis. This aids in determining store layout and merchandise plans, assists in establishing the amount of shelf space per item, and allows inventory to be replenished automatically.

There are two potential problems with the computerized checkout. First, customers may be unable to read prices on packages, if they are only posted on shelves. Because of this, several states have enacted laws making the placing of prices on in-

[30]See Bernie Whalen, "Acute Growing Pains Stifle Progress of Videotex Industry," *Marketing News* (November 25, 1983), Section 1, pp. 15–16; Jac L. Goldstucker, Thomas J. Stanley, and George P. Moschis, "How Consumer Acceptance of Videotex Services Might Affect Consumer Marketing," in Russell W. Belk et al. (Editors), *1984 AMA Educators' Proceedings* (Chicago: American Marketing Association, 1984), pp. 200–204; and Mike Connelly, "Knight-Ridder's Cutbacks at Viewtron Show Videotex Revolution Is Faltering," *Wall Street Journal* (November 2, 1984), p. 43.
[31]"CompuServe Unveils the 'Electronic Mall'," *Marketing News* (November 9, 1984), p. 3.

dividual packages mandatory. Additional states are considering legislation in this area. Second, the existence of both the Universal Product Code and the Optical Character Recognition systems, instead of a single code, will hurt manufacturers who sell through dual distribution channels.

Growing numbers of retailers are expanding beyond computerized checkouts to **electronic point-of-sale systems** which verify check and charge transactions, provide instantaneous sales reports, monitor and change prices, send intrastore messages, evaluate personnel and profitability, and store information. In most cases, point-of-sales systems are used in conjunction with a firm's retail information system.[32]

A variety of computer software firms are now developing packages tailored for retailers' use, as these examples show:[33]

- MTS (Minding the Store) software automates merchandise ordering, receiving, and pricing; and aids in merchandise planning, distribution, and open-to-buy calculations for small to medium-sized retailers.
- FSMA (Food Service Management Applications) software is used by restaurants to control food and inventory costs, process payrolls, and maintain accounting records.
- SIM (Store Item Management) software enables retailers to reorder merchandise, forecast sales, allocate inventory, control store deliveries, and so on.

Each of the preceding software packages costs about $1,000 to $1,200 and may be operated on an IBM PC. The National Retail Merchants Association has also published a directory listing almost 400 such packages.

Following are several illustrations of how retailers are developing uses of computers to upgrade operations:

- Capital Marine Supply in Baton Rouge, Louisiana, employs a Honeywell minicomputer system. "The core of the system is the inventory master file which permits you to see a current status report of any given item you have in your inventory. It tells you such things as the product's location, receipts to date, usages to date, current average cost, the retail valuation, markup, retail price, and currently owned quantities."[34]
- Super Valu has developed a computer-assisted design (CAD) program to aid its affiliated supermarkets in constructing or remodeling stores. CAD allows planners to draw and modify plans on computer monitors. "Eventually, we should be able to walk a retailer through a three-dimensional, full-color reproduction of his store. It's unlimited. You could never go back."[35]
- Dayton Hudson uses MCI Electronic Mail to speed external and internal transactions. Messages are transmitted over telephone lines and then laser printed in one of eighteen centers nationwide, or directly communicated with a receiver having the

---

[32]See Jules Abend, "Computer Uses," *Stores* (January 1983), pp. 83–90; and Saul Sands and Terry Guylay, "Supermarket Scanners: A Marketing Tool for the Eighties," *Business*, Vol. 34 (April–June 1984), pp. 12–15.
[33]"Software for Retailers Covers All the Bases," *Chain Store Age Executive* (February 1985), pp. 62–71; and "Roster of Retail-Oriented Programs Increases," *Chain Store Age Executive* (August 1984), pp. 71–75.
[34]"Keeping Inventory in Tow at Capital Marine Supply," *Chain Store Age Executive* (November 1984), pp. 66, 68.
[35]Robert E. O'Neill, "The Store Designer's New Best Friend," *Progressive Grocer* (October 1984), pp. 83–84ff.

Figure 17-6 An IBM Point-of-Sale System

The IBM 3680 Programmable Store System is a store-level terminal system
for small stores with a single point-of-sale station, as well as for larger establishments with multiple stations. It can collect data for processing in the
store in conjunction with an IBM host computer. Reprinted by permission
of International Business Machines Corporation.

Figure 17-7 A Giant Food Point-of-Sale System

Innovative supermarket chains, such as Giant Food, are using sophisticated point-of-sale systems that incorporate price scanning, weighing of produce, visual alphanumeric readouts, and
inventory control. Courtesy Giant Food.

required equipment. In the latter instance, a five-page letter can be transmitted in less than one minute for about $1.[36]

• Coupons a la Carte (CALC) has created an electronic, in-store coupon-distribution system which it installed in 240 New Jersey supermarkets in early 1985. The supermarkets include Acme, A&P, Grand Union, Shop Rite, and Pathmark outlets. CALC's machine features a video display offering coupons for up to thirty-two products. It is hooked up to a central computer and requires that consumers use a special card to activate it. The system reduces misredemptions and inefficiencies due to low responses to direct mail and other ads.[37]

Computers can either stand alone (the "intelligent" type) or be integrated with an in-store minicomputer. In both systems, keyboards, printers, scanners, wands, and screens can be utilized as needed by the retailer. See Figures 17-6 and 17-7 for examples of in-store computer systems.

Retail Institutions

The changes in demographics, life-styles, consumerism, the regulatory environment, and technology will undoubtedly have an impact on the nature of retail institutions. In addition, many retailers believe that profit margins are shrinking, as a result of intense competition and high costs. This shrinkage puts pressure on stores to tighten internal cost controls and to promote higher margin products and services while eliminating unprofitable items. Also, many retailers recognize that strategies must be modified as their retail institutions evolve over time.

In order to make sure that their organizations will be managed properly throughout the 1980s and 1990s, greater numbers of retailers will be hiring different types of people as executives than in the past. A recent study of the largest U.S. food retailers yielded these findings:

• The 1980s and 1990s manager "will oversee a store with more customers, higher sales volume, greater product diversity, and more capital investment. Managing this store will involve less of a hands-on approach with more attention given to delegation and management by exception."

• New responsibilities will include "building and maintaining a strong sense of the company's values and beliefs in store personnel, using automated information systems to develop plans and monitor results, and adapting the store's merchandise and services to its local customer base."

• In 1990, 42 per cent of potential supermarket managers will be recruited from college into a training program and rapidly moved from assistant to store manager, compared with 6 per cent in 1983. There will be much more analytical training and emphasis on teaching leadership skills.

• Better defined and attainable career paths will be needed, along with financial incentives. Authority will be more decentralized down to the store level.[38]

---

[36]Joyce A. Oliver, "Networking!" *Stores* (October 1984), pp. 35–38ff.
[37]Paul L. Edwards, "In-Store Coupon Machines Hit N.Y.," *Advertising Age* (February 14, 1985), p. 6.
[38]"Manager Challenges for 1985 and Beyond," *Progressive Grocer* (January 1985), pp. 22, 24.

Retail institutions will respond to the environment of the 1980s and 1990s through nonstore retailing, risk minimization, mass merchandising, positioned retailing, diversification and mergers, and adaptation strategies.

Nonstore Retailing

As indicated in Chapter 4, nonstore retailing, with sales of $174 billion in 1983, represents a major dimension of retailing. With the rapidly improving technology of video equipment, described earlier in this chapter, nonstore retailing promises to undergo large expansion in the 1980s and 1990s.

Nonstore retailing will enable firms to reduce personnel staff and costs, locate in less-costly sites, maintain low inventories, and appeal to specific target audiences. The new technology in telephones, electronic mail, order-processing equipment, and truck routing, as well as video equipment, will allow firms to reduce costs per transaction, speed up deliveries, and appeal to wider geographic markets.[39] Illustrations of advances in nonstore retailing follow.

Comp-U-Card is a computerized in-home shopping service that was begun in 1973. Today, Comp-U-Card has 1.5 million members who pay an annual fee of $25 to utilize the company's data bank. The data bank contains product specifications and prices on more than 60,000 products. Shoppers buying through Comp-U-Card receive discounts of 20 to 50 per cent over prices in typical retail stores. The company earns a 3 to 5 per cent commission on these sales. With the present system, subscribers receive information on their computer monitors (no graphics are displayed) and then order merchandise via the telephone or through their computers using a modem.[40]

At J. C. Penney in Kansas City, Missouri, there are well over 12,000 catalog customers. During peak hours, 7:30 A.M. to 9 P.M., Penney has twenty-seven telephone operators on duty to handle orders (at Christmas, this number rises to sixty). Throughout nonpeak hours, 9 P.M. to 7:30 A.M., Penney utilizes two dictaphone terminals, which are sophisticated enough to engage in back-and-forth conversations. Through its system, Penney then contacts customers to inform them when orders are ready.[41]

Risk-Minimization Retailing

Retailers will be more interested in limiting risks in the future. **Risk-minimization retailing** involves reductions in both initial investment costs and costs of operation.[42] In the future, risk minimization will be necessary for some retailers because of the rising number of off-price firms, the need to control complicated chain or franchise operations, higher investment costs (for land, construction, etc.), the volatility of the environment, and the interest in maximizing productivity.

[39]See "Direct Marketing," *Advertising Age* (January 18, 1982), Section 2; John A. Quelch and Hirotaka Takeuchi, "Nonstore Marketing: Fast Tracks or Slow?" *Harvard Business Review*, Vol. 59 (July–August 1981), pp. 75–84; and *Direct Marketing*, monthly.
[40]"The Computer as Retailer," *New York Times* (January 9, 1981), pp. D1, D4; Theodore Gage, "Two-Way TV Screening Out the Bugs," *Advertising Age* (January 18, 1982), Section 2, p. S-2; and Jeanne Saddler, "Computer Users Shop at Home over the Phone," *Wall Street Journal* (February 20, 1985), p. 35.
[41]"Teleshopping: The Future Is Now!" *Stores* (September 1980), pp. 71–72.
[42]Albert D. Bates, "The Troubled Future of Retailing," *Business Horizons*, Vol. 19 (August 1976), pp. 22–28.

Risk-minimization retailing can be accomplished through a combination of retail mix components:

- Emphasizing secondary locations, free-standing units, locations in older strip centers; occupying abandoned supermarkets or discount department stores (second-use locations).
- Moving to smaller towns where building restrictions are less stringent, labor costs are lower, and construction and operating costs are reduced.
- Using inexpensive construction materials, such as exposed rafters, bare cinder-block walls, and concrete floors.
- Using spartan fixtures and low-cost displays.
- Buying used equipment.
- Joining cooperative buying and advertising groups.
- Encouraging manufacturers to finance inventories.

Currently, a number of firms have risk-minimization strategies in their small-town stores. These include Dollar General (variety stores), Bi-Lo (food), Pamada (discount department stores), and Kentucky Fried Chicken.

In conjunction with risk minimization, some retailers are also turning to **rationalized retailing** programs that involve a high degree of centralized management control combined with rigorous operating procedures for each phase of business.[43] Each aspect of the company's operations is performed in an identical manner in every store outlet. Rigid control and standardization make this technique an easy one to implement and manage. In addition, a firm can add a significant number of units in a relatively short time period.

Radio Shack (part of the Tandy Corporation) and Toys 'R' Us are examples of firms applying rationalized retailing. Each of their stores is similar in size, the number of items carried, store layout, merchandising, and sales approaches.

In the future, rationalized retailing will increase and lead to more centralized management, sophisticated supplier evaluation programs, and formalized, computerized buying plans. Prototype stores will be particularly popular.[44]

Mass Merchandising

Mass merchandising involves retailers presenting a discount image, handling several merchandise lines, and having 10,000 square feet or more of floor space. In 1983, there were nearly 7,000 traditional mass merchandising outlets (discount stores, combination stores, superstores, and warehouse outlets). Retailers with 40 or more outlets own well over 80 per cent of all stores in this category.[45]

Because mass merchants have relatively low operating costs, achieve economies in operations, and appeal to price-conscious consumers, their continuing popularity is forecasted. The sales for traditional mass merchandisers are expected to remain level,

---

[43]Ibid.

[44]See "Prototypes: A Step Beyond Whimsey," *Chain Store Age Executive* (February 1985), pp. 22, 27.

[45]"A Look at Mass Merchandisers," *Nielsen Researcher* (Number 1, 1982), pp. 16–23; and H. R. Jones, "Mass Merchandisers: A Maturing Retail Concept," *Nielsen Researcher* (Number 3, 1984), pp. 14–20.

while the sales of newer forms (e.g., factory outlet malls, flea markets, and membership stores) rise:

> No matter what you call it, offering the right merchandise and with the right value is what counts. That's the name of the game.[46]

Positioned Retailing

An opposite approach to mass merchandising is **positioned retailing,** which consists of identifying a target market segment and developing a unique retail offering, designed to meet the segment's needs. The retailer positions the store for one specific segment and not the mass market. Positioning creates a high level of loyalty and shields a retailer from more conventional competitors.[47]

A good example of positioned retailing is the strategy followed by Limited Inc., a successful and growing women's apparel chain. Each of its store divisions appeals to a distinct market segment: The Limited, trendy clothes for fashion-conscious women aged 20 to 40; Limited Express, trendy clothing for women 15 to 25 years of age; Lane Bryant, Roaman's, and Sizes Unlimited, catering to full-size women; and Lerner, a budget apparel chain for young women.[48]

Positioned retailing will have a large impact in the future. It will lead some firms to nonprice competition and more specialized focusing by firms with broad target markets (such as department and discount stores), and it may force manufacturers to use multiple market-segmentation programs to meet the requirements of retailers with different market positions. The growth of boutiques, specialty stores, and compartmentalized department stores is expected to continue. And the department store concept of one-stop shopping may be changed to that of the one-stop shopping center.

Diversification and Mergers

In order to sustain or enhance sales growth, larger retailers will be turning more frequently to diversification and mergers during the 1980s and 1990s.

With diversification, retailers become active in businesses outside their normal operations. Diversification is an advanced form of scrambled merchandising, whereby distinctly new product or service categories are added. For example, K mart believed that it had reached a saturation point in traditional retailing; therefore, in order to thrive in the long run, the company decided to diversify. In 1984, K mart acquired WaldenBooks and Builders Square (formerly Home Centers of America). In 1985, it purchased Pay Less (a large discount drugstore chain) and began to expand the financial services offered in selected K mart stores (by experimenting with banks in Indiana

---

[46]"Whatever the Name, Value Is the Game," *Chain Store Age Executive* (February 1985), p. 47.

[47]See Leonard L. Berry, "Retail Positioning Strategies for the 1980s," *Business Horizons*, Vol. 25 (November–December 1982), pp. 45–50.

[48]"Limited Inc.: Expanding Its Position to Serve the Rubenesque Woman," *Business Week* (November 22, 1982), pp. 56, 58; Kathleen Deveny and Aaron Bernstein, "Limited Is Stitching Together a Fashion Empire," *Business Week* (February 25, 1985), pp. 78,80; and Cleveland Horton, "Limited Plans to Link 2 Chains," *Advertising Age* (December 17, 1984), p. 47.

stores, real-estate services in Michigan and Wisconsin stores, and consumer loan centers in Chicago outlets).[49]

Mergers involve the combination of independently owned retailers. Diversification mergers take place between retailers of different types, such as the one between K mart and WaldenBooks. Specialization mergers take place between similar types of retailers, such as two local banks. By merging, retailers hope to maximize resources, enlarge the customer base, limit weaknesses, and gain competitive advantages.

Adaptation Strategies

In response to the dynamic environment of the 1980s and 1990s, many retailers will develop adaptation strategies. Illustrations of these strategies follow.

Safeway supermarkets, the largest supermarket chain in the United States, is "going upscale" through a new Bon Appetit store concept. Its first Bon Appetit store was opened in early 1982; there are now three outlets. The Bon Appetit stores are quite different from Safeway's 2,000 other traditional supermarkets and superstores. They feature gourmet foods, a large selection of fine wine, choice meats, exotic produce items, and sizable floral departments. The Tiburon store (near San Francisco) offers 100 types of mustard, 65 vinegars, and 163 kinds of bulk cheese.[50]

Department-store strategies will focus on capital improvements for divisions showing the greatest profit and potential, expansion in the Sunbelt and Northwest, mergers, and the revival of downtown business districts. For example, in 1984, Macy's entered Houston with plans to open four stores by the end of 1986. It also scheduled new stores in various other locations throughout the United States. The Houston stores are extremely important to Macy's because total retail sales in the city almost tripled over the decade from 1975 to 1984. Macy's sees it as a real growth market.[51]

The rapid increase in the number of specialty stores selling computers means that there will be a shakeout in the future, as weaker firms close and several others merge. To be successful, computer stores must avoid price wars, carry IBM and Apple products, offer a full range of services (such as training and maintenance contracts), establish personal relationships with customers, and try to keep a satisfactory (but not excessive) inventory level.[52]

To stimulate consumer interest, some auto dealers are trying out new types of locations. For instance, Torrance Lincoln–Mercury now has a satellite dealership in the large Del Amo Fashion Center (a regional shopping center outside Los Angeles). The satellite showroom opens onto the center's main shopping aisle, is furnished like a boutique, uses soft background music, has a carpeted floor, and displays thirteen cars. As one analyst noted:

> The problem the domestic companies have, particularly here in California, is simply getting people to look at them. Shopping mall locations can be a very effective marketing technique in getting young people, in particular, to look at Detroit's products.[53]

[49]Doron P. Levin, "K mart to Buy Pay Less for $500 Million," *Wall Street Journal* (January 15, 1985), p. 7; and "K mart Says 31 Stores Will Offer a Range of Financial Services," *Wall Street Journal* (January 22, 1985), p. 42.
[50]Mary Ann Linsen, "Bon Appetit—Three Years Later," *Progressive Grocer* (February 1985), pp. 48–50.
[51]Daniel Kahn, "Shootout at the Retail Corral," *Newsday* (February 17, 1985), pp. 112, 106.
[52]David E. Sanger, "Shakeout in Computer Stores," *New York Times* (October 2, 1984), pp. D1, D10.
[53]John Holusha, "Shopping Mall Car Dealers," *New York Times* (January 26, 1985), pp. 31–32.

The International Environment of Retailing

The international environment of retailing encompasses both U.S. firms expanding into foreign markets and foreign retailers expanding into U.S. markets. In the future, more and more retailers will become international in scope, continuing the strong recent trend.

Opportunities and Risks in International Retailing

There are wide-ranging opportunities and risks in international retailing.

International retailing opportunities may exist for several reasons. One, foreign markets may represent better growth opportunities. Two, domestic markets may be saturated or stagnant. Three, the retailer may be able to offer products, services, or technology not yet available in foreign markets. Four, competition may be less in foreign markets. Five, foreign markets may be used to supplement, not replace, domestic sales. Six, there may be tax or investment advantages in foreign markets.

International retailing risks may also exist for several reasons. One, there may be cultural differences between domestic and foreign markets. Two, management styles may not be easily adaptable. Three, foreign governments may place heavy restrictions on operations. Four, personal income may be poorly distributed among consumers in foreign markets. Five, distribution systems may be inadequate (e.g., poor roads, lack of refrigeration, etc.).

In developing international strategies, retailers must pay particular attention to the concept of **standardization.** Can the strategy followed in the domestic market be standardized and directly applied to foreign markets; or, do personnel, physical structure of outlets, advertising, product lines, and other factors have to be adapted to local conditions and needs? For example, a study of store pricing behavior found that 63 per cent of the stores in India permitted bargaining, compared with 11.9 per cent in Brazil and 3.4 per cent in the People's Republic of China.[54]

U.S. Retailers and Foreign Markets

Many U.S. retailers are looking for sales and profit growth by expanding further into foreign markets. Southland, Safeway, Kentucky Fried Chicken, Jewel, and Sears are examples of U.S. retailers with high involvement in foreign markets.

Southland Corporation introduced the convenience store to Japan through its 7-Eleven stores in 1972. It offered operators of Japanese outlets inventory, financing, low-cost loans, partial payments for electricity, and name recognition. From fifteen Japanese stores in 1975, 7-Eleven reached 2,000 outlets in 1984; its leading competitor has about 800 stores. Its gross profit is over 27 per cent of sales. In addition to Japan,

[54]Laurence Jacobs, Reginald Worthley, and Charles Keown, "Perceived Buyer Satisfaction and Selling Pressure Versus Pricing Policy: A Comparative Study of Retailers in Ten Developing Countries," *Journal of Business Research*, Vol. 12 (March 1984), pp. 63–74.

Figure 17-8   Kentucky Fried Chicken in Seoul, South Korea

The exteriors of Kentucky Fried Chicken outlets in Seoul, South Korea combine the familiar company logo with Korean lettering in signs. Courtesy Kentucky Fried Chicken.

there are 7-Eleven outlets in Mexico, Sweden, Hong Kong, Taiwan, Australia, and Canada.[55]

Safeway has stores in Great Britain, Canada, Australia, West Germany, Saudi Arabia, Kuwait, Oman, Mexico, and other countries around the world. These markets are crucial to the company because of the higher profit margins supermarkets earn there. Overall foreign sales are about 25 per cent of company sales, but they contribute 52 per cent of net income. Canada alone accounts for 15 per cent of Safeway's sales and 32 per cent of its income.[56]

Kentucky Fried Chicken recently entered Switzerland, stating: "There's a real market for KFC here provided we can get across to people the fact that this is fast-food with a difference, not just another hamburger operation." It is also planning to have twenty-five restaurants in South Korea in time for the 1988 Summer Olympics.[57] Figure 17-8 shows a KFC outlet in Seoul, South Korea.

Jewel is a Chicago-based supermarket chain (recently merged into American Stores)

[55]Susan Chira, "7-Eleven Stores Find Favor with Japanese," *New York Times* (December 24, 1984), pp. 33, 36; and Valerie Mackie and Coleen Garaghty, "Southland Bid for Worldwide 7-11 Growth," *Advertising Age* (November 21, 1983), pp. 42, 44.
[56]Howard Sharman, "Safeway Holds U.K. Expansion Course," *Advertising Age* (September 5, 1983), pp. 32, 34.
[57]Bruce Vandervort, "KFC Wooing the Swiss Family," *Advertising Age* (January 25, 1982), p. 64; and Scott Hume, "U.S. Fast-Food Giants Moving In on France," *Advertising Age* (October 22, 1984), p. 54.

that owns about 40 per cent of Aurrera, Mexico's largest retailer. As a country, Mexico is undergoing rapid industrial and financial growth. Jewel has applied its retailing techniques to Aurrera, including point-of-sales displays, refrigerated meat counters, generics, professional management, and computerized financial controls.[58]

One of Japan's largest department stores, Seibu, is affiliated with Sears. Seibu is trying to expand its direct marketing sales by following some of Sears' techniques: "In the past Japanese catalogs were strictly commercial (merely listing the goods available and their prices), but we looked closely at Sears, which offers lots of information about the goods, and modeled our catalog after that. Our information catalog is now a major selling point." As a result, direct marketing yields almost 3 per cent of Seibu's total sales, in a country where less than 1 per cent of retail sales are made through direct marketing.[59]

Foreign Retailers and the U.S. Market

A large number of foreign retailers have entered the United States in order to appeal to the world's most affluent mass market. For example, in late 1984, Bigg's "hypermarket," a 90 per cent French-owned store, opened in Cincinnati, Ohio. Bigg's is a 200,000-square-foot combination discount grocery/department store with 40 checkout counters and 60,000 items in stock. The hypermarket concept originated in France, but as a Bigg's spokesperson stated: "Hypermarkets are popular all over the world. Consumers are the same everywhere. Americans are no different, so we're bringing them a new way of shopping."[60]

The following are some of the foreign companies having major ownership interests in American retailers:[61]

- Wienerwald of Switzerland, which owns Lums restaurants, International House of Pancakes (IHOP), Love's Wood Pit Barbeque restaurants, Copper Penny restaurants, and Ranch House restaurants.
- Tengelmann of Germany, which owns a majority interest in A&P.
- Imasco of Canada, which owns Hardee's fast-food restaurants, Shoppers Drug Mart, and Tinderbox tobacco stores.
- Hugo Mann of Germany, which owns Fed-Mart discount stores and supermarkets.

[58]"Jewel Cos.: Scoring in Mexico with U.S. Supermarket Techniques," *Business Week* (October 22, 1979), pp. 120–122.
[59]Terry Trucco, "Catalogs Gain with Changing Japan Shopper," *Advertising Age* (November 28, 1983), pp. M-32, M-34.
[60]Wendy Kimbrell, "French Superstore Opens in U.S.," *Advertising Age* (October 8, 1984), p. 60; Steven Greenhouse, " 'Hypermarkets' Come to U.S.," *New York Times* (February 7, 1985), pp. D1, D2; and Robert E. O'Neill, "Today Cincinnati, Tomorrow?" *Progressive Grocer* (December 1984), pp. 20–22.
[61]See Robert Ball, "Europe's U.S. Shopping Spree," *Fortune* (December 1, 1980), pp. 82–88; "Fast-Food Exec in U.S. Spree," *Advertising Age* (December 15, 1981), Section 2, p. S-7; Jennifer Pendleton, "IHOP Tests Conversion to Wienerwald," *Advertising Age* (February 1, 1982), p. 64; "A&P's Earnings from Lines Rose 22% in 1st Period," *Business Week* (July 12, 1984), p. 8; Tony Thompson, "Imasco Gaining Experience in U.S. Retailing," *Advertising Age* (November 30, 1981), pp. 4, 66; William Harris, "German Persuasion," *Forbes* (June 23, 1980), pp. 102–104; "Putting Some Pizazz into Marshall Field's," *Business Week* (August 22, 1983), pp. 87, 89; and John Tagliabue, "Secretive Brenninkmeyers," *New York Times* (September 5, 1983), p. 33.

- BAT Industries, a British conglomerate which owns Saks Fifth Avenue, Marshall Field, and Gimbel's.
- Brenninkmeyers, a West German/Netherlands firm which owns Ohrbach's, Kreeger & Sons, Miller's, and other U.S. retailers.

The Changing Environment of Retailing: A Summary

Many environmental trends will occur in the future, and these will have a strong impact on retailing. A far-sighted retailer must study demographic, life-style, consumerism, regulatory, technological, and institutional trends and adapt the retail mix to these trends.

Population forecasts show a low growth rate, a population increase of 40 million people between 1980 and 2000, and the importance of firstborn babies, later first marriages, and older consumer groups. Other important demographic trends are growth in the number of households (because of increases in one-person households), mobility, suburban communities, the number of working women, and the number of higher-income families.

Life-style trends will include different and expanding roles for women and increased consumer sophistication and confidence. Some consumers will experience a poverty of time and will seek convenience in shopping; other consumers will have greater amounts of leisure time and will purchase more entertainment and recreation products. In addition, consumers will be increasingly concerned with self-fulfillment.

Consumerism activities (those practices designed to protect consumer rights) have reached a level of maturity. Consumer groups will consolidate the gains they have made to ensure the consumer rights of safety, information, choice, and participation. Many retailers have already implemented voluntary plans to aid consumers. Government will also stress self-regulation and a deregulated environment.

The major technological trends will be concentrated in electronic banking (cashless transactions and debit cards), video-ordering systems (consumers ordering products from their homes after seeing them on television or video players), and computerization of operations (through computerized checkouts, point-of-sale systems, and other applications).

Retail institutional changes will occur because of the evolving environmental changes. In particular, nonstore retailing, risk minimization, mass merchandising, positioned retailing, diversification and mergers, and adaptation strategies will continue throughout the 1980s and 1990s.

International retailing, both U.S. firms in foreign markets and foreign firms in U.S. markets, will grow in the future. Opportunities and risks need to be evaluated, as well as the applicability of standardization.

Questions for Discussion

1. What impact will the change in age composition have on retailers?
2. If you operated a store in a central business district, how would you react to the statistics showing population movement to the suburbs?
3. Why will working women shop differently and select different merchandise than housewives?

4. Explain the concepts of poverty of time and increased leisure time.
5. How will consumer sophistication and confidence affect retailers? Will they affect all types of retailers? Explain your answer.
6. Will deregulation succeed? Why or why not? Take both a consumer's and retailer's perspective.
7. What are the pros and cons of debit-only transfer systems?
8. Will the time come when all consumer purchases are made through some form of video-ordering system? Explain your answer.
9. Distinguish between computerized checkouts and electronic point-of-sale systems.
10. What types of nonstore retailing will *not* grow in the future? Why?
11. Describe the advantages and disadvantages of rationalized retailing.
12. Differentiate between mass merchandising and positioned retailing. Give a current example of each.
13. How could a standardized strategy on the part of a U.S. retailer fail when introduced into Canada, a country with many similarities to the United States?
14. What are the opportunities and risks facing Kentucky Fried Chicken as it opens restaurants in South Korea in time for the 1988 Summer Olympics?
15. Why have so many foreign-based firms done well in retailing in the United States?

CASES

1. Dexter's Inc.: A Men's Clothier Tries Video-Ordering Systems*

Dexter's Inc. is the largest men's clothing store in North Dakota. Its one store is located in Grand Forks and has annual gross sales of about $2 million. In late 1985, Dexter's set up a direct marketing subsidiary named Elegant Clothiers and began advertising on Viewtron, a cable television video-ordering system operating in Southeast Florida. Viewtron subscribers use their home computers to order merchandise displayed on their televisions. Dexter's set up its subsidiary to reach a new market segment without adding store facilities, personnel, or inventory requirements.

Elegant Clothiers purchases space in the Viewtron system by the page, with each page corresponding to a full display on the television screen. The company regularly uses about sixty pages for its advertising. The first page includes Elegant's logo and an index of all the clothes the firm carries. The following pages contain product listings, graphical representations of products, text descriptions of products, and ordering instructions. In addition, an on-screen questionnaire is utilized to obtain information on tailoring preferences and clothing sizes. Once a customer provides this information to Elegant, it is kept on file and orders can be easily processed.

Since it started using Viewtron, Elegant Clothiers has promoted a broad range of clothing with little depth of assortment in terms of brands and styles so that the firm can better learn about consumer preferences. According to Dexter's president, "We'll start to narrow down the range and go into greater depth when we get a better feel for customer preferences. If dress shirts seem to be the hot thing, we'll try to have the most complete offering customers can find anywhere."

*The material in this case is drawn from "Screen Test," *Inc.* (July 1984), pp. 114ff.

In assessing the long-run potential of Elegant Clothiers using the Viewtron television ordering system, Dexter's management has these observations:

- There are 1.6 million people in metropolitan Miami alone, versus 45,000 people in Grand Forks, North Dakota. This is a large, prime market.
- Elegant can serve its customers 24 hours a day, seven days a week. No employees are required to take orders or wait on customers.
- By selling the same clothing lines as Dexter's, quantity discounts are possible when dealing with suppliers and one inventory location can serve both Dexter's and Elegant.
- Viewtron enables a small retailer to present the same type of image as a major retailer.
- Elegant can be an innovator and develop the loyalty of in-home shoppers.
- Currently, the Viewtron system operates over telephone lines. This negatively affects the quality of video reproduction.
- The video equipment, software, and networking need to be improved.
- Viewtron customers must purchase a control keyboard for $600. As of now, home computers are unable to receive video-ordering information directly.
- In 1985, a consulting firm estimated that 12 per cent of the U.S. households owning home computers had the modems required to process orders. The number should double by 1988.

At this time, Dexter's is uncertain about Elegant Clothiers. It does not know whether cable television video-ordering systems are too experimental to assess properly or if it should expand Elegant Clothiers to the video-ordering systems popping up throughout the country. Investment costs are quite low, but the firm's inclination is still to proceed cautiously.

Questions

1. What are the pros and cons of the Viewtron system for Elegant Clothiers?
2. Compare the retail strategies involved with Dexter's Grand Forks store and Elegant Clothiers video-ordering approach.
3. How do cable ordering systems put smaller retailers on a relatively equal footing with their larger competitors?
4. Should Elegant Clothier become involved in more video-ordering systems throughout the United States? Explain your answer. Are there other ways the subsidiary could be inexpensively expanded without video-ordering systems?

2. Miller's Place: Adapting to the Environment

Miller's Place is a chain of four record stores in Kansas City, Missouri. Bill Miller, a 42-year-old former record salesman, is the sole owner of Miller's Place. Miller started with one store in downtown Kansas City in 1970 and opened three other stores between 1975 and 1979.

Miller prides himself on long-run planning and adapting to the environment. In preparing his plans for the next five years, Miller examined a variety of factors and discovered the following:

- The population of Kansas City declined from 500,000 in 1970 to 450,000 in 1980. It has been relatively constant since then.
- The age of the Kansas City population has risen; 43 per cent of the population is age 35 or older. This trend is expected to continue.
- The 1981–82 recession greatly affected consumer expenditures. Unemployment remains relatively high.
- The sales of records and tapes have fallen drastically. This is due to alternative entertainment sources and the growth of taping music from stereos.
- Record prices have jumped. For example, LPs cost twice as much as 10 years ago.
- There is more competition from mail-order firms and department stores.
- Music tastes are constantly shifting.

Miller's Place is currently oriented toward the 12 to 30 age group. As such, it specializes in trends, such as the disco fad of the late 1970s and the new wave fad of the early 1980s. Miller's Place also relies on a large assortment of rock and roll, rhythm and blues, jazz, and "Grease" (1950s rock and roll) music. Classical, big band, opera, and other types of music are not stocked. Miller's market has money to spend (it is not uncommon for a sixteen-year-old girl to buy two records at $8.44 apiece) and likes to buy accessories (such as record and tape cleaners, posters, candles, and incense) at the store.

Within its music categories Miller's Place carries records, tapes, and cassettes. Special orders and one-of-a-kind orders are solicited. All products are priced close to list prices.

Each Miller's Place store has flashing neon lights in the window and interiors designed like discos. There are even small areas in the rear of the store for dancing. Customers are encouraged to browse and are not rushed. Store personnel are all young and are usually residents of the neighborhoods in which the stores are located.

Miller personally manages his original downtown store and employs three workers (one full-time and two part-time) in this branch. Each of the other three stores has a store manager, one full-time employee, and one part-time employee. Personnel decisions are decentralized, but all other decisions are made by Miller: store hours, store decor, buying, displays, pricing, and so on.

When buying merchandise, Miller relies on his past experience and intuition. He reads a number of trade publications, talks with customers, questions store person-nel, and meets with record and novelty salespeople. Most purchases are made through regular suppliers, with whom Miller has dealt for five years. He rarely deals with a new source of supply. Because of his bargaining position (as the owner of four stores), Miller is able to receive quick delivery. He keeps little surplus stock on hand, and readily transfers goods between stores.

Miller is aware that his strategy has some limitations. He works eighty-hour weeks. Store managers are unhappy because Miller makes all purchase decisions, despite the fact that branch stores are in significantly different types of neighborhoods than the downtown store and each other. There are many slow-moving items in inventory. Nonrecord merchandise planning is too haphazard.

Because of the environmental trends examined by Miller, he is concerned that his basic business will have limited growth potential in the future. He believes there is a 30 per cent chance that at least one branch store will not survive beyond 1987 in its present format.

Untapped by Miller is the growing market for classical, big band, opera, and other music which appeals to the 30-year-old-and-over market. Accordingly, Miller is weighing two alternative proposals to open a new store called Classics Unlimited. Under one option, Miller would refurbish the weakest branch outlet; under the other, Miller would close the branch outlet and open Classics Unlimited at a new uptown location. Miller would manage Classics Unlimited and switch the manager of his faltering branch to the well-entrenched downtown anchor store.

Questions

1. Based on the information presented in this case, is Miller correct about the future of his youth-oriented record chain? Explain your answer.
2. Which Classics Unlimited option should Miller select? Why?
3. Will Classics Unlimited be able to succeed? Why or why not?
4. Besides opening Classics Unlimited, what other actions could Miller take to improve his chain?

Comprehensive Cases

1. The Granzins: Deciding Whether to Purchase a McDonald's, Burger King, or Wendy's Franchise*

Introduction

Alice and John Granzin met while they were M.B.A. students at a large university and were married just after they graduated about eight years ago. Since that time, Alice has worked as an account executive for an advertising agency, specializing in the advertising campaigns of noncompeting local retailers. John has worked for a medium-sized management consulting firm, concentrating on human resource management. At present, Alice and John are considering career and life-style changes and are seriously interested in the purchase of a fast-food franchise.

They understand the long hours and financial investment involved, but feel that the chances of success, the personal satisfaction associated with ownership, and the opportunity to eventually operate multiple outlets far outweigh any disadvantages. The decision as to which franchise with which to affiliate is especially important: the dollar investment for a franchise unit varies widely; a noncompeting clause may forbid a

*The material in this case is drawn from *Burger King Corporation: Franchise Information;* "The Fast-Food War: Big Mac Under Attack," *Business Week* (January 30, 1984), pp. 44–46; Scott Hume, "Fast Food 'Dinosaur' On Attack," *Advertising Age* (January 21, 1985), pp. 3ff.; N. R.Kleinfeld, "Fast Food's Changing Landscape," *New York Times* (April 4, 1985), pp. B1ff.; "In Search of Diners," *Wall Street Journal* (March 14, 1985), p. 33; Scott Hume, "McDonald's Strategy: Drown 'em Out," *Advertising Age* (October 3, 1983), pp. 1ff.; Scott Hume, "Wendy's Aims to Get Better with Its Best," *Advertising Age* (April 30, 1984), pp. 4ff.; Arthur M. Louis, "Raymond Albert Kroc," *Fortune* (April 4, 1983), p. 147; *McDonald's Franchising;* Ralph Raffio, "Hamburger," *Restaurant Business* (March 20, 1984), pp. 134–137; "Restaurant Franchising in the Economy," *Restaurant Business* (March 20, 1984), pp. 167–170ff.; *Wendy's International Inc.: Prospective Franchise Application;* "Wendy's Will Enter Breakfast Business, Studies New Items," *New York Times* (August 31, 1983), p. 4; and Marci Jo Williams, "McDonald's Refuses to Plateau," *Fortune* (November 12, 1984), pp. 34–36ff.

franchisee from operating outlets in another chain (meaning that the franchisee must select the best franchising agreement and live with it); and growth and profit potential differ significantly.

The Granzins have narrowed their choices down to the three largest hamburger-based fast-food franchises: McDonald's, Burger King, and Wendy's. They have assembled data on franchising in the restaurant industry and on the individual companies. In addition, they have secured franchising requirements information directly from each of the firms.

Franchising in the Restaurant Industry

The restaurant franchise industry had total systemwide sales of $44.1 billion in 1984. The largest segment of the industry was comprised of firms emphasizing hamburgers, franks, and/or roast beef. This segment accounted for 48 per cent of total restaurant franchise sales, as shown in Table 1. The next largest segment, steak and full-menu restaurant franchises, represented 18 per cent of sales.

Despite the large sales volume for hamburger, frank, and roast beef establishments, they had lower-than-average growth between 1982 and 1984. The growth for all franchised restaurants was 29 per cent during this period, compared with 26 per cent for hamburger, frank, and roast beef establishments. Furthermore, chicken franchise sales rose by 50 per cent, sandwich restaurant sales rose by 48 per cent, seafood outlets' sales rose by 43 per cent, and pizza chains' sales rose by 38 per cent.

Tables 2 and 3 show the sales and number of units accounted for by company-owned and franchisee-owned hamburger, frank, and roast beef franchises from 1982 to 1984. Both the per cent of sales and the per cent of outlets represented by franchisees remained relatively constant during this time. However, average sales were slightly higher for company-owned outlets, which comprised 26.4 per cent of sales with 22.7 per cent of outlets in 1984.

Table 1
Restaurant Franchising Sales, 1982–84

Major Emphasis	Number of Firms	1984		1983		1982	
		Sales (thousands)	Market Share (%)	Sales (thousands)	Market Share (%)	Sales (thousands)	Market Share (%)
Chicken	32	$ 4,410,227	10.0	$ 3,569,907	9.2	$ 2,947,512	8.6
Hamburgers, franks, roast beef	102	21,315,390	48.3	18,961,299	49.0	16,862,890	49.4
Pizza	106	5,165,281	11.7	4,412,068	11.4	3,740,072	11.0
Mexican	33	1,734,457	3.9	1,500,828	3.9	1,258,054	3.7
Seafood	14	1,964,300	4.4	1,638,150	4.2	1,372,485	4.0
Pancakes, waffles	15	929,281	2.1	873,233	2.3	893,625	2.6
Steak, full menu	110	8,073,079	18.3	7,265,923	18.8	6,708,742	19.6
Sandwich and other	46	555,594	1.3	442,809	1.2	375,138	1.1
	458	$44,147,609	100.0	$38,664,217	100.0	$34,158,518	100.0

Source: "Restaurant Franchising in the Economy," Restaurant Business *(March 20, 1984), pp. 168–169. Reprinted by permission.*

Table 2
Retail Sales for Hamburger, Frank, and Roast Beef Franchises by Type of Ownership, 1982–84

		Sales (thousands)	Per Cent of Sales
1982	Sales by company-owned units	$ 4,482,780	26.6
	Sales by franchisee-owned units	12,380,110	73.4
	Total sales	$16,862,890	100.0
1983	Sales by company-owned units	$ 4,991,981	26.3
	Sales by franchisee-owned units	13,969,318	73.7
	Total sales	$18,961,299	100.0
1984	Sales by company-owned units	$ 5,634,977	26.4
	Sales by franchisee-owned units	15,680,413	73.6
	Total sales	$21,315,390	100.0

Source: *"Restaurant Franchising in the Economy," Restaurant Business (March 20, 1984), pp. 168–169. Reprinted by permission.*

A review of trade publications by the Granzins also yielded these findings:

- Good sites are becoming increasingly more difficult to find. In addition, with land and construction costs rising, these new sites need a high sales volume to pay for the leasing costs.
- Fast-food franchises are locating more outlets in nontraditional sites, such as college campuses and industrial plants. For example, Burger King now operates facilities at U.S. Army and Air Force exchanges, Woolworth stores, and Greyhound bus terminals.

Table 3
Ownership of Hamburger, Frank, and Roast Beef Franchised Outlets, 1982–84

		Number of Units	Per Cent of Units
1982	Company-owned units	6,100	22.4
	Franchisee-owned units	21,185	77.6
	Total units	27,285	100.0
1983	Company-owned units	6,430	22.5
	Franchisee-owned units	22,133	77.5
	Total units	28,563	100.0
1984	Company-owned units	6,952	22.7
	Franchisee-owned units	23,706	77.3
	Total units	30,658	100.0

Source: *"Restaurant Franchising in the Economy," Restaurant Business (March 20, 1984), p. 170. Reprinted by permission.*

- The burger market is becoming increasingly segmented. The Granzins feel that the niches in the market are rather small and that each niche will be able to support one or two medium-sized chains. As an illustration, "gourmet" hamburger franchises such as Flakey Jake's and Fuddruckers feature butcher shops and ground beef on the premises. At Flakey Jake's, customers can choose from a topping bar consisting of twenty items.
- For several reasons, hamburger chains are developing new products. First, new products are needed for defensive purposes; hamburger chains do not want to lose customers to other kinds of fast-food outlets. Second, new products are needed to attract breakfast customers and additional dinner patrons. It is also more efficient to have a steady stream of people throughout the day. Third, different market segments like different products. Females are more likely to desire chicken; diet-conscious people prefer salad bars; and so on.
- A significant amount of comparative advertising between Burger King and McDonald's (sponsored by Burger King) and Wendy's and McDonald's (sponsored by Wendy's) has recently occurred.

Background Information on Individual Fast-Food Franchises

The Granzins have assembled basic sales and outlet information for McDonald's, Burger King, and Wendy's, as shown in Tables 4 and 5. They used these tables to compute average sales per franchisee–owned outlet in 1983: McDonald's, $1,103,000; Burger King, $802,000; and Wendy's, $717,000. A thorough review of trade and company materials then yielded the following additional background information on the three firms.

McDonald's
- Is the largest food-service operator in the world. About 7 per cent of the U.S. population has a meal at McDonald's every single day.
- Has consistently and significantly boosted systemwide earnings during the two decades it has been a public corporation.

Table 4
1982–83 U.S. and Foreign Systemwide Sales for McDonald's, Burger King, and Wendy's (Millions of Dollars)

		McDonald's*	Burger King†	Wendy's*
1982	Sales by company-owned units	2,095	354	551
	Sales by franchisee-owned units	5,714	2,006	1,081
	Total sales	7,809	2,360	1,632
1983	Sales by company-owned units	2,170‡	422	666
	Sales by franchisee-owned units	6,430‡	2,388	1,256
	Total sales	8,600	2,810	1,922

*Calendar-year-end results.
†Fiscal-year-end results.
‡Estimates by *Restaurant Business*.

Source: "Restaurant Franchising in the Economy," Restaurant Business (March 20, 1984), pp. 168–169. Reprinted by permission.

Table 5
1982–83 U.S. and Foreign Franchise Unit Ownership for McDonald's, Burger King, and Wendy's

		McDonald's*	Burger King†	Wendy's*
1982	Company-owned units	1,846	488	827
	Franchisee-owned units	5,413	2,767	1,603
	Total units	7,259	3,255	2,430
1983	Company-owned units	1,949‡	525	922
	Franchisee-owned units	5,829‡	2,977	1,751
	Total units	7,778	3,502	2,673

*Calendar-year-end results.
†Fiscal-year end results.
‡Estimates by *Restaurant Business*.

Source: "Restaurant Franchising in the Economy," Restaurant Business *(March 20, 1984), p. 170. Reprinted by permission.*

- Adds one important new product about every five years. It is now testing a ⅓-pound gourmet burger, a salad bar, a cheeseburger with lettuce and tomato, and a sandwich version of chicken cordon bleu called "Chicken McSwiss." Although it is testing a salad bar, McDonald's really hopes to sell preportioned salads in containers instead. The company believes that salad bars are an operations headache.
- Has significant strengths in distribution and promotion due to its size. For example, one month after the national launch of Chicken McNuggets, McDonald's became the second largest chicken retailer in the United States. Its advertising budget is so large that it can drown out other messages.
- Plans to stick to burger-and-fries-based meals as the basic offering of the firm. It believes it knows this business best; detractors say that McDonald's is rigid and does not want to learn.
- Has an excellent control system. This assures consistency of offerings among locations. However, the chain is concerned that menu proliferation and made-to-order food may disrupt this consistency.
- Is eager to develop its dinner business, yet its association with the children's market deters some dinner customers.
- Has not promoted Chicken McNuggets to health-conscious consumers. A six-piece portion has only 310 calories.

Burger King

- Had some problems in the late 1970s as a result of management changes, strategy modifications, and expansion into such items as pizza and veal parmigiana sandwiches. These problems have since been resolved.
- Has done well with its relatively new salad bar and the salad-in-a-pita sandwich; together, they average about 6 per cent of total sales volume.
- Had a 1984 television advertising budget of $129 million, contrasted with $254 million for McDonald's. Wendy's spent $74 million.
- Uses more adult-oriented advertising than McDonald's.
- Started the "battle of the burgers" advertising campaign, claiming that its Whoppers were better than Big Macs because the Whoppers are flame broiled.

- Switched from Coke to Pepsi soda products in 1983 to gain a competitive distinction with McDonald's.
- Is affiliated with Pillsbury, which operates the company-owned outlets and sets franchise policies.
- Is testing ⅓-pound hamburgers and tacos.
- Is acknowledged as being less efficient than McDonald's. In a recent *Business Week* article, Burger King's chairman said that "McDonald's is still the best operated fast-food hamburger establishment."

Wendy's

- Is positioned as a quality, adult-oriented fast-food hamburger chain; however, only 40 per cent of sales are beef-based. Wendy's has the most diverse menu of the three chains and the largest proportion of female customers.
- Is trying out distinct meals for breakfast, lunch, and dinner. It is testing made-to-order omelets and French toast with toppings for breakfast. The dinner menu may eventually include chicken parmigiana, fish filets, and chopped beef with mushrooms. Wendy's was the first fast-food chain to introduce a salad bar.
- Baked potato products are rather unique. Toppings include broccoli and cheese, sour cream and chives, bacon and cheese, chili and cheese, and cheese alone. It also offers chicken sandwiches, bacon cheeseburgers, and taco salad.
- Is underrepresented in many large markets. For example, it has only 78 stores in New York and 146 in California (compared with 228 in Ohio). This means that Wendy's must count on customers who are willing to travel to its outlets.
- "Where's the beef?" advertising campaign was hugely successful. It generated a large amount of name recognition, helped position its image in consumers' minds, and resulted in substantial publicity.
- Used to sell only territorial franchise rights, under which franchisees agreed to open a specified number of outlets in an area. Today, individual franchise units are sold in territories where commitments have not been met or at sites falling between territorial areas.
- Uses only fresh meat and cooks all meals to order, unlike McDonald's and Burger King.
- Has decreased its budget for discount coupons. This has enabled Wendy's to significantly increase its television advertising budget.

Franchising Requirements

The Granzins have requested and received franchise application materials from McDonald's, Burger King, and Wendy's. The franchising requirements of each firm have a number of similarities. The franchisors want applicants to devote full time to their franchise outlets, have a net worth of $200,000 or more (not counting home, auto, and personal belongings), initially invest $120,000 to $150,000 in the franchise, and be willing to relocate. Application forms ask about business experience, education, personal references, personal finances, areas of geographic preference, and past business ventures.

Table 6 outlines the total required franchising fees for McDonald's, Burger King, and Wendy's. The amounts above the initial investment are to be paid out over a period of several years.

Table 6
Required Franchising Fees for a Single McDonald's, Burger King, or Wendy's Outlet

	McDonald's	Burger King	Wendy's
Technical assistance fee	$12,500	$5,000	$20,000
Land	—	—	$100,000–$300,000*
Building	—	—	$175,000–$225,000*
Site improvement	$18,000–$26,000	$35,000–$60,000	$50,000–$150,000
Equipment	$180,000–$201,000	$157,000–$220,000†	$135,000–$160,000
Miscellaneous (initial inventory, working capital, taxes, insurance, pre-opening expenses, etc.)	$65,000–$90,000‡	$50,200	$32,000–$49,000
Franchise fee	$23,000	$40,000	—
Total investment	$298,500–$352,500	$287,200–$375,000	$512,000–$904,000
Ongoing fees	11½% rent and services, 2% national advertising allowance	12% rent and services, 4% advertising allowance	4% services, 4% advertising allowance
Time period of agreement	20 years	20 years	20 years

*Franchisee owns land and building.
†Includes playground, but does not include sound system, security system, projector system.
‡$15,000 refundable security deposit.

Questions

1. What are the pros and cons of the Granzins operating a franchise outlet? Develop a checklist of factors they should consider in deciding whether franchising is right for them.
2. Evaluate the information contained in Tables 1-3. Do you agree with the Granzins' decision to concentrate on a hamburger fast-food outlet? Explain your answer.
3. Describe the fundamental differences in the strategies of McDonald's, Burger King, and Wendy's. Be sure to include an analysis of Tables 4 and 5 in your answer.
4. What are the benefits to choosing one franchisor over another? The disadvantages?
5. Why are Wendy's total investment requirements so much higher than those of McDonald's or Burger King?
6. What additional information should the Granzins acquire before making a decision? Provide several sources that they can use to gain this information.

2. Spiegel: A Direct-Marketing Retailer Aims for a New Target Market*

Company Background

Spiegel, Inc., the fourth largest direct marketer in the United States, was founded in 1865 by Joseph Spiegel (a German settler). The company began as a quality furniture store in downtown Chicago; it catered to affluent residents. However, by the early 1900s, Spiegel had expanded its merchandise selection and began issuing catalogs to appeal to the large number of lower-income immigrants who were attracted to Chicago. The firm was a pioneer in the concept of no-money-down credit plans, and continued to be successful through the Great Depression. Sales growth was strong until the mid-1970s, with Spiegel becoming almost exclusively a direct marketer.

In 1973, sales reached $319 million, but they fell to $266 million in 1976. According to Ted Spiegel, vice-president of marketing and a great grandson of the founder:

> Our market share was shrinking, and we were losing the low-end business to big discount chains and catalog giants like Sears and Ward that were better known and backed with actual stores.

Spiegel's me-too approach in merchandising did not allow it to have any competitive advantage, except in the area of credit. It had become "a last resort to a low-income group that was shrinking every day." Spiegel appealed to budget-conscious, low-income consumers who were concentrated in small rural communities in the South and Midwest. Spiegel accepted monthly installment payments as low as $7 per month. The "easy" credit terms became very expensive for Spiegel during this period.

At that point, Spiegel's parent company, Beneficial Finance (which had owned the retailer since 1965), hired a consulting firm to evaluate Spiegel's strategy and performance. The firm recommended that a new, more upscale target market be sought and a revised strategy implemented. To accomplish this, Henry Johnson (then the head of Avon Direct Products) was hired.

Immediately, Johnson sought to attract higher-income customers, many of whom came from two-income families and had little time to shop. A new marketing effort was aimed at women "who look for quality and value rather than the lowest price tag, and who want convenience." Spiegel wanted to become "a department store in print" for people who put a premium on time as well as the "fashion catalog of the country."

The transition has been a difficult one for Spiegel for a variety of reasons. First, it was hard to get existing employees and managers to think in terms of quality and

*The material in this case is drawn from "Direct Marketing Sales Far Outpace Estimates," *Marketing News* (November 23, 1984), pp. 1ff.; Christine Donahue, "A Dose of Class," *Forbes* (July 4, 1983), pp. 138–139; Richard Greene, "A Boutique in Your Living Room," *Forbes* (May 7, 1984), pp. 86–91ff.; Kevin Higgins, "Mail Order Industry Is Fighting the Old Sleazy Image on Several Fronts," *Marketing News* (July 8, 1983), pp. 1ff.; Frank E. James, "Spiegel Employs New Tactics to Fight Its Blue-Collar Past," *Wall Street Journal* (March 29, 1984), p. 31; Bernice Kanner, "Doing It by the Book," *New York* (May 14, 1984), pp. 17ff.; Sarah E. Moran, "Spiegel Hopes for Irish Magic, *Advertising Age* (September 13, 1984), p. 9; Eileen Norris, "Spiegel Takes Corporate Climb to the Summit," *Advertising Age* (April 2, 1984), p. M-18; Patricia Strand, "Spiegel Stretching Direct Response," *Advertising Age* (May 21, 1984), p. 38; and Winston Williams, "The Metamorphosis of Spiegel," *New York Times* (July 15, 1984), Section 3, pp. 8–9.

value—not just price. Many executives disagreed with the transformation strategy and either left Spiegel or were fired. Second, the initial customer mailing list dropped by 500,000 households, as lower-income customers were deleted. Yet it was hard to woo affluent consumers. Third, the closing of 200 order stores reduced sales, because some customers liked to view samples and place orders in a store environment. Fourth, some manufacturers that sold goods to department stores were not favorably disposed to Spiegel, due to its former image and customer base.

In 1982, Spiegel was purchased by Otto Versand, Europe's second largest catalog firm. The purchase price was a reported $49 million.

Spiegel's Current Strategy

Spiegel's current strategy can be described in terms of its target market, uses of marketing research, mailing-list generation, products available for sale, and catalog production and response.

Target Market

Today, about 85 per cent of Spiegel's customers are higher-income consumers with little time to shop. Its average customer is a 21- to 54-year-old working woman, from a two- to eight-member household with an annual family income of at least $38,000. There are well over 4 million Spiegel customers; and with 26 million U.S. households fitting its target market description, Spiegel has potential for future growth. Had Spiegel continued its old ways, its typical shopper would have been from a larger, less-educated blue-collar household with a family income of $18,000.

Uses of Marketing Research

Spiegel actively uses attitudinal research to determine if customer perceptions of the firm are in line with its goals. In particular, Spiegel is interested in building a general, continuous awareness of the company and its offerings. It recognizes that every advertisement and direct-mail piece contributes to a consumer's overall impression of Spiegel and helps in attracting awareness.

For example, in August 1983, research showed that 33 per cent of Spiegel's target market (upscale, working women) possessed an "unaided awareness" of the company as a fashion catalog retailer of women's apparel and home furnishings. Spiegel's goal was to reach 40 per cent in unaided awareness by the end of 1985.[1]

Mailing List Generation

The majority of Spiegel catalogs are sent to people who have previously ordered products. Forty per cent of new customers are introduced to Spiegel through a "Discover" catalog, which offers special prices on regular merchandise; these catalogs are mailed to several million potential customers. Twenty per cent of new customers are attracted through catalog request cards found in advertisements. The other 40 per cent of new customers are those who request company catalogs without any solicitation by Spiegel.

---

[1]Unaided awareness is surveyed when consumers are not given any prompting about a company. A typical question would be: "Please tell me what you know about Spiegel."

In 1984, Spiegel added a net amount of 700,000 active accounts. It started with 3.5 million names, added 1.8 million new clients, and dropped 1.1 million people who failed to order more than once. Spiegel increased its accounts in 1984 by spending $4 million on advertising and sponsoring "Spiegel Summits" in large cities. The Summits are conferences designed to help females with such skills as communication, leadership, and financial management. These seminars have enhanced Spiegel's image in cities where it has had relatively flat sales.

Products Available for Sale

Spiegel's product assortment has changed radically. While it still carries tools, vacuum cleaners, and cameras, it no longer stocks tires, curtain rods, pool tables, auto supplies, and a host of similar products. It does handle clothing, jewelry, housewares, furniture, clocks, and other merchandise that appeal to its target market.

These are some highlights of Spiegel's product assortment:

- Sheets and towels account for 29 per cent of company sales, compared with 5 to 7 per cent for an average department store.
- Designer merchandise is featured, including goods by Liz Claiborne, Pierre Cardin, Jean-Charles de Castelbajac, Ralph Lauren, and Gloria Vanderbilt. Spiegel is the largest seller of Laura Ashley products, with the exception of the designer's own stores.
- A typical catalog displays $550 black-onyx cuff bracelets, $225 women's tops, $1,799 grandfather clocks, and $5,695 red-fox coats among the thousands of items shown in its approximately 850 pages. A recent catalog was able to sell 1,500 $495 fur-lined raincoats and 800 Jackie Rogers Italian-linen envelope dresses.
- Children's wear and tailored men's clothes are selling well.

Catalog Production and Response

Spiegel produces two annual general catalogs, over twenty specialty catalogs, and the "Discover Spiegel" sample catalog (a 76-page book mailed to 30 million people). 700,000 general catalogs are sold each year at $3 each. This amount is refunded on the customer's first order; and one in four who buy a general catalog actually place an order. For all catalogs, the average order size rose from $50 in 1976 to $90 in 1984. The total for creating and producing all catalogs is $110 million; the general catalog alone costs $4.25 per copy to produce and distribute.

In order to effectively reach its target market, Spiegel has upgraded the paper, photographs, and merchandise presentation in its catalogs. These catalogs include the works of many of the country's most successful fashion photographers, do not have pages which are cluttered, and use bold and imaginative graphics. Once a shopper is drawn to the general catalog and his or her buying patterns are tracked, the shopper is offered specialty catalogs ranging from gourmet cookware to furs.

During late 1984, Spiegel began experimenting with a specialty catalog based on a foreign country theme, "Ireland—The Magic Is Here." The catalog featured women's and men's clothing, home furnishings, crystal, and crafts. If successful, Spiegel would consider introducing catalogs focusing on the Orient, Mediterranean countries, Scandinavia, and Australia.

Recent Financial Performance

Spiegel's revamped retailing strategy has led to positive results for the firm. From 1980 to 1983, sales rose from just over $300 million to $512 million annually. Spiegel lost money in 1980; by 1983, it was earning a pretax profit of almost $23 million. Between 1982 and 1983 alone, sales increased by 30 per cent and pretax profit more than doubled.

Despite these gains, Spiegel's 1983 pretax profit as a per cent of sales was only 4.5 per cent, less than the industry average. In comparison with total U.S. direct marketing sales, which increased by 260 per cent between 1975 and 1983, Spiegel's sales grew by 70 per cent during the same period.

Furthermore, despite its number four ranking among direct marketers, Spiegel is much smaller than the three firms positioned above it. Sears' direct merchandise group is over four times as large, J. C. Penney's direct marketing sales are three times greater, and Montgomery Ward is more than twice as large. See Table 1. These three firms appeal to broader target markets, have had more stable images and sales, and offer greater width and depth of assortment. A great variety of merchandise allows direct marketers to increase their average order size, an important factor in profitability and efficiency.

Table 1
The Largest Direct Marketing Firms in the United States, 1983

Company/Principal Merchandise	1983 Sales (millions)*	Per Cent Increase from 1982
Sears Merchandise Group/general	$2,092	11
J. C. Penney/general	1,652	7
Mobil	1,190	4
Montgomery Ward/general		
Otto Versand	512	30
Spiegel/general		
American Can	512	28
Fingerhut/general		
Figi's/food		
New Process/apparel	268	14
Horn & Hardart	215	54
Hanover House/general (22 specialty catalogs)		
LL Bean/apparel and sporting goods	205	7
American Express/high-ticket general	180	20
Quaker Oats	152	27
Herrschners/crafts		
Brookstone/tools and household		
Jos A Bank Clothiers/apparel		
Avon Direct Products/apparel	144	19
R.J. Reynolds	111	1
Jackson & Perkins/nursery		
Harry & David's/food		
Bear Creek/toys		

*Not all sales involve direct marketing.

Source: Direct Marketing Association, *based on figures provided by companies. Reprinted by permission.*

Strengths/Opportunities

Spiegel has several strengths/opportunities to consider and evaluate in planning its direct marketing efforts. These include:

* Direct marketing has some natural advantages over traditional store-based retailing. There are no parking difficulties, no lines, no traffic congestion. Direct marketing eliminates many of the inconveniences associated with traditional shopping. In addition, direct marketing enables customers legally to avoid paying state sales taxes if the mail-order firm has no outlets in the customer's home state.
* Versand's purchase of Spiegel has given the firm additional financial muscle. As a privately held company, Versand is less pressured for short-run profits at long-run expense. The firm's internal projections are that its sales will reach $1 billion by 1988.
* Since half of all households have not utilized direct marketing, a vast potential market exists.
* Spiegel is studying the possibility of mailing reminders of family birthdays and at other gift-buying times. This could increase its sales. The firm is also considering a system that would allow customers to order goods weeks before delivery is desired.
* Spiegel is contemplating a plan to sell high-status products in markets beyond the reach of manufacturers without broad distribution channels. Spiegel would identify the market, implement the mailings, and be paid on a commission basis. Spiegel's expertise in direct marketing could allow it to venture into new products (beyond its current product mix). Inventory would be held by the manufacturer.

Problems/Threats

Spiegel also needs to consider a number of problems/threats that could affect its future success. These include:

* Many customers are resistant to ordering by catalogs. Research by Simmons Market Research Bureau found that one-half of households in 1984 did some shopping at home; the balance did not use direct marketing. Among those using direct marketing, a Council of Better Business Bureaus study found that 62 per cent of complaints concerned delays in delivery or receipt of damaged goods. Credit and billing problems accounted for 18 per cent of complaints.
* Spiegel, like many other direct marketers, finds it difficult to plan inventory levels. Catalog development precedes distribution by several months; therefore, it is hard to forecast consumer acceptance, especially of high-fashion items. Sometimes, items must be drastically marked down to reflect poor acceptance; this affects profits. Recently, one of Spiegel's national surplus outlets had wool area rugs priced in a catalog at $399 on sale for $30; bamboo window shades, bedspreads, and designer sportswear were also heavily discounted.
* Spiegel acknowledges that it needs a better method for customers to return and exchange items. This is particularly important, since Spiegel's clothing, fabrics, colors, and fit may be hard for some customers to evaluate from a catalog.
* There is much competition in direct marketing. One study suggests that the number of catalog books is growing at a far faster rate than the number of catalog shoppers. Another study, by the Direct Marketing Association, found that in 1984 nearly 7

billion catalogs were mailed, nearly 80 per household on average. There is also much competition in Spiegel's market segment for upscale fashion and furnishing items.

- Spiegel's relatively narrow customer base is subject to intense competition from department stores and off-price chains. For example, a number of upscale department stores use fashion consultants to assemble clothing assortments for working women with limited time for shopping.

Questions

1. Evaluate Spiegel's shift from a "mass" to a "class" market.
2. Describe how consumers use the decision process when shopping by catalog. What trade-offs are consumers who buy from catalogs willing to make?
3. What marketing research projects should Spiegel conduct besides those noted in the case?
4. Do you agree with Spiegel's strategy to charge $3.00 for its general catalog? Explain your answer.
5. Suggest several additional methods for Spiegel to generate a mailing list.
6. Why are designer products particularly popular for Spiegel customers?
7. Assess Spiegel's long-term prospects. What must it do to maximize its chances for success?

3. Dodd's of Phoenix: A Merchandising Strategy for Boys' Clothing*

Introduction

Dodd's of Phoenix is an eight-store department store chain based in Arizona. Several times a year, Dodd's merchandise managers and buyers outline in detail their plans for subsequent seasons, in order to properly develop and implement a coordinated and progressive strategy. During the first week of May each year, final written approval for merchandising budget expenditures for the Fall season must be obtained by each of the chain's departments.

In the boys' clothing area, Dodd's has a senior buyer and two assistant buyers. They prepare merchandising plans for each of the categories in their product line and submit these plans to a divisional merchandise manager and a general merchandise manager. The plans must

1. Carefully justify and explain each segment of the product line.
2. Outline strengths and possible weaknesses.
3. Formally document assumptions and conclusions whenever possible.
4. Integrate information into a written statement of the "Strategy and Growth Potential, Fall Selling Season."
5. Be orally presented to the divisional merchandise manager and the general merchandise manager.

Merchandising Background of Boys' Clothing at Dodd's

Departments 452 and 453 at Dodd's represent a total boys' clothing effort by the chain, encompassing boys' sizes 8 to 20 and larger "husky" sizes. These two departments include every classification that makes up the men's clothing division. Dodd's overall objective is to be a dominant factor in boys' apparel and increase its share of the market. However, the level of sales for the two departments has been almost flat during the past four years. Sales at the downtown Phoenix headquarters store have decreased slightly over this period, while the Phoenix and Tucson branch stores have seen a small sales increase.

Prior to 1985, the two departments were maintained separately under two buyers, each of whom had one assistant. Then in eary 1985, the divisional merchandise manager and the general merchandise manager decided to consolidate the departments. One of the buyers, Carla Nickel, was promoted to senior buyer and retained the two assistant buyers. The other buyer was transferred to men's suits. For accounting and budgeting purposes, the two departments remain distinct.

Departments 452 and 453 are highly complementary in their merchandise lines. In fact, a substantial overlap exists in the sizes offered, even though they are divided by "style" and "look." The total merchandise lines are composed of boys' bottoms, tops, clothing, outerwear, accessories, husky styles and sizes, sports, and Levi clothing. See Table 1. Department 452 contains eleven product categories, while Department 453

*This case was prepared and written by Professor Jack Gifford, Miami University of Ohio, Oxford, Ohio.

Table 1
Departments 452 and 453 Merchandising Classifications by Merchandise Types

I. Bottoms	V. Accessories
A. Pants	A. Pajamas
1. Jeans	B. Underwear
2. Casual	C. Socks
3. Dress	D. Belts
B. Shorts	E. Ties
C. Swimwear	F. Hats and gloves
II. Tops	G. Gym supplies
A. Knits	VI. Husky
B. Cut and sewn shirts	A. Pants
1. Sport	B. Shirts
2. Dress	C. Clothing
C. Leisure wear	D. Outerwear
III. Clothing	VII. Sports
A. Sport coats	A. Shirts and jerseys
B. Suits	B. Outerwear
C. Leisure wear	C. Accessories
IV. Outerwear	VIII. Levi
A. Jean jackets	
B. Rainwear	
C. Regular seasonal outerwear	

has only four. See Table 2. About two-thirds of the selling space devoted to boys' clothing is allocated to products from Department 452.

A clearer picture of the boys' clothing operation can be seen by examining the layout of the two departments in Dodd's downtown Phoenix store. In this outlet, boys' clothing occupies a full floor and is displayed in five distinct selling areas, each of which is intended to project an identifiable personality and image. The five areas are Boys 8–20, Levi's, Preps 14–20, Husky, and Sports. See Figure 1. Each area is physically separated by aisles and square carpeted sections.

The individual personalities of the selling areas are maintained through differentiated merchandise colors in the carpeting, lighting, and displays. For example, the layout within the Preps area is formally structured. A rich, subtle color of carpeting is utilized. The fixtures are primarily round racks, stands, and tables presented in a modified grid layout. In contrast, the layout within Sports is basically free flow. The feeling of openness is maintained by using many hanging merchandise displays, as opposed to square bins and stacked goods. The space between displays is reasonably generous, providing a feeling or image somewhere between "fashion" and "budget."

Buying Policies

It is the stated objective of both departments to carry brand-name basics and fashions within each merchandise classification and offer a "value image" to the customer. It is both the policy of Dodd's as a whole and Department 452 and 453 management to concentrate buying with a limited number of vendors, given market availability and appropriate price points. This policy (1) helps obtain favorable vendor loyalty in terms

Table 2
Merchandise Categories by Department

Department 452		Department 453	
Category	Description	Category	Description
A	Cut and sewn shirts	C	Belts
B	Swimwear		Accessories
	Sweaters		Pajamas and robes
	Sweatshirts	AB	Underwear
D	Husky boys		Hosiery
E	Jeans	CC	Levi* pants and
F	All imports		tops
G	Sport coats	AC	Athletic clothes
	Suits		
H	Outerwear		
I	Knit shirts		
BB	Farah*		
BC	Donmoor*		
DD	Promotional pants		

*Because of the importance of these brands, they are designated as unique categories as if they are basic product categories.

of price, delivery, volume discounts, merchandise displays, and promotional terms; (2) ensures fashion-rightness; (3) improves communications with the market and specific vendors; (4) aids in solving problems through markdown allowances; and (5) provides generous return and exchange rights.

The concentration of buying from selected vendors has been very successfully practiced in both departments. The top ten vendors currently represent 66.0 per cent of purchases in Department 452 and 82.2 per cent in Department 453.

Customer Profile

As is the case in all the departments of Dodd's, a wide variety of customer types is drawn by the broad selection of merchandise. Departments 452 and 453 are no exception. However, even though the shoppers represent all ages, incomes, and life-styles, some generalizations can be made about the types of customers drawn particularly to the boys' clothing departments.

The largest percentage of potential customers entering these departments are female, middle income, and between the ages of 27 and 40. They have two or more children between the ages of 5 and 15. In many cases, particularly on weekends, the women are accompanied by their families.

The second largest group of potential customers is the young teenage boy between the ages of 11 and 15. This is a growing market for these departments, and one that deserves particular cultivation.

The remaining market is composed of a mixture of men and women of various ages and incomes. Because of the predominantly medium-price points for boys' clothing only a small number of low-income people actively shop in the department.

Interior Layout of Boys' Clothing at Dodd's Downtown Phoenix Store[1]

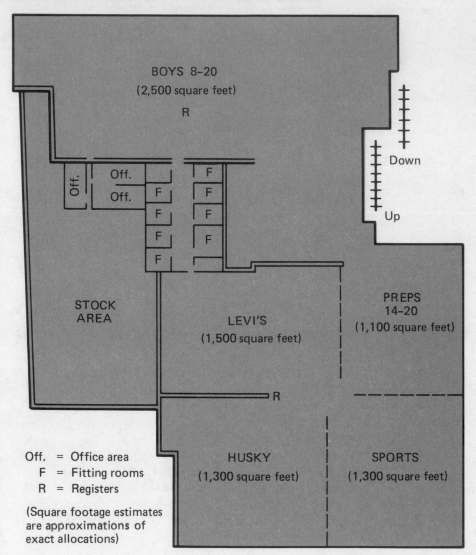

[1] These selling areas are comprised of merchandise from Departments 452 and 453.

Figure 1

Table 3
Selected Financial Data for Boys' Clothing, Most Recent Selling Year

Financial Measure	Department 452 at Dodd's	Department 453 at Dodd's	Median Department Store Performance for Infants', Boys', and Girls' Clothing and Accessories	Median Specialty Store Performance for Infants', Boys', and Girls' Clothing and Accessories
Per cent sales increase over prior year	+0.9	+1.3	+6.1	+0.8
Sales per square foot	$82	$94	$93.80	$104.30
Sales salaries and sales promotion costs (as a per cent of sales)	11.2	8.5	10.9	12.0
Maintained markup (gross margin as a per cent of sales)	40.5	43.0	41.6	41.7
Markdowns (as a per cent of sales)	20.7	14.0	17.5	18.1
GMROI (gross margin return on investment)	175%	249%	221%	245%
Stock turnover (times per year)	2.5	3.3	3.0	2.6

The motivation of customers to buy is almost entirely for specific, immediate needs. In particular, the needs are to replace outgrown or worn-out items, to wear or give at holiday times, or to add to boys' back-to-school wardrobes.

Financial Data

Dodd's managers annually analyze the financial performance of each department in the chain. These data are compared with previous years and with the industrywide statistics made available by the National Retail Merchants Association (NRMA), of which Dodd's is a member. The NRMA provides departmental data for department stores and for specialty stores. While the NRMA's classifications are broader than Dodd's would like, they may be used to assess the performance of Departments 452 and 453. Table 3 contains some of the most recent financial information compiled by Dodd's.

New Merchandising Opportunities

Carla Nickels and her assistants have identified a number of merchandising opportunities that they would like to pursue during the Fall selling season. These opportunities include

- Introducing a customized lettering program for organizations throughout Arizona.
- Clearly defining and strengthening the image of the Preps shop.
- Placing greater emphasis on Arizona State University clothing products.
- Expanding the Husky merchandise category.
- Adding jewelry products to complement clothing sales.

First, Carla believes there is a demand for lettering boys jackets with the names of the organizations (e.g., school, athletic, social) with which they are affiliated. Through vendors in New York, Dodd's can obtain embroidery at 67.5 cents cost per embroidery (to retail at $1.80) and silk screening of lettering, emblems, and so on, for $1.12 each (to retail at $3.60). The embroidery and silk screening are designed to be placed on jackets sold at $17.99 (light-lined) and $27.95 (pile-lined). Both of the jackets carry an approximate retail markup of 45 per cent. They come in a wide variety of colors and are presently stocked by all Dodd's outlets. The maximum time between the placing of a customer order and notification that a lettered jacket is ready for pickup is expected to be three weeks. To minimize cancellations, Carla recommends that a 20 per cent nonrefundable down payment be made when customers place orders.

A second strategy for growth involves strengthening the Preps shop concept. Preps has an older, more fashion-conscious look than other areas, focusing on sizes 14 to 20. It has all the basic merchandise classifications, with emphasis on cut and sewn shirts, knit shirts, pants, outerwear, sweaters, swimwear, and accessories. One of the merchandising opportunities is to more clearly separate the Preps from the image of the rest of the selling area. The atmosphere which might be created is that of a young university shop. Carla and her assistants are still thinking through certain questions concerning the Preps shop concept, such as: "How do we draw the appropriate customers' attention to this concept?" "How can we better separate this area from those surrounding it?" and "What sort of floor design, layout, advertising, and presentation techniques would maximize sales?" These and other questions have to be answered before meeting with the divisional merchandise manager and the general merchandise manager.

A third and unique opportunity, particularly for Dodd's stores in the Phoenix area, is the expansion of the sports selling area into the "A.S.U. Sports Shop." The sports selling area currently contains jerseys, sweatshirts, novelty T-shirts, outerwear, football pants, socks, and a wide line of accessories. Carla would like to expand the number of items carried in these categories, particularly in jerseys, accessories, and specialty products. It is felt that the key to success in this area is the variety of styles and colors. To give a special lift to this shop, Carla has made tentative plans for an all new A.S.U. football jersey to be carried exclusively by Dodd's. The estimated profit margin on the jersey, if sufficient volume is generated, would exceed the departmental target markup. However, Carla recognizes that larger sizes of sports-related clothing are also sold in Dodd's "University Shop" and that the buyer for this area may object to her plans for expansion.

The fourth major push being considered by Carla is the growth in assortment and depth of Husky merchandise, particularly in the branch stores. If this is to be successfully accomplished, it will be necessary to rotate new colors and styles through inventory to maintain both the newness and excitement for customers and sales personnel alike. There is an intuitive feeling among some managers that demand exceeds supply at the branches for this classification of goods; however, no research has been conducted at this time. Three particularly important problems which Carla feels must be overcome are floor space availability in the branches, sales personnel responses to selling an expanded line, and the primary types of clothing to add assortment and size ranges. Furthermore, there are a limited number of vendors who produce Husky sizes.

The fifth opportunity involves the introduction of an entirely new classification of goods: jewelry. The line would be limited initially and only cuff links, tie pins and bars, and rings would be sold. The jewelry would complement clothing sales, particularly for older boys. Due to the heavy workload of Carla and her assistants, very little research has been done on this opportunity. Potential vendors have been identified but not yet evaluated.

In addition to pursuing the preceding opportunities, Carla is planning to introduce a significant change in her approach to purchasing by placing smaller orders more often during the year. This will enable her to take advantage of styles, colors, and trends which "explode" when they hit the selling floor. The change will also provide customers and sales personnel alike with a greater variety of merchandise, thereby providing excitement and a feel of newness. The key to implementing the new approach will be careful evaluation of sales records and clothing trends, and effective communication with boys' clothing managers at branch stores.

Questions

1. Evaluate Dodd's decision to combine Departments 452 and 453 under one senior buyer and two assistant buyers.
2. Comment on the layout of boys' clothing at Dodd's downtown Phoenix store, which is shown in Figure 1 and discussed in the case.
3. Do you agree with Dodd's practice of concentrating on a limited number of vendors? Explain your answer.
4. Analyze the financial data contained in Table 3. What do you conclude?
5. Assess each of the five merchandising opportunities identified by Carla Nickels.
6. What do you think about Carla's plan to place smaller, more frequent orders throughout the year?
7. As the divisional merchandise manager, what other information would you want before approving a merchandising budget for boys' clothing?

4. Federated Department Stores: Developing and Adhering to a Comprehensive Strategy*

Introduction

Federated Department Stores is a diversified retail firm with department and specialty stores, mass merchandising stores, and supermarkets. It has nineteen operating units, which operated 550 stores in thirty-one states in 1983. Federated is the largest department store retailer in the United States. In 1983, total company revenues were about $8.7 billion and net income was $338.3 million (3.9 per cent of sales).

Table 1 lists 1983 sales data for each of Federated's operating units, organized on the basis of their major retail business. Most of these operating units are headed by a two-person senior management team, consisting of a chairman and a president. Each team has responsibility for day-to-day operations in all the stores in its unit. At the corporate level, each division is supervised by either Federated's chairman or vice-chairman.

As can be seen from Table 2, department and specialty stores account for more than 70 per cent of Federated's overall sales and almost 88 per cent of gross profit (gross margin in dollars). Federated operates two types of department stores: headquarters stores and upscale stores. Headquarters stores are broad-line outlets targeted at moderate to upper-moderate shoppers. These include Abraham & Straus, Burdine's, Rich's, Foley's, and Sanger Harris. Upscale stores are more selective in their merchandise offerings and are targeted at high-fashion and high-income shoppers. These include Bloomingdale's and I. Magnin.

Although Federated's performance is generally rated as quite good, it has had some problems, as these examples indicate. Between 1979 and 1983, revenues rose sharply as Federated expanded; however, income and profit performance were erratic during this period. See Table 3. The combining of Shillito's and Rike's came after four to five years of internal debate. Federated's MainStreet stores, first opened in October 1984, are a close copy of Dayton Hudson's Mervyn's (which was started many years previously). R. H. Macy is now viewed by many analysts as the leading department store innovator, a position previously occupied by Federated. For example, Macy's converted its basement area into a fashionable boutique many years before Federated followed.

In addition, department store chains such as Federated must now react to heightened competition. Off-price chains compete for the same target market but can outprice

---

*The material in this case is drawn from Isadore Barmash, "Filene's of Boston Enters New York with Queens Store, "*New York Times* (May 9, 1983), p. D4; *Federated Department Stores Annual Report 1983*; "Federated Stores Picks Chicago as a Base of Unit for Mid-Priced Stores," *Wall Street Journal* (September 7, 1983), p. 38; Howard Goldfeder, "New York Security Analysts Presentation," (December 6, 1984), pp. 1–15; Steven Greenhouse, "Federated's Bid for the Middle," *New York Times* (October 31, 1984), pp. D1ff.; *People and Places: Federated Department Stores 1984* (Cincinnati: Federated Department Stores, June 1984); Pat Sloan, "Bloomingdale's Future in Expanding Its Mystique," *Advertising Age* (October 3, 1983), pp. 3ff.; Jolie B. Solomon, "Federated Stores Sets to Catch Up to Rivals in Retail Revolution," *Wall Street Journal* (April 5, 1984), pp. 1, 24; "Going Middle Class: Federated Fashions a New Chain," *Business Week* (November 5, 1984), p. 129; and Subrata N. Chakravarty," Federated Chooses Not to Choose," *Forbes* (April 8, 1985), pp. 82ff.

Table 1
Sales Data for Federated Department Stores' Operating Units, 1983

Operating Unit	Location	1983 Sales (millions)	Gross Space (thousands of square feet)	Number of Stores	Annual Sales Per Square Foot
Department and specialty stores					
Abraham & Straus	NY, NJ, PA	$ 731.8	5,538	15	$132.14
Bloomingdale's	NY, NJ, CT, MA, PA, VA, ME, TX	787.9	3,784	14	208.22
Boston Store	WI	130.9	1,596	8	82.02
Bullock's	CA, AZ, NV	588.9	4,845	28	121.55
Burdine's	FL	630.3	4,536	25	138.96
The Children's Place	19 States	103.3	583	114	177.19
Filene's	MA, NH, ME, RI	292.5	1,901	14	153.87
Filene's Basement	MA, NH, NY, CT	151.2	605	14	249.92
Foley's	TX	625.9	4,077	15	153.52
Goldsmith's	TN	147.7	1,338	6	110.39
Lazarus	OH, IN, WV	420.4	3,812	17	110.28
I. Magnin	CA, OR, WA, AZ, IL, MD	276.0	1,730	25	159.54
MainStreet	IL	First outlets not opened until 1984			
Rich's	GA, AL, SC	509.1	4,101	17	124.14
Sanger Harris (including Levy's)	TX, OK, AZ	400.0	3,039	16	131.62
Shillito Rikes	OH, KY	359.9	3,824	14	94.11
Mass merchandising stores					
Gold Circle	OH, KY, NY, PA	590.1	5,770	51	102.27
Richway	GA, SC, NC, TE, FL	401.0	3,130	31	128.11
Supermarkets					
Ralphs	Southern CA	1,275.7	4,524	127	281.98

Source: People and Places: Federated Department Stores *(Cincinnati, Ohio: Federated Department Stores, June 1984),* pp. 3–18.

department stores. Specialty stores have taken much of the market in cameras, electronics, designer apparel, home-improvement items, and sporting goods. As a result, department stores must be more aggressive in dealing with vendors and in promoting their merchandise offerings.

Corporate Strategic Planning Emphasis

Howard Goldfeder, Federated's current chairman of the board, is the first person outside the Lazarus family to run the firm (after 35 years of control by the founding Lazarus family). Goldfeder has introduced Federated to corporate strategic planning.

Table 2
Federated Department Stores' Performance Data for Major Divisions, 1983

	Performance	Per Cent of Total
Net Sales (millions)		
Department and specialty stores	$6,224.8	71.6
Mass merchandising stores	991.1	11.4
Supermarkets	1,473.7	17.0
Total	$8,689.6	100.0
Gross Profit* (millions)		
Department and specialty stores	$ 644.3	87.8
Mass merchandising stores	39.5	5.4
Supermarkets	50.0	6.8
Total	$ 733.8	100.0
Gross Square Feet of Floor Space (hundreds)		
Department and specialty stores	45,309	77.1
Mass merchandising stores	8,900	15.2
Supermarkets	4,524	7.7
Total	58,733	100.0

*Does not include central office costs, interest expense, unusual items, or income tax.

Source: People and Places: Federated Department Stores *(Cincinnati, Ohio: Federated Department Stores, June 1984) p. 40.*

As a result of this planning, Federated has sold six shopping centers and is no longer in the business of developing them. It has also recently liquidated its marginally profitable Gold Triangle discount chain and Bullock's Northern California specialty stores, and closed twelve Ralph's supermarket units. "Before, every division's objective was to grow," said Federated's vice-chairman. "Now, the company has to reward a manager for shutting down."

Federated is being changed "from a series of independent, even rivalrous, fiefdoms into a nation-state" according to Goldfeder. In past years, Federated divisions such as Burdine's (Florida), Foley's (Houston), and Filene's (Boston) were viewed as independent; and it would have been unthinkable to have two separate divisions in the same city. Now Sanger Harris and Bloomingdale's are even in the same shopping center in Dallas.

Prior to 1983, Bloomingdale's had been limited to a few Eastern states (New York, New Jersey, Connecticut, Massachusetts, Pennsylvania, and Maryland). Now, Bloomingdale's will be the first full-line national fashion department store. The expansion will help Federated increase its overall market share in cities such as Dallas (where Fed-

Table 3
Selected Financial Data for Federated Department Stores, 1979–83

	1983	1982	1981	1980	1979
Revenues ($ billions)	8.7	7.7	7.0	6.3	5.8
Net income ($ millions)	338.3	232.8	258.3	276.8	202.3
Number of stores	550	508	369	358	346
Gross square feet (millions)	58.7	58.4	53.9	52.3	50.0
Net income (as a per cent of sales)	3.89	3.02	3.69	4.39	3.49
Average annual sales per square foot ($)	148.21	131.85	129.87	120.46	116
Change in sales over prior year (%)	+13.0	+10.0	+11.1	+8.6	+7.4
Change in net income over prior year (%)	+45.3	−10.9	−7.7	+36.8	+2.8

Source: Federated Department Stores Annual Report 1983.

erated has Sanger Harris units), Miami (where it has Burdine's units), Chicago (where it has MainStreet stores), and Los Angeles (where Bullock's is situated).

Federated has abandoned its "democratic theory of investing," wherein each division could lay claim to its share of investment dollars. Each division's spending allowances are now tied to its individual results and to Federated's overall corporate strategy. Federated's 1984–1988 capital-expenditure budget of $2.5 to $3.0 billion will be allocated as follows: department stores, 65 per cent; supermarkets, 10 per cent; mass merchandisers, 10 per cent; and others (The Children's Place, MainStreet, and Filene's Basement), 15 per cent. Over this period, 49 per cent of the total will go to new stores; 26 per cent for remodeling, expansion, and maintenance; and 25 per cent for support activities (such as point-of-sale systems and distribution centers).

The company now recognizes the need to focus on target customers and revise strategies regarding supplier selection, store services, store design, merchandise offerings, and personnel to reflect the target customers' needs. In particular, Federated's department stores are placing greater emphasis on professional women, aged 25 to 54, as a prime market segment. Federated's interest in this segment is based on several factors:

- Many professional women come from two-income households. These households have incomes that are 40 per cent greater than those for the average U.S. household.
- They are attracted to one-stop shopping.
- They spend 3½ times as much for apparel as their nonworking counterparts.
- This group is expected to expand in the future.

Consumer research conducted for Federated has determined the reasons why shoppers patronize conventional department stores in general and Federated stores in particular. Among the attractions of department stores are their role in determining fashion trends and fashion acceptability, their ability to demonstrate how and under what circumstances current fashion should be worn or used in the house, their pleasant shopping environments (store atmosphere), and the distinctive character of department stores. Federated's specific strengths are high consumer loyalty and prime locations.

Store Strategies

Federated has decided to use one broad overall strategy for all headquarters stores, since customer preferences are relatively similar. In contrast, upscale department store customer preferences are less similar; each of these operating units requires separate plans.

The headquarters store strategy seeks to build market share and return on investment by

- Efficiently allocating floor space. Federated has eliminated all its budget departments, despite the fact that they contained 1.5 per cent of total department store merchandise. This has freed up space for adding other product lines appealing to professional women.
- Expanding buying offices in New York. Federated is now developing its own brand names, such as Allen Solly, to exert more channel control and to reduce competition from off-price chains on traditional male and female apparal. At the same time, Federated plans to increase its business in branded fashion merchandise and to increase its cooperation with vendors.
- Improving store atmosphere through store remodeling and respacing.
- Reorganizing operations to provide better customer service.
- Regionalizing these stores. Foley's is adding stores in Austin and San Antonio; Sanger Harris is opening units in Tulsa, Tucson, and Albuquerque; and Rich's is adding stores in three Southeastern states.

There are some of the strategies being employed by Federated for its nonheadquarters stores:

- Regarding upscale stores, it plans to expand I. Magnin's national catalog business and open Bloomingdale's outlets in locations throughout the United States (as noted earlier).
- Ralph's supermarkets are following a more aggressive pricing policy.
- In late 1983, Filene's Basement was set up as a separate operating unit from Filene's department stores. Filene's Basement appeals to shoppers who are both value and fashion conscious. It is expected to be able to compete vigorously against other off-price chains, but not against traditional stores. Filene's Basement stores do not always have complete selections and items may not be in-season. As in Filene's department stores, Filene's Basement stores utilize an automatic markdown policy, whereby unsold goods are systematically reduced in price (based on the number of days the goods are on the selling floor) and given to charity if not sold in 30 days.
- MainStreet, Federated's new Chicago-based chain, is trying to carve out a niche between the medium- to low-priced mass merchandiser and the higher-priced traditional department store. MainStreet relies on brand-name merchandise and has 40 per cent more personnel per square foot than the average mass merchandiser. MainStreet is targeted at families with 25- to 40-year-old adults and annual household incomes of $20,000 to $40,000. While children's clothing and related products are featured, carpets, furniture, and major appliances are not carried by MainStreet.

Questions

1. Interpret the data presented in Tables 1, 2, and 3.
2. What type of organizational form is appropriate for Federated? Explain your answer.
3. How can Federated reduce the amount of potential conflict and the potential lack of coordination among its various operating units? Be complete in your answer.
4. Select any two of Federated's operating units and describe their target markets, store image, store atmosphere, store layout, customer services, advertising, personal sales force, sales promotions, and pricing orientation.
5. What special considerations must Federated take into account when opening Bloomingdale's in new cities? What criteria would you use to determine whether or not a city should get a Bloomingdale's outlet?
6. Evaluate Federated's 1984–88 capital-expenditure budget.
7. Comment on Federated's store strategies.

5. The Great Atlantic & Pacific Tea Company (A&P): Returning to Profitability*

Company Background and History

A&P was founded in 1859 as the Great American Tea Company. The firm began by purchasing tea directly from clipper ships at "cargo prices" and found customers eager to buy the tea at 50 per cent discounts from the regular prices at that time. The corporate name was later changed to the Great Atlantic & Pacific Tea Company (A&P) to mark the establishment of the transcontinental railroad and to separate the firm's retail store and mail-order operations.

For many years, A&P was considered an industry innovator. It was the first retailer to develop a dealer brand (for its tea blend and its Eight O'Clock coffee products in the 1860s). A&P was the leader in giving premiums to encourage customer loyalty and repurchases (in the 1870s). It was among the first retailers to sell prepackaged meats (in the 1920s). The company was the first food retailer to sponsor a radio program (1924). By 1936, A&P had 5,600 supermarkets, and it was the number one supermarket chain in terms of sales through 1972.

However, by the 1960s, many problems began to emerge:

- During the 10-year period from 1961 to 1970, A&P's share of the grocery business declined from 10 per cent to 6 per cent, and profits decreased from $57.5 million to $50 million. In 1975, the company lost over $157 million.
- Among the nation's five largest supermarket chains, only A&P failed to achieve large growth during the 1960s and 1970s.
- Between 1965 and 1980, A&P had six different chief executives. This resulted in little planning continuity.
- The firm overlooked suburban growth and had too many small inner-city stores.
- Most A&P stores did not stock highly profitable nonfood items and they did not encourage one-stop shopping.
- The company did not respond to consumer demand for national brands. This was partly due to A&P's extensive ownership of manufacturing facilities.
- A&P had very high labor costs. Seniority plans, high wage rates, and the lack of flexibility regarding its unionized employees performing other tasks (such as the inability to have checkout personnel unload merchandise from trucks when store traffic was slow) put A&P at a significant disadvantage with competing supermarket chains and nonunionized independent supermarkets.

---

*The material in this case is drawn from "A&P to Finish Closing Its Plus Discount Chain in the Next Few Weeks," *Wall Street Journal* (August 18, 1983), p. 12; "A&P: Story of a Turnaround," *Chain Store Age Executive* (September 1983), pp. 49–50; "Food Chains Get Hungry for Cost Cuts," *Business Week* (February 6, 1984), pp. 24–25; *The Great Atlantic & Pacific Tea Company, Inc.*, *Form 10K*, dated February 25, 1984; Doug Harris, "Repositioning in Black and White at the New A&P: Futurestore," *Supermarket Business* (November 1984), pp. 32–33ff.; Janet Guyon, "A&P's Earnings on Operations Jump Sharply," *Wall Street Journal* (December 19, 1984), p. 10; John Merwin, "A Piece of the Action," *Forbes* (September 24, 1984), pp. 146–148ff; Larry Schaeffer, "Fit and Feisty," *Progressive Grocer* (October 1983), pp. 65–66ff.; "Supermarkets," *Forbes* (January 14, 1985), pp. 202–203; and Ronald Tanner, "A Bold New Look," *Progressive Grocer* (January 1985), pp. 61–62ff.

Table 1
Selected Financial Data for A&P, 1978–83

Financial Measure	1983	1982	1981	1980*	1979	1978
Net sales (thousands)	$5,222,013	$4,607,817	$6,226,755	$6,989,529	$6,684,179	$7,469,659
Net income after tax (thousands)	$47,551	$31,211	$(101,633)	$(43,049)	$(3,807)	$(52,168)
Number of employees	53,000	40,000	45,000	60,000	63,000	72,000
Number of stores (at year end)	1,022	1,016	1,055	1,543	1,542	1,711
Total store area (square feet)	23,276,000	22,601,000	23,742,000	33,052,000	33,057,000	36,935,000

*Reflects 53 weeks. All other yearly periods are 52 weeks.

Source: The Great Atlantic & Pacific Tea Company, Inc. 1983 Annual Report, *p. 35; and* 1982 Annual Report, *p. 31.*

In 1979, Tengelmann of West Germany acquired a major interest in A&P. Tengelmann installed a new management team, headed by James Wood, in 1980. Under the direction of Wood, the number of supermarket outlets operated by A&P was reduced by about 500 (from 1,543 in 1980 to 1,055 in 1981 and 1,022 in 1983); all unprofitable manufacturing plants were closed; improved systems of control were implemented; and labor costs and overhead were reduced. In fiscal 1982, A&P was profitable for four consecutive quarters, the first time that had occurred in over a decade. During 1983, profitability continued and increased; in 1984, 85 per cent of A&P outlets were profitable. Cash flow projections indicate that between 1984 and 1987 internally generated funds should cover all remodeling and debt service. Table 1 shows selected

Table 2
Selected Financial Data for Major Supermarket Chains, 1979–84

Major Supermarket Chain	Return on Equity Rank, 1979–84	Average Return on Equity, 1979–84 (%)	Return on Equity, 1984 (%)	Net Profit Margin, 1984 (%)	Average Annual Sales Growth, 1979–84 (%)	Sales Growth, 1983–84 (%)
American Stores	1	25.0	26.1	1.5	41.3	15.3
Albertson's	2	23.5	19.6	1.6	13.6	9.3
Lucky Stores	3	22.3	16.8	1.3	12.1	8.1
Supermarkets General	4	21.6	17.1	1.2	11.3	7.9
Winn-Dixie	5	21.2	19.5	1.6	10.1	4.3
Stop & Shop Companies	6	18.3	19.3	1.8	9.0	19.6
Kroger	7	16.1	13.3	0.8	12.9	5.7
Safeway Stores	8	13.7	13.2	1.0	8.3	5.3
Great Atlantic & Pacific Tea	9	Deficit	10.1	0.6	-8.3	15.0
Median Performance		21.2	17.1	1.3	11.3	8.1

Source: "Supermarkets," Forbes *(January 14, 1985), p. 202. Reprinted by permission.*

financial data for A&P from 1978 through 1983. Table 2 compares A&P with other supermarket chains for the period 1979–84.

Current Strategy

There are several important components of A&P's current strategy. They include the planning structure, the target market, store renovation/enlargement planning, labor costs and relations, and sources of supply.

Planning Structure

The corporate planning structure consists of a management executive committee that meets monthly to study operating results, evaluate current programs, receive input as to future direction, and provide guidance as to future direction. The committee is headed by A&P's chief executive officer and is comprised of key people from all facets of the business. All members also serve on subboards, such as Finance and Administration, U.S. Retail Supermarket Operations, Warehousing and Distribution, Real Estate, and the Weekly Operations Review Committee.

In addition, planning is conducted at the manager level. Each manager formulates annual plans with growth objectives for his or her area; the manager is responsible for reaching these objectives. Computerized sales and inventory reports provide up-to-date store performance data that are useful in determining progress toward objectives and in developing sales projections.

Target Market

A&P executives now realize that the "average consumer" no longer exists. As recently as the 1960s, retailers could identify a mass market in terms of age, income, education, and life-style. Today, the market is becoming increasingly segmented. This is partly due to the rise in working women, smaller households and families, and the growth in single-parent households.

A&P is reacting to these developments in various ways. The use of alternative formats—superstores, warehouse stores, and inner-city stores—appeal to different market segments. Superstores encourage one-stop shopping, provide a large merchandise selection, offer gourmet and convenience foods (through in-store bakeries, custom butchers, fresh pasta displays, and take-out food counters). Warehouse stores satisfy consumers whose motivation is price and who are comfortable shopping in clean but nonego-gratifying environments. Inner-city stores serve the daily and fill-in needs of nearby residents.

The company is also continuously examining each store location on three dimensions of appeal: prices, product assortment, and service. It intends to modify these dimensions on a neighborhood basis to better serve shoppers.

Store Renovation/Enlargement Planning

The renovation/enlargement of existing stores is a key part of A&P's long-term growth strategy. Ideal candidates for renovation/enlargement are stores in superior locations, with sufficient space to satisfy A&P's new prototype plan. This plan involves installing an extensive deli, a modern in-store bakery, full-service meat and fish departments, and a service-oriented specialty foods island (offering imported cheeses, homemade pasta, gourmet ice cream, and exotic coffee beans).

In some cases, A&P is renaming its renovated stores to reinforce the new image sought; many company executives feared that shoppers would not give "A&P" super-markets another chance. Examples of this practice are Super Fresh (57 stores located in Philadelphia, Southern New Jersey, and Delaware), Kohl's Food Stores (62 outlets in Wisconsin), and Family Marts (23 stores in Southeastern states). James Wood recently acknowledged that these stores are doing better than the renovations that have kept the A&P name: "We haven't made the image improvements we would like in some of our A&P areas."

The company hopes its recently converted Futurestore in Baton Rouge, Louisiana, will serve as an upscale prototype. Among its features are

- An emphasis on fresh food, gourmet products, service departments, and perishables.
- A black-and-white background. The only colors that shoppers see are those involving the products on shelves.
- The use of pictographs to help guide people to the products they desire with a minimum of text. For instance, more than 25 pictographs of dairy products hang over this area and symbols of fish hang over the seafood department.
- Lights incorporated into display fixtures. There is little overhead lighting and great consistency throughout the store.
- Clusters of products with natural affinities, such as produce and flowers.

Another prototype store, which is still in the developmental stage, will be a hybrid of a warehouse store and superstore. Assortments will be extensive, including a full range of nonfood items. However, groceries will be handled as in a warehouse store; and there will be a strong price emphasis.

Table 3 lists the location of A&P stores in the United States and Canada as of the beginning of 1984.

Labor Costs and Relations

Labor costs are the largest single component of a supermarket's operating costs; they commonly account for 70 per cent of total operating costs. In the past, A&P's labor costs averaged 13 per cent of sales. They were about 11 per cent for major competitors. A&P's Philadelphia stores had labor costs that were 15 per cent of sales. This severely affected A&P's profitability. Each time A&P closed a store, its labor costs rose since veteran workers (at high wage rates) transferred to other outlets and few entry-level workers (hired at lower wages) were being employed.

The situation in Philadelphia became intolerable in 1981; and A&P closed eighty-three area stores after failing to win union concessions. Several months later, A&P (minus eighty-three stores) and the union (with 1,500 fewer members) negotiated an unprecedented arrangement. These are the important elements of that arrangement:

- A&P agreed to start a new free-standing chain, Super Fresh, in Philadelphia.
- Initial wages for Super Fresh employees were set 20 per cent below those at competing supermarkets.
- Regular meetings are held to solicit employee suggestions.
- If labor costs fall to 10 per cent of sales or less, employees earn 1 per cent of sales as a bonus.

Table 3
The Location of A&P Stores in the United States and Canada (As of the Beginning of 1984)

Location	Number of Stores	Location	Number of Stores
New England states		Southern states	
Connecticut	38	Alabama	20
Maine	5	Florida	31
Massachusetts	25	Georgia	34
New Hampshire	6	Kentucky	7
Rhode Island	3	Louisiana	49
Vermont	3	Mississippi	23
	80	North Carolina	70
		South Carolina	29
Middle Atlantic states		Tennessee	4
Delaware	10	Virginia	56
Washington, D.C.	1	West Virginia	15
Maryland	58		338
New Jersey	126		
New York	96	Total U.S.	915
Pennsylvania	52		
	343	Canada	
		Ontario	105
Central states		Quebec	2
Illinois	11		107
Indiana	9		
Michigan	55	Overall store total	1,022
Ohio	4		
Wisconsin	75		
	154		

Source: The Great Atlantic & Pacific Tea Company, Inc. Form 10K, *dated February 25, 1984, p. 4.*

- Each Super Fresh store's books are open to union officers.
- Work rules are relaxed (as to what tasks each employee can perform). This gives A&P greater flexibility.
- Seniority privileges are restricted to an employee's home store. If an outlet fails, its employees cannot bump more junior workers at successful stores. This also means that employees at successful stores do not have to fear being bumped.

In 1983, personnel at fifty-two of fifty-seven Super Fresh stores qualified for bonuses averaging just over $1 per hour. A similar arrangement at Kohl's Food Stores in Milwaukee resulted in 80 per cent of employees earning bonuses.

However, despite the success of this program in improving labor relations and increasing A&P's profitability, A&P executives believe that only an economic crisis in a specific one of its markets will get additional employees to agree to an arrangement similar to that being implemented at Super Fresh and Kohl's.

Sources of Supply

Until recently, A&P owned food-processing facilities as well as bakeries and a coffee manufacturing plant. In 1982, most of the food-processing facilities were closed. Today, A&P's only factory produces Eight O'Clock and Bokar coffees; and it sells more of its coffee through retailers located outside its market areas than through its own stores.

A&P now recognizes that it is a type of purchasing agent for its shoppers, and that it must stock the brands they desire. The private-label emphasis has been significantly reduced; and private labels are used to complement a good selection of national and regional manufacturer brands. A&P also stresses positive relations with suppliers and participates in a number of trade deals and cooperative-advertising programs.

Prospects

Although A&P has progressed a lot over the last few years, the firm still has a long way to go:

- Its 1984 net profit margin of six-tenths of 1 per cent is extremely low. The average for the nine leading chains shown in Table 2 was 1.3 per cent of sales.
- Its market share in major cities remains well behind competitors. In New York, Baltimore, Atlanta, Washington, D.C., and Detroit, it has not been among the top two firms. See Table 4 for 1983 market shares in these cities.
- Union concessions are in place in only 120 of A&P's 1,022 stores, with prospects dim for them being implemented elsewhere.
- Several of A&P's remaining stores are too small for nonfood items to be carried; and these stores do not have enough space for significant remodeling/enlargement.
- The A&P name still has a poor image in many consumers' minds.
- The renovation program is costly (averaging about $750,000 per store) and only half completed. A&P needs to generate sizable profits to be able to continue this program.

Table 4
The Market Share for A&P and the Sales Leaders in Five Major Cities, 1983

City	A&P's Market Share (%)	First Market Share		Second Market Share	
		Leader	Share (%)	Leader	Share (%)
New York	8.0	Pathmark	12.0	Shoprite	10.5
Baltimore	8.0	Giant Foods	20.5	Food-A-Rama	12.3
Atlanta	10.0	Kroger	24.0	Food Giant	21.0
Washington, D.C.	7.0	Giant Food	37.0	Safeway	32.0
Detroit	4.9	Farmer Jack	20.2	Kroger	11.7

Source: "Market Profile '83," Supermarket News (September 28, 1983). Copyright Capital Cities Media, Inc. Reprinted by permission.

Questions

1. Evaluate Table 1 to 4. What strengths and weaknesses of A&P can be seen from these tables?
2. Present a planning structure that A&P can apply at the store level. How would you coordinate this structure with the corporatewide format already in place?
3. Comment on A&P's strategy of using superstores, warehouse stores, and inner-city stores to appeal to different market segments. What are the pros and cons of modifying prices, product assortment, and service on a neighborhood basis to better serve shoppers?
4. Develop a checklist of criteria for A&P to consider in determining which existing stores merit renovation/enlargement. Should renovation/enlargement be completed on an area basis (remodeling all suitable stores in an area) or on a store-by-store basis (regardless of location)? Explain your answer.
5. What are some ways that A&P can further improve its productivity, even if its unions do not grant concessions in additional markets?
6. What are the advantages and disadvantages of A&P's now relying on outside suppliers for products? In the long run, will this practice lead to higher or lower prices for A&P? Why?

Appendix A

Careers in Retailing

Types of Positions

As indicated in Chapter 1, one of every six job positions in the nonagricultural workforce in the United States is in retailing. Figure 1 contains a comprehensive, but not exhaustive, listing of the types of positions available in this area. From the figure, one can see the diversity of employment opportunities in retailing. It should be noted that the more specialized positions are usually available only in large retail firms.

The evaluation of a retail career opportunity should center on these questions:

- What tasks do you enjoy performing?
- What are your strengths and weaknesses?
- What are your short-run and long-run goals?
- Do you want to work for a small, medium, or large retailer?
- Does the opportunity offer a clearly defined career path?
- Does the opportunity include a rigorous training program?
- Does the opportunity provide an attainable reward structure?
- Does the opportunity involve relocation?
- Will each promotion result in greater responsibility and authority?
- Is compensation fair?
- Can an exceptional employee gain faster recognition and rewards than an average employee?
- If ownership of a retail firm is a long-term goal, which opportunity will provide the greatest experience?

Career paths and compensation in retailing are highlighted in Chapter 1. Table 1 in this appendix shows selected data on retailing careers.

Selected Positions in Retailing

Job Title	Description
Accountant (Internal)	Records and summarizes the retailer's transactions. Verifies reports. Provides financial information, budgets, forecasts, and comparison reports.
Advertising manager	Develops and implements a retailer's advertising program. Determines media, copy, and message frequency. Recommends advertising budget and choice of advertising agency.
Assistant buyer	Works under the direction of a buyer, usually in a specific product category. Assists in sales analysis, handling reorders, purchasing goods, and setting up displays.
Assistant department manager	Works under the supervision of a department manager. Assists in managing personnel, controlling inventory, and other store operations.
Auditor (Internal)	Analyzes data, interprets reports, verifies accuracy of data, and monitors adherence to the retailer's regular policies and practices.
Buyer	Develops and controls sales and profit projections for a product category (generally for all stores in a chain); plans proper merchandise assortment, styling, sizes, and quantities; evaluates vendors; and supervises in-store-displays.
Catalog manager	Selects merchandise for inclusion in catalogs, works with vendors, orders catalogs, and monitors order fulfillment (particularly, timely shipments).
Commercial artist	Creates illustrations, layouts, and types of print to be used in the retailer's advertisements and catalogs as well as on private-label packages.
Credit manager	Supervises the retailer's credit process, including credit eligibility, credit terms, late payment fees, and consumer credit complaints.
Data processing manager	Oversees day-to-day operations of the retailer's computer facility. Generates appropriate accounting, credit, financial, inventory, and sales reports. Recommends computer hardware and software for the retailer.
Department manager	Responsible for a department's merchandise displays, analyzing merchandise flow, and the training and direction of the sales staff. Assists buyers in selecting merchandise for branch stores.
Divisional merchandise manager	Plans, manages, and integrates buying for an entire merchandise division (composed of several departments).
Fashion coordinator	Directs buyers in evaluating fashion trends. Orchestrates fashion shows.
Fashion director	Responsible for developing and maintaining a retailer's overall fashion perspective.
Franchisee	Purchases a business from a franchisor. Benefits by common format, joint advertising, and trouble shooting of franchisor. Operates under constraints set by franchisor.

Figure 1

Selected Positions in Retailing (continued)

Job Title	Description
Franchisor	Develops a successful business format and reputation, then licenses the right to utilize this format and name to independent businesspeople. Oversees franchises, maintains operating standards, and receives royalty fees.
Group manager	Manages a number of department managers in different merchandise classifications. Trains, supervises, and evaluates these department managers.
Management trainee	First position for most college graduates entering retailing. Involves company orientation, classroom and on-the-job training, and close contact with buyers and group managers. Leads to department manager or assistant buyer.
Marketing research director	Acquires and analyzes relevant and timely information that assists executives in making important decisions. Heavily involved in research methodology and data collection.
Merchandise administrator	Coordinates and evaluates the work of buyers in several related merchandise classifications (in a division).
Merchandise manager	Coordinates the selling efforts among different departments (merchandise categories). Acts as liaison between store managers and buyers. Similar to group manager, however there are expanded merchandise responsibilities.
Operations manager	Responsible for receiving, checking, marking, and delivering merchandise; customer service; workroom operations; personnel; and maintenance of the physical plant of the retailer.
Personnel manager	Develops a personnel policy. Analyzes long-run personnel needs. Recruits, selects, and trains personnel. Works on compensation scales and supervision rules
Public relations director	Keeps the public aware of the retailer's positive accomplishments. Measures public attitudes. Seeks to maintain a favorable image of the company.
Real estate director	Evaluates retail sites. Negotiates lease or purchase terms. Works with builders on major construction projects.
Salesperson	Assists customers in making appropriate choices. Handles minor complaints. Stocks some merchandise and sets up some displays. Notes understocked items. May also serve as a cashier.
Sales promotion manager	Plans and enacts special sales, themes, and sales promotion tools (such as contests).
Security supervisor	Responsible for minimizing pilferage among store personnel and customers. Recommends security systems and procedures. Supervises the retailer's security personnel.
Senior vice-president for merchandising	Responsible for developing and evaluating all merchandise categories' performance. Has direct accountability for growth and profit.
Store manager	Oversees all store personnel and operations in a particular outlet. Coordinates activities with other units in a chain.
Warehouser	Stores and moves goods within a retailer's warehouse. Maintains inventory records and rotates stock.

Table 1
Selected Data on Retailing Careers

- 52% of all retailing personnel are female.

- The largest employers in retailing are:
  1. Eating and drinking places — 4,820,000
  2. Food stores — 2,458,000
  3. General merchandise stores — 2,198,000
  4. Apparel and accessory stores — 942,000
  5. Furniture and home furnishings stores — 577,000

- These are the numbers of personnel in selected jobs:
  1. Sales workers — 3,367,000
  2. Store managers — 971,000
  3. Sales managers — 271,000
  4. Buyers — 172,000

- This is the outlook for growth in selected job categories:
  1. Store managers — Faster than average
  2. Sales managers — Faster than average
  3. Sales workers — Average growth
  4. Buyers — Average growth

Source: Occupational Outlook Handbook, *1984–85 Edition (Washington, D.C.: U.S. Department of Labor, Bureau of Labor Statistics, 1984), pp. 28, 195–196, 201.*

Making the Most of the Job Interview[1]

Preparing for the Interview

The employment interview is one of the most important events in a person's experience, because the 20 or 30 minutes spent with the interviewer may determine the entire future course of one's life.

Yet interviewers are continually amazed at the number of applicants who drift into job interviews without any apparent preparation and only the vaguest idea of what they are going to say. Their manner says, "Well, here we are." And that's often the end of it, in more ways than one.

Others, although they undoubtedly do not intend to do so, create an impression of indifference by acting too casually. At the other extreme, a few applicants work themselves into such a state of mind that when they arrive they seem to be in the last stages of nervous fright and are only able to answer in monosyllables.

These marks of inexperience can be avoided by knowing a little of what actually is expected of you and by making a few simple preparations before the interview.

Here are some of the things you can do to get yourself ready.

[1]Adapted from *Making the Most of Your Job Interview.* Reprinted with the permission of New York Life Insurance Company.

The Time and the Place

Find out the exact place and time of the interview. This may sound almost too basic for mention, but it's an unfortunate applicant who assumes that the interview is to be held in a certain place ("all the others were!") and then discovers two minutes before the hour that the appointment is somewhere else. Write the time and the full name and address of the company down and keep the notation with you. Don't rely on your memory. Be certain you have your interviewer's full name and find out how to pronounce it if it looks difficult.

Above all, be sure to be on time because late arrival for a job interview is almost never considered excusable.

Research

Do some research on the company interviewing you. It will be helpful to know how old the company is, what its products or services are, where its plants, offices, or stores are located, what its growth has been, and how its prospects look for the future.

Think about questions that you might wish to ask before you go to the interview. Bring a pen and a pencil with you and have some note paper with you. Keep it out of sight unless you are asked to take something down. You also should make a few notes immediately after you leave the interview.

There are a number of publications which provide information about prospective employers. Most of them can be found in any college or public library.

Your school's placement office is an excellent source for booklets and other material prepared by various firms to tell prospective employees about the opportunities they offer. You may find detailed information in the company's own literature that is unavailable in general registers.

Personal Appearance

The essentials of neatness and cleanliness when appearing for an interview scarcely need to be mentioned.

With regard to clothes, let your own good taste be your guide. Simply remember that you are looking for a job—not going to a ball game or a party.

It would be a mistake to become unduly worried over too many details. Be friendly, honest, and sincere and you will always make a good impression.

The Interview

You cannot rehearse your role in an upcoming interview because you don't know what cues will be given to you. Your best guide is to rely on your own courtesy and good sense. There are, however, some basic rules and situations common to most interviews which may help you if you know about them ahead of time.

Relax!

It is normal for many people to be nervous, particularly during an interview. A little nervousness is to be expected. Experienced interviewers discount a certain amount of nervousness, but try to avoid doing things which might make your nervousness more obvious. If you don't know where to put your hands, leave them in your lap and keep them still.

The interviewer on your campus is there to hire people—not to trip them up or embarrass them. Your interviewer wants to hire you if you have something definite to offer the company and if you will fit into the organization.

Initial Tips and Possible Questions

Greet the interviewer by name as you enter the office if you are sure of the pronunciation. Take your cues from the interviewer. Shake hands, but only if the interviewer makes the first gesture. Normally wait until a chair is offered before you sit down and don't smoke unless invited to do so. Don't chew gum during your interview.

You should be ready right at the start for at least one surprise question. A few interviewers favor one of the following openers:

1. What can I do for you?
2. Tell me about yourself.
3. Why are you interested in this company?

If you think these are easy questions to answer without some previous thought, just try them. This is where preparation counts.

If you are asked what the company can do for you, be as specific as you can—say that you would like to apply for a job that has prospects for advancement.

Suppose you are asked to talk about yourself. You have found out what the company sells and a little about how it operates. If you are wise, you have thought, "If I were in the interviewer's place, working for this company, what would I like to know about this applicant?" Tell those things about yourself which relate to the situation—your background, your education, and your work experience, if any. Don't learn a speech by rote, but have a number of points ready to discuss.

As for the third question, if you have studied the company's literature you will not be at a loss for something to talk about.

Answering Questions

Most interviewers follow a rather simple question and answer formula. If such is the case, your ability to answer quickly and intelligently is of great importance. If your answers are confused and contradictory your opportunity is lost. The best guard against contradictory answers is the plain, unembroidered truth. A frank answer, even if it seems a little unfavorable to you, is better by far than an exaggeration which may tangle you up in the next question.

Often a frank admission can be turned to your advantage. Frankness is admired and you may be able to recover in this fashion: you are asked, "Do you always pitch right into an assignment and get it done ahead of time?" You answer, "I don't always get assignments done before they are due. I sometimes tend to put things off until they have to be done. However, I have never turned in a major assignment or term paper that was late."

Keep following the interviewer's lead. Don't answer by just saying yes or no. On the other hand don't talk too much. Be informative without boasting or telling your troubles. If you find yourself talking too long, give the lead back by saying, "Perhaps you have some other questions to ask me?"

A few interviewers like to do most of the talking and judge you by your reactions—the interest, comprehension, and intelligence you show. Others hardly speak at all, and for an amateur these are the hardest to deal with. Their attitude is that it is your job to sell yourself. That is where you will have to call on your knowledge of yourself and your interest in the work the company does. In any interview, in the last analysis, you will have to sell yourself.

Even if the recruiter does much of the talking, remember that you can lead by asking questions which call in turn for a question you want to answer. Example: You are strong in extracurricular organizations. The interviewer hasn't mentioned that point and you want to go into a little detail you couldn't cover fully in your resumé. You simply watch for an opening and ask, "Are you interested in my extracurricular activities?"

Make sure that your good points get across. The interviewer won't know them unless you point them out—but try to appear factual and sincere, not bloated with conceit. If you can mention your best qualities in relation to something concrete, so much the better. For example, saying "I paid for 75 per cent of my college expenses" is better than saying "I am a hard worker and I want to get ahead."

Sit up in your chair and look alert and interested at all times. Don't look tense or relax so much that you appear slouchy. Show that you can be a wide-awake, intelligent listener as well as a talker, looking your interviewer directly in the eye from time to time during your conversation.

Be ready with an answer to the question, "What do you plan to be doing ten years from now?" It's a favorite. A popular alternative question is "How much money do you expect to be earning in ten years?" The purpose is to determine your ambition, ability to plan ahead, and the soundness of your thinking. Conduct yourself as if you are determined to get the job you are discussing. You have other irons in the fire, of course, and the recruiter is aware of that but still wants to think that you want a job with this company.

Wherever possible, apply for a specific job or field of work. If there is no opening in the line you suggest, the way you present what you have to offer may well lead the interviewer to suggest another job or department, perhaps even better than the one you were seeking. For this reason it is not advisable to get too far out on a limb by saying you will not consider anything but one certain job.

If the courses you took did not prepare you for a specific field of work, don't on that account pass up a chance for an interview. Some advance study on the talent a specific company may need will help you to present your broad qualifications for consideration.

Be careful not to make a slighting reference about a former employer or professor. If something went wrong, suggest that at least some of the fault may have been your own.

If you are asked if you've ever been fired—and you have been—again be frank in your answer. Admit you've learned from your mistakes. Also, there is the possibility you got into a wrong job through a misunderstanding.

Show the interviewer that you are interested in the company by asking some definite questions. Don't ask so many that the recruiter thinks you are afraid of work or are hesitating at the thought of joining the company. Have in mind two or three questions you want to ask about the company before you report for the interview. Also keep in mind two or three good reasons why you are interested in this particular employer. The chances are excellent that you will be asked for your reasons. If so, stick to the subject at hand. Don't let yourself wander away on a tangent because you like the sound of your own voice.

Should you get the impression that the interview is not going well and that you have already been rejected, don't let your discouragement show. You have nothing to lose by continuing the appearance of confidence and you may gain much. The last few minutes often change things. Once in a great while, an interviewer who is genuinely interested in your possibilities may seem to discourage you in order to test your reaction. If you remain confident and determined you have probably made a good impression.

Some Pointers and Questions

Don't take notes during an interview. This is annoying and distracting to some recruiters. The best policy is to note on paper immediately after you leave the interviewer everything you want to be sure to remember.

If you are given an application form, be certain that it is filled out completely and neatly. A messy application form can create as bad an impression as personal untidiness.

What if you so impress the interviewer that you are offered a job on the spot? This is very rare, but you should have an answer prepared. If you are absolutely sure it is the job you want, accept with a definite yes. If you have the slightest doubt or do not want to accept without further thought or further interviews, play for time. Be courteous and tactful in asking for time to think it over. Try to set a definite date when you can provide an answer. This will reassure the recruiter you are giving this offer serious consideration. Whether you decide to decline or accept, be sure to inform your interviewer of that decision as soon as possible.

On the other hand, don't be too discouraged if no definite offer is made or no specific salary is discussed. The recruiter almost always wants to communicate with superiors first or interview more applicants before making any offers.

If you accept more than one job offer, you will reflect badly upon yourself and your school. If you have accepted one job and a chance turns up suddenly to interview for a really irresistible position, turn to your placement officer for advice. Job engagements have been broken before. But the way it is done is most important. It frequently happens that in your job with Company B you will have dealings with Company A. Hard feelings are best avoided.

Don't make appointments in which you are not interested. You will find yourself in an extremely awkward position and you stand to lose the confidence of everyone involved.

You may be asked why you left your last two or three jobs. Return to school, better pay, more responsibility are acceptable reasons. Be careful, however, not to give the impression that you are a job jumper or shopper.

What about salary? Many people believe that an applicant has to ask for as much as the traffic will bear, or more, in hope of gaining a bargaining position. They feel that companies always offer as little as they can. However, where most college interviews are concerned, the company representative has arrived on campus with a certain number of jobs to be filled in definite salary brackets. The interviewer may not choose, unfortunately, to tell you what there is to offer.

It is possible that you may be asked how much you want in the way of salary. The usual answer in that case is to indicate that you're more interested in a job where you can prove yourself than you are in a specific salary. This politely passes the question back to the interviewer. In most cases, reputable corporations will offer the standard salary for the type of job in question. It is in your interest, of course, to find out what the rate is. You know, also, the level beneath which your needs and responsibilities will not permit you to go. Your placement officer can tell you what the normal range of starting rates will be for a person with your background.

Most interviews last between 20 and 30 minutes. Don't go on talking and talking. Some applicants talk themselves into a job and then right out of it. Be alert to signs from the interviewer that the session is almost at an end. (Watchlooking is a sure one.) If you still want the job, sum up your interest briefly, say you are interested, and stop.

Be sure to thank the recruiter for the time and consideration given to you. Resist the temptation to flatter. Even if the interviewer is the most fascinating person you've ever talked to, don't say so. You may be misunderstood. Smile, and show as much confidence in leaving as you did in arriving. Say something like: "If you have any other questions, or if there is anything you want me to do, I hope you will get in touch with me." Then say thank you and leave.

If you have answered the two questions uppermost in the recruiter's mind: why are you interested in my company? and what can you offer? Then you have done all you can.

Should you write a thank you letter? Ordinarily, no. You will have noted, soon after the interview, any further contact your interviewer suggested. Follow the instructions exactly and don't send unrequested correspondence.

The interviewer may have indicated that you would be contacted or truly seemed interested in you. Wait about a week and then write a brief note to remind the recruiter of your talk. Express appreciation for the time given you and explain in as few words as possible your continuing interest in the company. You have little to lose by refreshing his or her memory and you might get a favorable response.

In any event, if you do not get a flat rejection, or the polite no expressed in the type of letter that says, "We will keep your letter in our files and let you know if anything. . . ." keep in touch. Unless you make a nuisance of yourself you will thus be able to stay in the foreground if a vacancy appears.

As other questions or problems arise, take them to your placement officer. They work with all types of business, governmental, educational, and other organizations, and can be of great help to you if you work through their office. Be certain to notify them when you take a job or change your job.

If you don't connect immediately, remember that interviewers, companies, and jobs differ greatly. You will learn much from your first interview and you will almost certainly do better in succeeding ones. The important thing is to keep trying.

Your Resumé

Your school placement office may use a standard data sheet which you will be asked to fill in so that it may be used as a resumé of your activities and work experience. Some companies also may ask you to fill out such a sheet. In either case, be certain to do so accurately, fully, and neatly. Your data sheet will represent you to people who have never met you. If it is untidy you will be judged accordingly.

Some schools, and a number of companies, prefer you to develop your own resumé as a supplement to the face-to-face interview. For this reason we have included the following material on the resumé with the thought that it might be of help to you.

A self-prepared resumé becomes increasingly important if you change jobs in the years after graduation. In certain instances it is almost indispensable, such as application by letter, off-the-campus interviews, or an intensive job-hunting campaign in a major city.

The resumé must be neat. Careless erasures and misspelled words are inexcusable, and the latter, particularly, may cost you a good chance at a job.

A good resumé will go a long way toward helping you make a good impression. A bad resumé can seriously hurt the chances of an applicant who may seem desirable in every other way.

Contents and layouts of resumés vary as widely as the different individuals who apply for jobs. Interviewers and companies, also, differ as to what they want to see on a resumé. You will be safest, however, if you keep it simple and keep it on one page.

Your resumé should be typed. Multilithed, mimeographed, or otherwise duplicated copies are acceptable if they are well done.

Organizing the Resumé

Your use of white space is most important in creating an impression of neatness and orderliness. Space can be used to isolate important points to which you want to draw attention. Sufficient spacing between all elements helps to create a clean, inviting impression. Crowding too many details too close together results in a poor appearance, as well as a fine print look that repels a reader.

Be sure to use a good quality bond paper and keep carbon copies to save yourself a rewriting job if the original is lost.

Your method of organizing the separate elements of your resumé is not as important as the fact that you show some kind of orderly, reasonable process. Unless you have proven that you have a better idea, it is wise to stick to a conventional layout with straight lines and nonerratic paragraphing. Gimmick-type resumés have occasionally caught the interest of companies, but gimmicks can backfire.

If you make use of a resumé in a job-hunt a number of years after graduation your work experience will, of course, be highlighted. College activities will then ordinarily be reduced in the resumé to a statement of your university's name, the year graduated, your degree, and possibly your major.

Your own situation may call for a different approach from the examples given here. What is important to remember is that you must sell your value to a company as surely as that company sells its own products to the public. You must appeal to the employer's interest in what you have to offer. Never emphasize your personal problems or the personal advantages you will gain from employment.

References in the Resumé

References may or may not be included. Some interviewers prefer to see them on your resumé. Others assume that you have them readily available. References related to your work experience are preferred to those of social acquaintances. A professor in your chosen field of interest is a good choice if you are known well. (Not all of your references should be teachers, however.) Courtesy dictates that you ask your references' permission before using their names. Relatives are never used as references.

Work Experience in the Resumé

Work experience is an essential ingredient of any resumé. Dates should be given, along with the company addresses and a brief description of your work.

Your job list should ordinarily begin with the last job you held. It should include listings in reverse order, ending with the earliest. Some applicants have made strong cases for themselves because they have held jobs with the company for a considerable length of time. If you have been asked, for example, to return to the same company several summers in succession, by all means say so.

Other applicants, who have had successively more responsible jobs should emphasize that growing responsibility.

Since any company considering you likes to think that you will be a success, it is also good to note a promotion or recognition that has come your way as a result of success in a job. Be frank about your accomplishments, stating them briefly and factually. It is better, for instance, to say that you began as a shipping helper and were promoted to inventory clerk than just to list the latter position. Demonstrated ability and progress may mean more to an interviewer than the simple fact that you held a certain job. Also, significant minor experience, if it relates in any way to the job you are seeking, may help you, and should be included.

Since your major courses in school and your showing in those courses indicate your interests and abilities, you should have a section in your resumé touching on the highlights. Frankness is the wisest policy. Most companies do not limit themselves to seeking only students with stratospheric grade averages. Grades are an important part of the picture—but not the only part.

Extracurricular Activities in the Resumé

Include your extracurricular activities. Many jobs are especially fitted for a well-rounded individual. The fact that you have been chosen as a member by honorary groups or elected to professional societies in your field speaks well for your future in that field. If you belonged to purely social organizations, list them. A large part of anyone's success in a new job grows out of the ability to get along with other workers. A demonstrated social awareness can be a point in your favor. Further, if you participated in activities to an extent that you were recognized by awards or offices, mention those, too. Leadership quality is welcomed everywhere.

It is understood, however, that if you worked your way through school and maintained good grades you have little time for extracurricular activities. You should definitely state what per cent of your college expenses were personally earned, and how many hours per week were usually devoted to working.

Everyone has something to offer. Analyze your abilities, talents, and interests correctly and stress strong points as they relate to the job you are seeking.

Do that successfully in your resumé and follow through with it in your interviews. Sooner or later, you will find the organization which has been looking for you.

Figure 2 is an illustration of a resumé for a person about to enter a career in retailing.

Sample Resumé

Jennifer Marcus
17 Hart Drive
West Hartford, Connecticut 06117
203-200-7416

EMPLOYMENT OBJECTIVE: Assistant Buyer Position, Formal Training
Program Desired

EDUCATION: Bachelor of Business Administration, June 1985;
Hofstra University   Hempstead, New York 11550
Major: Marketing   Class Rank: Top 10%

SCHOLARSHIPS   Hofstra University Distinguished Scholar Academic Award
AND AWARDS: Member, Beta Gamma Sigma, National Business Honor Society

EXTRACURRICULAR
ACTIVITIES: Vice President, American Marketing Association,
Fall 1983 - Spring 1985; Hofstra Collegiate Chapter

Responsible for: recruitment of members, planning
of student career conference, and budget preparation
and control.

Member, American Marketing Association; New York
and National Chapters

WORK
EXPERIENCE:

January 1982 - Sales Clerk, Fashion World, 200 Main Street,
Present   Hempstead, New York
20 hours per week
Responsibilities include selling women's clothing,
setting up displays, and checking inventory in
high fashion ladies' specialty store.

July 1980 -   Cashier, Thrifty Drug Stores,
September 1981 Green Acres Shopping Center, Valley Stream, New York
Responsibilities included: setting up inventory
and displays, selling cameras, film, and radios.

Paid half of tuition expenses by working 20 hours per week
while attending college.

PERSONAL: Height — 5'5"   Date of Birth — September 6, 1963
Weight — 125 lbs.   Marital Status — Single
Health — Excellent

Willing to Relocate

REFERENCES: Will be furnished upon request.

Figure 2

Selected Firms Seeking College Graduates for Retail-Related Positions

Abraham & Straus
420 Fulton Street
Brooklyn, NY 11202
Division of Federated Department
 Stores
13,000 employees
Department store chain
East, South, Midwest

Albertson's
250 Parkcenter Boulevard
P.O. Box 20
Boise, ID 83726
34,000 employees
Supermarket chain
West

Allied Stores
1114 Avenue of the Americas
New York, NY 10036
62,000 employees
National department store group
Units located in 44 states

B. Altman & Co.
361 5th Avenue
New York, NY 10016
5,000 employees
Department store chain
East, Southeast

American Stores Co.
P.O. Box 27447
709 East South Temple
Salt Lake City, UT 84127
60,000 employees
Supermarket and drugstore chains
East and West Coasts

Ames Department Stores
2418 Main Street
Rocky Hill, CT 06067
5,200 employees
Discount department store chain
East

ARA Services
57 Executive Park South, NE
Atlanta, GA 30029
7,500 employees
Vending and food services firm
South, Southeast

Associated Dry Goods
417 5th Avenue
New York, NY 10016
60,000 employees
Specialty clothing and discount store
 chains
U.S.

Associated Merchandising Corp.
1440 Broadway
New York, NY 10018
860 employees
Affiliated with 30 department stores
Retail service organization
Northeast

Bamberger's
131 Market Street
Newark, NJ 07101
Division of R. H. Macy
3,000 employees
Department store chain
Mid-Atlantic, Midwest, Northeast

Block's
50 North Illinois Street
Indianapolis, IN 46209
Subsidiary of Allied Stores
2,000 employees
Department store chain
Midwest

Bloomingdale's
Lexington Avenue at 59th Street
New York, NY 10022
Division of Federated Department
 Stores
13,000 employees

Department store chain
East, Southeast, Southwest

The Bon
3rd and Pine Streets
Seattle, WA 98101
Subsidiary of Allied Stores
7,500 employees
Department store chain
California, Pacific Northwest

Bonwit Teller
1120 Avenue of the Americas
New York, NY 10036
Subsidiary of Allied Stores
2,500 employees
Fashion specialty chain
Mid-Atlantic

The Broadway–Southern California
3880 North Misson Road
Los Angeles, CA 90031
Subsidiary of Carter Hawley Hale
 Stores
16,500 employees
Department store chain
West, Southern California

Buffums Department Stores
301 Long Beach Boulevard
Los Angeles, CA 90802
Subsidiary of David Jones, Ltd.
2,000 employees
Department store chain
Southern California

Bullock's
800 South Hope Street
Los Angeles, CA 90014
Division of Federated Department
 Stores
9,000 employees
Department store chain
West Coast, Southwest

Burdine's
22 East Flagler Street
Miami, FL 33132
Division of Federated Department
 Stores
10,000 employees
Department store chain
Florida

Burger King
7360 North Kendall Drive
Miami, FL 33156
Subsidiary of Pillsbury Co.
1,700 employees
Fast-food franchisor
U.S.

Burroughs Corp.
Burroughs Place

Detroit, MI 48232
62,000 employees
Business machines, computer
 systems manufacturer
U.S.

Cain-Sloan Co.
5th Avenue and Church Street
Nashville, TN 37219
1,300 employees
Department store chain
Southeast

Canadian Tire Corp.
2180 Yonge Street
Toronto, Ontario, Canada
M4P 2V8
2,500 employees
Hardware, sports equipment, auto
 products retail chain
Canada

Carson, Pirie, Scott & Co.
1 South State Street
Chicago, IL 60603
8,000 employees
Department store chain
Midwest

Carter Hawley Hale
550 South Flower Street
Los Angeles, CA 90071
58,000 employees
Operates department store chains
Eastern and Western U.S.

City Stores
5 West 37th Street
New York, NY 10018
4,000 employees
Furniture store chain
East

County Seat Stores
Box 1442
Minneapolis, MN 55440
Subsidiary of Super Valu Stores
Retail apparel chain
Mideast, Midwest

Davidson's Golden Rule
601 Nicollet Mall
Minneapolis, MN 55402
Division of Allied Stores
2,700 employees
Department store chain
Midwest

Davison's
180 Peachtree Street, NW
Atlanta, GA 30303
Division of R. H. Macy
4,000 employees
Department store chain
Midwest, Southeast

Dayton Hudson Corp.
777 Nicollet Mall
Minneapolis, MN 55402
100,000 employees
Department store, discount store,
 bookstore, electronics store chain
U.S.

Dey Brothers & Co.
401 South Salina Street
Syracuse, NY 13201
Subsidiary of Allied Stores Corp.
1,060 employees
Department store chain
Northern New York

Dollar General Corp.
427 Beech Street
Scottsville, KY 42164
2,000 employees
Retail and wholesale general
 merchandise retailer
Southeast

Dominion Stores Limited
605 Rogers Road
Toronto, Ontario, Canada
M6M 1B9
25,000 employees
Retail food chain
Canada

Dun & Bradstreet
1 Diamond Hill Road
Berkeley Heights, NJ 07922
7,000 employees
Information advisory services
U.S.

Jack Eckerd Corp.
8333 Bryan Dairy Road
P.O. Box 4689
Clearwater, FL 33518
25,100 employees
Drugstore chain
East, Southeast

Edison Brothers Shoe Stores
P.O. Box 14020
St. Louis, MO 63178
20,000 employees
Women's shoe store chain
U.S.

Emporium-Capwell
835 Market Street
San Francisco, CA 94103
Subsidiary of Carter Hawley Hale
 Stores
10,000 employees
Department store chain
West Coast

Famous-Barr Co.
601 Olive Street
St. Louis, MO 63101
Subsidiary of May Department
 Stores
8,000 employees
Department store chain
Midwest

Fed-Mart Stores
3851 Rosecrams Street
San Diego, CA 92110
10,800 employees
Department store chain
Southwest

Federated Department Stores
7 West 7th Street
Cincinnati, OH 45202
124,000 employees
Department store, discount store,
 and supermarket chains
U.S.

Filene's
426 Washington Street
Boston, MA 01701
Division of Federated Department
 Stores
7,400 employees
Fashion specialty chain
Northeast

First National Supermarkets
17000 Rockside Road
Maple Heights, OH 44137
17,000 employees
Retail grocery chain
East

Fisher Foods, Inc.
5300 Richmond Road
Bedford Heights, OH 44146
15,000 employees
Supermarket chain
Midwest

Foley's
1110 Main Street
Houston, TX 77001
Division of Federated Department
 Stores
8,000 employees
Department store chain
Southwest

G. Fox and Co.
960 Main Street
Hartford, CT 06115
Subsidiary of May Department
 Stores
4,000 employees
Department store chain
New England, East

The Gap Stores Inc.
P.O. Box 60
900 Cherry Avenue
San Bruno, CA 94066
7,000 employees
Specialty store chain
U.S.

Garfinckel, Brooks Brothers, Miller &
 Rhoads Inc.
1629 K Street, NW
Washington, DC 20006
Department and specialty store
 chains
U.S. and International

General Distributors of Canada Ltd.
1370 Sony Place
Winnipeg, Manitoba, Canada
R3C 3C3
6,000 employees
Junior department and family
 clothing store chains
Canada

Genesco Inc.
230 Genesco Park
Nashville, TN 37202
16,000 employees
Manufacturer, wholesaler, and
 retailer of shoes and specialty store
 operator
U.S.

Genovese Drug Stores
80 Marcus Drive
Melville, NY 11747
1,800 employees
Retail drug chain
East

Giant Food Inc.
6300 Sheriff Road
Landover, MD 20785
12,900 employees
Retail food, general merchandising,
 and pharmacy chains
Maryland, Virginia, Washington, D.C.

Gimbels Midwest
101 West Wisconsin Avenue
P.O. Box 632
Milwaukee, WI 53201
Division of Batus
5,000 employees
Department store chain
Midwest

Gimbel's New York
33rd Street and Broadway
New York, NY 10001
Division of Batus
7,000 employees

Department store chain
East

Gimbel's Philadelphia
9th and Market Streets
Philadelphia, PA 19105
Division of Batus
3,300 employees
Department store chain
East, Midwest

Gimbel's Pittsburgh
6th Avenue and Smithfield Street
Pittsburgh, PA 15222
5,000 employees
Department store chain
East

Gold Circle Stores
6121 Huntley Road
Worthington, OH 43085
Division of Federated Department
 Stores
6,500 employees
Discount store chain
East, Midwest, West Coast

Goldblatt Brothers
333 South State Street
Chicago, IL 60604
7,900 employees
Department store chain
Chicago and vicinity

Goldsmith's
123 South Main Street
Memphis, TN 38143
Division of Federated Department
 Stores
3,000 employees
Department store chain
Mid-South

Grand Union
100 Broadway
Elmwood Park, NJ 07407
31,000 employees
Supermarket chain
East, Puerto Rico, Virgin Islands

The Great Atlantic & Pacific Tea
 Company
Box 418
2 Paragon Drive
Montvale, NJ 07645
53,000 employees
Supermarket chain
South, Central, Eastern U.S. and
 Canada

Hecht Co.
7th at F Street, NW
Washington, DC 20004
Subsidiary of May Department
 Stores

11,000 employees
Department store chain
East, Mid-Atlantic, Southeast

Heer's Inc.
Park Central Square
Springfield, MO 65801
Subsidiary of Allied Stores
200 employees
Department store
Missouri

Hennessy's Department Stores
140 South 24th Street, West
Billings, MT 59102
Subsidiary of Mercantile Stores
500 employees
Department store chain
Montana

Herp's
1 Monroe Mall, NW
Grand Rapids, MI 49503
Subsidiary of Allied Stores
600 employees
Department store
Michigan

Higbee Co.
100 Public Square
Cleveland, OH 44113
5,600 employees
Department store, sportswear, and
  women's shoe chains
Midwest

Hilton Hotels
9880 Wilshire Boulevard
Beverly Hills, CA 90201
31,000 employees
Hotel chain
Worldwide

Holiday Inns
3742 Lamar Avenue
Memphis, TN 38118
35,000 employees
Hotel chain and franchisor
Worldwide

Host International
34th Street and Pico Boulevard
Santa Monica, CA 90406
13,100 employees
Quick service and sit-down
  restaurant facilities
Michigan, Ohio

J. L. Hudson Co.
1206 Woodward Avenue
Detroit, MI 48226
Subsidiary of Dayton Hudson
14,000 employees
Department store chain
Indiana, Michigan, Ohio

Hudson's Bay Company
Hudson's Bay House
77 Main Street
Winnipeg, Manitoba, Canada
R3C 2R1
43,000 employees
Department store chain
Canada

IBM
1 Barker Avenue
White Plains, NY 10601
350,000 employees
Computer manufacturer
Worldwide

IHOP Corp.
6837 Lankershim Boulevard
North Hollywood, CA 91605
1,500 employees
Coffee shop chain
U.S. and Canada

Jewel Companies
O'Hare Plaza
5725 North East River Road
Chicago, IL 60631
37,000 employees
Supermarket chain (including self-
  service drug and department
  stores)
U.S.

Jordan Marsh–Florida
1501 Biscayne Boulevard
Miami, FL 33132
Subsidiary of Allied Stores
4,700 employees
Department store chain
Southeast

Jordan Marsh–New England
P.O. Box 2509
Boston, MA 02205
Subsidiary of Allied Stores
10,000 employees
Department store chain
Northeast

Joske's of Dallas
1900 Elm Street
Dallas, TX 75201
Subsidiary of Allied Stores
2,300 employees
Department store chain
Southwest

Joske's of Houston
4925 Westheimer
Houston, TX 77056
Subsidiary of Allied Stores
2,500 employees
Department store chain
Southwest

Joske's of San Antonio
By the Alamo
San Antonio, TX 78205
Subsidiary of Allied Stores
2,200 employees
Department store chain
Southwest

Joslin's
934 16th Street
Denver, CO 80202
Subsidiary of Mercantile Stores
Retail clothing chain
West

K mart
3100 West Big Beaver
Troy, MI 48084
250,000 employees
Discount department store chain
U.S., Puerto Rico, Canada, Australia

Kaufman's
400 5th Avenue
Pittsburgh, PA 15219
Subsidiary of May Department
  Stores
5,000 employees
Department store chain
Midwest

Kroger Co.
1014 Vine Street
Cincinnati, OH 45201
162,000 employees
Food and drug chain
Midwest, South, Southeast,
  Southwest

F. R. Lazarus & Co.
High and Town Streets
Columbus, OH 43216
Division of Federated Department
  Stores
8,000 employees
Department store chain
Midwest

Lerner Shops
460 West 33rd Street
New York, NY 10001
Subsidiary of Lerner Stores
Women's apparel chain
East

Levitz Furniture Corp.
1317 NW 167th Street
Miami, FL 33169
4,600 employees
Furniture and home furnishings
  chain
U.S.

Levy's of Savannah
201 East Broughton Street

Savannah, GA 31401
Subsidiary of Allied Stores
150 employees
Department store
Southeast

The Limited, Inc.
1 Limited Parkway
P.O. Box 16528
Columbus, OH 43216
7,000 employees
Women's fashion apparel chain
U.S.

Loblaws Limited
22 St. Clair Avenue East
Toronto, Ontario, Canada
M4T 2S3
10,000 employees
Retail food chain
Canada, Minnesota, New York

Loehmann's
3450 Baychester Avenue
Bronx, NY 10475
2,500 employees
Women's fashion apparel chain

Lord and Taylor
424 5th Avenue
New York, NY 10018
Subsidiary of Associated Dry Goods
7,000 employees
Specialty chain
East, Midwest, Southeast

Lucky Stores
6300 Clark Avenue
P.O. Box BB
Dublin, CA 94566
65,000 employees
Supermarket chain
U.S.

Maas Brothers
P.O. Box 311
Tampa, FL 33601
Subsidiary of Allied Stores
5,500 employees
Department store chain
Southeast

Mabley & Carew
5th and Vine Streets
Cincinnati, OH 45202
Subsidiary of Allied Stores
800 employees
Department store chain
Midwest

R. H. Macy & Company
151 West 34th Street
New York, NY 10001
48,000 employees
Department store chain

Midwest, Northeast, Southeast,
 West

I. Magnin
135 Stockton Street
San Francisco, CA 94108
Division of Federated Department
 Stores
3,500 employees
Specialty store chain
U.S.

Marks & Spencer Canada
3770 Nashua Drive
Mississauga, Ontario, Canada
L4T 3R1
4,000 employees
Department store chain
Canada

Marshall Field
25 East Washington Street
Chicago, IL 60690
30,100 employees
Department store chain
Northwest and Midwest

D&F May
16th at Tremont Street
Denver, CO 80202
Subsidiary of May Department
 Stores
3,000 employees
Department store chain
Southwest

May Co.–Cleveland
158 Euclid Avenue
Cleveland, OH 44114
Subsidiary of May Department
 Stores Co.
4,000 employees
Department store chain
Midwest, North

May Department Stores Co.
611 Olive Street
St. Louis, MO 63101
70,000 employees
Department store chain
U.S.

McDonald's
2111 Enco Drive
Oak Brook, IL 60521
117,000 employees
Fast-food franchise and restaurant
 chain
U.S. and International

Melville Corporation
3000 Westchester Avenue
P.O. Box 677
Harrison, NY 10528
68,000 employees

Shoe manufacturer and retail chain
U.S.

Mercantile Stores Co.
128 West 31st Street
New York, NY 10001
17,000 employees
Department store chain
Midwest, Northwest, Southeast,
 Northeast

Merry-Go-Round Enterprises
1220 East Joppa Road
Baltimore, MD 21204
2,000 employees
Specialty clothing chain
U.S.

Fred Meyer
3800 22nd Avenue
Portland, OR 97209
13,000 employees
Supermarket chain
Northwest

Montgomery Ward
1 Montgomery Ward Plaza
Chicago, IL 60671
79,000 employees
Department and discount store
 chain
U.S.

Morrison Inc.
P.O. Box 160266
Mobile, AL 36625
15,000 employees
Cafeteria, motel, and food service
 facility chain
South, Southeast

G. C. Murphy Co.
531 5th Avenue
McKeesport, PA 15132
16,000 employees
Variety store chain
East, Midwest, South, and
 Southwest

Nash Finch Co.
3381 Gorham Avenue
St. Louis Park, MN 55246
6,000 employees
Retail and wholesale food distributor
Midwest, West

National Convenience Stores Inc.
3200 Travis Street
P.O. Box 758
Houston, TX 77006
Subsidiary of Stop N Go Markets
5,200 employees
Convenience store chain
West, Midwest, Southeast

National Tea
9701 West Higgins Road
Rosemont, IL 60018
Subsidiary of Loblaw Limited
  Companies
Supermarket chain
Midwestern and South Central

NCR
World Headquarters
Dayton, OH 45479
68,000 employees
Manufacturer of electronic business
  equipment systems
Worldwide

Neiman-Marcus
Main and Ervay Streets
Dallas, TX 75201
Division of Carter Hawley Hale
  Stores
8,000 employees
Specialty store chain
U.S.

A. C. Nielsen
Nielsen Plaza
Northbrook, IL 60062
23,000 employees
Market research services
U.S.

Orbach's
5 West 34th Street
New York, NY 10001
2,200 employees
Fashion specialty chain
New York, New Jersey, Los Angeles

O'Neil's
226 South Main Street
Akron, OH 44308
Subsidiary of May Department
  Stores
2,800 employees
Department store chain
Midwest

Osco Drug
1818 Swift Drive
Oakbrook, IL 60521
Subsidiary of Jewel Companies
10,500 employees
General, merchandise, drug, and
  department store chain
Midwest, Northwest, New England

The Oshawa Group Limited
302 The East Mall
Islington, Ontario, Canada
M9B 6B8
12,700 employees

Department store and drugstore
  chains
Canada

P&C Food Markets
State Fair Boulevard
P.O. Box 4965
Syracuse, NY 13221
4,500 employees
Supermarket chain, franchisor
Northeast

J. C. Penney
1301 Avenue of the Americas
New York, NY 10019
175,000 employees
Department store and mail-order
  chains
U.S., Puerto Rico

Pizza Hut
9111 East Douglas
Wichita, KS 67207
Subsidiary of Pepsico
27,000 employees
Fast-food chain
U.S.

Plymouth Shops
125 West End Avenue
New York, NY 10023
Subsidiary of Allied Stores
1,000 employees
Women's specialty clothing chain
New York, New Jersey, Washington,
  D.C.

H. S. Pogue
4th and Race Streets
Cincinnati, OH 45202
Division of Associated Dry Goods
1,300 employees
Department store chain
East, Midwest

Pomeroy's Inc.–Harrisburg
326 Market Street
Harrisburg, PA 17105
Subsidiary of Allied Stores
1,440 employees
Department store chain
Pennsylvania

Pomeroy's Inc.–Levittown
500 Levittown Center
Levittown, PA 19059
Subsidiary of Allied Stores
1,982 employees
Department store chain
Pennsylvania

H. C. Prange Co.
727 Plaza 8

Sheboygan, WI 53081
6,000 employees
Department, discount, and specialty
  store chains
Midwest

Rapid-American Corporation
888 7th Avenue
New York, NY 10106
50,000 employees
Conglomerate with retail store
  chains
U.S.

Read's
Trumbull Shopping Park
Trumbull, CT 06611
Subsidiary of Allied Stores
1,800 employees
Department store chain
Northeast

Reitman's (Canada) Limited
250 Sauve Street West
Montreal, Quebec, Canada
H3L 1Z2
3,000 employees
Women's and misses' apparel chain
Canada

Rich's
P.O. Box 4539
Atlanta, GA 30302
Division of Federated Department
  Stores
8,000 employees
Department store chain
Midwest, Southeast

Richmand Gordman Stores
12100 West Center Road
Omaha, NE 68144
2,500 employees
Department store chain
Midwest

Richway Discount Stores
45 Broad Street SW
Atlanta, GA 30303
Division of Federated Department
  Stores
5,000 employees
Discount store chain
Southeast

Rose's Stores
P.H. Rose Building
Henderson, NC 27536
11,000 employees
Variety store chain
East, Southeast

Safeway Stores
Fourth and Jackson Streets

Oakland, CA 94660
162,000 employees
Supermarket chain
U.S. and International

Sanger Harris
303 North Akard
Dallas, TX 75201
Division of Federated Department
  Stores
10,000 employees
Department store chain
Midwest, South

Sav-On Drugs
1500 South Anaheim Boulevard
Anaheim, CA 92805
7,000 employees
Drugstore chain
West

Sears, Roebuck and Company
Sears Tower
Chicago, IL 60684
450,000 employees
Department store and mail-order
  chain
U.S. and foreign countries

Service Merchandise Co.
P.O. Box 24600
Nashville, TN 37202
12,000 employees
Catalog showroom chain
Midwest, Southeast, West

Sherwin-Williams
101 Prospect Avenue
Cleveland, OH 44115
17,000 employees
Manufacturer and retailer of paints
  and related products
U.S.

Shillito Rikes
7th and Race Streets
Cincinnati, OH 45202
Division of Federated Department
  Stores
4,000 employees
Department store chain
Midwest

Shoe Corporation of America
35 North Fourth Street
Columbus, OH 43215
4,000 employees
Operates retail shoe stores and
  leased departments

Sigmor
3643 East Commerce Street
San Antonio, TX 78220
5,245 employees
Gasoline and auto products chain

Skaggs Companies
310 Bearcat Drive
Salt Lake City, UT 84125
11,000 employees
Drugstore chain
Southwest, Midwest, West

Southland Corporation
2828 North Haskell Avenue
P.O. Box 719
Dallas, TX 75221
61,000 employees
Convenience food store chain and
  franchisor
U.S. and International

Steinberg Inc.
Alexis-Nihon Plaza
1500 Atwater Avenue
Montreal, Quebec, Canada
H3Z 1Y3
25,700 employees
Retail food market and self-service
  department store chains
Canada

Stern's
Route 4, Bergen Mall
Paramus, NJ 07652
Subsidiary of Allied Stores
5,700 employees
Department store chain
Metropolitan New York

Stewart Dry Goods Company
6790 Reistertown Road
Baltimore, MD 21215
Subsidiary of Associated Dry Goods
  Corp.
Department store chain
East, Midwest, South

Stop and Shop Companies
P.O. Box 369
Boston, MA 02101
28,000 employees
Supermarket chain
Northeast

Strauss
20 West Federal Street
Youngstown, OH 44503
Subsidiary of May Department
  Stores
2,000 employees
Department store chain
Midwest

Strawbridge and Clothier
Market East at 8th Street
Philadelphia, PA 19105
12,000 employees
Department store chain
Mid-Atlantic, New England

Super Valu
11840 Valley View Road
Eden Prairie, MN 55344
15,000 employees
Food wholesaler
Midwest, South

Supermarkets General
301 Blair Road
Woodbridge, NJ 07095
30,000 employees
Supermarket, drugstore, and home
  center chains
Northeast

Tandy Corporation/Radio Shack
500 One Tandy Center
Forth Worth, TX 76102
25,000 employees
Manufacturer and retailer of
  electronics
Nationwide

Thrifty Corp.
5051 Rodeo Road
Los Angeles, CA 90016
5,200 employees
Retail drugstores
West

Tiffany
727 5th Avenue
New York, NY 10022
Fine jewelry and accessories chain
U.S.

Titche Goettinger Company
1900 Elm Street
Dallas, TX 75201
Subsidiary of Allied Stores
2,150 employees
Department store chain
Southwest

Toys 'R' Us
395 West Passaic Street
Rochelle Park, NJ 07662
8,800 employees
Retail toy chain
U.S.

Troutman's
200 South Main Street
Greensburg, PA 15601
Subsidiary of Allied Stores
1,000 employees
Department store chain
Pennsylvania

Ups 'N Downs Stores
471 8th Avenue
New York, NY 10001
1,500 employees
Apparel specialty chain
East

Urban Decision Systems
P.O. Box 25953
2032 Armcost Avenue
Los Angeles, CA 90025
Retail site selection consultant

Venture Stores
615 Northwest Plaza
St. Ann, MO 63074
Subsidiary of May Department
  Stores
12,000 employees
Discount retail chain
Midwest

Volume Shoe Corporation
3231 East 6th Street
Topeka, KS 66607
Subsidiary of May Department
  Stores
6,000 employees
Family shoe store chain
34 states

Waldbaum
Hemlock Street and Boulevard
  Avenue
Central Islip, NY 11722
6,000 employees
Supermarket chain
New York, Connecticut,
  Massachusetts

Walgreen
200 Wilmot Road
Deerfield, IL 60015
28,000 employees
Restaurant and drugstore chain
U.S.

Wal-Mart Stores
702 Southwest 8th Street
P.O. Box 116

Bentonville, AR 72712
62,000 employees
Discount department store chain
South, Midwest

John Wanamaker
13th and Market Streets
Philadelphia, PA 19101
Department store chain
New York, Pennsylvania

Western Auto
2107 Grand Avenue
Kansas City, MO 64108
Subsidiary of Beneficial Finance
  Company
10,000 employees
Retailer and wholesaler of durable
  goods
U.S.

Western International Motels
Olympic Hotel
Seattle, WA 98111
20,000 employees
Hotel chain
Worldwide

Wickes Companies
3340 Ocean Park Boulevard
Santa Monica, CA 90405
44,000 employees
Retail lumber and building supplies
  chain
U.S. and Europe

Wiebolt Stores
1 North State Street
Chicago, IL 60602
4,900 employees
Department store chain
Midwest

Winn-Dixie Stores
5050 Edgewood Court
Jacksonville, FL 32203
67,000 employees
Supermarket chain
Southeast

Woodward and Lothrop
10th and F Streets
Washington, D.C. 20013
8,000 employees
Department store chain
Washington, D.C.; Maryland;
  Virginia

F.W. Woolworth
19th Floor, Woolworth Building
New York, NY 10279
115,000 employees
Variety and discount chain store
U.S.

Wren's
14 East Main Street
Springfield, OH 45501
Subsidiary of Allied Stores
120 employees
Department store
Southern Ohio

Zale Corporation
901 West Walnut Hill Lane
Irving, TX 75038
19,000 employees
Jewelry store chain
U.S. and International

Zayre Corporation
Speen Street
Framingham, MA 01701
28,000 employees
Discount department store and
  specialty store chains
Northeast, Southeast, Midwest

Glossary

AIO Life-style measurement based on activities, interests, and opinions of consumers.

Addition to Retail Percentage Measures a price rise as a percentage of original price:

$$\frac{\text{Addition to retail}}{\text{percentage}} = \frac{\text{New Price} - \text{Original price}}{\text{Original price}}$$

Additional Markup A further increase in an item's selling price when demand is high or costs rise.

Additional Markup Percentage The addition of a further markup to the original markup as a per cent of net sales:

$$\frac{\text{Additional markup}}{\text{percentage}} = \frac{\text{Total additional dollar markup}}{\text{Net sales (in \$)}}$$

Administered Pricing Occurs when retailers attempt to create strong loyalties on the basis of a distinctive retailing mix. If strong store differentiation is possible, a retailer can have control over the prices it charges.

Advertising Any paid form of nonpersonal presentation of ideas, goods, and services by an identified sponsor.

Affinity Occurs when a store is attracted to an area because of its ability to blend in and cooperate with the other stores in an area.

Agate Line Used in newspaper advertising; 1/14 inch deep by 1 column wide.

All-You-Can-Afford Promotional Budgeting Occurs when funds are first allocated to every element of the retail mix except promotion. Leftover funds are placed into promotion.

Ancillary Customer Services Those services that add a competitive advantage for the retailer. They do not have to be offered.

Application Blank Provides data on education, experience, health, reasons for leaving previous jobs, etc., for prospective employees.

Assortment Display An interior display in which a wide range of merchandise is exhibited. It may be open or closed.

Atmosphere The physical characteristics of a store that are used to develop an image and to draw customers.

Audit Form Lists the areas to be examined and the exact information required to evaluate each area.

Automatic Markdown Plan Controls the amount and timing of markdowns on the basis of the length of time merchandise remains in stock.

Automatic Reordering System Orders merchandise when a predetermined minimum quantity of goods in stock is reached. An automatic reorder can be generated by a computer on the basis of a perpetual inventory system.

Bait Advertising An illegal practice whereby a retailer lures a customer into the store by advertising products at exceptionally low prices and then tells the customer that the item is out of stock or is of inferior quality. In bait advertising, the retailer has no intention of selling the advertised item.

Bait-and-Switch Advertising *See* Bait Advertising.

Balanced Tenancy Occurs when the type and number of stores in a shopping area are related to the overall needs of the surrounding population. Common in shopping centers.

Basic Stock List The planned composition of staple merchandise that reflects the mix of merchandise available based on expected sales.

Basic Stock Method An inventory level planning tool wherein the retail buyer purchases an amount equal to planned sales plus a basic stock:

$$\text{Basic stock} = \begin{array}{l}\text{Average monthly stock at retail}\\ - \text{ Average monthly sales}\end{array}$$

Book Inventory System (Cost Method) Keeps a running total of all inventory on hand at cost at a given time. A perpetual system is maintained by adding purchases (at cost) to current inventory value (at cost) and then subtracting sales to arrive at the new current inventory value (at cost)

Box (Limited Line) Store A discount food store where strategy focuses on a small selection of items, restricted hours of operation, few services, and limited national brands.

Buying Club Straddles the line between wholesaling and retailing by selling goods to small businesses and individual consumers at low prices.

Buying Power Index (BPI) A measure of a geographic area's market characteristics expressed as

0.5 (the area's per cent of U.S. effective buying income)
+ 0.3 (the area's per cent of U.S. retail sales)
+ 0.2 (the area's per cent of U.S. population)

CBD *See* Central Business District.

COD (Collect on Delivery) Payment made when merchandise is delivered.

Canned Sales Presentation A memorized, repetitive speech given to all customers interested in a particular item.

Case Display Used to exhibit heavier, bulkier items than racks hold.

Central Business District (CBD) The hub of retailing in a city. It is the largest shopping area in a city and exists in that part of a town or city that has the greatest concentration of office buildings and retail stores.

Centralized Buying Organization All purchase decisions emanating from one office.

Chain Multiple retail units under common ownership that utilizes centralized purchasing and decision making.

Channel Control One member of a channel able to impose its will on other independent channel members through economic, political, or legal power, superior knowledge, or promotional tactics.

Class Consciousness The extent to which social status is desired and pursued.

Classification Merchandising Divides each department into related types of merchandise for data-reporting purposes for dollar control.

Cognitive Dissonance Doubt that occurs after a purchase is made, which can be alleviated by money-back guarantees and prompt service calls.

Collect on Delivery *See* COD.

Combination Store A conventional supermarket in which general merchandise accounts for 30 to 40 per cent of sales.

Commercial Cue A message that is sponsored by a retailer, manufacturer, wholesaler, or some other seller.

Community Shopping Center A planned shopping area that sells both convenience and shopping items to city and suburban dwellers. This center has a variety store and/or a small department store in addition to the outlets found in the neighborhood center. Twenty thousand to one hundred thousand people who live within 20 minutes of the center are serviced by this type of retail arrangement.

Company Department Manager Auditor Internal personnel whose prime responsibility is department management but who is also asked to participate in the retail audit.

Company Specialist Auditor Internal personnel whose prime responsibility is the retail audit.

Comparative Advertising Message that compares a retailer's offerings with those of competitors.

Compensation Includes direct monetary payments and indirect payments to employees and management.

Competitive Advertisement A persuasive message.

Competitive-Oriented Pricing A pricing approach in which a retailer uses competitors' prices as guideposts rather than demand or cost considerations.

Competitive Parity Method of Promotional Budgeting Technique that lowers or raises promotion expenditures according to the actions of competitors.

Computerized Checkout Checkout facility tied to a Universal Product Code or Optical Character Recognition system. As a cashier passes an item over or past an optical scanner, the computer instantly records and displays the sale; the customer is given a detailed receipt; and all inventory information is stored in the computer's memory bank.

Conglomerchant A multiline merchandising firm under central ownership.

Consignment Purchase Items not paid for by retailer until they are sold. The retailer can return unsold merchandise. Title is not taken until the final sale is completed.

Constrained Decision Making Excludes franchisees from or limits their involvement in decision making.

Consumer Behavior The process whereby individuals decide whether, what, when, where, how, and from whom to purchase goods and services.

Consumer Cooperative A retail establishment characterized by consumer ownership. A group of consumers invest, receive stock certificates, elect officers, manage the operations, and share the profits or savings that accrue.

Consumerism Involves the activities of government, business, and independent organizations that protect consumer rights.

Consumer's Decision Process The steps a consumer goes through in purchasing a product or service: stimulus, problem awareness, information search, evaluation of alternatives, purchase, and postpurchase behavior. Demographics and life-style affect this decision process.

Contingency Pricing Provides that the retailer does not receive payment from the customer until after a service is performed. Payment is contingent on the service being satisfactory.

Control Units Merchandise categories for which data are gathered.

Controllable Variables Those aspects of business that can be controlled by a retailer: store location and operations, product and/or service offerings, store image and promotion, and pricing. *See* Uncontrollable Variables.

Convenience Store A food store that is well located, keeps long hours, and carries a limited number of items. This type of retailer is small (1,000 to 4,000 square feet of floor space) and carries a balanced inventory of daily needs.

Conventional Supermarket A departmentalized food store that emphasizes a wide range of food and related items, with limited sales of general merchandise.

Cooperative Advertising Occurs when a manufacturer or wholesaler and a retailer, or two or more retailers, share advertising costs.

Cooperative Buying Procedure used by a group of independent retailers who get together to make a large single purchase from a supplier.

Corporation A retail firm that is legally incorporated under state laws. It is established as a legal entity separate from the individual stockholders.

Cost Complement The average relationship of cost to retail value for all merchandise available for sale during a given time period.

Cost Method of Accounting Requires the cost of every item to be recorded on an accounting sheet or coded on a price tag or merchandise container. When a physical inventory is taken, the cost of each item must be ascertained, the quantity of each item in stock is counted, and the total inventory value at cost is calculated.

Cost-Oriented Pricing A technique where a retailer sets prices by adding per-unit merchandise costs, retail operating expenses, and desired profits.

Cost-Plus Pricing Calculates price by adding a profit margin to merchandise or service cost.

Culture A group of people sharing a distinctive heritage. It affects the importance of family, religion, education, etc.

Curving Traffic Flow Constructs aisles and displays in a free-flowing pattern.

Customary Pricing A pricing practice in which a retailer sets prices for products or services and seeks to maintain them over an extended period of time.

Customer Space Area for shoppers to lounge, try on clothing, eat, park, etc.

Cut Case An inexpensive display, where merchandise is left in its original cartons.

Data Analysis Stage in the research process whereby secondary and primary data are examined.

Dead Areas Awkward spaces where normal displays cannot be set up, caused by corners, rest rooms, vertical transportation, etc.

Dealer (Private) Brand Contains the retailer's name. It is highly profitable, is controlled by the retailer, is less expensive for consumers, and generates store loyalty.

Debit-Only Transfer System A computerized system that immediately charges purchase prices against a buyer's account. Interest accrues from the day of the purchase.

Decentralized Buying Organization Allows purchase decisions to be made locally.

Deferred Billing Allows regular charge customers to buy merchandise and not pay for it for several months, with no interest charge.

Demand-Oriented Pricing A pricing approach that estimates the quantities demanded at various price levels and concentrates on the price associated with the stated sales goals.

Demographics Easily identifiable and measurable population statistics, such as age and income.

Department Store A store possessing the following characteristics: (1) at least 25 people are employed; (2) merchandise assortment includes some items in each of these lines: dry goods and household linens, family wearing apparel, and furniture, home furnishings, appliances, radios, and TV sets; (3) if sales are less than $10 million per year, no more than 80 per cent of the sales can come from any one of the lines. If sales are greater than $10 million, there is no limitation on the percentage of sales for any line as long as the combined sales of the smallest two lines are at least $1 million.

Direct Marketing A form of retailing in which a customer is first exposed to a nonpersonal medium or contacted by telephone and then orders products by mail or telephone.

Direct-to-Home Selling Involves sales through personal contact with consumers in their homes.

Disguised Retail Audit Employees not aware that an audit is taking place.

Disguised Survey Respondents not told the true purposes of a research project.

Distributed Advertising Effort Involves advertising throughout the year.

Diversionary Pricing A practice used by deceptive retailers. A low price is stated for one or a few products or services, which is emphasized in promotion, to give the illusion that all prices are low.

Dollar Control The planning and monitoring of the total inventory investment a retailer makes during a stated period of time.

Dump Bin A case display that houses piles of sale items.

EOQ *See* Economic Order Quantity.

Economic Base Indicates the source of income for a community's residents. The more diversified the economic base, the greater economic stability an area will generally have.

Economic Order Quantity The order quantity that minimizes the total costs of processing orders and holding inventory:

$$EOQ = \sqrt{\frac{2DS}{IC}}$$

where EOQ = Economic order quantity, in units
D = Annual demand, in units
S = Costs to place an order
I = Percentage of annual carrying cost to unit cost
C = Unit cost of an item

Electronic Banking Involves the use of automatic teller machines (ATMS) and the instant processing of retail purchases.

Electronic Point-of-Sale System An extension of the computerized checkout that verifies check and charge transactions, provides instantaneous sales reports, monitors and changes prices, sends intrastore messages, evaluates personnel and profitability, and stores information.

Ensemble Display Interior display in which coordinated merchandise is shown together.

Equal Store Organization Centralizes buying function and allows main store and branches to become sales units with equal organization status. There is complete separation of buying and selling responsibilities.

Evaluation of Alternatives Stage in the decision process where the consumer selects one product or service to purchase from a list of alternatives.

Experiment A type of research whereby one or more factors are manipulated under controlled conditions.

Extended Decision Making Occurs when a consumer makes full use of the decision process, usually for expensive, complex products or services.

Extensive Advertising Coverage An approach whereby advertising reaches many people with relatively low frequency.

FIFO A method of costing inventory which assumes that old stock is sold first and that new stock remains on the shelves.

Factory Outlet A manufacturer-owned store that sells manufacturer's closeouts, canceled orders, discontinued merchandise, and irregulars.

Fair Trade Protects smaller and full-service retailers against discounters by requiring uniform retail prices. Fair trade is now banned.

Family Two or more people residing together who are related.

Family Life Cycle Shows how a typical family evolves from bachelorhood to marriage to children to solitary retirement.

Feedback Signals or cues as to the success or failure of a retail strategy or some part of it.

Financial Merchandise Plan Specifies which products are purchased, when products are purchased, and how many products are purchased.

Financial Resources Funds needed for a retailer to operate. They must cover both business and personal living expenses.

Fixed Pricing Occurs when the government or a professional group controls prices.

Flat Organization An organization with a large number of subordinates reporting to one supervisor.

Flea Market   A retail institution located in sites not generally associated with retailing (such as race tracks, stadiums, and drive-in movie parking lots). Individual retailers rent space on a daily, weekly, or seasonal basis and charge low prices.

Flexible Pricing   A pricing policy that allows consumers to bargain over selling prices; those consumers who are good at bargaining obtain lower prices than those who are not.

Formal Buying Organization   Views the merchandise buying function as a distinct retail task; a separate department is set up.

Franchising   A contractual arrangement between a franchisor (who may be a manufacturer, wholesaler, or service sponsor) and a retail franchisee, which allows the franchisee to conduct a given form of business under an established name and according to a given pattern of business.

Free-Flow Traffic   *See* Curving Traffic Flow.

Frequency   Measures the average number of times each person who is reached is exposed to an advertisement during a given time period.

Fringe Trading Area   Includes the remaining customers not in primary and secondary trading areas. These are the most widely dispersed customers.

Full-Line Discount Store   A retailer characterized by (1) a broad merchandise assortment, including both hard and soft goods; (2) a relatively low operating-cost ratio; (3) relatively inexpensive building, equipment, and fixtures; (4) low-rent location; (5) emphasis on self-service; and (6) frequent use of leased departments.

Functional Classification   Divides jobs among functional areas such as sales promotion, buying, and store operations so that expert knowledge is utilized.

Functional Product Grouping   Categorizes and displays merchandise by common end uses.

Generic   An unbranded, no-frills brand stocked by some retailers. It receives secondary shelf space and little advertising and may be of lesser quality.

Geographic Classification   Divides jobs by area so that personnel in multiunit stores are adapted to local conditions.

Goal-Oriented Job Description   Outlines a position's functions, the relationship of a job to overall goals, the interdependence of positions, and information flows.

Graduated Lease   Sets exact rent increases in advance for a specified period of time.

Gridiron Traffic Flow   *See* Straight Traffic Flow.

Gross Margin   The difference between net sales and the total cost of goods sold.

Gross Margin Return on Investment (GMROI)   Shows the relationship between total dollar operating profits and the average investment in inventory by combining profitability and sales-to-stock measures:

$$\text{GMROI} = \frac{\text{Gross margin in dollars}}{\text{Net sales}}$$
$$\times \frac{\text{Net sales}}{\text{Average inventory at cost}}$$
$$= \frac{\text{Gross margin in dollars}}{\text{Average inventory at cost}}$$

Herzberg's Theory   Specifies that factors involved in producing job satisfaction (satisfiers) and motivation are distinct from those that lead to job dissatisfaction (dissatisfiers).

Hierarchy of Authority   An outline of the reporting relationships among employees.

Hierarchy of Effects   Steps a consumer goes through from awareness to purchase, in reacting to promotion. These steps include awareness, knowledge, liking, preference, conviction, and purchase.

Horizontal Cooperative-Advertising Agreement   Enables two or more retailers to share advertising costs and decision making.

Horizontal Price Fixing   Relates to agreements among manufacturers, among wholesalers, or among retailers to charge certain prices. Such agreements are illegal according to the Sherman Antitrust Act and the Federal Trade Commission Act, regardless of how reasonable the resultant prices may be.

Horizontal Retail Audit   Examines all of the elements that go into the retailing process, with particular emphasis on the relative importance of these elements and the mix between them.

Household   A person or a group of persons occupying a dwelling unit, whether related or not.

Image   How a retailer is viewed by consumers and others.

Implementation   Stage in the research process during which recommendations are put into practice.

Impulse Purchases   Involve products consumers do not plan to buy on a specific trip to a store.

Incremental Method of Promotional Budgeting   Adds or subtracts a percentage from this year's budget to determine next year's budget.

Independent   A retailer who owns only one retail unit.

Independent Channel Ownership   An arrangement in which manufacturers seek out wholesalers who seek out retailers to stock and sell products. Individual retailers or chains do not own manufacturing and wholesaling facilities.

Index of Saturation   A general ratio of store saturation combining the number of customers, retail expenditures, and size of retail facilities for a specific good or service in a trading area. The index of saturation equals

$$\frac{C_i \times RE_i}{RF_i}$$

where C_i = Number of customers in area i for the good (service)

RE_i = Dollar expenditures per customer in area i for the good (service)

RF_i = Total square feet in area i allocated to the good (service)

Informal Buying Organization   Does not view merchandising as a distinct retail function; existing personnel are also involved in buying.

Information Search   When a customer generates a list of alternative products or services to solve the problem at hand and then determines the characteristics of each alternative. Search may be internal or external.

Initial Markup (at Retail)   The difference between the original retail price and merchandise cost for an item, expressed as a percentage of the original retail price. This may be expressed as

Initial markup percentage (at retail)

$$= \frac{\text{Retail expenses} + \text{Profit} + \text{Retail reductions}}{\text{Net sales} + \text{Retail reductions}}$$

Inside Buying Organization   Staffs the buying function with store personnel.

Institutional Advertisement   Keeps the retailer's name before the public without an emphasis on product sales.

Intensive Advertising Coverage   Uses a high-frequency advertising campaign aimed at a selected audience.

Inventory Shrinkage   Comprised of customer shoplifting, employee theft, and inventory errors.

Isolated Store   A free-standing retail outlet located on either a highway or side street.

Item Price Removal   Practice whereby prices are marked only on shelves or signs and not on individual items.

Job Analysis   The gathering of information about the functions and requirements of a job. It is used in the selection of personnel, establishment of job performance standards, and salary administration.

Job Description   Contains the job's title, supervisory relationships, committee responsibilities, and ongoing functions.

LIFO   A method of costing inventory which assumes that new stock is sold first and that old stock remains on the shelves. It is preferred by most large retailers.

Law of Demand   States that consumers purchase more units at low prices than at high prices.

Layaway Plan   Allows customers to give the store a deposit to hold an item. Upon completed payment, the customer takes the item home.

Leader Pricing   Advertising and selling key items at less than their usual profit margins. The objective of leader pricing is to increase store traffic in the hopes of also selling regularly priced merchandise.

Leased Department   A department in a retail store, usually a department, discount, or specialty store, that is rented to an outside party.

Life-Style   The way a person lives and spends time and money.

Limited Decision Making   Occurs when a consumer uses each step in the purchase process but does not need to spend a great deal of time in each of the steps.

Loss Leader   Item priced below cost to draw customer traffic into the store.

Maintained Markup (at Retail)   The difference between net sales and the cost of goods sold, expressed as a percentage:

Maintained markup (at retail)

$$= \frac{\text{Actual retail operating expenses} + \text{Actual profit}}{\text{Actual net sales}}$$

or

$$= \frac{\text{Average selling price} - \text{Merchandise cost}}{\text{Average selling price}}$$

Maintenance Increase Recoupment   A lease provision providing for increases in rent if the property owner's taxes, heating bills, insurance, etc., increase beyond a given point.

Manufacturer (National) Brand   Produced and controlled by the manufacturer. It is usually well known, supported by advertising, somewhat presold to consumers, requires limited retailer investment, and represents quality to consumers.

Mapping   A technique to determine the trading area of a store by charting the distances consumers are likely to travel to get to the store, the population density of the geographic area surrounding the store, and the travel patterns and times from various locations.

Markdown   A reduction from retail selling price because of competition, overstocking, shopworn merchandise, odds and ends, and a desire to increase store traffic.

Markdown Control   Evaluates the number of markdowns, their proportion of sales, and their causes.

Markdown Percentage   Total dollar markdown expressed as a percentage of net sales (in dollars):

$$\text{Markdown percentage} = \frac{\text{Total dollar markdown}}{\text{Net sales}}$$

Market Penetration   A pricing strategy in which a retailer seeks to capture a large sales volume by setting low prices.

Market Pricing   Occurs in a competitive environment characterized by retailers pricing similarly to each other and each retailer having little control over price. Demand for a retailer is weak enough so that a number of customers will switch to a competitor if prices are raised.

Market Segment Product Grouping   Categorizes and displays merchandise according to target market.

Market Segmentation   Selling products or services to one specific group of consumers.

Market Skimming   A pricing strategy wherein a retailer charges premium prices and attracts those customers who are less concerned with price than with service, assortment, and status.

Marketing Research in Retailing   The systematic collection and analysis of data relating to retail strategy; a continuous process, yielding information for planning and control.

Markup   The difference between retail price and merchandise cost.

Markup Percentage (at Cost)   The difference between retail price and merchandise cost expressed as a percentage of merchandise cost:

Markup percentage (at cost)

$$= \frac{\text{Retail selling price} - \text{Merchandise cost}}{\text{Merchandise cost}}$$

Markup Percentage (at Retail)   The difference between retail price and merchandise cost expressed as a percentage of retail price:

Markup percentage (at retail)

$$= \frac{\text{Retail selling price} - \text{Merchandise cost}}{\text{Retail selling price}}$$

Marquee   A sign that is used to display the store's name and/or logo.

Mass Marketing   Selling products or services to a broad spectrum of consumers.

Mass Merchandising   Involves retailers presenting a discount image, handling several merchandise lines, and having 10,000 square feet or more of floor space.

Massed Advertising Effort   Concentrates advertising during peak periods.

Mazur Plan   Divides all retail activities into four functional areas: merchandising, publicity, store management, and accounting and control. Many medium-sized and large department stores are organized in a modification of the Mazur plan.

Memorandum Purchase   Items not paid for by retailer until they are sold. The retailer can return unsold merchandise. However, the retailer takes title on delivery and is responsible for damages.

Merchandise-Management Accounting   Plans markups in accordance with relevant cost information for individual items.

Merchandise Space   Area where nondisplayed items are kept in stock or inventory.

Merchandising   The planning and supervision involved in marketing particular merchandise or services at the places, times, and prices and in quantities that will best serve to realize the marketing objectives of the business.

Milline Rate   The cost to a retailer of one agate line per million circulation:

$$\text{Milline rate} = \frac{\text{Cost per agate line} \times 1,000,000}{\text{Circulation}}$$

Minimum Price Laws   State regulations preventing retailers from selling merchandise for less than the cost of the product plus a fixed percentage, which covers overhead. These laws restrict loss leaders and predatory pricing.

Mobile   A type of hanging display with parts that move, especially in response to air currents.

Model Stock Approach   Method of tabulating the amount of inventory and floor space necessary to carry a proper assortment of merchandise.

Model Stock Plan   The planned composition of fashion goods, which reflects the mix of merchandise available based on expected sales.

Monthly Payment Credit Account   Requires the customer to pay for a product in equal monthly installments; usually includes interest charges.

Monthly Sales Index   A measure of sales seasonality that is calculated by dividing each month's sales by average monthly sales and multiplying the results by 100.

Mother Hen Organization   All branch stores operated from headquarters. This plan works well when there are few branches and where the buying preferences of branch customers are similar to those of main-store customers.

Motivation   The drive within people to achieve goals.

Motives   A person's reasons for behavior.

Multidimensional Scaling   A statistical technique that allows attitudinal data to be collected and an overall store rating developed.

Multiple Segmentation   Selling products or services to two or more market segments at the same time, using different offerings for each.

Multiple-Unit Pricing   A policy wherein the retailer offers customers discounts for buying in quantity.

Multistage Approach   A technique for planning a broad price policy that helps a retailer generate a coordinated series of actions and a consistent image and that incorporates short- and long-run considerations.

Need-Satisfaction Approach   Sales technique based on the principle that each customer has a different set of wants and requires a different sales presentation.

Negotiated Pricing   Occurs when the retailer works out pricing arrangements with individual customers.

Neighborhood Business District (NBD)   Satisfies the convenience shopping needs of a neighborhood. This district contains either a supermarket or a variety store and is located on the major street(s) of a residential area.

Neighborhood Shopping Center   A planned shopping area that sells mostly convenience items. The largest store is a supermarket and/or drugstore. This center type caters to 7,000 to 70,000 people who live within 15 minutes' driving time.

Net Lease   Mandates that all maintenance expenses such as heat, insurance, and interior repair are to be paid by the retailer.

Never-Out List   Key items or best sellers that are separately listed (from a basic stock list and model stock plan) and separately planned and controlled.

Nondisguised Audit   Store employees aware that an audit is being conducted.

Nondisguised Survey   Respondents told the true purposes of a research project.

Nongoods Services   That area of service retailing not dealing with product elements but rather with an experience, or what might be called experiential possession.

Nonstore Retailing   Involves vending machines, direct-to-home selling, and direct marketing. These retailers do not possess conventional facilities (e.g., storefront, in-store selling, displays of merchandise).

Objective-and-Task Method of Promotional Budgeting   Technique whereby promotion objectives are clearly defined and then the size of

the budget necessary to satisfy those objectives is determined.

Objectives   The goals, long run and short run, that a retailer hopes to attain. Types of goals are sales, profit, satisfaction of publics, and image.

Observation   A form of research whereby present consumer behavior or the results of past consumer behavior are observed and recorded. Observation can be human or mechanical.

Odd Pricing   A pricing policy wherein retail prices are set at levels below even-dollar values, such as $0.49, $4.95, and $19.50.

Off-Price Chain   Features brand name apparel, footwear, linens, fabrics, and housewares and sells them at low prices in an austere, limited-service environment.

Off-Retail Markdown Percentage   The markdown for each item or category of items as a percentage of original retail price:

$$\text{Off-retail markdown percentage} = \frac{\text{Original price} - \text{New price}}{\text{Original price}}$$

One-Hundred Per Cent Location   The optimum site for a particular store.

One-Price Policy   A pricing policy wherein the retailer charges the same price for all customers who seek to purchase an item under similar conditions.

Open Credit Account   Requires the customer to pay the bill in full when it comes due.

Open-to-Buy   The amount a buyer has left to spend during any point in a month. The difference between a month's planned purchases and purchase commitments made by a buyer for delivery during a given month.

Optical Character Recognition (OCR-A)   An industrywide classification system for coding information onto merchandise that is utilized in nonfood stores. OCR-A is readable by both machines and humans and can handle greater information than the Universal Product Code.

Option Credit Account   A form of revolving account that allows partial payments. No interest is assessed if the consumer pays the bill in full when it is due.

Order-Getting Sales Personnel   Involved with informing and persuading customers.

Order Lead Time   The time span from the date an order is placed to the date merchandise is ready for sale (received, price marked, and put on the selling floor).

Order-Taking Sales Personnel   Involved with routine clerical and sales functions.

Organization   A system for achieving behavioral

objectives among employees so that they work together efficiently, achieve agreed-on goals, and gain satisfaction in performing the selected and required tasks.

Outshopping When a customer goes out of his or her hometown to shop.

Outside Auditor A consultant to a retailer who performs a retail audit.

Outside Buying Organization Involves the retailer's hiring outside buying services.

Overstored Area Has so many stores selling a specified good or service that each retailer is unable to earn an adequate return on investment.

Owned-Goods Services That area of service retailing dealing with the repair, improvement, or maintenance of a product owned by the consumer.

PMs Manufacturer's payments to retail sales personnel for selling specific brands.

Parasite A store that does not generate its own traffic and that has no trading area of its own.

Partial Vertical Integration Two channel members able to perform all production and marketing functions without the aid of a third. For example, a manufacturer and retailer may be able to ship and store merchandise without an independently owned wholesaler.

Partnership An unincorporated retail firm owned by two or more persons, each of whom has a financial interest.

Perceived Risk A consumer's belief about the probability and effect of making a wrong purchase decision, based on cost, performance, social acceptance, safety, and self esteem.

Percentage Lease Stipulates that rent is related to a retailer's sales or profits.

Percentage-of-Sales Method of Promotional Budgeting Ties the promotion budget to sales revenue.

Percentage Variation Method An inventory-level planning method wherein the actual stock on hand during any month varies from average planned monthly stock by only half of the month's variation from average estimated monthly sales. Under this method:

Beginning of month planned inventory level (at retail)

$$= \begin{array}{l} \text{Planned average} \\ \text{monthly stock at retail} \end{array}$$
$$\times \frac{1}{2} \left(1 + \frac{\text{Estimated monthly sales}}{\text{Estimated average monthly sales}} \right)$$

Performance How well a person carries out his or her roles (e.g., worker, consumer, citizen, parent).

Performance Measures Sales revenues, sales increases over prior periods, gross margin percentages, markdown percentages, stock turnover, stock age, employee turnover, financial ratios, profitability, and other factors.

Perpetual Inventory System Keeps a running total of the number of units handled by adjusting for sales, returns, transfers to other departments or stores, and receipt of merchandise shipments. This system can be maintained manually, by using merchandise tags that are processed by computers, or by using point-of-sale information tools such as optical scanning devices.

Personal Abilities The aptitude, education, and experience necessary for success in different types of retailing.

Personal Selling Oral presentation in a conversation with one or more prospective purchasers for the purpose of making sales.

Personality The sum total of an individual's traits which make that individual unique.

Personnel Space Area required for employees to change clothes, have lunch and coffee breaks, etc.

Philosophy of Business The firm's understanding of its role in the business system; a long-term commitment to a type of business and a place in the market.

Physical Drive Stimulation resulting from the senses being affected.

Physical Inventory System Involves an actual counting of merchandise. A retailer using the cost method of inventory valuation and relying on a physical inventory system can determine gross profits only as often as a physical inventory is conducted.

Pioneer Advertisement Provides information. Awareness is its objective.

Planned Shopping Center A group of store buildings centrally owned or managed, based on balanced tenancy, and surrounded by parking facilities.

Point of Indifference The geographic breaking point between two cities at which shoppers would be indifferent to shopping at either city.

Point-of-Purchase Display An interior display that provides consumers with information, adds to store atmosphere, and serves a substantial promotion role.

Point-of-Sale Perpetual Inventory Control System A system that feeds information from merchandise tags or product labels directly into computers for immediate processing. Some point-of-sale systems utilize optical scanners, which transfer information to a computer via a wand or stationary device that interacts with a sensitized strip on the merchandise; in others, merchandise classification data must be manually entered at the time of sale.

Positioned Retailing A retail program of identifying a target market segment and developing a unique retail offering, designed to meet the segment's needs.

Postpurchase Behavior Further purchases and/or re-evaluation based on a purchase.

Poverty of Time Occurs when greater affluence results in less free time, because the alternatives competing for the consumers' time rise significantly.

Predatory Pricing Large retailers attempting to destroy competition by selling goods at extremely low prices, which causes small retailers to go out of business.

Prestige Pricing Suggests that consumers will not buy products at prices that are considered too low.

Pretraining An indoctrination on the history and policies of a store and a job orientation on hours, compensation, chain of command, and job duties.

Price Adjustments Allow retailers to use price as an adaptive mechanism by taking additional markups and additional markdowns. Also included are employee discounts.

Price Elasticity of Demand The sensitivity of buyers, in terms of changes in quantities they will purchase, to changes in retail selling price:

$$\text{Elasticity} = \frac{\dfrac{\text{Quantity 1} - \text{Quantity 2}}{\text{Quantity 1} + \text{Quantity 2}}}{\dfrac{\text{Price 1} - \text{Price 2}}{\text{Price 1} + \text{Price 2}}}$$

Price Guarantee Protects retailers stocking merchandise against price declines. In the event a retailer cannot sell a product category at a given price, the manufacturer or wholesaler pays the retailer the difference between planned retail and actual retail selling price.

Price Line Classification A dollar-control classification system that analyzes sales, inventories, and purchases by retail price category.

Price Lining Sets a range of prices in which products or services are sold. Price points are created within the line.

Price–Quality Association The concept that consumers believe that high prices connote high quality and low prices connote low quality.

Price War Competitive reactions to price changes that result in retailers continually lowering prices below regular amounts and sometimes below merchandise costs to attract consumers.

Primary Customer Services Those that are considered as basic ingredients in the retail offering. These services must be offered.

Primary Data Information collected to solve the specific problem under investigation. Primary data can be gathered internally or externally through surveys, observations, experiments, and simulations.

Primary Trading Area Encompasses 55 to 70 per cent of a store's customers. It is the geographic area closest to the store and possesses the highest density of customers to population and per capita sales.

Private Brand *See* Dealer Brand.

Prize Money *See* PMs.

Problem Awareness Stage in the decision process where the consumer recognizes that the product or service under consideration may solve a problem of shortage or unfulfilled desire.

Problem Definition Step in the marketing research process that involves a clear statement of the topic to be investigated.

Product Classification Divides jobs along a product or service basis.

Product Life Cycle Shows the sales behavior of a product over its life. The stages of the cycle are introduction, growth, maturity, and decline.

Productivity The efficiency with which retail functions are performed.

Profitability Profits expressed in dollars or as a per cent of sales during a designated time period, usually a year.

Promotional Money *See* PMs.

Publicity Nonpersonal stimulation of demand for a product, service, or business unit by planting commercially significant news about it in a published medium or obtaining favorable presentation of it on radio, television, or stage that is not paid for by the sponsor.

Purchase Act The exchange of money or a promise to pay for ownership of a product or service. Purchase variables include the place of purchase, terms, and availability of merchandise.

Purchase Motivation Product Grouping Categorizes and displays merchandise according to the amount of time a consumer is willing to spend in shopping.

Push Money *See* PMs.

Rack Display Interior display used to hang clothing and other items.

Rationalized Retailing A retail program involving a high degree of centralized management control and rigorous operating procedures.

Reach Refers to the number of distinct people who are exposed to an advertisement during a specified time period.

Real Income Household income after adjusting for inflation.

Recognition of Shortage Occurs when a consumer realizes that a product or service needs to be repurchased.

Recognition of Unfulfilled Desires Occurs when a customer becomes aware that a product or service never purchased before is desirable.

Recommendations Stage in the research process during which the best alternative approach to solving a problem is selected.

Recruitment The activity whereby a retailer generates a list of job applicants.

Reference Group One that influences a person's thoughts and/or actions. There are aspirational, membership, and dissociative reference groups.

Regional Shopping Center A planned shopping area that sells predominantly shopping goods to a geographically dispersed market. This center type has at least one or two large department stores and as many as 100 small retailers. The market for the regional center is over 100,000 people who live within 30 minutes' driving time from the center.

Reilly's Law of Retail Gravitation A means of trading area delineation that establishes a point of indifference between two cities so that the trading area of each can be determined. The law may be expressed algebraically as

$$Dab = \frac{d}{1 + \sqrt{\dfrac{Pb}{Pa}}}$$

where d = Distance in miles along a major roadway between cities A and B
Pa = Population of city A
Pb = Population of city B
Dab = Limit of city A's trading area, measured in miles along the road to city B

Reminder Advertisement Geared to the loyal customer, emphasizing the store's attributes that have made it successful.

Rented-Goods Services That area of service retailing dealing with a consumer's right to possess and use a product through a rental arrangement.

Reorder Point The stock level at which a new order is placed:

Reorder point = (Usage rate × Lead time) + Safety stock

Resident Buying Office An inside or outside buying office that is located in an important merchandise center and provides valuable information.

Retail Audit A systematic, critical, and unbiased review and appraisal of the basic objectives and policies of the retail function and of the organization, methods, procedures, and personnel employed to implement those policies and to achieve those objectives.

Retail Balance The mix of stores within a district or shopping center.

Retail Catalog Showroom A retail operation where the consumer selects merchandise from a catalog and shops at a warehouse. Usually all the goods are stored out of the shopper's reach.

Retail Information System Anticipates the information needs of retail managers; collects, organizes, and stores relevant data on a continuous basis; and directs the flow of information to the proper retail decision makers.

Retail Institution Refers to the basic format or structure of a business. Retail institutions can be classified by ownership, retail strategy mix, nonstore retailing, and service versus product retailing.

Retail Life Cycle Theory which assumes that retail institutions, like products, pass through four identifiable stages: innovation, accelerated development, maturity, and decline.

Retail Method of Accounting A procedure wherein the closing inventory value is determined by the average relationship between the cost and retail value of all goods available for sale during the period.

Retail Promotion Any communication by a retailer that informs, persuades, and/or reminds the target market.

Retail Reductions Include sales, markdowns, employee discounts, and stock shortages.

Retail Strategy The overall plan that guides the firm: a framework of action for a retail establishment. It consists of the philosophy, objectives, overall and specific activities, and control mechanisms for a retailer.

Retailing Those business activities that involve the sale of goods and services to the ultimate (final) consumer for personal, family, or household use.

Retailing Concept Bases planning on these elements: customer orientation, coordinated effort, and profit orientation.

Revolving Credit Account Allows a customer to charge items during the month and be billed at the end of the month on the basis of the outstanding balance.

Risk-Minimization Retailing A strategy of reducing both initial investment costs and costs of operation in retail establishments.

Robinson–Patman Act Prohibits manufacturers from discrimination in price or terms of sale among retailers purchasing products of "like quality" if the effect of such discrimination is to injure competition.

Routine Decision Making Occurs when a consumer buys because of habits and skips steps in the purchase process.

Safety Stock Extra inventory kept on hand to protect against out-of-stock conditions because of unexpected demand or delays in delivery.

Sale-Leaseback The practice of retailers building new stores and then selling them to real-estate investors who then lease the buildings back to the retailers on a long-term basis.

Sales Objectives Those concerned with the sales volume of a retailer, such as growth, stability, and/or market share.

Sales Opportunity Grid A means of rating the potential of new products and/or store outlets across a variety of criteria.

Sales-Productivity Ratio Method for tabulating the amount of inventory and floor space for a product category based on sales or profits per foot.

Sales Promotion The marketing activities, other than personal selling, advertising, and publicity, that stimulate consumer purchasing and dealer effectiveness, such as displays, shows and exhibitions, demonstrations, and various nonrecurring selling efforts.

Satisfaction of Publics An objective to satisfy stockholders, consumers, suppliers, employees, and/or the government.

Saturated Area A geographic area having just enough retail facilities to satisfy the needs of its population for a specified good or service.

Scrambled Merchandising Occurs when a retailer increases its width of assortment by adding product lines that are unrelated to each other and to the firm's original business.

Secondary Business District (SBD) A shopping area in a city or town that is usually bounded by the intersection of two major streets. A secondary business district has at least a junior department store, a variety store, and several small service shops.

Secondary Data Data that have already been gathered for purposes other than solving the current problem under investigation. Internal secondary data are obtainable within the company. External secondary data are collected from sources outside the firm.

Secondary Trading Area A geographic area containing an additional 15 to 25 per cent of a store's customers beyond those in the primary trading area.

Self-Fulfillment A life-style concept whereby people express themselves by purchasing goods and services that are meaningful to them rather than symbols of conspicuous consumption.

Selling Against the Brand The practice of retailers carrying merchandise and placing very high prices on it so that rival brands (such as private labels) can be sold more easily.

Selling Space Area set aside for displaying merchandise, interactions between sales personnel and customers, demonstrations, etc.

Semantic Differential A disguised or nondisguised survey technique, whereby a respondent is asked to rate a store on several criteria by commenting on a list of bipolar adjectives.

Separate Store Organization Treats each branch as a separate store with its own buying responsibilities. In this system, customer needs are quickly identified, but there is duplication of effort by main store and branch managers.

Service Retailing Involves the sale of services rather than goods to the final consumer. Service retailing is characterized by intangibility, the inseparability of producer and services, and perishability of services.

Simulation A type of experiment that creates a complex model to resemble a real process or system, in which a researcher runs the model in the hope of learning something about the real system.

Situation Analysis The objective evaluation of the opportunities and potential problems facing a retailer.

Social Class System Ranking of people within a culture, based on income, occupation, education, dwelling, etc.

Social Cue A signal communicated through talking with friends, fellow employees, etc. It is interpersonal and noncommercial.

Sole Proprietorship An unincorporated retail firm owned by one person.

Sorting Process Involves the retailer's collecting an assortment of goods and services from suppliers and selling them to final consumers.

Specialty Store A retailer that concentrates on the sale of one merchandise line, such as apparel and its accessories, sewing machines, and high-fidelity equipment.

Standard Merchandise Classification A standardized dollar control product classification system developed by the National Retail Merchants Association. The use of this system enables retailers to compare their store's performance to that of others.

Standardization Depends on the applicability of a domestic retailing strategy in foreign markets.

Stimulus A cue (social or commercial) or a drive (physical) meant to motivate or arouse a person to act.

Stock-Counting System A unit control system that determines the number of units on hand at regular intervals by recording inventory on hand, purchases, sales volume, and shortages.

Stock Overage The amount by which a physical inventory exceeds the book inventory figures. This generally occurs when there are errors in taking a physical inventory or in compiling a book inventory.

Stock Shortage The amount by which a book-inventory figure exceeds a physical inventory. Stock shortages are the result of a magnitude of factors, including pilferage, unrecorded breakage, etc.

Stock-to-Sales Ratio An inventory-level planning method that assumes a retailer must maintain a specified ratio of goods on hand to sales.

Stock Turnover The number of times during a specified period, usually one year, that the average inventory on hand is sold. Stock turnover can be calculated in units or in dollars (at retail or at cost):

Annual rate of stock turnover (in units)

$$= \frac{\text{Number of units sold during year}}{\text{Average inventory on hand (in units)}}$$

Annual rate of stock turnover (in retail dollars)

$$= \frac{\text{Net yearly sales (in retail dollars)}}{\text{Average inventory on hand (in retail dollars)}}$$

Annual rate of stock turnover (at cost)

$$= \frac{\text{Cost of goods sold during the year}}{\text{Average inventory on hand (at cost)}}$$

Storability Product Grouping Categorizes and displays merchandise according to its level of storability.

Store Image The way in which a store is defined in a shopper's mind, partly by its functional qualities and partly by an aura of psychological attributes.

Store Loyalty Exists when a consumer regularly patronizes a particular store.

Store Positioning Enables a retailer to determine how consumers perceive the company relative to its retail category and its competitors.

Storefront The total physical exterior of the store itself, including marquees, entrances, windows, lighting, and construction materials.

Straight Lease Requires the retailer to pay a fixed amount per month over the life of the lease.

Straight Traffic Flow Constructs displays and aisles in a rectangular or gridiron pattern.

Strategic Approach Concentrates on planning to meet objectives and satisfy the retail concept.

Strategy Mix Composed of location, product, service, promotion, and price variables.

String A group of stores usually with similar or compatible product lines that has located along a street or highway.

Supermarket A self-service food store with grocery, meat, and produce departments, and minimum annual sales of $2 million. Includes conventional supermarkets, combination stores, superstores, box stores, and warehouse stores.

Superstore A retail institution that is much more diversified than a conventional supermarket and carries garden items, televisions, clothing, wine, boutique items, bakery products, and household appliances, in addition to grocery products.

Supervision The manner of providing a job environment that encourages accomplishment.

Survey A research technique whereby information is systematically gathered from respondents by communicating with them. A survey can be conducted in person, over the telephone, or via the mail.

Tactics Actions involving the daily and short-run operations of a retailer.

Tall Organization An organization with several levels of supervision. This leads to close supervision and few employees reporting to each manager.

Target Market The consumer group that a retailer tries to satisfy.

Terms of Occupancy Include ownership or leasing terms, operations and maintenance costs, taxes, zoning restrictions, and voluntary regulations.

Theme-Setting Display Interior display where the product offering is positioned in a thematic environment or setting.

Theory X A traditional view of motivation assuming that employees must be closely supervised and controlled.

Theory Y A modern view of motivation that assumes employees can use self-management and can be delegated authority.

Time Demands The time a retailer needs to spend operating a business. They vary by type of business.

Total Vertical Integration Successive stages of production and distribution contained under single ownership.

Trading Area The geographic area from which a store draws its customers.

Trading Area Overlap Occurs when the trading areas of stores in different locations encroach upon one another. In the overlap area, the same customers are served by more than one store.

Training Programs Used to teach new (and old) employees how best to perform their jobs or how to improve themselves.

Transfer of Title When ownership changes from supplier to buyer.

Trickle-Across Theory Occurs when a fashion is accepted by the general public and retains its basic form; within any social class there are innovative consumers who act as opinion leaders.

Trickle-Down Theory Occurs when a fashion is accepted by one market segment and then filters down to the mass market in three phases: distinctiveness, emulation, and economic emulation.

UPC *See* Universal Product Code

Uncontrollable Variables Those aspects of business to which the retailer must adapt: the consumer, competition, technology, economic conditions, seasonality, and legal restrictions. *See* Controllable Variables.

Understored Area A geographic area having too few stores selling a specified good or service to satisfy the needs of its population.

Unit Control Relates to the quantities of merchandise handled during a stated period of time.

Unit Pricing State regulations requiring certain sized food retailers in various states to express price per unit of measure as well as total price on some categories of merchandise.

Universal Product Code (UPC) An industrywide classification for coding information onto merchandise in the food industry. This system requires that manufacturers premark packages, through a series of thick and thin vertical lines. Product and inventory data contained in the UPC are not readable by employees or customers.

Unplanned Business District A retail location where two or more stores are situated together or in close proximity; this proximity is not the result of prior planning.

Usage Rate Average sales per day, in units, of merchandise.

Value Pricing Sets prices on the basis of fair value for both the service provider and the consumer.

Variable Markup Policy A policy whereby the markups for categories of merchandise and even individual products may differ.

Variable Pricing A pricing policy wherein a retailer alters prices to coincide with cost or consumer-demand fluctuations.

Variety Store A retail establishment selling a variety of merchandise in the low and popular price ranges, featuring a wide assortment of goods such as stationery, gift items, women's accessories, toilet articles, light hardware, toys, housewares, and confectionery.

Vending Machine A retail institution that involves coin-operated machinery. The vending machine eliminates the use of sales personnel, allows for around-the-clock sales, and can be placed outside as well as inside a store.

Vertical Cooperative-Advertising Agreement Enables a manufacturer or a wholesaler and a retailer to share advertising costs and decision making.

Vertical Price Fixing Refers to the right of manufacturers to control the retail prices of their products. All interstate fair trade regulations were terminated by the Consumer Goods Pricing Act of 1975. However, manufacturers still committed to controlling retail prices can do so by consignment selling.

Vertical Retail Audit Singles out certain functional elements of retail operations and subjects them to thorough searching study and evaluation.

Videotex Service A video-ordering system whereby a television channel displays graphic representations of products and services with accompanying text descriptions and ordering information.

Visibility A site's ability to be seen by pedestrian and vehicular traffic.

Visual Inspection System A unit control system that uses stock cards to monitor inventory levels.

Want Book A notebook in which store employees record items desired by customers but that are not in stock.

Want Slip A slip on which store employees record requested merchandise that is not in stock.

Warehouse Store A discount retailer that offers a moderate number of food items in a no-frills setting.

Weeks' Supply Method An inventory-level planning method wherein stock on hand is equal to several weeks' sales. This method assumes that stock carried must be in direct proportion to sales.

Under this method:

Beginning-of-month planned inventory level (at retail) = Average weekly sales × Number of weeks to be stocked

Weighted Application Blank A system whereby items that correlate with job success are given more weight than others. After a weighted score has been totaled for each application blank, a total score can be determined to use as a cutoff for hiring.

Wheel of Retailing Theory stating that retail innovators first appear as low-price operators with low-profit-margin requirements. As time passes, the innovators upgrade their product offerings, facilities, and services. As those innovators become more mature, they become vulnerable to new discount retailers with lower cost structures.

Name Index*

"t" indicates table; "f" indicates figure

635

Subject Index*

643

DATE DUE

MAY 2 2 2001			

Demco, Inc. 38-293

DEMCO

Top Ten Fast-Food Restaurant Franchises, Ranked by 1984 Sales

Franchise System	Total 1984 Sales ($ million)	Per Cent Sales Company-Owned Units	Per Cent Sales Franchised Units
McDonald's	9,900	26.3	73.7
Burger King	3,400	15.9	84.1
Kentucky Fried Chicken	2,850	30.9	69.1
Wendy's	2,490	34.9	65.1
Hardee's	1,917	33.2	66.8
Pizza Hut	1,700	50.0	50.0
Dairy Queen	1,391	0.2	99.8
Taco Bell	873	51.0	49.0
Big Boy	860	25.6	74.4
Arby's	760	12.5	87.5

Source: "Top 30 Franchise Restaurant Systems," Restaurant Business (March 20, 1985).

Selected Performance Data for Full-Line Discount Stores (1984)

Product Category	Per Cent of Industry Sales Volume	Annual Sales Per Square Foot ($)	Annual Inventory Turnover (times)	Per Cent Maintained Markup
Women's apparel	18.1	176	4.6	37.2
Men's and boys' wear	10.4	132	3.4	36.0
Housewares	8.0	135	3.2	30.2
Consumer electronics	7.4	316	3.2	19.4
Health and beauty aids	7.0	219	4.5	20.5
Automotive	6.6	279	2.6	28.7
Hardware	6.1	184	2.4	32.1
Toys	5.2	202	3.1	28.4
Sporting goods	4.8	187	2.0	26.9
Photo/camera	4.2	603	3.2	16.6

Source: "Census '84/'85: Merchandising Profiles," Discount Store News (July 23, 1984).

Selected Recent Acquisitions by Major Retailers

Firm Acquired	Acquirer
Caldor	Associated Dry Goods
Colonial Stores	Grand Union
Jewel Companies	American Stores
Lane Bryant	The Limited
Lerner Stores	The Limited
Linens 'n Things	Melville
Little Folk Shop	F. W. Woolworth
Loehmann's	Associated Dry Goods
Miller-Wohl	Petrie Stores
Pay Less Drug Stores	K mart
Service Merchandise	Best Products
WaldenBooks	K mart